THOSE WHO CAN, TEACH

NINTH EDITION

Kevin Ryan
Boston University

James M. Cooper
University of Virginia

Houghton Mifflin Company   **Boston**   **New York**

We dedicate this book to those readers ready to take up the great challenge and great privilege of teaching the next generation.

Senior Sponsoring Editor: Loretta Wolozin
Development Editor: Lisa Mafrici
Project Editor: Rebecca Bennett
Senior Production/Design Coordinator: Sarah Ambrose
Production/Design Coordinator: Jodi O'Rourke
Senior Manufacturing Coordinator: Marie Barnes
Marketing Associate: Carolyn Guy
Senior Cover Design Coordinator: Deborah Azerrad Savona

Cover Designer: Diana Coe / ko Design Studio
Cover Illustration: Diana Coe

Part Opening Photos: Part One: © Bob Daemmrich; Part Two: © Mary Kate Denny/
PhotoEdit; Part Three: © Elizabeth Crews; Part Four: CORBIS/Richard Hamilton Smith;
Part Five: © Bob Daemmrich

Other Photos: p. 377 (left): CORBIS/Bettmann; p. 377 (right): © Bob Daemmrich

Other Text Credits: p. 27 (definition of "vocation"): Copyright © 1996 by Houghton Mif-
flin Company. Reproduced by permission from *The American Heritage Dictionary of the
English Language*, Third Edition. p. 55 ("Ten Commandments for Successful Teaching"):
Copyright © Andy Baumgartner.

Printed in the U.S.A.

Library of Congress Catalog Card Number: 00-103024

ISBN: 0-618-04274-1

123456789-QUH-04 03 02 01 00

Brief Contents

Contents

v

PART THREE   Teachers

6   What Makes a Teacher Effective?

7   What Should Teachers Know About Technology and Its Impact on Schools?

PART FIVE   The Teaching Profession   467

14   What Are Your Job Options in Education?   468

15   What Does It Mean to Be a Professional?   496

Preface

This book, *Those Who Can, Teach*, is a book of questions. In fact, it was written in the first place to answer the question, "What are the things people beginning their formal study of education should know?" We have organized the chapters of our book around a series of questions that are likely to be of special concern to prospective teachers, and which we believe are keys to the central issues and concerns of teaching and learning. We hope that these questions provide direction and focus to readers' study well beyond the time they spend with this book. In addition, for those who are simply considering careers in teaching, we believe that the search for answers to these questions will help them clarify their career goals.

Purpose and Audience

Those Who Can, Teach is intended as a basic text for courses variously titled "Introduction to Education" or "Foundations of Education." We originally wrote this book because we couldn't find the kind of textbook our own students and the students of many of our colleagues needed and wanted—a book that involves prospective teachers in the real issues of schooling and education and that gives them a clear view of the skills and knowledge they will need to be successful professionals.

Content of the Ninth Edition

Those Who Can, Teach, ninth edition, presents a frank, contemporary examination of the field and foundations of education and, especially, the teaching profession. Although the text is firmly based in educational research and scholarship, it seeks to convey the important knowledge and issues in the field of education in a way that effectively bridges educational research and classroom practice. For this purpose, we rely heavily throughout the book on a narrative style, attempting to place the book's content in very human terms.

We have organized the book around five themes, each theme representing one of the five parts. Part One, "Schools," opens with an examination of the various motivations for teaching, and then tries to give the reader a behind-the-scenes look at what we know about the experiences of beginning teachers. This part ends with an examination of the dynamics of school life from many different angles to give the prospective teacher a multilayered view of schools. Part Two, "Students," attempts to provide the reader with a vivid grasp of the diverse and changing nature of today's students and examines the critical social issues that affect American students and schools today. Part Three, "Teachers," begins with the knowledge base about effective teaching and looks at what is taught and the growing role of technology in both teaching and learning. Part Four, "Foundations," contains chapters on topics that are "foundational" or basic to the practice of teaching: the economic and political issues underlying the control and governance of schools, the philosophy of education, the history of American education, and the ethical and legal issues facing teachers. It is in this mix of our educational past and current issues that we have placed an important chapter on educational reform. In Part Five, "The Teaching Profession," we present timely information on salaries and employment opportunities and, finally, examine teaching as a profession.

Features of the Revision

Teaching, learning, and the condition of our schools have been in the headlines almost continually in the three years since our last edition. Education is big news from Main Street to Pennsylvania Avenue. As the link between education and the well-being of both the individual and the nation becomes more obvious, both real change and proposals for change become apparent. In this edition, therefore, we—Kevin and Jim—try to sort out the most significant developments without losing sight of the enduring issues facing students and teachers.

Among the most significant changes in this edition are:

New "Policy Matters!" Feature   In recent years two things have happened. First, educational policies, emanating from either Washington, D.C., the state house, or parent and community groups, have had a great impact on everyone involved in our nation's schools. Second, many of these policies make profound differences in the everyday lives of beginning teachers. All chapters in this text now have a "Policy Matters!" section to help students be informed of current policy developments, highlighting key topics such as teacher standards, alternative licensure, and censorship issues.

New Conceptualization of the Educational Technology Chapter   Chapter 7, "What Should Teachers Know About Technology and Its Impact on Schools?" which was new in the eighth edition, has been completely updated and reoriented. In this revision, the chapter presents key technological tools within the context of the academic disciplines where they are being used to greatest advantage. This fits with all common themes and recommendations of major standards from national associations, states, and other specialized groups. This new focus will help readers make the link between the description of a tool and its application to actual teaching and learning. In addition, new technology resources, such as software programs, URLs, and references to standards found here and throughout the text, reflect technology's omnipresence in education today.

New Emphases on Diversity   The focus on diversity and multiculturalism, which we have emphasized from the earliest edition, has been expanded. Chapter 4, "Who Are Today's Students in a Diverse Society?" has been thoroughly revised to reflect the impact of changing demographics in schools today. This chapter now offers deeper analysis of the origins of today's diverse students and the implications for teaching and learning. Chapter 5, "What Social Problems and Tension Points Affect Today's Students?" has been refocused to include equality of educational opportunity, school choice issues, school violence, and gender issues.

Streamlined Coverage of Topics   This edition has merged the key concepts of two chapters on schools in the prior edition to form a new chapter entitled "What Is a School and What Is It For?"—thus eliminating overlaps in coverage and sharpening students' understanding of the complex phenomenon we call "schools." In addition, the "School Observations" feature is now found in the printed *Instructor's Resource Manual* and is also online where it can be used more flexibly by instructors and students, especially during the site-based component of this course.

New Beginning Teachers' Web Site   This brand-new site (http://college.hmco. com, select "Education") will provide access to self-testing opportunities, interactive activities, and selected articles from *Kaleidoscope,* ninth edition (our companion book of readings), that are annotated with links and critical thinking questions.

Learning Aids and Special Qualities

Although much is new in the ninth edition, many features have been retained. Chief among them is the book's informal writing style. We have tried to communicate the seriousness surrounding professional topics and, at the same time, weave in humor and create a sense of conversing directly with the reader. The text describes extensively the experiences of classroom teachers, often in their own words. Frequently, these experiences happened directly to us when we were teaching in public schools. We believe (and hope) that this writing style and heavy use of narrative give the text a greater sense of reality.

Many pedagogical features have been included to enhance the student's learning and the text's usefulness. Dialogues between the two authors appear periodically, both to highlight controversial points and to make clear to the reader that education is not a field where all issues are settled with cut-and-dried answers. Special inserts are included in each chapter to focus further on topics or research findings of particular interest to prospective teachers. Biographies of distinguished educators and teachers—such as Socrates, John Dewey, Anne Sullivan, and Jaime Escalante—have been placed throughout the text.

Further, the book is extensively illustrated with cartoons, color photographs, graphs, charts, and thought-provoking quotations. In addition, marginal notes highlight the important points of every page, and each chapter begins with a capsule overview and a list of key points. Each chapter concludes with a list of key terms, a series of discussion questions, and an annotated list of suggested readings and web resources. The book concludes with a glossary of terms and a very detailed text index.

Accompanying Teaching and Learning Resources

The ninth edition of *Those Who Can, Teach* is accompanied by an extensive package of instructor and student resources.

Kaleidoscope: Readings in Education, ninth edition, is a companion book of readings that can be used either in conjunction with the text or as a separate volume. This collection of more than seventy selections, approximately 30 percent of which are new in this edition, contains works by some of the most distinguished scholars in education, along with the writings of practicing teachers. A mixture of topical and classical studies, the readings include diary entries, letters, teacher accounts, journal articles, and reports. Many of the authors and reports of research cited in *Those Who Can, Teach* are included in this book of readings. Also, an easy-to-use chart in *Kaleidoscope* cross-references topics discussed in *Those Who Can, Teach* with the readings in *Kaleidoscope*.

Accompanying *Those Who Can, Teach* is an *Instructor's Resource Manual with Test Items*, prepared by Leslie Swetnam of Metropolitan State College of Denver, a highly skilled educator and a long time user of previous editions of this book. The *IRM* contains a transition guide from the eighth edition to the ninth; model syllabi; instructor and student support resources including annotated lecture outlines, media resources, sample chapter quizzes, activities, case studies, and a full bank of test items. The test items are also available in an easy-to-edit computerized test bank format, complete with online testing and ESAGRADE capability.

A set of eighty overhead color transparencies is free to instructors upon adoption of the text. The transparencies include figures from the text as well as new material generated specifically for the set.

The Real Deal UpGrade CD-ROM contains convenient links to web sites mentioned in the text, additional links to software evaluations, chapter outlines, a glossary of terms, chapter previews, and software demos.

Finally, the Beginning Teachers' Web Site (http://college.hmco.com, select "Education"), described previously, is an exciting new resource available to users of this edition. This site will contain original assessment opportunities, interactive activities, and enhanced articles from *Kaleidoscope*. For more information on instructional support resources for the ninth edition, please contact Houghton Mifflin.

Acknowledgments

Whenever any of us put pen to paper or fingers to the keyboard, we stand on the shoulders of others. This is certainly true of this book. We are indebted to many people. In the writing of this book, we are especially appreciative of the help given by the following individuals. Most notably, Lee McCanne and Brooke Graham contributed the new chapter on technology and the teacher, "What Should Teachers Know About Technology and Its Impact on Schools?" Additionally, we thank Larry Kaufman for his invaluable contribution to the research and writing of Chapter 11; William Etcher for writing one of the cases in Chapter 1; Steven Tigner for his portrait of Socrates and his helpful suggestions on the philosophy of education chapter. Special thanks go to our colleagues and students for their many good ideas and continuing support. A number of reviewers also made key contributions to the organization and content of this edition, most notably:

David Baker, Pennsylvania State University
Jeri A. Carroll, Wichita State University
June C. Edwards, SUNY College at Oneonta
Jerry C. Long, Emporia State University
Tom Lough, Murray State University
Cathleen Kinsella Stutz, Assumption College
Bernard R. Robin, University of Houston
Laura Wendling, California State University, San Marcos

A special acknowledgment is due to Marilyn Ryan for the substantial intellectual and psychological contributions she made to the several editions of this book.

Writing and revising a book is a multifaceted process. Many people provide advice—some solicited and some not. We believe, however, that our best source of advice on this book and its companion, *Kaleidoscope*, has been the team we've worked with at Houghton Mifflin. Lisa Mafrici, development editor, has been the one who has gracefully orchestrated the coming together of the many pieces of this book and *Kaleidoscope*. Rebecca Bennett, project editor, has deftly handled the copyediting process and all of the final stages of production. Ann Schroeder researched the wonderful, new color photos. Loretta Wolozin, senior sponsoring editor, has been with us for nine editions and has been a continuing source of support, good ideas, and new directions. Having an editor who believes in a book, particularly a book that has tried to be different, is a special blessing, and we feel blessed having Loretta on our side. The developmental editor for this edition has been Sheralee Connors, who has been a terrific source of good ideas, cartoons, quotes, and practical suggestions. A good revision editor has to have a fine sense of what to keep and what to drop. We are convinced that Sheralee is a gifted poker player because she truly "knows when to hold 'em and knows when to fold 'em." And, all of this with the greatest of tact.

Finally, we acknowledge the thousands of students for whom this book is written. Your new learning as you become teachers is central to our work as authors. We value your feedback on how we are doing and invite you to respond by sending us your comments through the Houghton Mifflin web site.

Kevin Ryan
James M. Cooper

PART ONE

SCHOOLS

Because schools have been so much a part of our lives, most of us think we know what schools are like. But our understanding of schools, often derived from the perspective of being a student, is not always accurate. These first three chapters attempt to sharpen our soft-focused image of schools and schooling.

1

Why Teach?

People take education courses for several reasons. Three in particular are common. First, as citizens, people need to know how a major institution like the school system works so that they can make informed choices within their communities and at the voting booth. Second, as potential parents, they need to know a great deal to be intelligent partners with the schools in their children's education. Third, those who are considering a career in teaching need to understand the profession they may enter. This text, by and large, is written with this third group in mind. And this chapter, more than any other in the text, focuses on those exploring the teaching profession. Its purpose is to help you answer a fundamental question: Why become a teacher?

As you read the cases of representative teachers that follow, we hope you come to understand more fully your own motivations for teaching. This chapter also emphasizes that

▶ A great variety of motivations lead people to select teaching as their occupation, and often the same person has more than one reason for choosing teaching.

▶ Teaching, like other occupations, often attracts people because of the rewards it offers them. The rewards of teaching can be divided into extrinsic and intrinsic rewards.

▶ In deciding whether to become a teacher, you can draw on a number of sources of useful experiences, including actual encounters with teachers and children, vicarious classroom experiences, guidance from friends and acquaintances in the profession, and—most important— your own personal reflections.

Examining Your Motives for Teaching

If you teach, it is likely that by the end of your second year of teaching you will have had both of the following experiences:

1. Someone at a party or some other social gathering will ask you what you do and how you like teaching. Soon the person will tell you that he or she has always wanted to be a teacher and regrets having become a stockbroker/computer programmer/bookkeeper/sales rep/flight attendant/disc jockey. He or she may still give it all up and become a teacher.

2. You will get to know an experienced teacher who confides in you that he or she deeply regrets having become a teacher. While in college, the person felt definitely cut out for teaching and actually enjoyed it in the beginning. But gradually he or she became fed up with the whole thing—bratty kids, pushy administrators, the same old faces in the teachers' lounge, the instant-expert parents, the boring curriculum. Now the person feels trapped in teaching and sees no way to get out.

The purpose of this chapter, then, is to keep you from becoming "the other person" in either of these two situations. It is to help you make a well-thought-out decision about what to do with your life, particularly if you are undecided about becoming a teacher.

Knowing Your Motives

Centuries ago, Francis Bacon told us "knowledge is power." Much earlier, Socrates (one of civilization's great teachers, about whom you will read more in Chapter 10) recognized the enormous power of self-knowledge when he urged, "Know thyself." Understanding one's motives in something as important as a career choice is crucial to good decision making.* A superficial motivation to teach can, and frequently does, lead to failure and disappointment. For instance, you may admire and want to emulate a former teacher. And you may, out of respect for this person, decide to teach without ever analyzing whether or not you have the ability, skills, attitudes, or drive to do so. Or you may think it is admirable to like

understand your real motives

---

*We ought to point out here a few idiosyncrasies in this book. For one thing, we sometimes speak to the reader in the third person, as in "One might argue . . ." or "The reader is warned . . ." At other times, when we are especially interested in getting the reader's attention (that is, *your* attention!), we use the second person, *you,* as in "You may not agree . . ." or "We would like you to . . ."

In presenting opinions and observations, we sometimes use *we* and sometimes don't directly identify the author of the remarks. When we use *we,* it is usually when we are stating our views on a subject. The "non-*we*" statements are intended to be more factual and less debatable.

Finally, when referring to individual teachers, we sometimes use *he* and sometimes *she.* Our major reason for doing so is that both sexes are, as you know, well represented in the teaching profession.

The best prize life offers is the chance to work hard at work worth doing.

—THEODORE ROOSEVELT

and help children. But in the process of actually working with, say, sixth-graders, you may discover that you can't stand sixth-graders or that you're not even particularly interested in children.

Clarifying your motives helps you to identify your strengths as a person and as a prospective teacher as well as to cope with your short-comings. Someone whose desire to teach grows out of a passion for art history has to know how to guard against hostility toward students who don't share that love of art. More than a few frustrated teachers have been heard to mutter, "Those ungrateful little whiners aren't worthy of Shakespeare" (or French infinitives, or the wonders of the protoplasmic process, or the niceties of quadratic equations). In any event, we have written this chapter—and, indeed, the entire book—in the hope that you will use it to gain a greater understanding of how you and a career in education might fit together.

make a list

We would like you to take a moment to write down, on the blank lines that follow, what you feel are your motives for wanting to be a teacher. If you are unsure whether you want to be a teacher (this probably applies to most readers), list your motives both for and against becoming a teacher. Incidentally, you may wish to save the list for future reference. More than a few readers have discovered that their motives for teaching have shifted dramatically as their classroom careers have unfolded.*

We use the plural, *motives,* for a particular reason. Most of us have mixed motives, some altruistic and some selfish, regarding what is important to us. Our motives often conflict, and sometimes they are incompatible. In any event, one motive is rarely enough to explain a choice as complex as the career in which we plan to spend a large part of our lives.

Why Become a Teacher?

Motives for   Motives against

_____   _____

_____   _____

_____   _____

_____   _____

_____   _____

_____   _____

*You may not wish to mark up your book, since that will make it more difficult to sell at the end of term. For this reason, and several other good reasons, you may wish to start keeping your own teaching journal so that you can reflect on the issues brought up in the chapters and other course-related experiences. This could be done in a spiral notebook, in a looseleaf binder, or on a computer. Realize, though, that if you do resell this book—instead of keeping it within arm's reach for your entire teaching career—well, we, your authors, will be personally hurt and very, very disappointed with you.

Engaging the Questions

If you did not stop reading to think about your motives for becoming a teacher or to commit yourself in writing, well, you're probably like many other readers. What kept you from seriously engaging the question? Your answer may tell you a good deal about yourself as a learner and, incidentally, about the educational system of which you are a product. Have you been trained to devour pages without really confronting the issues conveyed by the words? Have you learned to disregard your own views, even about issues quite central to you? If your answers to these questions are *yes,* you are like many other students. However, we hope this will be a different kind of book and a different kind of reading-questioning-thinking experience for you.

a different kind of book

We want it to be unlike so much else you read: things you pick up, spend time with, and put down again without having been moved or changed in any way. Because we are teachers, we want this book to have a very special impact on you and to help you make good decisions about whether you want to be a teacher and about what kind of teacher you want to become. For these reasons, you need to read this book in a different way. Take the book on fully. Encounter it. Fight with it. Laugh with it. Laugh at it. Improve it by adding yourself to it. You may be asked or nudged to do things that are not in keeping with your natural style of learning. Doing these things, however, should help you identify more clearly how you learn best and give you a sense of the various ways you can learn about and understand something. That old, tired cliché "You get out of it what you put into it" truly applies here. So, again, if you didn't think about and write down your motives, it might be good to go back and have a try at it.

This fifth-grade teacher is making reading books fun. (© Paul Conklin)

Motives for Becoming a Teacher

can you find yourself among these?

There must be nearly an infinite number of answers to the question "What are my motives for wanting to become a teacher?" Here are a few examples you might check against your own list:

▶ I really like the idea of having a positive influence on 25 (or 150) kids every day.

▶ I would rather be a big fish in a little pond than a little fish in some big corporation out there.

▶ I can't think of anything else to do with my major.

▶ Teaching seems to be a fairly secure, low-risk occupation with many attractive benefits and lots of vacation time.

▶ I always loved history (or mathematics, or science, or literature), and teaching seems to be a career that will allow me to work with a subject matter that I love.

▶ I can't imagine anything more important to do with my life than helping children with disabilities learn to cope with, and even overcome, their barriers.

▶ The instruction I had in school was incredibly bad, and I want to correct that situation.

▶ My parents would really be pleased if I were a teacher.

▶ Quite simply, I love children, especially the scruffy, unattractive ones everyone else ignores.

▶ I enjoy being in charge and having power and control over others.

▶ I really don't know what else I could do. I know about teaching, and I think I could do it.

▶ I'm concerned that society is falling apart, and I want to look out for the kids.

▶ One of my students might become a famous painter, or the president of a major corporation, or who knows what. It would be great to have a strong influence on just one significant life.

▶ I really want to become a principal (or a coach, or a guidance counselor, or a college professor, or an educational researcher), and teaching seems to be the way one has to start.

▶ Education seems as if it's going to be the action field of the future, and I want to be part of it.

▶ I have always felt I have a calling, a vocation, to be a teacher.

▶ Businesses are increasingly interested in training and educating their employees, and I want a career as a private-sector educator working in corporate America.

Motives for *Not* Becoming a Teacher

The door to teaching swings in and out. Each year two basic groups of teachers leave the profession. In the first group are the retirees, men and women who have toiled from twenty to fifty years and are now going on to other things—from gardening to totally new careers. In the second group are those who are leaving teaching because they have found it wanting.

In a 1995 survey of American elementary and secondary teachers, the researchers tried to understand why practicing teachers planned to stay in teaching or considered leaving the profession. First, the survey found a high level of job satisfaction, with only one in four teachers reporting that it is either "fairly or very likely" that he or she would leave teaching "in the next five years."[1] The survey also asked those teachers who *seriously* considered leaving for some specific new occupation to compare aspects of their present career (teaching) with their contemplated careers. Even among this group, as Figure 1.1 shows, teaching was judged to be better than the potential new occupations in a number of categories,

what drives people out

FIGURE 1.1   Aspects of Teaching Rated by Teachers Who Are Seriously Considering Another Occupation

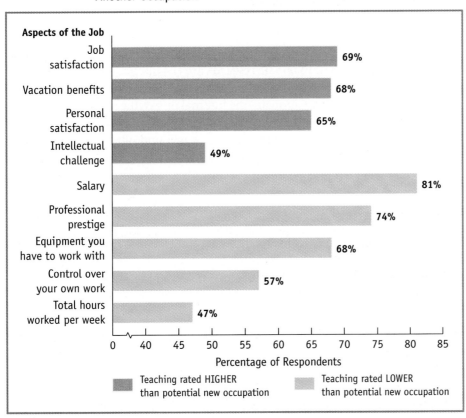

Source: Metropolitan Life Insurance Company, *The American Teacher 1984–95: Old Problems, New Challenges* (New York: Metropolitan Life Insurance Company, 1995), p. 62.

including job satisfaction, vacation benefits, personal satisfaction, and intellectual challenge. However, the dissatisfactions with teaching were revealed by the categories in which people rated other occupations higher than teaching: salary, professional prestige, "equipment you have to work with," "your control over your own work," and total number of hours worked each week.[2]

Though this survey focuses on "potential leavers," it does point to factors that ought to be considered in choosing a teaching career. We are convinced that a careful and realistic examination of the teaching career and the strengths and weaknesses you bring to teaching will substantially lessen the possibility of making a poor career choice.

The Rewards of Teaching

A person's response to the question "Why teach?" can run the gamut from "What's in it for me?" to "How can I help others?" Moreover, at different times and in different moods, our motivations may be quite different. As social psychologist Peter Drucker quipped, "We know nothing about motivation. All we can do is write books about it." On the other hand, the motivational *factors*—those qualities that reside within teaching—are clearer and relatively constant.

Those who educate children well are more to be honored than they who produce them; for these only gave them life, those the art of living well.

—ARISTOTLE

Researchers have identified a set of occupational rewards that can help us sort out both the attractive and the unattractive qualities of a career in teaching.[3] The two broad categories of rewards are extrinsic and intrinsic rewards. **Extrinsic rewards** are the public, external attractions of an occupation, such as money, prestige, and power. The **intrinsic rewards** of an occupation are the internal or psychic satisfactions one receives from one's work, such as a personal sense of accomplishment or an enjoyment of the work for itself. It will undoubtedly be no surprise to the reader that teaching is somewhat out of balance, receiving generally high marks on one set of rewards and low marks on the other.

Extrinsic Rewards

Teaching has rarely been cited for its abundance of extrinsic rewards. Although it offers more extrinsic rewards than occupations such as law enforcement and coal mining, when compared with other professions, teaching ranks low in extrinsic compensations.

Salaries   Teachers' salaries, as well as benefits such as retirement plans and health care, have improved substantially in recent years, and there are encouraging signs that steady gains can be expected. Nevertheless, compared with salaries in occupational fields with similar educational requirements (for example, a college degree, specialized training), teachers' salaries do not fare well. Whereas salaries in some professions usually begin low and then increase significantly, salaries for teachers may rise only modestly over the course of an entire teaching career. However, the importance of salary, like the whole issue of monetary

modest salaries

needs, varies enormously from one individual to the next. And, as we will see in Chapter 14, teachers' salaries vary significantly from one geographical location to the next.

Status   *Status* refers to one's position in a group, where one stands in relation to others. Whereas the status of a doctor or a beggar is rather clear, the status of a teacher is more difficult to discern. To young parents entrusting their child to the schools, the status of the teacher is quite high. To the same parents twelve or fifteen years later, on hearing that their child wants to become a teacher, the status may have diminished. However, our nation's current commitment to reform our educational system is having a positive effect on the status of teaching. A 1998 public survey asked which of eight professions (e.g., physician, lawyer, nurse, and journalist, among others) "provides the most important benefit to society." Respondents put teaching first, by close to a four to one margin over physicians (62 percent versus 17 percent). This is a significant change, since in a closely comparable poll in 1988, only 35 percent of respondents put teaching first.[4]

variable status

Power   As the answers in Figure 1.2 demonstrate, the same 1998 survey made it quite clear that the public sees the quality of teachers as the greatest influence on student learning.[5] Anyone who claims that teachers do not have power has forgotten what it was like to go to school without having done the assigned homework and to sit in fear of being called on by Mrs. Fisher. Any individual who can make another's day or ruin another's year has power. The power of the teacher is not a dollars-and-cents power, like that possessed by a corporate CEO. It is the power of the big fish in the small pond. And although power is not usually seen as one of the rewards of teaching, it nevertheless is a quality that "resides in the office." Yet, as sociologist Dan Lortie has observed, "Teachers are not supposed to *enjoy* exercising power per se."[6]

power over others' lives

Work Schedule   There is an old joke about a student in an education course being stumped on an exam by the question "What are the three best things about

FIGURE 1.2   Greatest Influence on Student Learning

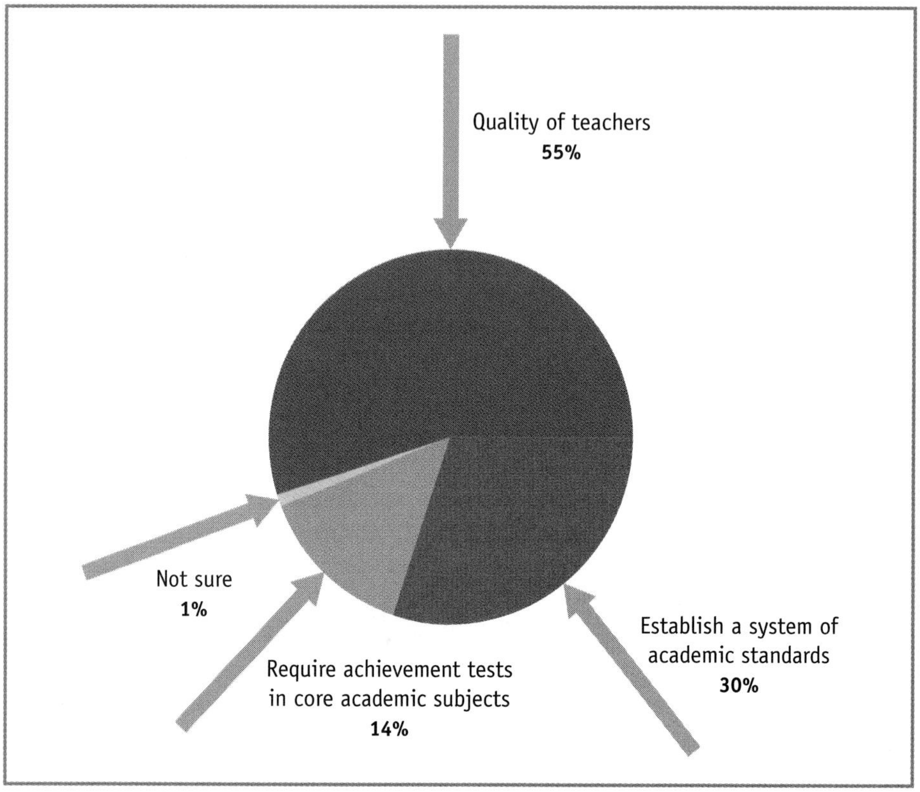

Source: From David Haselkorn and Louis Harris, "The Essential Profession: A National Survey of Public Attitudes Toward Teaching, Educational Opportunity and School Reform." Reprinted with permission.

teaching?" Finally, in desperation, he writes "June, July, and August." Compared with other workers, teachers spend much less time at their work sites. Ignoring what teachers do at home by way of preparing lessons, correcting papers, and checking homework, we can say they work six or seven hours a day for fewer than half the days of the year. Compared with those in the power and status occupations, such as corporate finance or medicine, teachers have less demanding work schedules. Also, teachers have much more flexibility and personal control over how they use their time. Teachers' work schedules are one extrinsic reward that clearly is in their favor.

flexibility and personal control over time

Intrinsic Rewards

Extrinsic rewards, such as company stock options or yearly bonuses, tend to be tangible. Intrinsic rewards are, by their very nature, in the eye of the beholder. What is one person's intrinsic reward, such as taking a busload of students on an overnight trip to the state capital, is another's living nightmare. However, the most satisfied teachers are usually those attracted to its intrinsic rewards.

TABLE 1.1   Principal Reasons Selected by All Teachers for Originally Deciding to Become a Teacher, 1976–1996

Reason	1976	1986	1996
Desire to work with young people	71.4%	65.6%	68.1%
Value or significance of education to society	34.3	37.2	41.9
Interest in subject-matter field	38.3	37.1	36.5
Influence of a teacher in elementary or secondary school	20.6	25.4	30.5
Never really considered anything else	17.4	21.0	19.3
Influence of family	18.4	22.9	19.3
Long summer vacation	19.1	21.3	20.3
Job security	17.4	19.4	18.1
Opportunity for a lifetime of self-growth	17.4	9.7	10.9

Source: From *Status of the American Public School Teacher* 1995–96, © 1997. Used by permission of National Education Association.

Students   The attraction of working with students has long been one of the strongest rewards perceived by teachers (see Table 1.1). The daily contacts, the conversations and exchanges, and even the struggles to motivate a student are a deep source of satisfaction for many teachers. Seeing children learn, grow, and develop—seeing them able to do things that they were unable to do at the beginning of the school year—is a genuinely fulfilling experience. Being important to others satisfies profound human needs, and teachers know about and appreciate this potential to affect the lives of others. When educational researchers Mihaly Csikszentmihalyi and Jane McCormack asked teenagers to tell who or what had influenced them to become the kinds of people they are, 58 percent—almost three out of five—mentioned teachers.[7]

This reward is particularly meaningful to elementary school teachers, who spend so much time with the same group of fifteen to thirty children. Secondary school teachers, who focus on a particular subject matter and see as many as 150 students in a day, identify working with students as an important attraction, but not always to the same degree as their elementary school counterparts do.

the joy of helping others

I believe the impulse to teach is fundamentally altruistic and represents a desire to share what you value and to empower others. I am not talking about the job of teaching so much as the calling to teach. Most teachers I know have felt that calling at some time in their lives.

—HERBERT KOHL

Performance of a Significant Social Service   In the award-winning film about early Renaissance England, *A Man for All Seasons,* Sir Thomas More says to Richard Rich, the man who eventually betrayed him, but who at the time was

contribution to society

The role of the teacher remains the highest calling of a free people. To the teacher, America entrusts her most precious resource, her children; and asks that they be prepared, in all their glorious diversity, to face the rigors of individual participation in a democratic society.

—SHIRLEY HUFSTEDLER

seeking a cushy job at court, "Why not be a teacher? You'd be a fine teacher. Perhaps a great one." Disappointed, Rich replies, "And if I were, who would know it?" More then says, "You . . . your pupils . . . your friends . . . God—not a bad public, that." To many teachers, the greatest satisfaction derived from teaching is the sense that they are doing important work for the common good. This realization buoys them up and helps them tolerate the less attractive aspects of teaching. Whereas workers in government and business are aware, in an abstract sense, that they are contributing to the social good, teachers have flesh-and-blood testaments to the importance of their service directly in front of them. As Figure 1.3 shows, members of the general public seem to agree that teaching provides valuable benefits for society. In our own classes, we see more and more college students not only seriously considering teaching as a career but also selecting teaching specifically because they see it as a way to pay back the country and to fulfill other service-related goals. For many teachers, the deeper motive behind the performance of important service for others is a religious one. They see teaching as a way to serve God through being of service to the young.

FIGURE 1.3   Profession That Provides Most Benefit to Society

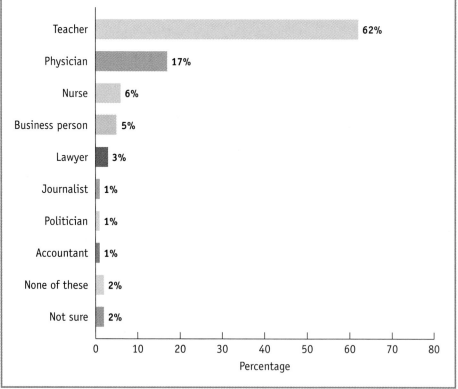

Profession	Percentage
Teacher	62%
Physician	17%
Nurse	6%
Business person	5%
Lawyer	3%
Journalist	1%
Politician	1%
Accountant	1%
None of these	2%
Not sure	2%

Source: From David Harolkorn and Louis Harris, "The Essential Profession: A National Survey of Public Attitudes Toward Teaching, Educational Opportunity and School Reform." Reprinted with permission.

Stimulation and Support from Fellow Teachers   When describing the work of teaching, researchers often report on the sense of isolation many teachers experience.[8] Nevertheless, for many teachers, their contacts and interactions with colleagues are an important intrinsic reward. Teachers enjoy the shoptalk and camaraderie that is a natural part of school life. Because teachers are seldom rewarded for their individual job performance or for their expertise, feelings of competition are less prevalent than among occupational groups such as salespeople or lawyers, who must establish and hold a clientele. Teachers know they are part of a cooperative venture.

collegiality

The Work of Teaching   For many teachers, the process of teaching is a meaningful reward in itself. Whether it is explaining an idea, working with small groups, or designing instructional units, the actual work is highly gratifying. Like a pianist moving through a favorite sonata or a lawyer cross-examining a witness, teachers often draw their deepest satisfactions in and from the act of applying their craft. Of course, teachers vary in which activities they find rewarding. Some draw their rewards from establishing a nurturing, cooperative environment, some from unraveling complicated problems for students, and some from seeing students work and learn independently. For these teachers, all else pales before their fulfillment in simply doing the work of a teacher.

teaching as pleasurable activity

POLICY MATTERS! Those Who Teach Know Policy Matters

In each chapter of *Those Who Can, Teach,* you will find a box like this, entitled Policy Matters! We have added these new boxes in this edition because it is vital for you, even at this early stage in your career preparation, to be aware of the effects that government policies will have on your day-to-day work as a teacher. Government bodies, from the national to the local level, are becoming increasingly concerned about education in our country. In response to numerous research reports and resounding public complaints about the schools, school boards, state legislatures, and even the president have suggested, or sometimes mandated, new policies. Many of these policies will change the way you will do your work in the classroom. The following questions summarize the effects of some key policy initiatives:

- *What is the policy?* What is the new law? What is its status? Has it already been adopted somewhere, or is it still under consideration? Which level of government is involved? Which teachers and students?

- *How does it affect teachers?* How does this policy work at the day-to-day level in the classroom? At the school level?

- *What are the pros and cons?* What are the arguments on both sides of the issue? We hope you will critically evaluate the evidence on each side before developing your own opinion.

- *What do* you *think?* The above questions should get you started on your own analysis of the issue. We hope they will lead to more questions for you and perhaps even inspire a lively discussion with your colleagues or classmates.

Rewards in Perspective

Around the world, teachers' intrinsic motives appear to be quite comparable. Whether one is teaching in Chicago or Krakow, the inner rewards are very similar. Not so the extrinsic rewards. Different countries reward teachers in vastly differing ways. In several European and Asian countries, teachers enjoy a great deal of status and attractive salaries relative to other occupations. Typically this occurs in countries that recognize that an investment in education reaps substantial economic benefits.

The issue of intrinsic and extrinsic rewards is captured by the story of a television reporter filming a documentary on the work of the late Mother Teresa and her community of nuns in the slums of Calcutta, India. After filming a young American nun cleaning the running sores, filth, and infections plaguing a dying beggar, the reporter looked down at the nun and declared, "I wouldn't do that for a million dollars!" Without taking her eyes off the dying patient, the young nun replied, "Neither would I." One of the great intrinsic benefits of a career in teaching—and one not shared by the vast number of other occupations—is the certainty that your work with the young is profoundly important. But be they extrinsic or intrinsic, the rewards we seek are expressions of our personal values.

Sources of Useful Experience

One of the major educational insights applied to schooling in recent years concerns individual differences. There is a new appreciation for the unique learning styles and often the unique learning problems of children and youth. As a result, the "one-true-way" approach to education is gradually slipping by the boards. The same insight about individual differences applies to making an intelligent career choice. Because people learn in such diverse ways and differ so much in what they already know and need to learn, we can give only sketchy guidelines here. We recognize four categories of experience that may help you answer the question "Should I teach?"

Real Encounters

People who plan to be teachers should test their commitment to teaching by putting themselves in actual school situations. As much as possible, students of teaching should observe in schools and participate in various activities that give them **real encounters** with children and adolescents. Many teaching candidates avoid actual contact with the young until they begin student teaching, only to find that young people are much different from the romantic images they have manufactured. "Those nasty little fifth-graders are so disgustingly . . . human!" one shocked student teacher said. Frequently, too, teaching candidates limit their encounters to typical elementary and secondary school students. They do not consider teaching children with mental or physical disabilities or even becoming

romantic images versus real children

a specialist such as a reading teacher. As a result of their past experiences, they have been exposed to only a narrow segment of the opportunities and challenges of teaching.

Increasingly, school districts are using college students as teacher aides and assistant teachers, both during the regular school year and in summer school. And a large number of teacher education programs have cooperative arrangements with schools that give college students opportunities to play various roles within the school, usually as part of their coursework in teacher education. Schools, however, do not exhaust the opportunities. There is much to be said for nonschool contact with children, such as camp counseling, playground work, after-school recreation projects, work in orphanages and settlement houses, and youth-related church work. Other possibilities include coaching a team or sponsoring a club. The opportunities are many. The important thing is to get your feet wet—to get the feel of working with children in a helping relationship.

ways to get your educational feet wet

Vicarious Experiences

Not all learning has to take place in the school of hard knocks. In fact, civilization itself requires that we be able to capitalize on the experiences of others. Artists and other talented people can make others' experiences accessible to us for enjoyment, edification, or both. Great fictional classics, such as *Good-bye, Mr. Chips* by James Hilton and *The Corn Is Green* by Emlyn Williams, portray teachers and schools, as do somewhat more contemporary novels such as Bel Kaufman's *Up the Down Staircase* and Evan Hunter's *Blackboard Jungle.* (All four of these books have been made into films.) There have also been some fine nonfiction accounts of teaching; among the best are Tracy Kidder's *Among Schoolchildren* and Samuel G. Freedman's *Small Victories* (both are cited in the For Further Information section at the end of this chapter).

the teacher in fiction and film

Films, such as *Mr. Holland's Opus, October Sky, Dangerous Minds, Dead Poets Society, Stand and Deliver,* and *Kindergarten Cop,* and some television shows are other sources of **vicarious experiences** that help us to both relive our own experiences in school and see school in a different light. However, that light is frequently distorting. Leslie Swetnam has reported on how the media, particularly film and television, twist the public's image of the teacher. Swetnam states, "Problems arise from the misrepresentation of who teaches, where they teach, how they teach, and what demands are placed on teachers, thereby creating an alarming distortion with consequences serious enough to warrant the concern of all educational professionals."[9] Her analysis of the most popular media presentations of teachers and schools shows that they overrepresent male teachers, secondary schools, minority teachers, and urban schools. Other distortions are that classes are small; teaching typically means the adult is talking (often with the skill of a stand-up comedian!) and, when the class finally gets around to it, learning is fun, fun, fun.[10]

If approached with a critical eye, these media images of teaching can prepare us for certain aspects of school life. We need to remember, however, that books,

> ### Last Day
>
> The last bell rang.
> The building filled with shouts and cheers
> And emptied soon. Yet one still sat.
> He looked at me, and I could see in that thin face
> An awful realization no other child had known:
> The year was gone.
> I knew, but I was older. I could bear
> The lost and sickish feeling of farewell
> From simple familiarity with it.
> I went back to where he sat;
> I said there would be other years.
> I said that I would write him letters in the summer.
> Somehow he knows, this child who had never had a letter in his life,
> That warm words are always somehow cold on paper,
> And never take the place of being close.
> Slowly he gathered up his books.
> Walking toward the door, he looked around the room.
> What did he see? What had this been to him?
> I knew, and yet I could not know.
> It was the end
> Of a year.
>
> *Source:* "Last Day," by Reese Danley Kilgo, *Phi Delta Kappan,* 51, no. 475 (May 1970). Reprinted by permission.

films, and television tend to portray school life at its extremes, featuring heightened situations well beyond the typical experiences of most teachers. The drama of teaching, on the other hand, is quiet, long term, and terribly real.

Guidance

advice from others

Another aid is the advice and counsel gained from those who know you. Besides parents and friends (who sometimes are too close to you to be objective), you can consult former teachers, career placement counselors, and your college professors. Your professors of education can be particularly helpful, because they usually are familiar with the realities of teaching. You should be somewhat cautious here, however. First, choose people who know you well rather than those who have seen you just at your better moments. Second, do not expect a comprehensive computer printout of hard data with a firm decision at the bottom line. If you get a few glimpses of insight from the person whose advice you are seeking, be satisfied. Third, be cautious, since many people are compulsive advice givers. Frequently people generalize on the basis of too little knowledge, and they are sometimes just plain wrong. Receive advice openly, but follow it cautiously.*

Reflection

The most important aspect of the real school encounters, guidance, and vicarious experiences you collect is that they provide you with data for reflection. By **reflection** we simply mean the process of thinking about your experiences and their implications for you. People are often so busy experiencing things, or getting ready to experience them, that they fail to reflect on what they have done in a manner that will ensure that they get the most from the experience.

taking time out to think

We cannot stress this point about reflection enough. It goes to the very heart of why we have written this book. Both of us are convinced that many people make sloppy decisions about becoming teachers. Often they have not asked some of the fundamental questions about themselves and about schools. This is precisely why we have organized this book around a series of questions such as "Why teach?" and "What is a school and what is it for?" It is also why, as you have seen, we periodically ask you to stop and reflect on a particular question. Occasionally we will ask you to commit yourself in writing, since doing so can help you clarify exactly what you think. We have also included case studies, anecdotal material, and actual accounts written by teachers. We hope you will use the material in the book to stimulate your own reflection. In effect, we are much less interested in telling you something than in presenting you with some tough, thought-provoking questions. Although questions such as "What makes a teacher effective?" may sound simple, their answers—if there *are* any answers—are frequently quite multifaceted. We hope you will use these questions not only to guide your career choice but also to help you reflect on the whole complex phenomenon of the teaching and learning process.

Our goal is not so much the imparting of knowledge as the unveiling and developing of spiritual energy.

—MARIA MONTESSORI

Case Studies in the Motivation to Teach

This section offers two case studies that illustrate common motives for going into teaching. Each case study is followed by a set of questions and a comment. The cases are intended as examples of how particular abstract motives take shape in teachers' lives. You may want to discuss the cases and the accompanying questions with other people. The shared experience of reading the cases and responding to the questions should help you probe and understand your own motivations. Finally, the cases and accompanying comments raise important issues about the nature of teaching.

---

*Although our good friend, Ernie Lundquist—about whom you will hear more later—has tried to claim credit for this thought, we believe that Shakespeare's Polonius beat him to it.

CASE STUDY **The Desire to Teach a Particular Subject**

Julia Tucker had been a star science student since junior high school. She received a partial scholarship to study chemistry in college and earned high marks in everything connected with science. She also derived a good deal of personal satisfaction from quietly showing her mostly male teachers and fellow students that a female could excel at science. When she graduated from college, she was heavily recruited by a chemical engineering firm. She immediately fell in love with her job. It took a little longer, two years, but she fell even more in love with Paul, a chemist, who was working on the same project. They got married, and a year and a day later Justin was born. Julia was back at work in six weeks. Both Paul and she hoped to have four children, but it didn't work out that way. There was no second pregnancy.

Julia was disappointed, but she took it philosophically. After all, she had a wonderful job, a loving husband, and a son who was the joy of her life. Everything was fine until Justin went off to middle school and began taking science courses. Julia couldn't wait to help him with his science homework. She stayed up late reading his science textbooks. She found all sorts of excuses to talk to his teachers about science education. She found herself daydreaming at work about how to teach various scientific concepts to children. And she was also quietly losing interest in the highly specialized type of chemistry she was doing. So, after a great deal of soul searching and several late-night conversations with Paul, she quit her job and went back to school to get a teaching license in chemistry.

a midlife career switch

That was over a year ago. Now Julia has a job, but hardly the job she fantasized about in her old lab or the teaching position for which she prepared. The only available position (other than ones that would force her to move the family) was at the elementary level, as a fifth-grade teacher. The school superintendent realized that Julia would be a real asset to his school district, but he did not have an opening in the high school for two more years, when the chemistry teacher was scheduled to retire. So he presented Julia with a proposition: take some methods courses over the summer (at district expense), become a fifth-grade teacher for two years, help establish a new elementary science curriculum, and be the coordinator of the annual science fair. At first, Julia was quite wary about this possibility. She thought it would mean throwing away a good deal of her specialized knowledge and risking failure as an elementary school teacher, even though it would be for only two years. But after talking it over with Paul and getting great support from her son, she reluctantly agreed.

And then a funny thing happened. During the summer, as Julia took the methods courses and prepared herself for her fifth-graders, she became more and more enthused about teaching children who she believed were "just becoming interested in the outer world." Once she started working with her fifth-grade students, she was hooked. They were so alive, so responsive, and so hungry to know about the world. What a challenge! Thoughts of ever becoming a chemistry teacher took a back seat to the elementary classroom.

Now, in November, however, Julia has misgivings. There is a flatness in her class that worries her. Much of the September curiosity has turned into an early case of the midwinter blahs. Moreover, her supervisor has conducted the first formal observation of Julia's teaching, and she is curious about the supervisor's opinion.

"So, Suzanne," Julia says at their postobservation conference. "How did I do? You were writing up such a storm, I thought you would need another notebook!"

AUTHORS' DIALOGUE

JIM: I'm having a little trouble with our list of motives for teaching and our case studies.

KEVIN: *Okay, but first we ought to clue the reader into what we're doing here.*

JIM: Sure. Often, in writing this book, the two of us have had differences of opinion about a particular issue. Rather than paper over those differences, we have decided to include some of them in these Dialogue inserts.

KEVIN: *Right. We hope these dialogues help make the point that many of the issues treated in this book—and really throughout education—cannot always be answered in neat, black-and-white terms.*

JIM: Yes, and I'm confident that after a few dialogues, acute readers will notice your flawed reasoning and the penetrating wisdom of my comments.

KEVIN: *Jim, your medication is wearing off again. Anyway, back to the discussion of motives. What's the matter? Can't you find your own motive in our list?*

JIM: Seriously, this issue of motives for teaching could be confusing the reader. For instance, the desire to have "power and control" over other people. This seems more likely to be an unconscious motive than the others.

KEVIN: *I agree, but some other motives can be hidden too, like the desire to choose a career our parents will approve. On the other hand, some people go into teaching to relieve the anxiety and discomfort they feel about particular social wrongs. They are consciously seeking to work out something that is a problem to them.*

JIM: All right, but I'm troubled about another thing. The way we've separated out these motives and the way we've written the cases make it appear that individuals are driven by a single, clearly visible motive. Life just isn't that way. We are driven by many motives, some of which may contradict one another.

KEVIN: *You're right. Even though we have stated that motives are mixed, our portrayal is somewhat simplistic. But if we tried to portray the full range of human motivations in each case, we'd have two novels instead of the two brief case studies coming up next. But you bring up a good point, and I hope the reader is forewarned.*

JIM: One final point. These pages may read like a summary of all possible motivations. We don't mean to give that impression.

KEVIN: *Right, we've left out all sorts of motives. For instance, some people go into teaching because they want to coach a state championship athletic team; some people use teaching as a second job so they can support themselves in what they really want to do, such as writing; and some people espouse a particular religious doctrine or economic system and are seeking converts. No, this list merely scratches the surface. We're just trying to get students to begin thinking hard about why they want to teach.*

Case Study cont'd

"Oh, I hope you didn't find that distracting. I probably should have warned you that I would be scribbling away."

"No, that's fine. I'm just curious to know how I did."

"I'd much rather hear what *you* think, Julia. How do you think the class went?"

"Well, I think pretty much as usual. They were a little quieter, perhaps because you were in there, but in general that was an average class."

"I did notice it being quiet, Julia. How do you feel about that?"

"As a matter of fact, I'm confused by it. Since September the decibel level has been steadily falling in all my classes, but particularly when we are doing science. I couldn't get them to shut up in September. They ate up everything I presented, especially science. They just seem to have lost interest."

"From what I just saw, and from what I have observed passing by your door these weeks, I'd agree. Interest looks low."

"Suzanne, I've really worked to find topics that will interest them. I built a whole unit on pollution last month with writing assignments and mathematics worked in. They said they were interested in heredity, so next month we're going to do family histories with interviews and collections of family facts and artifacts. They were all excited about this in September, but now I'm stumped. What is the matter?"

"Quite honestly, Julia, I had a feeling that this would happen."

"What do you mean?"

sometimes love for a subject gets in the way

"Well, when you came to interview last June, we were thrilled at the possibility of getting someone so knowledgeable and so experienced, and particularly someone who loves science so much. But those same qualities made us hesitant, too."

"I'm not getting you, Suzanne. I know we were all concerned that I didn't have traditional preparation for elementary teaching. You're not saying I know too much and I like science too much, are you?"

"Yes and no. No, you don't know too much. And your love of science is a terrific asset. But, at the same time, these qualities are keeping you from being the potentially fine teacher you can become. Julia, let me be honest with you. You are drowning these kids with information—and not just in science. It seems to me that you're doing all the work. What worked so well for you during your student teaching, with high school juniors and seniors, just doesn't work with these elementary school wigglers."

"Honestly, Suzanne, I'm not giving them high school material. This work is within their range. I don't mean to sound defensive, but really . . ."

"Julia, think 'romance.' "

"Romance? I thought you told me to do health and human sexuality in the spring!"

"No, no. Romance. Like in 'the romance of science' and 'the romance of writing.' Do you remember telling us during your interview how you fell in love—your words, Julia—fell in love with science in the fifth grade when you had to do a project for the science fair? Well, what I think you ought to do is a little time traveling and think about what caused *your* romance with science. Was it a fascinating question? An unsolved problem? The excitement of maybe solving a problem the adults couldn't? Or was it a teacher pumping facts and theories into you?"

"Oh-oh. I think the dawn is breaking. I've been so busy talking at them and trying to teach them some basic information, , , ."

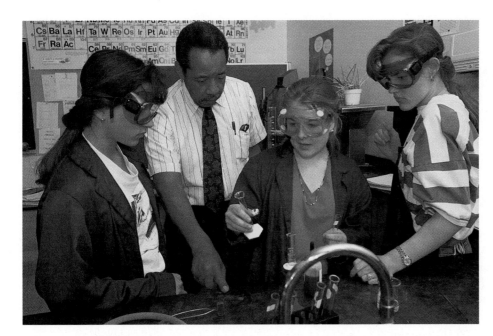

A chemistry teacher helps students with titrations.
(© Bob Daemmrich/ Stock Boston)

Case Study cont'd

"Right. You've been so busy telling them about what you love that you forgot romance. You forgot that romance is a two-way street. It's a classic mistake of rookie teachers, even ancient ones like you. Sometimes you can get away with it in high schools, but not with the wigglers. Not with elementary schools."

"So what do I do now?"

"Well, let me put aside these notes and let's see if you and I can put a little romance into the rest of the week's lessons."

"A little pedagogical seduction! Suzanne, I think you found the key!"

Questions

1. How would you characterize Julia's motivation to teach?

2. What sorts of things do you think her students were thinking and feeling about her classes?

3. Julia is clearly an outstanding resource to the school. What, however, are her liabilities?

4. What clues should Julia have been picking up?

5. What are some things Julia might do to stimulate romance for science in her students?

Jaime Escalante (b. 1930)

It is early in the fall term at Garfield High School in East Los Angeles, once a crime-ridden school filled with low achievers but now famous for outstanding calculus students. It is the morning after the second game of the World Series, and, as he enters the class, the teacher, known as *el professor,* shouts out his first question: "Who won the game?" After a pause, the students begin to chant enthusiastically, "Dodgers! Dodgers!" Having captured their attention, Jaime Escalante moves to the math lesson. Slapping a baseball into his mitt, he says, "As *X* approaches *A*, *F* of *X* is the trajectory. Could be a curve ball." And they are off—teacher and fifty-nine students—on a journey into the mysteries of calculus.

Jaime Escalante was born in La Paz, Bolivia, the son of an elementary school teacher, and began his own teaching career before age twenty. While he was a high school math and physics teacher, his students began to accumulate prizes, and soon he gained national recognition. Still in his twenties, he organized the first Bolivian national symposium of physics and math teachers. In 1963, amid growing social strife in Bolivia, Escalante, now married and with two sons, decided to take his wife and young family to the United States.

The next ten years were years of adjustment and struggle, years when Escalante learned English, went back to college, and worked as a busboy and a cook. When he finally graduated, he took a job in the fast-growing computer industry and studied for the California Teaching Certificate in his free time. When the news came that he had passed the test and would be assigned to a rundown, troubled high school in the *barrio,* Escalante turned his back on a substantially larger paycheck and headed for Garfield High School.

When the school's accreditation was threatened because of its students' low academic performance and high dropout rate, Escalante made his move. Supported by reform-minded administrators, he began setting high standards and making serious demands on students. They were not allowed into his class unless they proved that they had done their homework. He skillfully used the time-honored carrot-and-stick approach. The carrot was college and the world of opportunities higher education opened up for them. The stick was his constant challenging of them: "You *burros* have math in your blood! Our Mayan ancestors were the first to develop the concept of zero!"

Jaime Escalante, the subject of the Academy Award–nominated film *Stand and Deliver,* taught at Hiram Johnson High School in Sacramento, California. He has received numerous awards and has hosted the PBS series *FUTURES with Jaime Escalante,* produced by the Foundation for Advancements in Science and Education. But he is more than the man who has helped hundreds of Mexican American children discover self-discipline and learning and the enormous self-pride that comes with those accomplishments. Escalante is a tide turner. He has set an idea in motion, the idea that the poor and immigrant children in our country are capable of great intellectual feats. He has shown how remedial, slowed-down education can be replaced by demanding, accelerated education. "My skills are really to motivate these kids, to make them learn, to give them *ganas*—the desire to do something—to make them believe they can learn." He has always been clear about why he taught: his love of young people and his love of his subject. Now approaching seventy, Escalante recently retired and has been entered into the prestigious Teachers Hall of Fame.

Case Study cont'd

Comment

Love for a particular subject matter or content is an important and commendable motive for teaching. A major purpose of school is to pass on to the young the best of society's knowledge. Another important purpose is to develop in young people basic skills, especially a love for learning. A teacher who has a passion to convey subject matter is often quite effective at both of these goals. We probably all have had teachers whose excitement and enthusiasm for their subject were contagious. Such teachers often drive students very hard, but they are frequently the ones who make the greatest impact on us.

a balanced approach to subject matter

But carrying love for a particular subject to an extreme can cause trouble. Neither Julia's motive nor her problem is uncommon. Real learning is usually built on students' interest. This interest in or love of learning can be blunted when the lover (the teacher) is too overpowering or too insistent. The great teacher, like the great lover, knows how to draw out another's interest and help students "fall in love."

There is another danger for the teacher who is "blinded" by love of a subject. This teacher may be so busy teaching what she or he enjoys that the rest of the curriculum gets shortchanged. For example, the English teacher who loves interpreting literature often finds it easy to avoid slugging it out with grammar, punctuation, and other essential writing skills. The elementary school teacher who loves science, like Julia, may fail to give the other subjects their due. Although this tendency to focus on what we know and love and to avoid what we do not know or like is understandable, it is also irresponsible. It is unfair both to the students and to later teachers, who will expect students to have a command over the avoided or neglected content.

> *I love to learn in order that I might teach; and I get no joy from learning anything if I alone am to know about it.*
>
> —Seneca

covering all subjects responsibly

Teachers who are strongly motivated by the desire to teach a particular subject matter need to be somewhat cross-eyed. While keeping one eye on what they want to teach, they need to keep the other eye on the students and their day-to-day progress and needs. No one ever said it is easy to be a good teacher.

CASE STUDY | The Desire to Aid in the Renewal of Society

Fred Harvey was in his late thirties. His disposition was so pleasant, and a smile came so readily to his face, that one of the other teachers in the large metropolitan high school referred to him as "everybody's father." Fred had a remarkable ability to remain relaxed when everyone else was tense, and he frequently broke up emotionally charged situations with an appropriate quip or humorous question.

Each year Fred asked to teach the Curriculum II freshman history class. Of course, his request was always granted because the Curriculum II classes were considered the dumping ground for slow students and students who had given up. Some of the other teachers regarded the Curriculum II classes as "punishment." Year after year, Fred worked happily with children nobody else really wanted.

Fred's freshman history class was one of the most active in the whole school. He took his students beyond the walls of the school on expeditions to day court, to the police station and jail, and through industrial plants in the area, and most years he sneaked in a baseball game. Yet his classes were not characterized by fun and games. The students worked very hard on long and involved homework assignments, intricate discussions of problems, and demanding tests.

One year, Fred invited another teacher to speak to the class on shipbuilding in the eighteenth century. The talk went well, and after the session the other teacher, Todd Vincent, commented to Fred that the discussion following his talk had been very different from what he had anticipated; the questions were thoughtful and displayed observation of detail that the guest speaker had not expected from a "bunch of Curriculum IIs."

Fred laughed. "You know, Todd," he said, "they amaze me, too, sometimes. Most of these kids really have behavior problems, not intellectual ones. If you looked at their case histories, you'd find that the majority of them were 'dropped through the ranks.'"

"What do you mean?" asked Todd.

"I mean that they were in regular classes a good bit of their scholastic lives. But when they became problems in class, their teachers decided that the cause of their poor behavior was that the work was too hard for them. So most of the children in this class really represent the rebels, the nonconformists, the 'antisocials.' These are the kids who some teachers claim 'won't go along with the system.' They're the kids about whom teachers say, 'I don't care if they learn history as long as they become good citizens.'"

the danger of low expectations

"Yes, but you must admit that very few of them will go to college. Most Curriculum IIs just drop out," said Todd.

"Maybe you're missing my point," said Fred. "I guess I'm saying that people can't be 'good citizens' unless they are contributing members of society, and that they should contribute something they think is worth contributing. If they can't get the basic tools that make a person productive, how can they be good citizens? It's a lot more than getting jobs or making decent livings. As a matter of fact, I feel these kids are much more capable than the kids we send to the university."

"In what sense?"

"In the sense that they are the least accepting of society as it exists now," replied Fred. "If you talked to some of them for an hour or so, you'd find that they really feel the school is hypocritical in many ways, and they aren't afraid to point out the hypocrisies. They'll tell you, for instance, that there are two sets of rules in the school, two sets of discipline procedures, two sets of privileges, and all the rest."

double standards in schools

"But I hear the same thing from my 'honors' classes," Todd protested. "Those kids know about the double standard, too. They often tell me that an honors student here can get away with anything from cutting class to smoking in the john."

"You've got me wrong again, Todd. What these kids are saying is not that we expect too much of them, but too little. For instance, if a kid dropped from an A to a C in your honors history course, what would happen?"

"The kid would probably go in and see the counselor, by request."

Fred replied, "That's right. When a kid everyone believes is bound for college does poorly, people get concerned. They try to help the kid take a look at what's wrong. If one of these students goes from a C to an F, though, everyone says, 'Well, what more do you expect? The kid's only a Curriculum II and doesn't have the ability to sustain a

Computers can individualize instruction in many ways. (© Bob Daemmrich)

Case Study cont'd

C.' And they get all the inexperienced teachers and martinets in the school. Oh, they know that if they become real problems, they'll get counseling and possibly even better teaching. But that isn't their complaint. They know that the system isn't out to punish them. They know the system would rather they just float along and not bother anyone. That's the double standard in this school: those who are cared about and those who aren't. That's what these kids will tell you. It's not injustice, it's no justice at all."

"Is this why you request Curriculum II classes every year?" asked Todd.

"That's part of it," said Fred. "But it's not the whole reason. I'm not quite that altruistic. No, I see in these kids something that frightens me. They have capability, but if it isn't developed, it can become capability for hate, a hate based on fear. They're a mark for anyone who comes along with a hate message. They have to be taught to analyze critically, to think through problems, and to care about other people. In my mind, that is what good citizens do, and I think these kids need that capability developed even more than the kids in the honors classes do, because the attention the honors students get in the course of their day here will pull them through. Plenty of people challenge them, listen to them, and chastise them when they need it. But with these kids, it's a different story."

answering students' needs

Case Study cont'd

"You know," said Todd, "you're not just talking about the Curriculum II classes. I think the same thing is generally true of Curriculum I classes. It seems that a kid who's really bright gets a lot of attention, and so does the kid who is really slow, but it's that kid in the middle. . . ."

"Right," said Fred. "The kids in this class are the bottom of that middle group in terms of the concern they arouse from the system. And they know it. Yet, as you saw today, they are capable. We owe them a decent set of expectations. I've maintained high expectations for the kids. I would prefer to slightly overmatch them intellectually than undermatch them, because no development is possible when you're being undermatched constantly."

"Don't they complain about being pushed too hard?" asked Todd.

"Oh, sure! There's always a good deal of moaning, particularly in the early weeks, until they realize I don't dance to that tune. Pretty soon they settle in and decide to go along with the program. But then they realize that they are actually learning. At that point, they're hooked. They're mine, and I wouldn't trade teaching them for anything!"

"Well, Fred, this has been most instructive. I came to teach and I ended up learning."

"Me too. That's what keeps me going. And Todd, please come back next semester."

Questions

1. How is Fred's commitment to social renewal specifically shown in his classroom teaching?

2. According to Fred, what is the criterion for assignment to Curriculum II classes in his school? Was this true of your high school?

3. What is the double standard of which Todd Vincent spoke, and how do you explain it? What is the double standard of which Fred spoke, and how do you explain it? Did either of these double standards exist in your school?

4. How do Fred's expectations for his students differ from those of most teachers you have known? In what other ways is he different from most of the teachers you have known?

5. What do you think were Todd's major misconceptions as a teacher?

6. What does Fred see as the role of academic disciplines in education? If you had to, how would you argue against his position?

Comment

In addition to the serious injustice of underchallenging many of our students, Fred was reacting against the perversion of an important idea: teaching good citizenship. In Fred's school, as in many others, the idea of teaching good citizenship has been badly distorted.

Case Study cont'd

During the 1930s, in a reform started by the American educator and philosopher John Dewey, many schools adopted the policy of awarding a grade for citizenship. Dewey and many of his followers envisioned training for citizenship as a process of working out in class actual problems that arise in a democracy. They saw the schools as an appropriate place to teach students about democratic decisions and to give them low-risk but real practice in such decision making in a context where mistakes were not "for keeps."

As sometimes happens with reforms, educational and otherwise, the processes the reformers introduced to the classroom degenerated into empty forms. Good citizenship came to mean docility, doing what one is told. Students could earn "good citizenship" grades by "playing the game" and not bothering anyone. Citizenship became a code word among teachers. A teacher who was given a class of "low achievers" or "discipline problems" was sometimes told, "Don't worry about the academics with these children. Just make them good citizens." Parents were told that their child wasn't a very good student but was "an excellent citizen." This meant that even though he or she didn't learn anything, the child did without question everything that students were supposed to do.

misuse of citizenship grade

The use of a citizenship grade as a conduct mark is an absolute travesty of the system Dewey and the reformers designed, for in reality good citizens are not docile sheep who can be "conned" with impunity. The long-term effect of the misinterpretation of citizenship as conformity and docility has been to discredit it as an appropriate goal for schooling. Yet, in Fred's case, we see a person consciously attempting to develop educated citizens. Fred's visits to courthouses, legislative sessions, and factories, as well as the classroom study of major social problems, are very much in keeping with what Dewey—and, indeed, Thomas Jefferson and James Madison—had in mind when they spoke of educating for freedom.

Some Concluding Thoughts

When we were racking our brains for a title for this book, someone reminded us of the nasty comment George Bernard Shaw, the late-nineteenth-century Irish playwright, made about teachers: "Those who can, do. Those who can't, teach." While possibly true then (which we doubt), it certainly is false now. Throughout the twentieth century, the importance of education for the well-being of individuals *and* society became clearer and clearer. Much of America's power and prosperity resulted from our deep commitment to education. And teachers have been the keys to our educational achievements. As we move into the new millennium with its great promises and awesome challenges, one thing is crystal clear: we need even better schools and better teachers. G. B. Shaw was dead wrong. *Those who can, teach.*

Still, though, selecting a career is a personal decision and involves answering many questions, such as "Will I be happy?" "Will this career

Vocation n. 2. An inclination, as if in response to a summons, to undertake a certain kind of work.

—AMERICAN HERITAGE DICTIONARY

provide me with a satisfying lifestyle?" "Will I be up to the challenge, and will I find the work satisfying?" and "Will I grow in the experience?" People who are considering teaching as a life's work should grapple with these questions that surround the motives for choice. But they also need to scrutinize other, deeper motives.

teaching, a vocation

Teaching, like nursing, the ministry, and social work, is a service occupation. More correctly, teaching is a vocation. People are called to it. Built into teaching is the idea of contributing to the lives of others. For many people, the root of their decision to teach is deeper than a love of subject matter or an attraction to the life of a teacher. Many men and women select teaching for reasons that are, at heart, religious or humanitarian. In effect, they have a touch of the Calcutta follower of Mother Teresa. We suspect that teachers who are truly satisfied are people whose choice has been grounded in this deeper motivation. And although such religiously or humanistically based reasons for teaching are a private matter, it is a matter that each of us needs to explore very carefully. Of all the questions in this book, "Why teach?" is ultimately the most important one. How we answer determines not only whether or not we will teach but what we will actually *accomplish* as teachers.

KEY TERMS

extrinsic rewards (8)	vicarious experiences (15)
intrinsic rewards (8)	reflection (17)
real encounters (14)	

FOR REFLECTION

1. What questions about your own motivation for teaching has this chapter raised?

2. In your experience, did your teachers ever speak to you directly about their reasons for teaching? Did some teachers "tell" you by their actions what their motives for teaching were? Can you give an example?

3. What, to you, is the most compelling answer to the question "Why teach?" What is the most compelling reason *not* to teach?

4. If you are currently planning to teach, what events in your life have helped you discover why you want to teach?

5. How would you describe your personal thoughts about the power and the status of being a teacher?

6. Review the list of motives for teaching in Table 1.1 on page 11. Put an *E* before those expressing an extrinsic motive, an *I* before those reflecting an intrinsic motive, and a *U* for "uncertain."

7. Which intrinsic and extrinsic occupational rewards have the most bearing on your current thoughts about a career?

8. Do you think of teaching as a calling? As a social service? If you do, why? If not, why not?

FOR FURTHER INFORMATION

Collins, Marva, and Civia Tamarkin. *Marva Collins' Way.* **Los Angeles: Tarcher, 1982.**
This book takes the reader inside the world of one of America's most inspiring and controversial teachers. Marva Collins describes her method of educating the children others forgot.

Educational Resources Information Center. *AskERIC.* **World Wide Web site at http://ericir.syr.edu.**
AskERIC offers a gold mine of help to teachers, and its large bank of lesson plans can be of particular value to the new teacher.

Freedman, Samuel G. *Small Victories.* **New York: Harper and Row, 1990.**
This book chronicles life in a New York City high school in the late 1980s. It depicts the highs and lows of teaching in urban schools and vividly describes the major problems affecting life in these schools.

Kane, P. R., ed. *My First Year as a Teacher.* **New York: Penguin Books, 1991.**
This book is a collection of accounts by twenty-five teachers of their first year in teaching. The teachers describe their struggles and triumphs as they grappled with their new profession.

Kidder, Tracy. *Among Schoolchildren.* **Boston: Houghton Mifflin, 1989.**
The author spent the entire school year observing a fifth-grade teacher and produced a rich and fascinating account of a teacher's year. The book shows how one teacher shaped and moved the lives of her students.

Mathews, Jay. *Escalante: The Best Teacher in America.* **New York: Holt, 1990.**
This is the biography of Jaime Escalante, who is profiled in this chapter and is the subject of the film *Stand and Deliver.* Escalante wins over his students, largely urban Hispanics, with a combination of challenges to pride, demands of dedicated hard work, and demonstrated love.

SEARCH

2

What Can the New Teacher Expect?

Many new teachers are shocked and disappointed by the actual experience of being a teacher. In this chapter, we try to help prospective teachers anticipate some of the problems that lie ahead. All of the material comes directly from the experiences of beginning teachers. This chapter emphasizes that

▶ Although prospective teachers may feel that schools will hold few surprises, being on the other side of the desk is a very different experience and can cause a sense of culture shock.

▶ Administrators play an important but often confusing role in the life of the beginning teacher.

▶ Although fellow teachers are an enormous source of learning and support, they can also be a source of difficulty.

▶ New teachers learn much about the job in which they are supposed to be experts: instruction.

▶ Although the teachers' main purpose is to give service to children, students are also a source of both satisfaction and dissatisfaction.

▶ Some of the most intense satisfactions and disappointments confronting new teachers come from those they came to help: students.

▶ Working with parents can be surprisingly complex and is rarely what the new teacher has anticipated.

▶ Beginning teachers can follow specific strategies to mitigate problems and heighten their chances for a successful career start.

▶ Teaching invariably has hidden sweetness and secret joys.

We have good news and bad news for you. First, the good news: forecasters predict that as a result of retirements and population growth, our schools will need 2 million new teachers in the next decade.[1] Not since World War II has there been such a promising job market for teachers. As we will describe in Chapter 14, "What Are Your Job Options in Education?", young people entering the teaching profession in the first decade of the twenty-first century typically will have a rich variety of options and opportunities from which to choose. So much for the good news.

encouraging job reports

The bad news is that the first year of teaching can be a rough one— too rough for many beginners. Each year many new teachers walk into their classrooms with energy, high hopes, and rose-colored glasses. But unexpected problems cause them to give up on teaching or radically lower their sights about their capabilities as teachers. Rather than ignoring or, worse, sugar-coating these problems, we focus on them even at the risk of frightening some readers. However, to be forewarned is to be forearmed, and many of the problems discussed in this chapter can be either prevented or radically reduced in intensity.

But intense the first year is—intense because of the unexpected demands and the surprises that lurk in what was thought to be a familiar world: the classroom. Some of this intensity comes from the problems that confront the new teacher, but some also comes from the satisfaction in solving those problems and in succeeding as a professional.

Surprise is a big part of the first year, too. New teachers often report their astonishment at this or that experience or event. These surprises often come wrapped in everyday boxes; some contain sweet treasures and others hold booby traps. We have categorized these surprises in the following way:

surprises of the first year

▶ The school milieu: the shock of the familiar

▶ Administrators: mixed bag and many hats and many pressures

▶ Peers: a mixed blessing

▶ Instruction: so much to learn

▶ Students: friends or fiends?

▶ Parents: natural allies with different agendas

> *A teacher's day is half bureaucracy, half crisis, half monotony, and one-eightieth epiphany. Never mind the arithmetic.*
>
> —SUSAN OHANIAN

In this chapter, we will look at each of these categories and try to take some of the surprises out of the first year of teaching. We intend this chapter, then, to help you mobilize yourself by preparing for the problems, developing your strengths, and shoring up your weaknesses.

The School Milieu: The Shock of the Familiar

the strange and the familiar

One of the oddest occurrences related to becoming a teacher is the new teacher's sense of strangeness in what is, after all, a very familiar setting. People who become securities analysts, astronauts, or psychiatric social workers know they are moving into a strange environment, and they expect these new work worlds to present them with very different experiences from those they had as students. New teachers, however, are re-entering a familiar setting, even if their schools are not the same ones in which they were taught. The school routine of classes, periods, bells, tests, homework, and report cards is in their blood. So are the rituals and pageants: assemblies, Thanksgiving class presentations, honor society induction, and sports rivalries with other schools. The existence of cliques, in-groups, and out-groups among both students and faculty is no secret either. But despite all their experience and sophistication, beginning teachers are often overwhelmed by their initial exposure to school.

false sense of security

It appears that the new teacher's very familiarity with life in schools is a problem in that it lulls many into a false sense of understanding what is happening around them and thus a false sense of security. "School" is a very complicated series of structures, people, and interactions, and having "studied" school from the perspective of a student is hardly the same as understanding it as a teacher. Being one of twenty-five students sitting and listening to a teacher is quite different from being in front of twenty-five strange children and having responsibility for their learning. Also, new teachers have to learn not only a new set of school routines for their particular school but also how to administer them. They have to learn their way around a new building and find out how to requisition the supplies they need.

I am teaching . . . It's kind of like having a love affair with a rhinoceros.

—ANNE SEXTON

They have to get acquainted with their administration, their fellow teachers, and especially their students. And on top of all this, first-year teachers often have to develop lesson plans from scratch. They must build complete units, design bulletin boards, devise an evaluation system, and make up tests. The sheer volume of "newness" puts pressure and strain on the beginners.

Culture Shock

signs of stress

Beginning teachers' disorientation with what they thought would be the familiar turf of school often shows up in visible signs of mental and physical stress. In the early months of the school year, it is not uncommon for the new teacher to experience depression and self-doubt, outbursts of crying, physical exhaustion, insomnia, crankiness, inability to control temper, and even fits of vomiting before going to school in the morning. One anthropologist claims that the stresses and strains many new teachers experience are similar to the phenomenon known as "culture shock."[2]

school: a foreign culture?

Culture shock is the feeling of dislocation that people experience when they initially encounter a foreign culture. Peace Corps volunteers, foreign students, tourists, and newly arrived immigrants often report that when first thrust into the strange life patterns of a foreign culture, they feel numbingly disoriented, forced to assimilate too much too soon, and afraid they have made a drastic mistake by going to a strange country. It is easy to explain culture shock among Peace Corps volunteers and immigrants, but why teachers? Haven't we just said that teachers, as ex-students, are accustomed to the culture of school?

The following account by a new second-grade teacher speaks to the kinds of culture shock problems experienced by teachers in many situations.*

CASE STUDY **Karen Bohlin/Second Grade**

"The next time I hear someone say, 'Teaching is an easy job,' I think I'm going to slap their face . . . or cry! I can't believe how tired I am. I've been teaching for five weeks, and it seems as if it has been five months. I never realized that life on the teacher's side of the desk could be so different, so tiring. I remember seeing the old movie *Up the Down Staircase* and thinking it was exaggerated. My kids are younger and don't have the kinds of problems those high school kids in the movie had, but they still have problems, and they are so demanding. They all want my attention, and they all seem to want it at the same time. 'Miss Bohlin, someone took my pencil! Did you do it?' 'Miss Bohlin, Ralph and Maxine put gum in my hair.' 'Miss Bohlin, my father doesn't think we're doing enough arithmetic in this class and says I can tell the kids to shut up if you won't.' 'Miss Bohlin, I need to go to the nurse. I have a terrible nosebleed coming on!' And on and on.

"And the forms! They never end. Forms for shots. For lockers. For parent volunteers. For books. And we have an attendance procedure here that must have been designed by a sadist! It consumes hours of time. The principal's office continually wants information. I keep filling out forms and sending them in, only to be greeted with more forms. I can't imagine what they do with all the information.

"On top of all this, I'm supposed to teach! I leave school in the afternoon—always the last one out of the building—and I'm numb from the hairline down. On some nights, I can hardly unwrap a TV dinner. And I spend what little free time I do have staring at the TV set and having imaginary arguments with Sandra's know-it-all father (whom I have yet to meet) about why we actually are doing just the right amount of arithmetic. What is most discouraging is that Sandra's father wins the arguments.

"Clearly, this has been the most frustrating five weeks of my life. I feel as if I've been swimming in molasses. Student teaching was a breeze compared to this!"

swimming in molasses

pleasant surprises

But how do I feel at the end of each day? I feel proud of my students. I feel more knowledgeable about living, teaching, and learning. I feel lucky to be a teacher. I feel . . . full of sparks.

—IRASEMA ORTEGA-CRAWFORD

But many of the surprises of school life are very pleasant ones. There is much love and human warmth in the classroom. Some of the aspects of school life that one has dreaded never materialize. The content that one felt unsure of turns out to be one's strength. Also, within the four walls of the classroom, some people find a new self they didn't know existed.

---

*All the cases in this chapter that are not accompanied by specific citations are slightly altered or fictionalized accounts of situations and problems experienced by the authors or by beginning teachers with whom the authors have worked. The names have been changed to save us all from embarrassment.

The class clowns who were so amusing to you in high school are often a very different story when they reappear in your classroom. (© Elizabeth Crews)

CASE STUDY — Joan Gee/Office Management

"All through elementary and high school, I was bashful. In my high school graduating class, I won the 'Most Shy' award. I dreaded being called on, even when I knew I had the right answer! Part of it is that I blush so easily. So my approach was to be like the furniture or the wallpaper and hope that the teacher wouldn't see me. Still, I liked school and always liked my teachers, even the ones that had fun with my blushing. When I decided to become a teacher, I knew my shyness was going to be a problem, but I figured that I could pass my blushing off as a permanent sunburn.

personality transformation

"Something happened, though, when I became a teacher. I began to notice a change when I was student teaching, and once I had my own class, it was quite clear: I'm a different person in my class. I feel very outgoing, almost to the point of being aggressive. Also, I've discovered that I'm a ham actor. And what a stage my classroom is! I love it. My students seem to love it, too. It seems so odd that after all these years of trying to be invisible, now I'm discovering a whole new side of myself."

Administrators: Mixed Bag and Many Hats

As elementary and secondary school students, most of us had pretty simplistic notions of administrators. The superintendent was a vague presence we occasionally glimpsed in the hall talking to one of the staff or in front of a microphone on ceremonial occasions. The principal was much more a part of our school lives as someone beloved or feared, and occasionally both. Even though the principal was near at hand, our student's-eye view was rather one-dimensional. The principal represented AUTHORITY. In all but the rarest instances, the principal stood directly beyond the teacher, supporting the teacher and the system. When, as students, we went to the principal's office, it usually meant we were in trouble.

The Multiple Roles of the Principal

New teachers' relationships with their principals are not so simple, however. School principals loom quite large in the lives of beginning teachers, and the teacher-principal relationship (and relationships with vice principals, department heads, and master teachers) is many-faceted. The principal is, first, a *colleague,* a fellow educator joined with you in the common task of bringing civilization to the young. You are both professionals. You are both part of a common tradition. You probably share common goals (such as improving the educational opportunities of children) and attitudes (for example, that people engaged in the important work of educating the young need more support from the public than they receive).

principals as colleagues

Principals are the *official leaders*. They make decisions, or act as the funnel for the decisions of higher authorities. Decisions made by teachers or students are normally checked with principals. Principals speak for the school community to the superintendent, the press, and the local citizens. Nothing is ever quite "official" unless the principal has been involved.

as leaders

Principals are *helpers*. They can dispense information and materials, and, as experienced teachers, they are sources of tips, shortcuts, and helpful suggestions. Principals also visit classrooms and ordinarily hold conferences with teachers. They are there to aid beginning teachers who are encountering difficulties and confusion.

as helpers

Principals are *policymakers*. A school system is a bureaucracy whose long arm extends from the state commissioner of education, to the local district

as policymakers

You Know You're in Trouble When . . .

- You have threatened that if there is one more sound in the classroom, you will personally call every parent to complain—and you hear a sound.

- The principal asks you what you plan to be doing next year.

- You have your students correct their own tests and the lowest mark in the class is 96 percent.

- It is 10:15 and the class has ripped through three-quarters of the work you have prepared for the day.

- You return after being sick for three days and the students chant, "We want the substitute!"

- It feels like February and it's only late September.

- The teacher across the hall comes in and offers to show your kids how to behave.

- The parents of eleven of your students ask to see the principal and you are not invited.

- Unsolicited, your principal offers to write a recommendation for your placement file.

- You are convinced you have finally come up with challenging and interesting work for your class, and when you present it they chorus, "We did that last year."

- After sitting in your class for five minutes, your supervisor starts to look at the clock.

- You walk into your usually noisy classroom and immediately all the students get in their seats and smile at you.

superintendent of schools, to the individual school principal. The long arm is, in fact, educational policy, the ideas that are supposed to direct what happens in a school. Principals, in effect, act on behalf of the bureaucracy by introducing teachers to the policies and monitoring the policies' implementation. In addition, principals often set their own policies unique to their school building, such as discipline and dress codes, assembly activities, and a character education program.

as crisis managers

Principals are *crisis managers*. When something happens that a teacher cannot handle, the principal's office is where he or she naturally turns for help. A principal needs to know about crises in the school to try to deal with them effectively.

as facilitators

Principals are *facilitators*. Schools run on things: pencils, books, paper, heat, hot lunches, sanitary toilets, lights, construction paper, petty cash, and keys. It is the principal's job to keep teachers supplied so that they, in turn, can carry out the aims of the school.

as dispensers of rewards

Principals are *reward dispensers*. Principals assign classes to teachers, deciding what kind of children they will teach and whether the children will be at the level or in the subject for which particular teachers are prepared. Principals can also give or withhold compliments on teacher performance and give or withhold extracurricular duty assignments.

as judges

Principals are *judges*. Principals make the decision about a new teacher's qualifications to teach in their school and later decide whether or not the teacher's performance merits rehiring him or her. After all, first-year teachers are neither permanent members of the faculty nor permanently certified members of the teaching profession. Principals can write recommendations for or against teachers. They can enhance or destroy people's reputations as teachers. This role of judge is one that new teachers often don't appreciate until it is too late.

as buffers

Principals act as *buffers* between teachers and angry parents (or, occasionally, angry students). Teachers can be quite vulnerable to public attack. Parents hear tales from their children or from other parents and, if they have a question or a complaint to make against a teacher, often go directly to the principal, not to the teacher. The principal is the official "complaint department." This is a delicate position, requiring the principal to be open and responsive to complaints and at the same time support the position of the teacher involved. Such situations call for the skills of high diplomacy.

as sacrificial lambs

Finally, principals are the *sacrificial lambs*. Like new teachers, principals do not have tenure in their role. If the community, the teachers, or the school board become dissatisfied with what is going on in a particular school, the school's principal is vulnerable. No one suggests replacing the students! The tenured staff cannot be dismissed (except under very special circumstances). Thus, the principal, who may or may not be responsible for the reported problem, is likely to be chosen to pay the penalty. The ease with which the principal can be dismissed is, incidentally, a characteristic shared with beginning teachers.

multiple roles

The need to wear all these hats makes for a complicated existence. Today's school principal has a most difficult job, and to do the job well requires the strengths of a field general, a philosopher, a psychiatrist, and a saint. In light of the general shortage of these strengths, it is not surprising that new teachers sometimes find themselves in conflict with their principals. Principals have to make many quick and difficult decisions, frequently with insufficient information or time, and they are sometimes wrong. When principals observe in teachers' classrooms, they may appear to be there as *helpers,* but they cannot put aside their role as *judges*. At some time in the future, they must make recommendations about teachers to their superiors, and they obviously are influenced by what they have seen during their "helping" observations.

Therefore, confusion and potential conflict between the administrator and the new teacher may be expected. For one thing, beginning teachers often do not know how to work in a bureaucracy (that is, make it work for their ends) and sometimes are antibureaucratic, or overly critical and complaining. This can lead them into direct conflict with their administrators, whose job is to train beginners in bureaucratic procedures but whose primary responsibility is to make sure that the school, as a totality, runs smoothly. Amid these many roles the administrator plays, slippage and breakdown can occur. The following account illustrates such a case.

different priorities

CASE STUDY Steve Mellonwood/Junior High Social Studies

"During the special orientation meeting for new teachers, the principal told us all that whenever we have a problem we should come and see him. He didn't expect us to be perfect, and he felt his major job was to help new teachers. Later that week, he stopped me in the hall and warmly repeated his offer of help. I really took him at his word. So in early October, when I started having trouble planning and finding materials, I just went to see the principal. He was very cordial and, although he talked a lot about himself, he did give me some fairly helpful advice. I went to see him for three short visits. Just talking the problems out seemed to help. I started finding good materials, and my classes really improved. I felt I was really doing well, and I couldn't wait to get to school in the morning.

"Then, in early December, I started getting treated in an odd way by some of the senior teachers. They were always asking me whether or not they could help. Sort of like I had some incurable disease, and could they get me a glass of water. It was weird. Finally, I asked two of them in the lunchroom, 'Why all the concern?' Well, it came out that the principal had told them that I was having 'big trouble,' and he had told a number of the senior teachers to do what they could for me. He had not been in to observe me once. Later in the year he came in for two brief observations (to conform to minimum standards in our district), and he never had time for a conference. He did, however, write up supervisor conference reports. They were lukewarmish and had no specifics. He did mention in both reports that I was improving and overcoming early problems. What improvement? What problems? All he had to go by was what I told him. I got so mad that I wrote him a note to the effect that my self-reported problems had cleared up some time ago and that I felt my teaching was better than his report had indicated. I could see the handwriting on the wall, though. I started looking for another position, and got one without too much trouble. I liked the kids in my first school and many of the teachers. Somehow, though, early on I put myself in a box for the principal, and he wasn't going to let me out."

error of first impressions

An error of first impressions can also work the other way: the administrator who seems severe and distant can turn out to be warm and supportive, as described in the following case.

CASE STUDY **Victoria Klarfeld/Fourth Grade**

"Quite honestly, I was afraid of Mrs. Kelly when I first went for interviews. She seemed so businesslike and talked so much about high standards that I was sure that even if I got the job, I'd end up disappointing her. And after a few weeks with my fourth-grade wigglers, I was afraid I'd never get them to settle down and work on tasks. I was wrong on both counts. The kids settled down—some too much, so that now my biggest problem is getting them excited and alive. And, boy, was I really way off on Mrs. Kelly! She is a jewel! She has so many ideas and gives them to me in the nicest way. I never feel I have to use her suggestions, but in fact I think I've used every one.

solid professional support

"But what has meant the most is that she has treated me like an adult, a professional. Here I am, right out of college, and she is asking my advice about assembly programs and what to do about the cliques in our school. She has also made sure that the other teachers don't leave me out of things. I'm the only new teacher in the building this year, and they sometimes forget me. Mrs. Kelly has a great way of weaving me into things.

"I got very overtired and generally strung out after the Christmas vacation. I was depressed about my teaching and how little time or energy I had for any kind of social life. One day Mrs. Kelly intercepted me on my way to the lunchroom and took me around the corner to a sandwich shop. She knew exactly what was wrong with me and got right to the point, giving me super tips on how to organize my time and plan more efficiently. She even started me on a vitamin program that seems to give me much more energy. She has been terrific to me. She's made the year for me."

As the case above indicates, principals (and others who have supervisor responsibility over the beginning teachers, such as department- and grade-level chairpersons) can be a crucial source of professional expertise and moral support. In addition, research shows that supportive administrators actually help teachers to become reflective and solve their own problems.[3] But new teachers need to be proactive and not wait for the help to come to them. Among the potential kinds of help that administrators or supervisors can provide are the following:

types of help from administrators

▶ They may have valuable advice on dealing with specialized problems, such as an extremely reticent student.

▶ They can put you in contact with specialists in your building or elsewhere in the school district to help you on a range of issues, from curricular matters to dealing with disruptive students.

▶ They may be able to do demonstration lessons or special presentations in your class.

▶ They may be able to come to your classroom, observe you in action, and provide focused feedback on your early efforts to carry out a strategy such as cooperative learning.

While we suggest you seek help from administrators and supervisors, we also urge prudence. Do it honestly, directly, and somewhat sparingly.

Peers: A Mixed Blessing

New teachers are vulnerable to many outside forces and also to their own insecurities. If a supportive administrator can turn a potentially disastrous year into a year of growth, a beginning teacher's professional peers can be even more influential in the process of learning how to teach and how to survive in the classroom. The following example is a case in point.

CASE STUDY   Annmarie Laney/Sixth Grade

"I had a hard time finding a teaching job. I had hoped to teach in my hometown, but there were just no jobs at the level I wanted to teach. The best job was on the other side of the state, and when it became clear that there were no jobs on the local horizon, I took it. I was very excited about teaching; I really felt that I was starting out on an adventure. I was, however, also moving away from my parents. Being so far away from home meant that there were lots of things that were going to be new to me. I had to get a car, an apartment, establish a bank account, and take care of lots of other things, and all at once. It was literally like a crash course in being an adult. And that's what I felt like right from the beginning: an adult. It was so different from college and even student teaching. At my school people treated me like an adult, and they expected me to act like one. For the first months I felt as if I was play-acting at being a grown-up. Well, now I guess the role is comfortable. Or maybe I just have my act down pat.

"Although I made friends with a few people in my apartment building, I was really very lonely at first. I don't think I would have made it without Joan Silver. Joan teaches in the classroom next to mine. She's been, as she says, 'in the trenches' for eighteen years, but she's got more ideas and energy and dedication than any of us fresh troops. Joan was a lifesaver for me. She took me under her wing even before school started. She has been a source of ideas and a source of great materials and a source of inspiration. And she has never made me feel like a taker or a leech. And, actually, *I* taught *her* some things. That's one of the reasons I admired her so much. She really wanted to know about the new ideas I had learned in my education courses, and she put a lot of them to work in her class.

emotional support

"I guess we talked every day after school. A lot of the time we just spent the hour after school laughing. A couple of times the janitor came in thinking there was something wrong, but what he found was the two of us broken up with laughter. And about once a month she would drag me home for dinner. Joan always seemed to know when I was a little low, and that's when she'd insist that I come home with her for dinner.

"There's so much to learn in the first year, and not just about subject matter. Important things—like how to get information from the school secretary and how to stay on the right side of the janitor—that you can never learn in education courses. Joan was my guide on everything from how to fill out my planbook to which memos from the front office I had to pay attention to and which I could put in what she called the 'circular file.'

"It seems funny to say this, given the fact that Joan is twenty years older than I am, but I really think she's my best friend. She certainly has made this year a terrific one for me."

What Can the New Teacher Expect?

If you are worried about being isolated in your classroom with twenty-three third-graders who can't seem to fit into that terrific reading center program your cooperating teacher demonstrated so well for you during your student teaching, never fear. There is help on the way—at least if you are going to teach in California, Kentucky, Mississippi, Wisconsin, and several other states, plus a number of school systems, that have made a major commitment to the induction of new professionals.

For twenty years, California has been a leader in professional teacher induction programs. Our most populous state expects to hire over a quarter-million teachers in the next five years to teach its 6 million students. To launch them on their new careers, California has a statewide mentor program (with an annual budget of $80 million) and a new Beginning Teacher Support and Assessment Program (annual budget, $75 million). These programs are targeted at first- and second-year teachers and are closely geared toward helping new teachers to help their students reach the newly adopted statewide student achievement standards. Underlying these programs are two building blocks: the development of a common language about teaching between new and veteran teachers and a common set of thirty-five scales to describe teaching, aptly called Descriptions of Practice. These scales are

Well, in California, You Can Expect $5000 Worth of Help!

quite specific and observable, and therefore form the basis for down-to-earth discussions of how to improve classroom teaching.

As you can see from the numerous references and suggestions throughout this chapter, we strongly believe that your fellow teachers, your new colleagues, can be a tremendous source for your growth and development as a professional. In fact, they can be a gold mine of tricks of the trade on issues such as how to get students' attention and how to keep it; how to use your new school's PCs when you're MAC trained (or vice versa); how to lead a discussion and actually take it somewhere; how to organize your classroom for effective learning; and how to get those three girls in the back to stop giggling and passing notes. While your own initiative in getting to know your fellow teachers is important, the advent of programs for new teachers is good news indeed. More than just tea and sympathy (or a stapler and an aspirin), these new programs hold the promise of dramatically altering the rocky roller-coaster life of first-year teachers.

Source: Margaret Olebe, Amy Jackson, and Charlotte Danielson, "Investing in Beginning Teachers—The California Model," *Educational Leadership,* 56, no. 8, May 1999, pp. 41–44b.

colleagues more accessible than principals

Although there is increasing cooperation among teachers and greater access to specialists and aides, for the most part teachers work independently, in their own classrooms and with their own students. When they are engaged in their professional work, they typically are isolated from one another. However, although administrators are the official source of support and help for beginners, fellow teachers are a much more accessible and less threatening source of support. As the preceding case illustrates, a teacher's colleagues can be a powerful influence, especially in the beginning. They can be an ever-ready source of ideas and teaching tips, and can initiate the newcomer into the customs of the school. Like Joan Silver, a peer can be an inspiration and show by example what the phrase *teacher as professional* means.

KEVIN: *Are we in danger of giving the impression that all teachers struggle through an unhappy survival?*

JIM: Come to think of it, we probably are.

KEVIN: *Then we ought to correct it. Many teachers are quite skillful when they begin their careers. They have enough ability and training to perform at a high level of competence.*

JIM: As a matter of fact, I have known a few.

KEVIN: *Yes, so have I. The only problem for the ones I have known was that some of the older teachers became jealous.*

JIM: Yes, teachers share human nature, too.

On the other hand, other teachers can have a negative influence, undermining a beginning teacher's idealism, lowering his or her standards, and offering no help at all. The teachers' lounge is sometimes the venue for serious disillusionment. Many teachers use the lounge to "unwind." Unwinding often involves harsh criticism of students, mockery of administrators, and negative comments about teaching. Although not especially different from similar "off-camera" remarks in hospitals and businesses, such comments in the teachers' lounge can blunt the new teacher's idealism and enthusiasm. The lounge is a source of much learning for beginners, but in some cases the private side of colleagues can be a rude awakening for them.

possible negative influence

Although we strongly believe that the teaching profession has a larger percentage of dedicated, selfless people than any other profession (except, perhaps, the ministry), it also has its share of rogues and fools. Beginners should pick their way carefully among this field of new colleagues.

Instruction: So Much to Learn

Ultimately, a teacher's only real problem is his or her students' failure to learn and to develop. All other conflicts, triumphs, and defeats pale in significance if the children are learning and developing their human potential. The degree of the children's success as learners is the best measure of a teacher's success or failure. Although the closeness of the relationship between a teacher's instruction and a student's learning is frequently overstated, this relationship is crucial. Teacher effectiveness is an area in which there are few naturals. New teachers generally have much to learn in this area of instruction.

children's success most important

One major difficulty is the sheer newness of the role of teacher. After a little student teaching, you suddenly find yourself totally immersed. You are in charge of your own class and responsible for taking it from the first day of school to the last. One particularly vexing problem for the beginning teacher is the search for effective curricular materials, as the following example illustrates.

In this class, a new teacher's creative lesson on DNA is paying off in student interest. (© Bob Daemmrich)

CASE STUDY   Betty Dewey/Third Grade

"The overriding question of this year has been 'What works?' I'm in a constant search for materials. It is never-ending. My kids aren't especially brilliant, but they devour material and look at me as if to say, 'Well, what's next?' Our school's curriculum guide is only five years old, but it is terribly dated. The students know a lot of the stuff already. They learned it in lower grades or just picked it up. They are bored by a good bit of the rest, too. I'm constantly squeezing ideas and tips from the other third-grade teachers. They are helpful, but they are in the same boat I am. Sometimes I get a big buildup on a particular workbook or special unit by a teacher who had fabulous success with it. I try it and I fall on my face with it. Then there are the kids. They are so fickle! A couple of times I took their suggestions on things they wanted to study and work on. After much work and many late hours, I'd get these classes prepared and the very same kids who were so anxious to make the suggestions couldn't have cared less.

"My school district has curriculum specialists. Some of them are very good, too. Particularly the math specialist. He would give me *too* much material. I'd spend hours deciding about which approach to use to teach ten minutes' worth of material. The language arts specialist was a sweet lady but very rarely available, and most of her ideas were really out to lunch. I was on my own there. When you get right down to it, you have to make the curriculum and the materials *yours* before they are any good to you. Someone else's great materials are nothing until you have made them your own. This is hard to do the first year."

"owning" your own materials

Though the curricular and instructional aspect of teaching can be a thicket of difficulty for many beginners, for others it is very exciting and inspiring.

CASE STUDY Tom Middleton/Middle School Social Studies

"School has always been hard for me. But then again, if the truth be known, I've always worked hard. In high school I really got turned on to history, and I think it was then that I decided to become a teacher. In college I took every history course I could. I was way over the required number of history courses for certification. And I was lucky to teach at a very academic high school as a student teacher. I think I did well, too. At least that's what everyone said. I was really disappointed when I couldn't find any openings as a history teacher. I was getting very discouraged until I was finally offered a middle school job in the same school district where I had student-taught. My first thought was to let it go and wait for a 'real' history job. What they wanted me to teach was social studies. There was some history involved, but there was also a lot of other social science material to teach. What I really wanted to teach were the intricacies of the British parliamentary system and the rise and fall of Oliver Cromwell, and what they wanted was what seemed to me pretty low-level stuff. I was ready to hang it up. I could possibly work for the company my dad works for, or I could go back to school. Well, anyway, I decided I'd give middle school teaching a chance.

"The great surprise of teaching for me was not the kids or anything like that. It was, on the one hand, how little I knew about my strength—history—and, on the other hand, how intellectually exciting teaching in general can be. I had taken dozens of history courses and considered myself a super buff, but I had missed the essential meaning of history. That's what I have been learning these first two years, and it has been as stimulating as anything in my life. Now I feel I'm just beginning to understand the purpose of history and what should be taught. I came to teach and probably ended up learning more than my students.

"Incidentally, I was offered the position I thought I really wanted, a position on the high school history faculty. I turned it down. I couldn't be happier than I am here."

The love of nurturing and observing growth in others is essential to sustaining a life of teaching. This implies that no matter what you teach or how you present yourself to your students, you have to be on the learner's side and to believe that they can and will grow during the time that you are together.

—HERBERT KOHL

relearning one's subject

Students: Friends or Fiends?

Becoming comfortable and sensing that one is effective with children is a major concern for a new teacher. And well it should be: students are the main event! They make the good days good and usually make the bad days bad. The relationship between teacher and students is multifaceted. An important aspect of the relationship is based on how well the students are achieving.

CASE STUDY Edwina Bellatre/Fifth Grade

"I have enjoyed my students this year, probably more than I should have. It was a tremendous kick to have my own class. I was very worried about discipline. I think I jumped on the students so much in the first three weeks that they were shell-shocked until Thanksgiving. But I loosened up, and so did they. I've really liked the whole experience of being a

It's not what the teacher does that's important. It's what the teacher gets the children to do.

—PHIL SCHLECTY

Case Study cont'd

teacher. And I've worked hard. It seems that my whole life this first year has been school.

a moment of panic

"The one real down moment I had came right toward the end of the year. Something one of the sixth-grade teachers said really shook my confidence. She made some comment at lunch about how much fun-and-games was going on in my class. All of a sudden I began thinking that while I was having a great time—and maybe the kids were having a great time—they really weren't learning anything. I tried to think what I had taught them that was really important, and my mind was blank. I tried to think of particular students who I thought had really shown a lot of progress, and I couldn't think of anyone specific. I went around that way for a couple of days, and I got sort of panicky.

realization of student progress

"Finally, almost by accident, I came across one of the student's notebooks, which had all of his work from September, even his diagnostic tests. It was really enlightening. I could almost see the change from week to week in what he knew. The problems became more difficult, but he could master them. His compositions became more interesting, and the mechanics became sounder. His handwriting looked so much more mature. I figured, though, that maybe that was just one student. I asked to look at a few other students' notebooks, and there it was. They had changed. They were different. Not just different, but *better*. And I was an important part of that change."

There can be little doubt, however, that although students are the primary source of a teacher's success, they are also a source of failure. Three areas in particular cause problems: discipline, social distance, and sex. Behind each of these areas of difficulty is an inaccurate set of expectations the teacher holds about children.

changing views of children

One indication of these out-of-line expectations is the sharp change in attitudes people experience as they go through teacher education and into their first years of classroom teaching. Studies have shown that the longer college students stay in teacher education programs, the more positive and warm their attitudes toward students become. But among beginning teachers, positive attitudes toward students drop sharply. In fact, beginning teachers score significantly lower on attitude inventories than students just entering teacher education.

Why does this happen? Before going on, jot down some hypotheses about why beginning teachers' attitudes change in this way.

_____

_____

_____

Sources of a Distorted View

Our experience in working with college students (for more years than we care to report) convinces us that most students who are preparing to become teachers have high ideals in general and become particularly idealistic about children and

"HECKUVA DAY, WASN'T IT, MS. CARPENTER?
NO HARD FEELIN'S?"

© James Estes

education during their preparation. They believe that as teachers they should have warm relations with students, and they want to make the classroom more relaxed and more responsive to the needs of students than it normally is. As college students take more education courses and observe in classrooms, their views of children become more idealistic and, as a result, more positive. By graduation, the rose-colored glasses are firmly affixed.*

idealism

Also, college students have managed to shut out memories of many realities of their own childhood and adolescence. They forget things like the time they joined with the other seventh-graders to put four tacks on Miss Derriere's chair.

skewed view of students

*This analysis does not, we fear, account for the Lundquist Effect, named after our good friend Ernie Lundquist, whom you will hear from later in this chapter in the section on parents. Ernie deviated (as was his habit) from the normal. As Ernie progressed through teacher training, he began to dislike children more and more. By the time he graduated, he had a well-developed distaste for, as he called them, "the little creeps." But having few options and even less imagination, Ernie went ahead and got himself a teaching job. Failing at this, he quickly became an administrator. However, Ernie found sitting in his office quite lonely. The only people who came to see him were the children. As Ernie talked to the children about what his school was really like, he gradually came to like, and eventually love, the little creeps. But, on the other hand, as for the teachers . . .

They blot out all the juicy stories, most of which they knew were untrue, about the young home economics teacher. They forget about how they enjoyed reading (writing?) obscenities about their math teacher on the lavatory wall. They forget how cruel kids can be to kids. Somehow the dark side of human nature recedes from view during teacher education. But fear not: it reappears. Beginning teachers rediscover human fallibility, in their children and in themselves, and all too often the sad result is that their positive attitudes toward children plummet.

Normally, positive attitudes make a comeback, although they rarely regain the heights they reached during the latter stages of teacher training. Nevertheless, the beginner's unrealistic expectations are a great source of his or her problems. And although problems of this kind abound, we will look at just the three areas mentioned earlier: discipline, social distance, and sex.

Discipline

Classroom management, classroom control, or discipline (pick your euphemism) is one of those problems that shouldn't exist. After all, school is an opportunity for children. The teacher works hard to help them. It's simple: the teacher is there to teach, and students are there to learn. Unfortunately, though, things do not work out that way.

students expect discipline

The great majority of schools, whether kindergartens or high schools, are organized with the expectation that the teacher will be "in charge" of the class. You may not like this, and there are things you can do about it. But it is still what is generally expected of a teacher by the children, the administration, and peers. (We will return to this matter of expectations in the section on social distance.) Few (and lucky) are the teachers who do not have to come to grips with their role as disciplinarian.

lack of leadership background

Unaccustomed to Being in Charge   A discipline problem occurs when the expected pattern of classroom behavior is violated. Normally, a breach of discipline is an overt act by one or more students that distracts attention from or interrupts the performance of the task at hand. Few college students have had much opportunity to be "in charge," to give orders, to coordinate the activities of a group of people, or to say such things as "Quiet down" or "Stay in your seat!" In particular, many young women are still somewhat unaccustomed to leadership roles (although this has been changing in recent years). Students, on the other hand, are accustomed to being taught by experienced teachers who know how to control them, usually rather effortlessly.

Students can sense uncertainty and hesitancy in a new teacher. Moreover, school is not fun-and-games for children. They can get restless and bored. (Remember how long the school day was when you were in elementary and secondary school: how long you had to sit still at a stretch and how much you had to do that didn't interest you.) These conditions, plus the potential for friction in any group of so many people, make it almost inevitable that first-year teachers will have some trouble establishing the kind of productive relationship with students that they seek.

Sometimes a little "one-on-one" can clear up a discipline problem.
(© Elizabeth Crews)

As we have implied, many new teachers start out with a rather idealized picture of children as victims. They assume that misbehavior is a result of some condition external to the child, such as a disruptive home life or poverty. Often there is the suggestion that something in the teacher's class provokes or brings forth the problem. If only the teacher would "establish the right environment" or "reach out to the child in just the right way," the problem would be solved. This view is a subset of a larger view that people are not capable of evil, only social arrangements are capable of evil—an idea that had many adherents in education at one time and still has some advocates today. This idea that all children are innately good, combined with the first-year teacher's insecurities and search for approval, makes it difficult for many to deal confidently with their role as disciplinarian.

CASE STUDY Carole Green/Fourth Grade

"I was convinced that a good class was a happy class and that I wasn't going to be like those grouchy teachers I remember from my own elementary school. So, in the first part of the year, I let a lot of small infractions go unnoticed: talking during silent reading period, lateness on assignments, yelling out the window to students on the

faulty assumptions

Case Study cont'd

playground, and the like. It was a little hard on my nerves, but I thought I was establishing an open and creative environment. It soon became clear that it was open, but not particularly creative. In fact, I first discovered reality when a friendly parent suggested that the room was too noisy and disorderly for the children to get their work done. I tried to 'tighten up,' but the students were already used to my 'open and creative' environment. I just couldn't get them to settle down.

"Finally, the straw that broke the camel's back—and almost broke mine—was when the principal came in to observe. The kids behaved horribly. I felt as if they were trying to make me look bad. Whatever their intentions, the situation was not lost on the principal. During the follow-up conference, he was very frank with me, telling me that if I couldn't maintain better discipline, he might have to 'relieve me.' One thing I particularly remember him saying was 'Carole, if you can't *keep* school, you can't *teach* school.' Then he gave me some specific suggestions. Even with those good suggestions, though, I had a very difficult time working my way back in charge and establishing a more civil and orderly classroom."

Kevin and Jim's Guide to the First Day of School

1. *Teach your very best lesson.* Often teachers use the first day for filling out forms, assigning lockers, and essential but boring "administrivia." Such a day can set a tone for the students that this is going to be just like all the other years, like all the other classes. On the other hand, students will be fresh from the summer, carrying renewed expectations that this year may be different. Capitalizing on this attitude with a really interesting lesson will create important momentum for your class. You can catch up on the forms and other items later in the week.

2. *Establish class rules and procedures.* Although a good lesson is most important, getting classroom management under control cannot be stressed too much. On the first day, at least, let your students know you plan to have an orderly classroom with rules that foster respect and a healthy work environment. We do not imply that you lay down the law, but that you let your students know that any group needs to have clear rules and you are open to their suggestions or even codetermination of the rules.

3. *Start learning and using students' names.* As soon as you receive your class lists or rosters, start familiarizing yourself with the students' names. Once you meet your students, start matching names with faces, and, whenever possible, use their names. Nothing signals your interest in them and being on top of the situation like using their names on day 1.

4. *Be friendly but businesslike.* Often the insecurities of new teachers get the best of them. They vacillate between being Mr. or Ms. Nice Guy and Attila the Disciplinarian. The beginning teacher's early commitment to a friendly but task-oriented atmosphere is the key to its realization.

5. *Share with students your vision for the year ahead.* Students want to succeed. Even the ones with a history of difficulty with other teachers want the new school year to be better. Don't tell them how hard they are going to work. Tell them how much they are going to know at the end of the year and what they can do with this new knowledge.

6. *Establish procedures for communicating with parents.* You need parental support, and students want to know whether you'll contact parents about both good and bad events. Tell them you see their parents as your partners, as your coteachers.

Social Distance

Establishing an appropriate **social distance** from students occupies a good deal of a beginning teacher's attention and energy. Like disciplinary techniques, a correct social distance does not come with a teaching certificate or one's first job. Beginning teachers frequently take refuge in the two extremes of behavior. Many hide their insecurities by acting harshly strict and extremely businesslike, sometimes bordering on hostile. Others attempt to be completely "natural." They reject the stiff, "teacherish" image and seek to break down all barriers between themselves and their students. The first extreme, the overly strict teacher, can give rise to long-term difficulties, whereas the "natural" teacher usually has short-term problems.

The problem with playing the role of the overly strict, aloof teacher is that it may become a permanent habit. Acting like a Prussian officer may appeal to a hidden need to make others submissive. Also, one may begin to believe that "a quiet class is a good class."

overly strict behavior

The problem confronting overly "natural" teachers is that their view of natural behavior often clashes with the children's. The students expect their teacher to interact with them in certain recognizable ways; that is, they expect a certain degree of social distance. They are confused or put off when the teacher acts like "one of the gang." The crux of the problem, then, is that the beginning teacher often wants to be a friend or a pal, whereas the students expect and want the teacher to be an adult. Because they are uncertain and striving to be adults themselves, students seek strength and maturity in their teachers. Often they interpret the beginning teacher's efforts at naturalness and informality as weakness.

overly "natural" behavior

CASE STUDY ## Jane Candis/Seventh Grade

"Most of my year was spent alternating between being Wanda the Witch and sweet little Miss Muffet. I started out determined to be different from all those cold teachers I had had. I was going to be everyone's sweet Big Sister. I really was surprised when this didn't work. The children didn't respond. If anything, they seemed to be confused. Some of them started treating me like their big sister, and I found myself getting annoyed. They became very familiar and started asking me all sorts of embarrassing questions, both in and out of class. The final straw came when one of my boys—one of my favorites, too—came up to me in the hall while I was talking to a senior teacher. Smiling, he patted me on the back and said, 'How's it goin', Miss Candis?' I was mortified.

"After that little incident, I became tough. I was all business. If anyone got close to being familiar, I cut them off at the knees. I really said some nasty things. I was just so uptight that I overreacted. I guess I was hurt that my Big Sister routine didn't work. Later I realized that one reason behind my wanting to be Big Sister was simply that I wanted to be loved, at any cost. I guess my insecurities led me to seek love from my students. Anyway, I spent most of the year going back and forth on this issue—one week Wanda and the next Miss Muffet. It was really a strain, for me and the kids. Finally, toward the end of the year, things began to straighten out and I stopped playing a role. It was much more fun that way. I think everyone was relieved."

first-year insecurities

Sex

teacher-student attraction

Sexual attraction and romance between students, and even between teachers, is alive and well in the American school. And most people recognize this. But the idea of sexual attraction or romance between a teacher and a student wasn't talked about much, at least until the 1990s, when films like *The Election* and the celebrated case of Mary Kay LeTourneau, a thirty-four-year-old Seattle teacher who had two children fathered by a fifteen-year-old former student, brought the issue into the light. Nevertheless, sex between students and teachers generally remains a taboo subject.

Beginning teachers are more likely than experienced ones to confront this problem. For one thing, they are nearer in age to the students. For another, they are often single, new to the community, and lonely. The strain of the new job may increase their need for affection, and this need may find expression in their relationships with students.

In the same way, students often become attracted to their teachers. They sometimes get what is best described as a "crush" on their teachers, becoming emotionally attached to them, greeting them eagerly in the morning and walking them to their cars after school. This too can be a very awkward situation in that the student wants to be treated as special and to feel the affection is reciprocated. If the teacher rejects or embarrasses the student, the student can be hurt deeply.

Besides the platonic attachments teachers can form to young children, a twenty-two-year-old teacher quite conceivably can find a sixteen-year-old student sexually attractive. Thus, as the following account indicates, high school teachers are particularly vulnerable to sexual attraction or manipulation. Our only advice in this area is an emphatic *don't*.

CASE STUDY **Gary Cornog/English**

"In one class there dwelt a fair young creature who found me to be an easily flustered appreciator of her many charms. She was a coquette and, to my way of thinking, a dangerous one. She had me at a great disadvantage. While she could liltingly ask special favors of me (such as my continued toleration of her misbehavior in class), I could not cope with her in anything like a spontaneous way. Unless I was in a phenomenally commanding mood, I could expect to hear such daily entreaties as 'Oh, Mr. Cornog! Mr. Cornog! Could you come here and help me?' 'Mr. Cornog, I just don't understand!' (All this spoken in a voice of tender urgency.) She would have her left arm raised, her right arm aiding it, and would be leaning forward and upward from her desk so that (I thought) I would not fail to notice her finer endowments (I didn't).

"'What is it, Julie?' I would reply, hoping the fear in my heart would not be evident in my voice. It nearly always was.

"'Mr. Cornog, there's something here I don't understand. Could you come here and look at it?'

"*Don't*, I tell myself. *Don't*.

Case Study cont'd

"'Read it to me and I'll explain it.' (*From here,* I almost added, but that would be too obvious.) No. She's getting up.

"'I'll bring it up there.' *flirtation*

"She approaches. She arrives at my left side. I note a scent of lemony perfume; an attempt at makeup about the eyes. She leans over to place the book in front of me, and some of her long dark hair grazes my shoulder. By this time I feel thoroughly unwilling to answer any question regarding syntax. *What about private tutoring?* I hear my lecherous innards suggesting. Heaven forbid! My frustration causes me to blurt a response to her query, hoping that she'll return to her seat. The class by this time has observed me melting into a limpid pool behind the desk. She must be smiling triumphantly above me, her glory reflected in my devastation. If only she had been as innocent of malice in her manipulations as I had been tender in my innocence, then all would have been well. Alas, she was not. She thought it great sport to exercise her arts for the benefit of her friends, and I could think of no way to break the spell. I could not ignore her, because then the class would notice my attempt and think that she had really gotten to me. I could not allow her to continue to dominate me, for then the respect I sought would never appear. Who could respect a hen-pecked English teacher? The befuddled teacher doing battle with the temptress every day—what a tableau! What a cliché. It pained me to see myself in such a humiliating posture. It was so absurd."[4]

Some first-year teachers become terribly discouraged by their relationships with students. Most of us teach because we like young people and want to work with them. When we are rejected or make fools of ourselves, it is painful. Most problems with students are a result of inexperience, and the majority of second-year teachers find that most of their previous problems disappear and they feel very much at ease with their students. Developing satisfying relationships with students usually involves some initial uncertainty. However, previous experience with children as a camp counselor, settlement house worker, or tutor can ease the *experience as authority figure* transition. Contacts with children and adolescents before beginning teaching *helps* help you learn about how you relate best to children.

Parents: Natural Allies with Different Agendas

The parent and the teacher are natural partners. Both are working to help the child become a more fully developed person, and both want the child to be *shared goals* happy, sensitive, intelligent, and well balanced. Frequently, though, the relationship between teacher and parent runs amok and the natural allies become antagonists. Instead of devoting their energies toward understanding and aiding the child, they waste them on conflict with each other.

The great majority of parent-teacher conferences are cordial, constructive, and characterized by mutual respect. Although there may be initial problems of perception or communication, the parents' and teacher's shared interest in the child is enough to overcome these minor blocks. However, problems do develop—and they are not always the fault of the parents.

CASE STUDY Walter Connor/History

"In the late winter, we had our annual parents' night. All the teachers were to work with students on displays and projects. And, of course, we had to get lots of student work up on the board. The drab old school building looked like the Rose Bowl Parade by the big night. We met the parents in our rooms and gave them an overview of what we were doing for the year. I thought I would be nervous, but somehow I wasn't. I was so distracted and fascinated by their faces. I never suspected that they would look so much like their kids! Or vice versa.

"When I finished my talk, I handed out folders of the children's work and told the parents I would be happy to talk with them individually. Most of my students had been doing fairly well, so most of the evening went well. The parents of my two prize ding-a-lings didn't show, an event I greeted with mixed emotions.

"One set of parents hung back. I hadn't met them yet, but I knew immediately who they were. They were Bill Russell's parents. Bill is a great big happy kid. He is not bright, and he is quite lazy. All he likes to do is play his guitar, which he is pretty good with. The only time I have gotten any work from him was during a unit on the Civil War. I persuaded him to look up the folk songs and marching chants of the Civil War. He gave a 'singing and strumming' report to the class. But after that, nothing! Bill was carrying something between a D and an F at that time. Well, the Russells asked a lot of questions, and I stayed with the straight-facts-no-sugar-coating approach, which I was convinced was the right approach. Then Mr. Russell glanced anxiously at his wife, looked over his shoulder to see that none of the other parents was within earshot, and said, 'Tell me, Mr. Connor. We're both college men. My son, Bill: is he . . . you know . . . college material?'

"I didn't know what to say, so I said, 'What do you mean?'

"'We just want to know if we should be saving to send him to college. Is he . . . you know . . . college material?'

"All I thought of was that here was a guy who really wanted a straight answer, so I said, 'Well, no. I don't think so.' Then I looked at Mrs. Russell. I should have looked at her before answering. After the tears came the hostility. 'How dare you prejudge my boy! Admit it, you don't like Bill. You are trying to ruin his chances. We work hard to raise our only son, and then some young know-it-all teacher ruins everything!'

honesty to a fault

"Underneath the hysteria, which subsided in about five long minutes, she was right. I was way off base. I had no right to make that judgment. I had known their son for a half-year in one course that clearly didn't interest him much. I didn't have enough data. Well, I made another appointment with them. During that meeting, I saw that frightening intensity behind their desire to get my class's number-one guitar player into college. Some good things came out of this conference. Bill's work picked up. He actually ended the year with a C. I was the one who learned a good lesson, though. Wanting to be honest doesn't mean arrogantly abandoning good judgment."

The sources of teacher-parent problems are the same as those involved in any human relationship, but encounters are more highly charged than in most relationships. This is to be expected because a child and his or her future are at issue.

The following account of Brenda's mother and a new teacher illustrates some of the dynamics that are usually hidden from view.

CASE STUDY **Ruth Billsbury/Sixth Grade**

"It happened in late March. Ten days earlier, Brenda's mother called me. She said she wanted to talk to me and asked if there was any day that I stayed late at school. She didn't get off work until 4:30 and couldn't make it to school until 5:15. I often worked late at school, and so I made an appointment for ten days later.

"I was curious about why she wanted to see me, and I began to worry. Brenda had something of a reputation in the school. In September, during the teachers' workshop before the opening day, two teachers 'sympathized' with me when they heard I had Brenda Carson. They didn't go into great detail why, and I didn't want to ask. However, I was watching Brenda out of the corner of my eye during those first months, and I guess I paid particular attention to her. In recent months, I hadn't thought much about her—until her mother called.

"Brenda's mother showed up right on time, and after a few pleasantries she said, 'Well, I know you're busy, so I'll come right to the point. Three weeks after Brenda started kindergarten, Brenda's father and I separated. After a terrible on-again, off-again year, we decided to get a divorce. It was hard on both of us, but it was crushing for Brenda. She's an only child. Maybe she blamed herself for the breakup. I don't know. In any event, she went into a kind of tailspin. She was trouble at home, and she's been in trouble in school almost from the moment of the breakup. She's no genius, but she's bright enough to do better than she's done. She just dug in her little heels and wouldn't try. She wouldn't bring books home. She wouldn't do assignments. Every time I asked her about school, her standard answer was "I hate school." Once I got working and my life started to settle down, we were able to make a life together. But the school situation was still rotten. None of the other girls played with her. She was never invited to any parties. I even suggested that she invite one of her classmates to stay overnight one Friday night, and the kid refused. We were both heartbroken.

effects of divorce

"'Then you came along. I don't know what you did to her, but you certainly have turned her around. I sensed it the first day of school. She came home with a funny look in her eye and said, "This year is going to be different. I can just tell." She wouldn't say why, but after a few days I guessed. She was continually talking about you—from what you said to her to what kind of car you drive. Honestly, one weekend when we were out grocery shopping, she made me drive by your apartment, she was so curious to find out what it looked like.

unexpected praise

"'And I guess you know how she's doing in school. I don't think she's missed her homework once. I'm sure she's not your best student, but I know she's doing pretty well, particularly considering the hole she was digging for herself. You look surprised at all this. I figured you might be. Brenda can really keep her feelings to herself when she wants to. But honestly, you have touched that girl in a special place. The difference in her is like night and day. You can't imagine what all this has meant to me. Her pain was my pain, and now it's gone away. Brenda even has friends now.

"'Anyway, I just wanted you to know. I just wanted to see you and to thank you.'

"Brenda's mother was out the door before I could respond. It was so unexpected; I don't know what I could have said anyway. That one event has given me a great, great deal to think about."

Reasons for Parent-Teacher Problems

The two case studies you have just read illustrate a number of reasons that parents and teachers may have a difficult relationship with each other or even fall into direct conflict.

differences in perception

1. *Varied perceptions.* Teachers and parents are quite likely to perceive the same phenomenon in very different ways. The nerve-frazzled teacher perceives a child as a wild, undisciplined, raucous menace. The parents perceive their child as energetic, spontaneous, and sociable. An apparently quiet, shy child may turn out to be a chatterbox in the security of home.

evaluation: a sensitive area

2. *Judgments on students.* Evaluation is another area of difficulty. It is part of the teacher's job to make judgments about a child's performance, a process that can touch on some deep insecurities. It can wound the parents' hopes and aspirations, particularly in this age of anxiety when parents see education as their children's royal road to success. In our competitive society, being average is taken by some as failure. For these reasons, the teacher needs to be especially sensitive when dealing with issues of evaluation and would do well to stay away from judgments such as students being "above average" or "below average" or comparing certain children with other students.

social class and communication

3. *Differences of social class and experiences.* Issues of social distance have been at the hub of much parent-teacher antagonism in recent years. Since most teachers are middle class or aspiring to the middle class, they normally have little trouble communicating with middle-class people. But when they deal with parents from a lower or higher socioeconomic class or a different ethnic group, or both, the potential for communication difficulties heightens. Upper-class parents can look down on public schools and treat teachers condescendingly. Poor parents often have had unfortunate and unpleasant experiences with schools and, as a result, regard them with suspicion. Often these parents speak a different language or dialect than the teacher. What the teacher sees as a humble classroom is to them part of a huge, impersonal bureaucracy. In many urban areas, this impression of the school as a cold, unfriendly, and impersonal institution is supported by the evidence: the school doors are locked, and parents have to pass by police officers and assorted hall guards before receiving a pass to see the head secretary in order to see the teacher. The fact that many lower-class parents, as children, encountered prejudice in schools and found attendance at school more discouraging than helpful makes communication even more difficult.

mothers in work force

4. *Overburdened parents.* Another factor, as we note in Chapter 5, is the changing American family. Increasingly, mothers—who, in an earlier era, stayed home, kept house, and guided their children through school—are joining the work force. Currently, the great majority of women with school-age children work outside the home. The U.S. Department of Labor projects that by the year 2005, 80 percent of married women with children will be in the work force. Usually it is very difficult for working mothers to get off work to meet with their children's teachers or attend PTO meetings and after-school functions that would

put them in closer contact with teachers. Often these events are unwelcome chores in an already stressful life.

5. *The pain of change.* Finally, going to school changes children. School, in fact, exists to help children change in specified ways: to read, to speak a foreign language, to solve problems. And students do change. They master things. They acquire confidence. And they become increasingly independent of their parents. Some parents rejoice at their child's growing freedom from them. For others, this process of independence is painful. Hearing her little girl talk about how much she loves her teacher may arouse jealousy in a mother and cause her to act hostile when she meets the teacher. When a high school student comes home from school with political, social, or religious views that conflict with those of his parents, resentment and confusion can result. Thus, it is not uncommon for a parent to approach a conference with the teacher with a sincere mixture of appreciation and hostility.

students' independence causes pain

Surviving the First Year of Teaching

When one of the authors was about to begin his first year of teaching, his battle-scarred department chairman cryptically commented to him, "Promise yourself today that you will teach a second year." At the time, the meaning behind the remark was unclear. However, after the emotional yo-yo of that initial year had taken a few swoops and plunges, the meaning came into sharp focus. A person's first year of teaching is too unusual, too filled with extremes and emotional highs and lows to provide a sound basis for deciding whether or not teaching is the work on which one wants to spend one's life. Nevertheless, a whopping 30 percent of teachers leave the profession within their first five years,[5] presumably many of them first-year teachers. But statistics do not determine personal fate. Experienced teachers know that a novice teacher can do much to overcome or at least mitigate the problems of the first year of teaching. Andy Baumgartner, who was voted National Teacher of the Year in 1999, summarizes a great deal of valuable advice in his "Ten Commandments for Successful Teaching":

commit for two years

excellent suggestions from an excellent teacher

1. Make learning fun!

2. Enjoy the job of teaching or change your situation so that you will!

3. Speak out positively about the profession! Be honest about the concerns and praise the successes!

4. Look for the rewards in teaching on a daily basis! Give yourself a pat on the back for even the smallest of victories!

5. Care about the students! Appreciate their company! Advocate for their well-being! Treat them with dignity!

6. Stay clear of the watering holes frequented by the "old buffaloes" and the "naysayers"!

7. Don't be afraid to fail! Be willing to constantly try new things and to learn from mistakes!

8. Have a life outside of teaching! Play as hard as you work! Gather family and friends around you for support!

9. Find a mentor and a confidant who is trustworthy, and save all "soul baring" for that person!

10. Persevere and don't give up! In education, there are always second chances!

Let's look at some of these ideas more closely.

Begin Now

start to work on yourself

First, start now to prepare for the predictable events and problems of the initial year. Make a systematic study of your strengths and weaknesses, with an eye toward using those strengths in the classroom and gradually eliminating your trouble areas. For instance, if you have an especially good reading voice, plan to capitalize on it as a teacher. Students from preschool through college love to be read to. On the other hand, if you are painfully self-conscious and shy, develop a plan to overcome this shortcoming. Don't try to defeat your shyness with big, dramatic gestures, such as trying out for the lead in the college play. Take an incremental approach, using small steps. Plan to speak to someone standing in line next to you whom you don't know; volunteer answers in class. With problematic areas like this, but also with your strengths, seek the advice and help of trusted friends, family, and teachers. Realize that your shyness may never completely go away, but you will gradually feel more and more comfortable speaking and working with people if you push yourself to make small advances regularly.

Keep a Teaching Journal

benefits of a journal

A **teaching journal** can be any notebook that is large enough to hold your teaching thoughts and suggestions. Or, if you prefer working at a keyboard, a computer file can serve the same purpose. Although some teachers started such books in grade school when they first decided to teach, the beginning of one's formal preparation as a teacher is a very good time to begin a journal.

A teaching journal can be used to record all the useful ideas and strategies you discover, saving them for the time when you are actually teaching. It can include teaching skills learned in lectures or observed in the field, such as how to grade papers effectively or how to give students evaluative feedback on in-class presentations. In addition, it could include methods of disciplining in different situations, easy and efficient ways to take attendance, ways to present particularly difficult concepts, things to do when students get restless or overexcited, and sources of good curricular materials.

Having such a journal serves two functions. First, the teaching journal is a constant reminder that you are preparing to be actually in charge of your own classroom (a fact that often is not in sharp focus for preservice teachers). Second, the journal can be a lifesaver when you are struggling during the first year. A typical journal entry might look like this:

Tuesday, October 7
9th Grade English

Began the introductory lesson on Shakespeare and the Globe Theater today. The biographical info went over only minimally well. Brian and Mark loudly wanted to know why they needed to know when he was born and died and what difference it made. Some of the other kids looked bored as I went into my spiel, and I realized I was probably lecturing too much.

Next time I should review my information that I present, and figure out what's important for them to know and what's extraneous. Just because I'm fascinated with it doesn't mean that it's all appropriate or necessary for a ninth-grader's introduction to Shakespeare. Also, maybe some sort of question-answer sheet about Shakespeare would work better and get more involvement from the kids.

On the bright side, they all seemed to love the Globe Theater model. They really liked the way it opened, showing the cross-section with all the various stage areas. Brian and Mark were among the most interested in the model. The kids also seemed to be able to follow along on their photocopied drawing of the Globe. Jon and Elizabeth (who usually aren't impressed with anything) told me that it was "pretty cool." The next time, maybe I'll start with the theater and allow more time for them to explore it.

Besides offering professional advantages, the teaching journal can be a valuable personal record. One twenty-year teaching veteran in Massachusetts has kept a journal about his teaching experiences throughout his career. He finds that it has "captured the moment," recording what he was thinking and experiencing as he taught throughout the years.

An alternative form of this idea is to develop a card file of "teaching tips," either with index cards or in a similar computerized format. This file of tips can provide quick, easy reference for planning or problem solving.

The Proper Frame of Mind

It is important to have the right frame of mind during your first year of teaching: that of someone who is untested and who has a great deal to learn. Humility is a virtue that has been all but drowned out in our modern, "We're Number One" culture. Zen masters and teachers of the spiritual life urge the beginner to assume an attitude of submissiveness before what is to be learned. Not weakness, but humility. Many new teachers strive hard to *avoid* humiliation, not realizing that a humble person cannot be humiliated. Instead of assuming a false confidence, one can acknowledge that there is much to learn and open oneself up to that learning.

cultivating humility

Making use of this suggestion is somewhat tricky. The humble frame of mind we are urging is one of alertness and quiet observation of your new context, expecting difficulties of some sort but being quietly confident that solutions will

POLICY MATTERS!   Teacher Induction Programs

What's the Policy?

Recently the issue of special help for new teachers is becoming an important question for many local school districts and state legislatures. Every job has a break-in period, a time when the beginner learns the ropes and makes the connections between theory and practice. Adjustment and adaptation are the watchwords of life in the new workplace. Teaching is no exception. School districts and state legislatures are looking for ways to provide help for new teachers in a programmatic way, rather than individual experienced teachers lending a hand to newcomers.

How Does It Affect Teachers?

Most of the new programs and those on the legislative drawing board include mentoring assistance and targeted in-service help designed to augment formal teacher preparation, helping beginners to make the link between what they learned on the campus and the very concrete world of their new classrooms. Experienced teachers are affected as well, because they are often cast in the role of mentor.

What Are the Pros?

Programs that offer special help for new teachers represent a major opportunity for the teaching profession to ensure that beginners are not swamped and discouraged, but rather are given the opportunity to make a smooth transition into their chosen occupation.

For years the plight of the new teacher has commanded attention in the educational press and journals. Experts estimate that 30 percent of all new teachers leave the field within their first five years, and that many of these are one- or two-year teachers. Systematic help for new teachers could help reduce the loss of early-career teachers. In addition, students will benefit if their teachers get the help they need to do an effective job on their first assignments.

What Are the Cons?

Among the issues surrounding special help for new teachers are three, in particular: first and foremost, that old favorite, money; second, who gets the special help; and third, who gives the special help.

▶ *Money.* The costs of new teacher assistance programs are typically between two to five thousand dollars a year per teacher. And, while that may seem like a fine investment, there are arguments on the other side. First is the competing-options argument. A district that adopts a new teacher training program may be choosing to forgo a new swimming pool or banks of computers in every classroom. Or, the state legislators may want to use those same funds for special education or a new statewide testing initiative. Second, there are those who worry about "wasting funds" on people who are "just passing through." They cite the 30 percent new teacher turnover statistics, arguing that it is more prudent to spend precious staff development monies on those who represent a long-term investment.

▶ *Who gets the help?* Most of the teacher assistance programs now being considered were conceived when teaching positions were scarce. They were designed to help graduates from teacher-preparation programs make the transition from the college classroom to leading their own classrooms. Now new teachers are a scarce commodity and school districts are forced to hire people with little or no teacher preparation. The in-service programs are becoming "on-site and in-flight" substitutes for unprepared teachers. For example, a Greater Los Angeles school district, Montebello Unified schools, recently came to the realization that of the 160 new teachers in its new professionals support program, only 19 had regular state credentials.

Policy Matters! *(cont'd)*

▶ *Who does the helping?* This issue can become a political football. Ideally, the best person to help a new teacher is a master teacher, experienced at the same grade level or in the same subject area, and who has talent as a teacher of teachers. In the actual world of schools, however, it does not always work out that way. Being designated a mentor teacher or having special responsibilities to help neophytes is both a professional honor and a professional plum. And plums are not always distributed on merit or worth. Among the alternative fruit distribution methods are:

- having those in power (superintendents, principals, supervisors, or school board members) decide;

- having the local teachers union decide and thus be tempted to hand out assignments to the most loyal members or those with the most seniority;

- having a faculty member in a particular school building decide, which runs the possibility of turning it into a popularity contest; and, finally,

- having the new teachers themselves select, which, among other problems, could again fall into the popularity trap.

While everyone seemingly wants to see new teachers succeed, the issue is hardly an educational policy slam-dunk.

What Do You Think?

1. In the arena of competing educational dollars, how high a priority would you put on support for new teachers?

2. Do you believe that these new teacher support programs should focus on the most needy, even if they become end-runs around regular teacher education programs?

3. Specifically, where do you believe that you, as a beginning teacher, will need the most help?

Source: Jeff Archer, *Education Week,* March 17, 1999, pp. 1, 221–222.

---

come. In a way, the new teacher should be like a good apprentice: working hard, eyes open, asking questions, and being eager to learn everything possible about the craft.

Find a Mentor

A first-year teacher can have no greater gift than a good **mentor,** an experienced teacher who is willing to act as a guide and confidant through the first year. Besides all of the information and tips that a mentor can give you, a good mentor is an interpreter-guide on what is essentially foreign turf. A mentor can tell you which pieces of paper from the principal's office need to be responded to immediately, who has the formal power and who has the real power, what the administrators emphasize most in teacher evaluations, and which teachers are most willing to share ideas and which ones are not. Perhaps even more important, a mentor is a friend. Seventy percent of teachers who have been mentored claim that the experience significantly improved their teaching. On the other hand, only one in five teachers reports having received such guidance.[6] However, in recent years many school districts have developed special arrangements to help beginning teachers. Some have special induction programs, some have mentor programs, and some have both. In situations where there is no induction program or a mentor is not assigned, we urge you to find a mentor on your own.

values of mentor

Home-school communication at its best!
(© Michael Newman/
PhotoEdit)

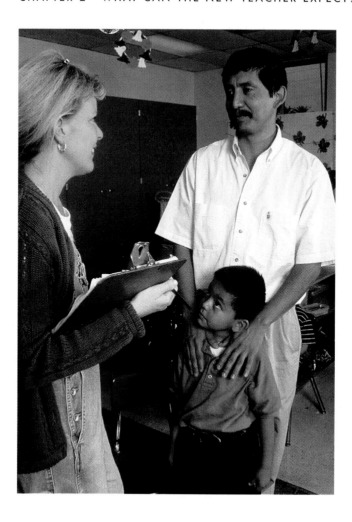

Make Your Students' Parents Your Allies

We suggest that all teachers, but particularly new teachers, take a very proactive, positive approach to parents. Instead of having them get to know you indirectly through the often distorting eyes and mouths of their children ("My new teacher, Miss Sniddly, hates me. And besides, she can't teach. How come I got stuck with a new teacher?"), help them to get to know you and what you will be doing with their children this school year.

establish communication with parents

One way to do this is to prepare a short statement to be carried home and signed, introducing yourself to parents and outlining your major goals for the year. Stress that you and they are in a partnership to help their child have a productive year. Further, let them know how to get in touch with you and that you are looking forward to meeting them. One new first-grade teacher we heard about sent a letter with a snapshot of herself to her first-graders and their parents once she received her class list in the summer. She wrote a little about herself, told them some of the things they would do during the coming school year, and (for the parents) explained her approach to teaching. Besides being exciting for the students, this technique helped the new teacher start the year (and, more important, finish the year) with her students' parents as strong allies.

A second suggestion is that once you have established disciplinary and homework policies, a copy should be sent home for parental sign-off.

Third, on the first day, get the home and office telephone numbers of each student's parent or parents. The fact that you possess these valuable bits of information will not go unnoticed by your students.

Fourth, it is a good idea to call all parents early in the fall. In particular, call the parent(s) as soon as a student appears to be falling behind, tuning out, or misbehaving: "Mrs. Tate, this is Philip's teacher. Philip's performance has begun to slip. What can we do to get him back on track?" "Mr. Fisher, this is Kathleen's teacher. Kathleen just won't stop talking in class. It is interfering with other students and keeping her from doing the work she is capable of. What can we do to make this the good year we all want for Kathleen?" The key word in dealing with parents is *we,* as in "What can *we* do?" Phone calls should be made and brief notes sent home for positive reasons as well. Such a "good news" call can make a parent's month!

Finally, if problems persist, insist on a parent visit. There is no surer way to get children's attention than to have them realize they are the reason their parents had to leave work early to come to school. And although this is an upsetting bother for many parents, it is usually worth it because of the positive effect it can have on their child's school experience.

Take Evaluation Seriously

The news that they are to be evaluated by their principal or some other administrator is often a surprise to novice teachers. Even more shocking is the revelation that the related evaluation reports are sometimes the cause of not being rehired.

Typically, it is a major job responsibility of principals and other district administrative personnel to visit systematically and evaluate the performance of new teachers. Depending on the district and the conscientiousness of the administrator, this can take place anywhere from once to a dozen times during the first year. Usually, though, there are three or four evaluative visits, followed up closely by feedback conferences during which the administrator goes over his or her observations. Together these evaluative visits play an important part in the school district's decision to rehire the teacher or terminate his or her employment.

preparing for and responding to feedback

It is important, then, for new teachers to understand thoroughly how their work will be evaluated. Before you accept a teaching position, be clear about how and when your work will be evaluated. Most school districts have an official evaluation and feedback form, and you should know this well. If the evaluator gives you advance notification of a visit, prepare for the occasion. Find out from your mentor teacher what the administrator really stresses in teaching. And do your best. If the evaluator raises issues or makes suggestions for improvement, take them seriously. You do not necessarily have to agree, but you should not casually ignore the issues. In most cases the comments are legitimate, and the new teacher should strive to repair or strengthen the area that was criticized.

Take Care of Yourself

physical health

One of the greatest surprises of full-time, fully responsible teaching, as opposed to student teaching, is how tiring it is. Teaching is physically, mentally, and emotionally draining, particularly until one gets conditioned to it—that is, until one gets into "teaching shape." This is true for many jobs. The stress and strain of new employment wear newcomers down and set them up for colds, flu, and other mild ailments. The problem is compounded in teaching because it is such an "in your face" occupation (referring to all those coughing, sniffling, and wheezing faces you encounter every day). A classroom is a magnificent germ factory, with viruses claiming new victims regularly. The teacher who is exhausted, run-down, and staying up late reworking lesson plans and correcting papers is a prime target for whatever is circulating in the environment.

mental health

The stress and strain of a new teaching position also can cause mild depression. In their first year, few teachers are what they had hoped to be. Often new teachers

---

Kevin and Jim's Seven Additional Rules for Surviving the First Year of Teaching
(or Seven Compelling Reasons Why Future Teachers Should Not Try to Resell This Book to the Evil Used-Book Buyers)*

1. *When in doubt, think.* Instead of simply fretting about problems or panicking, use your best tool: your mind. Problem-solve. Try to identify the problem, possible solutions, and what seems best, and then act and judge whether or not that option helped the situation.

2. *Don't look for love in the classroom.* Maybe respect, but not love. Don't even expect to be appreciated—that may not come from your students for ten or twenty years.

3. *Deal with your authority problems before entering the classroom.* Come to terms with the fact that you will be responsible for maintaining an orderly and civil environment, and think about how you will accomplish this feat.

4. *If you are not organized, get organized.* Coping with the planbooks, student papers, office memos, attendance records, grades and report cards, and on and on requires much more organization than many beginners have practiced.

5. *Love thy school secretary and custodians.* Many beginners fail to realize how important the school secretary and custodians are in enabling teachers to do an effective job and how important they are in the "informal communication network" of the school.

6. *Focus on learning.* Many beginners fail to concentrate on making sure their students really learn something and thus have feelings of accomplishment. Students will put up with a great deal of "beginning teacheritis" if they sense they are learning.

7. *Don't—we repeat, don't—get married two weeks before the start of your first teaching job.* For reasons unknown to the authors, each year thousands of new college graduates decide to jump at the same time into two of life's most difficult undertakings: beginning a career and starting what they hope will be a lifelong relationship.

*The authors promise that if you follow these seven rules faithfully, you will survive the first year of teaching. You may even like it! On the other hand, if you do not survive the year, return the unused portion of the book to your instructor for a refund.

are away from their regular support system of family and friends. Having not yet established realistic standards, they really don't know if they are succeeding or failing. A bad class or even one resistant or disrespectful student can emotionally unseat them.

To counter this vulnerability to sickness of body and spirit, new teachers need to give special attention to their health. Instead of getting overtired and run-down, beginners need to take special pains to get enough rest, eat well, and get adequate exercise.

A Final Word

Much of this chapter has dealt with the trials of being a new teacher. Nevertheless, most new teachers have a great sense of accomplishment and are proud of themselves at the end of their first year. They have learned an enormous amount in nine or ten months. Along with the trials, teaching has its pleasures and bright moments, making it a rewarding and fulfilling occupation for most. English novelist Joyce Cary has written that human joy comes not from the great events but from the little, everyday things, like a good cup of tea. The joys and satisfactions of teaching can lie in mundane happenings and small surprises. As a teacher, you may find joy in the following:

▶ Experiencing those electric moments when you can *feel* the children thinking and *see* them making new connections

▶ Watching two lonely kids whom you brought together walk down the hall side by side, now friends

▶ Getting your planbook back from the supervisor with the comment "These are *excellent* lessons"

▶ Finding in your box, on a rainy Friday afternoon, a note written in a childish scrawl: "You are my most favorite teacher. Guess who?"

▶ Shopping downtown and meeting one of your students, who proudly introduces you to her mother as "my teacher," and being able to tell by the mother's response that you are respected in their household

▶ Having a former student call to tell you that he has a problem and needs your advice

▶ Chaperoning a dance and having what you thought was your most hostile student smilingly introduce his girlfriend to you

▶ Hearing in the teachers' lunchroom that your supervisor called you "a real professional"

▶ Being observed by the principal and having your students make you look terrific

▶ Surviving until June, being bone-tired but proud of what you and your kids have been able to do

▶ Cleaning out your desk on the last day of school after the kids have been dismissed and finding a box of candy with a card signed by the whole class

▶ Realizing—be it daily, weekly, or monthly—that what you are doing with your life *really does make a difference*

KEY TERMS

culture shock (32)
social distance (49)
teaching journal (56)
mentor (59)

FOR REFLECTION

1. Think of a time when you experienced culture shock, and try to remember, in as much detail as possible, how it made you feel.

2. Can you remember any beginning teachers you have had who fit the scenarios described in this chapter or got into similar situations?

3. How do you explain the different attitudes toward students of teachers in training and first-year teachers?

4. Where do you stand on the issues of discipline and social distance? Do you believe the school should be concerned with discipline? What is your concept of an effective degree and method of discipline? How much social distance do you believe is appropriate for you?

5. If you were to begin teaching tomorrow and were free to evaluate your students in any way you chose (or not to evaluate at all), what would you do?

6. What do you expect to be the major problems you will encounter as a beginning teacher?

7. What can you do now to begin solving those problems?

FOR FURTHER INFORMATION

Codell, Esme Raji. *Educating Esme: Diary of a Teacher's First Year*. Chapel Hill, NC: Algonquin Books, 1999.
This book is the account of a new fifth-grade teacher in a Chicago inner-city school. Hip, imaginative, and irreverent, the book takes the reader through the teacher's triumphs and travails with students and a particularly dense administrator.

Dollase, Richard. *Voices of Beginning Teachers: Visions and Realities.* New York: Teachers College Press, 1992.

Using the stories of four beginning teachers, the author weaves their voices and insights into an examination of many key themes confronting new professionals.

Kellough, Richard D. *Surviving the First Year of Teaching: Guidelines for Success.* Columbus, OH: Merrill/Prentice Hall, 1999.

Designed specifically as a survival guide for beginners, this manual is filled with practical tips from first lessons to conducting conferences with parents.

Pitsco's Launch to Lesson Plans. World Wide Web site at http://www.pitsco.com

This web site offers a wealth of information for new teachers, particularly for lesson plans and teaching ideas.

"Supporting New Teachers," *Educational Leadership* [special issue], 56, no. 8, May 1999.

This special issue has several articles focusing on the plight of first-year teachers and how schools can help them get over their initial difficulties.

What to Expect Your First Year of Teaching. World Wide Web site at http://www.ed.gov/pubs/FirstYear/index.html

This web site is an excellent resource for beginning teachers. It combines many of the practical tips and much of the advice in this chapter with several resources helpful to beginning teachers.

Wong, Harry K., and Rosemary T. Wong, *The First Days of School: How to Be an Effective Teacher.* Sunview, CA: Harry Wong Publishing, 1998.

This handbook abounds with tips and strategies to help the new teacher get a strong start through motivation and minimizing discipline and the other problems that plague new teachers.

3

What Is a School and What Is It For?

In this chapter, you will look at the nature and purposes of schools and hopefully get a renewed sense of the life that goes on in schools. In addition to deepening your understanding of your own schooling, you will encounter several models of schools with different characteristics and purposes. This chapter emphasizes that

▶ Education is a large, all-encompassing endeavor, whereas schooling is simply one aspect of education.

▶ The purpose of school determines much of what happens in school. You can determine the aims of school by reading formal statements of purpose and relying on your own experiences in and observations of schools.

▶ You can define schools by comparing them with models, or abstract representations of reality.

▶ Schools are cultures and therefore play a critical part in passing on a society's values to the young.

▶ Research is giving us more accurate answers to the age-old question "What is a good school?"

What is a school? This may not sound like a profound question; in fact, it probably seems rather tame. School is an everyday thing. We have spent vast stretches of our lives there. Much of what we are—intellectually, socially, and emotionally—can be traced to our experiences in school. School is just . . . school. However, behind the familiar words and images lie thorny issues that have baffled theoreticians and practitioners of education for years. Quiet communities have been split into warring camps because of their inability to agree on an answer to this question. Let us see if *you* can answer the question "What is a school?" In the space below, jot down a definition or two of *school*.

_____

_____

_____

_____

_____

_____

Your reaction to this question reflects who you are and what your experience with school has been. Perhaps you responded in one of the following ways:

▶ A school is an agency that weans children from the protective warmth of the family and trains them for what society has decided is useful work.

▶ A school is a place where they fix your mind so you think like everyone else.

▶ A school is where children fall in love with learning.

▶ A school is a tax-supported baby-sitting agency.

▶ A school is a place where young savages have a chance to become civilized by engaging the world's most precious wisdom.

▶ A school is a place where we explore who we are and how we can become full, creative human beings.

▶ A school is a fun place.

▶ A school is a tax-supported institution where the dead wisdom and worn-out skills of the past are force-fed to the young.

▶ A school is where education takes place.

Each of these descriptions says a great deal about the school experience of the person who formulated it. Our conviction is that your definition of *school* is a cognitive map that greatly affects how you think about schools. Again, reflect on your definition of *school*. What does it say about you and your past experience?

Education and Schooling

It has been quipped that today children interrupt their educations to go to school. The distinction between schooling and education implied by this remark is important. Like school, education has myriad definitions. We have sprinkled a few such definitions here and there throughout the book for you to sample. Before we go further, though, we should look at the two concepts in more detail.

Education

definition of education

For the moment, let us say that **education** is a process of human growth by which one gains greater understanding and control over oneself and one's world. It involves our minds, our bodies, and our relations with the people and the world around us. Education is also characterized by continuous development and change. The end product of the process of education is learning.

takes place everywhere

Education is much more open-ended and all-inclusive than schooling. Education knows few bounds. It includes both the formal learning that takes place in schools and the entire universe of informal learnings, from hooking a worm on a line to burping a baby. The agents of education can range from a revered grandparent to the guests on a late-night television talk show, from a child with a disability to a distinguished scientist. Whereas schooling has a certain predictability, education quite often takes us by surprise. We go to the movies to relax and come home with a vivid sense of poverty's corrupting influence. We get into a casual conversation with a stranger and discover how little we know about other religions. Education is a lifelong process; it starts long before we begin school and should be an ongoing part of our entire lives.

> *All of us have two educations: one which we receive from others; another, and the most valuable, which we give ourselves.*
>
> —JOHN RANDOLPH

Schooling

definition of schooling

In contrast to education, **schooling** is a specific, formalized process whose general pattern traditionally has varied little from one setting to the next. Throughout the country, children arrive at school at approximately the same time, take assigned seats, are taught by an adult, use the same or similar textbooks, do homework, take exams, and so on. The slices of reality that are to be learned, whether the alphabet or our governmental system of checks and balances, usually have been mandated in advance. Finally, schooling tends to be limited to the young. Many people, including numerous teachers, administrators, and parents, are attempting to forge new practices and expand this standard understanding of schooling—a topic we will return to later in the book, especially in Chapter 13. As of now, however, schooling remains a formalized process following certain patterns that tend to be similar throughout the United States.

> *I have never let my schooling interfere with my education.*
>
> —MARK TWAIN

The Role of the School

Schools are created for the express purpose of providing a certain type of educational experience, which we call the *curriculum*. The curriculum, to be discussed more fully in Chapter 8, represents what a community believes young people need to know to develop into good and productive adults—or, at least, it includes what the school policymakers in a particular community believe young people need to know. In effect, the curriculum represents a social bet. It is what the older generation thinks the young will need to live well in the twenty-first century. If the curriculum turns out to be a losing bet, the individual and social consequences are severe.

curriculum as a social bet

Teachers receive preparation and are employed to fulfill the purposes of schooling as defined by the curriculum. In simpler, premodern societies, when a boy could learn to be a man by following his father around and imitating the men of the village and a girl could learn to be a woman by doing the same with her mother and the other women, schools were not necessary. Formal schooling became a social necessity when the home and the community were no longer effective or competent at training the young through informal contacts. Most modern societies have realized that education is too important to be left to chance. Whereas important things are sometimes learned on street corners, and grandparents often are excellent teachers, the formal educative process is simply more reliable. There are nagging doubts, however, that herding youngsters into school buildings five days a week is the most effective way to educate our children.

Keeping the differences between education and schooling clearly in mind is often particularly difficult for the people who should be most sensitive to them, that is, teachers who "do" education "in" schools. People enter teaching because they wish to educate others. They may be committed to a particular educational philosophy. Usually, however, the everyday experiences of working in a school cause their allegiances to shift from abstract educational ideals to the network of personalities and ideas surrounding the particular schools where they teach. They become invested in schooling, in the way things are—the routines of homework, quizzes, and detention—and, to varying degrees, they forget education. For this reason alone, it is important for the teacher to keep alive the questions "What is a school for?" and "What is my contribution to this child's or this class's education?" But more on this topic when we get to examining your ideas and philosophy of education in Chapter 10.

Discovering the Purposes of School

By distinguishing between education and schooling, we may have clarified the question "What is a school?" but we have not yet answered it. We need to think further about the goals of a school. The following sections describe some ways to search out a school's purposes and functions.

Formal Statements

The most direct approach is to read official statements of purpose. Like most institutions, our schools have occasioned many official attempts to explain what they are all about. In 1986, a report sponsored by the Carnegie Corporation, *A Nation Prepared: Teachers for the 21st Century,* reasserted an old theme about American education—the link between education and the common good:

high-level statements . . .

> From the first days of the Republic, education has been recognized as the foundation of a democratic society for the nation and the individual alike. . . . School must provide a deeper understanding necessary for a self-governing citizenry. It must provide access to a shared cultural and intellectual heritage if it is to bind its citizens together in the common will. It certainly must enable the citizens of this Republic to make informed judgments about the complex issues and events that characterize life in advanced economies. . . . The cost of not doing so might well be the gradual erosion of our democratic birthright.[1]

Limitations of Formal Statements   Formal statements such as this one are typically eloquent and valuable, but they are also quite remote from the daily grind of life in schools. They do not help a teacher to select just the right story when students are restless or bored, or to decide how to deal with a distraught child whose parents are in the midst of a traumatic divorce.

. . . versus reality

Finally, statements of purpose may mask contradictory practices. What we say and what we actually do are not always the same. One therefore needs to look beyond the formal statements on paper to see the true, operational purposes of schools. Take, for example, the contradictory messages teachers receive about what to do to help their students. In a study entitled *Teachers at Work,* one researcher describes the frustrations of teachers who are caught between their desire to teach what they feel the children need and the drive by school boards and school administrators to have tangible evidence that students are making progress in areas such as mathematics and reading. One method of stimulating teachers to attend to student achievement is to make the results of standardized tests publicly available. The researcher quotes one teacher who was angered by recent comparisons of achievement scores in local newspapers:

> We just had all the state testing at grades three, seven, and eleven. A year ago, when all this was introduced, it was: "This is to help you better understand what you're doing for the kids. It is not designed for comparison." Yet in the last three weeks . . . all they did was compare. It is extremely depressing to pick up the newspapers and read about schools being weighted by their CAT scores, their SAT scores, when at the same time, we're being told by so-called experts . . . that we have to do more hands-on work with the kids, get out of the schools more. It's the same people saying these things. "Scores have to go up. Get them out in the world." Yet, if I don't have them here and can't sit down and work with them, I can't help them with their skill problems.[2]

Personal Experiences

If formal statements by official groups, even presidential and other blue-ribbon commissions, can be misleading, why can't we simply rely on our own experiences to discover the true nature and purpose of a school? After all, we have all spent a large portion of our lives in schools, and each of us has a rich mental storehouse of ideas and impressions to draw on. Although personal experience is a very important source of data to help us define what a school is, it has two limitations: the uniqueness of the schools that we, individually, have attended and the uniqueness of our own personal experiences in those schools.

limitations of personal experiences

The Variety of Schools   The United States is a huge, continental nation with a great mix of religions, races, and social and economic groupings. For better or worse, our schools vary substantially. Before going further, put down the book and jot down five or six phrases that you believe capture your high school. Then contrast the word picture of your school with these two images:

▶ strong smell of disinfectant and human sweat in the air / gritty sound of chalk scraping blackboard / fear of getting beat up on the way home / drab, greenish paint everywhere / asphalt playground with basketball backboards, but badly bent hoops

▶ bright colors and cheerful, sunny rooms / same alphabet cards as grade school on top of board / knowing everyone—all 105—in the school / bonfire pep rally for whole community before regional football championships / rows of computers in each classroom

Clearly, the authors of these word pictures went to different schools. The first description suggests a rundown school in an urban slum. The second could be a new school in a rural area. The point is that the same word, *school,* conjures up different images in two minds. This is because schools vary so enormously in our country. The resulting difficulty is that since each of us has known a very narrow range of schools, each of us has a narrow range of vision, which constricts our ability to understand fully the purpose of a school.

Our Personal Angle of Vision   Besides our narrow range of vision, there is a problem with the uniqueness of our angle of vision, the way each of us sees and interprets our school experience. For instance, note the differing angles of vision of one seventh-grade history class we once observed. Many students finished the year confused and upset because their teacher had raised serious and unanswered questions about the widespread homelessness and structural poverty in our country. But the teacher felt that unsettling the students and goading them to ask new questions was exactly what should have been accomplished. The principal, on the other hand, thought the teacher was turning the students into malcontents. A foreign visitor observing the class saw a teacher who told the students "so little and asked them too

multiple angles of vision

School is not preparation for life, but school is life.

—JOHN DEWEY

A student volunteer helps out with a reading group.
(© Paul Conklin)

many questions." And parents, who had to rely on their children's perceptions (or secondhand angles of vision), had wildly divergent views of the true purpose of that classroom.

The simple word *school* conjures up a great variety of people, motives, activities, and outcomes. But the narrowness of our experience and the angle from which we perceive it color both what we see in a school and the judgment we make about it. We have to make up somehow for these limitations if we are to really know what a school is. However, the school experiences of people in this country share many commonalities, and we will explore these areas later in this chapter and throughout this book.

Models of Schools

A *model* is a representation of reality. All of us create mental models to help us sort out the sounds and sights we encounter daily and to organize them into sensible patterns. Scientists use theoretical models to predict events and to explain why certain things have occurred. Models can also be useful as we attempt to answer the question "What is a school?" The following paragraphs briefly describe a few such models. As you read, think about how well each model describes the schools you know.

descriptive models

The School as Trainer of the Good Worker   The school's essential task is to turn children into good, productive workers, adults who will contribute to the current economic system. Students are gradually fashioned, like raw material, into the finished product: docile workers. Their teachers are their first real supervisors, who ready them to obey happily and unquestioningly the orders of the "higher-ups." When America was primarily an industrial power, the school was a minifactory, getting students ready to take their place on the production line. Now that we are more and more a service economy (as in "Do you want fries with that?"), students are being trained to be productive workers in service jobs.

The School as Preparer for College   The school prepares the student for more schooling. In particular, the goal of the American school is to ready the boy or girl for admission to college. As a result, the here and now is not nearly as important as the future. Using this model, the curriculum of the secondary school is justified to the degree to which it prepares students to do college-level work. Likewise, the elementary school curriculum is justified to the degree to which it prepares students for success in secondary school. Students' needs and interests are given slight attention because the focus is on the demands of the curriculum at the "next level up."

The School as Shopping Mall   The school, particularly the high school, is a large structure made up of different customer-oriented enterprises, all competing for the student's "business." College-bound students frequent the academic boutiques. Students interested in particular occupational opportunities frequent the vocation-oriented specialty shops. Other students just drift around, casually shopping and socializing.[3] And teachers are the sales personnel, trying to get the student customers to buy their wares.

The School as Social Escalator   In this model, the school is seen as the vehicle by which one rises in society. School is the royal road to economic well-being and social prominence. Success in school is the ticket to the upper rungs of the community. Although athletic or artistic success in school escalates some students to prominence, academic achievement provides the boost for most. Failure or poor performance in school acts as a "de-escalator" for many students.

The School as Social Panacea   Here the school becomes the society's problem solver. If poverty exists or parents are neglecting their responsibilities, the school takes on the problem and acts as a panacea. Whereas schools once were limited to passing on the moral and intellectual heritage to students, schools in this model "do what is needed." Driver's education, multicultural education, sex education, drug education, and AIDS education are all examples of the school attempting to solve new social problems.

Reprinted with special permission of King Features Syndicate.

The School as Developer of Human Potential

The school attempts to ensure that each individual develops her or his capacities—intellectual, social, and physical—to the fullest possible measure. The teachers are specialists in identifying students' strengths and needs and in matching the instructional program to these strengths and needs. The cornerstone of the school is the uniqueness of each child, and the school is designed to be flexible and have a positive impact on the child. By focusing on the individual child, the school runs the risk of preparing self-oriented, highly individualistic students.

The School as Acculturator

The school brings together people of divergent backgrounds who must accommodate themselves to one culture. The school's role in the United States, therefore, is to teach "the American way of life" and to pass on the customs, values, and social patterns of the dominant group to immigrants and others who have been excluded from full participation in this society. According to this view, the school is a melting pot whose function is to minimize the influence of minority ethnic, racial, and religious influences. More about this later.

The School as Family

As the American family weakens, the school helps to pass on to the young the skills and knowledge they need to become effective in the world. The school-as-family model focuses on establishing a caring commu-

AUTHORS' DIALOGUE

JIM: Isn't this something of a simplistic picture?

KEVIN: Simplistic? What are you talking about?

JIM: Describing something as integrated and multifaceted as a school in terms of this model or that model . . .

KEVIN: Well, I'm giving the readers a little credit. They know a model is just a tool for understanding.

JIM: Well, we should put in a cautionary note that these models can't describe an entire school, and that models are not reality.

KEVIN: Okay, that little point may help—but, you know, you are getting very picky.

JIM: It's another one of my charms.

nity in which the child's emotional and familial needs are addressed. More than just a great baby-sitter, the teacher nurtures the students' development not only in the intellectual arena but also in the social, emotional, and moral arenas.

Schools as Cultures

A *society* is a grouping of individuals bound together by various connections. Some of the connections might be shared geographic space or similar racial features. But what really connects people is their shared culture. A *culture* is composed of beliefs about what is right and wrong, good and bad. It also includes the dominant ideas, stories and myths, artistic works, social habits, and organizations of a group. Another key aspect of culture is language and the ways people use it in relationship to one another. Every group of people who live together in relative harmony can be said to share a culture. Someone once defined culture as simply "just the way we are 'round here." Without a common culture, every time we walked into a room or passed someone on the street, we would grope for a way to respond. Our culture tells us what to do.

meaning of culture

All sorts of cultures exist. A family possesses a culture. The U.S. Marine Corps possesses a culture. After a few weeks and months, a college dorm assumes a distinctive culture. And so, too, a school possesses a culture. Think about it. Each school you have attended has had its own culture—a set of beliefs, values, traditions, and ways of thinking and behaving—that distinguishes it from other social institutions and from other schools.

Cultures—including **school cultures**–can be good or bad, leading to good human ends or poor ones. A strong, positive school culture engages the hearts and minds of children, stretching them intellectually, physically, morally, and socially. A weak, negative school culture may have the same type of physical plant, the same teacher-student ratio, and the same curriculum as a neighboring good school, but fail to engage students. Everyone, students and teachers, goes through the motions, but with few of the positive effects that the strong-culture school provides.

Socialization

Since a human being comes into the world vulnerable and "not quite ready for prime time," adults play a crucial role in the child's survival. Besides food, shelter, and loving care, adults pass their culture on to their young. A major part of that culture is the skills and attitudes necessary to function in that particular society. The task of passing on a society's culture to the young is called **socialization,** defined as the general process of social learning whereby the child learns the many things he or she must know to become an acceptable member of a particular social environment. Besides the family and the school, the major socializing agencies in the life of a young person are peer groups, religious institutions, youth organizations, political and economic institutions, the mass media, and, in some cases, work environments. Each of these agencies has its own values, norms, and mores that it attempts to teach so that the individual child will know how to act

POLICY MATTERS!   School Uniforms

What's the Policy?

No issue in education is of greater concern than student behavior or discipline. One of the leading school policy options in this area is the adoption of school uniforms.

In the wake of the Columbine High School shootings in 1999, in which the killers dressed in "Goth" or "trench-coat Mafia" outfits, came a rash of suspensions across the nation over inappropriate dress. The tragedy also fueled interest in school uniform policies. Currently 20 percent of the nation's school districts use uniforms, although most of these districts have a voluntary school uniform policy.

How Does It Affect Teachers?

The way students conduct themselves in school is of intense interest to everyone, whether a parent, an administrator, or a teacher. Many schools, such as those in Long Beach, California, which has had a very successful uniform policy for years, attribute dramatic declines in school violence and misbehavior to uniforms. If students are not distracted by their own or others' misbehavior, both they and teachers are able to spend more time on the teaching and learning tasks that are central to education.

What Are the Pros?

Proponents say that school uniforms offer a concrete and visible means of restoring order and discipline to the schools. Instead of kids fighting one another over designer jackets or the latest hot sneaker, or creating an economic pecking order based on who can afford the "in" clothing, there is greater economic equality since everyone wears the same clothes.

Also, requiring uniforms for public school students appeals to an intuitive belief that increased structure will improve students' behavior, attitudes, and learning. In this country, school uniforms are associated with private and Catholic schools, which are perceived to be more orderly and safe as well as offering a better learning environment than public schools.

What Are the Cons?

Those opposing school uniforms see this policy as un-American, attempting to stifle children's individuality and sense of distinctiveness. They see uniforms as part of a larger move: the "vanilla-ization" of America. Still others see wearing an inoffensive, individually selected outfit to school as a student's right.

Opponents of uniforms can point out that research results are mixed. One recent study of five thousand tenth-graders, for example, found that "sophomores in schools requiring uniforms were no less likely than their more casually dressed peers to fight, smoke, drink alcohol, take drugs, or otherwise get in trouble in schools."

Still, the movement toward school uniforms is building up steam, and much more research will be done to determine its effects.

What Do You Think?

1. Have you had any firsthand experience teaching or observing students who are required to wear school uniforms? If so, what did you observe?

2. Do you favor a schoolwide uniform policy? Why or why not?

3. What do you anticipate future research on this policy topic will reveal?

Sources: Jessica Portner, "Schools Ratchet Up the Rules on Student Clothing, Threat," *Education Week,* May 12, 1999; Debra Viadero, "Uniform Findings," *Teacher Magazine on the Web,* January 1999.

and behave in a manner acceptable to other agency members. Some agencies, such as the school, are formally created and organized, and some, such as the peer group, are informally created and organized. Every school attempts to socialize children by getting them to value those things the school teaches both explicitly and implicitly. The more successful students tend to accept these values, whereas many of the less successful ones reject the ways of thinking and behaving that the school tries to teach.

What students learn in the environment of the school extends beyond the planned curriculum of courses or subjects they will take. The planned content and objectives of language arts, mathematics, science, and all the other subject areas available to students constitute this **formal** or **explicit curriculum.** In Chapter 8, we will look at what schools generally intend students to learn from this curriculum. But classroom observers have noted that the schools also teach an **informal** or **implicit** (or **hidden**) **curriculum** through which the classroom and school, as learning environments, socialize children to the values that are acceptable to the institution and to society at large.

formal and informal curriculum

What are these values, and how are they communicated to students? One researcher suggests that schools value several specific ways of thinking and behaving.[4] One is compliant behavior as opposed to personal initiative. Students soon learn to give the teacher what she or he wants or expects. Reward systems used by schools teach students to "read" both the teacher and the system to determine just what is expected to get the grade, the teacher's attention, or the sticker with the smiling face. Similarly, competitiveness is learned through the examples of athletics, grading systems that compare students to one another, and ability grouping to separate students into classes according to their achievement. The many ways in which students learn what a school values include how the school allocates time to subjects of study, the rules established for the school, and even the architecture of the school.

Perhaps the greatest of all pedagogical fallacies is the notion that a person learns only the particular thing he is studying at the time.

—B. BRADFORD BROWN

As future teachers, you should work to be able to *read cultures.* What rules of behavior, rituals and ceremonies, and accepted patterns of teacher and student interaction are communicated to students at these schools? Does the "climate" of the classroom and the school suggest warmth, support, and nurturing of individuals, or do observers describe a mood of disinterest, regimentation, and antipathy among staff and students? And, most important, what is the school's deeper message about what stance its students should take toward the current culture?

reading school cultures

Schools as Transmitters or Re-creators of Culture

Underlying the various models of school discussed earlier are different purposes and therefore different curricular emphases. Two models are especially prominent on the American educational scene: the school as the social institution where the young receive from the older generation the very best of their culture and the school as the social institution where the young learn skills and become agents of social change.

Transmitting Culture

In the model of the school as acculturator, schools exist to advance society by ensuring that the young know and appreciate the dominant ideas and values of their society's culture. The goal of cultural transmission in the American public schools is to teach the American way of looking at the world and the American way of doing things. Without even being conscious of it, our teachers instruct our young in our version of reality and our way of handling the real world. And so, too, do the schools of other countries. Schools in northern India, for instance, differ markedly from those in Ghana, and both have sharp differences from their counterparts in the United States. However, the schools of each country are attempting to perform a similar function: to transmit the unique culture of the country to its newest members, the young.

schools reflect culture

This desire to ensure that the young share the common culture may explain why in many U.S. school systems we teach American history in the third grade, the seventh grade, and again in the eleventh grade. It can also explain why, for instance, we give little attention to the history of China, even though China is the most populous nation on earth and has one of the world's oldest and richest cultural heritages.

Acculturation and Diversity   Several dangers lurk in this tendency of schools to concentrate on transmitting the dominant culture. If schools offer the young an understanding of only the prevailing culture, the result may be an attitude of smug cultural superiority, which frequently leads nations and individuals to foolish actions. In cultural terms, what we do not know we frequently do not respect, and without mutual respect people easily become enemies.

need to understand other cultures

In recent decades, instantaneous electronic communications, missile-delivered nuclear weapons, and interdependent national economic structures have increasingly made the world a global village, and our students must learn how to function in this new world.

arrival of new cultures

Moreover, in recent decades the United States has experienced an enormous immigration from Southeast Asia, the Middle East, Central America, and elsewhere. These new Americans tend to be young. They and their children are hungry for education. Although they are eager to learn American ways and American culture, teachers and students need to be respectful of the cultures these students bring with them. Indeed, the presence of new Americans can be a valuable resource in the effort to increase multicultural understanding and appreciation. Therefore, although American schools need to transmit American culture, we must realize that what we call "American culture" has always embraced many cultures. We will return to this thorny issue when we discuss multiculturalism later in the text.

Reconstructing Society

Some of the issues just mentioned—including the threat of terrorists with nuclear weapons, a highly interdependent world economy, large numbers of immi-

Where in the world is Lisbon, Portugal?
(© Elizabeth Crews)

grants, and the hunger, suffering, and social injustices rampant in our modern world—have led some educators to the view that schools must become the tool of social reconstruction. They envision a school that acts as a leaven to the society. Instead of seeing schools as places where the collective wisdom of the past dribbles down to those who have the capacity and interest to make use of it, these educators assume a much more active, even assertive role for the school.

school as social leavener

These **social reconstructionists** see the school forming the young into agents of change and also participating in the decision about how society needs to change. They have little reverence for the accumulated wisdom of the past and more concern for the world's problems and the necessity to create a new order. They see the successful student not so much as a cultivated person but as an autonomous citizen ready to join with others to tackle the world's ills and help in the reconstruction of society.

But even among social reconstructionists, there is a wide range of emphases and views. Social reconstructionists fall into two broad categories: one we will call *democratic reconstructionists* and the other *economic reconstructionists*.

In the course of history, education has served every purpose and doctrine contrived by man. If it is to serve the cause of human freedom, it must be explicitly designed for that purpose.

—GEORGE S. COUNTS

Democratic Reconstructionists   **Democratic reconstructionists** see the solution to certain trends and current issues, such as racism, poverty, and the destruction of the ecosystem, in an aroused and skilled citizenry.[5] The school's mission, then, is to prepare students for vigorous participation in their government. The focus of schooling is on developing knowledge of democratic processes, critical thinking skills, and group process skills so the student can fruitfully work with others for social improvement. In more active programs, students actually select, study, and work on a community environmental problem, such as the polluting of landfills with unrecycled garbage.

Economic Reconstructionists   **Economic reconstructionists** tend to take a harsher view of the dominant culture and see schools as the pliant servants of those in power. Instead of humanistic institutions attempting to free individuals from their own lives' limitations, schools are institutions operating for the economic powers-that-be. The influence of corporate values is seen in many phases of school life, from the way textbooks are used to our widespread use of testing.[6] Because of their deep suspicions of—and sometimes outright disgust with—capitalism, economic reconstructionists are often called neo-Marxists.

Paulo Freire

One noted economic reconstructionist is the Brazilian educator Paulo Freire. Freire's first book, *The Pedagogy of the Oppressed,* describes his work with poverty-stricken, illiterate peasants in his native Brazil.[7] As Freire tried to teach these adults to read, he saw they were trapped in an economic and social web over which they had little control. He saw, too, that the normal mechanisms of education, such as grading and control by the teacher, imposed on the peasants passivity and subservience to authority. For Freire, the typical methods and routines of schooling are a form of oppression in that they keep people from becoming fully human. To counter this, Freire taught literacy by helping the peasants to (1) name their problem (such as polluted water supply), (2) analyze the problem (sewage contamination of the springs), and (3) collectively take action (design and build a new sewage system) to solve the problem. In this manner, education becomes a tool both to develop the human potential of people (such as the ability to read) and to free them from oppressive conditions (lives of poverty and disease).

Although both democratic and economic reconstructionists focus on social problems and try to foster in students the attitudes and skills necessary to solve them, the economic reconstructionists question more deeply the fundamental economic and social arrangements in a society. They see education as a necessary means for restructuring the power structures in a society. For them, money, power, and control of education are tightly bound together. Critics of the social reconstructionists' approach to education see it as naive and wrong-headed. Our current economic and social relations, the critics emphasize, are too fragile and serious to be toyed with by children.

critics of social reconstructionism

As we gingerly enter the new millennium, a relatively new concept of the world as a highly interrelated and interdependent community is emerging. The Cold War concepts of ten or so years ago have been replaced by globalization, a new reality brought on by peace, free trade, the Internet, and an explosion of life-changing technologies. National borders are being ignored by global economic partnerships, and ancient and modern cultures are being integrated in new ways. We have all seen advertisements showing a Tibetan weaver with a cell phone and Bedouin camel drivers with laptops. This is the face of globalization, and increasingly our students need a larger understanding of culture than simply a North American one.[8] They need to be educated in terms of this global interconnectivity, clearly drawing on the best ideas of the past, but also to be ready to address the fresh demands of a new world. For our educators, that is a big job!

the new globalization

What Do Studies Reveal About the Nature of Schools?

Researchers often look at the everyday events of human life and see patterns of which the rest of us may be only vaguely aware. In the next several pages we present a few of these studies, focusing first on elementary schools, then middle schools and junior highs, and finally high schools, and examine the patterns the researchers noticed.

Life in Elementary Schools

One of the best perspectives on how time is usually spent in the elementary classroom is provided by Philip W. Jackson's classic study *Life in Classrooms.*[9] Anthropologists have taught us that the humdrum aspects of human existence have cultural significance and that we must look at the most routine events in an elementary classroom if we are to understand what happens there. Are certain trivial acts repeated many times? How often do they occur? What is their cumulative effect on the child? What do they teach the child? Jackson's observations of elementary school classrooms show how revealing the answers to these questions can be.

Jackson's study

Have you ever figured out how many hours a child spends in school? In most states, the school year is 180 days. The day typically begins at eight-thirty and ends at three, a total of six and one-half hours. Thus, if a child doesn't miss a day of school, he or she spends over a thousand hours in school each year. Including kindergarten, the average child will spend over seven thousand hours in elementary school. How are those hours typically spent?

You may think first of the curriculum—so many hours of reading and language arts, so many hours of mathematics, science, play, social studies, music, art, and so on. But what do students really *do* when they are studying these subjects? They talk individually, to the teacher, and to one another. They read silently and aloud. They yawn. They look out the window. They raise their hands. They line up. They stand up. They sit down. In short, they do a number of different things, many of them commonplace and trivial. To understand why some of these things happen, we first need to look at what the teacher does.

The Teacher's Role Jackson has observed that the elementary school teacher engages in as many as a thousand interpersonal interchanges each day. The teaching-learning process consists, for the most part, of talking, and the teacher controls and directs discussion. The teacher acts as a *gatekeeper,* deciding who shall and who shall not speak. (One may debate whether or not this *should* be the teacher's role, but clearly most teachers function this way.)

controlling discussions . . .

The teacher also acts as a *dispenser of supplies.* Since both space and resources are limited and the number of students wishing to use them at any one time is likely to be greater than the supply, the teacher must dole them out. A related function is the *granting of special privileges* to deserving students: passing out the milk, sharpening pencils, taking the roll, or operating the videocassette player. Although little teacher time is involved in awarding these special jobs, they are

. . . supplies, privileges

important because they help to structure the classroom socially as a system of rewards and punishments.

. . . time

Timekeeping is another teacher responsibility. It is the teacher who decides when a certain activity ends and another begins, when it is time to stop science and begin spelling, and when to go outside for recess. In some schools, the teacher is assisted in timekeeping by bells and buzzers that signal when a "period" is over. As Jackson observes, things happen because it is time for them to occur and not because students want them to.

result of crowded conditions

All these teacher functions can be seen as responses to the crowded conditions in the classroom. If the teacher were dealing with one student at a time in a tutorial situation, gatekeeping, dispensing supplies, granting special privileges, and timekeeping would not be necessary. But since a tutorial setting is not possible, much time and energy are spent keeping order. The resulting atmosphere has unavoidable effects on the students. What are some of the consequences for students in crowded classroom conditions?

What Students Experience   One inevitable outcome for students that results from the teacher's "traffic management" functions is *delay*. Since students' actions are limited by space, material resources, and the amount of teacher attention they can command, there are definite limits on their freedom in class. In addition, since the class ordinarily moves toward a goal as a group rather than as individuals, its slowest members often determine the pace of progress.

waiting

Waiting is therefore a familiar activity for elementary school children—waiting in line to get a drink of water, waiting with arm propped at the elbow to be called on to answer a question, waiting to use the scissors, waiting until others have finished their work to go on to the next activity, waiting until four other students have finished reading aloud for a chance to do so.

denial of desire

Denial of desire is another common experience for the elementary student. A question goes unanswered, a raised hand is ignored, talking out of turn is not permitted, relief of bodily functions is allowed only at specified times. Some denial is necessary, and some is probably beneficial, but one thing is certain: delayed gratification and denied desire are learned in school, and a certain amount of student frustration is bound to develop.

interruptions

Students also experience frequent *interruptions* of many sorts—interruptions of seatwork by the teacher to give additional instructions or to clarify one student's question, interruptions when messages from the principal's office are read aloud to the class, interruptions for fire drills, interruptions when the teacher is working with one student and another student misbehaves, and so on. Students are expected either to ignore these intrusions or to quickly resume their activities. The emphasis on an inflexible schedule contributes to the sense of interruption by making students frequently begin activities before their interest has been aroused and stop at the height of their interest when the schedule dictates that they must begin another task.

social distraction

A related phenomenon is *social distraction*. Students are often asked to behave as if they were in solitude when in fact they are surrounded by thirty or so other people. During assigned seatwork, for example, communication among students

Waiting and delayed gratification are frequent occurrences in elementary school classrooms.
(© Elizabeth Crews)

is often discouraged, if not forbidden. To be surrounded by friends, sometimes seated across from one another at a table, and not be allowed to talk is a difficult and tempting situation. As Jackson remarks, "These young people, if they are to become successful students, must learn how to be alone in a crowd."[10]

Delay, denial, interruption, and *social distraction,* then, are characteristic of life in elementary classrooms. How are children affected by these classroom facts of life? It is difficult to measure their effect because they are present to a greater or lesser degree in every classroom. Also, different students have different levels of tolerance for these phenomena. It would seem, however, that the student who either possesses or quickly develops patience would find school more tolerable *patience is a necessity* than the student who lacks it. The ability to control desires, delay rewards, and stifle impulses seems to be characteristic of successful students, whereas less successful students exhibit less patience and more impulsiveness.

Life in Middle and Junior High Schools

We know much less about the routines and roles of students and teachers in the *little descriptive information* middle grades than we do about those in elementary grades. One reason is that educators have been somewhat late in focusing on students in the middle grades. However, in the late 1980s, several reports emerged identifying the needs of early adolescents and recommending some educational remedies for students in the middle grades. They do not, however, provide comprehensive descriptions of what actually goes on in the middle grades. Perhaps, though, the most obvious

many grade configurations

issue is the variety of grade-clustering patterns evident in our schools. A national survey of middle-grade practices and trends found that schools around the country enrolled seventh-grade students in about thirty different grade spans. For example, some schools were structured to educate all students in grades K–12; others served primarily elementary and middle grades, such as K–8; and yet others served middle to high school students, such as grades 7–12. Some schools were structured just for students in the middle grades, but even within this group there was great variety. "Middle schools" mainly contained students in grades 6–8, but also in 5–8, 5–7, and 6–7. Other schools were strictly "7–8" schools. And another grade configuration of "junior high" schools structured students in grades 7–9, 6–9, or 5–9.[11]

What difference does it make where students in the middle grades are educated? Researchers at Johns Hopkins University found direct relationships between grade configuration and such important educational characteristics as school goals, report card entries, course offerings, instructional practices, relationships between students and staff, and other trends in middle-grade practices.[12] One factor related to the organization of middle grades was size. In the various schools examined, enrollment in grade 7 ranged from 5 students to more than 2,250. Consider for a moment the very different educational experiences these students will have in their middle school years in regard to familiarity with peers, class size, teacher contact, and so forth.

varying school sizes

School goals were also examined across different grade configurations. Regardless of the grade span of their schools, most principals identified mastery of subject matter and basic skills as the most important goals at their institutions. However, secondary goals of educational importance varied by the school organization. As might be expected, principals of K–12 schools assigned more importance to higher-level skills such as reasoning, problem solving, and creative thinking. Principals of K–8 schools put less emphasis on personal growth and developmental issues, such as self-esteem and self-knowledge, than principals of middle schools.[13] Though students in the middle grades are being educated in each of these types of settings, it becomes clear that the educational goals and expectations of students in the middle grades are greatly influenced by the organization or grade configuration of the school.

varying school goals

The goals that schools set for students influence middle school education in other ways as well, including the curriculum offered and the instructional methods used. The same study found that schools serving younger students (K–8, for example) typically offered fewer elective courses, such as home economics or keyboarding, for students in the middle grades. Seventh- and eighth-grade teachers used drill practices more frequently and made less use of higher-order thinking activities such as writing essays, using computers, and discussing controversial issues. These schools, however, also reported greater use of such methods as peer- or cross-grade tutoring.[14]

Another distinction among schools of different grade configurations was seen in staffing patterns. Classroom structure for students in the middle grades varied from completely self-contained classrooms, in which one teacher taught one group of students all major subject areas, to completely departmentalized schools in which each teacher specialized in a single subject area and taught several different classes of students. As you might expect, schools serving younger students (K+) had a larger percentage of self-contained classrooms, whereas middle schools showed a greater percentage of departmentalized staffing.[15] Teachers also differed by type of licensure held. Teachers with secondary licensure were more likely to be "subject matter–oriented," and middle-grade students who were taught by subject-matter "experts" showed higher levels of achievement. On the other hand, teachers who were licensed in elementary education were likely to be more "student centered" and tended to focus on both the academic and personal development of individual students. The research indicated that relationships between students and teachers in self-contained classrooms tended to be more positive.[16]

staffing patterns

licensure patterns

So we see a variety of educational experiences occurring along a number of dimensions in the middle grades. Is one means of educating students in the middle grades best? Probably not. The many aspects of diversity we have just examined—from grade configuration to school goals to teacher orientation—appear to present a series of trade-offs in educating students in the middle grades. What is consistently being identified as important for educating students in the middle grades, however, is that the developmental needs of early adolescents must be acknowledged and considered in developing and organizing programs.

Life in High School

No aspect of our public educational system has recently received more study than our high schools. This is probably because we are worried about our teenagers and dissatisfied with the educational experiences we are providing them. Nevertheless, the studies, some of which are hardly new, provide fresh insights into how students and teachers live and carry on in our high schools. For instance, in 1983 the Carnegie Foundation for the Advancement of Teaching released a study intended to guide discussion about needed reforms in American secondary education. In this investigation of fifteen supposedly unique schools, the researchers found striking commonalities among them.[17] Typically, a school day is divided into six or seven 50-minute periods (although in recent years, high schools around the nation have been experimenting with a wide variety of class-time structures). Hall passes, dress codes, and rules against smoking are often part of

high school similarities

life in a high school. From most principals' points of view, absenteeism, class cutting, and parents' disinterest are moderately serious problems; fights, thefts, and vandalism are less serious problems.[18] High school is a place where young people experiment with growing up, find the support that may not be available at home, and attempt to accomplish a variety of goals ranging from marking time to finding social acceptance to preparing for intellectual challenges. While some high schools have departed from this picture, this description still fits the great majority of our schools.

Multiple Purposes   Tracing the history of the high school, Ernest Boyer, the lead researcher in the Carnegie study, concluded, "high schools have accumulated purposes like barnacles on a weathered ship."[19] Americans seem to want high schools to accomplish everything. The resulting confusion of goals is evident in the variety of goal statements adopted by the states for their schools, in the written goals found in teachers' manuals or school district curriculum guides, and in teacher and student responses when asked about school goals.

multiple goals

In an attempt to accomplish these multiple purposes, high schools have developed a comprehensive curriculum with many elective courses. How do students decide what to take and what not to take among dozens or, in some cases, hundreds of courses? Students report that their choices are guided more by parents and peers than by guidance counselors or teachers.[20] Boyer and his colleagues conclude that students' academic programs may be shaped most decisively by the "tracks" in which they are enrolled. *Academic* tracks stress the traditional subjects—English, mathematics, science, and foreign languages—as preparation for college. A *general* track usually allows a greater number of elective courses and less rigorous versions of the traditional subjects. *Vocational* tracks may include a combination of academic and job-related courses; students in these tracks are preparing for a job after graduation. Because of the variations in courses required for these different tracks and the differing standards for student achievement among them, a high school education can take on myriad meanings.

influence of tracking

The Shopping Mall High School   Another group of researchers suggest that the high schools' characteristics resemble those of a shopping mall, with an emphasis on variety and choice for the consumer,[21] a model mentioned earlier in this chapter. Given a diverse student body with many different interests, high schools have offered a diverse curriculum in an attempt to provide something for everybody. Students are expected to make their own course selections; the schools maintain neutrality in regard to students' or parents' choices among the many alternatives offered. The customer has the final word.

emphasis on variety and choice

Staying with the shopping mall metaphor, the study found that some customers (students) are serious about buying, others are just browsing and looking for ideas on what to buy, and still others are at the mall to meet their friends and "cruise." Faced with customers with such different levels of commitment, teachers reach accommodations or "treaties" that promote mutual goals or keep the peace. For example, some teachers make their deals crystal clear when they advise students, "Don't get into my class if you don't want to work." If students don't want to play by these rules, they don't have to take the course.

classroom "treaties"

Most classroom treaties are not this formal or public, however; rather, they are *tacit* arrangements made to accommodate students and teachers in a manner satisfactory to all. If teachers preach or push too hard, some students resist. To avoid resistance, individual teachers strive to find the appropriate balance in their classrooms between requiring academic rigor and allowing students to opt out of learning entirely. As one teacher commented, "I think I get along fairly well with most of the kids, but to be perfectly truthful I think I get along because I don't put a lot of pressure on them."[22]

Within the shopping mall high school can be found "specialty shops," the niches for students and families wanting more learning and school engagement. These can include top-track programs, special education programs, vocational and technical education programs, and extracurricular programs like band or football. Because the students in these programs have been designated as special, they tend to receive special attention. In contrast, the average or unspecial students are generally ignored by the specialty shops; they do not receive the additional commitment of time, personal relationships, and intensity of learning generally given to specialty-shop students.

specialty shops

Although school personnel were not precise about who the middle students were—using terms such as *average, general, normal,* and *regular*—the researchers concluded, "few characteristics of the shopping mall high school are more significant than the existence of unspecial students in the middle who are ignored and poorly served."[23] These students have no important allies or advocates. Their treaties are characterized by avoidance of learning, not engagement. Schools may try to nurture these students' self-esteem but do not make academic demands on them. As a result, parents of these students occasionally demand a specialty program for their children or transfer them to private schools where purposes are more focused and attention is

Kids may do poorly in school not simply because they aren't motivated to study or because they lack ability, but because they are intent on maintaining their standing in a crowd that regards academic achievement as uncool.

—B. BRADFORD BROWN

more personal. Without these opportunities to experience the purpose, push, and personalization of a specialty shop, the unspecial students become the losers in the educational marketplace.

As one reviewer of this study notes,[24] the researchers' evidence supports generalizations made by previous high school observers. For example, although students may have equal access to a high school education, enormous differences may exist in the opportunities available to them within their schools. "Effective" schooling is marked by a consensus of purpose, high expectations for students, and a supportive climate, and the "treaties" notion of this study emphasizes the power that teachers and students have to negotiate the quality of education. What can schools and teachers do to help *all* students be winners? The suggestions are many, but reading *The Shopping Mall High School* study may provide a starting point for thinking about the problem.

differences in opportunities

Inside Classrooms   What happens in classrooms during those typical six- or seven-period days? In a review of instructional practices in American classrooms, Larry Cuban concluded that the high school of today is *remarkably similar to the high school of the 1890s.*[25] While gathering descriptions of more than twelve hundred classrooms, Cuban examined how classroom space was arranged, the ratio of teacher talk to student talk, the manner of grouping the teacher used for instruction (whole-class, small-group, or individual), the presence of learning or interest centers used by students as part of a normal school day, and how much physical movement students were allowed within the classroom. Cuban found that just as in the 1890s, today's high school classes are characterized by whole-class instruction, teachers talking most of the time while students listen, little student mobility, and a narrow range of activities completed by the entire class at one time.

same as in 1890

The dead might as well try to speak to the living as the old to the young.
—WILLA CATHER

Boyer's classroom observers found similar characteristics. They noted, for example, a standardized use of classroom space: rooms equipped with rows of desks for thirty or more students, a teacher's desk at the front of the rows, and the traditional black or green chalkboard. The use of time is also routine, consumed by procedural tasks like taking attendance and keeping records, although relentlessly interrupted by announcements on the intercom, pep assemblies, photo sessions, and many other distractions.[26] Boyer also describes teachers' powerlessness over the factors that influence the quality of instruction they can deliver: the number of students in a class, the lengths of school days and periods, the formats of report cards, the courses that will be taught, and even the textbooks that will be used. Pressures of time and heavy student loads invite traditional, teacher-centered instruction: lecturing, question-and-answer sessions, and routine homework assignments. Too often, students play passive roles in classrooms dominated by regimentation and conformity.

pressure on teachers

exceptions to the norm

These pictures of life in high school classrooms contrast with glimpses of teachers who challenge their students to think, to express themselves creatively, and to struggle with difficult questions. Students in such classes are pushed to perform as individuals; their teachers share a vision for them that includes high expectations of success. Which picture is more characteristic of high school life? Did the reform movements of the 1980s create conditions in schools that will encourage teachers to teach well in the new millennium? At the time they finished their study, Boyer and his team believed the time was ripe for a true renewal of high school education. By the late 1990s, however, this renewal had yet to take place in most high schools, and new calls for reform were emerging.

A New Call for High School Reform

In 1996, the Carnegie Foundation for the Advancement of Teaching and the National Association of Secondary School Principals released a joint report entitled *Breaking Ranks: Changing an American Institution*. This national study offered many suggestions for improving the quality of American high schools. Among the factors cited for particular attention were personalization, coherence, time, and technology.[27]

Personalization Finding American high schools too large, impersonal, and rigid, the report recommends that high schools break into units of no more than six hundred students so that teachers and students can get to know one another better. Each teacher should be responsible for no more than ninety students each term. Every student should have a "personal adult advocate" who knows him or her well and follows the student's progress throughout high school. No student should be able to remain anonymous, and each student should feel "special" to some adult in the school. Each student should have a "personal progress plan." Just as every student with a disability must have an IEP (individualized education program, described in Chapter 4), a student's progress plan would set learning goals that are continually reevaluated.

personal adult advocate

Coherence High schools should identify the essentials that all students must learn to graduate. Instead of organizing the school by disciplinary departments, the report calls for a reorganization that more closely links the various subject matter areas so that learning makes more sense to students in terms of the real world and the application of what they know. Tests must also be aligned with what is taught so that both are consistent with each other.

connect subjects to real world

Time Flexible, innovative scheduling should replace the fixed fifty-minute periods that dictate the amount of instructional time devoted to each course. The Carnegie unit (the standard type of course credit) should be abandoned or revised so that it no longer equates seat time with learning. Instead, high schools should identify a set of "essential learnings"—in literature and language, math, social studies, science, and the arts—in which students must demonstrate achievement in order to graduate. Furthermore, schools should operate twelve months a year.

identify essential learnings

Technology High schools should develop long-term plans for using computers, CD-ROMs, videodiscs, and other technologies in all aspects of learning and teaching. Each high school should have a technology resource person to consult with and assist the staff.

develop technology use

One thing we can be certain of is that the American high school will continue to be a center of controversy and concern. Worrisome achievement scores and outbursts of violence such as those in the late 1990s will keep public attention focused on this segment of our educational system. Reform, a topic we will turn to in Chapter 13, is in the air.

What Is a Good School?

school as human "product"

First, not all schools are good schools. Second, good schools do not just happen. They are made. A school is the product of people's intellectual and physical energies, and, at any particular moment, the way a school happens to be reflects efforts that have gone into creating and maintaining it. Like towns and civilizations, schools also rise and fall. They are human creations—dynamic and continually on the move.

No school—at least in the authors' experience—is "right" or "good" for all students. But although we believe this is true, we also believe that some schools are strikingly better than others; that is, some schools provide a significantly better education for a much larger percentage of their students than do others. These schools—referred to in the educational literature as **effective schools**—are the focus of this section.

Achievement consists of never giving up. . . . If there is no dark and dogged will, there will be no shining accomplishment; if there is no dull and determined effort, there will be no brilliant achievement.

—HSUN TSU, CHINESE PHILOSOPHER

One major problem associated with this question of effectiveness is what criteria to apply. Effective or good in what dimension? In happy students? In a teaching staff with high morale? In the percentage of students who get promoted or graduate? Who go on to colleges? What kinds of colleges? How many succeed in business or professional life? In athletics? Socially? Ethically? *Effective,* as currently defined in most of the educational research literature, refers to students' achievement test scores in basic skills (for example, reading and mathematics). Although such tests measure skills that are hardly the only objectives of education, achievement in these academic areas is an important and widely acclaimed outcome of schooling. Also, achievement in reading and mathematics is easier to measure than good citizenship, artistic development, or interest in ideas.

Characteristics of an Effective School

definition of effective schools

Beginning over twenty years ago, a number of educational researchers began looking for the qualities of effective schools.[28] Among the most significant characteristics they found to be correlated with high achievement in the basic skills were high expectations for student performance, communication among teachers, a task orientation among the staff, the ability to keep students on task, the expenditure of little time on behavior management, the principal's instructional leadership, the participation of parents, and the school environment.

high, "can-do" expectations

The Teacher's Expectations   Through their attitude and regular encouragement, teachers in effective schools communicate to students their belief that the students will achieve the goals of instruction. In effect, the teachers get across to students a "can-do" attitude about learning.

Communication Among Teachers   Teachers in effective schools do not operate in a vacuum, each in his or her isolated classroom. Instead, they talk among themselves about their work. They converse about one another's students. They know the curricular materials and activities that go on in one another's classrooms. And they are helpful to one another. In short, effective schools have teachers who are good colleagues.

high degree of colleagueship

Task Orientation   The faculties of effective schools are highly task oriented. They begin instruction early in the class period and end instruction late in the period. The staff approach their teaching responsibilities with a serious air and waste little time in class. Whether the classes are formal or informal, underneath the surface of events lies a seriousness of purpose that is communicated to students.

serious attitude

Academic Engaged Time   *Academic engaged time* (or *academic learning time*) refers to the amount of time students are actually engaged in relevant content-related activities. Research has demonstrated a tight link between the amount of time devoted to academic learning tasks and students' achievement.[29] This characteristic involves the ability of a teacher to get students engaged in academic tasks (such as reading or solving math problems) and to keep their attention on these instructional activities.

keep students working

Behavior Management   We have all been in classrooms with teachers who spent huge chunks of time trying to quiet students to get them "on task" or who, in the course of correcting one student, disturbed all the rest, causing a ripple of distraction throughout the room. Teachers in effective schools have learned techniques to minimize the time devoted to managing students. They are efficient both in handling discipline problems and in implementing the learning activities. In addition, these teachers do not routinely resort to corporal punishment, because they use other techniques to deal with student behavior.

maintain classroom order

The Principal   Principals play an important role in effective schools. Instead of being faceless bureaucrats aimlessly shuffling papers, the principals of effective schools are instructional leaders. They have strong views on the purposes of education and are vitally concerned about the quality of teaching and learning in their schools. Still, though, the principal is perceived as democratic in approach and cooperative in relationships with faculty. The effective principal gains teachers' confidence and clearly communicates to them a vision of what the school should accomplish and how each teacher can contribute toward this end.

principal as instructional leader

Parents   An effective school reaches out and draws in parents instead of ignoring them or keeping them at arm's length. Parents are treated as key members of the learning team, as partners with the professional staff in helping their children

parent involvement

Good communication among teacher, student, and parents is key to good teaching. (© Bob Daemmrich/The Image Works)

achieve academic success. In addition to aiding in students' intellectual achievement, the involvement of parents can help to improve their children's self-concepts, work habits, and attitudes toward school.

The School Environment   A school that is unsafe, hostile, and generally unruly is rarely a place of learning—academic learning, at least. On the other hand, an environment that is calm, safe, pleasant, and orderly is conducive to learning.

environment conducive to learning

Different studies often come up with different characteristics. A ten-year study of 140 schools in the Chicago area, which looked for more holistic measures of effectiveness (rather than just academic achievement), came up with a quite different list. Among the characteristics the study found to be associated with successful schools were coherence, good communication within the school community, vital subgroups of teachers (work groups with meaningful responsibilities), a wide range of student incentives (prizes and other forms of recognition), a clear disciplinary policy, and an extracurricular program stressing service to others.[30]

another view

Attempts to answer the question "What is a good school?" are still incomplete, however. The characteristics cited are those identified by several extensive research projects. And studies continue. We have a strong suspicion that a number of qualities besides those mentioned here dramatically contribute to the making of a good school. Among these characteristics are a pervasive sense of curiosity, a passion for excellence, a strong belief in students' capacity to grow, and an environment of kindness and support. Perhaps the reason the research does not demonstrate these as characteristics of effective schools is that there are not enough schools where these qualities prevail.

other possible qualities of effective schools

Nevertheless, it appears that whether one is measuring school effectiveness by test scores on math and reading tests or by the more holistic measures, certain features stand out in the schools that most successfully socialize students to behave in ways that the school values. The principal, faculty, and staff in such schools

▶ Agree on what they are doing and why something is being done

▶ Clearly communicate their expectations to students

▶ Consistently enforce rules

▶ Provide an environment conducive to the accomplishment of learning tasks and the regular monitoring of students' academic progress

The Unfinished Work of the Schools

It is probably clear by now that there is no single satisfactory answer to our question "What is a school?" This and many other questions that we ask in this book are too large and elaborate to be adequately answered here. We pose them and talk about them anyway to aid you in forming your ideas about the issues that lie behind them. It seems unlikely that you can make a good career choice if you lack a fundamental understanding of the institution you are considering entering. And if you hope to survive and be happy within an institution, you will need to know how it works. For example, you need to know what the institution says it is doing ("We are training future workers" or "We are educating well-rounded citizens prepared to excel in college") and what it actually does. You need to know a particular school's expectations of you as a teacher so that you can decide how to respond or if you wish to respond at all. Finally, if you hope to improve the schools—that is, make them better because of your involvement with them—you need to have a realistic view of what is now going on in the schools and develop your vision of what the schools can and should become.

understand your school

We cannot stress enough that schools are human inventions. People bring schools into being for particular social purposes. The overall purposes of schools are to advance the common good and to help people live happy and successful lives. However, if schools are to serve a society, they must at least keep pace with that society. Many people who are concerned about our schools feel that the schools are moving very slowly while the rest of society experiences dynamic change. In effect, the schools are out of step with the society, usually being either

Teachers play an important role in the invention of their school's culture.
(© Elizabeth Crews)

too far ahead (which is the rarity) or lagging behind (the more common situation) the needs of the people they exist to serve.

need for balance

As happens frequently in times of tension, views polarize in the manner suggested in this statement by John Gardner, who was imagining the reactions of future scholars looking back at our age:

> The twenty-third century scholars made another exceptionally interesting observation. They pointed out that twentieth-century institutions were caught in a savage crossfire between uncritical lovers and unloving critics. On the one side, those who loved their institutions tended to smother them in an embrace of death, loving their rigidities more than their promise, shielding them from life-giving criticism. On the other side, there arose a breed of critics without love, skilled in demolition but untutored in the arts by which human institutions are nurtured and strengthened and made to flourish. Between the two, the institutions perished.[31]

Nevertheless, the purposes for which schools are brought into being are still vital. People still desire good schools for their children, and, as you will see later in this book, many excellent ideas are being generated and movements are under way for the renewal of our schools.

Your Challenge

today's challenges

Some readers may be uncomfortable with the idea that it is their job to renew the schools. Many may feel that becoming a good classroom teacher is sufficient.

Teachers, however, are more than technicians in charge of their classrooms. As professional people, they and their colleagues must have a strong and clear voice in deciding how they render their services. It follows that the teacher is not simply responsible for his or her own performance but bears responsibility for the total educational enterprise. To live up to this responsibility requires a deep understanding of the schools and much hard work, but it is the very critical nature of the problems confronting the schools that makes teaching such an exciting occupation today. In the immediate future, education is where the action will be. You have a chance to complete this unfinished work of the schools.

KEY TERMS

education (68)

schooling (68)

school cultures (75)

socialization (75)

informal (implicit or hidden)
  curriculum (77)

formal (explicit) curriculum (77)

social reconstructionists (79)

democratic reconstructionists (79)

economic reconstructionists (80)

effective schools (90)

FOR REFLECTION

1. Can you think of some pieces of information you picked up on the street that you later "unlearned" in school? Can you think of some things you learned in school that your experience later taught you were untrue? Which has happened more often? What is your reaction?

2. To what extent did the schools you attended serve the purposes suggested by the various models we described? Can you suggest any models we have overlooked?

3. Look at the cartoon on page 74. Is it appropriate to any of the models of schools that we have discussed? Does it seem to you an apt comment on your own education?

4. How do you feel about the school as transmitter of the culture rather than of "the truth" or "just the facts"? What are some problems with the school being a transmitter of cultures? What happens if the national government takes a very strong hand in this? What examples from history can you think of in which a government used schools to promote a particularly dangerous culture?

5. How would you describe the cultures of the schools you have attended?

6. This chapter cites several factors that are associated with good schools. Which five factors are, in your opinion, the most important, and why do you think so?

FOR FURTHER INFORMATION

Boyer, Ernest. *Basic School: A Community for Learning.* Princeton, NJ: The Carnegie Foundation for the Advancement of Teaching, 1995.
This was the final book of one of education's great practitioners and spokespersons. Practical wisdom is woven into a clear description of the kind of schools we can and should have.

SEARCH

Eisenhower National Clearinghouse. *ENC Online.* World Wide Web site at http://www.enc.org
ENC is a rich resource of research-based ideas about school improvement and curricular materials for classroom teachers from kindergarten through twelfth grade, particularly in mathematics and science.

Pritchard, Ivor. *Good Education: The Virtues of Learning.* Washington, DC: Judd Publishing, 1998.
Pritchard's book explores the purpose of education and schooling, giving particular attention to the frequently neglected mission of the schools in character and moral education.

SEARCH

Shiney, Lee, and Lajean Shiney. *Teacher's Edition Online: Tools for Teachers.* World Wide Web site at http://www.teachnet.com/
This web site contains many resources for teachers, including links to information on such topics as classroom management, advice to student teachers, attention deficit disorder, drugs and violence in schools, and gangs.

Sizer, Theodore R. *Horace's Hope: What Works for the American High School.* Boston: Houghton Mifflin, 1996.
The third book in Sizer's Horace trilogy, this book embodies the principles espoused by the Coalition of Essential Schools, a reform-oriented association of secondary schools.

PART
TWO

STUDENTS

The makeup of children in America's schools is changing dramatically. Our culture is becoming increasingly diverse, especially in its ethnic and racial composition. About 36 percent of the children enrolled in our schools are minorities, and the percentage increases each year. Children are also innocent victims of many of society's ills—poverty, drug abuse, disorganized and disintegrating families, to name a few—that greatly affect schools' ability to teach youngsters effectively.

As a new teacher, you must understand these social factors because they may affect your own and your students' ability to respond to their intellectual, physical, emotional, and ethical needs. All of these variables make the task of teaching challenging.

Who Are Today's Students in a Diverse Society?

4

In some ways, children never change. The pictures of children in our classic literature are as true today as when they were first written. Look at the conniving, mischievous Tom Sawyer, or the overly curious Alice in Wonderland, or the tenacious Mafatu in *Call It Courage*. These characters are endearing to us in part because we have all known children like them. And yet we are also products of our present society. The world around us shapes our daily experiences and influences our understanding of ourselves. As our society changes, so does the context, the social milieu, in which our children are raised and brought up to understand and form expectations of the world. Children have been called barometers of change. More than any other segment of society, children are affected and shaped by emerging social conditions.

This chapter emphasizes that

▶ Studies of the demographic makeup of the country indicate shifts in ethnic composition.

▶ All children have basic needs. Being aware of and understanding these commonalities helps us understand the diverse needs of students.

▶ Students have many strengths and abilities that extend beyond the traditional emphasis in our schools on linguistic and analytic abilities. Approaches that recognize multiple views of intelligence and differing learning styles emphasize the great diversity in student learning and ability.

▶ Schools address the individual needs of students through multicultural, bilingual, special education, and gifted and talented programs.

- Cooperation between the school and various support agencies, such as community health, child care, and social services, is increasing.

- To cope in today's classroom, teachers must be aware of many dimensions of student diversity.

The children of today are very much like the children of yesterday or the children of tomorrow. Certain stages of cognitive, social, emotional, and physical development have been identified, and a similar progression through these stages occurs for everyone. We all have basic psychological and physical needs that cut across racial, cultural, age, and gender boundaries. Understanding these stages of development and areas of common needs gives the classroom teacher insight into student behavior and so helps the teacher develop appropriate classroom experiences. You learn a great deal about these subjects in your courses in child development and educational psychology.

However, it is also important to be sensitive to the great differences among students and to factors in our society that are directly affecting their lives. In this chapter, we hope to make you more fully aware of the diversity in our society and our classrooms, the range of abilities among your students, and the schools' attempts to address all this diversity. We also hope to make you more deeply sensitive to the sorts of issues, potential problems, and benefits related to this diversity.

Student Diversity

Children in schools are a mirror of society. In public institutions, therefore, many types of diversity will be represented in varying degrees. You will see this diversity in your students along a number of dimensions, including who the students are, what they need, and their various kinds of abilities.

Racial, Ethnic, and Cultural Backgrounds

Students in your classroom are likely to come from a variety of racial and ethnic backgrounds, representing many different cultures and ways of looking at the world. With the development of a richer, more varied society, differences in values and family expectations are more and more evident. For example, some families may place a premium on school and higher education, whereas other families may emphasize early entry into the workplace. But even though you will encounter a range of familial expectations for school achievement, all children deserve the best educational experience they can get while in school. Recognition of racial and ethnic differences can provide the understanding and insight needed for more effective instruction.

racial and ethnic diversity

Diversity in the classroom means that your students will come from a wide range of cultural backgrounds, may speak a first language other than English, and may have a variety of learning abilities and learning styles.
(© David Young-Wolff/ PhotoEdit)

Languages Other Than English

non-English-speaking students

Some of your students may speak a primary language other than English. More than 3.4 million **limited English proficient (LEP)** students are enrolled in public or nonpublic elementary and secondary schools—about 7 percent of the total enrollment—and the number has increased every year for the last decade.[1] Seventy percent of all LEP students are concentrated in the states of California (42 percent), Texas (15 percent), New York (7.8 percent), and Florida (5 percent).[2] About one in seven of the nation's five- to seventeen-year-olds speaks a home language other than English, and the percentage of such young people is growing two and one-half times faster than the general school population.[3] More than 2 million immigrant youths enrolled in U.S. schools in the past decade, many of them non–English speakers. As these children and youth enter schools, most will need to make sense of a new language, a new culture, and possibly a new way of behaving. An important function of teachers and schools is to offer a source of stability for students who are experiencing rapid change in their lives. Some school systems have used teacher aides who speak the child's language to help connect the child and the school. The use of bilingual peer tutors may also help provide a greater sense of stability.

Socioeconomic Status

Students come from families with varied economic, educational, and occupational backgrounds. **Socioeconomic status (SES)** is the term used by the U.S. Bureau of the Census to measure economic conditions of people using the family's occupational status, income, and educational attainment as measures of status. Individuals high in income, occupational prestige, and amount of education are considered to be high in socioeconomic status, and are usually seen by others to be upper-class people who are influential in their communities. In contrast, people low in socioeconomic status are seen as being lower-class people who have little prestige or power. The benefits of being a child from a high-SES family show up in school performance, as such a child typically does much better academically than a student from a low-SES family. Teachers and schools are challenged to help overcome the debilitating effects of low SES on students from these families. This topic is discussed in more detail in Chapter 5.

SES related to school performance

Gender

Boys and girls are different even when they come from the same socioeconomic, racial, or ethnic group. They are raised differently, and often society has different expectations of them. Treating boys and girls equitably as individuals and not as gender stereotypes is a constant challenge for both male and female teachers. We will discuss this topic in more detail when we look at gender issues in Chapter 5.

avoiding gender stereotypes a challenge

Sexual Orientation

You are likely to have gay and lesbian students in your classroom, especially if you teach at the middle or high school level, and you are apt to encounter gay and lesbian parents of students at any level. Schools typically have not been welcoming environments for young homosexuals. Gay and lesbian students have often experienced taunting, harassment, and even violence because of their sexual orientation. As a teacher, you will be challenged to establish and maintain a safe and supportive classroom environment for these and all of your students. See Chapter 5 for a more detailed discussion of this topic.

schools often hostile toward gay/lesbian students

Diverse Needs

Psychologists and educators have identified a number of basic needs that all individuals experience, including needs for belonging, safety, and self-esteem. However, students in your classroom will develop at different rates and probably will display *diverse needs*. Students will also bring their own individual histories, backgrounds, and conditions that have influenced how and whether certain needs have been satisfied. For example, a child from a stable, secure home may have different needs than a child who has not had this kind of security. Recognizing diverse needs will help you to better understand some student behaviors and perhaps increase your insight into how to respond.

students with differing needs

Diverse Abilities

Another dimension of diversity will be seen in the academic *abilities, achievements, and learning styles* of your students. Some students will enter the school environment and immediately do well. Other students will appear not to respond to your teaching. One of your biggest challenges as a teacher will be to provide a variety of experiences and learning encounters to accommodate your students' diverse learning styles and abilities.

academic diversity

As we delve further into the topic of today's students in a diverse society, you will discover that you need to be aware of these sources of diversity to address the educational needs of your students. Let's examine each of these sources in more detail and consider how they will influence your ability to teach effectively.

Racial, Ethnic, and Cultural Diversity

"melting pot"

Though American society has always been composed of various races, ethnicities, and cultures, today we are experiencing great cultural diversity. At one time, the United States was considered a "melting pot" of many different kinds of people. Immigrants were expected to give up the language and customs of their homelands and adopt the language and customs of their new country. During the nineteenth and early twentieth centuries, schools contributed to the concept of the melting pot by socializing and acculturating immigrant children to American ways while discouraging them from maintaining the ways of their homelands. Many states even passed laws forbidding instruction in any language but English. The basic idea was to produce a society with one dominant culture. This process of incorporating an immigrant group into the mainstream culture is often referred to as *enculturation* or **assimilation.** Many European immigrant groups were easily assimilated into the dominant American culture, but people of color were often prevented from doing so.

cultural pluralism

The concept of the melting pot has generally been replaced by the notion of **cultural pluralism,** which calls for an understanding and appreciation of the cultural differences and languages among the nation's citizens. The goal is to create a sense of society's wholeness based on the unique strengths of each of its parts. Cultural pluralism rejects both assimilation and separatism. Instead, it seeks a healthy interaction among the diverse groups in our society; that is, each subculture maintains its own individuality while contributing to our society as a whole. As some commentators put it, cultural pluralism argues for replacing the melting-pot metaphor with that of a "mosaic" or "tossed salad," in which the individual parts are still distinct but combine to make a unique whole.

demographic changes

Cultural pluralism is becoming an increasingly important concept in our society as the demographic composition of public school classrooms continues to change as we enter the twenty-first century. While about 28 percent of the total population are members of minority groups, 36 percent of school-age children are minority, a figure that will continue to increase in the coming years.[4] Birth rates among minority groups are higher than those of white Americans, and immigration patterns are contributing to the increasing size of the minority population.

A statistical breakdown by individual youth groups reveals some interesting trends and projections, as shown in Table 4.1. Compared to the 1995 population, nonwhite youth are expected to increase by 7.6 million by the year 2010, and white youth are expected to decline by 2.9 million. These national averages disguise the fact that minority groups are unequally distributed across the

TABLE 4.1 Projections of the U.S. Population Age 0–17, 1995–2010 (millions)

Youth	1995	2010	Change
Total youth*	69.1	73.6	+4.5
White, non-Hispanic	45.9	43.0	−2.9
Hispanic (of any race)	9.5	13.6	+4.1
Black†	10.3	11.7	+1.4
Other races†	3.3	5.4	+2.1
Increase in total nonwhite youth = +7.6 million			
Decrease in total white youth = −2.9 million			

*May not add exactly because of rounding.
†Includes small number of Hispanics; "other races" are primarily Asian and Native American.
Source: Youth Indicators 1996 (Washington, DC: U.S. Department of Education, National Center for Education Statistics, September 1996), p. 16.

country. The fastest-growing states also have high percentages of minority youth. For example, the four states of California, Texas, New York, and Florida will have more than one-third of the nation's young people by 2010, and the youth population of each of these states will be more than 52 percent minority. By that same year, about twelve states will have more than 50 percent minority youth populations.[5] In the forty-seven urban school districts that constitute the "great city schools," including those in New York City and Chicago, an overwhelming majority of students are from minority groups.

increasing minority school population

As might be expected with increasing cultural diversity, teachers will encounter more students whose native language is not English and whose ethnic and cultural backgrounds reflect a Hispanic or Asian heritage. Although you might think that these non-English-speaking youngsters are from recent immigrant families, a surprisingly large number of them were born and raised in the United States but have not learned English at home or in their community. Many of them also lack basic skills in the language spoken at home, which makes it more difficult to teach them English at school.

Not There Yet

Although many people have promulgated cultural pluralism as a desirable goal, it does not currently exist in the United States. Although racial, ethnic, and cultural diversity does exist, equality among the various groups does not. In general, racial and ethnic minorities do not share equal political, economic, and educational opportunities with those of the dominant culture, even though our society espouses such equality. Many minority groups have been excluded from full participation in American society.

cultural pluralism not a reality

Acting White

Two researchers, Signithia Fordham and John Ogbu, studied a predominantly African American high school in Washington, DC, to see how students' sense of collective identity enters into the process of schooling and affects academic achievement. They conclude that many African American students underachieve academically because they are afraid of being accused of "acting white."

Fordham and Ogbu argue that historically subordinate minorities like African Americans have developed a sense of collective identity, or sense of peoplehood, in opposition to the social identity of white Americans. Because African Americans have been excluded from true assimilation in economic, political, social, and psychological arenas, they develop an oppositional cultural frame of reference that includes protecting their identities and maintaining boundaries between themselves and white Americans. For African Americans to behave in a manner that falls within the white cultural frame of reference is to "act white" and is negatively sanctioned by the peer group.

The teenage peer group at "Capital High School" (99 percent African American student body) exerted strong pressure to reassure one another of black loyalty and identity by discouraging students from engaging in certain behaviors that were interpreted as "white." Being an academic high achiever was one such unacceptable behavior. Fordham and Ogbu found that many students succumbed to peer pressure and purposely underachieved academically. Many of these students were afraid of being labeled "brainiacs," a term meaning that a person was smart but also a jerk. Worse yet for male students was to be known as a "pervert brainiac." To be known as a brainiac was to question a male student's manhood, but to be known as a pervert brainiac left little doubt and was the kiss of death among peers.

Students who wanted to achieve academically and still be considered an accepted member of the peer group tried various strategies to avoid antagonizing their peers, including engaging in athletic activities, acquiring the protection of "tough guys" in return for assisting the latter in their schoolwork and homework, and clowning. These students were careful not to brag about their academic achievements or to bring attention to themselves. But even in these instances, the researchers conclude, the students would do much better if they did not have to divert their time and attention into strategies to conceal their academic pursuits.

What are the implications of these findings? Clearly, schools must find ways to reinforce black identity that are compatible with academic achievement. Similarly, the African American community must convince black children that academic pursuit is not synonymous with acculturation into white society. If the community can demonstrate that academic achievement is valued and appreciated, the children will get a different message.

Source: Signithia Fordham and John U. Ogbu, "Black Students' School Success: Coping with the Burden of 'Acting White,'" *The Urban Review* 18, no. 3 (1986), pp. 176–206.

Unfortunately, schools have too often been run for the benefit of those in the dominant cultural group, excluding minority groups from receiving the full range of benefits. Schools that embrace cultural pluralism seek to promote diversity and to avoid the dominance of a single culture. Their curricula are infused with the histories and contributions of diverse groups. These schools attempt to use the cultural patterns of the students to provide instruction and promote learning. The goal is for students to be comfortable operating both within their own cultures and in others as well. Students from all racial, ethnic, and cultural groups are urged to participate in the school's various social, athletic, and governmental activities. These schools seek to eradicate the academic achievement disparities among the various racial, ethnic, and cultural groups. In short, the goal for schools that aim for cultural pluralism is that no particular cultural group either dominates or is excluded from those activities and accomplishments that schools value.

Many people, however, resist the notion of cultural pluralism as a desirable goal. These people argue that cultural pluralism will undermine our country's common traditions, historically derived from western European cultures. We discuss these issues later in the chapter when we talk about multicultural education.

Diverse Needs

In addition to the diversity of racial, ethnic, and cultural backgrounds we have discussed so far, another element of diversity occurs within each individual. We all have basic physical and psychological needs that may vary in their prominence and expression because of individual circumstances. One way to understand the diverse needs of students is to see how one prominent psychiatrist and educator, William Glasser, has conceptualized the basic needs of all individuals.

Glasser's Choice Theory

Glasser begins with the premise that each of us is born with fundamental needs for survival, love and belonging, power, freedom, and fun.[6] Throughout our lives, our motivations, actions, and behaviors are attempts to satisfy these needs. This premise, called **choice theory,** holds that if we understand and identify these needs within ourselves, we can make conscious choices about how best to meet them. The recognition of our ability to make choices results in personal empowerment: we have control over how we choose to react to external events and information.

choice theory

Glasser believes that teachers should empower their students through the use of choice theory. He states that effective teachers combine the needs of students with classroom assignments or activities. By understanding and incorporating basic human needs into the classroom structure, the teacher is teaching in a way that also meets those needs. The more students are convinced that their schoolwork satisfies their needs, the harder they will try and the better work they will produce. For example, when asked what is the best part of school, many students respond, "My friends." According to Glasser, this expresses the students' built-in need for friendship, love, and belonging. Rather than structure classroom settings to suppress this need, such as by emphasizing independent seatwork or teacher lectures, teachers should find ways to let students associate with others in class as a planned part of learning. Glasser refers to this kind of cooperative grouping as the use of *learning teams.*

Teaching students in cooperative learning teams also meets students' needs for power. Using the term *power* synonymously with *self-esteem* or *sense of importance,* Glasser explains that to fulfill this need students must have the sense that

learning teams, power needs

someone whom they respect listens to them. Unfulfilled needs for power often result in a number of undesirable attention-getting behaviors. Glasser believes these inappropriate behaviors are often misguided efforts to achieve power and are the source of 95 percent of discipline problems in school. In accordance with choice theory, he suggests that teachers structure opportunities for students to fulfill needs for power appropriately during the school day, such as by providing a forum for students to be heard. In addition to learning teams, in which students interact and listen to one another in the learning process, Glasser suggests that teachers provide opportunities for student input and self-evaluation of homework, classwork, and tests. He believes that students need to be encouraged to set their own standards for quality work and to evaluate whether they are meeting those standards. This helps to satisfy the need for power and instills an internal standard for quality education and work.

Understand and be confident that each of us can make a difference by caring and acting in small as well as big ways.
—MARIAN WRIGHT EDELMAN

Glasser proposes that students' needs for freedom and fun, though important, are not at the core of problems in schools. Students generally understand the need for some structure in dealing with large groups of people and the resulting rules and regulations that must govern behavior in school. Though fun is an essential need, students who have a sense of belonging in school and a forum for personal power are already likely to be experiencing fun.

Glasser's theory of personal empowerment provides one interesting way of viewing and identifying a wide variety of student needs. Other approaches, such as Abraham Maslow's hierarchy of needs theory, may also be useful. The most important point is that teachers must be aware of their students' varying needs and respond accordingly in the classroom.

Schools help students meet social, as well as academic, needs. (© Bob Daemmrich)

Adolescent Subcultures

Teenagers often satisfy their needs for belonging, power, and fun by forming crowds, or groups that share common characteristics. Most schools have crowds of elites, average students, and outcasts, with various terms used to describe them: *jocks, preppies, brains, druggies, burnouts, nerds/geeks/dweebs,* and *goths.* Each crowd has attitudes, behaviors, or dress characteristics that distinguish it from all other crowds. As members of these adolescent subcultures, teenagers can express their own attitudes, explore personal relationships, and test themselves against others. Often teens don't even select a group as much as they are placed into one because of their image among their peers.

how crowds are labeled

Elite groups, such as the jocks and preppies, are the "leading crowd," who enthusiastically participate in, and receive the endorsement of, the school. The outcasts, such as the burnouts or the goths, tend to have an adversarial rather than cooperative relationship with the high school because they believe school doesn't serve their needs well. The outcasts are contemptuous of the elites' interest in student government and athletics, while the elites reject the outcasts' resistance to authority and achievement. Clothing and adornment are probably the most powerful symbolic indicator of category membership, although each crowd also tends to stake out particular territories of the school as its own.

symbols of membership

Membership in teenage subcultures begins to form in the middle and junior high schools as cliques develop around particular interests such as athletics, academics, student government, drugs, and tastes in music and cars. These groups strengthen as the teenagers begin to move away from their families, and peer membership becomes a type of new family where youngsters find comfort and support. By senior year, however, the hold of the subcultures on students has weakened. The students develop more self-confidence, and they seek greater freedom. At this point, the friendship group becomes a drag on their autonomy. Until that happens, however, the teen subcultures exert a strong influence on the values of their members.

Most high schools have done a reasonably good job of making academically and socially oriented students an integral part of school life. They have been less successful with subcultures like the various outcast groups. In fact, because groups like the burnouts or goths reject the schools' values, the schools may be reinforcing their alienation. Finding ways to bring members of alienated subcultures into participation in their schools, bring the loners or outsiders into greater contact with their peers, and channel peer influence as a positive force is a major challenge for high school and middle school educators.

Diverse Abilities

In some ways, many of our schools today are not structured to address students' diverse abilities. Most of our schools tend to emphasize a curriculum that specifically targets the predominantly linguistic and analytic abilities needed to do well on commonly used standardized tests. This constricted focus on a limited

traditional focus on small range of abilities

range of abilities results in an education system that teaches and reinforces only certain types of achievement. Children who are strong in linguistic and analytic tasks are likely to be successful in school and feel a great sense of achievement. Other children, however, who may be very competent or even gifted in non-traditional school tasks may experience frustration or failure in school. Children do not enter school as failures; rather, they acquire this debilitating label from a system that is strongly oriented toward a limited range of student abilities.

As a teacher, it is important to be aware of and help nurture a broad spectrum of abilities and strengths in your students. In the following section, we look at the theory that students may have many abilities and talents not tapped by traditional schooling. We also explore learning styles to see how different students learn and perhaps broaden your views on approaches to teaching. Then we briefly examine characteristics of students along a range of disabilities and talents.

Multiple Intelligences

Howard Gardner, a leading psychologist, proposes that we should move toward educating **multiple intelligences,** of which linguistic and analytic abilities are only two facets. In Gardner's books, *Frames of Mind* and *Multiple Intelligences: The Theory in Practice,*[7] he explains that we all have strengths, weaknesses, and unique combinations of cognitive abilities. Gardner proposes that people have at least eight distinct intellectual capacities that they use to approach problems and create products:

eight different abilities

1. *Verbal/linguistic* intelligence draws on the individual's language skills, oral and written, to express what's on the person's mind and to understand other people.

2. *Logical-mathematical* intelligence understands principles of some kind of causal system, such as the way a scientist does, or can manipulate numbers, quantities, and operations, the way a mathematician does.

3. *Spatial* intelligence refers to the ability to represent the spatial world internally in the mind, the way a chess player or sculptor does.

4. *Bodily-kinesthetic* intelligence is the capacity to use your whole body or parts of your body to solve a problem, make something, or put on some kind of production, such as an athlete or a performing artist does.

5. *Musical* intelligence is the capacity to "think" in music, to be able to hear patterns, recognize them, remember them, and manipulate them.

6. *Interpersonal* intelligence is the ability to understand other people, an ability that we all need but is particularly important for teachers, salespeople, and politicians.

7. *Intrapersonal* intelligence refers to having an understanding of yourself, of knowing your preferences, capabilities, and deficiencies.

8. *Naturalist* intelligence refers to the ability to discriminate among living things (plants and animals) as well as sensitivity to features of the natural world, such as rock formations and clouds.[8]

Traditionally, schools have tended to reinforce a learning profile emphasizing verbal/linguistic and logical-mathematical abilities and de-emphasizing or excluding other possible intelligences.

Teaching Implications   In Gardner's theory, abilities in diverse areas would be valued as indicators of intelligence and be considered worthy of further nurturance and development in school. To address these varied intelligences, Gardner emphasizes learning in context, particularly through apprenticeships. Student development in an area like music should be fostered through hands-on practice and experiences. Even traditional subjects should be taught in a variety of ways to address the varied intelligences of both students and teachers. For example, the history of an era might be taught through a number of media and methods, ranging from art and architecture to biographies and dramatic reenactments of events. Assessments should also be tailored to different abilities and should take place in the learning context as much as possible.

The theory of multiple intelligences emphasizes the highly individualized ways in which people learn and recognizes that each of us has unique intellectual potential. Acknowledging and fostering individual abilities in a variety of areas is one way teachers can help students. This is an emerging idea in education. The Multiple Intelligences Menus, shown in Table 4.2, offer some ideas for expanding instructional repertoires and infusing variety into lessons. Currently a number of schools across the country are applying the theory in the classroom on a day-to-day basis. The multiple intelligences theory provides a framework for enhancing instruction and a language to describe the efforts. It provides teachers with a complex mental model from which to construct curriculum and improve student learning. These efforts should contribute to our knowledge and skills in this area.

fostering diverse abilities

Differing Learning Styles

Another approach to individual abilities and differences is the theory of learning styles. A **learning styles** approach to teaching and learning is based on the idea that all students have strengths and abilities, but each student may have a preferred way of using these abilities. Learning style models focus on the process of learning, that is, how individuals absorb and think about information. Some researchers have identified four basic learning styles[9]:

varieties of learning styles

1. The Mastery style learner absorbs information concretely; processes information sequentially, in a step-by-step manner; and judges the value of learning in terms of its clarity and practicality.

2. The Understanding style learner focuses more on ideas and abstractions; learns through a process of questioning, reasoning, and testing; and evaluates learning by standards of logic and the use of evidence.

TABLE 4.2   Multiple Intelligences Menu

Linguistic Menu _Speeches_	Musical Menu
Using storytelling to explain _____	Give a presentation with appropriate musical accompaniment on _____
Conduct a debate on _____	Sing a rap or song that explains _____
Write a poem, myth, legend, short play, or news article about _____	Indicate the rhythmical patterns in _____
Create a talk show radio program about _____	Explain how the music of a song is similar to _____
Conduct an interview of _____ on _____	Make an instrument and use it to demonstrate _____
-List of Books Read. -Journals	
-Intropersonal	
Logical-Mathematical Menu	**Interpersonal Menu**
Translate a _____ into a mathematical formula	Conduct a meeting to address _____
Design and conduct an experiment on _____	Intentionally use _____ social skills to learn about _____
Make up syllogisms to demonstrate _____	Participate in a service project to _____
Make up analogies to explain _____	Teach someone about _____
Describe the patterns of symmetry in _____	Practice giving and receiving feedback on _____
Others of your choice _____	Use technology to _____
Bodily-Kinesthetic Menu	**Intrapersonal Menu**
Create a movement or sequence of movements to explain _____	Describe qualities you possess that will help you to successfully complete _____
Make task or puzzle cards for _____	Set and pursue a goal to _____
Build or construct a _____	Describe one of your personal values about _____
Plan and attend a field trip that will _____	Write a journal entry on _____
Bring hands-on materials to demonstrate _____	Assess your own work in _____

3. The Self-Expressive style learner looks for images implied in learning; uses feelings and emotions to construct new ideas and products; and judges the learning process according to its originality, aesthetics, and capacity to surprise or delight.

4. The Interpersonal style learner, like the Mastery learner, focuses on concrete, palpable information; prefers to learn socially; and judges learning in terms of its potential use in helping others.

TABLE 4.2   Multiple Intelligences Menu *(cont'd)*

Visual Menu	Naturalist Menu
Chart, map, cluster, or graph _____	Create observation notebooks of _____
Create a slide show, videotape, or photo album of _____	Describe changes in local or global environment _____
Create a piece of art that demonstrates _____	Care for pets, wildlife, gardens, or parks _____
Invent a board or card game to demonstrate _____	Use binoculars, telescopes, microscopes, or magnifiers to _____
Illustrate, draw, paint, sketch, or sculpt _____	Draw or photograph natural objects _____

Source: Reprinted with permission from Linda Campbell, "How Teachers Interpret MI Theory," *Educational Leadership, 44* (September 1997), p. 18.

It's important to understand that various styles are neither good nor bad, just different. It's also important to know that individuals are not locked into any one style but can vary styles to fit different situations and tasks. Whereas Gardner's theory of multiple intelligences centers on the *content* and *products* of learning and has its roots in an effort to rethink the theory of measurable intelligence, learning styles theory addresses differences in the *process* of learning and the different ways people think and feel as they solve problems, create products, and interact.

Though key advocates and researchers of a learning styles approach to education agree that individual strengths and abilities should be emphasized, they disagree on how to put the theory into practice. Some educators call for a formal assessment of each student's learning style and then a prescription for appropriate teaching methods for that individual. Others believe that students should be assessed and matched with teachers having similar learning styles. Still others warn that current tests are not yet technically adequate and that using these tests may actually harm students because they may result in improper labeling of individuals and their so-called learning styles.

disagreements over implementation

Teaching Implications   A learning styles approach to teaching is currently receiving a great deal of attention in education. Though few schools adhere strictly to any one "model," the approach is being applied in varying forms and intensities in many schools. Rather than label students as having a particular learning style, many educators argue that curriculum and instruction should offer varied lessons that appeal to a range of strengths, abilities, and learning preferences over time. Teachers need to accommodate different learning styles by systematically varying teaching and assessment methods to reach all students. Flexibility and variety are the keys: don't assume that all students learn the way you do, and don't undervalue students just because their learning styles differ from yours. Technology can help in varying instruction and assessment methods.

keys for teachers

As teachers become more familiar with new technology, they are making use of CD-ROMs, video/audio World Wide Web sites, and other multimedia tools that offer students varied ways to access materials and learning experiences.

Students with Disabilities

types of disabilities

Within the range of diversity your students will display, some will have disabilities. The types of disabilities you may encounter are many. For example, you may have students with mental retardation, emotional disturbance, learning disabilities, attention deficit disorders, speech or language impairments, multiple handicaps, autism, traumatic brain injuries, orthopedic impairments, visual impairments or blindness, and hardness of hearing and deafness. Figure 4.1 shows the percentage and number of students in each of these categories. During the 1996–97 school year, 5.2 million students, ages six to twenty-one, received federal aid for their disabilities; these students represented 11 percent of the total public school population. About 560,000 additional children, ages three to five, also received federal aid for their disabilities. In 1997, the federal government distributed approximately $3.1 billion to the states for students with disabilities.[10]

Teaching Implications   Students with disabilities will likely be in your classroom for varying amounts of the school day depending on the types and amount of support services they are receiving. How will you deal with the different needs of these children? Most important, remember not to stereotype them. Certainly

FIGURE 4.1   Specific Disabilities Among Children Age 6–21: Total and Percentage for Each Category

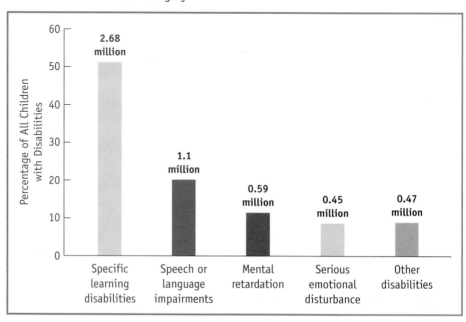

Source: Twentieth Annual Report to Congress on the Implementation of the Individuals with Disabilities Education Act (Washington, DC: U.S. Department of Education, 1998), p. II-16.

different disabilities will have different implications for student learning. For example, a student with mental retardation may require repetition and practice to master simple concepts, whereas a student in a wheelchair may learn even the most difficult material quickly. Even within the parameters of each type of disability, however, you will probably encounter a wide range of differences. Consider two students identified as having learning disabilities. One may display a low-average IQ and have extreme difficulty in mathematics; the other may have an extremely high IQ and have difficulty in reading. Both of these students have a learning disability, but you would not provide the same instruction for each of them or have the same expectations.

The point is, you should approach instruction for these children as you would for other students in the classroom: expect diversity, anticipate a range of abilities, and look for the particular strengths and learning profiles of each student. A helpful resource for recognizing student abilities and suggesting instructional strategies will be the special education teacher(s) in your school. The more you and a special education teacher can coordinate instruction and services for your students with disabilities, the better the students' educational experiences are likely to be.

expect diversity

Gifted and Talented Students

One of the most challenging types of students is the gifted or talented child. The gifted child is extremely bright, quickly grasping ideas and concepts you are teaching and making interpretations or extrapolations that you may not even have considered. Gifted children may also have a creativity that shows itself in original thinking or artistic creations.

Students who are gifted and/or talented are sometimes overlooked when educators talk about students with special needs. However, as one educator says, "Highly gifted children are as far from the norm in the direction of giftedness as the severely retarded are in the other direction."[11] Therefore, they do have special needs.

Although special educational care and services for students with disabilities have long been recognized and accepted, American education has been slow to accept the notion that gifted children require special adaptations in both curricula and teaching methods. Because the idea of giftedness implies an elitism to many Americans, it seems undemocratic to provide special services to children who already enjoy an intellectual advantage.

As a result of neglected needs, gifted and talented students drop out of school at rates far exceeding the rates of dropout for their nongifted peers. Many of those who stay in school feel unchallenged and become bored and apathetic. The result is that many of our brightest and most talented minds are being turned off or underdeveloped. Only recently have school districts begun to make serious efforts to identify gifted children and develop special programs for them.

high dropout rate

Identifying Gifted Students   How do educators decide whether a student is gifted? A survey of definitions of the terms *gifted* and *talented* used by the education departments in each state reveals wide variations. The areas in which states

meanings of gifted and talented

identify gifted and talented students can range from intellectual to psychomotor to artistic, with many variations. But the term *talented* most often refers to an ability or skill (musical or artistic talent, for example) that may not be matched by the child's more general abilities, whereas the term *gifted* usually includes intellectual ability. However, this definition of giftedness is shifting away from an emphasis on general intellectual ability toward the recognition that giftedness occurs in a variety of areas, such as mathematics, language, spatial ability, and kinesthetics. Through its evolution, the study of giftedness has moved increasingly toward more *inclusive* definitions and away from more *exclusive* ones. Intelligence is now thought to be composed of many factors, not just one or two as was previously thought. Howard Gardner's work on multiple intelligences cited earlier in the chapter demonstrates this more inclusive thinking.

reliance on scores and grades

In their assessments of students' intellectual abilities, school districts have, in the past, tended to rely heavily on general intelligence and achievement tests, as well as on teacher recommendations and grades earned in school. There is a danger of letting the tools used to identify the children become synonymous with the *definition* of gifted and talented. To avoid this danger, teachers and administrators must study and interpret the data the tools provide rather than take the

avoid cut-off points

data at face value and use them for hard-and-fast cut-off points. Whether or not to recommend a child for a special program is a decision that should be made by the responsible teacher and other professional educators on the basis of their objective and subjective appraisals of the student, the nature of the gifted program or activity, and the atmosphere in which the student lives and goes to school. Parents should be a significant part of these discussions. The point is that the complexity of the variables involved requires that individual decisions be made by professionals using their best judgments rather than according to arbitrary, predetermined cut-off points on tests.

The problem of identification is especially acute for bilingual children and children adjusting to a new culture, as well as for children in other minority groups. A major concern in the identification of gifted and talented students

minorities underrepresented

centers on the underrepresentation of economically disadvantaged students and certain minority students. In a national survey of eighth-graders enrolled in gifted and talented programs, only 9 percent of the students were in the bottom quartile of family income, while 47 percent of program participants were from the top quartile in family income.[12] Asian American students are well represented in gifted and talented programs, but African American and Hispanic students are underrepresented in terms of their proportion in the total school population. Thus, educators and parents are concerned that the measures being used to identify gifted and talented youngsters may work to the disadvantage of African Americans, Hispanics, and children from low-income families.

Teaching Implications   If your school or school district has special programs for gifted and talented students, you may be expected to work with resource teachers to help prepare individualized education plans for these students. Or, if you want to teach gifted students, your state may be one of the twenty or so that require you to receive a gifted endorsement to your teaching license. It is more likely, though, that you will discover certain students in your class to be gifted or talented and, lacking any special program, you will be responsible for teaching these students as part of your regular class. What do you need to know?

1. Recognize that gifted pupils generally learn the standard curricular skills and content quickly and easily. They need teaching that does not tie them to a limited range, that is not preoccupied with filling them with facts and information but allows them to use the regular class as a forum for research, inquiry, and projects that are meaningful to them.

2. Realize that these students are persistently curious. They need teachers who encourage them to maintain confidence in their own ideas, even when those ideas differ from the norm.

3. Teach these pupils to be efficient and effective at independent study so that they can develop the skills required for self-directed learning and for analyzing and solving problems independently. Allow students of varying abilities to work together in areas of high interest, such as social action research projects.

4. Help students apply complex cognitive processes such as creative thinking, critiques, and pro and con analyses.

5. Expand your ideas concerning what instructional materials are available. Consider businesses, religious groups, national parks, and resource people as sources of potential instructional materials in addition to the textbooks and reference books available in the school. Be sure to investigate any technological resources that are available, including World Wide Web sites and other electronic links to information and to knowledgeable people outside the school.

6. Use various instructional strategies, such as flexible grouping, "tiered" assignments (in which all students explore the same topic but the level of questions or products produced varies depending on students' abilities), learning centers, student contracts, and mentorships.

7. Implement *curriculum compacting,* in which teachers test students on what they already know on upcoming units. Students who demonstrate mastery in advance are allowed to accelerate through the material or pursue enrichment activities while the unit is being taught to the rest of the class.

8. Match students with *mentors* to help develop talent and engage students in relevant and applied problem solving. Mentoring programs encourage independent growth, increased self-confidence, and a willingness to reach out into new, untried areas.

guidelines for teaching gifted and talented students

If 2 + 3 is always going to be 5, why do they keep teaching it to us?

—A GIFTED FIRST-GRADE STUDENT

The School's Response to Diversity

You may be getting concerned about whether you can handle the range of diversities you may face in your classroom. Be assured, however, that you are not in this alone. Besides other teachers and administrators to help you, most schools have specialists who often can give you valuable advice or direct help to your students. At one time, the only business of schools was to educate students. But now, because of the increasing complexity and diversity of our students' lives, other needs are being addressed and incorporated into the way schools are approaching "education."

Various assistance systems have been devised to help the teacher respond to the range of student needs. Some of this assistance is in the form of support personnel such as nurses, school psychologists, counselors, and administrators. A growing number of parent councils involve parents in giving advice and helping to deal with problems. Teacher aides may be community members who speak the language of substantial minorities in the schools. Interns or students from the local college may help as well, providing another adult in the classroom.

In addition to support personnel, schools have tried to provide special programs to address some dimensions of student diversity. Multicultural and bilingual education, special education, and programs for gifted and talented students have all evolved out of concern that certain types and degrees of student diversity require different educational strategies to ensure an equal opportunity for intellectual stimulation and growth.

Multicultural Education

definition and goals

Multicultural education represents one approach to meeting the educational needs of an increasingly diverse student population. **Multicultural education** values cultural pluralism and seeks to enrich the cultural perspectives of all students. Spurred by the civil rights movement of the 1960s, multicultural education is a response to economic inequality, racism, and sexism in American culture. Originally used in conjunction with improving the lot of "people of color," the term has been broadened to include gender, disability, and other forms of diversity. Its goals include reducing prejudice and fostering tolerance, improving the academic achievement of minority students, building commitment to the American ideals of pluralism and democracy, and incorporating minority groups' perspectives into the curricula of our schools. Like the concept of cultural pluralism on which it is based, multicultural education rejects the notion of the melting pot, whereby minority groups are expected to abandon their group identities and become assimilated into a homogeneous American culture. Equally, multicultural education rejects separatist philosophies that would have each cultural group go its own way without trying to fit into an overall American culture.

different approaches

At least five different approaches to multicultural education have been identified, which helps to explain why the term often has very different meanings for different people:

1. "Teaching the exceptional and culturally different," which helps students achieve academically and socially within currently existing schools by building bridges between the students' backgrounds and the schools to make the curriculum more "user friendly."

2. "Human relations," which attempts to build positive relations among members of different racial/cultural groups and between males and females.

3. "Single-group studies," which focus on programs that examine particular groups, such as African American studies or women's studies.

4. "Multicultural," which promotes cultural pluralism by reconstructing the whole educational process around the perspectives of diverse racial, ethnic, cultural, and social classes.

5. "Multicultural and social reconstructionist," which teaches students to examine inequality and oppression in society and to take action to remediate these inequalities.[13]

Multicultural education is not just for members of minority racial or ethnic groups but for all students, including those with western European heritage. True multicultural education does not consist of only black history or women's history

United Feature Syndicate

months. Instead of simply adding on information about particular groups, leaving the rest of the curriculum untouched, real multicultural education presents multiple perspectives and viewpoints to help students understand how events and facts can be interpreted differently by various groups. In addition to valuing cultural diversity, multicultural education is based on the concept of *social justice,* which seeks to do away with social and economic inequalities for those who have been denied these benefits of a democratic society. African Americans, Native Americans, Asian Americans, Hispanic Americans, women, individuals with disabilities, people with limited English proficiency, people with low incomes, members of particular religious groups, and individuals with different sexual orientations are among those groups that have at one time or another been denied social justice. Educators who support multicultural education see establishing social justice for all groups of people who have experienced discrimination as a moral and ethical responsibility.

social justice

An Ongoing Debate   Many school districts are attempting to permeate their curricula with a multicultural emphasis, believing that attention to multicultural education is our society's best way to combat the prejudice and divisiveness among the different subcultures of our nation. By developing mutual respect for and appreciation of different lifestyles, languages, religious beliefs, and family structures, students may help shape a better future society for all its members.

concerns and controversy

Some educators, however, are concerned about what they believe are potential dangers of multicultural education in the schools. They fear that it may destroy any sense of common traditions, values, purposes, and obligations; that it may divert the schools' attention from their basic purpose of educating for civic, economic, and personal effectiveness; that it attacks the problem of minority students' underachievement by advocating an emphasis on self-esteem rather than hard work; that it substitutes "relevance" of subjects studied for instruction in solid academics; and that it may undermine a sense of morality because no universal moral positions are considered acceptable to all elements of our society. These critics do not argue against the need to preserve and value the achievements of the diverse ethnic and racial groups of our country, but they reject the position that everything is of equal value, that the schools have a responsibility to teach every possible belief and value, and that behavior is moral if it is believed to be so by any group.[14] These critics assert that there are limits to pluralism and that those limits must be articulated by schools and school leaders. Other critics of multiculturalism completely reject the concept of cultural pluralism, preferring an assimilationist perspective whereby schools are charged with forging one dominant American culture in which English is the only acceptable language.

Thus, the major thrusts of multicultural education are not without controversy. Multicultural education has often been cast as a reform movement, designed to address inequity and discrimination resulting from the race, religion, socioeconomic status, sex, age, exceptionality, or language of students.[15] As with any attempt to solve social problems, excesses and overexuberance can occur. Nevertheless, schools do need to accommodate larger minority populations in a way that removes barriers while preserving the basic purposes of schooling.

Bilingual Education

Students whose native language is not English constitute one of the most conspicuous failure groups in the American educational system. Because of their difficulty in speaking, writing, and understanding English, many of these limited English proficient (LEP) students fall further and further behind in school, and overwhelming numbers drop out before finishing high school.

The Government Response To cope with this problem, Congress passed the Bilingual Education Act in 1968, and subsequently amended it five times, to provide federal funds to develop bilingual programs. Much of the expansion of bilingual programs in the 1970s can be attributed to a series of court cases, the most notable of which was the 1974 U.S. Supreme Court case of *Lau* v. *Nichols*. The case involved a class action suit on behalf of Chinese-speaking students in San Francisco, but it had implications for all of the nation's non-English-speaking children. The Court found that "there is no equality of treatment merely by providing students with the same facilities, textbooks, teachers, and curriculum; for students who do not understand English are effectively foreclosed from any meaningful education." Basing its ruling on the Civil Rights Act of 1964, the Court held that the San Francisco school system unlawfully discriminated on the basis of national origin when it failed to cope with the children's language problems.

Lau v. Nichols

Although the *Lau* case did not mandate bilingual education as the means to solve the problem, subsequent state cases did order bilingual programs. With the advice of an expert panel, the U.S. Office of Civil Rights suggested guidelines for school districts to follow, the so-called Lau Remedies. The guidelines "specified that language minority students should be taught academics in their primary home language until they could effectively benefit from English language instruction."[16]

Bilingual Education Models Several types or models of **bilingual education** programs exist. In the *immersion model,* students learn everything in English. Teachers using immersion programs generally strive to deliver lessons in simple and understandable language that allows students to internalize English while learning academic subjects. The extreme case of immersion is called *submersion,* wherein students must "sink or swim" until they learn English. Sometimes students are pulled out for *English as a Second Language (ESL)* programs, which provide them with instruction in English geared toward language acquisition.

different models

The *transitional* model provides intensive English-language instruction, but students get some portion of their academic instruction in their native language. The goal is to prepare students for regular classes in English without letting them fall behind in subject areas. In theory, students transition out of these programs within a few years.

Maintenance or *developmental* bilingual education aims to preserve and build on students' native-language skills as they continue to acquire English as a second language.

The Battle over Bilingual Education

What's the Policy?

In 1998, voters in California passed Proposition 227, an initiative that called for ending bilingual education in the state, and a similar effort is under way in Arizona. The California law, which took effect in the fall of 1998, requires schools to teach limited English proficient students almost entirely in English except when at least twenty students in a given grade level are granted waivers to the law. If an insufficient number of students receive waivers in a given school, the school district must allow students to transfer to another school that offers bilingual education. Educators and legislators in other states will be closely following the progress of California's students as they consider implementing similar plans.

How Does It Affect Teachers?

Many teachers are withholding judgment on the effects of Proposition 227 until they have a sense of what it will mean in the long run for Latino student achievement. School districts vary greatly in their strictness or leniency in granting waivers to allow bilingual education programs. School districts that supported bilingual education before Proposition 227 have found ways to keep at least some bilingual classrooms, whereas in school districts without such support, bilingual education has been either eliminated or severely restricted. In the Oceanside school district in San Diego County, for example, of the 159 waiver requests received, only 5 were approved, which effectively meant that no bilingual programs needed to be offered. Even within a district, waiver rates vary tremendously from school to school. Some schools have even seen an increase in the number of students enrolled in bilingual classes since Proposition 227 was passed.

What Are the Pros?

Many teachers at Ditmar Elementary School in the Oceanside school district report surprise at how well their LEP students have progressed academically in English immersion. Some report rapid gains in students' oral English skills and in their requests to read books in English in the school library.

What Are the Cons?

Some teachers report that their students tune out as the day goes on because they can't keep up in English, while others say they have slowed the academic pace of their classes because it takes much longer to convey information. Still other teachers state that fewer students in their classes are ready to read compared to last year because the students' English vocabulary is much more limited than their Spanish vocabulary. Teachers in the upper elementary grades say they often pull students out of subjects such as science to do extra work in English so they can read their textbooks.

Lynn Gonzalez, a second-grade bilingual teacher at Ditmar, says, "This has been the hardest year of my life." She feels "enormous pressure" to make the school district look successful by producing English-proficient students by the end of the year, even though her training taught her that such proficiency takes at least three years. "I'm implementing something that goes totally against my beliefs," she says.

What Do You Think?

1. Do you support the intent of Proposition 227 to do away with bilingual education models other than structured English immersion? Why or why not?

2. If you were teaching LEP students who had had only one year of English instruction, what concerns would you have?

3. What might be some motivations for parents to request waivers to Proposition 227?

Source: Lynn Schnaiberg, "Calif.'s Year on the Bilingual Battleground," *Education Week*, June 2, 1999, pp. 1, 9–10.

Controversies   Students with a native language other than English have two goals in school: learning English and mastering content. But the debate over how students can best reach those goals has become a divisive political battle.

While some educators believe students who use English as a second language should be educated in their native language as well, critics insist such an approach doesn't work. The critics believe the best path to academic achievement for language-minority students in most cases is to learn English and learn it quickly. Too many bilingual programs, they say, place LEP students into slower learning tracks where they rarely learn sufficient English and from which they may never emerge. These critics basically support an immersion model of bilingual education but oppose the transitional and maintenance models. But supporters of transitional and maintenance models argue that students can best keep up academically with their English-speaking peers if they are taught at least partly in their native languages while learning English.

critics support immersion model

The transitional and maintenance models of bilingual education are in growing jeopardy, as first California and now other states threaten these bilingual programs (see Figure 4.2). In 1998, California voters passed Proposition 227, which called for LEP students to be taught in a special English-immersion

California abandons bilingual education

FIGURE 4.2   State Bilingual Education Requirements

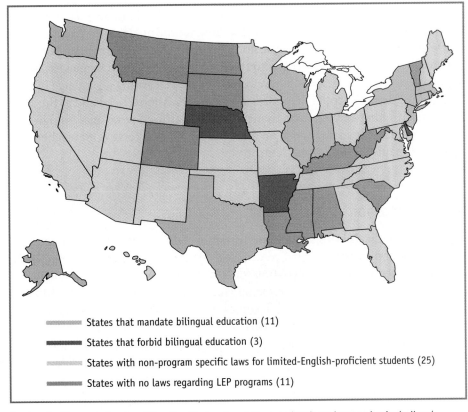

━━━━━ States that mandate bilingual education (11)

━━━━━ States that forbid bilingual education (3)

━━━━━ States with non-program specific laws for limited-English-proficient students (25)

━━━━━ States with no laws regarding LEP programs (11)

Reprinted with permission from *Education Week* as found at www.edweek.org/context/topics/gallery/biling1.htm

program in which nearly all instruction is in English, in most cases for no more than a year, before moving into mainstream English classrooms. Proposition 227 basically ended transitional and maintenance models of bilingual education in California, except when sufficient numbers of parents specifically request that their children continue in them. Many parents, administrators, and teachers are concerned that all children, not just LEP students, will be affected as mainstream teachers grapple with students who may be unprepared to deal with grade-level work in English after one year in immersion. The legality of Proposition 227 is also being challenged in the courts. One year after voters approved Proposition 227, it appears that bilingual education continues to flourish in pockets across the state, but overall only about 20 percent of the students who were previously enrolled in such programs have requested to continue in bilingual education.[17]

many still support bilingual education

Whereas in the early 1970s language-minority speakers and their advocates fought for bilingual education as their right, today many of them are expressing doubts about the effectiveness of bilingual programs. Civil rights and cultural issues are giving way to concerns that non-native English speakers are just not sufficiently mastering the English language. But advocates say it is not fair to blame bilingual education for the slow progress some students are making. They cite research indicating that instruction in the native language concurrent with English instruction actually enhances the acquisition of English.[18] The problem is not bilingual education, they say, it's that becoming proficient in any second language takes longer than just one or two years. And they point out that there is a shortage of well-qualified, fully bilingual teachers, so that in many cases the problem with bilingual classes is not the curriculum but the quality of instruction.

need for bilingual teachers

Despite this controversy, many school districts are in desperate need of bilingual teachers, particularly those who speak Spanish and Asian languages. If you speak a second language or still have time to include learning a language in your college program, you could help meet a serious educational need and at the same time greatly enhance your employment opportunities. Speaking a foreign language, especially Spanish, is also an asset for the regular classroom teacher who may have Spanish-speaking students in class.

Special Education

Students with disabilities are another group in our schools who have received special attention to ensure equal educational opportunities. The term **special education** is often used as a designation for services designed for these students.

Public Law 94–142

In 1975, the federal *Education for All Handicapped Children Act (PL 94–142)* established the right of all students with disabilities to a "free appropriate public education." The law specified that each such student must be provided with an **individualized education program (IEP)** outlining both long-range and short-range goals for the child. Since that time, a number of other federal laws have reinforced and extended the commitment to special education.

early intervention

Preschool Legislation The *Education of the Handicapped Act Amendments (PL 99–457)*, passed in 1986, provided for early intervention for children from

© Lynn Johnston Productions, Inc./Dist. by United Feature Syndicate, Inc.

birth to age two who are developmentally delayed. For states that choose to participate, programs must include a multidisciplinary assessment of the child's needs, a written **individualized family services plan (IFSP),** and case management. Services may draw from a variety of areas, such as special education, speech and language pathology, occupational or physical therapy, or family training and counseling, depending on the developmental needs of the child.

PL 99–457 also stated that a "free appropriate public education" must be extended to children with disabilities ages three to five years. Although state and local education agencies administer these programs, they may contract with other programs, agencies, or providers to provide a range of services, such as programs that are home based for part of the day. Families are recognized as playing a particularly important role in preschool education, and instruction for parents is to be included in the IFSP whenever that is appropriate and the parents desire it. When students reach school age, they are covered by the provisions of IDEA, discussed in the next section.

IDEA and ADA   In 1990, Congress passed two significant federal laws: the *Individuals with Disabilities Education Act (IDEA)*, subsequently amended in 1997, and the *Americans with Disabilities Act (ADA)*. IDEA amended the 1975 Education for All Handicapped Children Act. ADA ensures the right of individuals with disabilities to nondiscriminatory treatment in aspects of their lives other than education.

Six principles provide the framework of IDEA around which education services are designed and provided to students with disabilities:

basic provisions of IDEA

▶ Free appropriate public education (FAPE)

▶ Appropriate evaluation

▶ An individualized education program (IEP)

▶ Least restrictive environment (LRE)

▶ Parent and student participation in decision making

▶ Procedural safeguards

Special education laws and practices have given disabled students many more opportunities to participate in activities from which they previously had been excluded. (© Tony Freeman/ PhotoEdit)

IEP's function

Because of the wide variety of disabilities and infinite degrees of severity in which these conditions may be found in individual students, IDEA mandates that an "appropriate education" be defined on an individual basis, using the written IEP first mandated in 1975. The IEP states the child's current levels of educational performance, short-term objectives and annual goals, services to be provided, and criteria and schedules for evaluation of progress. Thus, the IEP helps to ensure that the educational goals designed for the child are appropriate to individual learning needs and that these plans are actually delivered and monitored. Provisions must be reviewed and revised annually, and more often if necessary. Teachers, parents or guardians, special educators, other professionals, and (whenever appropriate) the child are all involved in the development and approval of the IEP. IDEA also requires that all older students with a disability (usually ages fourteen to sixteen) have an individualized plan for making the transition from school to work or additional education beyond high school through age twenty-one.

least restrictive environment

Like the original 1975 act, IDEA further stipulates that services for students with disabilities be provided in the **least restrictive environment (LRE),** meaning students with disabilities should be educated with children who are nondisabled to the greatest extent appropriate. Determination of what constitutes an appropriate environment has been subject to great debate. The social and academic benefits of the regular classroom must be weighed against unique educational needs and individual circumstances for each child. The term **mainstreaming** has long referred to the practice of placing special education students in general education classes for at least part of the school day while also providing additional services, programs, or classes as needed. More recently, the term **inclusion** has been used to mean the commitment to educate each child, to the maximum extent appropriate, in the regular school and classroom.

mainstreaming

inclusion

Compared to mainstreaming, inclusion—particularly *full inclusion,* as it is sometimes called—generally indicates an even greater commitment to keeping students with disabilities in regular classrooms. Thus, it usually involves bringing the support services to the child rather than moving the child to services located in separate rooms or buildings.

Controversy over Inclusion   Advocates of full inclusion argue that segregated education for students with disabilities is inherently unequal and therefore a violation of the rights of the children who are segregated. They also argue that traditional special education programs have resulted in a costly special education bureaucracy that has not shown the expected benefits in terms of academic, social, or vocational skills. Among the benefits of full inclusion for children with disabilities, they say, are higher expectations and better socialization, as well as greater acceptance of human differences by nondisabled children.

pros and cons of inclusion

Critics, on the other hand, say that both teachers and students are being hurt in the rush to embrace inclusion. Teachers have complained that they are given inadequate resources and training to deal with students with disabilities. Cases are cited in which teachers have been given sole responsibility for a class of thirty students, as many as ten of whom have disabilities. In too many instances, critics say, when children with disabilities are moved from resource rooms and self-contained classrooms into regular classrooms, the necessary supports don't follow. One reason is that some school districts use the cover of inclusion as a way to cut costs for special education services. Since 1967, when local and state expenses for special education services constituted 4 percent of all school expenditures, these expenses have increased more than fourfold.[19] With voter reluctance to increase school taxes and many school districts facing budget cuts as a result, some school boards and administrators see the inclusion movement as a way to save money by reducing funding for special education.

special education costs

Ideally, when students with disabilities are included in regular classrooms, their teachers receive special training as well as help from a special education teacher who serves as either a co-teacher or a consultant. True collaboration between general education and special education teachers is essential for inclusion to work effectively.

Even when such collaboration is possible, some special educators voice concern that full inclusion may result in diminished or inadequate specialized services for students who have special needs. They point out that the regular classroom may not be the best setting for every child. Violent or emotionally disordered children, for example, may pose a threat to themselves and their classmates. These educators are wary of eliminating the range of service delivery options currently available in favor of a pure inclusion model. Furthermore, they argue, there is little evidence that inclusion programs strengthen students' academic achievement. (However, the same criticism could be made of many special education programs.)

One thing is certain: inclusion of children with disabilities is becoming increasingly common in American schools. More and more students with disabilities are taking part in regular classroom life with their nondisabled peers. Inclusion seems to thrive in schools that have a shared vision of the school's

inclusion becoming widespread

The Personal Side of Inclusion

Cecelia Pauley is a sixteen-year-old sophomore in a Montgomery County, Maryland, high school. Last year was the first time she had ever attended regular classes like other students her age. As a result of her parents' insistence that she be educated as a regular student, Cecelia, who has Down syndrome, completed her freshman year but not without great effort on her part and with the help of her teacher and other students in her class.

Initially, Cecelia experienced great difficulties. She was always late for class, interrupted her teachers, and often asked inappropriate questions. She was often frustrated with the work and felt isolated from her peers. Because Cecelia had spent most of her academic career in special education courses with other students with severe disabilities, she was not used to the pace and expectations of a regular class. Nor were the other students used to someone like Cecelia.

A special education teacher became Cecelia's "case manager," whose responsibilities included figuring out how to meet Cecelia's needs without disrupting the classroom atmosphere. To assist in this process, Cecelia's parents contacted a private, nonprofit organiza-

tion that trains nondisabled people to deal with those who have disabilities. This organization worked with students in her classes to help Cecelia stay focused on tasks, to hold her to high expectations, and both to encourage and to scold her on appropriate occasions. In each of Cecelia's classes, one student was identified as her "buddy" to help her manage her affairs. Cecelia succeeded in overcoming her initial difficulties and has made friends and succeeded in her schoolwork. Her teachers credit Cecelia and her parents with her success. Cecelia hopes to achieve a certificate of attendance, since the level of her work would not qualify her for a high school diploma.

In spite of Cecelia's success story, her teachers doubt that they could handle more than one severely disabled student in a class, and they question whether full inclusion would work for all severely disabled students.

Source: Stephen Buckley, "Making Room in the Mainstream," *The Washington Post,* June 12, 1993, pp. A1, A10. Copyright © 1993 *The Washington Post.* Reprinted with permission.

purposes; strong lines of communication among teachers, administrators, and parents; and cultures of innovation and reform. In many schools with successful inclusion programs, the presence of students with disabilities has sparked other reform initiatives such as cooperative learning, peer teaching, team teaching, authentic assessment, and interdisciplinary instruction.

Assistive Technology   Just as many students use contact lenses or glasses to help them compensate for poor eyesight, students with disabilities may rely on a variety of technology-based innovations to help them learn better. The term **assistive technology** refers to the array of devices and services that help people with disabilities perform better in their daily lives. Devices such as motorized chairs, remote control units to turn on appliances, voice recognition systems, ramps to enter and exit buildings, and computers can all assist people with severe disabilities. Computers are especially important in allowing many students with disabilities to participate in normal classroom activities that would otherwise be impossible. Assistive technologies also exist for students with mild disabilities, including special software and multimedia materials to help them develop higher skill levels in spelling, reading, or math concepts.

Congress incorporated definitions of assistive technology in IDEA, declaring that such technology must be provided whenever necessary as an element of free and appropriate public education. Thus, assistive technology must be considered a potential component of the IEP for each student with disabilities.[20] As a new teacher, you should be prepared to encounter situations in which a child uses technology as a medium for interaction and engagement within your classroom.

assistive technology incorporated into IDEA

Implications for Teachers   How can you as a regular education teacher be effective in teaching children with disabilities in your classroom? Here are a few suggestions:

guidelines for teaching students with disabilities

▶ First, be open to the idea of including students with disabilities in your classroom.

▶ Learn about each child's limitations and potential, and about available curriculum methodologies and technologies to help the child learn.

▶ Insist that any needed services be provided.

▶ Pair students with disabilities with children who can help them.

▶ Use a variety of teaching strategies, including hands-on activities, peer tutoring, and cooperative learning strategies.

▶ Avail yourself of opportunities for co-teaching with a special education teacher.[21]

Programs for Gifted and Talented Students

Programs for gifted and talented students exist in every state and in many school districts, but the exact number of students served cannot be determined because not all states and localities collect this information. We do know, however, that by 1994, thirty-two states reported serving almost 2.4 million K–12 gifted students and spending almost $500 million on gifted and talented programs.[22]

Current educational programs for gifted and talented students are quite varied. Some programs establish special schools that are designed only for gifted or talented students and have special admission requirements. In such schools, stimulating courses can be devised and taught without concern for students who might be unable to keep pace, and teachers as well as students can be recruited on the basis of their talents.

Other programs adapt and enrich the regular school curriculum for gifted and talented children by grouping these students together for all or part of their instruction. This option normally is more flexible and practical than special schools. Classes can be established on a continuing or short-term basis, in any subject area, with the intention of either enriching or accelerating the student.

various approaches

Although special programs and special schools for gifted and talented students do exist, these students are most likely to receive all, or nearly all, of their education in regular classrooms. In many school districts, in fact, separate programs for gifted students are being curtailed or phased out. There are two *inclusion of gifted students*

primary reasons for this trend. One is the spread of a philosophy that favors mixed-ability grouping; the other is a lack of funds for separate gifted programs.

The move to meet gifted students' needs within the regular classroom is parallel to the inclusion movement in special education. Some advocates for gifted education programs are disturbed by this trend, concerned that gifted students will be shortchanged in the regular classroom. They fear that teachers will concentrate their efforts on struggling students or that gifted students will be drafted to serve as tutors for these students rather than working to their own potential. Supporters of the current trend, however, believe that most gifted students' needs can be met in the regular classroom if teachers can differentiate curriculum and instruction for them and increase the level of challenge.

Still others argue that it is important to keep a continuum of programs and services available for gifted students. Along with the regular classroom, these educators argue, the options should include pullout programs, special classes, and separate centers and schools. A range of giftedness exists, and whereas some students will do just fine in a regular classroom, others can benefit from different programs.

Nontraditional Programs

All of the school programs discussed so far in this section address student diversity in a somewhat "traditional" way; that is, they have evolved from the notion that the role of the school is to address issues that arise for children in a standard school setting during the course of the school day. However, a number of social conditions may complicate the issue of diversity. Social problems such as poverty, homelessness, or inadequate health care are such pervasive influences in some students' lives that we will discuss them in more detail in the next chapter. The more we examine "today's children," the more we realize that societal conditions and problems affecting our students cut across traditional lines of services delivery.

social services provided through schools

Interagency Cooperation   In acknowledgment of the complexity and pervasiveness of these conditions and problems in the lives of children, programs are emerging that emphasize interagency cooperation in meeting the needs of individuals. For example, the coordinated school health initiative responds to the risk factors that threaten children and youth by providing coordinated school health services related to student health and success in school. The initiative assesses the health problems in particular school communities, builds consensus on what services should be provided, and puts together a comprehensive approach to improving children's health using agencies that address health, mental health, dental health, social services, recreation, and youth development. The guiding principle of the coordinated school health movement is that schools and communities can do much more with their current resources if they work together in partnership rather than as separate, isolated agencies. At least nine hundred school-based health centers are operating in the United States.[23]

The Comer Model   James Comer, a public health physician and psychiatrist at Yale University, developed an initiative in New Haven, Connecticut, that emphasized structuring the environment to facilitate learning and development rather than placing blame and trying to change children. The "Comer model" attempts to change the climate of demoralized schools and to create a sense of community and direction by bringing together the principal, teachers, aides, and parents to form a school planning and management team. Services of the school social worker, the psychologist, special education teachers, and counselors are coordinated to provide a consultation team to support individual students and teachers as well as the school planning and management team. Comer notes, "Kids don't learn in pieces. That's why it is essential to address the entire social system of the school because of the way the many variables interact and because attitudes, morale, and hope all affect school performance."[24] (See the box on page 130 for more on Comer and his model.)

changing the school environment

Diversity: A Complex Phenomenon

The school programs described in this section have been designed to address student diversity and create a more equal educational opportunity for children in our school systems. An inherent danger in these approaches to addressing diversity, however, is the tendency to label children and form stereotypic images of who they are. Remember that student performance in school is affected by many factors, including social and cultural trends.

differences, not deficits

We encourage you, as a teacher, to remember that we are talking about *differences* in students, not necessarily deficits. The educational groupings we have been discussing are an administrative convenience, not a naturally occurring segmentation of children. Within each of these groups, each child will vary along a number of dimensions and have very different learning profiles of strengths and weaknesses.

The Teacher's Response to Diversity

So far in this chapter, we have presented a great deal of information about the diversity of the children you will be teaching. Ultimately, how these children are educated will come down to you and your daily interactions with them in your classroom. How will you deal with diversity?

Teacher-Student Disparity

Consider what we know about the typical teacher today. Women and whites predominate in the teacher force; 73 percent of all public school teachers are women, and 87 percent of those teaching in public schools are white.[25] Profiles of preservice and beginning teachers show similar gender, racial, and ethnic patterns.

the typical teacher

James P. Comer (b. 1934)

James Comer is a public health physician and psychiatrist who, through his work with low-income New Haven, Connecticut, schools, has shown that it is possible for low-income African American children to achieve at high academic and social levels.

After receiving his M.D. from Howard University in 1960, Comer entered the public health service. He became interested in the study of how policies and institutions interact with families and children, and began to see the school as the place to improve the life chances for children from difficult home situations. He decided that a career in psychiatry would enable him to address the social problems that plagued the people with whom he worked, and in 1964 he began his psychiatric training at Yale University.

At Yale, Comer worked with the inner-city New Haven schools to find out why they were not helping African American children and how they could be made to do so. He wanted to give these children the same opportunities in life that education had given him. The more he worked with children, the more he came to believe that schools were the only places where children trapped in poverty and failure could receive the support their families could not give them.

With the help of a Ford Foundation grant, Comer became the director of the School Development Program with the New Haven public schools. A team of educational and mental health professionals consisting of Comer, school administrators and teachers, a social worker, a psychologist, a special education teacher, and other support staff worked to involve parents in developing a social skills curriculum that integrated academic disciplines. The curriculum included four major areas: politics and government, business and economics, health and nutrition, and spiritual and leisure time, all areas in which the students would need proficiency to succeed in school and to lead productive lives. Through the curriculum, the students became more aware of their community and of how their involvement in it could make a difference.

By adopting child development and behavioral science research, the team concentrated on problem solving rather than blame fixing and made decisions based on consensus. This consensus process gave each team member a sense of participation and ownership of decisions. The project was a great success: students' standardized test scores rose dramatically, project schools had higher attendance rates than other New Haven schools, and students graduated to become school leaders in their later schooling.

The "Comer model" emphasizes the social context of teaching and learning. No academic learning is possible, Comer asserts, unless there is a positive environment at the school where teachers, students, parents, and administrators like one another and work together for the good of all children. Built around three elements—a school governance team, a mental health team, and parental participation—Comer's model seeks to create schools that offer children stable support and positive role models. With the school and parents working successfully together, no conflict arises between home and school. The students learn desirable values, disruptions at school are reduced, and both teachers and students have more time and energy to focus on academic and social skills learning.

Among the many sites that have successfully implemented Comer's approach, now known as the School Development Program, are Washington, DC; Dade County, Florida; Dallas; Chicago; Detroit; San Diego; and New Orleans. Many school districts have chosen this program's structure and processes as a way to implement site-based management.

Teachers who are socially and culturally different from their students require solid pedagogical training to help them understand how to overcome these differences to promote student learning in effective ways. (© Elizabeth Crews)

Most of these teachers, moreover, come from relatively stable family backgrounds. The majority of teachers and future teachers in our classrooms, then, come from very different backgrounds than many of the students they teach. Despite efforts to increase the number of minority teachers (see Chapter 14), this gap between teachers and students is likely to continue for some time.

As we mentioned in Chapter 3, the more alike students and teachers are in social and cultural characteristics, the more they share tacit expectations about behavior and academic performance. But as social and cultural characteristics become increasingly disparate, teachers need to rely on solid pedagogical training to overcome these differences. The discrepancy between the cultures of today's typical teacher and the increasingly diverse students of the future emphasizes the growing importance of pedagogical training in sensitizing incoming teachers to the commonalities and differences among students, as well as in providing specific methods and techniques for addressing the plurality of culture and learning styles. Too often white educators have been reluctant to recognize that their own backgrounds and the culture of the school have an effect on learning. Rather than thinking of minority students as having a culture that is valid albeit different from theirs, they sometimes think of these students as deficient. Teachers are challenged to recognize the diversity of cultures represented by their students and to address these cultures in their teaching.

preparing for student diversity

Implications for Teachers

Given this profile of the cultural discrepancy between students and teachers, how can prospective teachers best prepare? Here are some steps you can take now:

▶ Seek out experiences to broaden your understanding of societal and cultural commonalities and differences; for example, travel to foreign countries.

▶ Spend time in communities whose residents differ from you in terms of ethnicity, culture, or language.

▶ Volunteer in schools that differ from those you attended.

Once you have your own classroom, what can you do to address diversity there? Here are some guidelines:

▶ Learn about and appreciate the values and backgrounds of your students.

▶ Teach to your students' strengths rather than making them feel incapable or deficient.

▶ Provide a variety of educational experiences, and find ways for all students to achieve recognition from you and peers for being good at something.

▶ Involve your students' parents and other professional staff at the school to coordinate expertise and support so that students get a consistent message.

▶ Recognize that the schools' traditional emphasis on middle-class values such as individual learning and competition may clash with the values represented by their students' cultures. Teachers can provide opportunities for students to learn ways to succeed in today's dominant culture, but they must also respect the value systems in students' home lives and help them, in positive ways, to bridge the gap between the two worlds.

A Final Word

A major goal of this chapter has been to make you aware of the complexity of issues that directly affect many children's lives and their ability to get an adequate education. In our complex society, it is no longer feasible for the teacher to try to attend to all students' needs alone. You will need to use all the resources available to you, including parents and other professionals. Some teachers may initially feel threatened by this involvement or have a sense that the classroom is their "turf." But as we have seen throughout this chapter, our students need the coordinated expertise and support of all school professionals and the crucial link with parents to be given a fair shot at acquiring the good education that is their due.

KEY TERMS

limited English proficient (LEP) (100)   assimilation (102)
socioeconomic status (SES) (100)   cultural pluralism (102)

choice theory (105)
multiple intelligences (108)
learning styles (109)
multicultural education (116)
bilingual education (119)
special education (122)
individualized education program
   (IEP) (122)

individualized family services plan
   (IFSP) (123)
least restrictive environment (LRE)
   (124)
mainstreaming (124)
inclusion (124)
assistive technology (126)

FOR REFLECTION

1. How do you compare to the profile of the typical teacher described at the end of this chapter?

2. How can you help prepare yourself for the diversity you are likely to encounter in the classroom? What experiences with diversity will you bring to the classroom?

3. What are the pros and cons of living in a pluralistic society? In your opinion, is this preferable to a "melting-pot" or assimilationist approach to diversity?

4. What are the general characteristics of your learning style? How can you capitalize on them in your teaching? How will you account for various learning styles in your students?

5. Have you had any contact with individuals with disabilities (for example, a relative or neighbor)? What did you learn from this relationship that might be helpful in your teaching?

6. Would you like to be a teacher of gifted or talented children? Why or why not?

7. What other elements of diversity will you find in your students that have not been discussed in this chapter? How will you be sensitive to these differences?

FOR FURTHER INFORMATION

Cole, Robert W., ed. *Educating Everybody's Children: Diverse Teaching Strategies for Diverse Learners.* Alexandria, VA: Association for Supervision and Curriculum Development, 1995.
This text presents research-based but practical instructional strategies for teaching diverse students.

Delpit, Lisa. *Other People's Children: Cultural Conflict in the Classroom.* New York: The New Press, 1995.
Asking why schools have such a hard time making school a happy place for poor children and children of color, the author concludes that most classrooms are dominated by a white perspective and too few teachers acknowledge that children of color have perspectives of their own.

Gardner, Howard. *Multiple Intelligences: The Theory in Practice.* **New York: Basic Books, 1993.**

A mixture of previously published articles and lectures, as well as chapters written specifically for this book, all explain the theory of multiple intelligences and how it can be applied in today's schools.

Nieto, Sonia. *The Light in Their Eyes: Creating Multicultural Learning Communities.* **New York: Teachers College Press, 1999.**

This book draws on research in learning styles, multiple intelligences, and cognitive theories to portray the ways in which students learn. It also discusses the social context of learning and the influence of culture on learning.

Pugach, Marleen C., and Cynthia L. Warger, eds. *Curriculum Trends, Special Education, and Reform: Refocusing the Conversation.* **New York: Teachers College Press, 1996.**

Arguing that the reform agenda must address the needs of all children, including those with disabilities, this volume gives practical suggestions for doing so in different curriculum areas.

SEARCH

University of Virginia. *Office of Special Education: A Web Resource for Special Education.* **World Wide Web site at http://curry.edschool.virginia.edu /go/specialed**

This web site at the Curry School of Education, University of Virginia, contains much information about special education, including the history of the field and types of disabilities. It also offers discussion groups, electronic addresses of special educators, and much more.

5

What Social Problems and Tension Points Affect Today's Students?

Rarely a day goes by on which educational issues fail to make headlines in newspapers across the country. Violence in schools, rampant teenage drug use, inequality of educational opportunity, sex education programs, and youth suicides are only a few of the issues that we read about daily. Underlying these issues are problems that complicate young people's efforts to get an education, such as crippling poverty and child abuse and neglect. This chapter explores some of the most sensitive and controversial issues in American education. Naturally, in such a short space we can treat each topic only briefly. However, we urge you to pursue additional reading on each issue.

This chapter emphasizes that

▶ Some critical problems affect many school-age children, directly influencing their lives and frequently spilling over into the classroom. Among these problems are severe poverty, homelessness, teenage pregnancy, child abuse, alcohol and drug abuse, and adolescent suicide.

▶ Violence and vandalism are not confined to urban schools; they are major problems in all of our schools and in our society.

▶ School dropout rates, although improving, reflect disparities among various groups and foreshadow future societal problems.

▶ Access to equal educational opportunity for poor and disadvantaged youth is an elusive goal in American education.

▶ Charter schools and school voucher plans are controversial forms of school choice.

- Sexism and gender bias is a real, though often overlooked, issue in our schools.

- Sex education remains as controversial as ever, although concern about AIDS has strengthened the argument for proponents of sex education.

social class differences

As we discussed in the last chapter, most teachers come from relatively stable backgrounds. Although this situation can be a source of strength, it also means that children often inhabit different worlds than their teachers. Often there are gaps in social class and in personal exposure to major social problems. Many teachers may have difficulty recognizing and adapting to those differences that contribute to the problems some children bring to the classroom.

The children who stream into a teacher's classroom each September bring their own personal histories. Although they may wish to start afresh with the beginning of the new school year, much of who they are is wrapped up in their past and their current out-of-school lives. It is likely that some of these students bear deep scars from their past experiences and that some are currently caught up in desperate widespread social problems. We are not suggesting that you should be Mr. or Ms. Fix-It, taking in troubled children and, with a few quick adjustments to their psyches, sending them out into the world cured. Rather, we wish to make you more fully aware of and more deeply sensitive to the sorts of problems your students will bring to your classroom. We also want you to recognize the healing power of education, which gives structure, purpose, and hope to youngsters whose daily lives often lack these stabilizing and motivating influences.

Social Problems Affecting Students

In Chapter 4, we talked about changes in our society resulting in increased diversity among today's students. These conditions will affect many students' lives, but they do not necessarily prevent them from getting an education. However, some changes or trends in society do pose a more direct threat to the performance of students in school. In our discussion we deal with several difficult conditions and problems, including poverty, homelessness, child abuse, alcohol and drug use, teenage pregnancy, adolescent suicide, violence, and school dropout. As you will see in the following discussion, these pervasive societal problems do not occur in isolation but actually tend to cluster or overlap. In real life, it is difficult to separate out discrete sources of social problems. The compounding of risk factors contributes to the incredible scope of these problems and places a number of students at risk for not completing or succeeding in school. For such **at-risk students,** as they are often called, the chances are great that they will have difficulty getting an adequate education.

problems tend to cluster

What are some of these risk factors? Six key measures include the following:

▶ The child is not living with two parents.

▶ The household head is a high school dropout.

▶ Family income is below the poverty line.

▶ The child is living with a parent or parents who do not have steady, full-time employment.

▶ The family is receiving welfare benefits.

▶ The child does not have health insurance.

America is losing sight of its children. In decisions made every day we are placing them at the bottom of the agenda, with grave consequences for the future of the nation.

—ERNEST BOYER

We know that these family variables do not necessarily compromise children. Many children from families with these risks overcome the odds to succeed in school and in life. But research indicates that when several of these risk factors are present, fewer children make it. As one prominent author states, "The research . . . shows that the more risk factors are present, the greater the damaging impact of each. But the impact is not just additive—risk factors multiply each other's destructive effects."[1] Nationally, 9.2 million children are growing up with four or more of these risk factors (see Figure 5.1). Nearly 30 percent of African American children and almost 25 percent of Hispanic children are in the high-risk category, compared to only 6 percent of white children (see Figure 5.2).[2]

risks multiply with each added factor

FIGURE 5.1 Number of Risk Factors Experienced by Children, 1998

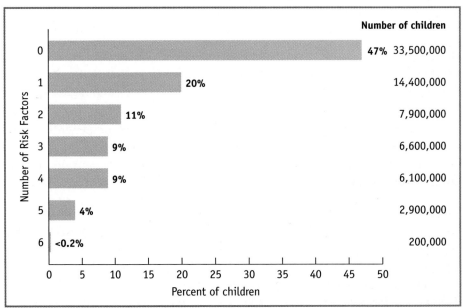

Source: Kids Count 1999 (Baltimore: The Annie E. Casey Foundation, 1999), p. 10. Reprinted by permission of the Annie E. Casey Foundation.

FIGURE 5.2 Percentage of Children in High-Risk Category by Race/Ethnicity and Location*; 1998

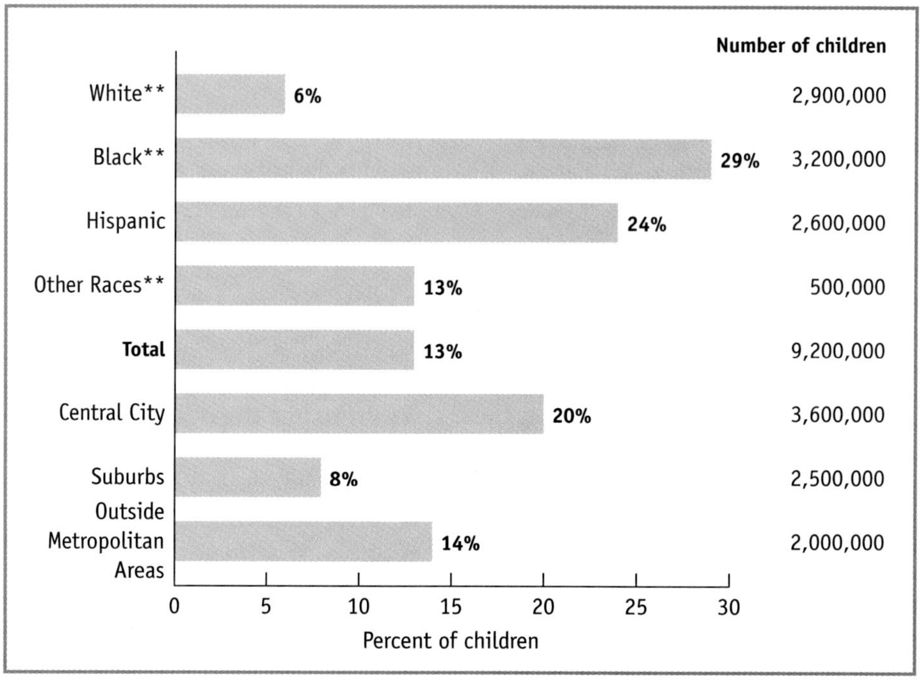

Bar chart titled "Number of children":

Category	Percent	Number of children
White**	6%	2,900,000
Black**	29%	3,200,000
Hispanic	24%	2,600,000
Other Races**	13%	500,000
Total	13%	9,200,000
Central City	20%	3,600,000
Suburbs	8%	2,500,000
Outside Metropolitan Areas	14%	2,000,000

x-axis: 0 5 10 15 20 25 30 — Percent of children

Source: Kids Count 1999 (Baltimore: The Annie E. Casey Foundation, 1999), p. 11. Reprinted by permission of the Annie E. Casey Foundation.
*There were 9.7 million children whose location could not be determined; 1.2 million of the children were high-risk children.
**Non-Hispanic

Compounding the problem is the fact that multiple-risk families are often concentrated in economically and socially isolated communities that have limited job opportunities, poor schools, low-quality public services, and higher levels of crime and drug use.

Let's examine some of these risk factors in more detail, starting with the changing patterns of the American family.

New American Family Patterns

no "typical" family

In recent decades, our society has experienced dramatic changes in how families are structured. The once common image of the "breadwinner" father, a housewife mother, and two children of public school age now accurately describes only 6 percent of households in the United States.[3] So what is the typical family of our students like today? Actually, there is no longer one "typical" family pattern. Rather, a number of economic and societal trends have resulted in families that come in many forms that, in turn, have a pervasive influence on children in school.

Family Composition   An increasing number of children are being raised by single parents. The rate of divorce has influenced the composition of our families, particularly among couples who have children. Over half of today's new marriages will end in divorce. Twenty-four percent of all children live only with their mothers, 4 percent live only with their fathers, and 4 percent live with neither parent.[4]

In addition to divorce, other factors, such as births to single parents, separation, and death of a parent, contribute to the number of children living in single-parent households or possibly with grandparents or aunts and uncles. A breakdown of the figures by racial group reveals that almost 25 percent of white children, 65 percent of African American children, and 36 percent of Hispanic children live in single-parent families.[5]

single-parent households

Being a child in a family in which the parents' marriage is conflict ridden and unhappy may be less preferable in some ways than living in a single-parent family, but single-parent families have one major disadvantage: lower incomes. In 1997, the median income for single-mother households was just over $19,700; for married-couple households, the median income was just over $54,500.[6] Single-mother families have been called "the new poor." It is not just the absence of one parent but the loss of a two-parent income that puts a special burden on these families. More difficult to pin down is the effect of only one parent bearing the daily chores of monitoring, supporting, and guiding the school-age children.

Another result of high divorce rates is the increasing number of children living in blended families with stepparents, stepsiblings, and/or half-siblings. In some cases, divorced parents share physical custody of the children, with the result that the children must split their time between parental households.

Changes in American family patterns will likely influence your interactions with students and their parents in a number of ways. For example, in divorce situations it may be difficult to keep both parents informed of their child's progress. Or a single parent may have a very heavy workload and be unable to attend parent-teacher conferences at the usual times. Varied family patterns will also require more sensitivity in daily interactions, such as when asking students to bring a note from "your mother." It would perhaps be better to say "your parent" or "the person who takes care of you."

teaching implications

Family Relationships   The composition of families influences the way family members relate to one another. Two-career families must balance the needs of childrearing and family life with the demands of two work environments. Single-parent families must meet these same needs with the increased pressure of only one adult income. Thus, family composition affects the amount of time children and their parents have to spend with each other and can also affect the quality of that time. For a single parent, the combination of a job with the necessities of maintaining a family, such as cooking, cleaning, and grocery shopping, does not allow for a great deal of leisure time to spend supervising and enjoying the children. For single parents with young children, finding and paying for good child care is also a major concern. Many single parents do a fine job of raising their children, but the hardships are considerable.

working parents

Even in two-parent families, many mothers now go to work or return to work when their children are very young. One result of the mother's work demands is that she is less involved than she traditionally has been in raising her children—that is, in attending daily to her children's social, intellectual, and moral development. Neither Mom nor Dad is as available as she or he used to be. In 30 percent of two-parent families, both the mother and father worked all year, full time.[7] Sixty percent of today's students live in families in which both parents work or the only parent works.[8] Now, when many children return home from school, they watch television rather than talk with their mothers. Coming home to an empty house or apartment after school is standard for an estimated 4 million "latch-key" children in our country.

"latch-key" children

For parents of younger children not yet in school, working outside the home raises the issue of adequate child care. If both parents or the only parent is working full time, who is taking care of the children? Grandparents and extended family used to pitch in and help, but today it is less and less common for a family to settle in one location near relatives for extended periods of time. Parents who have to work can easily be caught in a bind, and they often must settle for whatever child care they can find.

child care issues

In addition to limiting the amount of time children spend in close contact with their parents, the trend toward two-career and single-parent families also has a direct impact on the schools. Whereas in the past young people were actively involved outside of school in family and community, today the school is being urged to play a larger role in expanding and guiding the limited experiences of children. Schools are being asked to deal with the new problems being brought to them by the facts of modern family life and our changed economy. For example, many schools have responded to child care needs by offering both before- and after-school programs. In the past, teachers could count on more support from families; now teachers often find it difficult to even get in contact with many parents. In this situation, the more dramatic social problems, such as poverty and homelessness, take on even greater urgency for the schools.

schools play a larger role

> *America's future will be determined by the home and the school. The child becomes largely what it is taught, hence we must watch what we teach it, how we live before it.*
>
> —*JANE ADDAMS*

Poverty

"The rich are getting richer and the poor are getting poorer." This well-known phrase describes the extremes of different socioeconomic levels in our society today. The poorest 40 percent of American citizens receive less than 13 percent of the national income, while the wealthiest 40 percent receive almost 73 percent.[9] The increase in earners of extremely high or extremely low incomes has resulted in the shrinking of America's middle class. By 1998, the number of impoverished Americans was 34.5 million, slightly less than 13 percent of the population.[10]

the widening income gap

Numerically, the majority of poor Americans are white; however, the rate of poverty is higher among minorities. Less than 11 percent of whites, 26 percent of African Americans, 25.6 percent of Hispanic Americans, and 12.5 percent of Asian Americans live below the poverty line ($16,600 for a family of four in 1998).[11]

Although poverty rates have recently declined because of a booming economy, the problem of poverty is still pervasive, and the prospects for breaking its grip on children are particularly bleak. Slightly less than 19 percent (13.5 million) of American children live in poverty, the highest rate among all age groups and the highest in any industrialized country. This percentage has been relatively stable since 1981. Whereas children make up about one-fourth of the population, they constitute 39 percent of the poor. Almost half of the children in families headed by females are poor; more than 55 percent of the children in African American female-headed families are poor[12] (see Figures 5.3 and 5.4).

1 in 5 children are poor

In the past, poverty was assumed to be the result of unemployment, and for many this is still true. Nearly 20 million American children, or 28 percent, are growing up in households in which no parent has a full-time, year-round job.[13] However, many people do hold regular jobs but still find themselves in poverty. After World War II, many high school graduates could get manufacturing jobs that required minimal education yet paid quite well. A high school graduate could support a family of four, buy a house, own two cars, and live comfortably. But the American job market has changed. Many manufacturing jobs can now be done more efficiently and effectively by machines, and many of those that are still done by people have been moved to countries with low-wage workers. The U.S. job market for unskilled workers today is found mostly in fast-food establishments and service jobs that typically pay minimum wage and offer no benefits.

the working poor

FIGURE 5.3   Percentage of Children Under 18 Living in Poverty, by Race/Ethnicity and Year

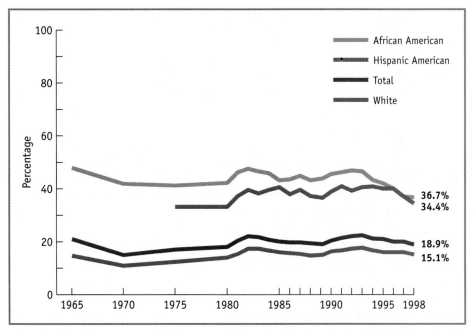

Source: U.S. Bureau of the Census, *Historical Poverty Tables—People*, Table 3: Poverty Status of People by Age, Race, and Hispanic Origin from 1959 to 1998. http://www.census.gov/hhes/poverty/hispov/hispov3.html

FIGURE 5.4 Percentage of Children in Poverty Who Live with a Female Householder, by Race/Ethnicity and Year

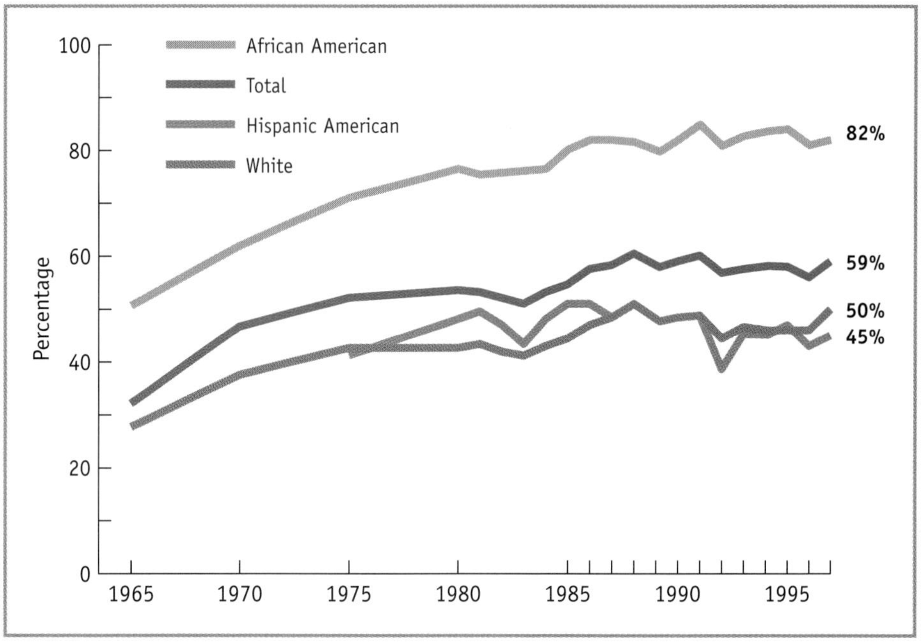

Source: U.S. Bureau of the Census, *Current Population Reports,* Series P-60, Table 1: Age, Sex, Household Relationship, Race and Hispanic Origin—Poverty Status of Persons in 1997, 1996, and 1995. http://ferret.bls.census.gov/cgi-in/ferret?&time=14:39:13

Full-time employment at the current minimum wage is not enough to support a family above the poverty line.

With poverty so prevalent, schools have a challenging problem, partly because they are not designed to serve poor children. The schools in this country were created and continue to be supported by the middle class to perpetuate the middle-class way of life. There is nothing particularly startling about this. Middle-class people want their children to be like themselves, or possibly somewhat better. Therefore, they have built and continue to pay for a school system that reflects their values and supports the way of life with which they feel comfortable.

two views of schooling

Many people in our society have thought that we could eliminate poverty through education and that, through schooling, it would be relatively easy to free people from the chains of impoverishment. The efforts have been well intentioned but often too little, too late, and, in retrospect, sometimes naive. On the other hand, some critics see our schools as part of an enslavement system. They claim that the schools not only do not help develop the individual talents and strengths of poor children but also make these children believe they are losers. After eight to eleven years of schooling, many of these young people see themselves as unable to fit into the middle class and as people who, at best, will do society's menial work. Although some of these critics see this system as a conscious plan of our society, we do not. Such a cynical view suggests that the teachers who are toiling in the urban and rural slums are either people of evil intentions or simply dupes. In our view, many of the teachers who are most heroic and alive are struggling to aid people oppressed by poverty.

Our past and present inadequacies in educating the children of the poor tempt some to turn away and devote their energies to more solvable problems. We cannot do this. Ours is an evolving society. As a people, we are not finished with our own development. Eradicating the ravages of poverty and its withering effect on children should be at the top of our agenda as citizens of this nation and as educators. Although there are many important and solvable problems to work on, we cannot afford—in justice—to ignore this one.

Homelessness

For families close to poverty, the threat of homelessness is very real. Families in poverty often pay more than one-half of their annual incomes in rent. With such a large percentage of income consumed by rent payments, one incident or emergency in the family can disrupt the tenuous equilibrium and jeopardize the family's ability to maintain a home. Imagine, for example, the domino effect that could occur from mechanical difficulties with the one family car. Even minor repairs costing $50 to $100 may be beyond the family's budget. Without a car, the family breadwinner may be unable to get to work and the children unable to get to day care. It does not take long in such a situation to lose a job or a long-awaited slot in a day care center. It is easy to see why housing, which consumes so much of annual income, is a particularly vulnerable area for families in poverty.

There are about 1 million homeless children and youth in the United States, and more than 750,000 are of school age.[14] Imagine the obstacles for a homeless child trying to get an education. Uprooted from their homes, many live in shelters or other locations in distant parts of town. Attending school may require extensive transportation, which parents are not likely to be able to afford. Enrolling children in a school near a shelter may be a difficult and intimidating process for parents struggling with daily survival. Many parents, believing they will be homeless only for a short time, may not even try to transfer their child's enrollment. As days turn into weeks and months, the child may miss a great deal of school. If the child is fortunate enough to attend school, other difficulties may arise, such as the stigma of wearing dirty and ragged clothes, being unwelcome by other children or school officials, or being unable to stay awake in class.

obstacles for homeless schoolchildren

Some homeless children are on their own, having run away from home or been ejected from their families. Many of these chronically homeless youth have been physically or sexually abused, and many suffer from drug or alcohol abuse, poor nutrition, inadequate sleep, exposure to the elements, and lack of health care. School can be a stabilizing force in the lives of these children, but it can also exacerbate their problems. In 1987, Congress passed the Stewart B. McKinney Homeless Assistance Act, with subsequent amendments, to provide protection for the educational needs of homeless children and youth. The legislation provides grants to states to provide for the educational needs of homeless children and requires states to ensure that these children are educated with the rest of the youth in their area and not isolated and stigmatized.[15]

Whom You Will Teach

Percentage of ninth- to twelfth-graders who admitted carrying a weapon at school in the previous year: 9.

Percentage of ninth- to twelfth-graders who reported being in a physical fight in the previous year: 37.

Percentage of teens ages sixteen to nineteen who were high school dropouts: 10.

Percentage of three- to five-year-olds who were read to every day in the last week by a family member: 57.

Percentage of children under age eighteen who are living in poverty: 19.

Percentage of high school seniors who report having used an illegal drug in the past year: 41.

Percentage of students age twelve to seventeen who reported gangs at their schools: 28.

Percentage of young people who will not attend college: 42.

Percentage of students in grades nine through twelve who had drunk alcohol during the previous thirty days: 51.

Percentage of high school students who have jobs: 31; percentage who work twenty or more hours per week: 11.

Percentage of children under eighteen living in single-parent households: 25.

Percentage of thirteen-year-olds who watch television three to four hours per day: 42; five hours or more: 31.

Percentage of sixteen- to nineteen-year-olds who participate in volunteer activities for schools and other organizations: 13.

Percentage of tenth-graders absent from school seven days or more each year: 26.

Percentage of students with disabilities who are served by federal programs: 12.

Percentage of eighth-graders who agree or strongly agree with the following statements:

▸ Teachers are interested in students: 75.

▸ Teachers praise my effort when I work hard: 63.

▸ I often feel "put down" by my teachers: 22.

▸ I don't feel safe at this school: 12.

▸ Students get along well with teachers: 67.

Sources: The Condition of Education 1995, 1996, 1997, and *1998* and *Digest of Education Statistics 1998* (Washington, DC: National Center for Education Statistics); *Youth Indicators 1991, 1996* (Washington, DC: U.S. Department of Education); *1999 Kids Count Data Book* (Baltimore: The Annie E. Casey Foundation, 1999).

homeless children require teacher's support

You may have homeless children in your classroom; if so, they are likely to require support and understanding from you. Some may be malnourished and physically dirty because they lack access to shower or tub facilities. They may show emotional needs. Other children may make fun of them. Your support and caring could provide them with hope and be crucial in improving their chances for success. Hundreds of local and federal programs serve runaway and homeless youth, and these agencies will help you work with these youngsters. More than anything else, homeless children need homes.

Teenage Pregnancy

The bad news is that each year almost 900,000 American teenagers get pregnant and give birth to some 500,000 children, by far the highest teenage birthrate among the world's developed countries. The good news is that between 1991 and 1996, the birthrate among girls ages fifteen to nineteen declined from 62 to about

As pregnant teenagers struggle with the decision of whether or not to drop out of school, educators are finding ways to encourage pregnant teenagers and young mothers to stay in school and graduate. (© David Young-Wolff/PhotoEdit)

54 births per 1,000.[16] Still, the annual cost in public funds for teenage pregnancies in America is estimated to be over $7 billion.[17]

Most of these teenage mothers are not married and so are particularly vulnerable to poverty. When we combine the difficulties of single parenthood with the likelihood that teenagers will have poor work skills and limited employment experience and, if they find work, will receive low wages, we gain some understanding of the finding that almost half the children from households headed by a female live in poverty.

relationship of teen pregnancy and poverty

Teenage parents face not only the enormous task of juggling childrearing and employment but often a premature baby, which is more likely to have health problems and possible learning difficulties. Moreover, poverty often correlates with worse nutrition, less health care, more homelessness, and less education than for more advantaged families.

To lessen this problem, many schools are working with local health officials to ensure that pregnant teenagers receive prenatal care and parenting advice. They are also encouraging these young women to stay in school and graduate. In many cases, the schools are permitting young mothers to bring their babies with them to school. To prevent teenage pregnancies, some schools have established clinics where birth control devices can be obtained, and sex education programs (discussed later in the chapter) have become common as well as controversial. One thing seems certain, however: Americans are caught in an epidemic of careless sexual behavior and negligent childrearing practices.

steps taken by schools

Abused and Neglected Children

The education of the young brings us into contact with humanity's best impulses. Occasionally, however, we see the wreckage of its darkest and most vicious urges. For many years, the phenomenon of child abuse was known only to a small percentage of social workers and law enforcement people. More recently, we have become aware of the magnitude of this problem and the variety of forms abuse can take, including physical or mental injury, sexual abuse, negligent treatment, and maltreatment.

many cases unreported

Because of the hidden nature of child abuse and neglect, reliable figures on it are somewhat difficult to obtain. Professionals in the field acknowledge that most cases are unreported. Nevertheless, in 1996 about 3 million incidents of child abuse or neglect were reported to child-service agencies. Slightly more than 1 million of these reported cases were substantiated, an increase of 18 percent since 1990. Half of the victims of maltreatment suffered from neglect, about one-fourth experienced physical abuse, and about 12 percent were victims of sexual abuse.[18] Parental substance abuse was reported as a major contributing factor in child abuse cases.

effects of abuse

The toll that abuse and neglect take on children's physical, emotional, and psychological development is difficult to assess. Children subjected to violent treatment also sustain injuries that cause serious learning problems in school. These children may be withdrawn or have trouble concentrating. They suffer enormous stress, and their self-esteem is low. They sometimes have excessive needs for control because they have experienced such helplessness. Ironically, they may be more likely to abuse their own children in the future.

the teacher's responsibility

The classroom teacher will not directly encounter the problem of abuse very often. However, in all fifty states, educators are legally responsible for reporting suspected cases of child abuse. Teachers must be aware of potential signs of abuse and know school policy and procedures for reporting suspected abuse. (See Chapter 12 for a discussion of teachers' legal obligations regarding suspected child abuse.) Potential signs of abuse include the following:

▶ Repeated injuries such as bruises, welts, and burns

▶ Neglected appearance

▶ Sudden changes in academic performance

▶ Disruptive or passive, withdrawn behavior

▶ "Supercritical" parents who remain isolated from the school and community[19]

The abused-child syndrome is not a problem that we can always do something about directly. Teachers need to realize that even after an abusive situation has been reported and perhaps disclosed, these children's problems in school will not suddenly end. Children who have been abused have a continuing need for emotional safety and stability. They need capable adult role models who can provide varied but predictable activities and measurable classroom achievement. They need trustworthy praise, concrete rewards, and constructive ways to control their classroom environment.

Alcohol and Drug Abuse

Many of the trends we have talked about so far in this chapter can severely stress the functioning of families, provoking self-destructive responses. Substance abuse is a particularly destructive response. It may involve the use of alcohol or various other drugs. It may be the act of parents or children. But when one family member gets entangled in substance abuse, the entire family is usually a victim.

Alcohol is the most commonly abused substance, and the first use of alcohol may occur at a young age, sometimes in elementary school. Historically, the greatest number of alcoholic teenagers have been male students, especially those with low grades, but the gap between males and females seems to be closing. The problem of alcohol abuse among high school students is widespread. A 1998 survey revealed that there were over 10.4 million current alcohol drinkers between ages twelve and twenty. Of these, 5.1 million were binge drinkers (five or more drinks) and 2.3 million were heavy drinkers.[20]

alcohol, a major problem

After a long period of decline, teen drug use has increased since 1992 (see Figure 5.5). In 1998, the percentages of eighth-, tenth-, and twelfth-graders who reported using an illicit drug during the past year were 21, 35, and 41 percent, respectively. Marijuana use in particular continued the strong resurgence that

drug use

FIGURE 5.5 Student Drug and Alcohol Use: Percentage of High School Seniors Reporting Use in the Previous 30 Days, by Year and Substance

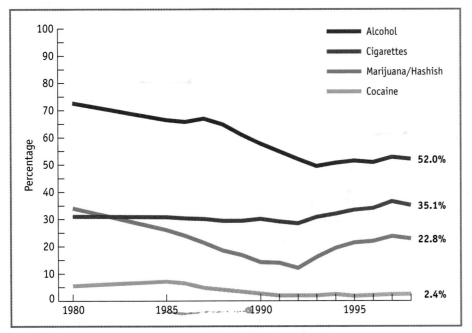

Source: University of Michigan, Institute for Social Research, *Monitoring the Future*, various years, available on the World Wide Web at: http://www.isr.umich.edu/src/mtf/pr98t4.html.

physical and emotional damage

began in the early 1990s.[21] Drug and alcohol abuse remain massive problems. Substance abuse by parents has increased, with devastating results for children. As indicated in the previous section of this chapter, many child abuse and neglect cases involve parental substance abuse.

Adolescent Suicide

Suicide is third only to motor vehicle accidents and homicide as a leading cause of adolescent death in the United States. According to the most recent figures available, each year about 4,200 people in the fifteen-to-twenty-four-year age group take their own lives. Seven percent of high school students in one survey reported that they had attempted suicide within the previous twelve-month period, and 29 percent said they had thought about it.[22]

suicide patterns

Studies of young people who have attempted suicide and those who have succeeded reveal several patterns. Among those who attempt suicide, the vast majority are female. Girls attempt suicide about three times more often than boys, but boys complete suicide about five times more often than girls.[23] Recently the suicide rate for blacks ages fifteen to nineteen increased dramatically from 3.6 in 1980 to 8.1 per 100,000 today, but that is still lower than the rate for whites, which is 11 per 100,000.[24]

risk factors

What puts young people at risk for attempting suicide? Factors include family violence or disruption, mental illness, unemployment, a history of substance abuse, and stress in school or social life. To add to the tragedy, young people sometimes engage in copycat suicides. In this "cluster" syndrome, a wave of adolescent suicides plagues an area. In response, hundreds of school districts now offer programs in suicide prevention.

warning signs

Educators often have the opportunity to recognize children and youths who are suicide risks and to help them get the advice and support they need. Although suicidal behaviors are complex and the warning signs can be ambiguous or misleading, it is important to realize that most young people who commit suicide give warning first to signal their need for help. The American Academy of Child Psychiatry recommends that parents, teachers, and counselors watch for these signs:

- ▶ Changes in eating and sleeping habits
- ▶ Withdrawal from friends, family, and regular activities
- ▶ Violent or rebellious behavior
- ▶ Running away
- ▶ Drug or alcohol abuse
- ▶ Unusual neglect of personal appearance
- ▶ Radical change in personality

▶ Persistent boredom, difficulty concentrating, or a decline in the quality of schoolwork

▶ Frequent complaints about physical symptoms that are often related to emotions, such as stomachaches, headaches, or fatigue

▶ Loss of interest in previously pleasurable activities

▶ Inability to tolerate praise or rewards[25]

If you observe such potential indicators of suicidal tendencies, do not try to handle the burden alone. Seek a support network of the guidance counselor, the school social worker, and/or the school psychologist. Recognizing symptoms and getting professional help for students who behave in this way may prevent their suicides and help them develop coping behaviors to deal with their problems.

School Violence and Vandalism

"Massacre at Columbine High School in Littleton, Colorado—15 Die," "Gunman shoots 8th-grader in L.A. . . . ," "Sixth-graders plot to kill their teacher . . . ," "Student, 14, shoots security guard in D.C. . . . ," "Fifteen-year-old shoots and kills classmate . . . ."

As these headlines indicate, America has become a dangerous place for its children. In urban areas, crime and violence from surrounding neighborhoods have spilled over into the schools, affecting children, staff, and teachers alike. In the

Although school shootings, such as the one that occurred at Columbine High School in Littleton, Colorado, are truly tragic events, school violence is actually declining.
(© Pamela Salazar/Liaison Agency)

suburbs, we have seen some horrible examples of students killing other students. How extensive is the problem of school violence and crime?

Despite the headlines just given, serious violent crime constitutes a small percentage of the total amount of school crime, and homicide is extremely rare. Students ages twelve through eighteen are 2.6 times more likely to be victims of serious violent crime away from school than at school.[26] Although the number of multiple homicide events at school has increased and receives national media coverage when it does occur, the chance of suffering a school-associated violent death is less than one in a million. But even that is too much. For example, during the 1997–98 school year, six multiple-victim homicide events killed a total of sixteen people. During the Columbine High School shootings in 1999, fifteen people were killed.

Consider the following statistics:

school crime statistics

▌ Of crimes reported to police, the most common types of middle and high school crimes were physical attacks and fights without weapons.

▌ Theft accounts for about 62 percent of all crime against students at school. As with students, most crime at school against teachers is theft, with a rate of 46 thefts for every 1,000 teachers.

▌ About 4 out of every 1,000 elementary, middle, and high school teachers were victims of serious violent crime at school. Serious violent crime differed little among teachers in urban schools (5 for every 1,000), suburban schools (3 for every 1,000), and rural schools (3 for every 1,000).

▌ About 3 percent of high school seniors reported carrying a gun to school at least one day during the previous four-week period. This percentage has remained fairly stable since 1994. During the 1996–97 school year, more than 5,000 students were expelled for possession or use of a firearm.

▌ Schools in cities were at least twice as likely to report serious violent crime as those in towns and in rural locations, although the rate among city schools was not significantly different from that among urban fringe schools. Seventeen percent of city schools and 11 percent of schools in urban fringe areas reported at least one serious violent crime, compared to 8 percent of rural schools and 5 percent of schools in towns.[27]

Concern over school crime and violence has prompted many public schools to take various measures to reduce and prevent violence and ensure safety in schools. Such measures include adopting zero-tolerance policies regarding weapons (that is, carrying a weapon to school will result in expulsion); requiring students to wear uniforms; employing various security measures, such as requiring visitor sign-in and using metal detectors; having police or other law enforcement officials stationed at the school; and offering students and staff various types of violence prevention programs. Theories about why school violence occurs abound, including easy access to guns, moral decay among our youth, vio-

Reprinted with special permission of King Features Syndicate.

lence portrayed on television and in video games, and abdication of parental responsibility. All are probably contributing factors to greater or lesser degrees.

Gangs   Severe violence is often associated with gangs. Once confined to inner-city areas, street gangs are now present in smaller urban areas and suburbs, although in smaller percentages. In 1995, urban students were more likely to report street gangs at their schools (41 percent) than were suburban students (26 percent) or rural students (20 percent).[28] The proportion of young people who actually join gangs is quite small, however. The Justice Department estimates the number of gang members at about 250,000 out of the nearly 47 million Americans ages twelve to twenty-five, the years most closely associated with gang activity.[29]

Children and teenagers join gangs for a variety of reasons: the excitement of gang activity, peer pressure, physical protection, attention, financial gain, a sense of belonging, and sometimes because they feel ignored by the people they should be close to, usually one or both parents. In many cases, youths are not actively discouraged from gang involvement by their parents. Often parents are unaware that their children are engaged in gang activity. Gangs often display clothing, jewelry, or graffiti that distinguish and identify their members. The character of gang activity has become more violent because increasingly gangs are involved in drug dealing and other criminal activities. The easy accessibility and spread of guns, and the greater tendency to use extreme violence to settle disputes or to revenge even the smallest acts of "disrespect," have also contributed to increased violence. Although gang members are often stereotyped as lower class, some are children of middle-class, suburban families who commit acts of vandalism, robbery, and drug dealing out of boredom or feelings of alienation from family and friends.

increasing violence

How can educators minimize the negative influences of gangs? Useful actions include the following:

combating gang influence

▶ Establish and enforce clear codes of school conduct that stress the unacceptability of gang behavior and the prohibition of weapons.

▶ Establish programs that stress positive youth involvement as alternatives to gang membership.

▶ Assimilate gang-oriented students into the mainstream—academically, socially, and through extracurricular activities.

▶ Create school programs that focus on nonviolent conflict resolution and gang prevention.

▶ Take quick, decisive actions when instances of gang activity occur on school grounds.

Costs of Vandalism and Violence   Costs resulting from vandalism or violence include the costs of building repairs, skyrocketing premiums for liability insurance, and human costs in terms of injuries to students and teachers, and, in extreme cases, even deaths.

Many teachers are injured while attempting either to break up student fights or to halt robberies. Student-teacher disagreements also provoke attacks. Still other teachers are injured not by students but by intruders who may be dealing drugs or who see the elementary schools as buildings with little security and populated by women and children.

Steps to Reduce School Violence   Several aspects of school organization can contribute to student aggression, including high numbers of students occupying a small space, imposition of routines and conformity that may anger some students, and poor building designs that may contribute to the commission of violent acts.[30] On the other hand, students who enjoy positive interactions with faculty and staff, are academically successful, or participate productively in school activities are less likely to commit acts of violence. What, then, can schools do to reduce school violence?

how to reduce violence

▶ Principals can establish common goals and elicit commitment to the goals from teachers, students, and parents.

▶ Establish a firm, fair, and consistent system for running the school.

▶ Establish high expectations for the behavior and performance of students and staff.

▶ Create a curriculum that supports the values of honesty, integrity, kindness, and respect for others.

▶ Use a variety of security measures to keep intruders and weapons off school grounds.

▶ Establish the school as neutral territory for students, control rumors, and squelch loitering and tardiness.

▶ Create alternative schools for serious offenders.

▶ Provide students and teachers with training in effective communication.

What can teachers themselves do to prevent violence and vandalism?

▶ Establish a classroom environment centered on respect and kindness where "put-downs," ridicule, and sarcasm are not tolerated.

▶ Learn how to defuse conflict in ways that save face for both students and teachers.

▶ Develop intensive skill in classroom management.

▶ Use peer counseling or peer mediation to train students to handle problems before they become serious.

▶ Involve students in decision-making processes in areas such as finding methods to handle offenders.

The encouraging news is that although school violence and vandalism are a serious problem, they still affect a relatively small percentage of teachers and students in the public schools. The problem probably reflects as much on societal malaise as on the schools. Boredom, frustration, alienation, despair, and low self-concept are characteristics that teenagers may experience in their homes and in society in general, as well as in school. The disintegration of the traditional family and the increasing depiction of violence in the media and in popular music are cited as two major causes of violence in the public schools. As long as violence prevails in society, we may be unable to expect anything different in our schools.

School Dropout

National dropout rates have declined over the last decade, but they are still substantial. Each year 300,000 to 500,000 tenth- to twelfth-graders leave high school without their diploma.[31] Overall, according to the most recent statistics, the dropout rate for sixteen- to twenty-four-year-olds stands at 11 percent. When we break down this figure to look at subgroups, we find considerable variance among ethnic and racial groups (see Figure 5.6). Hispanic youth are much more likely to become dropouts than African Americans, who in turn are more likely to drop out than whites. Comparable data for Asian Americans and Native Americans are not available, although the dropout rate for Native Americans is estimated to be similar to that for Hispanic Americans. Dropout rates are also strongly related to income levels. Youth from high-income families are highly unlikely to drop out, whereas 13 percent of those from low-income families drop out.[32] Dropout rates are highest in schools with a larger proportion of students from low-income families.

different dropout rates

Reasons for Dropping Out   Besides poverty, what contributes to high dropout rates? Students report poor grades, dislike for school,

> *I am often asked whether I approve of compulsory education, and I usually reply that I do and that I wish we had it; we only have compulsory attendance.*
>
> —JOHN BREMER

FIGURE 5.6   Dropout Rates for 16- to 24-Year-Olds, by Race and Ethnicity

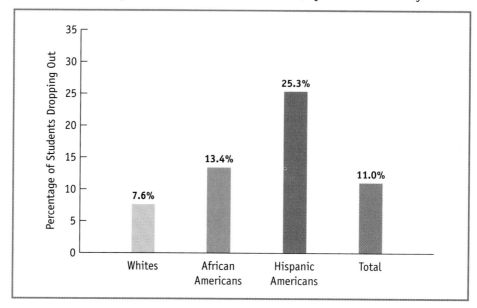

Source: *Dropout Rates in the United States: 1997* (Washington, DC: National Center for Education Statistics, 1997), p. iii.

alienation from peers, marriage or pregnancy, and employment as common causes for leaving school. The most frequently reported factor is poor academic performance. Warning signs include increased absences, lethargy in completing work, and preoccupation with things outside of school. Teachers can discourage students from dropping out by showing interest and care in their students and by talking to and encouraging them. Knowing your students well can help you detect changes in their attitudes and work habits.

One cause of dropping out is unrealistic expectations about the world of work. Many students with high hopes for the imagined luxury of a regular income fail to realize that wages in the service sector of employment have deteriorated. Other teenagers may envision starting at the bottom of the work hierarchy and, through hard work, eventually climbing the ladder of success. However, many of them lack job search skills and usually end up in entry-level jobs with limited potential for advancement. Despite this reality, the strong motivation to work often proves too powerful an incentive and results in a student leaving school. The immediate rewards of the workplace lure some students away from the more remote incentives for attaining an education and staying in school.

Tension Points in American Education

This section explores opposing positions on some of the most controversial topics in American education today. Our goal is to equip you, as a teacher, with an understanding of and sensitivity to the exposed nerve endings of American education. Keep in mind the significance of these tension points; they are the result of an attempt to educate children in a pluralistic society. Tension points are inevitable when diverse groups and individuals with different objectives for the schools try to achieve those objectives. Since teachers have a deep responsibility to the schools, it is important that they provide leadership in seeking enlightened solutions to the problems arising from these complex and touchy issues.

One warning: our coverage of these tension points will acquaint you with some of the key aspects surrounding these issues, but it is not very deep. You should not be satisfied to stop here. It is your responsibility to dig below the surface to find out what these issues really involve. Obviously, all of the tension points in American education cannot be explored in this chapter, but a number of them are addressed in other chapters. For example, equitable school funding issues, certainly a "hot button" topic, are addressed in Chapter 9, "How Are Schools Governed, Influenced, and Financed?" In this section, we focus on three topics that have generated considerable controversy and debate: access and equality of educational opportunity, school choice, and gender issues.

Before we proceed, take a few moments to assess your own position by answering the following questions about these three controversial topics in American education:

assessing your own position

▶ What constitutes equality of educational opportunity? Should it be determined by students having equal access to similar resources or by achieving comparable academic results?

▶ Do you believe in providing preferential treatment to members of groups to compensate for unequal educational opportunities resulting from their race, social class, or financial situation?

▶ Do you believe parents should be free to choose the public school their child attends, regardless of whether they live in that school's district? Are you in favor of providing parents with state-funded vouchers that they can use to pay their child's tuition at a private or religious school?

▶ Do schools treat boys and girls equally? What evidence can you provide to support your position?

▶ Should schools teach sex education? If so, what should be the focus of such programs?

Opinions on these issues are extremely diverse because they touch on our religious, political, or philosophical convictions. Whatever your views, you may find it stimulating and thought provoking to compare your responses with those of your classmates.

Access and Equality of Educational Opportunity

America is a multiracial, multiethnic, and multiclass society. Many people consider it to be one of the most successful mixed societies the world has ever seen.

However, it is far from perfect, and many children born into poor or minority-group families face severe disadvantages in their attempts to live decent lives and to climb the ladder of success. Schooling is intended to help individuals in this process. Whether or not the schools have been helping or hindering the progress of these children has been a source of raging debate for decades.

One fact seems clear: large numbers of poor and minority-group students are leaving school without the academic and occupational skills necessary to function effectively in American society. Who, if anyone, is to blame for this situation? The schools? Teachers and administrators? Or is the responsibility that of society as a whole, and are the schools merely being made a scapegoat? Talk to five different people and you will probably hear five different opinions about where blame should be fixed. But assessing blame is not our function here.

changing definitions of access and equal educational opportunity

The debate revolves around the ideas of *access* and **equality of educational opportunity.** These are hardly new concepts in American education, but their components have changed dramatically in recent decades. In the nineteenth century, the goal of educational access was to build schools where children lived and to enroll as many of them as possible. By the beginning of the twentieth century, that goal was augmented by a focus on giving students curricular choices, including vocational training, to help prepare them for their different economic and social roles. In the 1930s, 1940s, and 1950s, access to equal educational opportunities focused on removing legal, racial, and economic barriers to schooling. The federal government's role in removing these barriers to school access increased dramatically, especially after the landmark 1954 Supreme Court

Brown *v.* Board of Education

decision in *Brown* v. *Board of Education*. This decision held that segregated schools are inherently unequal because the effects of such schools are likely to differ (see Chapter 11, "What Is the History of American Education?", for more on desegregation efforts). Thus, a new component was introduced into the concept of educational opportunity: that equality of educational opportunity is defined in terms of the effects, rather than the provision, of schooling. In the *Brown* decision, the Supreme Court found that even when the facilities and teacher salaries provided were identical, "equality of educational opportunity" did not exist in segregated schools.

Equality is the result of human organization.

—HANNAH ARENDT

Prior to *Brown*, the community and educational institutions were expected only to provide equal resources (teachers, facilities, materials), and responsibility for the best use of those resources lay with the child and the child's family. In the decades since *Brown*, many people have come to consider it the responsibility of the educational institution, not the child, to create achievement.

During the 1960s through the 1970s, access and educational opportunity were redefined as they became increasingly tied to results. The removal of racial, linguistic, mental, and physical discrimination as the basis for expanded access was augmented by a focus on measuring learning outcomes among different groups as a test of whether improved access led to real educational opportunity. Others do not accept this assertion, arguing that the school should do its best to provide equal educational resources for all its students but cannot be held accountable for differences in student learning. As one noted educational historian has stated,

When all students are expected to meet high academic standards, access to comparable learning resources is a critical part of equal educational opportunity. (© A. Ramey/ PhotoEdit)

Each redefinition incorporated the view that schools had fallen short of meeting existing goals or that the goals themselves needed modification. This duality was itself revealing. On the one hand, inequalities by region, social class, race, gender, and disability meant that access—in any of its meanings—was always incomplete. On the other hand, even when goals were substantially met . . . new expectations were added to what the schools should accomplish. By the end of [the twentieth] century, those expectations had shifted to an emphasis on academic achievement and a de-emphasis on issues of equity.[33]

Although it is agreed that many poor minority children in our schools are not learning at a rate comparable to white middle-class children, opinions vary considerably as to the locus and cause of the problem. At one extreme are those who think the problem resides in the so-called deficiencies of minority children. Their impoverished home life, their particular cultural milieu, or even their mental capacities are cited as the sources of unequal results in school. At the other extreme are those who claim the problem is in the schools, which neither stimulate nor instruct the minority child with the intensity that is needed. Teachers expect minority children to do poorly, they claim, and this becomes a self-fulfilling prophecy. As described in Chapter 4, this position assumes that it is the school's obligation to diagnose the learner's needs, concerns, and cognitive and affective styles and to adjust its program accordingly. As with most controversies, the answer probably lies somewhere in between: many minority students do have certain deficiencies, but the schools need to learn how to overcome them.

opinions vary regarding poor achievement

In addition, numerous court cases have challenged the school finance systems in various states, charging that when educational spending in rich school districts exceeds that of poor districts by two or three times, students in the poor districts

Maria Montessori *(1870–1952)*

Maria Montessori became a proponent of preschool education, an urban educational reformer, and a believer in equal opportunities for women sixty years before any of these issues were matters of widespread concern.

As a child, Montessori excelled in mathematics and thought of becoming an engineer. Later she became interested in medicine and overcame tremendous criticism to become the first woman to enroll in the University of Rome's medical school. After graduating, she lectured on anthropology at the university and became associated with the psychiatric clinic. She developed an interest in children with mental retardation and, suspecting they were far more capable of learning than was commonly believed, founded and headed the Orthophrenic School, where she achieved remarkable results with these children.

But not until she was thirty-six years old did Montessori find her life work. Believing that her methods could be even more effective with normal children, she opened her first school, the Casa dei Bambini (Children's House), to the preschool-age street urchins of Rome. Montessori's school was run on the principle of allowing children freedom within a carefully designed environment and under the sensitive guidance of a trained director. The materials and toys available in the school were prescribed, but the children could handle or ignore them as they wished. The teachers were instructed simply to wait until the child became interested in a particular game or project. A child who was concentrating deeply on a ritual with a toy was not aided or corrected by a teacher unless she or he asked for help.

Montessori discovered that certain simple and precise educational materials evoked sustained interest and attention in young children. Children under five years would concentrate on a single task, oblivious to distraction, from fifteen minutes to an hour, and afterward seemed refreshed rather than tired. Montessori's close observations of children led her to conclude that from birth to age six, all children have "absorbent minds" that equip them to learn more quickly and easily than at any later period in their lives. Montessori recognized that small children learn through their senses, and she developed methods of stimulating the child's senses in ways that would improve learning. For instance, children were taught the alphabet with sandpaper letters that they could manipulate with their fingers. Montessori was the first to use flashcards as a sensory stimulus, and she even introduced the hula hoop, which became a fad in the United States in the 1950s. When severely criticized for ignoring discipline, she replied that in the conventional schools she had visited, children were "not disciplined, but annihilated."

Montessori's teaching methods have aroused considerable interest in the United States as a result of recent psychological research that verifies many of her theories. Psychologists and educators have come to agree with her that the period of early childhood is critical in determining a person's intellectual potential. Teachers of underprivileged or poor children in particular claim great success with Montessori techniques. The day care center movement and the early childhood movement in general have been significantly influenced by Maria Montessori's views. In many ways, hers was one of the first compensatory education programs.

are not getting access to equal educational opportunities. In a number of cases, courts have ordered legislatures to redesign the school finance system. (See Chapter 9 for more on the topic of equitable school finance.)

As we begin a new century, the goals of access and educational opportunity have become exceedingly complex as they encompass multiple meanings. Even as America has achieved success in creating greater access to schooling, those very successes have bred discontent and changed expectations as to what access and educational opportunity mean. The current emphasis on elevating academic outcomes for all students has essentially displaced the historic commitment to removing barriers to universal attendance and high school graduation as measures of access. The controversy over access and equity is best seen in the contentious debates about affirmative action. Although affirmative action centers primarily on admission to college, it is also being tested in admissions to select private schools and magnet schools. The issue centers on whether awarding minority students special status in admissions decisions is either appropriate or legal. The larger issue is whether any group defined as "in need" should receive preferential treatment designed to compensate for unequal educational opportunities resulting from their race, social class, or financial situation. These changed expectations have made the concepts of access and equal educational opportunity a major tension point in American education.

controversy over preferential treatment

School Choice

America is recognized around the world as a consumer's paradise. Whether it is soft drinks in the supermarket, jeans in a clothing store, or sports cars at the auto dealer, the principle of choice rules—except in K–12 schooling.

Technically, all parents have a choice as to where they wish to have their children educated. If they do not like the public, state-supported school to which their children are assigned, they can send them to a private or religious school (that is, if there is one in their locale). Or they can move to another community where the schools are more to their liking. The only problem with this theory is that not everyone can put it into practice. For the large percentage of parents without the resources to pay tuition at private or religious schools, there really is no choice at all. Many people are touting school choice as an important aspect of access and educational opportunity. They argue that poor parents should have a choice in the schools their children attend as wealthier parents do. Being able to choose the school your children attend, they argue, is an important way to ensure access to educational opportunity. If the neighborhood school isn't doing an adequate job, shouldn't parents have alternative choices of schools?

constraints on parental choice

The advocates of **school choice** see our current system as monopolistic and want to revolutionize the way we organize education. They want to transfer the decision of where a child must go to school from the school system to the child's parents. They want *market forces* to regulate the schools instead of the educational monopoly that they claim currently operates.

Parents as Educational Consumers   Advocates for choice say that the current public schools have no real incentive to better serve students, since salaries and benefits are unaffected by either good or poor student results. The teacher who works sixteen hours a day and gives heart and soul to the school is on the same salary scale as the teacher who is the first one out of the parking lot at two-thirty. On the other hand, if the parent can act as a consumer, choice advocates argue, schools will have an incentive to improve. Free-market principles suggest that "More choice equals more competition equals better products at lower prices." Here the phrase "better products" means better-educated students.

Supporters of school choice say further that the group getting the worst public education today, our urban minorities, stands to benefit the most. As an example, they point to one of the longest-running choice experiments in the country, District 4 in New York City. Central Park East secondary school and the area's elementary schools are part of a network of schools from which parents can select. Not only has parents' satisfaction increased, but, more important, the students' achievement has improved substantially. Poor families that would have had little or no choice now have some options.

The choice concept is definitely gaining support across the country. There are at least three kinds of school choice. The least controversial form allows parents to choose from among the various public schools that a school district operates. Many school districts have created a variety of schools with different goals and purposes, and allow parents to select the one they want their child to attend. The next, more controversial form of school choice is the charter school concept, and the most controversial form is school voucher plans. The major political parties have staked out positions on the choice issue, with Democrats favoring choice within the current public school system and Republicans tending to support voucher plans. Charter schools draw support from Republicans and many Democrats.

Public School Choice   Many public school systems are offering parents and students options, in addition to the traditional neighborhood school, as to which schools students attend. Some schools have a particular specialty, such as mathematics or science. Others are "alternative" schools designed for youth who don't seem to fit well within traditional schools. There are several varieties of public school choice, most of which are fairly noncontroversial. "Districtwide," or "intradistrict," choice allows parents to select among the schools within their home district. These school choice options are offered in numerous school districts around the country, including Boston, Seattle, Minneapolis/St. Paul, and District 4 in New York City. "Statewide," or "interdistrict," choice allows students to attend public schools outside their home school district. By 1999, fourteen states, led by Minnesota, had accepted statewide choice plans, and over twenty states had considered them.[34]

Magnet schools represent another form of public school choice. During the 1970s, a number of urban school districts began implementing magnet school programs as a way to reduce "white flight" from the inner cities and as an alternative to forced busing for desegregation purposes. Magnet schools are alternative schools that provide high-quality instruction in specified areas as well as in the basic skills. Magnet schools differ from regular schools in three principal ways: (1) magnet schools have a unified curriculum based on a special theme or method of instruction, (2) enrollment is open to students beyond the geographic attendance zone, and (3) students and parents choose the school. They are designed to attract (like a magnet) students of all racial and ethnic groups from all areas of the school district; thus, they offer quality education in integrated classrooms.

Magnet schools have been established with considerable success in many areas of the country. Once limited to a few large cities, today magnet schools number more than 2,600 elementary and secondary schools, serving more than 1.5 million students.[35] Offering parents a choice of what school their children will attend is a key factor in the popularity of magnet schools. Another factor is the millions of dollars spent by the federal government to get magnet schools up and running in over 100 school districts. In many cases, magnet schools have been established as a method of voluntary desegregation by offering quality education to students who meet admission criteria, regardless of the neighborhoods in which they reside.

magnet schools popular

Magnet school programs are diverse. Some emphasize academics: science, social studies, foreign languages, college preparation, and so on. Others stress fine arts or performing arts. Some magnet schools address students with special needs, such as gifted and talented students. Still others take a career or vocation, such as engineering or the health professions, as their focus. Elementary magnet schools are often identified with a particular teaching style: emphasis on basic skills, Montessori methods, or open classrooms. Besides diversity, most magnet school programs offer quality.

diversity among magnets

Although originally designed to achieve voluntary desegregation, magnet programs have also been found to help stem enrollment declines, raise achievement levels, and allay community doubts over the general quality of education. These programs have been linked with reduced school violence and vandalism and improved pupil attendance, as well as more positive student attitudes toward school.[36] However, a more recent study found no evidence that magnet schools in themselves contribute significantly to districtwide desegregation.[37] In fact, one researcher argues that considerable segregation occurs inside many magnet schools' classrooms.[38]

effectiveness of magnets

Despite these doubts, magnet schools are likely to continue to flourish in the future. Virtually all magnet schools now have long waiting lists, despite the facts that in many schools students have to travel long distances to school, the class day is longer, and the work is harder than in nonmagnet schools. Their successes have been numerous, and they offer parents and students school choice within the public school system. The secret of their success seems to be an environment with high interest, motivation, and learning for students, along with support and satisfaction for parents.[39] By providing quality education to students of all types, magnet schools offer a promising step in the direction of equal educational opportunity.

▶ In some proposals, the vouchers are worth only $1,000 to $2,500 per student, limiting the choices of schools for which these amounts would pay the actual costs of tuition.

public funding for religious schools?

▶ In Cleveland and Milwaukee, religious schools have been the major beneficiaries of the vouchers, which raises concerns about whether spending public dollars for students to attend religious schools violates the principle of church and state separation.

teacher unions oppose vouchers

▶ Many voucher opponents, including the two largest teacher unions, suggest that if voucher plans become widespread, the public schools will lose much-needed revenue and be forced to educate children with great needs, whom the private schools would not accept, while lacking the resources to do a good job.

▶ Finally, voucher opponents contend that applying market forces to educational institutions doesn't make sense because schools should be driven by the need to serve the public good, not the need to earn profits.

Those who support voucher plans offer counterarguments to many of these objections. For example, although funding private and religious schools with public money is very controversial in the United States, it is less so in many other countries. The United States is one of the few developed nations with such strict limits on parental choice of schools. Most other Western democracies fund private or religious schools with public money, although if these schools accept public money, they usually have to meet certain conditions required by the government.

religious schools already get some public money

Voucher supporters also point out that while many people believe U.S. tax dollars fund only public schools, private and religious schools already benefit from public money. The major breakthrough for private and religious schools was the passage of the Elementary and Secondary Education Act of 1965, which funneled millions of dollars into private schools through federal programs. In addition, private schools in many states have been receiving assistance ranging from pupil transportation, textbooks, health services, and general auxiliary services to salary supplements for teachers. In general, state assistance in areas other than transportation, milk, school lunch programs, and textbooks has been attacked in the courts.

private schools relieve burden on public schools

Another argument in support of voucher plans is that the private schools, which provide education for 5 million students a year, are lightening the burden of the public schools. If, for example, the Catholic school system collapsed, over 2.5 million new students would enroll in the public schools, creating a massive shortage of space, teachers, and money. Advocates of private school aid argue that by partially subsidizing private schools to keep them in operation, the public schools can avoid a deluge of students whom they would be unable to assimilate readily. Private elementary and secondary schools spent $27 billion during the 1997–98 school year.[41] If these schools were to shut down, the public schools would incur a substantial portion of these costs.

The issue of school choice is likely to remain a contentious one for some time to come.

Gender Issues

Another multifaceted tension point in American education centers on issues of gender, particularly equality between the sexes, sexual harassment, sexual orientation, and sex education. Our ideas about the roles of men and women and how each should be treated, how schools should behave toward gay and lesbian students, and what role schools should play in educating youth about sex are all closely tied to moral, ethical, and legal issues. As a result, considerable disagreement surrounds these complicated issues. This section explores some of these controversial positions.

Equality Between the Sexes   Earlier in this chapter, we made the point that racial and ethnic groups have been denied equal educational opportunities throughout our country's history. Another social group also has suffered discrimination and denial of equal educational opportunities: women. Many women assert, and rightfully so, that societal values and mores have discriminated against them as a class and have significantly limited the development of their human potential. Indeed, strong evidence supports the contention that historically women in our society have been denied educational and employment opportunities routinely extended to men. Whether that condition continues to exist is a matter of controversy.

historical discrimination against females

Early Differences in Socialization   Women and men experience very different kinds of socialization in our society. From very young ages through adulthood, society holds different expectations for males and females. These expectations, in turn, generate different patterns of behavior toward boys and girls. Whether it's blue versus pink clothes, G.I. Joes or Barbie dolls, video games or drawing kits, or football helmets versus ballet slippers, boys and girls get different messages from society about what is expected of them. Society tolerates aggressive behavior more in boys than in girls. Boys are encouraged to be independent, whereas girls often are expected to conform to accepted norms.

differences in socialization

This situation is not confined to the home. The American Association of University Women (AAUW) issued a controversial report in 1992, *How Schools Shortchange Girls,* describing various ways in which girls are adversely treated in schools.[42] The report contends that the educational system is not meeting girls' needs. Although boys and girls enter school roughly equal in measured ability, by the end of high school girls have fallen behind males in key areas such as science, higher-level mathematics, and measures of self-esteem. Yet, the report argues, very little of the discussion or action on school reform includes gender equity issues. The dominant culture of schools, especially of secondary schools, is masculine. The AAUW report challenges policymakers, educators, parents, and citizens to rethink old assumptions and to act now to stop schools from shortchanging girls.

AAUW report

Several researchers have charged that gender bias abounds in the schools and is even taught informally in the curriculum. Textbooks, other reading materials, and educational software, despite recent attempts at improvement by publishers and authors, often still portray females as more helpless than males. Although

gender bias in schools

sexism has decreased in many texts, these researchers argue, examples of gender stereotyping, tokenism, and omission still occur frequently in references to girls and women.

males dominate interactions

Classroom Interactions   Numerous observational studies have concluded that teachers treat boys differently than girls, often to the girls' detriment, although teachers are generally unaware of their behaviors that favor boys.[43] For example, at all levels of schooling, male students have more interactions with teachers than do female students. Males are more likely to dominate classroom discussions, whereas females sit quietly. Boys are more likely to call out, and when they do, teachers are apt to accept the call-out and continue with the class. When girls call out, a much less frequent occurrence, the teacher's typical response is to correct the inappropriate behavior. As a result, boys receive more attention simply by demanding it. As Myra and David Sadker, two leading researchers in gender equity research, report, "As victims of benign neglect, girls are penalized for doing what they should and lose ground as they go through school. In contrast, boys get reinforced for breaking the rules; they are rewarded for grabbing more than their fair share of the teacher's time and attention."[44] Although boys receive more criticism from teachers than do girls, they also receive more praise. Boys also receive more precise feedback from teachers than do girls.

Boys often dominate classroom discussions unless teachers take steps to ensure participation on the part of girls.
(© Myrleen Ferguson/ PhotoEdit)

Implications of Classroom Findings   What are the implications of the findings on gender interactions in classrooms? In subtle and not so subtle ways, female students get the message that boys are more important than girls because teachers pay more attention to boys. One explanation is that boys demand more attention than girls, but cultural influences are also at work.

The long-term effects of gender bias taught or reinforced in schools are potentially many: fewer women in professions and occupations that emphasize mathematics and science, such as engineering and medicine; fewer women in executive leadership positions in business, government, and education; and lower earning power for women because of their smaller representation in positions of leadership. However, some observers challenge the assertion that schools discriminate against girls. They cite the fact that the large gaps between the education levels of women and men that were evident in the early 1970s have essentially disappeared for the younger generation. Although females still lag behind males in science and higher-level mathematics achievement, high school females on average outperform males in reading and writing, take more credits in academic subjects, are more likely to attend college after high school, and are as likely to graduate with a postsecondary degree. If schools were really so biased against females, they argue, why are women doing so well academically?

effects of gender bias

not everyone agrees

Certainly women have made tremendous progress in educational attainment. What remains to be seen, however, is how these attainments will be rewarded in the marketplace. The average earnings of female high school graduates age twenty-five to thirty-four are more than one-third lower than those of male graduates of the same age. Similarly, female college graduates earn, on average, salaries that are only 80 percent of what their male counterparts receive.[45] Women have made important advances recently in gaining equal educational opportunities with men, but our society still seems to favor males when it comes to prestigious jobs and salaries.

Title IX   In 1972, Congress passed **Title IX** of the Educational Amendment Act, which states, "No person in the United States shall, on the basis of sex, be excluded from participation in, be denied the benefits of, or be subjected to discrimination under any education program or activity receiving Federal financial assistance." Although the fine print required interpretation, the large print was clear: gender discrimination in educational programs receiving federal financing is against the law.

The law has been interpreted to ban gender discrimination in physical education, athletics, vocational education, financial aid, pension benefits, employment and compensation of staff, facilities, and counseling. Athletic programs have received the most public attention. Included under Title IX have been regulations requiring that equal opportunity be provided in all facets of physical education and athletics, such as facilities, game and practice schedules, coaching, travel and per diem allowances, equipment, and supplies. Separate teams have been permissible in contact sports, such as boxing, football, and ice hockey. Whenever a school has had a team in a given noncontact sport for one sex only and athletic opportunities for the other sex have been limited, members of the other sex must be allowed to try out for the team.

effects of Title IX

POLICY MATTERS! Single-Sex Education in Public Schools

What's the Policy?

Despite potential legal challenges, a number of public schools are experimenting with offering all-boys and all-girls classes. As part of the choice movement, some policymakers and educators believe that parents should be able to have their children educated in classes of like gender. In 1996, California initiated an experimental program of single-sex academies, and similar schools or classes have sprung up around the country. Although single-sex schools and classes have long existed in private education, legal complications have discouraged public schools from providing separate education for boys and girls.

How Does It Affect Teachers?

One of the main reasons for separating the sexes is to reduce distractions and to provide equitable educational opportunities. Research indicates that in co-educational classes, boys receive much more attention than girls. Teachers who teach single-sex classes often report fewer discipline problems and greater attention to academics. Whether these results are because of the separation of the sexes or smaller class sizes isn't clear.

What Are the Pros?

For boys, single-sex classes offer a learning environment without the distraction of trying to impress members of the opposite sex. Some single-sex classes have targeted African American boys, often a population with a high risk for dropping out of school. These classes often have an African American male teacher at the elementary grades, hoping to provide the young boys with a positive role model. For girls, single-sex classes offer the opportunity to speak out freely. Many believe that by separating the sexes, girls will participate more in class, have more opportunities to provide leadership, and focus more on academics rather than trying to impress boys.

What Are the Cons?

A major concern is the questionable legal status of single-sex education in public schools. Although the U.S. Supreme Court's only action on the issue dates to 1976, when the justices let stand an appeals court's ruling that Philadelphia's single-sex high schools did not violate the equal-protection clause of the Fourteenth Amendment, a lower federal court in 1991 forced three all-male public schools in Detroit to admit girls. In 1988, the U.S. Department of Education's office for civil rights cited racial and sex discrimination in killing a plan to hold separate classes for African American boys in Miami. The office is now investigating whether the Young Women's Leadership Academy in New York violates Title IX, the federal law barring sex discrimination in schools receiving federal aid, by discriminating against boys. In addition to the legal issue, many researchers say there is no substantial evidence that single-sex education produces the results its supporters advocate.

What Do You Think?

1. Should public schools be allowed to experiment with single-sex schools or classes? Why or why not?

2. Have you or anyone you know attended a single-sex school? If so, what advantages or disadvantages can you report?

3. If public schools are to offer single-sex education, what safeguards would you want instituted to ensure discrimination did not occur?

Your Role as a Teacher Title IX regulations and the overall attention given to gender bias have greatly helped to correct inequities resulting from gender discrimination. It is still clear, however, that the elimination of gender bias and gender-role stereotyping in schools will be a complex procedure requiring the cooperation of teachers, administrators, school boards, counselors, educational publishers, teacher educators, and parents. Your role as a teacher will be especially important. As you interact with your pupils and as you select and use instructional materials, your sensitivity to this problem will help determine the attitudes of our future generations. Here are some steps you can take to address gender inequities: *steps you can take*

▶ Be aware of your own behavior toward boys and girls in your classes.

▶ Organize classes so students don't segregate themselves by sex.

▶ Examine instructional materials to ensure that they are not sex biased and that they include features on girls and women.

▶ Place less emphasis on competition and speed and more emphasis on cooperative activities to ensure that everyone understands and completes the assignment.

▶ Increase the focus on practical, real-life applications of mathematics and science.

▶ Structure learning activities so girls will have equal opportunities to participate.

▶ Help to promote a school culture in which gender and ethnic bias are not tolerated.

Much remains to be done. Remember: as with all the other issues we have addressed in this chapter, if you're not part of the solution, you're part of the problem.

Sexual Harassment In 1993, the AAUW commissioned a national survey to investigate a national problem of sexual harassment—unwelcome verbal or physical conduct of a sexual nature imposed by one individual on another—in our schools.[46] Although girls are not always the victims of sexual harassment, in most cases a boy is harassing a girl. Surprisingly, however, 76 percent of the boys responding to the survey reported at least one instance of sexual harassment compared with 85 percent of the girls. The psychological effects of harassment seem to be most profound among girls. Teenage girls responded with stories of pervasive and overt sexual harassment. Girls described sexual jokes and taunts; attempts to snap their bras, lift their skirts, and grope their bodies; and other unwanted physical attention. Most of the harassment occurred in plain view of others—in hallways, lunchrooms, classrooms, assemblies, and playgrounds, and on school buses.

Sexual harassment is prohibited by law, but sex-biased peer interactions appear to be tolerated in our schools. Too often school authorities treat the matter *prohibited by law* as a joke. However, as the 1992 AAUW report states, "When boys line up to 'rate' girls as they enter a room, where boys treat girls so badly that they are reluctant to enroll in courses where they may be the only female, when boys feel it is good fun to embarrass girls to the point of tears, it is no joke."[47] Boys and girls get the message that girls are not worthy of respect and that it is OK for boys to exert power over girls. And, as we'll see in the next section, harassment related to sexual orientation is commonplace in our schools.

In 1999, the U.S. Supreme Court ruled that school districts may be sued for damages under Title IX of the Educational Amendment Act of 1972 in cases involving student-on-student sexual harassment if they fail to respond to student sexual harassment of other students. The Court emphasized that districts could be found liable only if they were "deliberately indifferent" to information about "severe, pervasive, and objectively offensive" harassment among students. In a separate case involving sexual harassment of a student by a teacher, the Court ruled similarly that a school district could be sued for damages only if district officials were aware of the teacher's harassing behavior and were deliberately indifferent to it.[48] School officials are worried that these rulings may trigger an avalanche of lawsuits against school districts, which could end up costing districts millions of dollars.

All our students, boys and girls, have the right to attend schools whose environments are free from such harassment. As a teacher, you cannot ignore such instances when you see them occur. Choose to make such times "teachable moments" by helping students learn to appreciate the dignity of others and ensuring that the classroom is a welcoming environment for all students. Schools can address the problem by drafting a sexual harassment policy; requiring training programs for administrators, teachers, and students; acting quickly when confronted with sexual harassment; enlisting the support of parents; and instituting disciplinary actions against repeat harassers.

Sexual Orientation   Another controversial aspect of gender issues centers on sexual orientation. Regardless of your own beliefs on the subject of homosexuality, if you are going to teach in the public schools, you may very well teach gay and lesbian students.

schools hostile to homosexuals

There is considerable evidence that school is often a hostile environment for young homosexuals. The teen environment tends to ridicule differences in general and homosexuality in particular. Gay and lesbian students are often verbally and physically abused by classmates. Teachers and administrators who condone such name calling as "queer" or "faggot" while prohibiting profanity or racial slurs are also sources of hostility toward homosexual youth. In fact, there have been recent cases where gay students won lawsuits against school officials for failing to maintain a safe school environment and to discipline students who regularly tormented them.

The hostility that gay and lesbian youth encounter in school is mirrored in the larger society, which bombards them with messages that they are outcasts. This hostility leaves many of them isolated, frightened, and uncertain about their own worth. As a result, gay students are a high-risk population. Many run away from

gays a high-risk population

home or are thrown out by parents, abuse drugs and alcohol, suffer from depression, or attempt suicide. One youth risk behavior survey conducted in Massachusetts found that more than one-third of self-identified gay, lesbian, or bisexual teenagers reported having attempted suicide in the previous twelve months.[49] The National Education Association, the American Federation of Teachers, and the Association for Supervision and Curriculum Development have all passed resolutions calling on their members and school districts to acknowledge the special needs of homosexual students, provide supportive services such as counseling and support groups, and implement anti-harassment measures. In 1993 Massachusetts became the first state to ban anti-gay discrimination in public schools and establish a statewide "safe schools" program, and in 1997 the U.S. Department of Education issued guidelines spelling out that "gay or lesbian students" are covered by federal prohibitions against sexual harassment.[50]

However, the issue of homosexuality is extremely controversial, and actions urged by these organizations are certain to provoke opposition by some community members who believe such steps would signal that the schools are condoning homosexuality. Some people believe that while touting tolerance, gay and lesbian organizations are actually seeking to promote homosexuality among students. In spite of such controversy, all students, regardless of sexual orientation, have the right to a safe and supportive learning environment. As educators, we also have the responsibility to promote the emotional well-being of all of our students.

Sex Education

"Sex education is more than just knowledge of the mechanics of the sex act and the development and birth of a baby. The physical aspect should not be emphasized at the expense of its psychological and social aspects."

"Sex education should communicate that sexuality is normal, is healthy, and has many variations."

"Sex education reduces one of life's most profound and mysterious activities to something akin to plumbing, and ends up promoting irresponsible sexual activity."

"Sex, love, birth, and family life are all one package and should be discussed in the reassuring warmth of the parents' presence."

"Runaway teenage pregnancy rates and the wildfire spread of AIDS make it imperative that the schools teach sex education, especially since parents don't teach it."

Sex education is a headline grabber in newspapers throughout the country. *controversial topic* The preceding statements represent five different attitudes about sex education and give evidence of the controversy surrounding it. Though most people agree that children should be given information about sex, the controversy centers on two issues: (1) is the school the appropriate institution to offer such instruction? and (2) if so, should it limit instruction to strictly factual information, or should the psychological, social, health, and moral aspects of sex also be included in the curriculum?

Some people argue that because sex is such an intimate topic and is closely related to religious and moral beliefs, sex education is the responsibility of the home and the church. Advocates of sex education in the schools respond that they would agree with that position if parents did in fact provide adequate sex information for their children. They argue that, unfortunately, this simply is not the case. The majority of parents fail to assume the responsibility to teach their children about sex. According to advocates of sex education, the public school is the only institution that has access to most children over an extended period of time, and the responsibility must fall to the school because of the demonstrated failure of the home, church, library, and medical profession to provide effective sex education. Courts have supported state boards of education and local school boards' right to offer sex education in the curriculum.

what kind of program?

Arguments over the kind of sex education the schools should offer are equally heated. Some support comprehensive sex education programs that convey sexual activities as a natural and healthy part of life, be it heterosexual or homosexual expression. Others believe this approach negates certain moral or religious beliefs; they would recommend an abstinence-based curriculum that teaches students to abstain from homosexuality and sex outside of marriage. Advocates of the abstinence approach argue that when sex education programs teach both abstinence and the use of contraceptives, students receive a mixed message. The only message they should receive, say these people, is abstinence.

Teenage Pregnancies   Preventing teenage pregnancies is a major goal of any sex education program. As we discussed earlier in the chapter, besides endangering babies, early pregnancies are placing the future lives of great numbers of teenage girls in serious jeopardy, interrupting and usually terminating their education. In spite of special counseling and accommodations made for teenage mothers to stay in school, the majority drop out, thus drastically reducing their job and career opportunities.

dropout problem

Sexually Transmitted Diseases (STDs)   Another issue relating to sex education is the incidence of sexually transmitted diseases. It has been estimated that about 3 million American adolescents are newly infected with a sexually transmitted disease each year, with chlamydia and gonorrhea being the most commonly acquired diseases.[51] With the alarming spread of AIDS (acquired immunodeficiency syndrome), preventive measures have become a matter of life and death. Almost 50 percent of high school students reported ever having had sexual intercourse (49 percent of males and 48 percent of females), but only 57 percent of the teenagers who were sexually active in the previous three months reported using condoms, which, aside from abstinence, is the only relatively safe protection against AIDS.[52] It is estimated that one-fourth of all new human immunodeficiency virus (HIV) cases occur in people ages thirteen to twenty-one, half are among people under age twenty-five, and the majority of these infections are sexually transmitted.[53]

risk of AIDS

Some believe that the large number of sexually transmitted diseases, especially AIDS, has strengthened the position of those who argue for comprehensive sex education programs. Providing children with the sex education that will help them understand the risks they face and how to prevent or minimize those risks makes a great deal of sense. Still, some object that sex education, by exciting interest in sexual experimentation, will lead to more promiscuity and increase the risk that it is supposed to reduce. In fact, in programs that provide information about both contraception and abstinence, evaluators have found no increase in sexual activity. A review of forty-seven diverse programs found that sex education not only tended to delay the onset of sexual activity but also appeared to reduce the number of sexual partners, the number of unplanned pregnancies, and the rates of sexually transmitted diseases.[54] Unfortunately, those are not the kind of sex education programs students typically receive.[55] Most sex education programs aren't long enough in duration to be effective; don't provide enough nitty-gritty information about how to minimize risks; begin too late in adolescents' development; rely too heavily on ineffective teaching methods, such as lecturing; and don't treat human sexuality as part of our ethical responsibilities to one another.

research reports

Successful HIV education programs must focus on students' behavior, for that is what puts them at risk. Teenagers report that they know what they should and should not do to avoid transmission of HIV, but their physical urges are stronger than their common sense. This speaks to the need for advice on how to handle sexual feelings and how to evaluate relationships. Students need to be helped to gain the self-control and strength of character to avoid risky and irresponsible behavior.

In the meantime, it is possible that you will have students in your class or school who are known to be HIV infected. It is important for you and your colleagues to know school district policy regarding these children and the ways in which the disease can be transmitted. Safeguarding other children while also attending to the rights and needs of the infected child requires knowledge, care, and understanding.

be aware of district policy

A Final Word

Given the range of social problems that we have discussed in this and the preceding chapter, it is not surprising to find the schools bearing an ever-growing burden to guide young people's decision making. How well equipped are the schools to handle this task? Too often public education has merely reflected the inequities of our society in its treatment of women, racial minorities, individuals with disabilities or disadvantages, individuals who are culturally different, and so on. Many of the tension points in American education touch on questions of values: Can equity and excellence coexist? If not, which is more important? Can the rights of the majority and minority receive equal protection? The problems implied by these questions are not easily solved, and these tension points will likely be with us for a long time to come.

KEY TERMS

at-risk students (136)

equality of educational opportunity
  (156)

school choice (159)

magnet schools (160)

charter schools (162)

site-based decision making (162)

school vouchers (162)

Title IX (167)

FOR REFLECTION

1. How does poverty affect the lives of students from poor families? What is the teacher's responsibility to children burdened with poverty?

2. What aspects of our culture contribute to the high incidence of child abuse in the United States?

3. Should schools assume responsibility for educating children about alcohol, drugs, sex, and suicide? Why or why not? If so, what aspects of the current curriculum should be dropped to make room for these topics?

4. Were you aware of the problem of school violence and vandalism before you read this chapter? Will it be a major factor in your decision regarding whether or not to teach?

5. Do you agree that equality of educational opportunity should be defined by its effects rather than by its provisions? Can you think of an analogy to support your case for or against this position?

6. Do you support the use of school vouchers? Why or why not?

7. Can you recall any gender-biased behavior that you have observed in schools? Do you think gender bias and gender-role stereotyping are problems in our schools?

FOR FURTHER INFORMATION

AAUW Report: How Schools Shortchange Girls. **Washington, DC: American Association of University Women, 1992.**
This report examines the various ways in which girls are treated detrimentally in schools, including the formal and informal curriculum, teacher-student interactions, and sexual harassment.

Comer, James P., Norris M. Haynes, Edward T. Joyner, and Michael Ben-Avie, eds. *Rallying the Whole Village: The Comer Process for Reforming Education.* **New York: Teachers College Press, 1996.**
In this text, James Comer and his colleagues describe the process they have employed to coordinate various resources to create effective school communities in areas of low socioeconomic status.

Education Week on the Web. **World Wide Web site at http://www.edweek.org** SEARCH
Published forty-one times a year, *Education Week* is the nation's newspaper devoted to educational issues, preschool through secondary school. Many of the issues discussed in this chapter are reported on in this periodical, and its web site contains an archive section that permits searches for particular topics and issues. The site also includes the archives of *Teacher Magazine.*

Levine, Daniel U., and Rayna F. Levine. *Society and Education,* **9th ed. Needham Heights, MA: Allyn and Bacon, 1996.**
The authors summarize recent research examining many of the social issues touched on in this chapter.

Nathan, Joe. *Charter Schools: Creating Hope and Opportunity for American Education.* **San Francisco: Jossey-Bass Publishers, 1999.**
The author, a long-time proponent of charter schools, provides the historical background on the charter school movement, gives examples of successful schools, and offers specific guidelines for people who want to develop and operate their own charter school.

PART
THREE

TEACHERS

What exactly do good teachers do, and how do they do it? In recent decades, educators have been developing a deeper understanding of what makes a teacher effective. There are many new teaching methods, new technologies, and new approaches to curriculum. In this section, we aim to give you insights into the issues, challenges, and opportunities for teachers.

6

What Makes a Teacher Effective?

Effective teaching is much more than an intuitive process. A teacher must continually make decisions and act on those decisions. To do this effectively, the teacher must have *knowledge,* both theoretical knowledge about learning and human behavior and specific knowledge about the subject matter to be taught. A teacher also must demonstrate a repertoire of teaching *skills* that are believed to facilitate student learning and must display *attitudes* that foster learning and genuine human relationships.

This chapter emphasizes that

▶ Teachers are required to make many decisions as they plan for instruction, implement teaching strategies, and evaluate outcomes of their planning and strategies.

▶ Four major types of teacher attitudes affect teaching behavior: (1) attitude toward self, (2) attitude toward children, (3) attitude toward peers and parents, and (4) attitude toward the subject matter.

▶ A teacher should have an intimate knowledge of the subject matter being taught, both the instructional content and the discipline from which it derives.

▶ To be able to recognize and interpret classroom events appropriately, a teacher should be familiar with theoretical knowledge and research about learning and human behavior.

▶ Effective teachers demonstrate a repertoire of teaching skills that enable them to meet the different needs of their students. Research has identified a number of these skills in, to name a few areas, classroom management, effective questioning, and planning techniques.

We once knew a teacher who was described as having not twenty years of experience but one year's experience twenty times. The message was that this teacher had stopped growing and developing as a professional after the first year. As someone just starting in your teaching career, this may seem like a remote possibility. After all, there's so much that you know you don't know, and you're eager to learn as much as you can. It is relatively easy, however, to fall into comfortable patterns of teaching, especially after you have gained a few years of experience. How can you avoid this complacency and stagnation?

One way is to maintain your curiosity and develop habits of inquiry and reflection. More and more teacher educators are coming to believe that although it is important to prepare beginning teachers for initial practice, it is even more important to help them develop the attitudes and skills to become lifelong students of teaching. Ideally, rather than relying on authority, impulse, or unexamined previous practice, teachers will continually examine and evaluate their attitudes, practices, effectiveness, and accomplishments. This process of examination and evaluation is often called **reflective teaching**. Reflective teachers ask themselves such questions as "What am I doing and why?" "How can I better meet my students' needs?" "What are some alternative learning activities to achieve these objectives?" "How could I have encouraged more involvement or learning on the part of the students?" Even when lessons go well, reflective teachers analyze the lesson to determine what went well and why, and how else things might have been done.

developing the habit of reflection

Developing the habits of inquiry and reflection should begin in the teacher education program. Experiences with schools, teachers, and students will give you many opportunities to reflect on what has occurred. The use of journal writing, observation instruments, simulations, and videotaping can help you examine teaching, learning, and the contexts in which they occur. Comparing your perspectives with those of classmates, professors, and school personnel will broaden your interpretations and give you new insights. As you reflect on your experiences, you will come to distrust simplistic answers and explanations. Nuances and subtleties will start to become clear, and situations that once seemed simple will reveal their complexities. Moral and ethical issues are likely to be encountered and thought about. By practicing reflective teaching, you will grow and develop as an effective, professional teacher.

This chapter will discuss some basic characteristics of effective teachers that you can use as a starting point for your own reflections. We begin with a case study of a new teacher who faces problems that many classroom veterans will find familiar.

CASE STUDY Carol Landis: A Case of Classroom Decision Making

As an example of how ordinary teaching situations can lead to useful reflections about effective teaching, consider the case of Carol Landis. Carol is beginning her first year of teaching. She prepared to be a high school social studies teacher, graduated, and accepted a job in her own community, a small city in the Northwest. Most of her students come from solidly blue-collar, working-class backgrounds.

the case of Carol Landis

Case Study cont'd

Carol has been assigned three periods of world geography and two periods of American history. We'll join her as she prepares the first lesson of a new unit in world geography.

Carol plans to require her ninth-graders to work in groups to prepare panel discussions about a country of their choice. She wants the groups to research the relationships among the geography, political history, and culture of a country and share what they find in panel discussions with the rest of the class. Carol sets these goals for her students: that they work together in groups and that they make effective oral presentations of their research.

Carol's questions

When planning how to present the assignment to her classes, Carol has many questions. Do these students know how to use the library? If not, will she need to provide directions for using reference materials? Maybe the librarian has already done this, and they'll just need a review. Do these students know what *culture* means or understand general concepts that will help them look for relationships among culture, history, and geography? What background do they need before they start researching a specific country? And do these students know how to work in groups? Have they ever participated in a panel discussion? In planning how to help her students complete this assignment, Carol bases her decisions on what she thinks she knows about them as learners.

Although Carol has already planned this assignment to fit into the social studies curriculum, she is concerned about whether the books in her room and the library will provide the information her students need. What other resources are available? She knows that other teachers have back issues of *National Geographic,* for example. Maybe she could help students use the World Wide Web to access hypertext links that would tie together geography, political history, and culture for their respective countries.

In addition to the panel discussions, Carol has considered having each student submit a written report. But for this first research assignment, she decides that an oral presentation by the group is appropriate. Later, she'll work with the classes on report writing. In the beginning, she wants her students to enjoy her classes, to feel a part of a group, and to get to know one another. And Carol prefers listening to her students to grading written reports anyway, so this assignment fits her style of teaching.

Despite her planning, when Carol reflects on her second-period class after the first day of library research, she wonders what went wrong. One group argued the whole period and never did select a country. Maybe she should have assigned groups and not let students choose their own partners? She tried to ignore the group, believing they should work out their own differences and come to a group decision. But what if they never work together? She noticed that another group was completely dominated by one of the top students. He decided what country they would research, he assigned the topics, and he told the others where to look for information. When Carol urged the other members to share equally in the group decisions, they asserted, "Tom always gets A's. We don't mind if he tells us what to do." Carol didn't know how to respond to their concern for grades without insulting Tom. So she said nothing.

incident with Tom

Later in the period, Tom asked her what religion predominated in Indonesia. Carol wasn't sure but was afraid to admit her lack of information, so she told him, "Just look

Case Study cont'd

it up." Tom responded, "So you don't know either?" Carol testily told Tom that she was not his personal encyclopedia. Now she wonders if she overreacted. Maybe she should have admitted she didn't know. Was Tom challenging her authority, or was he just reacting to the sharp tone in her order to look it up? Did she turn Tom and his group against her?

Carol also wonders whether the other groups worked productively. She spent so much time watching the arguing group and Tom's group that she didn't have time to notice whether the chatter from the other groups was work or play. Maybe it didn't hurt to let the other groups have some fun today, anyway. She can direct her attention to them tomorrow.

There is so much to watch and monitor when students work in groups, Carol realizes. And so many questions: "Where do I find this?" "Mr. Shaw won't lend me his magazines; what do I do now?" "This library stinks. Why do we have to do this assignment anyway?" "Miss Landis, what did you do this weekend?" Carol wonders if she will ever learn to field all her students' questions and comments and distinguish the words on the surface from the real messages. And what to do about Ron, who started reading a novel about life in Siberian concentration camps? Carol thinks it is the only book she has ever seen him read. But it won't help his group do their project on Zaire.

Carol's frustrations

Maybe this assignment wasn't such a good idea in the first place, Carol thinks. Or maybe she just wasn't up to working with her classes in groups. The stares from the librarian and the study hall teacher indicated that they didn't think she could handle her classes. And Carol hasn't even thought about how she will grade her students' panel discussions. Just thinking about it all exhausts her. How will she ever get through another day with that second-period class?

The Teacher as Decision Maker

We present Carol's case to illustrate that the teacher's role can be described as one of *decision maker*. Indeed, some educational researchers have identified skill in decision making as the most important teaching skill. Some decisions are made as teachers quietly deliberate curricular and instructional goals; many more must be made almost instantaneously as teachers and students interact. Let's look at some of the particular decisions that Carol made or will make, dividing them into three basic stages: planning, implementing, and evaluating.

Carol as decision maker

Planning Decisions   Carol wants her students to understand the relationships among geography, history, and culture. But what exactly does she want them to know about these relationships? She must decide the particular kinds of understanding she wants her students to achieve, and this decision affects her choice of teaching techniques.

From a variety of possible techniques, she has chosen independent group work. She has also decided that a panel discussion will provide evidence of her students' learning. These decisions reflect Carol's personal preferences, her goals for her students' learning, and her skills in methods of evaluating their learning. Her decisions are also based on a series of judgments about her students' ability to do research, work in groups, and present panel discussions, as well as on judgments about how long they will need to work together and what resources they will need.

Implementing Decisions   As Carol teaches this lesson or series of lessons, she has to decide when and how to intervene with some of her groups, whether to allow Ron to continue reading a novel, and what responses to make to students' questions.

Evaluating Decisions   After the first day's library work, Carol examines her interactions with the students, facing decisions about what adjustments to make in her strategies for the next day. As the groups continue to work, she will also face decisions about how to evaluate the impact of her planning and instruction on her students' learning.

In each of these planning, implementing, and evaluating stages of instructional decision making, Carol chooses among alternative concepts her students could learn, approaches to help them learn the concepts, ways to manage the classroom to encourage their learning, and ways to measure their learning. Could her decisions improve with more adequate knowledge, skills, and attitudes?

Aspects of Effective Decision Making

In the rest of this chapter, we will explore the areas of competence that help teachers make more effective decisions. We, along with many other educators, believe that to be effective decision makers, elementary and secondary school teachers need to have attitudes, knowledge, and skills particular to the teaching profession. Teachers must ask themselves not only "What am I going to teach?" but also "What should my students be learning?" "How can I help them learn it?" and "Why is it important?" To answer these questions, teachers must be familiar with children and their developmental stages. They must know something about events occurring outside the classroom and about what society requires from the young. They must have enough command of the subject they teach to be able to distinguish what is peripheral from what is central. They must have a philosophy of education that guides them in their role as teacher. They must know something about how human beings learn and about how to create environments that promote learning.

areas of teaching competence   What are the specialized skills and attributes of the effective instructional decision maker? The four areas of competence that we consider essential for a teacher are the following:

1. Attitudes that foster learning and genuine human relationships

2. Knowledge of the subject matter to be taught

3. Theoretical knowledge about learning and human behavior

4. Skills of teaching that promote student learning

Differences Between Expert and Novice Teachers

A number of educational researchers have tried to identify expert and experienced teachers and compare them with ordinary or novice teachers. These studies have identified various ways in which novice and expert teachers differ.

We can think of an expert teacher as similar to an expert chess player. Expert chess players quickly spot trouble areas in any chessboard pattern; likewise, expert teachers quickly recognize trouble spots in a classroom setting. Experts in chess or teaching draw on their hours of experience to build a repertoire of recognizable patterns. In one experiment, expert and novice teachers were asked to look at a photograph of a classroom and identify the class activity. Experts were better able to "read" the classroom, making inferences about what was happening in the picture. When observed in action, expert teachers also show greater ability to gather information in a short time for multiple purposes. For example, an expert teacher may be able to accomplish many tasks in an opening review session: gather attendance information, identify who did or did not do the homework, and locate students needing help with the next lesson.

In comparison, novice teachers described the surface characteristics of the classroom pictures they saw. And when presented with descriptions of student problems, the novices relied again on the literal features of the problems to suggest solutions. Their analyses did not correspond with the higher-order classifications used by expert teachers.

Experts differed from novices in their approaches to planning as well. In a simulated task of planning, experts focused on learning what students already knew about the subject matter to be learned, while novices planned to ask students where they were in their textbooks and then present a review of important concepts. In other words, experts planned to gather information from the students, whereas novices planned to give information to them.

The research suggests that experts in any field demonstrate skill in planning and in classifying problems and formulating solutions. This is no less true for teachers: the expert teacher shows problem-solving skills like those of other experts, whether in chess, bridge, or physics. The studies also indicate that the process of moving from novice to expert teacher takes considerable time because extensive experience is necessary to develop enough episodic knowledge to interpret information about classrooms.

Sources: David C. Berliner, "Expertise: The Wonder of Exemplary Performances," in *Creating Powerful Thinking in Teachers and Students*, ed. J. N. Mangiere and C. C. Block (Fort Worth, TX: Harcourt Brace College Publishers, 1994), pp. 161–186; Greta Morine-Dershimer, "Instructional Planning," in J. M. Cooper, ed., *Classroom Teaching Skills*, 6th ed. (Boston: Houghton Mifflin, 1999), pp. 32–33.

Teachers draw on their competence in these four areas to inform the many decisions they make as they plan instruction and as they spontaneously interact with the students in their classes. Figure 6.1 indicates the relationship of these areas of competence to the process of instructional decision making. In the remainder of this chapter, we'll examine these areas of competence, now and then referring to the instructional decisions that Carol made and the attitudes, knowledge, and skills influencing her decisions.

What Attitudes Does the Effective Teacher Possess?

Many people believe that the teacher's personality is the most critical factor in successful teaching. If teachers have warmth, empathy, sensitivity, enthusiasm,

FIGURE 6.1   Relationship of Teacher-Competence Areas to Process of Instructional Decision Making

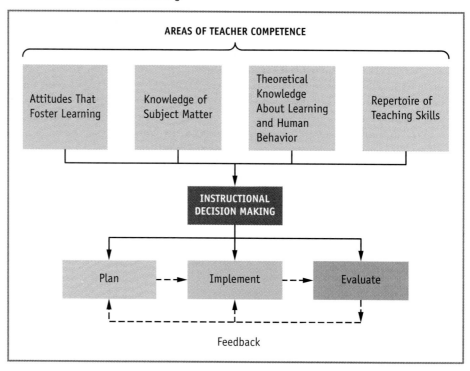

Source: From James M. Cooper (ed.), "The Teacher as a Decision Maker," in *Classroom Teaching Skills*, Sixth Edition. Copyright © 1999 by Houghton Mifflin Company. Reprinted with permission.

and humor, they are much more likely to be successful than if they lack these characteristics. In fact, many people argue that without these attributes, an individual is unlikely to be a good teacher.

For years, educational researchers sought to isolate the characteristics essential to good teachers. In one comprehensive study, the researcher concluded that effective teachers are fair, democratic, responsive, understanding, kindly, stimulating, original, alert, attractive, responsible, steady, poised, and confident. Ineffective teachers were described as partial, autocratic, aloof, restricted, harsh, dull, stereotyped, apathetic, unimpressive, evasive, erratic, excitable, and uncertain.[1]

But this information is not very useful. After all, what human interaction wouldn't be improved if the participants possessed only positive traits? Two researchers, summarizing fifty years of research on teachers' personalities and characteristics, conclude, "Despite the critical importance of the problem and a half-century of prodigious research effort, very little is known for certain about the nature and measurement of teacher personality, about the relation between teacher personality and teaching effectiveness."[2]

definition of attitudes

A person's *attitudes,* or predispositions to act in a positive or negative way toward people, ideas, and events, are a fundamental dimension of his or her personality. Although the relationship between general personality traits and teacher

Anne Mansfield Sullivan *(1866–1936)*

The proof is in the pupil. In this case, Helen Keller, a blind and deaf pupil, was a terror. Wily and mean, Helen was also animal-like. Nevertheless, her teacher, Anne Sullivan, enabled her to become an international celebrity.

Sullivan pioneered the teaching of individuals without sight and without hearing. Today we speak of a *deaf culture,* but this term was not used in the era of Anne Sullivan. "Teacher," as Helen always called her, is credited with making it possible to reach students who were thought to have mental retardation.

The daughter of Irish immigrants, Sullivan was born in Feeding Hills, Massachusetts, on April 14, 1866, and entered the almshouse at eight when her mother died and her father abandoned her and her brother. Half-blind herself, she went to the Perkins School for the Blind in Boston at age fourteen without a toothbrush, hat, or coat; her only possessions were a shirt and stockings tied in a bundle.

At age twenty-one, Sullivan took a job offered by the Keller family in Tuscumbia, Alabama, to teach the Kellers' daughter, Helen. Helen Keller was an angry and frustrated child, but not stupid. Sullivan saw this and began her assault on Helen's locked mind. Within a month, she made contact with Helen in the now famous pump story, immortalized in the drama *The Miracle Worker.* Sullivan fingerspelled words into Helen's hand, each word suiting an action. Finally, Helen, feeling water over her hand, realized the connection between word and object. She had broken the code and realized that everything had a name.

Sullivan's methods were practical. She taught Helen to play through games and exercises, stimulating her to ask the names of the motions. She kept a menagerie of animals for Helen to help her understand movement. She progressed to abstractions like peace and God as soon as her pupil was ready.

Sullivan wanted to make Helen as normal as possible, giving her every experience she could. She worked at teaching her to sit, stand, and walk properly. As soon as Helen could distinguish between right and wrong, "Teacher" sent her to bed for misdeeds. Laziness, carelessness, untidiness, and procrastination were dealt with by ingenuity, humor, and light sarcasm.

Helen used the manual alphabet for three years before she began to speak. When Helen was nine, Sullivan was rewarded with the words "I am not dumb now." It was one of the most dramatic achievements in the history of teaching.

Sullivan's great discovery was that a child should not be taught each word separately by a separate definition but instead should be given endless repetition of language he or she does not understand all day long. Sullivan continually spelled words into Helen's hand to mimic the way a hearing child in the cradle absorbs words. This method had never before been put into practice in the education of a deaf child, especially a deaf-blind one.

When Helen attended a school for deaf pupils in New York, Annie Sullivan went along. At Cambridge School and Radcliffe, Sullivan attended classes, interpreting instruction and looking up words for Helen. She made herself eye and ear to Helen and supplied knowledge to a starving mind as she fired her pupil's drive to study hard. After college, Sullivan accompanied Helen on worldwide lecture tours as Helen became a famous author and personality. Extraordinarily close, teacher and pupil spent much of their lives together. The name "Teacher" has been enriched by Annie Sullivan's dedicated life, persistent high standards, and creative instruction.

Source: Marilyn Ryan.

A teacher's positive attitude toward self and students can help create an environment conducive to learning. (© Elizabeth Crews)

effectiveness has proven elusive, almost all educators are convinced of the importance of teacher attitudes in the teaching process. Attitudes have a direct, though often unrecognized, effect on our behavior in that they determine the ways we view ourselves and interact with others.

four categories of teacher attitudes

We believe four major categories of attitudes affect teaching behavior: (1) the teacher's attitude toward self, (2) the teacher's attitudes toward children and the relationship between self and children, (3) the teacher's attitudes toward peers and pupils' parents, and (4) the teacher's attitude toward the subject matter.

The Teacher's Attitude Toward Self: Self-Understanding

If teachers are to help students have meaningful experiences, develop their aptitudes and abilities, face their inner difficulties, and accept themselves as people, they need to know and understand those students. But before teachers can do that, they must work at knowing and understanding themselves. Empirical evidence from psychology indicates that people who deny or are unable to cope with their own emotions are unlikely to be capable of respecting and dealing with others' feelings.

recognize own needs as well as students'

For example, unless teachers recognize their own needs and anxieties, they will be unlikely to understand and empathize with their students' needs or expressions of anxiety. They may not recognize that students' inabilities to learn, inattentiveness, impudence, or irritability may be the result of anxiety. Teachers also need to recognize that their own anxieties may make them irritable, causing the students in turn to feel anxious and to show similar symptoms.

Ways to Achieve Self-Understanding   How can one achieve understanding of self and, after achieving it, accept it? A number of potential resources can help promote self-understanding. For example, books by sensitive and compassionate people who have made progress in their own struggles to know themselves can be a valuable aid in self-examination. For prospective teachers, such books might include Sylvia Ashton-Warner's *Teacher,* an account of her teaching experience in a Maori infant school in New Zealand; Tracy Kidder's *Among Schoolchildren;* Herbert Kohl's *36 Children;* and Lisa Delpit's *Other People's Children.*

books about teachers

Another method is **participant observation,** the process of observing a class and recording what you hear, see, and feel as you observe. You then compare your record with the records of other observers. This experience may show you that what you notice in any given situation is determined largely by habits of thought that you take for granted. It may also show that your "objective" perceptions are often projections of your own subjective state, and so may tell you more about yourself than about the people you have observed.

observing in classrooms

Some colleges offer sessions run by trained leaders, as well as personal counseling sessions, to help you face and cope with feelings of limitation, insecurity, inferiority, or confusion, the need to be liked and approved of, lack of direction,

college and self-examination

What Would You Do?

1. You are a woman, a beginning teacher in a ninth-grade English course. As the first semester proceeds, you realize that one of your students, Fred, has a crush on you. He is always volunteering to help you pass out papers, and he lingers after class each day to talk to you. He finds out your home address and comes to visit you one Saturday morning. His actions are becoming obvious to the other students, who are starting to kid him about his infatuation.

   What would you do?

2. You are generally recognized as one of the most popular teachers in your school. The students look upon you as a friend who can be trusted, and you have told them that if they ever have problems, school-related or personal, they should feel free to come to you. One day Maryanne, a junior in one of your classes, seeks you out. Close to hysteria, she tells you she is ten weeks pregnant. You are the first person she has told. She begs you for advice, but insists you do not tell her parents.

   What would you do?

3. You are a sixth-grade teacher. Until recently, you have been quite comfortable in your class of twenty-seven children. About three weeks ago, you had to speak to Debbie. Although she is the bright-est student and the natural leader in your class, she was continually talking when you were trying to address the class. Since then she has been as cool as ice to you. But, more worrisome, she has turned the class against you. They seem hostile, and there are continued signs of lack of cooperation. The principal wants to talk with you because she has heard many complaints recently.

   What would you do?

4. You are a white teacher in a somewhat racially tense school. There are seven African American students in one of your classes. Because you fear alienating the African Americans and being accused of prejudice, you make special efforts to treat them fairly. One day three of your white students come to see you and accuse you of coddling the African Americans and discriminating against whites.

   What would you do?

5. You teach in a school that uses a letter grading system. You have assigned your students a term paper. You know that one student has spent hours and hours on his report, but its quality is quite poor. The student has already expressed his hope that you will take effort into account when grading the reports.

   What would you do?

and other problems. We urge you to regard self-examination as a serious commitment and to undertake it, *as a prospective teacher,* in an effort to make a good decision about whether to teach and to become the best teacher you are capable of becoming.

Carol's self-concept

Remember Carol's attitude toward Tom when he asked for information she didn't have. And recall her seeming "live and let live" attitude toward the argumentative group and the student reading a novel. What may these attitudes about student behaviors indicate about Carol's self-concept? Is she afraid to admit limitations in her knowledge? Does she hesitate to discipline off-task behavior because she thinks her students will no longer like her? How strong is her need for approval? Maybe Carol overreacts to Tom's request for information because she is insecure with the role of teacher and feels threatened by his authority among his peers. Although Carol's case does not give enough information to answer these questions, we can say with confidence that her self-concept will influence her behavior toward her students. As Carol develops a realistic understanding of herself and her needs and anxieties, she will change her attitudes toward her students and improve her relationship with them.

The Teacher's Attitude Toward Children

Children are sensitive observers of adult behavior, and they often see, and become preoccupied with, aspects of the teacher's attitude toward them of which the teacher may be unaware. Consider how a teacher's effectiveness might be reduced by these feelings or attitudes toward students:

negative attitudes

- A strong dislike for particular pupils and obvious fondness for others

- Biases toward or against particular ethnic groups

- A bias toward certain kinds of student behavior, such as docility or inquisitiveness

- An uneasiness in working with children who have disabilities

Few teachers are entirely free of negative attitudes at the outset, and self-awareness can be the crucial factor distinguishing a teacher who is able to control and change these attitudes. Thus, it is important that prospective teachers confront their own attitudes early on, perhaps through case studies, group discussions, role playing, or behavioral records of teaching experiences. When we become aware of our attitudes, we can often control our behavior better, but even then change is neither easy nor automatic. It is difficult to admit to feelings and attitudes that might be considered inappropriate or unprofessional. For example, most teachers would like to believe that they like all their students equally, but this is almost never the case. You will have some students you find charming and others who rub you the wrong way. The important thing is that teachers treat students fairly, which usually means treating them differently. Each child has different needs, and the best way to address these needs equitably is to address them

treat students fairly

PEANUTS reprinted by permission of United Feature Syndicate, Inc.

uniquely, including taking into account such factors as race, ethnicity, and gender. As one educator puts it, "If teachers pretend not to see students' racial and ethnic differences, they really do not see the students at all and are limited in their ability to meet their educational needs."[3]

Teacher Expectations   In general, a teacher's expectation that *all* students can succeed seems to make a difference in students' achievement. As a teacher, you need to believe that all your students are capable of high academic achievement and base your beliefs and behavior on the needs, abilities, and aspirations of each individual student.

cultivating positive attitudes

Teachers do form expectations about a student's performance, and these expectations seem to relate to the student's achievement. The source of a teacher's expectations may vary: a student's social class, race, or sex; information from previous teachers; test scores; or family background information. Research indicates that some teachers expect certain behaviors from students on the basis of stereotypes that they have about particular racial, ethnic, or socioeconomic groups.[4] For example, Asian American students may be encouraged to study mathematics or science because teachers believe they are "good" in those subjects. Or teachers may expect more from middle-class students than from lower-class students. Often teachers do not recognize these attitudes and beliefs but communicate them nevertheless in both overt and subtle ways, including the use of praise or criticism to guide a student's performance.[5]

stereotypes

If a teacher expects a student or group of students to behave in a certain way, the teacher's attitude may serve as a **self-fulfilling prophecy:** that is, the students may behave in the predicted manner in response to the teacher's attitude and not as a result of the other factors on which the teacher's expectations are based. Thomas Good and Jere Brophy have suggested a process by which teachers' expectations may encourage certain levels of achievement.[6]

self-fulfilling prophecies

First, the teacher forms expectations of specific behavior and achievement for individual students. Then the teacher's behavior toward these students differs according to the expectations. The students perceive the teacher's expectations from how they are treated; this perception affects their self-concept, motivation to achieve, and aspiration to excel. Over time, students of whom much is expected will perform well, and students of whom little is expected will perform poorly. Thus, the result seems to justify the original expectation and fulfill the teacher's unspoken prophecy. The process is not automatic; teachers' expectations are not always fulfilled. But research indicates that teachers can influence which children do or do not achieve in the classroom.

Carl Rogers's Views   At this point, let us consider the position—most eloquently expressed by Carl Rogers, a noted counselor, psychologist, and therapist—that significant learning depends on certain "attitudinal qualities" in the personal relationships between the facilitator and the learners.[7] Rogers used the term *facilitator* rather than *teacher* because he believed that it emphasizes what happens to the learners rather than the performance of the teacher. The term *facilitator* also implies significantly different functions than does the term *teacher*.

teacher as facilitator

According to Rogers, an effective facilitator possesses the following three attitudinal qualities:

three important attitudes

1. *Realness* or genuineness. This is the attitude most basic to the learning relationship. The facilitator must be a real person, one who "is *being* himself" and who is free to be enthusiastic, bored, interested, or angry instead of presenting a front or playing a role.

2. *Valuing* the learners. To develop effective relationships, the facilitator must respect the learners—their feelings, their opinions, and their persons—as worthy in their own right, accepting both their imperfections and their potentialities.

3. *Empathic understanding.* This is the ability to understand the learner without judging or evaluating. Recall the student who said to Carol Landis, "This library stinks. Why do we have to do this assignment anyway?" An empathic, nonevaluative response by Carol might be "You don't care for the library, and you don't understand why you have to do the assignment. What do you find the most troublesome about the assignment?" Rogers urged that a teacher initially set the goal of making one nonevaluative, accepting, empathic response per day to a student's demonstrated or verbalized feelings. By doing so, he believed, the teacher will discover the potency of this approach.

Rogers's approach is intended to create a classroom environment conducive to self-initiated learning. He maintained that the teacher's skills, knowledge of the field, curricular planning, lectures, and selection of books and other learning aids are all peripheral; the crux of the learning situation is the relationship between the facilitator and the learner, which should be characterized by *realness, valuing,* and *empathy*. In the absence of these three attitudinal predispositions, Rogers contended, the learning environment is sterile and cannot produce significant learning.

facilitator-learner relationship

There is little question that if you have empathy for your students, value them as unique individuals, and are secure enough to be yourself without playing a

How Do Teachers Treat Low Achievers?

Researchers have not definitely established why some teachers treat students they perceive as high and low achievers differently. But observations of many classroom teachers reveal that they often behave differently toward these two groups of students. Good and Brophy have summarized these differences:

1. Teachers wait less time for lows to answer a question.

2. Teachers give lows answers or call on someone else for the answer instead of giving clues or providing additional opportunities to respond.

3. Teachers reward lows for inappropriate behaviors or incorrect answers.

4. Lows are more often criticized for failure.

5. Lows are praised less frequently for success than highs.

6. Lows may not receive feedback for public responses.

7. Generally, teachers interact less often with lows, paying less attention to them.

8. Teachers call on lows less often for answers to questions.

9. Teachers seat lows farther from the teacher.

10. Less is demanded from lows.

11. Lows receive more private than public interactions; their activities are more closely monitored and structured.

12. When teachers grade tests and assignments, they give highs but not lows the benefit of the doubt in borderline cases.

13. Lows experience fewer friendly interactions, including fewer smiles and other nonverbal signs of support.

14. Lows receive shorter and less informative feedback to their questions.

15. Teachers make less eye contact and respond less attentively to lows.

16. Teachers make less use of effective but time-consuming instructional methods with lows when time is limited.

17. There is less acceptance and use of lows' ideas.

18. Lows are exposed to an impoverished curriculum.

Source: "How Do Teachers Treat High or Low Achievers?" from *Looking in Classrooms,* 8th ed. by Thomas L. Good and Jere E. Brophy. Copyright © 2000 by Addison-Wesley Educational Publishers, Inc. Reprinted by permission.

role, you will be a more successful teacher. In addition, the atmosphere in your classroom will make possible for you and your students a joy, an excitement, and a closeness absent from many classrooms.

The Teacher's Attitude Toward Peers and Parents

Much of what we have already said about teachers' attitudes toward themselves and toward children also applies to their attitudes toward peers and parents. Some attitudes enhance a teacher's effectiveness, and others detract from it.

Authority/Collaboration   One source of conflict may be the teacher's attitude toward those who represent authority (ordinarily administrators but, for prospective teachers, the university supervisor or cooperating teacher). Teachers

problems with authority

may find it hard to be themselves while dealing with people who outrank them in position or prestige. Sometimes teachers find they yield too readily to demands from those in authority, and as a result they feel guilty about complying rather than standing on their own convictions. When this occurs, the result is often a continuing undercurrent of resentment toward the person in authority.

If teachers can assume a role of collaboration with those in authority, seeing themselves as part of a valuable partnership in the enterprise of education, they may be able to overcome any predispositions to hostility or any anxiety unwarranted by reality. Resentment of those in authority only prevents communication and understanding.

Competition/Cooperation   Some teachers develop a strong drive to compete with other teachers for recognition from both authority figures and students. They try to have the best lesson plans, to be the "most popular teacher," or to maintain the friendliest relationship with the administration. Such teachers are striving to be recognized and rewarded. As a result of this attitude, they sometimes cut themselves off from much-needed help and severely limit their ability to be of help to others. Carol Landis has taken an important first step by enlisting the help of other teachers to get the necessary resources for her students. For the benefit of staff and students, teachers need to cooperate and share ideas.

need for recognition

Superiority and Prejudice/Acceptance   One attitude that never fails to cause trouble for teachers is a feeling of superiority to other teachers or parents of students. They may feel intellectually superior to colleagues, socially superior to students' parents, or both. Some teachers simply have little tolerance for people who differ from them in values, cultural background, or economic status, and, as a result, they treat others with disdain and contempt rather than patience and respect. Again, effective teachers—those who work well with colleagues and parents to empower children to achieve—show attitudes of acceptance. In their dealings with other teachers and parents, teachers can again benefit from Carl Rogers's advice: be real or genuine, value other people as worthy in their own right, and show empathy.

lack of tolerance

The Teacher's Attitude Toward the Subject Matter

This section is short because our message is simple: it is most important that whatever subject matter you teach, you feel *enthusiasm* for it. Just as students usually can discern the teacher's attitude toward them, they are also very sensitive to the teacher's attitude toward the subject matter. One of the most striking characteristics of the excellent teacher is enthusiasm for what she or he is teaching, or facilitating. The bored teacher conveys boredom to the students—and who can blame them for failing to get excited if the teacher, who knows more about the subject than they do, doesn't find it engaging?

must feel enthusiasm

Some teachers find it difficult to feel enthusiasm for a curriculum they haven't constructed themselves, or don't identify with, or don't want to teach. The surest way to guarantee that teachers are enthusiastic about what they are teaching is to allow them to teach what they are enthusiastic about. And we do not mean this

**Teacher enthusiasm
is usually contagious.**
(© Bob Daemmrich)

as a mere play on words. We would rather see an enthusiastic teacher teaching a minor historical topic or macramé than an uninspired teacher teaching Shakespeare. As one student put it, "There is nothing worse than sitting in a lesson knowing full well that the teacher is dying to get rid of you and rush back to the staff room to have a cup of coffee." Unfortunately, as more and more states adopt learning standards for students, the latitude that teachers once had to choose content is being greatly curtailed. States expect teachers to teach to the standards, and the high-stakes assessment tests given to students exert considerable pressure on teachers to be certain they "cover the content" contained on the assessments. If you have to teach something you would rather not, try to develop a positive attitude toward the subject. Enthusiasm: if the teacher has it, life in the classroom can be exciting; if it is missing, there is little hope that students will learn much of significance.

I touch the future. I teach.
—CHRISTA MCAULIFFE

What Subject-Matter Knowledge Does the Effective Teacher Need?

Very simply, prospective teachers need to understand the content of the subjects they teach, as well as the methods of teaching the specific content. The content is learned by studying subject-matter courses taken in college and studying the actual curriculum taught in the schools. Teachers need to understand the subjects they teach well enough to analyze and convey their elements, logic, possible uses, and social biases. That is, teachers need to understand the structure of the subjects they teach.

structure of the discipline

Unfortunately, most college courses in the specific disciplines don't prepare prospective teachers to actually teach the knowledge that students are expected to learn. Much of what prospective teachers learn from their study of the academic disciplines is not taught to children and so is not directly applicable to teaching. This is particularly true for elementary school teachers, who are called on to teach content that is rarely taught in universities. For example, a mathematics major preparing to teach elementary school may never have occasion to use differential equations or calculus in the content she or he teaches to elementary-age children. Thus, although studying and understanding specific disciplines is crucial, it is not sufficient for effective teaching. The teacher must also understand the content of the school curriculum that pupils are expected to know.

curriculum content

pedagogical content knowledge

Another type of knowledge shown by effective teachers is **pedagogical content knowledge,** the knowledge that bridges content knowledge and pedagogy. Pedagogical content knowledge represents the "blending of content and pedagogy into an understanding of how particular topics, problems, or issues are organized, represented, and adapted to the diverse interests and abilities of learners, and presented for instruction."[8] The skilled teacher draws on the most powerful analogies, illustrations, examples, explanations, and demonstrations to represent and transform the subject so that students can understand it. For example, a physics teacher who possesses pedagogical content knowledge might use the analogy of water flowing through a pipe to explain how electricity flows through a circuit, but he or she would also know the limitations of such an analogy. Education methods courses in the specific subject areas are where you are most likely to learn pedagogical content knowledge.

all three types of knowledge essential

These three types of knowledge—of discipline content (including the structure of the discipline), of curriculum content, and of pedagogical content—are, we believe, essential for effective teachers. Did Carol Landis have such knowledge? We suspect not, at least not to the degree that she could communicate information and concepts to her class with the authority and expertise required for effective teaching. In the next section, we'll examine more closely another area of the effective teacher's knowledge: theoretical knowledge about learning and human behavior.

What Theoretical Knowledge Does the Effective Teacher Need?

Theoretical knowledge about learning and human behavior equips the teacher to draw on concepts from psychology, anthropology, sociology, and related disciplines to interpret the complex reality of the classroom. The teacher who lacks a theoretical background will have to interpret classroom events according to commonly held beliefs or common sense, much of which is, unfortunately, based on outmoded notions of human behavior.

Theories-in-Use

Let's return for a moment to the case of Carol Landis. In the incident described, Carol operated on the basis of certain ideas, or what some call *theories-in-use,* which differ from pure theories.[9] A *theory* is an unproved explanation of why something happens the way it does. In its simplest form, a theory is a hypothesis designed to bring generalizable facts, concepts, or scientific laws into systematic connection. On the other hand, a *theory-in-use* is something people have in their heads and apply in their dealings with people and the world. Theories-in-use are often unexamined.

We all have these theories-in-use, and they guide us as we make our way through our daily lives. You eat certain foods because you have an idea that they have a healthy effect on the body. Or you decide to take a summer job in a public playground, believing that you'll get to know children better and that future prospective employers might be pleased or impressed when they hear you've had that kind of experience.

typical theories-in-use

As you may have observed, Carol Landis has several theories-in-use. For example, Carol has the theory-in-use that groups should operate democratically and not be dominated by one student. She also has a theory-in-use that some children will perform better in school than others; as a result, she expects certain behavior from certain kinds of students. She also has a classroom management theory-in-use that she should give students some leeway before she resorts to firm discipline. Some of Carol's theories-in-use are clearly questionable. A few may have contributed to her problems that day in the library, and some may cause her more problems further down the line. But notice that Carol was not worried about her theories-in-use. She was worried about what she did and what she will do. She didn't question some of her conceptions. Theories-in-use were the last things she had in mind, but they in fact caused some of her problems.

Carol's theories-in-use

Why Study Educational Theory?

The fact that Carol did not reflect on the truth or falsity of her theories-in-use or try to recall some theories she had learned during her teacher education is not uncommon. Indeed, many teachers question the basic usefulness of theory. Many a beginning teacher has been told by a senior colleague, "Forget all that theory they've been giving you in college. Here's what works in the real world." Further, preservice teachers often complain that courses are too theoretical. They want to get out to schools, where the action is. This desire (perhaps it is your own desire) for things that work and ways to cope with real situations is vital, and we do not want to diminish it. As a teacher, you will need practical techniques and solutions to real problems. But to need practical tools does not mean that educational theory is less important.

POLICY MATTERS!   Raising Standards for Teachers

What's the Policy?

Along with the push to raise academic standards for students in elementary and secondary schools, most states are raising the standards expected of would-be teachers.

How Does It Affect Teachers?

States are now requiring higher grade point averages for students entering teacher education programs. Also, as a prospective teacher, you will most likely have to pass some form of standardized test to become licensed to teach in your state. Candidates for teaching licenses usually must achieve passing scores on examinations that test general literacy and mathematical knowledge, subject-matter knowledge, and professional teaching knowledge.

What Are the Pros?

Teachers are increasingly seen as the missing element in the drive to raise academic standards and increase public confidence in K–12 schools. The perception is that you can raise standards for children and youth, but if you don't have good teachers, you won't make progress.

What Are the Cons?

Higher standards could contribute to a teacher shortage. States are increasing the standards for becoming a teacher just as the demand for teachers is increasing, and many are predicting a shortage of teachers over the next decade. Nationwide, 2.2 million new teachers will be needed in the next decade to meet rising student enrollments and replace retiring teachers. Passing state tests is not always automatic. For example, in the spring of 1998, Massachusetts introduced its first-ever licensure exam, and nearly 60 percent of the test takers flunked. The bar for becoming a teacher has been raised, with the predictable result that fewer people will get over it.

The increasing standards may also discourage people from pursuing teaching as a career for fear that they will spend four or five years of teacher education, only to be denied the opportunity to teach because they failed an exam. There is also concern that the exams don't really measure teaching effectiveness, merely general knowledge. Also, some people who would be fine teachers just don't test well. Finally, many people are concerned that these tests will diminish the pool of minority candidates, who historically have not tested as well as white candidates.

What Do You Think?

1. Is your decision on whether or not to become a teacher influenced at all by the requirement to pass a test to become licensed? Why or why not?

2. Professions such as law and medicine require tests for licensure. Do you support the idea of testing teachers for licensure? What concerns, if any, do you have about teacher competency tests?

3. What alternative methods can you suggest for states to use to determine teacher competence?

The case of Carol Landis illustrates how lack of theoretical knowledge of classroom management can lead to inappropriate behavior on the teacher's part. Both theory and empirical research support the notion of being consistent in your expectations of student behavior, whereas Carol thought it was all right to let students behave as they wished until they crossed her tolerance threshold, at which point she came down hard on them. Carol probably would not have encountered such trouble if more of her theories-in-use had been challenged.

why theoretical knowledge is necessary

Like Carol, you may have your own theories-in-use, and these need to be challenged and tested. The best way to do this is to pit them against other theories and ideas. We believe, moreover, that theoretical information *is* practical. The problem is not that theory is wrong or unworkable but that many teacher education programs offer students few opportunities to apply theory to practical situations. As the great American educator John Dewey said, "Nothing is so practical as a good theory."* Finally, by giving attention to theoretical knowledge now, we are looking ahead to the future. In other words, even if it doesn't interest you much at this point, we want you to know that at a later stage of your development, you will encounter theories that will enlighten and enrich your work with the young.

good theories are practical

How Can Theoretical Knowledge Be Used?

A teacher's theoretical knowledge can be used in two ways: to interpret situations and to solve problems. (Practical knowledge, on the other hand, is more limited in applicability and is used primarily to respond to familiar situations.)[10]

An Example of Using Theoretical Knowledge   Let's consider an example of how theoretical knowledge can help a teacher interpret classroom events and solve the problems arising from them. In educational psychology, there is a concept known as the **zone of proximal development,** a range of tasks that a child cannot yet do alone but can accomplish when assisted by a more skilled partner. In other words, the child is on the verge of being able to solve a problem, but just needs some structure, clues, help with remembering certain steps or procedures, or encouragement to try. (This assistance, called **scaffolding,** allows students to complete tasks they can't complete independently.) This zone is where instruction can succeed and real learning is possible. The concept of the zone of proximal development derives from the theoretical work of the Russian psychologist Lev Vygotsky, in which he theorized that a child's culture shapes cognitive development by determining what and how the child will learn about the world.

zone of proximal development

Education must bring the practice as nearly as possible to the theory.

—HORACE MANN

Now suppose that a student, John, is experiencing difficulty doing some percentage problems in math. You, the teacher, understand that the zone of proximal development is influenced by reasoning ability, background knowledge, and motivation. Therefore, you assess John's ability to understand the problems by

*For the moment we will downplay the fact that John Dewey was primarily an educational theorist.

Teaching: Art or Science?

One of the pioneering investigators of research on teaching, N. L. Gage, professor emeritus at Stanford University, sees teaching as a blend of both art and science. Teaching can be considered an art because teachers must improvise and spontaneously handle a tremendous number of factors that interact in often unpredictable and nonsystematic ways in classroom settings. Teaching cannot be reduced to formulas or recipes for action, in Gage's opinion.

On the other hand, Gage contends that teaching is also a science. Although science can't offer absolute guidance for teachers as they plan and implement instructional strategies, research can provide a scientific basis for the art of teaching. For example, the research on academic engaged time has demonstrated the importance of keeping pupils on task with intellectually challenging, but not too difficult, subject matter.

These two components of teaching, art and science, interact. Empirically derived knowledge of the relationships among teacher behavior, pupil behavior, material to be learned, and desired student learning can guide teachers as they make artistic decisions about their teaching. That is, teachers use their knowledge of the research on these relationships to accomplish the artistry of moving a unique classroom of unique students toward the intended learning.

Is teaching an art or a science? The answer is "yes."

Source: N. L. Gage, *Hard Gains in the Soft Sciences: The Case of Pedagogy* (Bloomington, IN: Phi Delta Kappa, 1985), pp. 4–11. Copyright © 1985.

---

forming hypotheses and investigating

watching him try to solve one of them. You ask him to explain to you what he is thinking as he attempts the solutions. Is he missing some important understanding, or is he making some procedural error? Are the problems too difficult, or should he be able to solve them with some assistance? If the latter, what kind of assistance does he need? Who should give him the assistance, you or another student?

You decide that John is not lacking any fundamental knowledge but is very close to understanding the correct procedures. You ask Mary, a student who understands percentage problems pretty well, to come over and think aloud as she works on one of the problems. By thinking aloud and having John follow along, Mary provides John with insight into how she goes about solving the problem. You encourage John to ask Mary questions as she goes over her solution. You now ask John to work a similar problem, also thinking aloud as he tries to solve it. This time he gets the problem correct. You ask him to do a couple more problems and to raise his hand when he finishes so you can check to see if his understanding carried over to the new problems.

using theoretical knowledge

How did the theoretical knowledge about the zone of proximal development assist you in helping John? First, you had to determine whether John was close to understanding or missing some fundamental knowledge. Was he in the zone of proximal development where additional coaching or assistance would help him, or would you have to reteach some important knowledge that he didn't have? Second, what sort of scaffolding would benefit John? By having both Mary and John think aloud as they solved the problem, mistakes or errors could be easily determined and, if solved correctly, provide a model for John. An understanding of the zone of proximal development and its related scaffolding strategies represents the kind of theoretical knowledge that can help you interpret and solve classroom problems.

This example helps to show that a teacher needs much more than a common-sense understanding of human behavior. The capable and effective teacher uses theoretical knowledge drawn from various education-related disciplines to formulate and test hypotheses about human behavior in the classroom. In our opinion, the translation of theory into practice cannot be left to chance; you must constantly take advantage of opportunities that allow you to apply theoretical concepts to classroom situations and to receive guidance and feedback from your instructors about the application of these concepts. The field of cognitive psychology, in particular, has recently provided fertile research findings and theoretical concepts for teachers.

taking advantage of opportunities

What Teaching Skills Are Required of an Effective Teacher?

Knowing Versus Doing

Simply knowing something does not guarantee the ability to act on that knowledge. There is a profound difference between *knowing* and *doing*. Teachers may know, for example, that they should provide prompt feedback to their students on written assignments, but they are not always able to act on that knowledge. Or teachers may know how important it is to hold high expectations for all children, regardless of race, ethnicity, or social class, but not act on that knowledge. No teacher education program can afford to focus only on theoretical knowledge at the expense of the practice, or "doing," dimension of teaching, just as no individual teacher can rely solely on knowledge of subject matter. All prospective teachers need to develop a repertoire of *teaching skills* to use as they see fit in varying classroom situations.

> *A master can tell you what he expects of you. A teacher, though, awakens your own expectations.*
>
> —PATRICIA NEAL (ACTRESS)

Among the skills that many educators believe are essential to effective teaching are the following:

some essential skills

▶ The ability to ask different kinds of questions, each requiring different types of thought processes from the student

▶ The ability to plan instruction and learning activities

▶ The ability to diagnose student needs and learning difficulties

▶ The ability to vary the learning situation to keep the students involved

▶ The ability to recognize when students are paying attention and to use this information to vary behavior and, possibly, the direction of the lesson

What Are Some Characteristic Behaviors of Effective Teachers?

In a broad study, educational researcher David Berliner attempted to provide an answer, based on contemporary research on teaching, to the question "What is an effective teacher?" His answer focuses on teacher behaviors that give students the opportunity to spend sufficient time engaged in and succeeding at tasks that help them achieve intended learning. Several behaviors seem to distinguish effective teachers:

- They monitor students' independent work, checking on their progress and providing appropriate feedback, to maintain a high level of student engagement with the task at hand.

- They structure lessons to let students know what is expected of them and what procedures to follow.

- They pace instruction rapidly to deliver a maximum amount of the curriculum to students.

- They ask questions requiring students to analyze, synthesize, or evaluate, demand answers at the same level as the question, and wait at least three seconds for students' answers.

- They communicate high expectations for student success.

- They provide a safe and orderly classroom. Deviant behavior is managed sensibly, and academic achievement is rewarded.

- They foster a convivial atmosphere in their classrooms.

- They capitalize on the instructional and motivational uses of tests and grades.

- They provide feedback to students through praise, the use of student ideas, and corrective forms that allow students to respond appropriately.

This list is not comprehensive; these nine categories of teaching behaviors are only examples of behaviors that distinguish effective teaching. But the relationship of this collection of attitudes, knowledge, and skills to a research base indicates their importance in the repertoire of the professional teacher.

Source: David C. Berliner, "Effective Classroom Teaching: The Necessary But Not Sufficient Condition for Developing Exemplary Schools," in *Research on Exemplary Schools,* ed. Gilbert R. Austin and Herbert Garber (Orlando, FL: Academic Press, 1985), pp. 127–154. Copyright © 1985.

- The ability to use technological equipment, such as computers, to enhance student learning

- The ability to assess student learning

- The ability to relate learning to the student's experience

importance of overlearning

The list of skills just given is far from complete. It does make it clear, however, that teachers need a large repertoire of skills to work effectively with students with varying backgrounds and different educational experiences. Varied approaches are necessary to meet the many needs of students. Such skills must be overlearned to the point of becoming automatic; otherwise teachers will have difficulty calling up these skills in the classroom's complex and rapidly paced setting. As Figure 6.1 illustrated, effective use of teaching skills, along with appropriate attitudes, knowledge of subject matter, and theoretical knowledge, leads to better instructional decision making.

Classroom Management Skills

No other dimension of teaching causes more concern for beginning teachers than managing the classroom and maintaining discipline. "Will I be able to manage and control my class(es) so I can teach effectively?" is a question most beginning teachers ask themselves. Because there is such a great concern about this aspect of teaching, we have chosen to spend some time on this skill area first, before turning, somewhat more briefly, to two others: questioning and planning skills.

Classroom management is "a process—a set of activities—by which the teacher establishes and maintains those classroom conditions that facilitate effective and efficient instruction."[11] Developing teacher-student rapport, establishing productive group norms, and rewarding promptness are examples of managerial behavior. Managerial behavior also includes housekeeping duties like recordkeeping and managing time and resources in the classroom.

definition of classroom management

As with most complex teaching skills, classroom management requires a thorough understanding of theoretical knowledge and research findings, as well as practical experience. The knowledge or theory comes primarily from educational, social, and humanistic psychology. As with many other areas of investigation, there is no consensus regarding the one most effective approach to classroom management. Instead there are different philosophies, theories, and research findings, each tending to address particular dimensions or approaches to classroom management. Table 6.1 gives a brief overview of some of these approaches.

no one approach

The last twenty-five years or so have produced significant new knowledge about effective classroom management practices. The following sections describe some of those findings.

Academic Engaged Time   Research that focuses on student behaviors—primarily academic engaged time—reveals some interesting insights on effective teaching skills.* **Academic engaged time** (also known as *academic learning time*) is the time a student spends being successfully engaged with academically relevant activities or materials. Several research studies indicate that academic engaged time in reading or mathematics is strongly related to achievement in those subjects.[12] Simply put, the more time elementary students spend working on reading or mathematics activities that provide them with successful experiences, the more likely they are to achieve in those areas. Although this finding may not seem very startling, observations indicate that tremendous differences exist in the amount of time individual students spend engaged in academic activities, both across classrooms and within the same classroom.

research findings

---

*On-task behavior, time on task, and academic engaged time are related concepts. *On-task behavior* is student activity that is appropriate to the teacher's goals. *Time on task* refers to the amount of time students spend engaged in on-task behavior. *Academic engaged time,* discussed here and in Chapter 3, adds the dimensions of a high success rate and academically relevant activities or materials to the concept of time on task.

TABLE 6.1   Different Approaches to Classroom Management

Name	Major Developers	Characteristics
Behavior modification	B. F. Skinner	Originates from behavioral psychology. Modify student behavior by consistently and systematically rewarding (reinforcing) appropriate student behavior and removing rewards for, or punishing, inappropriate student behavior.
Socioemotional climate	Carl Rogers William Glasser Haim Ginott	Originates in counseling and clinical psychology. Emphasis on building positive interpersonal relationships between students and teachers.
Group process	Richard Schmuck and Patricia Schmuck Lois Johnson and Mary Bany	Originates in social psychology and group dynamics research. Emphasis on teacher establishing and maintaining effective, productive classroom group. Unity and cooperation, as well as group problem solving, are key elements.
Authority	Lee Canter and Marlene Canter	Views classroom management as a process of controlling student behavior, primarily by using discipline. Emphasizes establishing and enforcing rules, using soft reprimands and orders to desist. *Assertive discipline* is a popular manifestation of this approach.

Source: Wilford A. Weber, "Classroom Management," in *Classroom Teaching Skills*, Sixth Edition by James M. Cooper (ed.). Copyright © 1999 by Houghton Mifflin Company. Reprinted by permission.

The research on academic engaged time clearly indicates that a primary goal of elementary teachers (and probably secondary teachers, although the research has been limited mostly to elementary schools) should be to keep students on task. We know that classes that are poorly managed usually have little academic learning time. A major task of teachers is to learn how to manage their classes so that students are productively engaged.

Numerous studies indicate that the most efficient teachers are able to engage their students about thirty minutes a day longer than the "average" teacher. If the most efficient teachers are compared with the least efficient, daily differences of an hour in academic engaged time appear. If this is spread out over 180 days, students of efficient teachers get 90 hours more of academic engaged time than

differences among teachers

students of average teachers and 180 hours more than students of inefficient teachers! Differences of this magnitude may help explain why students in some classes learn more than students in others.

Kounin's Research   Jacob Kounin's research on classroom management in the elementary school grades explains which skills can help teachers improve their classroom management and keep pupils on task.[13] Kounin discovered that effective managers kept students involved in academic tasks, minimized the frequency with which students became disruptive, and resolved minor disruptions before they escalated into major ones. Of the concepts Kounin identified to describe teacher classroom management behavior, three seem particularly useful. The first concept he termed *withitness*. Teachers who are "with it" are those who communicate to pupils, by their behavior, that they know what is going on. Teachers who are "with it" pick up the first sign of misbehavior, will deal with the proper pupil, will ignore a minor misbehavior to stop a major infraction, and so forth.

"withitness"

The second and third concepts concern the problems of lesson flow and time management. *Smoothness* involves the absence of behaviors initiated by teachers that interfere with the flow of academic events. Examples of teacher behavior that do not reflect smoothness occur when a teacher bursts in on children's activities with an order, statement, or question; when a teacher starts, or is engaged in, some activity and then leaves it "hanging," only to resume it after an interval; and when a teacher terminates one activity, starts another, and then initiates a return to the terminated activity.

smoothness

The third concept, *momentum,* concerns the absence of teacher behaviors that slow down the pace of the lesson. Kounin conceptualized two types of slow-down behaviors: *overdwelling* (when a teacher dwells too much on pupil behavior, on a subpoint rather than the main point, on physical props rather than substance, or on instructions or details to the point of boredom) and *fragmentation* (when a teacher deals with individual pupils one at a time rather than with the group or unnecessarily breaks a task into smaller parts when the task could have been accomplished in a single step).

momentum

Kounin found strong correlations between teachers' use of withitness, smoothness, and momentum and their pupils' work involvement and restraint from misbehavior. He discovered that teachers who are effective classroom managers emphasize the prevention of disruptions rather than having to deal with them after they occur. Good managers do this by keeping the students engaged in lessons and assignments through effective application of the skills related to withitness, smoothness, and momentum.

Other Research Findings   Many researchers have replicated and extended Kounin's work on classroom management. Here are a few other important recommendations arising from the research:

important recommendations

1. *Establish clearly defined rules and routines.* Clear rules and routines decrease the complexity of the classroom, minimize confusion, and prevent loss of instructional time. Moreover, having students help make the rules increases their commitment to abide by them.

Kevin and Jim's Suggestions for Classroom Management Problems

1. *When students misbehave, check your instruction.* Many behavior problems result from problems with instruction. Students are bored or confused, and their response is to get off task and into trouble.

2. *Take the time to ensure that students fully understand your classroom's rules and procedures.* As the old adage has it, "You have to keep school before you can teach school." At the beginning of the year, and again if and when things begin to break down, teachers need to fix in the minds of their students how the class is to be ordered.

3. *Regularly monitor the entire class.* Successful classroom managers frequently scan the class, noticing what each student is doing. Although the teacher need not react to every sign of off-task behavior or deviation from the established procedure, it is important for students to know that what they are doing is being noted.

4. *Move in on repeated or flagrant breaches of conduct quickly and directly.* Do not let things drift. Students will think you are afraid to confront them, and they may end up confronting you!

5. *Correct in private.* As much as possible, deal with student misconduct in private. Don't disturb the rest of the students and get them off task simply to get one or two students back to work. Also, public reprimanding may backfire and get you involved in a game of escalating remarks with a student.

6. *Don't make empty threats.* Do not say you are going to "do" something to a student or the class unless you have thought it over carefully and are really ready to do it. For instance, do not threaten to call the parents of every child in the room and tell them what rotten children they have unless you have a good deal of time—and alternative plans for next year.

7. *Don't put a hand on a student in anger or even annoyance.* Do not even think of striking a student, no matter how much you are tempted. When a situation is emotionally charged, even your well-intended gesture can be misinterpreted. On the other hand, if students are fighting, you may need to restrain them physically for their own good.

8. *Think through behavior problems.* When your class or an individual student is not behaving up to your expectations, treat the event as a problem-solving activity. Do not flail around or get panicky or discouraged. Coolly identify exactly what the problem is, consider possible causes, and test some possible solutions.

9. *Get help.* If management problems persist and you cannot solve them on your own, get help from a colleague or an administrator. Do not let things fester. Do not be shy about asking for help, particularly about discipline problems, which are so common for many beginning teachers.

10. *Be sure there is a back-up system.* If you need to remove a student from your room, you need to know there is a system in place that will back you up.

11. *Be sure your rules accord with schoolwide expectations.* For example, if the school has decided that chewing gum is tolerable and you crack down on it, you can expect to have more trouble than the issue is probably worth.

2. *Ensure students' compliance with rules and demands.* To encourage students to comply willingly with the rules and routines, teachers must gain students' co-operation by establishing positive relationships, sharing responsibilities, and using rewards. In addition, teachers must be willing to administer consequences for repeated misconduct in a way that is not threatening or punitive.

3. *Involve families.* When families understand what the teacher is trying to achieve, they can provide valuable support and assistance, including helping to develop and carry out successful behavior management plans.

One school of thought rejects the notion of effective classroom management as a system of rewards and punishments, because these are seen as instruments for controlling people. In this approach, instead of teachers seeing themselves as being in charge and taking steps to maintain that control, they should give up some of the control and help students work together to decide how to be respectful and fair; that is, teachers should help students develop an internal sense of *developing students'* how to work together in a community.[14] The approach may involve times of *responsibility* chaos and uncertainty, but advocates believe that students will learn ethics and democracy in action. One of your responsibilities as a teacher will be to develop a philosophy and a way of operating in the classroom that make sense to you and that accomplish what you value. Your attitude toward the use of rewards and punishments will be part of that development.

Overall, we are learning more about what constitutes effective classroom management behavior. Understanding the related theories and research and practicing the skills that this body of knowledge has identified as effective will help you establish and maintain the conditions that promote student learning. Effective classroom management is a skill that can be taught and learned.

Questioning Skills

The questioning process is a central feature of most classrooms. Studies indicate that teachers may ask hundreds of questions in a day's lessons, but they often fail to ask questions that require students to process and analyze information, and *ineffective questioning* their questions require only a rote response of memorized facts. They also tend to rush students' responses, not giving them adequate time to provide varied and thoughtful answers. Some teachers do not direct as many questions to certain groups of students—minority students, girls, "slower" learners—and thus deprive them of the opportunity to interact actively in classroom learning.[15] Mastery of questioning skills contributes to students' learning and thus is important for effective teaching.

Wait-Time   Good questioning behavior requires that the teacher provide students with sufficient time to think about and respond to questions. What do you think is the average amount of time a teacher waits for a student to respond to a question she or he has asked? Mary Budd Rowe, a science educator, determined in a series of studies that the teachers she observed waited less than one second before calling on a student to respond. Furthermore, after calling on a student, they waited only about a second for the student to answer before calling on someone else, rephrasing the question, giving a clue, or answering it themselves! How can students think carefully or deeply when they have only one second to respond to a teacher's question?

results of wait-time training

Rowe followed up these observations with studies designed to train teachers to increase their **wait-time** after questions from one second to three to five seconds. She reported amazing results, including the following: (1) an increase in the average length of student responses, (2) an increase in unsolicited but appropriate student responses, (3) an increase in student-initiated questions, (4) a decrease in failures to respond, (5) an increase in student-to-student interaction, and (6) an increase in speculative responses. In short, she found that longer wait-times led to more active participation on the part of more students and an increase in the quality of their participation. Subsequent research by others replicated her findings. If questions require students to think about material or generate original responses, they need a longer time to think about their answers than if they are being asked only to recall information from memory.[16]

Effective Questioning Techniques   In addition to wait-time, those who have studied the relationship between questioning strategies and student achievement have identified a number of other techniques as signs of effective teaching. This

useful techniques

research suggests that teachers do the following:

1. Phrase questions clearly. Avoid vague questions.

2. Ask questions that are purposeful in achieving the lesson's intent.

3. Ask brief questions, because long ones are often unclear.

Effective questioning strategies engage students in verbal discourse and promote genuine learning. (© Paul Conklin)

4. Ask questions that are thought provoking and demand original and evaluative thinking.

5. Encourage students to respond in some way to each question asked.

6. Distribute questions to a range of students, and balance responses from volunteering and nonvolunteering students.

7. Avoid asking "yes-no" and "leading" questions.

8. To stimulate thinking, probe students' responses or demand support for their answers.

9. Provide students with feedback about their responses, both to motivate them and to let them know how they are doing.[17]

With knowledge and practice, teachers can learn questioning strategies that engage all students in the verbal interaction that supports learning.

Planning Skills

Another skill related to a teacher's effectiveness is skill in planning. The plans teachers make for lessons influence the opportunity students have to learn, because plans determine the content students will experience in a lesson and the focus of the teaching processes. Effective teachers base their plans on a rich store of perceptions of classroom events and of their students' progress toward educational objectives. This store of perceptions—ways of looking at students and classroom activities—also helps the teacher make adjustments during instruction when plans must be adapted to the immediate situation.

Teachers do four basic types of planning—yearly, unit, weekly, and daily—and all are important for effective instruction.[18] Research shows that experienced teachers don't plan the way curriculum experts recommend, that is, by beginning with instructional objectives and then selecting instructional activities to meet those objectives. Instead, many elementary school teachers begin by considering the context in which teaching will occur (for example, the materials and time available); then they think about activities that students will find interesting and that will involve them; finally, they ponder the purposes these activities will serve. Secondary school teachers, on the other hand, focus almost entirely on the content and preparation of an interesting presentation.[19] This doesn't mean experienced teachers don't have goals; rather, it suggests that the interest and involvement of their students are paramount. Since research shows that student achievement is related to academic engaged time, planning should include consideration of how to involve students.

types of planning

Good teaching is one-fourth preparation and three-fourths theatre.

—GAIL GODWIN

We have looked at three skill areas—classroom management, questioning, and planning—that researchers have identified as competencies demonstrated by effective teachers. (Another important skill relates to the use of technology, to which we devote the next chapter.) Principals and other school evaluators assess beginning teachers' competence in these as well as other skills areas as part of their observations of beginning teachers. Therefore, developing classroom management, questioning, and planning skills should be an important concern for those preparing to teach.

A Final Word

We think this chapter is an important one because it provides an overview of what a truly effective teacher needs to know and be able to do. It may have been a frustrating chapter if you concluded that there is no way you can achieve the ideal we describe. We share that frustration, since we ourselves have not attained this ideal in our own teaching, and we're not certain that we ever will. Nevertheless, we continue to aspire to be the type of teacher we have detailed in this chapter. If you too can fix your sights on this conceptualization of an effective teacher and continually work toward this ideal, you are certain to observe positive and rewarding results in your own classroom.

Although we can detail the various proficiencies teachers need, noted educational author Jonathan Kozol cuts to the chase in his description of what he would look for in a teacher:

> . . . obviously we want people who can teach [their subjects]. . . . But if I had to narrow it down to one characteristic, I would always hire teachers whom I wouldn't mind getting stuck with on a long plane flight to California. I would look for people who are capable of making the world seem joyful, people who are a delight to be with, people who are contagiously amusing human beings. To me, that's more important than almost anything else. I would put the emphasis on the capability to create contagious enthusiasm for life. There are a lot of teachers like that, but not enough."[20]

KEY TERMS

reflective teaching (179)
participant observation (187)
self-fulfilling prophecy (189)
pedagogical content knowledge (194)
zone of proximal development (197)

scaffolding (197)
classroom management (201)
academic engaged time (201)
wait-time (206)

FOR REFLECTION

1. Has reading about Carol Landis and her theories-in-use helped you identify any of your own theories-in-use or those of teachers you have known? If so, what are some of those theories-in-use?

2. Do you have negative feelings or expectations about any group or type of people? Can you identify the basis of those feelings? Do you want to change them? If so, how might you try?

3. Do you agree that having an enthusiastic teacher teach an unimportant subject is preferable to an uninspired teacher teaching a crucial subject? What implications do you see in this remark? On what assumptions about teachers, students, and subject matter is it based?

4. Carl Rogers argues for a teacher who "is *being* himself" and shows feelings. Do you agree? Have you known any teachers who did so? Do you think children can cope with any reaction from the teacher as long as it is honestly expressed? Do you think this kind of teaching requires any particular prior training?

5. What is the difference between common sense and theoretical knowledge?

6. We have maintained that decision-making skills are important for teachers. What do you think you can do to improve your ability to make good decisions as you plan and deliver instruction?

7. Which of the skills listed on pages 199–200 seem most important to you? What skills would you add to the list? What skills would you subtract from it?

8. Do the research findings on academic engaged time surprise you? If you think the findings reflect common sense, why do you suppose teachers vary so much in their ability to keep students engaged?

9. We have included a number of suggestions for managing a classroom. Which seem most useful to you, and why? Which do you believe you would find most difficult to use, and why?

FOR FURTHER INFORMATION

Cooper, James M., ed. *Classroom Teaching Skills.* 6th ed. Boston: Houghton Mifflin, 1999.
This self-instructional book is designed to help teachers acquire basic teaching skills such as writing objectives, evaluation skills, classroom management skills, questioning skills, and interpersonal communication skills.

Danielson, Charlotte. *Enhancing Professional Practice: A Framework for Teaching.* Alexandria, VA: Association for Supervision and Curriculum Development, 1996.
This useful book, organized around a framework of professional practice, is based on the PRAXIS III criteria, including planning and preparation, classroom environment, instruction, and professional responsibilities.

Good, Thomas L., and Jere E. Brophy. *Looking in Classrooms.* 8th ed. New York: Longman, 2000.
This excellent book provides teachers with concrete skills that will enable them to observe and interpret the classroom behavior of both teacher and students.

Joyce, Bruce R., Marsha Weil, and Emily Calhoun. *Models of Teaching.* **6th ed. Boston: Allyn and Bacon, 2000.**
This text describes numerous teaching models based on different assumptions about teaching and learning.

SEARCH

Teachers.Net. World Wide Web site at http://www.teachers.net/
This excellent site has an online reference desk, an active chat board, and a lesson plan exchange.

Weinstein, Carol Simon, and Andrew J. Mignano, Jr. *Elementary Classroom Management: Lessons from Research and Practice.* **2d ed. New York: McGraw-Hill, 1997.**
This practical book, based on sound research findings, addresses the major issues in establishing and maintaining effective learning environments. Ms. Weinstein has a secondary version entitled *Secondary Classroom Management* (1996), also published by McGraw-Hill.

7

What Should Teachers Know About Technology and Its Impact on Schools?

The use of technology in the classroom is gaining increased attention as an issue in education. As our society continues to embrace new forms of communication, networking, and computer technologies, our schools are scrambling to keep up. In this chapter, we will explore what teachers should know about technology and its use in the educational setting, what roles technology may take in education, and how those roles may change what students and teachers do in the classroom.

This chapter emphasizes that

▸ Technology is not new to the field of education.

▸ Schools are being pressured from many sides to incorporate contemporary technologies into instruction.

▸ Students can use computers not just for drill but in ways that promote creativity and higher-order thinking.

▸ Technologies can help teachers change their role from dispensers of information to facilitators of students' learning.

▸ Teachers can also benefit from the productivity of computers in areas ranging from recordkeeping to staff development.

▸ The placement of technology within the educational setting affects how it can be used.

▸ Issues involving equity, teacher education, infrastructure, and budgeting will need careful consideration as technological tools become more and more integrated into classroom instruction.

Jan Whitland: Using Technology to Innovate in Her Classroom

Jan Whitland issues a challenge to her eighth-grade class: "Where should the next landfill be built in our state?" The students are interested in this topic, which they have heard their parents discuss. To find a solution, Jan's class works with local city officials, who coach them on the mechanics of a geographic information system, or GIS. A GIS, in simple terms, is a collection of electronic tools that translate data to a digital map. The power of a GIS comes from its ability to electronically display several layers of maps on the computer screen at a single time. For example, students can look at a map showing population density and then at another that depicts distance from urban areas. They can also view these two maps together as they struggle to choose the site of their landfill. The GIS tools allow students to zoom in and out on an area as they begin to narrow down their choices for the site. Then they can search the GIS database to make sure they will not disturb any known historic or archaeological sites.[1]

After two weeks of investigation, Jan's class divides into teams to present their choices. Three sites are offered, and a different group presents the case for each location. The culminating activity requires students to role-play a city council meeting, assuming such roles as city councilor, mayor, geologist, and angry citizen.

Two years later, Jan's students are still using GIS, but now they are in the field collecting water samples near the landfill that was built. Students meticulously record data, which are transferred to a GIS database. They still work with municipal officials to continually monitor the safety of the landfill.

This project has many educational benefits. The partnership between city government and middle school classrooms lets students learn about the workings of government while contributing to a worthwhile cause in their community. Furthermore, Jan's students learn marketable skills to take with them into the job force. The nature of Jan's lesson is a problem-solving activity. Students work collaboratively to consider things like water leakage. They incorporate their math skills to calculate the slope of different areas and see how the results might affect the landfill. Finally, the nature of GIS means that it integrates learning from several different subject areas. The GIS technology allows Jan to innovate. Posing a dilemma such as the landfill problem would be possible without technology, but the GIS tools allow her students to do what scientists do with the same question: use sophisticated equipment, consider multiple perspectives, and grapple with real, scientific data.[2]

Jan Whitland's role in the classroom is far from the traditional view of the teacher as sole dispenser of information. Instead, Jan functions as a facilitator. As she wanders around the room, she challenges her students to consider how they can convince an area's citizens that their backyards are the best place for the landfill. She knows the technology skills required by GIS software, but she relies on the expertise of the municipal officials who use it daily to teach her students while she facilitates. Jan is one reference point along with others, including technology, municipal officials, and other students. She allows her classroom to become an active laboratory where students take charge of their learning and hypothesize about solutions.

Case Study cont'd

Has Jan been replaced by the computer? The answer is no. Teachers, in fact, have an expanded role in this technologically enriched environment, though this role differs from the traditional one. Later in the chapter, we will explore in more detail how teachers can use computer technologies in instruction and what changes this approach can bring to the roles of both students and teachers. First, though, to put contemporary changes in perspective, let's look at the way technology has affected American schools in the past.

A Brief Look at Education's Technological Past

Today people usually equate educational technology with computers. In fact, this chapter's discussion of current technology refers mostly to microcomputer applications. But technology in a more general sense is by no means new to education.

In the early 1800s, a technological innovation was introduced to classrooms that would prove to have a profound impact on teaching. Though advocates called this new tool "invaluable" and it was installed in classrooms throughout the country, many teachers ignored it at first. Schools had to encourage use of this new technology by preparing training manuals with step-by-step instructions to help teachers integrate the device into their lessons. The newly forming

a high-tech wonder of the early 1800s

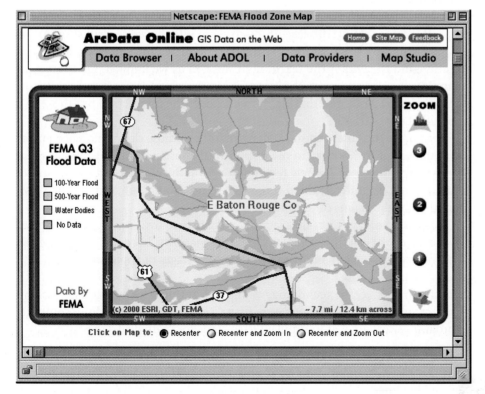

GIS software allows users to create customized maps such as the one shown here.
(ArcData Online screen capture provided courtesy of ESRI. Copyright © 2000 ESRI, EDT, FEMA. All rights reserved.)

normal schools also incorporated courses on its use. What was this technological wonder? The chalkboard!

In the old one-room schoolhouses, where students of different ages worked on various individual lessons, the function of a chalkboard was not immediately apparent. During the nineteenth century, however, classroom structure began to evolve from a one-room orientation to the graded classrooms we know today. When teachers began to teach the same lesson to an entire group of students, the chalkboard came into its own.[3]

filmstrips introduced in schools

The twentieth century brought a variety of technological devices that helped teachers use pictures in the classroom. In the early 1900s, the stereograph allowed students to view three-dimensional photographs. After 1910, the filmstrip projector, the overhead projector, and the motion picture all provided new ways for teachers to integrate visual images into their lessons.[4] Such changes were viewed as so significant that technological proponent Thomas Edison stated, "Books will soon be obsolete in the schools. Scholars will soon be instructed through the eye. It is possible to teach every branch of human knowledge with the motion picture. Our school system will be completely changed in ten years."[5]

TV reaches the classroom

In the 1950s, educational television was introduced as a possible method of handling teacher shortages caused by the baby boom. This technology could bring instruction into classrooms and homes from even the most remote distances. Proponents became quite excited. But funding could not be sustained, and as a result educational television has had a relatively small impact on daily classroom instruction.

microcomputers become affordable

In the 1980s, another wave of innovation occurred when microcomputers became affordable. Many software products were introduced to drill students on basic skills, and some educational visionaries predicted the end of classroom instruction and the end of the teaching profession as we know it. Of course, the technology never lived up to the hype. Today the most effective and promising technologies are not those that claim to take over the instruction but those that help with it.

Over the years, as these episodes show, many grandiose claims have been made about the use of technology to revolutionize the instructional process. But the eventual acceptance of the new technology, from the chalkboard to the microcomputer, has been determined more by the needs and demands of the classroom than by the claims of technology advocates.

typical stages of technology

Once a technology enters the classroom, the uses to which it is put are affected by what we might call the technology's level of maturity. In education, as in other fields, new technologies tend to go through three stages of application:

1. In the first stage, the technology is applied to things we already do. For instance, when microcomputers were first introduced into education, computer programs were created to simulate flash cards for math drill.

2. As a technology moves into the second stage, it is used to improve on the tasks we do. As an example, a more sophisticated math software application can provide remedial instruction when a student makes the same mistake more

than once. It can also expand to cover more math topics and increase motivation by using gamelike activities.

3. In the third stage of maturity, the technology is used to do things that were not possible before. An excellent example is the GIS software that Jan used in our opening example. Among other things, the GIS software helps students pull together their knowledge and skills from different disciplines in a collaborative manner to solve a problem in their local community. This kind of application uses technology in a way that is innovative rather than just allowing us to do old things in new ways.

Following this pattern, the role of any technology in the classroom will tend naturally to change as the technology matures. In addition, teachers follow a similar progression as they become more comfortable with various technologies. Teachers who are just beginning to use technology may start with applications, like drill and practice software, which are similar to something they already do. As they begin to learn about technology's possibilities, they will move on to applications that allow them to innovate. As we examine different technologies, ask yourself at which stage they can be applied and at which stage you would feel comfortable using them. Will the excitement about computers in education eventually fizzle as it did for educational television, or will computers go the way of the chalkboard, being seamlessly integrated in a meaningful way?

How Are Schools Being Pressured to Change?

Computer and networking technologies are an integral part of our society. It is hard to imagine a world without ATM machines, email, and pay-at-the-pump gas stations, a world with no microprocessors to run your microwave, TV, VCR, automobile, toaster oven, and cellular phone. Now imagine a classroom with no TV, no VCR, no phone, and no computer. This classroom scenario is easily imagined, for we have all experienced it. Most people agree that schools should prepare students for life in our society. If pervasive use of technology is a fact of life, should the classroom be an exception?

do schools prepare students for modern life?

No wonder, then, that schools are feeling pressure to increase their use of technological tools. The pressure is coming from many sources:

sources of pressure

1. Parents are placing pressure on schools to use technologies in the classroom. They see a discrepancy between what is taught to their children and the real-world activities they perform every day at work. An example is the debate over the importance of cursive writing as opposed to keyboarding skills: is instruction in handwriting important if most adults will soon be using a keyboard? Parents are concerned not only that their children have access to technology in the classroom but also that the students learn technology skills to allow them to compete in a job market increasingly powered by technology.

> *Technology is not only a product of a given culture; it also shapes the culture that created it.*
> —HOWARD D. MEHLINGER

2. Students are placing pressure on schools by knowing more about current technologies than many of the teachers.

3. Teachers are placing pressure on schools because they need both access to technology in their classrooms and training to use the technology effectively. New teachers in particular, who have used technological tools in college and at home, want to use them in their classrooms. Peer pressure and the desire to share information with colleagues increase the need for change.

4. Businesses are placing pressure on schools and governmental agencies to adequately prepare future employees. In the early twenty-first century, 60 percent of all jobs in the nation will require computing and networking skills.[6] Computer-based information processing power is doubling every two to three years, and the pace of change in technology is several times faster than even the pace in business, let alone that in education.[7] The pressure on schools to keep up therefore is intense.

5. Another pressure stems from the perception that America is falling behind the world in educational attainment. Business and governmental agencies march to the drum of global competition: "If America is to compete with the world, America's schools must be the best!" Regardless of their truth, rallying calls like this add to the pressure on schools to use technology.

6. Governmental agencies are now moving to support federal, state, and local initiatives to acquire technologies, including steps to ensure access for K–12 students. Many state departments of education have written "technology skills" into teacher licensure requirements, and national organizations are moving toward specific subject-area technology standards for K–12 students.*

Although we have been speaking of "pressures" for change, they can also be seen as opportunities. Many educators welcome the chance to try new curriculum materials and methods in their classrooms. There are also new opportunities for teachers with skills in technology, now an important competitive edge in the job market. Most important, perhaps, there are tremendous opportunities for students, as the next section describes.

change equals opportunity?

How Are Technologies Affecting Student Learning?

As our example of GIS software shows, many new technologies have been introduced into the educational setting in the last decade. To facilitate our discussion of these new technological tools, we will group them into content-specific categories, even though some examples will cross disciplines and join subjects, such as social studies and math. Many disciplines use some of technology's tools, but how, for example, a teacher uses telecommunication in science will differ from how another uses it in English.

Some computer applications can be classified as **cognitive tools** when they are used to engage and enhance thinking.[8] These tools are applications that manage information in ways that allow users to think more clearly, creatively, and critically. For example, they allow users to organize information in new ways, evaluate it, and construct personally meaningful representations of it. They derive their power from their flexibility and their ability to unleash creativity and foster significant cognitive processes. In the words of one team of researchers, "we learn best 'with' technology rather than 'from' it."[9] Cognitive tools are not necessarily meant to make learning easier. Instead, they often require students to think harder, more critically, or more creatively than without the tool.[10] Much of the working world uses cognitive tools for everyday tasks, and we believe that all teachers and students should have similar opportunities. There are many computer technologies that we might consider cognitive tools. Our discussion will

learning "with" rather than "from" technology

*For one example, see ISTE's National Educational Technology Standards (NETS) at http://cnets.iste.org/.

TABLE 7.1   Types of Technology Tools

Technology Tool	Educational Benefits	Example
Word processor	• Easy cut-and-paste procedures and the ability to save and return to a document later encourage editing. • On-screen spell checkers, dictionaries, and thesauruses aid accuracy.	*Alpha Smart,**a portable and user friendly word processor, is especially popular with teachers who work with younger writers.
Multimedia presentation software	• Combining text, audio, video, and virtual environments helps to communicate complex ideas. • Caters to a variety of learning styles.	*PowerPoint* allows students to easily combine a variety of media or even publish a presentation on the Web.
Drill and practice	• Similar to an interactive worksheet that provides feedback for the user and teacher. • Progress through the program depends on mastery of previous level. • Effective at reinforcing a concept.	*Reader Rabbit* is a popular program to reinforce letter recognition, rhyming words, and word families.
Database	• Organizes and stores complex sets of information. • Users can sort through information and filter unwanted data.	The *Valley of the Shadow* web site offers students access to a variety of searchable databases from two communities during the Civil War.
Simulation	• Interactive in nature, simulations allow students to reenact an event. • Students assume roles in the story, making decisions to which the software responds appropriately.	*Decisions, Decisions: Local Government* lets students play the role of a mayor facing a dilemma about the city's economic future.
Spreadsheet	• Allows users to form multiple calculations and to see all answers simultaneously. • A powerful tool to manipulate large sets of data. • Includes easy tools to graph.	Students can study a graph of population demographics in a community and use a spreadsheet program, like *Excel,*† to predict future changes in that society.

*AlphaSmart is a product of IPD, Inc. (web site: http://www.alphasmart.com/; phone: 1-888-274-0680).
†Microsoft produces *Excel* (web site: www.microsoft.com; phone: 425-882-8080).

TABLE 7.1   Types of Technology Tools *(cont'd)*

Tutorial	• Provides the initial instruction for a topic in a self-controlled, self-paced environment.	*Intermediate Algebra* allows teachers to individualize their students' instruction in math.
	• Monitors progress and evaluates the student once instruction is complete.	
	• Students' location within the tutorial can be saved.	
Telecollaboration over the Internet	• Allows for fast, inexpensive worldwide communication and collaboration.	The GLOBE program supports a project that uses data on acid rain and waste disposal collected and submitted by students around the world.
	• Organizations support these projects, allowing students to participate in legitimate research.	

include word processors, databases, spreadsheets, telecommunications tools, tutorials, simulations, multimedia software, drill-and-practice programs, and presentation and publishing tools. Table 7.1 summarizes these tools and their educational benefits.

Today most educational software applications use a combination of instructional techniques—for example, tutorial, simulation, and interactive multimedia—to achieve the desired outcomes. It would be relatively rare to find an application that neatly fits into only one of these categories. Moreover, teaching approaches that use educational software normally draw from two or more of these categories.

combining instructional techniques and technologies

As you read the following sections, consider how teachers are using particular tools. At which of the stages discussed earlier are teachers making use of these technologies? Are teachers applying the tools to things they already do? Does the technology enhance the teacher's ability? Are teachers innovating with the tools?

English/Language Arts Education

Teachers of many disciplines will find the tools for developing literacy useful. In this section, we will examine word processors, different software applications to develop reading skills, multimedia presentation and communication tools, and ways to combine technologies across disciplines.

Writing with Word Processors   While technology has vastly broadened the avenues of expression available to students, writing ability is still highly valued in our culture, and today many students write using word processing software. The **word processor** provides many benefits over paper and pencil. Editing is less tedious when you don't have to laboriously erase several lines of text or even start

ease of editing and rewriting

over. Using a word processor, students can experiment with different sequences for their paragraphs with little effort. In fact, students who learn to write using word processors are more likely to revise their work and make more substantial revisions than students who learn to write without the tool.[11] Built-in spelling and grammar checks in most word processing software help struggling students to focus on their ideas, and the keyboard itself avoids the handwriting obstacle many students face. These aids are controversial, however; they are not foolproof, and some educators believe they are often a crutch. Nonetheless, the more students edit their writing, the more they learn about the writing process. In this respect, the word processor engages students and enhances thinking, making it a cognitive tool.

new kinds of literacies

finding a better match between instruction and learning style?

Communicating in Multimedia   With technology's expanded definition of media, students are now becoming literate not just in the written word but also in video, audio, and multimedia* productions. In Chapter 4 we discussed Howard Gardner's theory of multiple intelligences and the concept of learning styles, emphasizing that different individuals learn best in different ways. Students who struggle with written expression may enjoy the chance to publish a web page or create a multimedia presentation instead of submitting a traditional five-page essay. Presentation tools such as *PowerPoint* can combine text, graphics, audio, video, and virtual environments to communicate complex ideas. Older students can use multimedia authoring programs like *HyperStudio* to create their own interactive presentations. Younger students can use applications such as *Kid Pix* to illustrate and present stories they have written.[†]

These programs allow students to use their strengths in expressing themselves while they become familiar with valuable tools for the future. It is relatively easy to publish student work via the **World Wide Web,** and knowing their work may end up in the public domain motivates students to care more about their creations.[12] Like word processors, presentation tools are used across the disciplines—from a presentation on the Depression that includes music from the era and clips from Roosevelt's Fireside Chats to a hurricanes project with graphs, images, and links to the National Weather Service web site.

Learning to Read   Multimedia technologies also give students an advantage in learning to read. The *Living Books* series[‡] consists of children's literature titles available on CD-ROM in which the story is represented in many forms or media. For example, the student reads the text on the screen, the computer reads it to the

---

*Multimedia productions combine various media such as text, graphics, video, music, and voice narration.

†*PowerPoint* is a product of Microsoft (web site: http://www.microsoft.com/; phone: 425-882-8080). For *HyperStudio*, contact Roger Wagner Publishing (web site: http://www.hyperstudio.com; phone: 1-800-497-3778). Bröderbund offers *Kid Pix* (web site: http://www.broderbund.com/; phone: 1-800-685-6322).

‡*Living Books* are published by Bröderbund (web site: http://www.broderbund.com/; phone: 1-800-685-6322).

"Edutainment" Software

A software application that is both entertaining and educational is referred to as "edutainment." Ordinary drill-and-practice software is repetitive by nature, and children can easily lose interest in such mundane tasks. Therefore, software developers added gamelike characteristics to their applications in the hope of motivating users to complete the task. These features also helped to sell the products to students and parents looking for educational activities for the home.

Today most edutainment software is designed and marketed for the parents of school-age children, not specifically for classroom use. Nevertheless, some software applications with gamelike features, such as *Math Blaster* and *Oregon Trail,** manage to bridge the gap, proving useful in both the home and the classroom. Since parents often ask teachers to recommend software applications for the home, it is a good idea to know what applications available for home use would complement the school's curriculum.

**Math Blaster* is manufactured by Davidson Associates (web site: http://www.bradfordlicensing.com/pages/davidson.html; phone: 973-509-0200). *Oregon Trail* is a product of The Learning Company (web site: http://www.learningcompanyschool.com/school/products.htm; phone: 1-800-685-6322).

student, and the student sees interactive video and still images illustrating the concept. Multimedia technologies can improve the match between the instruction and students' learning styles, offering a great opportunity to encourage literacy.[13]

Drill-and-practice programs are the earliest form of educational software or educational game. First used as an interactive worksheet, the software provided feedback to the user, usually by labeling an answer right or wrong, and then presented the next task. These products generally increase the fluency of a skill rather than actually teaching it.[14] Drill-and-practice programs, such as the *Reader Rabbit* series,* are popular for reinforcing young children's reading skills. These programs focus on letter recognition, rhyming words, and word families. Many programs monitor the students' progress so they do not move on until they have mastered the current concept. Teachers also use drill-and-practice programs such as *Reader Rabbit* to diagnose students' ability in reading, as well as other subjects, and assign them to the appropriate group.

Combining Technology and Crossing Disciplines Technology can facilitate interdisciplinary connections in a powerful way. An example combining several types of technologies as well as crossing content areas is the *I Lost My Tooth* project.[15] First-grade students around the world use email to share stories and myths about losing their teeth. Using these rich and diverse stories, teachers develop interdisciplinary activities. For example, students use maps to locate the countries where other children live and ask their "e-pals" about the weather and local heroes of their regions. Students use drawing software to illustrate their tooth fairy

**Reader Rabbit* is a product of the Learning Company (web site: http://www.learningco.com/home.html/; phone: 1-800-685-6322).

enhancing what teachers do

stories and graphing software to chart the number of teeth lost. Technology draws the disciplines together easily and provides a unique cross-cultural exchange. In this project, technology is functioning at the second stage we described: facilitating and enhancing what teachers can do.

Science Education

As the example at the beginning of this chapter showed, technology can allow students to do legitimate scientific investigations on a scale that would be impossible without technology. Although the equipment to conduct many of these experiments is costly, there are ways around these financial obstacles. For example, most city governments own GIS software and many are interested in partnering with a local school to share their expertise. Many organizations support collaboration between scientists and schools; for a reasonable membership fee, schools receive the technical support they need and an opportunity to work with experts. This section discusses some of these opportunities, ranging from conducting sophisticated local research that contributes to an organized database to collaborating with NASA scientists via teleconferencing technology. Technology is enabling teachers to use a constructivist approach to education in which students engage in building their own knowledge on the basis of their experiences. (See page 233 for a boxed discussion of constructivism.) Putting these technologies in students' hands can allow learning to become an active process in which students do the experiments themselves, draw conclusions, and engage in problem solving rather than merely reading about an investigation and memorizing the results.

doing "real" science

Scientific Hardware   Imagine conducting class beside a stream behind your classroom and having the technology to collect a water sample; instantly and accurately find the pH, temperature, and amount of dissolved oxygen in it; and graph the data on the spot. Revolutionary technology in the form of affordable handheld computers such as the PalmPilot* and accompanying probes, thermometers, and sensors allow this to happen. No longer are teachers forced to demonstrate stale experiments in the sterile environment of a lab; now students can collect the data, do the calculations, and test the hypotheses themselves with relatively low-cost equipment.

some concerns

Not everyone is a fan of such projects, however. Some caution, for example, that the many bells and whistles technology offers can reduce science to a "spectator sport" where students sit back and watch machines do the calculations. Furthermore, the complicated calculations that technology allows are often beyond the comprehension of the students involved. They understand the results but not the process required to get there.[16] Educators must address these problems as technology continues to progress.

*PalmPilots are produced by 3Com (web site: www.palmpilot.3com.com; phone: 1-800-638-3266).

Communication with Other Scientists   The students doing the stream experiment could take their results a step further and **telecollaborate** with students and scientists around the nation and the world to examine the effect of acid rain or waste disposal on the earth's water quality. The GLOBE (Global Learning and Observations to Benefit the Environment) program* coordinates such a project. GLOBE allows students to collaborate with expert mentor scientists who will answer questions, engage in the analysis of data, and help students place their measurements in the broader context of global environmental issues. Students and teachers work with other classrooms to collect data at the same time and send it into a computer that aggregates it and returns analyses of all the classrooms' data. The program is a dynamic, legitimate scientific investigation without preprogrammed answers. Students must interpret the results and develop an understanding based on their own experiments.

Telecollaboration projects are becoming more popular across the disciplines and making it increasingly easy to connect with schools, universities, experts, and organizations around the world. Many teachers can now choose to use text-based email. Some even opt for videoconferencing, in which students and teachers exchange live audio and video. Imagine the thrill of announcing to your class that they will be attending a videoconference in which they can ask a NASA mentor scientist questions about their project on black holes! Organizations such as Global Schoolhouse provide the technical support and organizational framework to connect students, teachers, and experts using telecommunications.[17]

Enhancing Problem Solving   Teachers would love to understand the cognitive processes students use as they solve problems, and technology is providing some unique insights into these phenomena. At Palisades Charter School, students use the True Roots program† to play the role of forensic scientists trying to determine if a girl is correct in asserting that she was switched at birth in the hospital. Using genetic data, students must try to deduce whether or not the girl is related to the parents who have raised her. The computer's combination of media and technological tools allows students to easily interact with the complex data. More innovative, however, is the program's ability to track students' decisions so that the teacher can later analyze the problem-solving strategy students used. Teachers instruct students not to guess or proceed randomly but to have a systematic plan. To reinforce the idea that problem solving should be a logical exercise, classes often use the program two times over three days. Teachers take the middle day to show students the graphs of their problem-solving strategy. Students try again and are graded on their improvement.[18] Here technology is functioning at the third stage of progress: offering teachers unique insight into their students' cognitive processes, which would not be possible without this sophisticated technology.

understanding students' cognitive processes

*GLOBE can be found at www.globe.gov.
†True Roots is produced by IMMEX (Interactive Multimedia Exercises) at UCLA (web site: http://www.immex.ucla.edu; phone: 310-825-9121).

GalapagosQuest: Darwin Meets the Internet

GalapagosQuest is an educational Internet project organized by Classroom Connect. In 1999, a team of scientists and explorers retraced Charles Darwin's 1835 journey to the Galapagos exploring the animal, plant, and geological components of this chain of islands. Armed with sea kayaks, camping equipment, laptop computers, digital cameras, and a satellite uplink, the team investigated the impact of the earth's changes on the Galapagos Islands. For example, they studied the earth's only marine reptiles and the effects of El Niño on penguin colonies. Focusing on grades four through eight, the scientists posted pictures of animals and habitats as well as logs from their journals on the *GalapagosQuest* web site as they tried to unlock the secrets of this unusual environment. This interactive project allowed students around the world to vote on the course the team followed. Teachers and students theorized about the evolution of both animal species and the natural habitat, and conversed with the scientists via email. Curriculum materials and lesson plans are available for classrooms that subscribe to the project. The technology provides a means to bring together the context of the Galapagos Islands, the expertise of the scientists, and students around the world for an extraordinary learning journey. Check it out for yourself at http://quest.classroom.com/galapagos1999/splash.asp.

Social Studies Education

Not traditionally a field at the forefront of technology integration, social studies is beginning to realize the power of technology across its broad range of subjects. Among other tools, social studies teachers are making use of databases, online archives, electronic simulations, virtual fieldtrips, and spreadsheets.

organizing knowledge using databases

Databases   **Databases** are powerful tools for organizing information. A database software program stores information in the form of records (analogous to a 3″ by 5″ index card) and fields* of data within each record (analogous to the individual lines of data on the index card). The database user is able to sort quickly through the "cards," shuffling them in different orders. For example, if the database contains information from a census, you can view it by last name, age, race, and so on. The computer will also allow the user to filter out those records not relevant to the task—for instance, hiding all records except those of African American women. Database software allows the user to search for information that would otherwise prove too tedious to gather. For instance, a database could be used to compare several decades of infant mortality rates. Done by hand, this task might take several hours; by computerized database, it would take a few minutes. An extremely powerful tool for organizing data, the database is used across many content areas.

---

*A *field* is a container for one piece of information. For example, a first-name field would store the first name for each record.

In addition, the computer's ability to filter information into discrete categories, then sort that information by various criteria, allows the user to manipulate data in ways that are purposeful and useful beyond the data itself.[19] A middle school class studying socioeconomic statistics could use a world atlas database to examine the relationships between literacy and life expectancy, population and land mass, or average income and crime rates.[20] In these ways, the database can become a cognitive tool allowing students to enhance their thinking rather than a mere collection of information.

Online Archives   Social scientists are digitizing* immense archives and publishing them on the World Wide Web. Without the computer to help organize and manage such large amounts of information, a teacher would be limited to using several photocopied diary entries to expose students to primary sources.† Giving students access to a rich archive that is organized by databases allows them to broaden their understanding of history and do the work of historians. *doing the work of historians* For example, the *Valley of the Shadow* web site‡ contains detailed databases of census results, church records, newspaper articles, military records, and letters about two communities, one southern and one northern, during the Civil War. Users can investigate the answers to questions they pose, such as what was the average number of slaves people held or how did occupations differ in the North and South. Students can incorporate the details they discover into their larger picture of the Civil War, building a richer understanding of the event than facts alone could provide. The role of the teacher changes from dispenser of knowledge to guide through the archives, helping students learn to ask the right questions and examine the sources critically. Students and teachers construct history together. *teacher as guide through the archives*

Simulations   A **simulation,** a representation of an activity or environment, is a time-honored and effective teaching technique. Long before software developers began to use the technique, teachers had their classes simulating a newspaper business or a famous court case. A simulation can be a fun way to explore an environment or a concept that would be too expensive, or possibly dangerous, to handle in reality. For this reason, simulations have proven to be a fertile field for educational software developers. A large variety of computerized simulations are available for classroom use in practically every field, and more are coming.

Decisions, Decisions: Local Government§ is a simulation game in which users assume the role of the mayor of a community facing a dilemma. The town's main *students assume the role of mayor*

---

*The digitizing process stores documents in an electronic format that allows them to be viewed on the Web and stored in a more permanent form.

†A primary source is a firsthand account. For example, a soldier who fought at the battle of Gettysburg and described it in his diary provides a firsthand account or primary source.

‡The University of Virginia's Valley of the Shadow web site is: http://jefferson.village.virginia.edu/vshadow2/.

§The *Decisions, Decisions* series of software titles is available from Tom Snyder Productions (web site: http://www.tomsnyder.com/index.html; phone: 1-800-342-0236).

employer, a mining company, wants to greatly expand production to include the mining of an alternative fuel for cars. The mayor must choose between improved employment opportunities with increased development and keeping the quality of life while risking economic stagnation. The mayor must listen to advisers and weigh the options. The program allows for use with the class as a whole, using only one computer or multiple small groups at individual computers. After students input their decisions, the software reacts and presents them with the results. For example, if the mayor raises taxes, she or he must accept some public dissatisfaction. To come up with every possible scenario and consequence manually would be an overwhelming task for any teacher, but the computerized simulation manages that information easily. The software frees the teacher to be more involved with the students and to mediate instruction.

Virtual Fieldtrips   **Virtual fieldtrips** provide a wealth of opportunities to extend learning. Not limited to social studies, virtual fieldtrips can be used to provide information about a site that students are unable to visit.[21] It is unlikely you will manage a class outing to the Amazon rainforest, for example, but National Geographic's Jason Project* provides a "fieldtrip" via the computer. Hundreds of similar sites are produced by teachers, agencies, governments, and students. Student-produced virtual fieldtrips are often used in connection with local history. Students conduct interviews and use digital cameras to take pictures of important sites and people in their community. Digital cameras use a disk instead of film to capture an image. By using photo-editing software such as *Photoshop,*† the image can be manipulated or enhanced on the computer screen. Students can put their images of local sites into a multimedia presentation program such as *HyperStudio* or *PowerPoint* and add descriptions. These can then be published to the World Wide Web and viewed by others. Students can see themselves as historians who are contributing to the preservation of their community's story.

Using Spreadsheets to Connect Disciplines   Though social studies and math are not two subjects that people naturally connect, technology helps to facilitate such interdisciplinary relationships by providing easy access to rich data. For example, students who visit the National Center for Health Statistics web site‡ can find data on the number of live births in the United States, create a spreadsheet to display the information, and analyze the trends based on their knowledge of U.S. history.[22] A **spreadsheet** is a software program that allows users to perform multiple calculations. A calculator, the infant sibling of a spreadsheet, limits the user to viewing only one answer at a time, and for more complex scenarios, this is too limiting. But a spreadsheet will allow the user to see all the numbers and formulas at once. Any change is immediately reflected in the entire sheet. Using the above example, students are able to calculate whether

exploring environments beyond the classroom

students contribute to local history projects

---

*The Jason Project's Amazon tour can be found at: http://www.jasonproject.org/front.html.

†*Photoshop* is available from Adobe (web site: http://www.adobe.com/; phone: 1-800-833-6687).

‡The National Center for Health Statistics maintains a web site at: http://www.cdc.gov/nchswww.

The teacher helps a student use a Photoshop program as others watch. (© David Young-Wolf/ PhotoEdit)

the number of live births increased or decreased over time. As a tool for forecasting and predicting, a spreadsheet might help students understand the consequences of population changes. For example, during a hypothetical epidemic, students can predict the future population changes and hypothesize the societal effects. Technology facilitates these interdisciplinary connections: the World Wide Web offers easy access to numerous sets of rich, real-world data, while the spreadsheet provides a powerful tool to manipulate the data. Social studies problems are analyzed using mathematical skills, and students are challenged to synthesize data, make predictions, and construct knowledge.

forecasting and predicting changes in society

Mathematics Education

From slide rules to calculators, math teachers have relied on technology for years. This section deals with some of the newer uses of technology in math education, including tutorial software, other software, and graphing calculators.

Tutorial Software   **Tutorials** are educational software applications designed to provide the initial instruction on a given topic and are used in most disciplines. Unlike drill and practice, tutorials present the skill or concept, then check for understanding throughout the process, and evaluate the learner's grasp of the topic once the program is completed. More narrative in nature than drill and practice, tutorial software often has the feel of a book placed on computer.

Somewhat controversial, tutorial software is intended to replace the teacher as the primary agent of instruction for a particular topic. To achieve this, the software is self-contained and self-paced. Small chunks of information are delivered to the learner in a careful sequence of instruction designed to achieve success and

self-contained, self-paced software

adjust to students' needs. The software may be turned off and the user's location in the program saved for a later time. One popular tutorial is *Intermediate Algebra.** Users move through algebraic concepts at their own pace; topics are explained, reinforced, and tested. Generally more flexible than drill-and-practice applications, this type of software is a powerful tool for individualizing instruction and monitoring student progress.

Other Math Software   Certain mathematics-specific software enhances what teachers can do. For example, *The Geometer's Sketchpad*† allows students to explore the relationships among points, lines, planes, and angles in an environment conducive to experimentation. Users are offered a palette of tools for drawing and deriving geometric concepts. This cognitive tool enables the user to explore, question, learn, theorize, fail, succeed, and grow.[23]

Graphing Calculators   Schools are trying to heed the National Council of Teachers of Mathematics' advice that, for students in grades 9–12, "scientific calculators with graphing capabilities will be available to all students at all times."[24] Many students find it difficult to make connections among the graphical, numerical, and algebraic representations of mathematical functions, but the speed and ease with which graphs can be generated and manipulated using these calculators help students to understand those relationships. Learning becomes more active, and students consult with both technology and the teacher.[25]

making connections among multiple representations

Foreign Language Education

The **Internet** and **telecommunications** applications open up vast opportunities in foreign language education. Compare assigning a sterile article about French food published in a textbook to connecting your students with e-pals in French-speaking Africa so they can ask about the cuisine themselves. Furthermore, the World Wide Web offers a wide array of current foreign language publications that would be far too difficult and expensive to obtain otherwise. Students will find extensive online newspaper collections in languages as different as Arabic and Portuguese, as well as live radio from Guatemala.

A **news group** is a feature of the Internet that can be compared to a large wall full of messages in chronological order. When you subscribe to a news group, you join an online discussion that occurs as people post messages and reply to one another. Teachers nationwide log in to these resources to share ideas, find keypals for their students, and converse with other professionals in their field. For example, ESPAN-L‡ is a news group for teachers of Spanish, and discussion ranges from cultural notes to grammatical points. Students can also log on to news

connecting professionals and students

**Intermediate Algebra* is available from Boxer Learning, Inc. (web site: http://www.boxerlearning.com/; phone: 1-800-736-2824).

†Key Curriculum Press produces *Geometer's Sketchpad* (web site: http://www.keypress.com; phone: 1-800-995-MATH).

‡The address for this discussion group is: ESPAN-L@TAUNIVM.BITNET.

groups and join a discussion in a foreign language. To participate in this real, interactive chat, students are required to put their communication abilities to the test. These engaging ways of learning foreign languages are changing the way we teach and encouraging us to be creative and flexible.

Distance Education

School districts can vary greatly in location, size, budget, composition of populations, and graduation requirements. Such differences often create educational inequities, particularly when a school district simply cannot afford to provide the quality and variety of courses offered by larger or more affluent districts. **Distance education** is a fast-growing alternative for schools trying to overcome such constraints.

Distance education involves using technology to link students and instructors in separate locations. As we have seen, two-way audio and video allows live interaction between individuals who are hundreds or thousands of miles apart, while the Internet allows the rapid exchange of data over distances. Thus, distance education can allow schools to increase educational opportunities by offering courses otherwise prohibited by cost or other constraints.

A congressional report found that distance education can help reverse some of the effects of the nation's long-term population shift from rural to metropolitan areas. This population loss has caused many districts to close or consolidate schools, forcing many rural students to travel long distances.[26] Ironically, the decline of rural populations has often been accompanied by state educational reforms that pressure schools to broaden programs and offer more courses. Many schools find themselves in the awkward situation of having to offer elective subjects for which neither funds nor teachers are available.

An explosion in the availability of online courses has alleviated some of this pressure. The Virtual High School (VHS)* first offered courses in 1997–98 and estimates that by the fall of 2000, it will offer more than 100 courses to more than 2,000 students.[27] Students from around the country use their courses' web sites as their starting point. From there they obtain readings and assignments. Students log on to a daily discussion group in which the teacher conducts a *netseminar*. This flexible arrangement accommodates a variety of school schedules as well as time zone differences. Students do telecollaborative projects for the course by exchanging information over the Internet. All the makings of a traditional class are present without the face-to-face interaction. The convenience of logging on at any point and the additional time for reflection make the netseminar particularly appealing. Furthermore, schools in more isolated areas or with limited resources can vastly expand the courses they offer to include such diverse classes as Eastern philosophy and the history of aviation. Students below the college level can explore nontraditional academic avenues and connect with peers who have similar intellectual interests.

helping to equalize the quality and quantity of courses offered

---

*The Virtual High School is a project of the Concord Consortium (web site: http://vhs.concord. org/).

an alternative to the traditional high school experience

While the VHS intends to enhance the traditional high school experience, the University of Nebraska–Lincoln Independent Study High School* offers a complete four-year high school curriculum of more than 130 core and elective courses in 16 subject-matter areas, all of which are online. Students who are homebound, have difficulty in a traditional classroom, are overseas, or want to return to complete their high school diploma can take advantage of this online program.

Technology for Students with Special Needs

Technology tools can be of especially great assistance to students with special needs. For those with disabilities, the tools can help level the playing field by presenting information in a manner best suited to a student's learning style and particular needs. While using a software program does not replicate the experience of learning from a teacher, the computer is not constrained by the human variables of limited patience and classroom distractions. Using the right software, an alternative, individualized curriculum can be created for students with special needs, paralleling the standard school curriculum.

assistive technology

In addition to its direct instructional uses, technology plays a second, very important role for special-needs students. The term **assistive technology** describes the array of devices and services that help people with disabilities perform better in their daily lives. (See Chapter 4 for a further discussion of assistive technology and special education.) Such devices include motorized chairs, remote control units and lasers that turn appliances off and on, artificial arms that respond to muscle signals, and ramps that help people get into and around buildings. Students with disabilities may rely on a variety of these innovations to help them achieve successful inclusion in regular classrooms.[28] At the present time, however, the computer has become the most prominent technology used to assist students with disabilities.[29]

vastly improving the quality of life and education for special-needs students

Computers can allow students to participate in normal classroom activities that would otherwise be impossible. User-friendly keyboard enhancements simplify typing, and assistive technology can be used to control most basic computer applications. ERICA (Eyegaze Response Interface Computer Aid System) is one revolutionary technology that opens up opportunities for special-needs students. With ERICA, an extremely immobile student with only the ability to move his or her eyes suddenly has a powerful tool for communicating with the world. Using ERICA's system that tracks and records the user's eye movements and pupil dilation across a computer display, the mouse can be controlled with eye movement alone.[†]

---

*To learn more about UNL's Independent Study High School, visit its web site at: http://www.unl.edu/conted/disted/ishs.html.

†To learn more about ERICA, visit the web site at: http://www.ericainc.com/main.htm or phone 804-982-2065.

This computerized voice synthesizer is reopening the world to this mute accident victim. (© Spencer Grant/The Picture Cube)

The variety of tools to help special-needs students fully participate in school is constantly expanding. The options include a word-predictor feature* that facilitates keyboarding. After the student types a letter or two, the computer presents a list of likely words, and the student simply selects the correct word rather than typing it out completely. Other aids, such as voice input devices, which translate a student's spoken words into text on the computer screen, or programs that will read text aloud,† can make writing a satisfying experience for students who struggle in this area.[30] Blind students and their teachers can use braille software, which provides easy-to-use, sophisticated print-to-braille and braille-to-print translations.‡

How essential is technology in the education of students with disabilities? In 1990, Congress incorporated definitions of *assistive technology* into the Individuals with Disabilities Education Act (IDEA). The U.S. Department of Education's

---

*One such product is *Co-Writer* by Don Johnston Inc. (web site: http://www.donjohnston.com/; phone: 1-800-999-4660).

†*DragonDictate* is a popular voice-input program available from Software Maintenance, Inc. (web site: http://www.ddwin.com/dictate.htm; phone: 888-343-3773). *IntelliTalk* is a talking word processor from IntelliTools (web site: http://www.intellitools.com/IntelliTalk.html; phone: 1-800-899-6687).

‡Duxbury Systems offers a wide range of software for braille (web site: http://www.duxburysystems.com/index.html; phone: 978-692-3000).

required by IDEA

Office of Special Education Programs views assistive technology devices and services as important parts of the educational program required by the IDEA. Assistive technology must be provided whenever necessary as an element of free and appropriate public education for children with disabilities. Thus, assistive technology must be considered a potential component of the individualized education program required under law for each child with a disability.[31] As discussed in Chapter 4, regular classrooms now often include students with disabilities as well as other students with special needs. This is one of the opportunities and challenges of teaching, and you should be prepared to work with children who use assistive technology in your classroom.

How Are Technologies Affecting Teaching?

movement toward standards

As a teacher, you can expect your students to have to meet some standards relating to technology. Currently thirty-eight states have these requirements. Eleven of those states have a set of standards exclusively for technology, and five have a set that combines technology with some other subject. North Carolina requires the most of its students by having them demonstrate their technology skills. Beginning with the class of 2001, North Carolina high school seniors will have to pass an assessment of technology competency before graduating.[32] In line with the current nationwide move toward standards (see Chapter 13), the International Society for Technology in Education (ISTE) has produced technology standards. For example, before completing fifth grade, students should have basic keyboarding skills;[33] however, ISTE encourages teachers to teach these skills within the context of their academic curriculum. To this end, they are currently working with content specialists to incorporate the ISTE technology standards into the subject standards.

This trend is encouraging; however, for technology to be truly integrated as an important part of classroom instruction, several additional shifts must take place in current practices and attitudes. The impact of technology on learning depends more on how teachers use the technology than on the characteristics of the technology itself.

A Different Role for the Teacher

Integrating technology into your teaching can change the way you deliver content to your classes. Think back to the scenario at the beginning of this chapter. Jan Whitland, a technology-assisted teacher, was *facilitating* instruction as needed to bring about a deeper understanding and relevance for students. Because of the technology the students employed, she was relieved from many tasks related to dispensing information. By using technology to present basic factual and historical information, the teacher is freed to become much more involved in higher-level evaluation of performance. Teachers can monitor students' projects, guiding their efforts and providing feedback. Instead of being a teller and a tester, the teacher can be a leader and a co-learner.

teacher as leader and co-learner

Cognitive Tools and Constructivist Teaching

In the constructivist approach to teaching (discussed in Chapter 10), learning is recognized as an active process. Students engage in constructing their own knowledge on the basis of their previous experiences instead of passively absorbing knowledge as presented by the teacher. This approach to instruction celebrates the differences among students instead of continually trying to build similarities.

Constructivist teachers can find cognitive tools especially helpful. Since cognitive tools do not try to instruct, they do not assume a particular learning style or methodology. A spreadsheet is a good example of this. The student must bring the goals—and the content to achieve them—to the tool, and then the tool will facilitate the student's discovery of knowledge and construction of meaning.

It is important to note that it is *how* the tool is used that makes it constructivist, not necessarily the tool itself. Although cognitive tools are an excellent match for constructivist methods, many software applications can be used in a similar manner. As with many other aspects of teaching, it is the learner's and teacher's ingenuity, creativity, and experience that set the limits of a tool's educational use, not the tool itself.

Many schools and teachers have been slow to implement the real potential of new technologies, but some new trends are emerging. Teaching technology skills in isolation is giving way to a new model of embedding technology skills within the context of the content.[34] For example, a teacher will teach the mechanics of a program such as *HyperStudio* when asking students to create a virtual fieldtrip as described earlier in the chapter. The students are not learning the skills without having a content-related task. The subject matter is driving the technology rather than vice versa.

incorporating technology within the content

the subject matter drives the technology

To better use the available technology, teachers must move from whole-class instruction toward smaller group projects and activities that are conducive to active, engaged learning and student interactions. This is not a shift all teachers warmly embrace. In some cases, teachers must change their fundamental view of the classroom and learning. Smaller group work may mean that students learn different things at different times rather than an entire class learning the same material together. In many ways, this resembles the days before chalkboards and full-class instruction. In such environments, teachers must view themselves as "coaches" or "facilitators" who, using the constructivist approach discussed in Chapter 10, guide students as they use technology to discover facts and concepts. Classrooms that effectively use technology evolve into cooperative rather than competitive social structures, and student assessment shifts from pencil-and-paper testing toward the evaluation of products and progress in meeting established criteria.[35]

technology takes us full circle

Florida's Project CHILD (Computers Helping Instruction and Learning Development)* demonstrates how classrooms can effectively incorporate technology in teaching by changing some common teaching practices and attitudes

*To learn more about Project CHILD, visit the web site at: http://www.ifsi.org/.

toward learning. Elementary classrooms in this project have been transformed into learning resource rooms for three hours each day, focusing on one of three subject areas: reading, language arts, or math. Teachers within a cluster (K–2 or 3–5) work together in teams, with each teacher having a particular area of expertise. A typical classroom has a computer station with three to six computers, a teacher station for small-group activities, and stations for textbook-based and written work. Students spend one hour per day in each of the three classrooms. For the rest of the day, they are with one of the teachers whose classroom serves as their home base. Through this rotation, students have access to computers every day in one subject or the other, and a systematic approach ensures equitable computer time for all.

Project CHILD combines traditional and constructivist views of education

    Project CHILD combines both traditional and constructivist views of instruction. The use of technology and students' cooperative activities at workstations allow students to become active in their own learning and to construct their understanding of a concept. Students keep a written "passport" that records progress and organizes their instruction as they move from classroom to classroom, working at different learning stations. Children often work together to foster collaboration as well as to have maximum computer time. While students are using their station time, teachers circulate to facilitate learning. In addition, teachers offer some traditional instruction when they pull out small groups for extra help or enrichment. Teachers can individualize instruction by examining students' passports and specifying where students begin working each day. Project CHILD aims to help teachers shift from being the single source of knowledge in their classroom to being a facilitator and coach. Even though the activities and assessments in Project CHILD differ from traditional schoolwork, students who participated in the program for a full three-year cycle scored better on standardized tests than their peers in conventional classrooms with similar computer-student ratios.[36] These results suggest that an important variable is not simply how many computers students have access to but how those computers are used. Technology can be more effective in a teaching environment where computers help to facilitate instruction and foster a constructivist approach to learning.

technology as a facilitator for change?

    The connection between technology and constructivism is not clear, but some researchers are beginning to understand elements of it. We know that teachers who have changed to a more constructivist approach in their classrooms are the same teachers who have used computers consistently and in meaningful ways in their classrooms. These teachers are more willing to discuss subjects in which they are not experts and tend to assign longer, more complex projects. It appears not that the technology makes teachers change but that the technology facilitates changes that teachers already wanted to make.[37] However, change in education is rarely swift. Even highly motivated teachers who regularly used technology took substantial amounts of time over three to five years to become comfortable with new technology and able to fit it into their classroom goals.[38] With increasing pressure on schools to incorporate technology and with other supporting factors present, such as sufficient funding and on-site technical support, we can expect to see changes in teachers' pedagogy as they become more comfortable with the power of technology.

Professional Resources and Communication

In the past decade, we have witnessed a boom in communications. Facsimile machines, cellular phones, satellite broadcasting, and the tremendous growth of the Internet have been shrinking our world. With these tools a teacher can communicate with colleagues worldwide, both quickly and cheaply.

Voice Mail Technology's advantages are not confined to extremely expensive and complicated arrangements. A sophisticated, easy-to-use message system can facilitate communication. For those schools and parents who do not yet have a powerful, efficient Internet connection, technology still provides ways to ease communication. The Bridge Project is a voice messaging system every teacher in a school can use to post a message on a voice "bulletin board" for his or her class. Parents can access this message twenty-four hours a day, seven days a week. Teachers can leave a description of the week's activities as well as reminders for upcoming events. Parents can also leave a message for the teacher, or students can check homework assignments. In schools that use the Bridge Project, the number of daily teacher-parent contacts increased from three to fourteen per teacher in the project's first year.[39]

a less expensive technological modification

Email Email is an excellent medium for teachers to use in sharing ideas, materials, and resources. Besides being fast and cheap, email can be sent with attachments for sharing documents. It can also be sent to large groups of recipients as easily as to one, making it much more efficient than the telephone or mailings. Teachers can also communicate with parents via email, and vice versa, without the disruption of ringing phones and answering machines. Within the school setting itself, email has the potential to change the work environment. Principals can distribute faculty announcements and even conduct administrative tasks through this communication channel, reducing staff meetings and mounds of accumulated paper.

the changes accompanying email

The Internet and World Wide Web The World Wide Web connects teachers to professional organizations in their field and to vast databases of lesson plans and teaching materials throughout the world. The list of web sites in the "For Further Information" section at the end of this chapter is just a small sample of an incredibly large and growing resource. As described in the accompanying box, **search engines** can help you find more information specific to your needs. In addition, Internet news groups, described earlier, offer teachers a source of resources and collegial communication. Many professional organizations host online discussions of relevant topics. These forums can reduce feelings of isolation by building a sense of community among professionals.

teacher resources on the Web

reducing teachers' isolation through technology

Specific computer networks are also providing an innovative medium for the professional growth and support of teachers. The Lighthouse Project* is an

*The Lighthouse Project web site is located at: http://www.soe.unc.edu/lighthouse/home.htm.

Search Engines

When you need information immediately, posting a question to a news group will not do. Instead, you can use a search engine to pinpoint where you might find the information on the World Wide Web. A search engine is a large database that has searched through many millions of web pages and indexed the text within them. Most web browsers have an icon that will call up a search engine automatically. To employ a search engine, type in a few words or phrases about which you would like to find more information. Just as with a library card catalog system, the more specific your criteria, the more focused the result. Submit your search and the search engine will provide you with a list of web addresses to look through.

It is important to remember that the Web has no form of quality control. A published web page only means that the author has access and privileges to transfer information. It does not mean the information has been evaluated by anyone other than the author. All sorts of information, from lesson plans to bibliographies, can contain numerous inaccuracies, so be a cautious consumer.*

*For some helpful questions to ask yourself when evaluating a web site, see *Elizabeth E. Kirk's Guide to Evaluating Information on the Internet,* found at http://miltonsweb. mse.jhu.edu:8001/research/education/net.html.

Teachers have discovered that the Web makes possible new levels of individualization, and encourages collaborations that take students far beyond the classroom.

—ODVARD EGIL DYRLI

Internet-based peer support and problem-solving community for new teachers. Beginning teachers use these online forums to pose dilemmas they face in their classrooms. Education faculty and accomplished teachers participate in the electronic discussion along with other new teachers to help encourage collaboration. The forum is a place to provide suggestions, offer support, and exchange resources. New teachers enthusiastically support the program and enjoy the immediate support they receive from a safe community of professionals.[40] Additional newsgroups and real-time scheduled conversations* that focus on issues of more veteran teachers are available on the Internet.[†]

Management: Teacher Productivity Tools

Teaching involves many complex tasks. Organizing learning activities, creating or gathering the materials needed, keeping records, managing conduct, and delivering instruction—all of these together add up to a big job. A teacher may have from 25 to 150 or more students every day, with attendance records to be kept and grades recorded for each one. Although no technology will take on all these tasks for teachers, tools are available to help in organizing them.

---

*A real-time conversation, or synchronous communication, occurs when people from around the world join in a "live" conversation at a scheduled time. It simulates a real conversation as if you were all in the same room: you "hear" people's thoughts when they appear on your screen, and you can immediately type in your response.

†Talk with Teachers is one example. It can be accessed at: http://www.teachnet.org/docs/talk/ index.htm.

Gradebooks   A software gradebook, also referred to as an *electronic gradebook,* is a hybrid application of a spreadsheet and a database. The database functions keep records of student and parent information such as mailing addresses, phone numbers, locker numbers, book numbers, and other details. The spreadsheet functions calculate grades and provide the teacher with statistical information regarding assignments, tests, and performance of students over time. The computer's ability to handle these calculations and information retrieval tasks can save hours of work for teachers. It can also give teachers new ways to identify a student's strengths and weaknesses. Gradebook software will even allow the teacher to print charts of a student's academic performance over time (quarters or semesters) for the student or parent to inspect.

software gradebooks save time

Other Teacher Productivity Tools   Test generators and question bank software allow teachers to create a database of questions and then construct tests from them. The teacher can easily create two or three versions of the same test with the questions in a different order or with slightly different questions. This is particularly useful for pre- and postassessments or for giving a different test to students absent on test day. Lesson-planning software can help teachers organize their repertoire of lesson plans and orchestrate them to meet curriculum objectives. Individualized education program (IEP) software helps to manage the paperwork involved in the individualized programs required in special education. Time management tools, such as schedule or calendar software, can help teachers keep track of appointments and schedules. Grant-writing software can help teachers find alternative sources of funding and organize the process of applying for grants. Tools such as these allow teachers to spend more time at the art of teaching and less time dealing with paperwork, organization, and materials management.

software to help teachers

How Are Computer Technologies Organized for Student Use?

Computer technologies generally operate in several different arrangements within the school setting, and it is useful to think of these arrangements across a continuum from concentrated to infused, as shown in Figure 7.1. When technology is *concentrated,* students are given intense exposure to computers from time to time. Technology that is integrated smoothly into the daily classroom experience is described as *infused.* Several common computer setups exist along this continuum.

Computer Labs

Computer labs, which usually feature a number of computers in a single room, offer a concentrated arrangement in which all the students use computers at the same time. This setup is ideal for technology education—teaching about the

advantages of labs

FIGURE 7.1   Arrangements for Computer Technologies

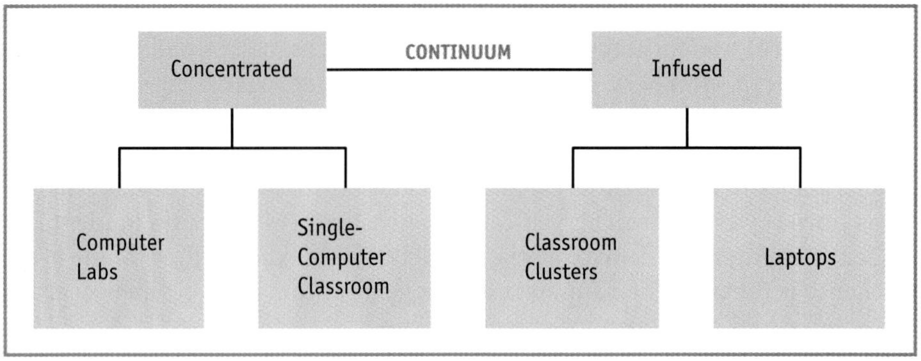

One way to think about the different ways of arranging computer technologies within a school is to consider where each arrangement fits along a continuum, from concentrated to infused. If the arrangement is concentrated, students are exposed to computers in an intense way from time to time, whereas technology that is integrated smoothly into the daily classroom experience is considered infused.

computer or how to employ a particular application. A large display station for the teacher facilitates the demonstration of skills for more effective whole-class instruction. Forty-three percent of computers in American schools are found in computer labs and 48 percent are found in classrooms, according to a 1998 national survey.[41]

disadvantages of labs

However, most computer labs do not lend themselves to interdisciplinary or cooperative group projects because of a lack of open table space. In addition, the lab setting may not include the kinds of resources that are conducive to effective group work. Access to computer labs is another key factor in their use by teachers. If many classrooms share one computer facility, there may be little lab time for each class, and visits to the lab must always be planned. For these reasons, computer labs tend to foster technology education rather than what we might call education *with* technology, that is, education that uses technology to facilitate learning about other subjects.

Single-Computer Classrooms

In a slightly more infused arrangement, the single-computer classroom might have the computer on the teacher's desk or rolled into the room on a mobile cart. In the first case especially, the teacher can use it for recordkeeping and other administrative tasks.

productive uses for a single computer

Although a single computer makes it difficult to use the technology for active instructional tasks, additional computers can be rolled into the classroom for lessons. Also, a display station can be attached to project the monitor's image on a large screen for classroom presentations and demonstrations. With software designed for the single-computer classroom, such as *Decisions, Decisions: Local Government,* discussed earlier in the chapter, the computer can even be used to facilitate cooperative groups. However, schools using this level of technology integration usually also have computer labs available for class use.

Classroom Clusters

In a more infused situation, a cluster is usually a table or an area of a classroom where three to five computers are available for use at any time by the students in that class. Clusters provide convenient access to computer technologies for a variety of tasks. For example, a teacher might use two of the computers to allow cooperative groups access to cognitive and communication tools and the others as learning stations for specific subjects.

clusters are a flexible arrangement

Providing a cluster of computers in each classroom generally requires more of an investment in technology than the other arrangements we have described. Whereas a computer lab of twenty-five computers may afford access for ten classrooms, clusters might require thirty to fifty computers. If a school can afford them, clusters offer a very flexible use of technology in the classroom setting. Teachers can plan to use them in instruction and can set up each computer to fit their needs. This arrangement genuinely fosters education *with* technology. It is not particularly good, however, for technology education, since not every student has access simultaneously.

Laptops and Handheld Computers

Partnerships between business and education have made the dream of a laptop computer for every student a reality in some places around the nation. In the fall of 1996, Microsoft and Toshiba began a Laptop Pilot Program at twenty-nine "pioneer" school sites across the United States. Participating students acquired Toshiba notebook computers loaded with Microsoft Windows and Microsoft Office software to use regularly at home and at school. This arrangement facilitates active, collaborative learning and encourages the teacher to assume the role of facilitator.[42] The laptop arrangement and the even more compact and affordable handheld computer, described earlier in the chapter, offer the most infused arrangement for a classroom and can provide seamless integration with the curriculum.

laptops as the most infused arrangement

What Are the Key Issues in Educational Technology?

You probably realize by now that many features of educational technology have given rise to serious debate among educators, policymakers, and the general public. To achieve the best use of available technology, schools need to reach some consensus on several key issues.

Infrastructure and Budgeting

Before technology can be used as an educational tool, schools must have in place the infrastructure to support it—that is, the basic facilities that make the technology usable. At the most fundamental level, the physical plants of American schools are often ill equipped to handle the demands of technology. Of course, a

Acceptable-Use Policies: Censorship or Good Sense?

What's the Policy?

As more and more schools provide students with access to the World Wide Web, parents and teachers have become concerned about how to protect students from exposure to inappropriate web sites. As a result, many schools are adopting *acceptable-use policies (AUPs),** which are signed by teachers, students, and administrators and state the guidelines for the use of computer technology.

One way to protect students includes the use of web-filtering software.[†] This software disables access to web addresses that are known to be inappropriate, such as pornographic or hate sites. The software updates the filters daily by searching the Web for new inappropriate sites. Although not foolproof, web-filtering software is an effective way to monitor the burgeoning amount of information on the Web.

How Does It Affect Teachers?

When teachers assign students research projects using the Web, they need to realize that when web-filtering software is being used at school, the students may be unable to access certain sites that would be relevant to their research. On a day-to-day basis, teachers must be aware of the parameters set for the web-filtering software their schools use. Suppose, for example, that you are teaching a unit on AIDS and you have designed an activity in which students use the Internet to search several sites to find up-to-date research. All the sites work when you develop the idea at home, but at school none of your students can access them. The reason is that your assignment is incompatible with the web-filtering software in use at your school.

What Are the Pros?

One problem with using the Internet in the classroom is the possibility of coming across incorrect or inappropriate information. From pornography to hate literature to directions on how to make a bomb, the Web is an unknown and unmonitored entity with the potential to cause extreme damage. The global nature and design of the Internet make it almost impossible to enforce any code of moral or academic ethics. No registry is required to publish a web page; anyone with access can create his or her own home page, and the information it contains is not necessarily subject to accountability. This lack of quality control concerns many teachers and makes them hesitant to use the Internet without "safety nets," such as web-filtering software and AUP guidelines, in place.

One additional consideration must be the school's liability. Some teachers and administrators worry that if a child encounters dangerous information and then uses that information to act unlawfully, the school could be held responsible. They suggest that an AUP that errs on the side of restraint and protects the school from liability is better than one that allows unrestricted access to all the information available.

What Are the Cons?

This debate brings up censorship and First Amendment rights (see Chapter 12 for more on this subject). Some teachers believe that even though the Web contains a great deal of inappropriate information, students should have unlimited access but be closely monitored. This strategy models trust and teaches proper researching skills instead of withholding valuable information.

Policy Matters! *(cont'd)*

What Do You Think?

1. In this scenario, if your school were reviewing its acceptable-use policy, would you vote to remove the web-filtering software? Why or why not?

2. How would you answer a parent who complains that her child came across pornographic information while researching the project you assigned?

3. How would you modify your lesson about online searching if a parent refused to sign his child's permission slip to use the Internet at school?

*An example of an AUP can be found at http://www.jefferson.k12.ky.us/aup/policy.html.
†One popular example of web-filtering software is Surf Watch (http://www1.surfwatch.com/; phone: 1-800-458-6600).

discussion of infrastructure problems immediately raises issues of money, both the initial costs of new technology and the yearly allowances that must be made in school budgets. This section offers a quick survey of infrastructure and budgetary issues and the ways in which they interrelate.

Electrical Problems   One basic obstacle to technology integration has been inadequate power supplies. For many years, classrooms were designed with only one electrical outlet at the front of the room. A cluster of computers will not run safely from one outlet. Rewiring has cost both time and money as schools join the information age.

inadequate power supplies

Network Wiring   Network wiring has been another roadblock on the information superhighway. The Telecommunications Act of 1996 defined equal access to "universal service" to include electronic networking and provided a fund to help reduce the price of wiring each classroom to form a schoolwide network. This fund of just under $2 billion per year is used for local and long-distance phone charges, high-speed data lines, and Internet access in schools. Depending on how needy a school district is, discounts can be as high as 90 percent.[43] Much progress has been made in networking schools: nearly eight in ten schools have a local area network,[44] and 90 percent of all schools have some sort of Internet access.[45]

expense of wiring

Access   The ratio of students to computers has dramatically improved in K–12 schools in the last fifteen years, dropping from about 168 to 6. On average, six students share one computer.[46] While this trend is encouraging, significant gaps remain in terms of the quality of equipment. For example, most school computers cannot run multimedia software and therefore are very limited in the graphical features, such as pictures or video, they can display from either software programs or the Internet.[47] The new challenge in education is not to simply get technological equipment into schools but to keep it up to date and usable in a daily classroom situation.

student-to-computer ratios improving

continued need for up-to-date equipment

Technology Budgets   Although costs of personal computers have dropped considerably since they first entered schools, information technology is expensive, especially when it is implemented on the immense scale of public education. Targeting large funds to technology often means underfunding or eliminating other programs. In 1998 all but eight states provided funds for educational technology, ranging from $500,000 in Vermont to $230 million in California.[48] The current national investment in educational technology is around $5 billion,[49] and estimated costs to make our schools "technology rich" are $15 billion.[50]

range of technology budgets across the states

Beyond the basic issue of providing the needed hardware, school administrators must plan for an ongoing technology budget that includes such items as repair costs. Maintaining a network, within a school or among schools, can be a time-consuming task requiring highly trained personnel. Although many such tasks can be contracted out to local businesses, this factor must be accounted for in yearly budgeting.

budgets to include repair, maintenance costs

Support Personnel   Besides repair personnel to keep the system running, teachers should have access to training and support personnel. Even the most advanced technologies are useless if teachers are not comfortable with their operation. Teachers who encounter technological difficulties may become discouraged and find it easier to avoid using technology altogether. Educational technology specialists who work on-site (in the school itself) are especially important. A technology specialist can act as a safety net for the integration of technology into teaching. Teachers may be more likely to take a risk and try something new if they know help is readily available.[51]

specialists need to support teachers

Education of Teachers

Because of the excitement and demands generated by new technology, pressures have risen to improve both the preparation of new teachers and the staff development options for in-service teachers.

Teacher Preparation   Over 2 million new teachers will be hired over the next decade,[52] and schools of education, much like elementary and secondary schools, are struggling with how to develop competent teachers who will use the latest technology in powerful and innovative ways. Faculty indicate that even with the recent emphasis on computer literacy, instructional technology is not adequately modeled for future teachers.[53] Schools of education are continuing to rethink their programs and are gradually using modern technology to enhance what they offer. For example, professors can use two-way interactive video to observe, but not interrupt, education students during their practice teaching.

struggling with technology issues

Vanderbilt University's Peabody College of Education is at the forefront of technology integration. It has forged unusually strong connections among technology, education, and the arts and sciences departments at the university level. As an exemplary illustration, six education students worked collaboratively to produce an interactive multimedia program that they would use in their student teaching. Their final product, a CD-ROM entitled *Billie's Story* about a young

connecting technology, education, and arts and sciences

Using ERIC

ERIC is a federally funded national information system that provides access to a variety of services and products dealing with education-related issues. The ERIC database is the primary resource for locating research on teaching and learning. In addition, ERIC creates digests of research on important topics to help educators traverse the research landscape. ERIC is available to libraries on CD-ROM or to anyone with access to the Internet at http://ericir.syr.edu/.

AskERIC is an Internet-based question-answering service for teachers, library media specialists, administrators, and anyone else with questions about education. Just send an email message to askeric@askeric.org, and the AskERIC staff will draw on its extensive resources to answer your question, usually within forty-eight hours. You can also visit the web site mentioned above. In addition to these important services, ERIC offers hundreds of lesson plans, a virtual library, and links to many other educational services.

child with cystic fibrosis, combined their content knowledge about such topics as gene therapy, their pedagogical skills in teaching science, and their technological expertise in combining the information in a multimedia format. Technology did not drive the project, but it facilitated a powerful interdisciplinary experience for these future teachers.

As an education student, you can expect to take three or more credit hours of information technology courses, and you will receive approximately the same amount of technology instruction within your other education courses.[55] When you graduate, you can count on having to demonstrate your skills in technology. Thirty-eight states have technology requirements for teacher licensure, and four of those states require coursework in technology (see Chapter 15). Requirements vary widely, and some states' tests include hands-on components.[56]

technology requirements for licensure

Staff Development   Similarly, some states are adding more stringent requirements for teachers to renew their licenses. Three states require teachers to participate in technology training as part of the relicensure process, and by 2001 Idaho districts must show that 90 percent of their teachers are competent technology users to receive state accreditation.[57] However, the training programs have not yet kept pace with the new requirements. Most school districts have not prioritized training, giving it only 15 percent of the technology budget.[58] Teachers received an average of around thirteen hours of training in technology use in 1997.[59]

keeping up to date

Experts do not agree on exactly how training should be offered. Some believe it should be ongoing at teachers' convenience, whereas others advocate an intensive, off-site course with follow-up seminars. With the advent of widespread telecommunications networks, many professional development courses are now offered online.* Teachers can log on at night or during the summer to work

*One example is Classroom Connect (web site: www.classroom.com).

Educational information at your fingertips.
(© Elizabeth Crews)

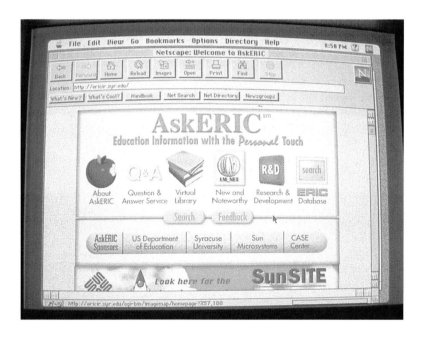

in-service and pre-service teachers learn from each other

through self-paced lessons. Accompanying discussion groups allow time for reflection.

The Curry School of Education at the University of Virginia offers an innovative program for professional development that incorporates pre- and in-service teachers. In the Technology Infusion Project, or TIP, each pre-service teacher enrolled in the Introduction to Classroom Computing course is paired with an in-service teacher who has an interest in educational technologies. During their collaboration, the in-service teacher provides insight about curriculum and classroom practices while the pre-service teacher shares the new skills he is learning, such as hypermedia applications or skills in telecomputing. As both teachers become more familiar with new technologies, they jointly explore instructional possibilities, culminating in a long-term project that they teach together in the classroom. Pre-service teachers gain a valuable classroom perspective from a veteran in the field and ground their technology learning in classroom practice. Whereas technology workshops often intimidate in-service teachers, TIP's collaborative nature makes it a more comfortable experience.

Parents

E-mail seems the best possible way to bridge the parent-teacher communication gap.

—JOYCE KASMAN VALENZA

Technology can be a "hook" to get parents involved or a quick deterrent to send them running. Parents who are not familiar with technology may be intimidated by or fearful of their child's computer use. Technology can become an obstacle between you and your students' parents, but several initiatives are aimed at breaking down these barriers while also educating parents.

Since 1987, Indiana's Buddy System Project has supplied every student and teacher in selected schools with computers, modems, printers, and software, both at home and at school. The program currently serves 6,000 families. Parents are encouraged to place the computer in a family room where all will have access to it. Extensive training is part of the program; for example, a mother and a daughter might attend a special summer camp together to learn more in-depth Internet searching skills. Parents teach other parents, children teach parents, and children teach one another. The Buddy System extends the child's learning opportunities beyond the classroom walls while creating a special opportunity for the family to become involved as well. With sensitive training, technology can "hook" parental interest in education.[60]

parents and children learning together

Eighty percent of families with household incomes over $100,000 per year have a computer at home, while only 25 percent of families making less than $30,000 have a home computer.[61] Initiatives such as the Buddy System help to equalize the technological playing field that income levels can divide.

the digital divide

Equity

Some critics argue that programs like the Indiana Buddy System are the exception, and current patterns of technology use in schools contribute to the disparity in educational quality between the affluent and the disadvantaged. At school, data indicate that poorer students are at a disadvantage.[62] Only twenty-two states target technology funds to underprivileged schools or districts.[63] The equalization of computer density is significant progress, but the digital divide still exists in terms of quality of equipment and type of instruction. Underprivileged children are more likely to use computers in a rigid drill-and-practice format rather than in more flexible formats that build higher-level cognitive skills and promote more positive attitudes toward technology.[64] Besides the basic question of fairness, these inequalities will have implications when these students graduate and look for jobs without the computer skills of their more affluent peers.

Gender differences also have emerged from the use of technology in education. For example, in 1996 only 17 percent of high school seniors taking the Advanced Placement Computer Science exam were female.[65] Researchers argue that certain types of technologies aggravate the differences between boys and girls. For example, many commonly used applications value speed, aggression, and efficiency[66]—qualities that boys tend to display—whereas technology tends to be more interesting for girls when it's used for a legitimate problem-solving exercise and not as an end in itself.[67] Although researchers may argue about whether these differences arise from natural differences between girls and boys or from cultural and social influences, there is little doubt that girls receive less exposure and training in technology during their school experience than boys. However, with the growth of telecollaboration in both education and business, girls' skills may become more valued. Tasks that require versatility and collaboration may invite girls to participate.

gender inequities

Teachers can do a lot to dispel inequities within their own classrooms. Students with little computer experience can be teamed with more experienced

what teachers can do

users. Classrooms and computer labs can be made available to students before and after school, and teachers can promote gender equity through modeling, attitude, and expectations. Technology need not become a wedge widening the gap between the "haves" and the "have-nots"; but without awareness of the problem, the potential for increased inequity is very real.

Integration into the Curriculum

For computer technology to become a genuine part of school life, as it has in the business world, the tools of technology must be *integrated* into school behaviors. Integrating technology means bringing the tools of technology into daily learning and teaching activities, just as teachers already do with chalkboards and books. This is not an easy task. Much of this chapter has focused on how computer technologies can be used as tools for student learning, but we have also seen that many support systems must be in place.

essential conditions

What conditions must be present in a school "to create learning environments conducive to powerful uses of technology"?[68] Among other conditions, schools must have the following:

▶ Student-centered approaches to learning

▶ Access to contemporary technologies, software, and telecommunications networks

▶ Educators skilled in the use of the technology for learning

▶ Technical assistance for maintaining and using technology resources

▶ Ongoing financial support for sustained technology use

▶ Content standards and curriculum resources

▶ Community partners who provide expertise, support, and real-life interations

▶ Proactive leadership from the education system

As this list* indicates, real change in education and technology cannot be the job of a lone teacher who is a whiz on the Internet or a solo school board member who votes for new software. It must be a systemic change coming from a critical mass of individuals who are committed to the integration of education *with* technology.

*From *National Educational Technology Standards—Connecting Curriculum and Technology.* Copyright © 2000, ISTE (the International Society for Technology in Education), 800.336.6191 (U.S. and Canada) or 541.302.3777 (International), cust_svc@iste.org, www.iste.org. Reprinted with permission.

A Final Word

One key issue that we have not fully addressed is whether all the "hype" about technology will simply go the way of the filmstrip. Are we spending billions of dollars on fancy hardware, ripping up ceilings in schools to install fiberoptic cables, and asking veteran teachers to change their ways without reason? What do we lose when we incorporate technology into our teaching? With increased access to vast amounts of up-to-date information and powerful new technologies, are students learning "the basics" as well as they do in more traditional classrooms?

words of caution

When "techno-reformers" talk about their grand plans, they have one purpose in mind: preparing future employees in a technology-driven work environment.[69] Teachers, on the other hand, have a broader focus: they want to develop healthy bonds with their students that will lead to intellectual growth. Teachers hope to produce responsible, educated citizens who have every opportunity open to them. When teachers see the rapidly changing world of technology in which machines sometimes break, certain applications take a long time to learn, and some programs are not flexible enough to meet their needs, they hesitate to take part in it.[70] While policymakers rush to move schools into the information age, it's important not to forget that teachers make up a crucial part of the integration question.

Certainly new technologies are no panacea for the classroom, but they offer tools that can help change the classroom from a teacher-centered to a more cooperative and student-centered environment. Students can use technological devices as tools—not toys—in the same ways that they will likely use technology in their future lives. We believe that all teachers should have the opportunity to gain skill in educational technologies, and in particular we believe it would behoove new teachers to develop these skills in the context of their preservice work. Most important, we want you to consider how technology will affect your future classroom. Ask yourself where technology can enhance what you do and where it can allow you to innovate. If it is not accomplishing these goals, ask yourself why you are using it.[71]

technology is not the panacea

is technology worth it?

KEY TERMS

cognitive tools (217)
word processor (219)
World Wide Web (220)
drill and practice (221)
telecollaborate (223)
databases (224)
simulation (225)
virtual fieldtrips (226)

spreadsheet (226)
tutorials (227)
Internet (228)
telecommunications (228)
news group (228)
distance education (229)
assistive technology (230)
search engines (235)

FOR REFLECTION

1. How have recent developments in technology affected you and your family?

2. Do you think parents should be concerned about the role, or lack of it, that technological tools play in the education of their children?

3. What technologies should students have access to within the classroom?

4. What technologies should teachers have access to?

5. What skills in using media and technology do you think teachers should have?

6. In what ways have you witnessed technology being used in the classroom? How would *you* use educational technology in your classroom?

7. What reservations do you have about the integration of technology in education?

8. What support systems do the teachers you know have for using technology in instruction? Whom do they ask when they have questions?

FOR FURTHER INFORMATION

Forcier, R. C. *The Computer as a Productivity Tool in Education.* Englewood Cliffs, NJ: Prentice Hall, 1996.
This is an introductory book in the use of computers as a tool in education.

Grabe, M., and C. Grabe. *Integrating Technology for Meaningful Learning.* 2d ed. Boston: Houghton Mifflin, 1998.
Taking active learning in classrooms as its pivotal theme, this book is a useful resource for integrating technology into daily instruction.

Heinich, R., M. Molenda, J. D. Russell, and S. E. Smaldino. *Instructional Media and Technologies for Learning.* 6th ed. Upper Saddle River, NJ: Merrill, 1999.
Now in its sixth edition, this is one of the seminal books on the "how to" of using media in the classroom.

Jonassen, D. H. *Computers in the Classroom: Mindtools for Critical Thinking.* Englewood Cliffs, NJ: Prentice Hall, 1996.
Centering on the use of software applications to foster thinking skills, this is a useful book for learning how to integrate "mindtools" into instruction.

Maddux, C. D., D. L. Johnson, and J. W. Willis. *Educational Computing: Learning with Tomorrow's Technologies.* 2d ed. Needham Heights, MA: Allyn and Bacon, 1997.
This text combines history, theory, and practice to provide a strong base of knowledge for applying educational technologies in classroom instruction.

Saettler, P. *The Evolution of American Educational Technology.* **Englewood, CO: Libraries Unlimited, 1990.**

This text is an almost encyclopedic volume of the *who, what,* and *when* of educational media and technology history.

Tapscott, D. *Growing Up Digital: The Rise of the Net Generation.* **New York: McGraw-Hill, 1998.**

This text is a good source for understanding the unique characteristics of the generation that has grown up with digital media.

In addition to these printed materials and the web sites listed within the chapter, the following list offers some educational web sites for you to look through. Remember, however, that these sites are only starting points. For specific information, use a search engine. Also, keep in mind that web addresses can change without warning. If your web browser cannot locate an address, one trick that sometimes works is to shorten the address to the next root level. For example, if http://www.iste.org/Research/Background/Online.html does not work, try http://www.iste.org/. If you still have trouble, try an Internet search engine and use some descriptive keywords.

ISTE's Electronic Resources: **http://www.iste.org/Research/Background/Online.html** SEARCH

A superb list of links that covers a wide range, including standards, distance education, corporate partnerships, curriculum, and government support.

Kathy Schrock's Guide for Educators: **http://discoveryschool.com/schrockguide/** SEARCH

A very well-organized list of useful links, with an especially helpful section categorized by subject area.

Judi Harris's Virtual Architecture Web Page: **http://ccwf.cc.utexas.edu/~jbharris/Virtual-Architecture/** SEARCH

An excellent resource for teachers who want to explore telecollaborative projects.

Learning and Leading with Technology Journal: **http://www.iste.org/L&L/index.html** SEARCH

A monthly journal available online that offers great suggestions from teachers for teachers on how to use technology effectively in the K–12 classroom.

California Instructional Technology Clearinghouse: **http://www.clearingouse.k12.ca.us/** SEARCH

This site allows teachers and parents to search for objective reviews of quality educational software.

disABILITY Links: **http://www.irsc.org/disability.htm** SEARCH

A helpful site for information and resources about a wide range of disabilities and health conditions.

SEARCH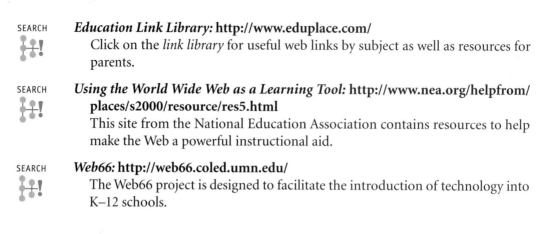

Education Link Library: **http://www.eduplace.com/**
Click on the *link library* for useful web links by subject as well as resources for parents.

SEARCH

Using the World Wide Web as a Learning Tool: **http://www.nea.org/helpfrom/ places/s2000/resource/res5.html**
This site from the National Education Association contains resources to help make the Web a powerful instructional aid.

SEARCH

Web66: **http://web66.coled.umn.edu/**
The Web66 project is designed to facilitate the introduction of technology into K–12 schools.

8

What Is Taught?

What knowledge is most worth knowing? What should be taught in the schools? The answers to these questions take the form of curricula, and they are often a source of tension among teachers, school boards, education professors, textbook publishers, policymakers, and parents. Currently these groups are seeking to raise academic standards through common curricular emphases, while also accommodating various cultural and ethnic groups' demands for representation in the curriculum. This chapter emphasizes that

▶ The school curriculum, which has evolved over time as a result of shifting purposes, consists of all the organized and intended experiences of the student for which the school accepts responsibility.

▶ The 1980s and 1990s marked a time of renewed public attention to the purpose of schooling. Among other issues, many commission reports and national studies addressed the shape of the formal or explicit curriculum, and educators pondered what learning should be common for all.

▶ The present curriculum in most subject areas is in a state of flux as reformers try to set standards and raise academic expectations.

▶ Textbooks have such a strong impact on what is taught in the classrooms that some people argue that texts represent a national curriculum.

▶ Major innovative instructional approaches used across the curriculum include interdisciplinary teaching, cooperative learning, critical thinking and problem solving, writing across the curriculum, and block scheduling.

▶ The relevance of the schools' curricula to individual and societal problems is a continually debated issue.

Baseball, debating, reading, and biology—along with love, tolerance, and independence, frustration as well as mathematics and dramatics, values and ceramics, woodshop and poise, history and boredom, computer science and leadership—all are learned in school, some intentionally and others incidentally or in spite of the teachers' intentions.

definition of curriculum

We define the **curriculum** as all the organized and intended experiences of the student for which the school accepts responsibility. In other words, the curriculum is not just the intellectual content of the subjects taught but also the methods used to teach them, the interactions that occur among people, and the school-sponsored activities that contribute to the "life experience."

formal vs. informal

During your high school years, many daily activities may have been considered "extracurricular." The formal courses of study—history, science, mathematics, English—were curricular, whereas participation in the football team, cheerleading, the Future Teachers Club, or the band belonged to another, lesser category. Chapter 3 looked at what is often called the "informal curriculum," the school and classroom environments that shape the students' experience of life in school. In this chapter we examine the formal curriculum, those subjects that are taught in schools and some of the forces and instructional approaches that influence how they are taught.

All that is taught is a commitment to what is thought valuable.

—R. S. PETERS

The typical school curriculum is organized according to subject-matter divisions, and most of the efforts that go into curriculum development are still concentrated around traditional subject matter. Some historical background may help explain the current strong emphasis on these traditional subject-matter areas.

Where Does the Existing Curriculum Come From?

Throughout their history, American schools have changed in structure and curriculum to reflect various visions of what children should learn. Let's look at how the question "What is most worth knowing?" has been answered over the years. Following is a brief overview of the country's changing educational goals that have promoted major curriculum changes. Table 8.1 summarizes the key events and trends.

Shifting Purposes: From Colonial Times Through the 1970s

Seventeenth to Nineteenth Centuries During the colonial period of our history (from about 1620 until the 1770s), knowledge of the community's concepts of right conduct and religious belief was considered the most important thing children should learn. During the 1770s, the time of the Revolutionary War, the schools began to focus on political ends. Although not available to all, education was seen as essential to produce a populace literate enough to continue the democratic form of government. Schools extended their curricula beyond the Bible teachings of earlier years to include knowledge necessary for trade and commerce or a university education.

The purpose of the common school, which developed in the mid-1800s (as described in Chapter 11), was to produce a literate and moral citizenry. The curriculum emphasized conservative republican virtues and moral values; these were molded by teachers and by the *McGuffey Readers,* a series of popular books that guided the learning of millions of American children during the nineteenth century.

Changes in the Twentieth Century   As American society experienced rapid changes in the twentieth century—massive immigration, depression, world wars—the definitions of the formal curriculum reflected equally rapid changes. Those who thought the schools should prepare students for entry in the world of work tried to shape the curriculum for that purpose. Others who held a progressive philosophy thought the schools' curriculum should help children gain knowledge of themselves, develop as individuals, and acquire democratic social competence to reform society. During the so-called progressive education era of the 1920s, 1930s, and 1940s, many elementary schools emphasized citizenship and self-adjustment and followed a primarily **child-centered** or **society-centered curriculum;** that is, they tended to stress the needs and development of the individual student rather than the mastery of fixed subject matter. (See Chapter 11 for more on progressive education.) This by no means was universally true; many schools during the progressive education era maintained a strong subject-matter focus, especially at the secondary level. By the 1950s, the curriculum of the schools had become broad and diverse in response to these competing demands for vocational preparation, reconstruction of society, and personal development.

child-centered . . .

Critics of American education in the 1950s used the 1957 space launching of the *Sputnik* satellite by the Soviet Union as evidence that American schools were deficient. The American public, which had complacently believed American schools to be far superior to any other country's, reacted against the perceived "softness" of the curriculum and demanded a return to the "meat and potatoes" of learning: the academic disciplines, with particular emphasis on science and mathematics. As a result, curriculum development during the 1950s and 1960s became largely subject matter centered. The pendulum swing from child-centered to **subject-matter–centered curriculum** and back again is an ongoing theme of American curricular change.

. . . vs. subject-matter–centered

Prosperity was a major factor in the extensive curricular changes of the 1950s and 1960s. Because the public was willing to spend increasing amounts of money for children's education and because of concern for national defense and world-wide prestige, the federal government poured huge amounts of money into curriculum development projects, teacher-training workshops, and research. The influence of the federal government on the development of new curricula during this period cannot be overestimated.

massive federal support

TABLE 8.1   Curriculum Trends in American Education

Time Period	Key Events and Trends	Curriculum Characteristics and Emphases	Dominant Educational Philosophies
1620–Revolutionary War	Education limited by sex and socio-economic class Northwest Ordinance, first national education law	Religious training Moral development Reading, writing, arithmetic basics Bible teaching	Perennialism
1770s–1820s	Revolutionary War (1775–1783) U.S. Constitution ratified (1788) War of 1812 (1812–1815)	Moral development Knowledge necessary for either trade/commerce or university education Literacy to continue democratic form of government	Perennialism
1820s–1880s	Establishment of common schooling Civil War (1861–1865) Morrill Land Grant Act (1862)	Basic tools of literacy for practical education Conservative virtues and moral values (*McGuffey Readers*) Cultivation of American identity and loyalty Melting-pot theme	Perennialism
1880s–1950s	World War I (1914–1918) World War II (1939–1945) Great Depression (1930s)	Child-centered, not subject-centered, curriculum Activities and experiences rather than verbal and literacy skills Cooperative rather than individual learning activities Citizenship and self-adjustment	Progressivism
1950s–1970s	Launching of Soviet satellite *Sputnik* (1957) Cold War *Brown* v. *Board of Education* (1954)	*1950s–1960s* Structure of the discipline Discovery method of teaching	Existentialism Essentialism

TABLE 8.1 Curriculum Trends in American Education *(cont'd)*

Time Period	Key Events and Trends	Curriculum Characteristics and Emphases	Dominant Educational Philosophies
1950s–1970s	Elementary and Secondary Education Act (1965) Vietnam War and protests Education for All Handicapped Children Act (PL 94–142) (1975)	*1970s* Career education Mainstreaming Multicultural education Flexible curriculum— many electives	
1980s	America's pre-eminence in world economy declines Educational reform reports End of Cold War	Back-to-basics movement Core curriculum Strengthening of academic requirements Inclusion Multicultural education	Essentialism Perennialism
1990s	Recession during 1990–1992, followed by unprecedented boom in the economy Growing teacher shortage NEA and AFT fail in merger talks	Standards movement High-stakes testing for students Technology emphasis Growing rejection of bilingual education	Essentialism

The tremendous postwar knowledge explosion forced new approaches to curriculum planning and made many areas of existing curricula, such as geography, seem obsolete. In addition, a combination of social and political factors encouraged a new approach to the educational needs of the country, including new emphases on multicultural and bilingual education.

Structure of Disciplines Approach   The approach to teaching specific disciplines underwent significant changes during the 1960s and 1970s. Instrumental in leading these changes was the publication of Jerome Bruner's book *The Process of Education.*[1] Bruner's basic thesis was that any discipline could and should be studied, at any level of complexity, in terms of its "structure." Bruner defined the structure of a discipline as the concepts and methods of inquiry that are its most basic parts. Instead of studying random facts or incidental phenomena, students should learn the principles that constitute the heart of a discipline; in this way,

Bruner—structure of disciplines

discovery (inquiry) method

they will *learn how to learn.* Teachers were encouraged to let students discover meanings for themselves using a *discovery* (or *inquiry*) *method.* The concepts fundamental to the discipline's structure would be studied over and over throughout the school years, but each time from an increasingly complex point of view. The curriculum of the discipline would resemble a spiral; as students moved upward along the spiral, they would re-encounter familiar concepts in more complex forms.

Any subject can be taught effectively in some intellectually honest form to any child at any stage of development.

—JEROME BRUNER

Bruner's **structure of disciplines approach** was used in numerous curriculum projects that had considerable impact on the public secondary schools' curricula, particularly in the areas of mathematics, biology, chemistry, physics, and foreign languages. But these new projects had less impact at the elementary level; elementary school educators objected to planning from the top down, believing that such an approach failed to take sufficient account of the developmental processes of young children and that it separated rather than integrated the disciplines.

By the late 1970s, reaction against the structure of disciplines approach became more vocal. The new curriculum projects seemed to work for the bright, college-bound students but did not seem to prepare students for the world of work. As youth made demands for freedom of choice in the educational system, secondary schools responded with a more flexible curriculum and a proliferation of electives, with little focus or balance. For a time, in some schools, it seemed that no particular knowledge was considered any better than any other knowledge.

Curriculum Reform in the 1980s and 1990s

rigorous, traditional curriculum

Back-to-Basics Movement   During the late 1970s and early 1980s, a perceived decline in the quality of education, as evidenced by declining scores on standardized tests and attributed to students' choice of so many electives considered to be "soft" academically, led to a **back-to-basics movement.** The spokespersons for this movement were among both the very best educated and the least educated people in the country. Although their goals were not always clear, their disenchantment with the public schools and their desire to return to a more rigorous, more traditional curriculum were evident and often stated quite sharply. Proponents urged more emphasis on basic subjects, particularly reading, writing, and arithmetic, but also science, history, geography, and grammar. They wanted the schools not only to teach content but also to help children learn to work hard. They believed that to create a society made up of strong citizens, our schools must turn out individuals able to take on difficult tasks that they can see through to completion. They wanted the schools to demand more orderly and disciplined student behavior. They wanted the authority and centrality of the teacher to be reasserted, and they desired a more structured teaching style. Finally, back-to-basics advocates often wanted the schools to return to the teaching of basic morality and, in particular, the virtue of patriotism. In many ways, the back-to-basics movement was a reaction against the personal freedom movement of the 1970s, which emphasized drug use and sexual freedom, symbolized by the culture of the "hippies."

Elementary school teachers must build basic understanding in key subjects such as mathematics if students are to succeed in later grades.
(© Elizabeth Crews)

Although the term *back-to-basics* is heard less often today, many more educators than were involved in that movement have called for similar kinds of school reforms in the name of "excellence in education," a concept discussed further in Chapter 13. The recommendations for greater academic rigor in public school education have been adopted by many state legislatures. The early advocates of the back-to-basics movement offended many educators with their pressure tactics, hostile language, and the deep strain of idealistic nostalgia in their desire to return to a simpler society. But behind much of their rhetoric were ideas and aspirations that most educators also believed. Many people inside and outside education believe that the schools have tried to be "all things to all people" and that it shows. If nothing else, then, the back-to-basics movement, as subsumed in the more recent excellence-in-education movement, has refocused the public and educators on the primary mission of the schools: to help children develop the necessary knowledge and skills to live good and productive lives and contribute to the well-being of society.

excellence in education

The best education for the best is the best education for all.
—ROBERT MAYNARD HUTCHINS

Curricular Issues and Reform Reports   As our brief historical review shows, American schools have been subject to many varying demands and expectations—

more than they can possibly fulfill. In response to the realization that the schools had been asked to do too much, curriculum reformers of the 1980s tried to define some unifying major purposes for the schools. These reformers, including Ernest Boyer, John Goodlad, and the very influential report of the National Commission on Excellence in Education, *A Nation at Risk,* strongly supported higher academic standards and the development of students' academic competencies in mathematics, science, literature and language, history, arts, foreign languages, and technology. Emphasis would be placed on developing ways of knowing, reasoning, communicating, and problem solving. These reformers wrestled with traditionally troublesome curricular questions: What knowledge is best for all? Should schools have a core curriculum, and, if so, of what should it consist?

emphasis on higher standards

Many discussions of curriculum reform during the early 1990s involved issues of centralization or decentralization. In contrast to many other countries, the United States has traditionally had a decentralized system of state and local curricula. The national government has had little influence on what is taught in our nation's schools. During the early 1990s, however, spurred by concern about the nation's economic competitiveness with other countries, a strong movement emerged toward national curriculum standards, national testing and assessment, and the establishment of national goals. A 1994 law, the Goals 2000: Educate America Act, codified eight national goals (listed in Table 13.1, page 456) to guide future educational initiatives and funded different academic groups to develop national standards in the various subject-matter fields. By 1996, though, these centralization efforts had lost steam, giving way to a growing consensus that the setting of standards and curriculum should remain the prerogative of the individual states and that the federal government should downplay its attempts to influence curriculum standards. Interestingly, many states were using the national standards developed by different academic groups in formulating their own state standards. By the beginning of the twenty-first century, virtually every state had developed its own standards for student learning, and many states backed up their new standards with rigorous accountability measures for both students and educators. Chapter 13 discusses national education standards and assessment in more detail.

centralize or decentralize?

Goals 2000

What Is the Present Curriculum?

In looking at the courses of study prescribed by the fifty states, we will see that the similarities far outweigh the differences. Parts of this chapter discuss some reasons for this phenomenon, such as the influence of national reform movements and the uniformity of available textbooks. But for now, let's examine what is presently taught in elementary and secondary schools across the country. At both levels the curriculum is organized into subject-matter areas, which ordinarily are language arts and English, mathematics, science, social studies, foreign languages, the fine arts, physical education and recreation, and electives and vocational education.

Language Arts and English

The *language arts* program seeks to develop in children the skills of reading, writing, speaking, and listening, as well as a knowledge of culture as represented in literature. The importance of language arts cannot be overemphasized, since no subject can be successfully studied without adequate language skills. In elementary schools, most language arts programs focus on helping students develop written and oral communication skills, comprehension and problem-solving strategies, creativity, and appreciation for language and literature. At the secondary level, English courses focus on integration of the language arts using literature as the prime motivator. Among the most commonly read works are *Romeo and Juliet, Julius Caesar, The Scarlet Letter, Macbeth, Huckleberry Finn,* and *The Great Gatsby.*

> *I have often reflected upon the new vistas that reading opened to me.... As I see it today, the ability to read awoke inside me some long dormant craving to be mentally alive.*
>
> —MALCOLM X

Issues and Trends   Teachers today are selecting literature that is relevant to student interests yet representative of an accepted literary tradition; balancing classic literature selections with works by and about minority groups; instructing

"They're words, Eddie. Assembly required."

© Martha Campbell

POLICY MATTERS!   Teaching by Script or Improvisation?

What's the Policy?

Schools and school districts around the country have adopted or considered standardized programs for teaching reading—such as DISTAR, Success for All, and Reading Mastery—that have excellent records in promoting reading success among children, but relegate the teacher to a functionary role devoid of creativity.

How Does It Affect Teachers?

Instead of giving teachers suggestions and guidelines on how to use the materials provided, prescriptive reading programs are actually scripted, with specific instructions for how teachers should proceed, including what to do and say. If a student's response is A, then you are to go to question 2; if his response is B, then you go to question 3. Teachers have almost no flexibility to deviate from the program's procedures and questions.

What Are the Pros?

Several of the most well-known reading programs are very effective, and can boast proven track records of helping children, even those from impoverished backgrounds, to learn to read. One elementary school principal in Houston, for example, brought his low-income students from near the bottom in reading and math to ranking twelfth among his district's 182 elementary schools. He attributes the success to implementing the DISTAR program, a highly scripted direct-instruction program.

What Are the Cons?

A Rice University researcher criticizes these programs as dishonoring the professional craft of teaching. "Educators do not find in this program, or any other package, the depth and breadth and variety of reading styles that they need to get all their kids to read and to find reading purposeful and fun."

Teachers who use these programs are not expected to diagnose students' difficulties, matching their interests and styles with materials selected by the teacher. In contrast, critics suggest, the teacher's role in these programs is to do what the program dictates, with little difference between the master teacher and a bright teaching aide.

What Do You Think?

1. What position do you take regarding the use of these prescriptive programs? What additional information would you like to have about these programs?

2. What would you do if your school or school district adopted one of these programs, even if you were personally opposed to them?

3. What position do you think the parents of your elementary-aged children would take regarding this issue?

Source: William Raspberry, "Classroom Riffs," *The Washington Post*, June 25, 1999, p. A29.

students in critical thinking; encouraging writing across the curriculum (discussed later in this chapter); integrating the various language arts by, for example, linking reading and writing or speaking, listening, and reading; and maintaining a balance between composition and literature in the curriculum.

Major disagreements exist in the field of reading education. The basic debate is whether reading instruction should emphasize the integration of language arts skills and knowledge in a literature-based approach, commonly known as the

whole language approach, or focus on **phonics** instruction, an approach to reading that teaches the reader to "decode" words by sounding out letters and combinations of letters. During the 1970s and 1980s, whole language approaches to reading displaced the phonics approach in many schools. However, discontent with declining reading scores in states that emphasized a whole language approach, notably California, spurred a renewed interest in phonics. In fact, the issue has become politically charged, with conservatives supporting phonics and liberals supporting whole language approaches. Although both the whole language and phonics camps have their strong believers, recent research suggests that explicit phonics instruction is an essential ingredient in teaching many— perhaps most—children to read. The research concludes that it is important to teach explicit, systematic phonics within a context of meaningful literature.[2] *Phonemic* awareness, the understanding that sounds make up language, seems to be crucial in the development of good readers. Thus, a balanced use of both approaches, rather than one over the other, seems to be the key to reading instruction.

phonics vs. whole language

issue

Mathematics

Before the 1950s, schools emphasized student mastery of basic computational skills. In the 1960s, a new type of mathematics curriculum, known as the *new math,* emerged. It saw mathematics as a language that both communicates ideas about numbers and describes the quantitative aspects of ideas and objects. As a result, the new math stressed *structure* rather than drill and computational skills. The new math tended to be abstract, and for the average student its conceptual theories were of little practical use.

"new math"

Today the traditional approach featuring drill and practice, computation, and memorization tends to be used in courses for non-college-bound students. College-bound students, after studying algebra and geometry, often take optional fourth-year courses that place strong emphasis on structure, learning by discovery, definitions, properties, sets, rigor, statistics, calculus, trigonometry, and other abstract concepts.

Issues and Trends   Mathematics at the elementary level emphasizes the use of hands-on manipulatives to aid students in learning about patterns in mathematics and our base-ten system. Reason and argument rather than the teacher's authority and the textbook is being urged, consistent with the popular constructivist approach to learning, which is based on psychological theories suggesting that people must construct knowledge and meaning for themselves, rather than receiving knowledge passively from teachers or textbooks. (Constructivist approaches to learning are discussed further in Chapter 10.) Even at the elementary level, and especially in later years, calculators and computers are increasingly common as mathematics education focuses less on computational skills and more on developing concepts, relationships, structures, and problem-solving skills. Moreover, the use of computers and computer programming in mathematics classes adds a great deal of practical utility for many students. Not only do

Math- Ele- hands on Reason & Argument

use of computers

computers create interest in the curriculum, but students receive valuable experience that may prove useful as they seek jobs. Graphing calculators are seen as important tools to help students understand complex mathematical relationships.

A 1998 national study examining the use of computers in schools concluded that the $5 billion being spent each year on educational technology is actually hurting many children in mathematics because the computers aren't being put to good use. The report found that computers can be an important learning tool when used in simulations and real-life applications of math concepts, but using computers for repetitive math drills actually hurt students' math scores.[3]

In addition to using technology and emphasizing problem solving, mathematics programs have been moving away from the traditional compartmentalization of arithmetic, algebra, geometry, calculus, and so on. As newer topics, such as probability, statistics, and computer science, are emphasized, course designers have begun to integrate a variety of mathematics skills and topics in one course or across several courses. The blending of mathematics with other subject areas, including consumer economics and personal finance, will continue as part of the trend toward broadening students' applications of their mathematical understandings and skills.

integration of skills

Science

Science in the elementary grades takes advantage of children's natural curiosity about the world around them—plants, seasons, color, light, sound, and animals. In the upper elementary and middle school grades, the curriculum includes weather and climate, the solar system, electricity, and health-related topics. The secondary school science curriculum is still centered around year-long courses: general science, biology, chemistry, and physics.

Issues and Trends   Two major questions drive science education reform: where will the next generation of scientists come from, and how can all students be prepared to make informed judgments about such critical and science-based issues as environmental pollution, energy sources, and biotechnology?

For reformers, there has been both good news and bad news concerning science education in the United States. The bad news is that American youth don't know much science. The good news is that the country is reaching consensus on how to remedy the problem. The science curriculum has been undergoing dramatic redirection as a result of Project 2061 (named for the year in which Halley's comet is expected to return), an initiative of the American Association for the Advancement of Science. Inquiry-based learning and a hands-on approach are strong elements in science reform efforts. Addressing both elementary and secondary science, the association's recommendations include the following:

Project 2061

▶ Reducing the boundaries between academic disciplines

▶ Emphasizing ideas and thinking skills rather than specialized vocabulary and memorization

Performing well-designed experiments fosters a deeper understanding of key scientific concepts and methods. (© Bob Daemmrich/Stock Boston)

▶ Helping students develop a cogent view of the world by including such key concepts and principles as the structure and evolution of the universe; basic concepts related to matter, energy, force, and motion; the human life cycle; medical techniques; social change and conflict; and the mathematics of symbols.[4]

In the science classroom, wondering should be as highly valued as knowing.
—*2061 SCIENCE CURRICULUM*

The work of Project 2061 appears to have had a strong effect on both the national standards for science education and many state curriculum frameworks, but as yet it has had little impact on how science is taught in the schools.

Social Studies

Social studies—the study of people and their ideas, actions, and relationships—is not a discipline in the same sense as mathematics or physics, although it draws on the various social science disciplines (history, geography, political science, economics, psychology, sociology, and anthropology), as well as on religion, literature, and the arts, for its content and methods of inquiry. (A *discipline* has been defined as an area of inquiry containing a distinctive body of concepts and principles, with techniques for exploring the area and for correcting and expanding the body of knowledge.)[5]

history dominates

History has traditionally been the leading discipline of the social studies at both the elementary and secondary levels, and although other disciplines have made some inroads, it still remains dominant. Recently efforts have been made to restore geography to the social studies curriculum following assessments that pointed out students' inability to locate countries on maps. Government is also a staple of the social studies curriculum. Altogether, however, the social studies curriculum at both the elementary and secondary levels is a hodgepodge of approaches.

Issues and Trends   Currently a major debate rages over whether the social studies curriculum overemphasizes European history and culture at the expense of Asian, African, and Latin American history and culture. Another concern is the representation of women's roles in the history curriculum. Although many textbook publishers are making efforts to include greater representation of women and people of color in their books, critics argue that the efforts seem feeble and contrived. At all levels, textbooks dominate the social studies curriculum.

concern for non-European cultures

Civic learning or **civic education** is another issue gaining the attention of social studies educators. Advocates of this new focus call for courses that will acquaint a racially and culturally diverse student population with the heritage common to the American democratic tradition. These new courses would extend the basic study of American law and government to include trends in history, issues in contemporary society, and questions of character and values. Through critical study of case histories and current news reports, students would learn to apply principles of democracy to everyday concerns they will face as citizens. Practical experiences in civic, cultural, and volunteer activities are also strongly recommended. The "new civics" courses may help to unify educators calling for issues-centered, traditional historical, critical thought, and character education approaches to the teaching of social studies.

the "new civics"

Standards have been developed by the various national organizations representing history, geography, economics, civics, and social studies. Unfortunately, none of these standards relate to one another, so fragmentation of the social studies curriculum is likely to continue.

Foreign Languages

Compared to citizens in other nations, Americans are woefully unprepared to speak foreign languages. Only about 38 percent of students in U.S. public high schools are enrolled in a foreign language course, and most of them take a foreign language for only two years.[6] On the bright side, more and more elementary schools are offering foreign language programs in recognition of the ease with which young children learn foreign languages.

Issues and Trends   Foreign language departments in the public schools are trying to make the study of foreign languages more attractive by expanding their course offerings and integrating language study with concerns for international and multicultural education. The Internet assists students and teachers to gain greater access to current materials from other countries, thus facilitating teaching and learning. Leaders in the field emphasize the cultural foundations of language, asserting that language study increases linguistic competence and cultural sensitivity. Alternative secondary schools, such as international schools, schools-within-schools, and magnet schools, have also begun to integrate international studies and foreign language study. Attention to techniques used in elementary bilingual education—immersion, partial immersion, or the Foreign Language in the Elementary Schools Program—has focused instruction on developing fluency in speaking, writing, and comprehension. Proficiency-oriented instruction that focuses on what the learner can do with language rather than what the learner knows about language marks modern-day language teaching.

cultural understanding

Early introduction of foreign languages continues to gain support, and concern about U.S. competitiveness in a global economy has led many business leaders and politicians to urge greater emphasis on foreign language instruction. More and more states are responding to these pressures.

The Arts

The arts include visual arts, music, dance, and theater. Art and music in the elementary school are ordinarily taught by regular classroom teachers, although some schools hire specialist teachers in one or both areas. Dance and theater are largely ignored in the elementary school, although children of this age are less inhibited and seem to enjoy these activities more than do secondary students. The small amount of instruction provided in the arts for elementary students contrasts with high school offerings such as drama clubs, orchestras, bands, and dance groups. In most instances, instruction in music or dance during a child's elementary school years takes the form of private instruction outside the public school.

Art is humanity's most essential, most universal language. It is not a frill, but a necessary part of communication.

—ERNEST L. BOYER

Issues and Trends   Programs in the arts have tended to emphasize the creation of an art object or the development of a performance, but newer programs center on aesthetic education and art as a way of knowing and perceiving the world. For most students, this trend will be useful.

aesthetics emphasis

Curriculum specialists have suggested integrating the arts with other subject matter to show the usefulness of the arts. There is little doubt that the arts play a crucial role in the development of cultured, educated individuals and that they respond to a deep instinct in humanity. In spite of this recognition, however, the arts remain an endangered species whenever budget cuts occur and when high-stakes assessments of standards in language arts, math, science, and social studies dictate what teachers should emphasize in their classrooms.

Physical Education, Health, and Recreation

Physical education—education by and through human movement—contributes to physical fitness, skill and knowledge development, and social and psychological development. Currently physical education curricula are responding to four

emphasis on fitness

needs: (1) to develop aerobic capacity to maintain acceptable cardiorespiratory efficiency, (2) to achieve appropriate levels of body fat, (3) to acquire strength to perform expected tasks of living, and (4) to achieve flexibility and abdominal strength to avoid lower back injuries. To address these needs, sports skills are alternated with fitness development through such activities as swimming, jogging, bicycling, and cross-country skiing. Students are given information on exercise and nutrition so they can understand how to balance caloric intake and maintain an appropriate body fat level.

health education

The health curriculum addresses such topics as injury prevention and safety, prevention and control of disease (including AIDS), substance abuse, nutrition, family life (sexuality), consumer health, and mental and emotional health. More than most academic subjects, health education strives to change students' attitudes and behaviors to get them to take fewer risks and take preventive measures.

Elective Courses

Most high schools today offer their students a number of options regarding the courses they take. Whereas the average high school student graduates with about twenty units—a year-long course representing one unit—large high schools may offer as many as one hundred courses. The average student, then, will probably choose among optional courses according to individual interests and academic or career ambitions.

non-college-bound students

Issues and Trends   Although college preparation has been the major goal of many high schools, recently increased effort has been made to provide comprehensive programs for students not planning to attend college. This trend is especially evident in rural areas, where small, local high schools are being replaced by comprehensive regional high schools. Some of the courses involved, such as technology education, distributive education, home economics, business education, and agriculture, are specifically vocational. Others, such as driver education and consumer education, have been added to the curriculum because of an obvious societal need or in response to student interest.

more graduation requirements

A trend disturbing those who teach elective courses is the increase in requirements for graduation from high schools, which leaves less time for elective courses. Some argue that a common general education provides the best foundation for future work or academic study; others hope to maintain a large percentage of the curriculum as electives. Issues raised by teachers of elective courses focus attention on the purpose of comprehensive schooling and on what is "basic."

Vocational Courses

recent criticism

Vocational education has come under fire from those who note its inadequacy in preparing students for careers in high-technology fields or in the country's now dominant service economy. In 1991 the U.S. Department of Labor issued the Secretary's Commission on Achieving Necessary Skills (SCANS) report, which called for all high school students to develop a set of higher competencies and a foundation of skills to be better prepared for the world of work.[7] The report recognizes that both education and businesses will have to change if America is to have a well-prepared work force. The report urges teachers to help students see the relationships between what they study and its applications in real-world contexts, and to emphasize real-life problem solving. The federal government also supports a School-To-Work program designed to help students who are not going on to college to develop skills and understandings that will prepare them to adapt to the changing needs of the workplace.

A liberal education is the only practical form of vocational education.
—Cardinal John Henry Newman

Issues and Trends   Some educators and labor officials urge that the line between academic and vocational education be blurred and that all youngsters be provided with more applied learning experiences. *issue* Further, they argue that the "general education" track in high school, which falls between a college-preparatory track and a strictly vocational track, should be eliminated. Although just 42 percent of all high school students are enrolled in a general education track, nearly two out of three high school dropouts come from that track. In addition, apprenticeship programs such as those in Germany are being praised. In such a program, students receive on-the-job training with a company for four days a week and participate in classroom instruction on the fifth day. Such programs are designed to help youth move from school to work.

more apprenticeship programs?

Another promising trend is the development of "tech-prep" programs that link high school and postsecondary study. Tech-prep programs typically involve the last two years of high school and the first two years of college (usually at a community college) and provide an attractive alternative for students who do not plan to attend a four-year college.

"tech-prep" programs

trend

Assessing Student Academic Performance

Both supporters and critics of contemporary curricula often focus on the results: what do students actually learn from their studies of language arts, math, science, and so forth? The methods of assessing results are themselves highly controversial, but in this section we will look at both national and international studies that attempt to judge the academic performance of American students.

National Assessment of Educational Progress

"By the year 2000, all students will leave grades 4, 8, and 12 having demonstrated competency over challenging subject matter including English, mathematics, science, foreign languages, civics and government, economics, arts, history, and geography. . . . " Thus states Goal 3 of the National Education Goals, established by President George Bush and the nation's governors in 1990. A National Education Goals Panel reports annually on the progress toward all eight of these goals, drawing on a variety of data sources, including the National Assessment of

Educational Progress (NAEP), a congressionally mandated survey of educational achievement of America's students.

Even though the United States did not meet its ambitious education goals by the 2000 target date, at the time of this writing the National Education Goals Panel was urging Congress to keep the eight education goals in place without setting any deadline for their achievement.

"nation's report card"

Since their introduction over thirty years ago, NAEP assessments have been conducted periodically in reading, mathematics, science, writing, history, geography, and other fields. Administered to a representative national sample, the NAEP assessments are the primary source on educational achievement in the United States, and they have become known as "the nation's report card." Assessment occurs at three grade levels: fourth, eighth, and twelfth. Achievement levels are defined as *basic* (denoting partial mastery of knowledge and skills fundamental for proficient work), *proficient* (representing solid academic performance over challenging subject matter for the grade level), and *advanced* (signifying superior performance).

how are students doing?

So how are American students doing? Over the past twenty years, student achievement on the NAEP science and mathematics tests has improved slightly for all ages and racial and ethnic groups. African American, Hispanic, and Native American students continue to score significantly lower than white and Asian American students. Although few differences exist between the achievement scores of males and females on NAEP science and mathematics tests, males score significantly higher than females on college entrance examinations in those areas.[8]

ignorance of history and geography

Further NAEP assessments reveal that American students are woefully ignorant of history, geography, and civics. In the 1994 history assessment, a significant percentage of students—36 percent of fourth-graders, 39 percent of eighth-graders, and 57 percent of twelfth-graders—failed to achieve the expectations for the basic level. The percentages of students who reached the proficient or advanced levels at the fourth, eighth, and twelfth grades were only 17, 14, and 11, respectively.[9] In geography, the percentages of students who reached the proficient or advanced levels at the fourth, eighth, and twelfth grades were 22, 28, and 27, respectively. Similarly, in the 1998 reading assessment, the percentages of students who reached the proficient or higher level for the same grade levels were 31, 33, and 40, respectively.[10] Figure 8.1 summarizes these statistics.

In every subject field, therefore, a large majority of American students are failing to achieve the proficient level in the NAEP assessments. Clearly, if National Goal 3 is to be met at any time in the near future, much needs to be accomplished.

International Comparisons

Compared to the academic performances of students from other developed countries, American students have tended to do poorly, especially middle and high school students. In 1995, the Third International Mathematics and Science Study (TIMSS) tested the mathematics and science knowledge of half a million

TIMSS

FIGURE 8.1 Percentage of Students Scoring at the Proficient or Advanced Level on NAEP Assessments in Various Subject Fields

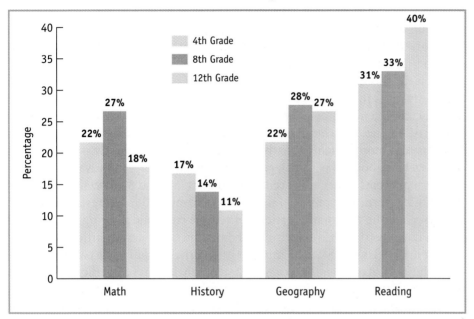

Source: The Nation's Report Card, web site: http://nces.gov/nationsreportcard/site/home.asp.

students at three grade levels—fourth, eighth, and twelfth—in forty-one countries. TIMSS was the largest, most comprehensive, and most rigorous international comparison of education ever done. The general finding of TIMSS is that U.S. students start out performing at high levels in fourth grade, but by the time they graduate they are performing at unacceptably low levels in both math and science. The two main messages of TIMSS are that (1) U.S. students don't start out behind, they fall behind; and (2) by the time U.S. students finish high school, they are not achieving at the international standards demanded by a global labor market.[11] Of the twenty-one nations that participated in the twelfth-grade tests, the United States outperformed only two, Cyprus and South Africa, in general math and science knowledge. Even our most advanced students, those taking advanced mathematics and physics, scored at the bottom when compared to their counterparts in other countries. And none of the Asian countries, which led the eighth-grade performances, even participated in the twelfth-grade assessments.[12]

poor U.S. performance

The TIMSS is not without its critics. A number of nations in the study did not heed the quality control guidelines in selecting the students who would participate. For example, some countries only tested students in programs concentrating on mathematics and science. As a result, TIMSS may tell us more about the differing educational systems than about the students.[13] In spite of the criticisms, it is difficult to find much in the U.S. TIMSS data to cheer about.

A number of explanations are possible for the differences in mathematics and science achievement test scores between U.S. students and those from high-scoring countries, including cultural differences that result in greater value being placed on education in some countries than in the United States, lower expectations for American students, and more American students holding jobs. Moreover, the TIMSS study revealed that the content of U.S. mathematics and science classes is not as challenging or focused as that of other countries. Many middle school students in the United States are still doing elementary arithmetic and introductory science while their international counterparts are studying algebra, geometry, physics, and chemistry. By the senior year of high school, many of our students have stopped taking math and science altogether. Many students never study algebra (about 15 percent), geometry (about 30 percent), advanced algebra (about 40 percent), other advanced mathematics (around 80 percent), chemistry (about 45 percent), or physics (almost 75 percent).[14] TIMSS researchers have characterized the U.S. mathematics and science curricula as being "a mile wide and an inch deep"; that is, they cover many topics, but devote little time to any one topic. The United States is number one in the world in one category, however: the size of the textbooks, which tend to be encyclopedic rather than focused! U.S. teachers, supported by the textbooks they use, teach more topics but in less detail than teachers from high-scoring countries. Furthermore, when contrasted with Japanese teachers, they focus much more on procedures and skills and much less on concepts, deductive reasoning, and understanding. Surprisingly, however, U.S. teachers assign more homework and spend more class time discussing it than do teachers from Japan and Germany.[15]

Another factor is the total amount of time spent on academic pursuits. At the high school level, American students spend much of their school day in such nonacademic activities as counseling, gym, homeroom, driver training, pep rallies, and education about personal safety, AIDS, consumer affairs, and family life. An average of only 41 percent of secondary school time needs to be devoted to core academic work to earn a high school diploma[16]—and that's probably the way most American parents want it. Both parents and students downplay a "nerdish" emphasis on strong academics in favor of preparing "well-rounded" individuals, making it difficult for schools to strengthen their academic requirements beyond a certain point. As long as a majority of Americans feel this way, it seems unlikely that we will see a radical restructuring of schools to emphasize strong academics.

We believe there are several lessons to be learned from TIMSS. First, we need to continue setting clear, high standards for what we expect students to know and be able to do in mathematics and science. Second, we need to align everything else we do with those standards: initial preparation of teachers, selection of texts and other curriculum materials, design of assessments, and the continuing professional development of teachers. The difficulty, of course, is that unlike most of the other countries participating in the TIMSS, the United States is highly decentralized in its educational decision making, thus making it extremely difficult to align the various educational components with the standards.

Additional Influences on Curriculum

Although we can examine what is taught in the schools independently in terms of the subjects offered, the curriculum as students experience it is affected by a number of other factors. The individual teacher, of course, is a major variable in what students actually learn. The classroom and school context also affect the delivery of the curriculum, as does the academic track to which the student is assigned. We will focus on two other major influences on the curriculum that is actually delivered to students: textbooks and emerging instructional approaches.

Textbooks

Education in the United States is constitutionally the domain of the various individual states; that is, the states are empowered to establish curricula and to organize and finance school systems. Unlike in many other countries, there is no national curriculum established by the federal government and implemented throughout the country. Some educational observers assert, however, that we do have a national curriculum of sorts, called textbooks. Several recent studies have concluded that most of what teachers and students do in classrooms is textbook related. For example, the objectives and goals for student learning are defined by the textbook (even the text you are now reading), learning activities and materials are provided to teachers as part of the textbook package, and tests geared to the textbook's objectives are usually prepared for the teacher's use.

no national curriculum

Critics claim that textbooks are dry, devoid of concepts, and "dumbed down" to meet readability standards. In spite of the criticism, textbooks are prevalent in America's classrooms. (© Jeff Dunn/Stock Boston)

Over twenty states, mainly in the Sunbelt, have a textbook adoption process in which citizens have the opportunity to examine textbooks being considered for statewide adoption and to express their objections to particular books. Because textbook adoption is a multimillion-dollar business, publishing companies must be careful not to include material that influential groups and factions may find offensive.

call for better textbooks

A wave of educational reform is directing attention to the quality of the textbooks that determine the curriculum. Some critics claim that texts are "dumbed down" to meet readability requirements; the writing style, designed to meet arbitrary criteria for lengths of words and sentences, can be awkward and stiff. Others believe that textbooks try to include too much material and so lack depth of coverage, a criticism certainly supported by findings from the TIMSS. Critics also complain about typical textbook emphases on skill development instead of the stimulation of students' interest and intellect; these emphases, they say, create texts that are dry, barren of ideas, devoid of concepts, and lacking in the vigorous style that stirs students to comprehend and retain what they read.

Critics have noted the shortcomings of many adoption systems that allow too little time and money to support the selection of excellent texts by qualified personnel. Whereas some curriculum personnel call for schools to spend more money on textbooks, many others claim that teachers and curriculum developers rely too much on textbooks and not enough on primary sources.

multimedia texts

A recent modification of the traditional textbook involves the use of electronic laser discs. The state of Texas offers school districts the option to use an elementary science program on laser discs instead of textbooks, and about one-half of the districts choose to do so. The multimedia system, called *Windows on Science,* contains eleven discs, plus printed lesson plans and suggested activities for students. The producer of the program, Optical Data Corporation, regularly updates the information on the discs and distributes the new discs to adopters of the program. Besides keeping information current, the technology provides access to rich materials and interesting projects, such as using the videodiscs to engage in simulated scientific experiments that otherwise would be impractical. The videodiscs also provide alternative assessments by permitting students to answer questions and follow directions on the disc. Whether laser disc systems or other electronic media will make major inroads into textbook adoptions in other subjects remains to be seen. While lacking the technological pizzazz, conventional textbooks are less expensive and more portable, and do not break down. One thing appears certain: textbooks, in paper or electronic form, are one of the major determinants of our nation's elementary and secondary school curricula, and that situation does not appear likely to change in the near future.

Innovative Instructional Approaches

Curriculum and instruction are intimately related, and the instructional approaches teachers use clearly shape how students experience the curriculum. Although these approaches have remained amazingly constant since the 1890s, especially at the secondary level, some alterations to traditional teacher-centered instruction have taken hold.[17] Educators are constantly searching for new ways to deliver the curriculum more effectively. All of the trends discussed here can be used in a variety of subject areas with students of many age and ability levels. We will look at five nontraditional instructional influences on the curriculum: interdisciplinary curriculum, cooperative learning, critical thinking and problem solving, writing across the curriculum, and block scheduling.

Interdisciplinary Curriculum Students, particularly secondary students, are often critical of the traditional curriculum, which seems irrelevant to their lives outside of school. They often fail to see how English, history, mathematics, and science relate to them. The curriculum they experience is fragmented and isolated. As one student explained, "Math isn't science, science isn't English, English isn't history. A subject is something you take once and need never take again. It's like getting a vaccination; I've had my shot of algebra. I'm done with that."[18]

Many teachers agree. Noting that the real world is not organized by disciplines but contains situations and problems that cut across disciplinary boundaries, these teachers are returning to an old idea of organizing and teaching the curriculum in an integrated and interdisciplinary fashion. Although numerous definitions of **interdisciplinary** or **integrated curriculum** exist, the terms are often used synonymously to mean a curriculum that cuts across subject-matter lines to focus on comprehensive life problems or broad-based areas of study that bring together the various segments of the curriculum in meaningful association.

There are many approaches to developing integrated, interdisciplinary curricula. One of the simplest is for two or more teachers from different disciplinary backgrounds to plan and teach their respective subjects together, seeking different disciplinary perspectives on a particular unit of study. For example, an English and social studies teacher might team together to integrate the study of the nineteenth century through the history and literature of that period.

teaming teachers from different disciplines

Another approach is *thematic* in nature. A cross-departmental team chooses themes as overlays to the different subjects. "Inventions," for example, is a theme that could combine science and mathematics in the study of machines and their mechanics, reading and writing about inventors in language arts, and designing and building models in industrial arts. Another example, "health," would permit a number of different subjects to be used to better understand specific health topics (see Figure 8.2). Still another thematic approach is to identify concepts that apply in different subjects, such as examining how symmetry, patterns, evidence, and proof apply in mathematics, art, science, social studies, and language arts.

thematic teaching

Proponents of interdisciplinary curricula argue that the merits far outweigh the extra expenditure of time and effort required. Students benefit by experiencing coherence in the curriculum and connections to real-world situations. Critical thinking and problem-solving skills are developed within contextualized situations rather than in isolation. Teachers benefit by having students who enjoy learning and by working collaboratively with other teachers. Although interdisciplinary teaching is enjoying a resurgence of popularity, particularly in middle schools, the disciplinary approach to curriculum in the secondary schools is well

arguments for interdisciplinary teaching

FIGURE 8.2   Sample Interdisciplinary Approach

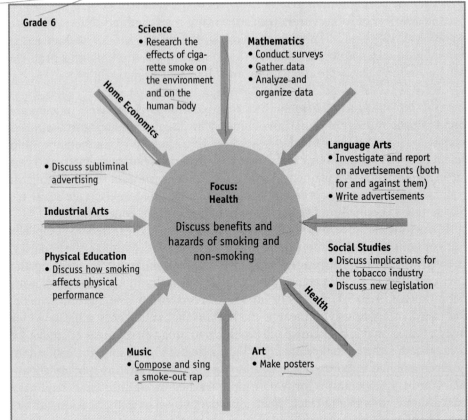

Source: Palmer, Joan (1991). "Planning Wheels Turn Curriculum Around," *Educational Leadership* 49, 2:58. Reprinted with permission of the Association for Supervision and Curriculum Development, and the author. Copyright 1991 by ASCD. All rights reserved.

entrenched and is being reinforced by the development of national standards within each discipline rather than across disciplines. The tension between disciplinary and interdisciplinary approaches to curriculum development will continue for some time.

Cooperative Learning   Cooperative learning in classrooms is another trend influencing what is taught in the schools. Those who have analyzed the "hidden" curriculum, or the implicit teachings that schools communicate to their students, have observed that American schools tend to reward competitive or individual accomplishment more than cooperative effort.[19] Arguing for cooperative learning techniques, some educators maintain that such techniques can change the ways students learn, their attitudes toward what they are taught, and their perceptions of themselves and others.

What is **cooperative learning?** There are many different forms, but all involve students working in small groups or teams to help one another learn academic material. Cooperative learning strategies are organized, highly structured methods that usually involve formal presentation of information, student practice and coaching in learning teams, individual assessment of mastery, and public recognition of team success. Table 8.2 summarizes several such strategies. By their structure and individual assignments, cooperative learning strategies avoid the problem of letting the hard-working students in the group do the work while the other students get a free ride. Cooperative learning strategies have proven successful across grade levels and in different subjects. The effectiveness of cooperative learning, particularly for achievement outcomes, depends on the particular approach used, but overall positive effects have been found on such diverse outcomes as self-esteem, intergroup relations, acceptance of academically handicapped students, attitudes toward school, and ability to work cooperatively.[20]

definition of cooperative learning

The success of cooperative learning strategies comes from three important characteristics: group goals, individual accountability, and equal opportunity for success. *Group goals* usually take the form of rewards based on team success in academic tasks. To achieve team success, each member of the group must coordinate the completion of his or her assigned task with the other group members; each team member is indispensable. *Individual accountability* involves assessing each student's mastery of the content, with the results usually given back to the group and the individual. Teammates practice together and support and coach one another, but individuals are assessed in the usual ways. The team's success is often judged by how much each team member improves over earlier assessment. In that way, even the least-achieving student can contribute to the team's success by improving over the first assessment. *Equal opportunities for success* are ensured by team scoring systems based on individual improvement over prior performance. This feature reinforces the perception that student effort, not just innate ability, counts.

three key characteristics

Cooperative learning has been found to be a particularly effective instructional tool in teaching at-risk students who benefit from immediate feedback for their learning attempts. It works well because it offers students more involvement in and control over their learning activities. As many schools attempt to do away with tracking and to encourage heterogeneous grouping, cooperative learning provides a means to make all students feel they are essential to the classroom learning process. It enables students to recognize that they all, when given a chance, have something to contribute to everyone's learning. Cooperative learning has quickly become a major instructional method in the United States, particularly in elementary and middle schools.[21]

helps at-risk students

Critical Thinking and Problem Solving

A growing interest in helping students become better thinkers and problem solvers is evidenced by the sudden flurry of publications, workshops, curriculum study institutes, journal articles, and course requirements addressing the topics of thinking and problem solving. Although many people favor

A great many people think they are thinking when they are merely rearranging their prejudices.

—WILLIAM JAMES

TABLE 8.2 Selected Cooperative Learning Strategies

Name	Brief Description	Function
1. Student team learning a. Student Teams Achievement Divisions (STAD)	Four-member mixed learning teams. Teacher presents lesson, students work within teams to make certain all team members have mastered the objectives. Students take individual quizzes. Points awarded based on improvement over previous quizzes.	Appropriate for teaching well-defined objectives with single right answers in most subjects.
b. Teams-Games-Tournament (TGT)	Uses same teacher presentations and teamwork as in STAD, but replaces quizzes with weekly tournaments.	Same as STAD
2. Jigsaw	Each student on team becomes "expert" on one topic by working with members from other teams assigned same topic. Upon returning to home team, each expert teaches the group, and students are all assessed on all aspects of the topic.	Acquisition and presentation of new material, review, informed debate. Promotes interdependence, status equalization. Used in social studies and other subjects where learning from text is important.
3. Jigsaw 2	Same as Jigsaw, except instead of each student being assigned a particular section of text, all students read a common narrative. Each student receives a topic on which to become expert.	Same as Jigsaw
4. Group investigation	Students work in small groups using cooperative inquiry, group discussion, and projects. Students form two- to six-member groups. Groups choose subtopics from a unit, break subtopics into individual tasks, and prepare group reports.	Develop skills of planning, investigating, and reporting.
5. Think-pair-share	Students think to themselves on a topic provided by teacher; then pair with another student to discuss it; then share their thoughts with class.	Generating and revising hypotheses, inductive reasoning, deductive reasoning. Fosters participation and involvement.

teaching it, definitions of **critical thinking** vary widely. At the heart of these definitions, however, is the intent to help students evaluate the worth of ideas, opinions, or evidence before making a decision or judgment.

Some educators favor approaches that help students detect bias or identify a wide range of propaganda strategies. The teaching of philosophy is also proposed as a way to provide criteria by which students can judge others' thinking. Still other approaches identify component skills (making inferences, testing hypotheses, identifying assumptions, for example) within the realm of critical thinking and advocate direct instruction in each skill. Socratic questioning (a style of questioning that elicits a clear expression of truth that was implicitly known by the person being questioned) is also suggested as a way to teach the art of thinking.

different approaches

Problem solving is an element of critical thinking that has received increasing attention and use. **Problem solving** generally refers to the process of either presenting students with a problem or helping them identify a problem and then observing and helping them become aware of the conditions, procedures, or steps needed to solve it. The problem may range from putting puzzles together, to solving simple science or math problems, to solving more complex mental, logical, or social dilemmas. It may be presented as an individual activity, such as when independently predicting outcomes in a reading passage, or may be used with a group, such as when simulating wilderness "survival" activities that require group cooperation. In the many diverse ways of teaching problem solving, the emphasis is on the *process* of reaching a solution. Proponents of problem-solving instruction point out that if students become more aware of their mental processes, they will be able to exercise greater control over their own learning and thinking in future situations. In group problem-solving activities, students may also benefit from interacting with

problem solving

A closed mind is a dying mind.

—EDNA FERBER

Technology now plays a major role in promoting student problem-solving abilities. (© PhotoEdit)

one another and being exposed to the variety of approaches used by peers in solving the same dilemma.

What is the role of critical thought in the curriculum? At one time, educators debated whether students can best learn effective thinking through separate courses or as an integrated part of every course. Greater agreement now exists that although students do benefit from stand-alone courses in critical thinking, they must also learn to think within the context of each discipline. The integration of critical thinking into subject areas appears to be the direction of the future, especially since the curricula of the schools are already so crowded.

integration with subject areas

Writing Across the Curriculum

The **writing across the curriculum** movement has been a center of curricular interest for a growing number of English educators since the 1960s. Also called writing to learn or writing to learn in the content areas, the idea emphasizes writing as a tool for students' learning, not only in English classes but in all subject areas.

writing as aid to subject-matter learning

How can teachers use the act of writing as the medium through which subject-matter learning takes place? Students in social studies classes may be asked to take a written stand on school issues, moral questions, or political problems. Music students may write their own ballads. Students in science classes may work together to predict the future in story form or to write futuristic headlines and news features. Children in math classes can create their own word problems and keep records of what they have learned, their questions, and their observations. Art classes can write scripts for slide shows and cartoon strips or create illustrated guides and storybooks. Teachers at many grade levels and in many subject areas can ask students to keep informal journals or "learning logs." In these journals students record their responses to what they have read and studied, and so can interact with text material and with the teacher's responses to their queries and remarks. These are just a few examples of the many ways teachers use writing as a thinking tool for students to use and apply their knowledge in the content areas.

Block Scheduling

A 1994 report by the National Education Commission on Time and Learning, an independent panel temporarily convened by Congress, called time "the missing element in the school-reform debate." The report urged that the traditional six-hour school day and 180-day year "be relegated to museums as an exhibit of our education past." Advising schools to be less rigid in how they use time, the report also recommended the use of block scheduling and an extended school year.[22] As the accompanying box describes, in another innovative twist on the traditional school year, some schools are trying out **looping,** a practice that lets teachers stay with the same students for more than a single year.

what is block scheduling?

Block scheduling is a "less is more" approach in which students take fewer classes each school day but spend more time in each class. In theory, block scheduling carves out more time for instruction by reducing the amount of time students spend going from class to class and the time teachers spend taking roll and settling classes down. Though it was relatively rare a decade ago, now at least 14 percent of high schools nationwide use some form of block scheduling, including more than 40 percent of the high schools in North Carolina and Vir-

Looping or Multi-year Teaching

Suppose someone offered you an educational innovation with the following benefits: better teacher/student relationships, improved teacher job satisfaction, extra teaching time, a richer curriculum, increased student attendance, increased student development in social skills and a sense of community, and easy implementation at very little cost. Sound good? Proponents of an old but increasingly common practice called *looping* claim these as among its benefits.

Looping, or multi-year teaching, is a simple concept in which the teacher is promoted with his or her students to the next grade level and stays with the group for several years, typically two but sometimes as many as five. Although not much quantitative research exists on the benefits of looping, qualitative research supports the benefits just mentioned. By keeping the same group of students together with the same teacher, everyone gets to know one another well and feel comfortable in the group. Teachers get to know their students' strengths, weaknesses, and interests. Forging bonds of trust and understanding between teachers and students is at the heart of looping. Teachers who loop have fewer transitions to make at

the beginning of the school year and can introduce curriculum topics right away at the start of the second year. They don't have to spend precious instructional time at the beginning of the new year to establish classroom routines and expectations. Instead, teachers can spend the gained time exploring curriculum topics in greater detail.

Administrators argue that looping isn't for everyone, so implementation should be on a voluntary basis. Some administrators urge teaming teachers to implement looping. In that way, students can benefit from different teacher strengths, and if a student has a problem with one particular teacher, another teacher can compensate.

Sources: "Looping—Discovering the Benefits of Multiyear Teaching," *Education Update* 40, no. 2 (March 1998), a publication of the Association for Supervision and Curriculum Development, pp. 1, 3–4; *Looping: Supporting Student Learning Through Long-Term Relationships,* Themes in Education (Brown University: LAB–Northeast and Islands Regional Educational Laboratory, 1997).

ginia.[23] Although block scheduling is not an instructional approach in itself, it does allow and encourage teachers to use cooperative learning, interdisciplinary teaching, critical thinking and problem solving, writing across the curriculum, and other innovative instructional strategies.

Several models of block scheduling exist. The trimester approach may have classes lasting an hour and twenty minutes; instead of students taking the traditional six classes per semester, they take four each trimester. Courses that used to last a semester now last a trimester, and courses that used to last a year now run for two trimesters. In the 4 × 4 plan, students take four 90-minute classes a day and complete them in a semester rather than a full year. In the A/B plan, students take eight 90-minute classes each semester, but classes meet every other day, four on day A and four on day B. And still more models exist.

models of block scheduling

The research on block scheduling so far is relatively scarce, and what does exist is often contradictory. Anecdotal evidence indicates that students like the new schedule if teachers are good and keep students' interest through various learning activities. But if teachers rely primarily on lectures, which are longer under block scheduling, students complain. The key seems to be to work with teachers to change their teaching models to make better use of the additional time they have each day the class meets. Teachers seem to like the block schedules because they have fewer students each term—for example, 90 instead of 150—and, as a result, they get to know those students better. In addition, block scheduling allows teachers more in-school preparation time. Teachers of certain disciplines, such as music and foreign languages, tend to dislike those models of block scheduling that don't allow students to work each day on those subjects, arguing that developing skill in their subjects requires daily practice. On the other hand, science teachers tend to like block schedules that allow for longer laboratory periods. Some parents and students are concerned about student absences, which in some forms of block scheduling mean they miss more material and find it difficult to make it up.

Current Curriculum Controversies

Given a highly pluralistic society and many different educational philosophies represented in America today, it is little wonder that the questions of how and what schools should teach generate much controversy and debate. In this section we'll touch briefly on two of the most highly charged curriculum issues.

Core Versus Multicultural Curriculum   American schools have traditionally played a central role in instilling the ideas and attitudes that maintain our pluralistic society as "one nation." They have helped to weave the many ethnic and religious strains together to make a seamless national garment. At least that's the theory. Questions are now being raised about whether schools today provide a shared understanding of our culture, history, and traditions. Does the current curriculum of our schools reflect our national diversity to the exclusion of our national unity? Or is the reverse true?

Proponents of a **multicultural curriculum** argue that minority students, whose representation in the public schools is about 36 percent and increasing every year, experience a Eurocentric (that is, Europe-centered) curriculum that gives short shrift to the literary and historical contributions of other parts of the world and to minorities within the United States. As a result, the proponents of multiculturalism argue, youngsters of color see the schools' curricula as being irrelevant to them, not reflective of their cultures or backgrounds. Some multiculturalists take the position that the current school curriculum needs to be broadened to better reflect the contributions of people of color. Cultural pluralism, a fact of our society, needs to be a fact of our school curriculum, they assert.

A more extreme position is taken by those who demand that the whole curriculum be oriented to a particular ethnicity. For example, some advocates of an Afrocentric curriculum claim that black schoolchildren can learn effectively only in an environment that recognizes and amplifies their African heritage. The theory is that if students learn of the accomplishments of those who share their ethnic identities, their self-esteem will improve, which will promote learning. When schools emphasize the achievements of African cultures, especially ancient Egyptian culture, and of individuals of African descent, students will have a greater sense of pride and be more motivated to learn. Afrocentric curricula are currently being used in a number of large-city school districts.

shared understanding?

multicultural curriculum

ethnocentric curriculum

The man who doesn't read good books has no advantage over the man who can't read them.

—MARK TWAIN

AUTHORS' DIALOGUE

KEVIN: *I have very mixed feelings about the cultural literacy and core knowledge movement.*

JIM: How so?

KEVIN: *I agree that the country and its people need a common identity, a sense of who we are as Americans. But don't you remember how narrow the curriculum was before the seventies, when minority history and literature started appearing in textbooks? I don't want to go back to those days.*

JIM: I know what you mean. Before the seventies, students weren't able to read about African American scientists, or Hispanic authors, or women athletes, for that matter. But maybe we've gone too far. It's hard to communicate with somebody who isn't acquainted with the basics of America's history, literature, music, inventions, sports— what makes America America.

KEVIN: *OK. But isn't part of "what makes America America" its interweaving of diverse cultures? After all, wouldn't life in America be different without tacos and Crispus Attucks and LeRoi Jones and Kate Chopin and . . .*

JIM: We agreed, though, that the schools can't teach everything. Besides, I think that Hirsch's core curriculum does reflect contributions to our common culture from different minority groups, and since it is designed to be only 50 percent of the curriculum, lots of flexibility is left to meet local needs. Also, Hirsch's core knowledge curriculum is geared only through the eighth grade. After that, students should be free to pursue different interests and courses. So maybe a core curriculum ought to be in effect through the middle grades.

KEVIN: *Good point!*

In contrast, proponents of a **core curriculum**—that is, a course of study every student would be required to take—argue that ever since the 1970s, schools have focused on celebrating national diversity and pluralism but have failed to help students develop a shared national identity and common cultural framework. Some advocates of a core curriculum, such as Mortimer Adler (*The Paideia Proposal*, 1983), promote the great literary works that have endured over the years as the basic elements of a core curriculum.

core curriculum

E. D. Hirsch, Jr., also endorses the great literary works, but goes beyond them in his push for **cultural literacy** (now called **core knowledge**).[24] Hirsch sees a culturally literate person as someone who is aware of the central ideas, stories, scientific knowledge, events, and personalities of a culture. Hirsch does not restrict his idea of a core curriculum to the great works of "dead white males," a criticism made of many core curricula; rather, he sees American culture as incorporating the contributions of many ethnicities and subcultures. Hirsch believes that privileged youth gain much of their cultural literacy at home, but since many poor, minority, and immigrant children do not receive cultural literacy at home, it is especially important that they receive it in school. Hirsch and his colleagues, through the Core Knowledge Foundation, have developed grade-by-grade guidelines for a core knowledge sequence for grades K–8, as well as a series of books entitled *What Every 1st [2nd, etc.] Grader Needs to Know.* Currently about 1,000 schools across the country have adopted the core knowledge curriculum.

cultural literacy

The debate between those who advocate a common curriculum to ensure that all students learn what society has determined is important and those who favor state, local, and individual choice in what is learned will likely continue indefinitely.

Tracking   The curriculum that a student receives is influenced by many factors, including aspirations for further schooling, academic ability, motivation, and vocational interests. Based on these and other factors, students are often placed into academic program tracks that determine what courses they take. The track in which a student is placed can open or close future academic and vocational options. The three most common tracks are academic (stressing the traditional subjects of English, science, mathematics, and foreign languages), general (allowing more electives and less rigorous versions of the traditional subjects), and vocational (preparing students for the world of work with a combination of academic and job-related courses). Each track has variations in courses required and different standards for student achievement. Within the academic track further options exist, including advanced placement (AP) and honors.

three common tracks

During the 1970s and 1980s, tracking came under attack. Several prominent educational researchers produced studies showing that students placed in the lower tracks received an inferior curriculum and less stimulating instruction than students in the academic tracks. Furthermore, these researchers found that poor and minority students were disproportionately placed in the lower tracks, where they had less qualified teachers, thinner curricula, and poorer instruction than students in the upper tracks. These researchers also reported that students in the upper tracks did no better than if they had been in mixed-ability classrooms.[25] *Tracking* became a dirty word, and detracking efforts ensued.

tracking harmful to poor and minorities

Other educational studies found conflicting evidence that while detracking does help the educational performance of low-achieving students, high-achieving students are hurt academically.[26] Parents of these high-achieving students exert considerable pressure to ensure that their children have access to honors and AP classes, resisting efforts to detrack the schools. Furthermore, teachers who teach the high-track students often resist efforts to detrack, enjoying the intellectual challenge and prestige that come from teaching these students. The general sense is that tracking benefits high-ability students while hurting low-ability students, whereas the reverse is true of detracking. Where do you stand on this issue?

strong support for tracking

Reprinted with special permission of King Features Syndicate.

Is the Existing Curriculum Relevant to Today's Society?

People often raise questions in one way or another about the relevance of the education provided to today's students. But before anyone can determine whether a particular curriculum is relevant to today's needs, some difficult issues must be addressed. In Chapter 3, we discussed the purposes of schools and different models of schooling, particularly the school as a transmitter of culture and the school as an agent of social reconstruction. In Chapter 10, we discuss four schools of educational philosophy: perennialism, progressivism, essentialism, and existentialism. In judging curriculum relevance, all of these matters come into play, because the relevance of a curriculum depends very much on one's basic beliefs about schooling.

In a society as large and pluralistic as the United States, many philosophies and notions of school purpose have committed supporters. How can the schools incorporate in their curricula such diverse ideas of what a school should do? If a certain philosophy is dominant within a given community, the curriculum of the community's schools is likely to reflect that set of beliefs, and those who don't agree will remain dissatisfied. On the other hand, some communities are responding to these diverse philosophical conceptions of the curriculum by providing alternative schools, each with a different curricular emphasis.

The main issues of contention can be framed in terms of two basic oppositions: the intellect versus the whole child and perennialism versus progressivism. That is, should schools emphasize the intellectual training of children (the *intellect*), or should they be concerned about children's overall development (the *whole child*)? Should the school curriculum emphasize tried-and-true knowledge (*perennialism*), or should it focus on the students and their interests and needs (*progressivism*)?

two basic oppositions

For example, if one considers the school's primary objective to be the intellectual training of students, any curriculum that does not emphasize scholarship will be judged to be irrelevant. Conversely, if one believes the school should emphasize the development of the "whole child"—the child's emotional and social, as well as intellectual, growth—a curriculum devoted exclusively to English, history, the sciences, mathematics, and foreign languages will be considered inappropriate for many students and thus irrelevant. What one considers to be a relevant curriculum, then, depends on the philosophical position one takes. At the present time there are conflicting trends in the academic curriculum, each representing a different philosophy.

relevance depends on philosophy

The Curriculum in a Changing World

Our society and our environment are presently undergoing change at a rate unprecedented in human history. The population of the world, now numbering about 6 billion, is expanding at a tremendous pace and exerting severe pressure on the environment. We are consuming natural resources at an alarming rate; agricultural surpluses fail to reach the most needy, and many starve. Acid rain

The Saber-Tooth Curriculum

In his classic satire on curriculum irrelevance, Harold Benjamin—using the pseudonym J. Abner Peddiwell—describes how the first school curriculum was developed in the Stone Age. The earliest theorist, according to Benjamin's book, was a man named New Fist, who hit on the idea of deliberate, systematic education.

Watching children at play, New Fist wondered how he could get them to do the things that would gain them more and better food, shelter, clothing, and security. He analyzed the activities that adults engaged in to maintain life and came up with three subjects for his curriculum: (1) fish-grabbing-with-the-bare-hands, (2) woolly-horse-clubbing, and (3) saber-tooth-tiger-scaring-with-fire. Although the children trained in these subjects enjoyed obvious material benefits as a result, some conservative members of the tribe resisted the introduction of these new subjects on religious grounds. But, in due time, many people began to train their children in New Fist's curriculum and the tribe grew increasingly prosperous and secure.

Then conditions changed. An ice age began, and a glacier crept down over the land. The glacier brought with it dirt and gravel that muddied the creeks, and the waters became so dirty that no one could see the fish well enough to grab them. The melting waters from the approaching ice sheet also made the country wetter, and the little woolly horses migrated to drier land. They were replaced by antelopes, who were so shy and speedy that no one could get close enough to club them. Finally, the new dampness in the air caused the saber-tooth tigers to catch pneumonia and die. And the ferocious glacial bears who came down with the advancing ice sheet were not afraid of fire.

The thinkers of the tribe, descendants of New Fist, found a way out of the dilemma. One figured out how to catch fish with a net made from vines. Another invented traps for the antelopes, and a third discovered how to dig pits to catch the bears.

Some thoughtful people began to wonder why these new activities couldn't be taught in the schools. But the elders who controlled the schools claimed that the new skills did not qualify as *education*—they were merely a matter of *training*. Besides, the curriculum was too full of the standard cultural subjects, fish-grabbing, horse-clubbing, and tiger-scaring, to admit new ones. When some radicals argued that the traditional subjects were foolish, the elders said that they taught fish-grabbing not to catch fish but to develop agility, horse-clubbing to develop strength, and tiger-scaring to develop courage. "The essence of true education is timelessness," they announced. "It is something that endures through changing conditions like a solid rock standing squarely and firmly in the middle of a raging torrent. You must know that there are some eternal verities and the saber-tooth curriculum is one of them!" (pp. 43–44)

The Saber-Tooth Curriculum was written in 1939, but its continuing applicability seems to be one of the "eternal verities."

from industrialization threatens vegetation and wildlife; pollutants contaminate the air we breathe and the water we drink. At the same time, we are destroying huge tracts of vegetation that provide us with oxygen. Diseases such as AIDS, whose cure is yet unknown, are sweeping the globe with alarming rapidity. Racial, ethnic, and gender prejudices, which had gone unchallenged for decades, are no longer being endured by their victims. Nations possess the power to annihilate one another at the push of a button. Bands of terrorists can alter tenuous balances of power among countries. In short, we have reached a point at which *all* human beings must work together to survive another century on this planet.

What are the best survival strategies for a society influenced by such rapid external changes? Perhaps the most basic function of all education is to increase the survival chances of the group. As long as the environment remains stable or changes very slowly, the skills necessary for survival seem to remain constant. In such times, when a culture is proven able to ensure the survival of the group, education can be content to transmit that culture. In times of change, however, educators face questions about which concepts and skills remain useful for survival and which should be discarded in favor of new ideas. Just because the environment is changing, should the curriculum change too? Are there essentials that students of every time and situation should learn? Can the schools preserve a common culture in times of increasing technological and social change?

which curriculum for survival?

As we enter the twenty-first century, educators and the public are debating what curriculum adaptations to make, if any, to new environmental characteristics. Whatever the outcome may be, the debate itself is important. We must continually examine the relevance of the school's curriculum. We must challenge ourselves and our curriculum developers to answer this question: how can the curriculum sustain ideas and ideals of enduring value, yet make the necessary adaptations to ensure that we survive?

KEY TERMS

curriculum (252)
child- (or society-) centered
   curriculum (253)
subject-matter–centered curriculum
   (253)
structure of disciplines approach
   (256)
back-to-basics movement (256)
whole language approach (261)
phonics (261)
civic learning (civic education) (264)
interdisciplinary (integrated)
   curriculum (273)

cooperative learning (275)
critical thinking (277)
problem solving (277)
writing across the curriculum (278)
looping (278)
block scheduling (278)
multicultural curriculum (280)
core curriculum (281)
cultural literacy (core knowledge)
   (281)
tracking (282)

FOR REFLECTION

1. In your opinion, should the curriculum emphasize cultural learning common to all Americans, or should it stress the pluralistic nature of our diverse cultural backgrounds? Is it possible to do both?

2. With which of the curriculum reforms discussed in this chapter do you agree? Disagree?

3. What is your view of the recent developments in your favorite subject field?

4. In your opinion, is the prevalent use of textbooks in the schools a positive or negative influence on teaching and learning? Can you see both the benefits and the dangers? If so, what are they?

5. Which of the instructional approaches described in the chapter appeal to you, and why?

6. What would you do to improve the curriculum of the public schools?

7. Are there aspects of our current curriculum that you would equate with the Saber-Tooth curriculum? If so, what are they?

FOR FURTHER INFORMATION

Eisner, Elliot W. *The Educational Imagination*. 3d ed. New York: Macmillan, 1994.
The author presents a stimulating, controversial book regarding forces influencing today's curriculum.

SEARCH

Hirsch, E. D., Jr. *Cultural Literacy: What Every American Needs to Know.* Boston: Houghton Mifflin, 1987.
This provocative treatise asserts that literacy requires the early and continued transmission of specific information—the common knowledge that enables students to make sense of what they read. (See the Core Knowledge Foundation web site at: http://www.coreknowledge.org.)

SEARCH

Mid-continent Regional Educational Laboratory. World Wide Web site at: http://mcrel.org.
One of ten regional educational laboratories supported by the federal government, this lab has a great set of materials in different subject areas, as well as research reports on effective practice. The web site also offers links to other useful sites.

Rothstein, Richard. *The Way We Were? The Myths and Realities of America's Student Achievement.* New York: Twentieth Century Fund Press/Priority Press Publications, 1998.
This analysis of student academic achievement concludes that American students are steadily getting better rather than worse.

Slavin, Robert. *Cooperative Learning: Theory, Research, and Practice.* 2d ed. Boston: Allyn and Bacon, 1995.
This excellent, comprehensive book was written by one of the leading researchers on the topic.

Walker, Decker F., and Jonas F. Soltis. *Curriculum and Aims*. 3d ed. New York: Teachers College Press, 1997.
This brief book on curriculum and the aims of education is designed to stimulate thinking about what teachers teach in school and what purposes schooling serves.

The following journals and web sites contain many interesting and helpful items for teachers in the respective subject-matter fields.

Science: *The Science Teacher; School Science and Mathematics;* Eisenhower National Clearinghouse web site at http://www.enc.org; *Blueprints for Reform: Science, Mathematics, and Technology Education* at http://project2061.aaas.org.

Mathematics: *The Mathematics Teacher; School Science and Mathematics;* Math Forum web site, particularly Ask Dr. Math at http://forum.swarthmore.edu/dr.math.

Social studies: *The Social Studies; Social Education;* History/Social Studies web site for K–12 teachers at http://execpc.com/~dboals/boals.html.

Reading and language arts: *Language Arts; The Reading Teacher;* Children's Literature Web Guide at http://www.ucalgary.ca/~dkbrown/.

Elementary and early childhood: web site of ERIC Clearinghouse on Elementary and Early Childhood Education at http://ericeece.org/.

English: *English Journal;* web site of ERIC Clearinghouse on Reading, English, and Communication at http://www.indiana.edu/~eric_rec; National Council of Teachers of English web site at http://www.ncte.org.

Foreign languages: *Modern Language Journal;* web site of ERIC Clearinghouse on Languages and Linguistics at http://www.cal.org/ericcll/; University of Wisconsin Letters & Sciences web site (contains lots of language links) at http://polyglot.lss.wisc.edu/lss/lang/langlink.html.

Physical education: *Journal of Health, Physical Education and Recreation;* web site of the American Alliance for Health, Physical Education, Recreation and Dance at http://www.aahperd.org/.

Music: *Music Educators' Journal;* Music Education Resource Links (MERL) web site at http://www.cs.uop.edu/~cpiper/musiced.html.

Art: *Art Education; Arts and Activities; School Arts;* web site of ArtsEdge at the Kennedy Center at http://artsedge.kennedy-center.org/.

Vocational education: *Industrial Education; Journal of Home Economics; Business Education Forum; Business Education Review;* web site of ERIC Clearinghouse on Adult, Career, and Vocational Education at http://ericacve.org/.

Special Education and Gifted Education web site at http://www.cec.sped.org/ericec.htm.

PART

FOUR

FOUNDATIONS

Just as the subjects of anatomy and chemistry are essential to the practice of medicine, certain areas of organized knowledge are essential to the practice of education. These areas, called the foundations of education, provide the intellectual underpinnings of educational practice.

This section covers several of these key areas: school governance, finance, philosophy, history, the law, and ethics. Truly professional teachers ground their daily practice in the wisdom gleaned from these foundational areas. The section concludes with a chapter on recent movements for educational reform, in which all the foundational components come to bear in the effort to improve our schools.

How Are Schools Governed, Influenced, and Financed?

9

Very few beginning teachers are concerned about issues related to school governance and finance. The topic seems remote to them; it is something administrators and representatives of teacher organizations care about, but it does not seem particularly vital for beginning teachers concerned with learning how to survive in the classroom. We feel differently; we believe beginning teachers must have some understanding of the way schools and school systems operate, since they will be affected personally by governance and financial decisions. Not understanding how these decisions are made and how they might affect you as a teacher will reduce your effectiveness as a professional.

This chapter emphasizes that

▶ Legal responsibility for school governance belongs to the state. Traditionally, however, policy decisions and administration have been delegated to local school boards.

▶ In addition to local school boards and state governments, many other groups exercise some measure of influence on educational decisions, either through legal authority or through less formal means. These other groups include professional education organizations, parents, teachers, the business community, the designers of standardized tests, the federal government, and the courts.

▶ Court rulings in some states have shifted the responsibility for public school financing from dependence on local property taxes to greater reliance on state support.

How would you explain the fact that

▶ A very popular high school teacher was not given tenure?

▶ The average job expectancy of superintendents in large urban school districts is less than three years?

▶ The sex education program being planned in your hometown was never implemented?

▶ A textbook with a fresh approach to the curriculum was removed from circulation after a year, even though the teachers favored its use?

▶ A coalition of superintendents from poor school districts in your state sued the state government for increased financial support?

▶ Legislators in New York State banned schools from subscribing to Channel One, a free television news service for school-age children?

▶ Members of Citizens for Excellence in Education, a conservative Christian organization, have actively opposed states' efforts to design an "outcomes-based" curriculum?

It is quite likely that at least one of these questions applies to your local school district or state. They all reflect the struggle for governance, control, and influence over the public schools. This chapter explores how the American educational system is organized, governed, and financed. Although there are legal authorities for the schools and organizations established to exercise this authority, the educational system is strongly influenced by interest groups that do not appear on any organizational chart. We first examine the legal governing authority that exists in most states and then discuss special-interest groups that influence educational policy. Then we look at how the American educational system is financed and how disparities between rich and poor school districts are generating strong challenges to current financing policies.

Who Legally Governs Public Education?

In most countries, the public schools are a branch of the central government, federally financed and administered and highly uniform in curricula and procedures. In the United States, however, responsibility for the public schools has evolved as a state function as a result of the Tenth Amendment to the U.S. Constitution. Each of the fifty states has legal responsibility for the operation and administration of public schools within its own boundaries. In most aspects of public education (we will discuss certain exceptions later), the authority of federal, county, and city education agencies is subject to the will of the state authorities.

education as a state function

state vs. local control

Although legal responsibility for school governance belongs to the states, policy decisions and administration have usually been delegated to local school boards, which exist because Americans have come to insist on control of schools at the local level (see Figure 9.1). Recently, however, states have been reasserting their policymaking prerogatives.

State Offices and Administrators

At the state level, educational services can be influenced by a variety of actors, from the governor through the many employees of the state's department of education.

governors play leadership role

The Governor and the State Legislature   Policy analysts agree that the state legislatures are the most influential actors in establishing educational policy because they make the laws that govern and affect education within their states. In recent years, because of the high profile of educational issues, legislatures' interest in educational policy has increased, particularly in the areas of school finance and minimum competency testing. Many governors, too, have played more prominent roles, beginning with the educational reforms of the 1980s. President Clinton and his education secretary, Richard Riley, for example, became nationally visible as governors through their educational leadership in Arkansas and South Carolina, respectively. Like legislatures, the governor's office has the power to affect educational policy, but often chooses to do so only on limited issues.

the "Golden Rule"

On financial issues, the roles of governor and legislature are especially obvious. Governors propose and legislatures act on budgets that contain funding for school districts. Governors and legislatures can increase or decrease the amount of money that goes into supporting public education, including any new initiatives. This is, as one wag has stated, the "Golden Rule": "Whoever has the gold makes the rules." When state economies are strong, more tax revenues are available to invest in public education, as occurred during the mid- and late 1990s. However, when recessions occur, state governments, facing a loss of tax revenues, cut back on their educational commitments and initiatives, forcing school districts to cut budgets. In either scenario, governors and state legislatures have tremendous influence over educational policy and expenditures.

policymaking function

The State Board of Education   The state's legal responsibility for public education requires it to establish an organizational framework within which the local school districts can function. The result is the establishment of a **state board of education** to exercise general control and supervision of schools within the state. The state board of education is the state's policymaking body. It typically sets goals and priorities for education in the state; formulates education policy and curricular offerings, including establishing academic standards and their assessment; establishes and enforces rules and regulations for the operation of educational programs; represents the public in matters regarding the governance of education; reports to the public on accomplishments and needs; and makes recommendations to the governor and/or state legislature for the improvement

FIGURE 9.1 Organizational Structure of a Typical State School System

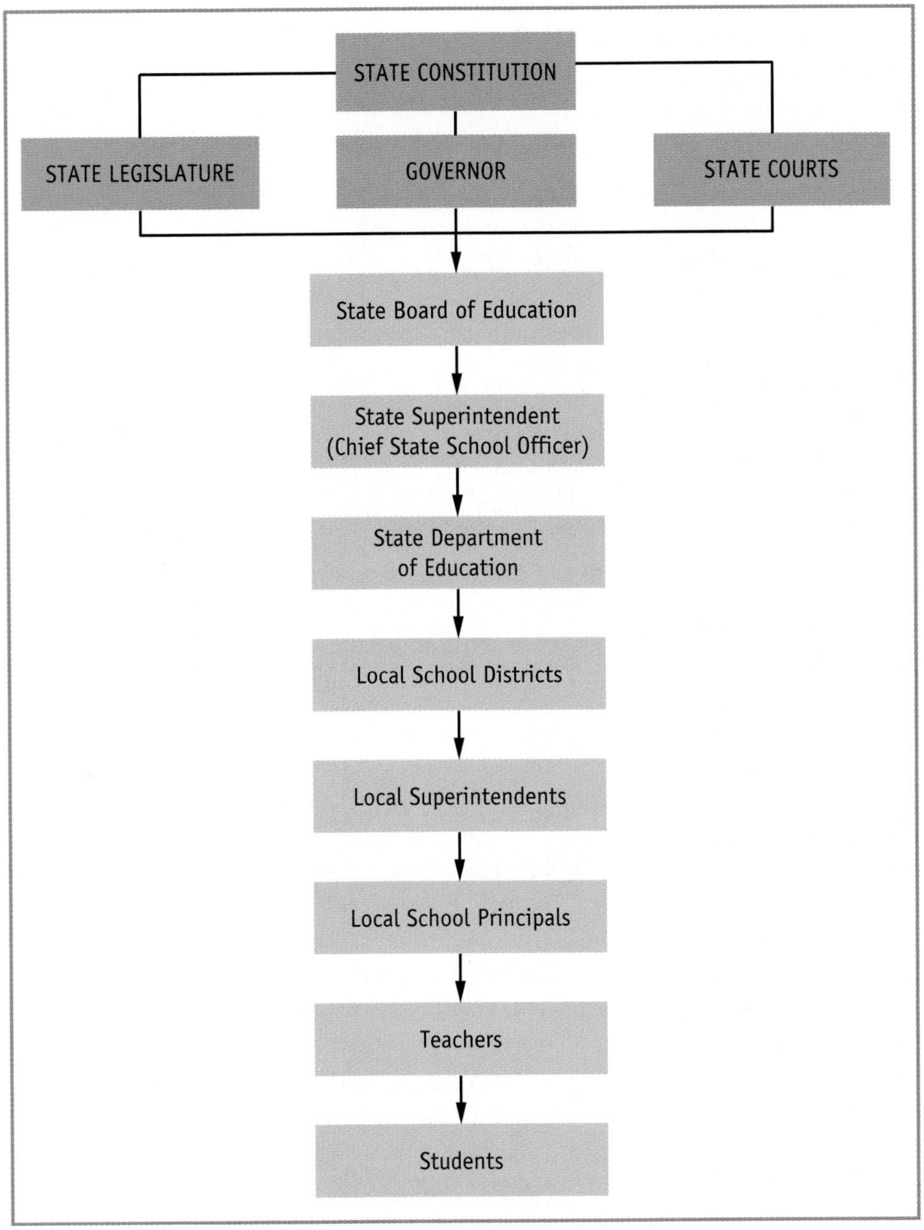

of education. The state board of education also establishes and enforces minimum standards for the operation of all phases of elementary and secondary education from the state to the local school system level.

Despite these responsibilities, state boards of education are relatively weak policy actors. They usually cannot hire or remove the chief state school officer, are often poorly staffed, and frequently lack political lines to the legislature and governor.

relatively weak

Who Should Be Accountable for Getting Results?

What's the Policy?

As a condition for spending more money on elementary and secondary education, legislatures and state boards of education are increasingly demanding that educators be accountable for achieving results. No longer content to measure quality schooling by its inputs (school facilities, dollars spent, teacher-pupil ratios, number of books in school libraries, and educators' salaries, for example), policymakers in a number of states are insisting that educators get results, and results are narrowly construed as increased student achievement test scores. In many areas, school report cards are publicized to inform communities about how well their schools are performing in terms of test scores.

How Does It Affect Teachers?

Some states are implementing steps to reward educators whose schools produce more student learning than expected and punish those whose schools fail to meet the accepted standard. For example, in Virginia, by year 2006, 70 percent of the students in each school must successfully pass the statewide assessments of student learning for the school to maintain its accreditation. In other states, educators are being given pay bonuses if the students in their schools exceed expectations.

What Are the Pros?

Advocates of accountability argue that input measures are at best indirect and that the true test of a school's effectiveness is how well its students learn the knowledge and skills it is attempting to teach. They contend that only by looking at the results of students' schooling, as measured by student test scores, can we ascertain the worth of schools.

What Are the Cons?

Many educators are concerned about using test scores for accountability purposes. Most assessments encompass learning standards across two or more grades. Should individual teachers be accountable for what their students were supposed to learn from teachers in previous grades? Should the quality of a school be judged on the basis of a single criterion: test scores? Should all schools be judged on the basis of the same test even if they differ dramatically in terms of the resources available and the challenges faced by the children they serve? Schools serving poorer communities face many more challenges in educating their students than do schools located in wealthier areas. Scores on these standardized tests may reflect the socioeconomic status of the communities served more than they indicate the quality of the schools.

What Do You Think?

1. Do you think states should publicly issue school report cards that reflect how well students in a given school performed on statewide assessments of learning standards? What are the advantages and disadvantages of doing so?

2. Can each educator's contribution to a child's learning be determined and distinguished from that of other educators? If so, how?

3. How should other important learning outcomes for which schools are responsible, such as good citizenship, be taken into account in determining a school's effectiveness? Or should they?

The procedure for selecting state board members varies from state to state. In most states members are appointed by the governor, but in about one-third of the states members are elected by the people or the people's representatives. The number of members on a state board of education varies from state to state, but a board of nine to fifteen members is typical.

selection of members

The Chief State School Officer   The executive officer of the state board of education, the **chief state school officer,** usually is responsible to the state board of education for the administration of public education. (The actual titles for this position, which vary from state to state, include *superintendent of education, commissioner of education, secretary of the state board of education,* and others.) The responsibilities normally involve teacher and administrator licensure, organization of the program of studies, curriculum revision, application of the state finance law, approval of school sites and buildings, collection of statistical data, and direct supervision of elementary and secondary educational programs. This officer exercises little direct administrative authority over local educational officials, but his or her indirect influence is widely felt at the local level. In some states the officer is elected by the voters, in other states appointed by the governor, and in still other states appointed by the state board of education.

duties of chief state school officer

The State Department of Education   The **state department of education** (sometimes called the *state department of public instruction*) usually operates under the direction of the state board of education and is administered by the chief state school officer. The state department of education is responsible for carrying out the policies of the state board of education and the laws passed by the state legislature. It consists of a large bureaucracy of officials, often numbering in the hundreds.

Originally organized to provide statistical reports, state departments of education have grown in size, power, and influence. Their primary responsibilities usually include administering and distributing state and federal funds, licensing teachers and other educational personnel, providing schools with technical assistance in improving curriculum and teaching, providing educational data and analyses, providing administration for special programs, and accrediting college and university educational licensure programs. Most schools, school districts, and colleges of education are strongly affected by the policies and actions of these state departments. School and college personnel, including public school teachers, serve on advisory committees and task forces to assist the chief state school officer and the state department of education in their decision-making processes.

influence of state departments

The Local School District

To facilitate local control of education, the state creates local school districts for the purpose of carrying out education in conformity with state policy. The school district is thus a unit of the state government and is usually distinct from the local municipal government.

The School Board   The policymaking body of the school district is the **local school board,** which represents the citizens of the district in setting up a school program, hiring school personnel to operate the schools, determining organizational and administrative policy, and evaluating the results of the program and the performance of personnel. Although school board members are usually elected by the citizens of the local district, they are officially state officers (not simply local representatives), and they must follow the guidelines and policies established by the legislature, the state board of education, and the state department of education. The tension between states' efforts to regulate educational policy and local districts' desire to determine their own policies has increased as states have taken the initiative in the recent educational reform movement.

board members are state officers

Methods of selecting school board members are usually prescribed by state law. Over 90 percent of the school boards are elected by popular vote, and the remainder are appointed. When board members are appointed, the responsibility for making appointments falls most often to the mayor or city council.

selection of members

What does the composite profile of school board members look like? As Table 9.1 indicates, the majority of today's school board members are male, white, and between ages forty-one and sixty—demographic characteristics that have changed little in recent years.[1] However, the proportion of women serving on boards has increased from 12 to around 40 percent since 1972. Representation of minorities continues to be small. At least 82 percent of members have annual family incomes over $40,000. Two-thirds of them have at least bachelor's degrees. Most are professionals, managers, or business owners, have children in public school, and consider themselves to be conservative. These figures indicate that in many ways, school board members are not typical of the public they serve. Whether or how this atypicality influences their values and decisions is not known. Can you think of any ways in which it might?

school boards lack diversity

> *Just as war is too important to be left to the generals, education is too important to be left to the educators.*
>
> —PAUL WOODRING

The Superintendent of Schools

The **superintendent of schools,** a professional educator selected by the local school board to act as its executive officer and as the educational leader and administrator of the school district, is undeniably the most powerful officer in the local school organization. A superintendent's duties are many. The superintendent must recruit, select, place, and promote personnel. In addition, the superintendent has responsibility for providing and maintaining funds and facilities. Often, too, the superintendent plans the budget and supervises the maintenance, construction, and renovation of buildings. Decisions about how to improve educational opportunities, including all aspects of curriculum and instruction, may originate with the superintendent. And the superintendent generally has responsibility for maintaining harmonious relations with the community by communicating the mission of the schools to the public and marshaling support for district programs.

duties of superintendent

Theoretically, the superintendent's role is administrative and executive—he or she (only 11 or 12 percent of the nation's superintendents are female) keeps the

TABLE 9.1   Profile of School Board Members

Characteristic	Percentage
Gender:	
Male	54.1
Female	39.1
No response	6.8
Ethnic background:	
Black	6.5
White	81.3
Hispanic	3.1
Asian	0.3
Other/no response	7.8
Age:	
Under 25	0.7
26–35	3.7
36–40	6.1
41–50	46.6
51–60	24.2
Over 60	14.6
No response	4.1
Family income:	
Under $40,000	10.9
$40,000–$59,999	15.3
$60,000–$79,999	21.0
$80,000–$99,999	17.3
More than $100,000	28.0
No response	7.5

Note: Because of rounding, some totals may not add up to 100 percent.

schools functioning—whereas the local school board of education retains policy-making responsibilities. In practice, however, the superintendent has become the major policymaker in the school district.

Superintendents Versus Local School Boards   The way a school board and superintendent operate together to control a school district may depend on their relationship. According to independent observers, this relationship often is one of conflict.

conflict

One observer, Larry Cuban, asserts that "conflict is—and always has been—the essence of the superintendency."[2] Cuban describes the conflict between the superintendent and the school board, or between the superintendent and local private groups, as one of seeming competitors seeking to achieve their goals at the expense of the other participants. Such conflict is inevitable, he writes, when individuals have incompatible goals, resources are scarce, and misperceptions occur among those influencing policy decisions. Although school boards hire and fire them, superintendents are expected to lead the board. If they fail to do so, board members are likely to act independently, often with disastrous consequences.

> *But one thing about today's superintendent is almost a given . . . he must indeed be a political animal.*
>
> —ARTHUR BLUMBERG

high turnover rate

One measure of conflict between superintendents and school boards is the turnover rate: how often superintendents change their jobs. Currently 56 percent of all superintendents have had their jobs for five or fewer years[3] (see Figure 9.2). The average tenure for superintendents in urban districts is only 2.75 years, compared to a national average of 5.6 years among all superintendents.[4] Cuban maintains that the issues over which boards and administrators disagree may change as a result of shifting political concerns, changes in school funding or demography, or constantly changing coalitions of teachers or local constituencies. But the relationship remains one of conflict regardless of particular issues.

FIGURE 9.2   Superintendents' Years of Experience in Current Job

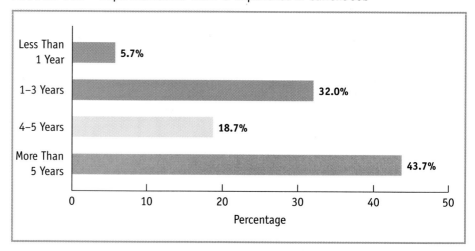

Source: Reprinted with permission from *American School Board Journal,* December 1996. Copyright © 1996, National School Boards Association. All rights reserved.

School boards and superintendents search constantly for local constituencies to provide the funding and support for school programs. And with every school board election, new points of view may be brought to the governance of the district. Superintendents must weather these changes in points of view and the emerging coalitions resulting from board member turnover. Sympathies with the schools' mission may be in a constant state of flux, requiring superintendents to exercise coalition-building skills. Their survival as nonelected public officials rests on their ability to mobilize support and manage conflict.

The School Principal   For the schools within a school district, the superintendent and the local school board of education select professional educators to serve as principals. High schools and middle schools may have a staff of administrators to assist the principal, including assistant or vice principals with specific responsibilities for discipline or curriculum and instruction. At the elementary level, on the other hand, principals may be responsible for more than one school building or may serve part-time as teachers. Whatever the pattern of administrative assignments, those who act as principals are generally considered to be a part of the administrative organization, directly accountable to the superintendent and the local school board of education. (See Table 9.2 for a profile of school administrators.)

As administrators, principals usually interview prospective faculty members and make faculty assignments, supervise and evaluate staff members, schedule students and classes, manage school budgets, administer district discipline policies, and procure and dispense supplies. The tasks are many; to list them all would be impossible. Historically, the role of the principal has included management, supervision, and inspection duties.

responsibilities of principal

Effective principals promote a productive working and learning environment. They do so by understanding the mission of the school, communicating it to the

A principal's leadership style and values set the tone for the way a school functions. (© Bob Daemmrich/The Image Works)

TABLE 9.2 Profile of School Administrators (in Percentages)

	Superin-tendents	High School Principals	Junior High & Middle School Principals	Elementary School Principals
Sex:				
Male	89.0%	90.1%	75.2%	57.0%
Female	11.0	9.9	24.8	43.0
Ethnic background:				
White	96.3	91.4	88.0	83.8
African American	1.7	4.6	6.0	10.2
Hispanic American	1.0	1.3	4.0	4.2
Asian American	—	1.3	1.0	0.6
Native American	0.7	0.7	1.0	0.6
Other	0.3	0.7	—	0.6
Highest degree earned:				
Bachelor's	—	0.7	1.0	0.6
Master's	31.3	72.2	60.0	66.7
Specialist	28.3	15.9	28.0	22.0
Doctorate	40.0	11.3	11.0	10.7
Salary (12 month)	$106,122	$76,768	$71,499	$67,348

Note: Because of rounding, some totals may not add up to 100 percent.
Sources: Reprinted with permission from *American School Board Journal,* December 1996. Copyright © 1996, National School Boards Association. All rights reserved.

staff and students, and rewarding excellent performance. They also represent the school to parents and the community. Involving parents and community members in the school's activities and securing their support for these activities is an important function of the principal.

In schools led by effective principals, teachers and students say that the school pulls together, values learning, and is a supportive place. Effective principals establish a feeling of community and work to accomplish the goals they establish, constantly gathering information about the progress toward the goals and helping teachers and students in their efforts.[5] Thus, the principal can play a key role in establishing relationships among faculty and students and in setting standards for the accomplishment of student and teacher objectives.

Researchers are predicting a shortage of principals during the first decade of the new millennium. The shortage exists in all types of schools—rural, urban, and suburban—and at all levels, elementary through high school. Why the anticipated shortage? The number one reason is that teachers who might want to become principals believe that principals don't get paid enough for the responsibilities they must shoulder. Other reasons include the belief that the job is too stressful and time consuming and the perceived difficulty in satisfying the demands of parents and the community.[6]

shortage of principals predicted

Who Influences American Public Education?

It is not our intention in this chapter to examine in detail the authority and power that enable various groups to influence certain aspects of public education. However, a brief look at the interplay of influence exercised by professional education organizations, parents, business, standardized testing, the courts, and the federal government yields some fascinating insights into how decisions about public education are actually made.

Professional Education Organizations

Among the most influential forces on the schools are professional education organizations, in particular the National Education Association (NEA) and the American Federation of Teachers (AFT).

In recent years, the role of teachers' organizations in determining educational policy has greatly increased. At the national level, the NEA and the AFT exert considerable influence on educational policy and legislation. Moreover, the state affiliates of the NEA and AFT are among the most effective lobbying groups in their respective states. (See Chapter 15 for more on these two teacher organizations.) The NEA and AFT affiliates have well-articulated positions on selected issues, represent thousands of teachers who can be mobilized to vote for or against particular legislators, and spend considerable amounts of money to make their positions known. State politicians pay considerable attention to these teachers' organizations because of their power and influence. At the local level— largely as a result of collective bargaining techniques, including work stoppages or the threat of them—teachers' organizations have won more and more power over educational policy.

teacher organizations are powerful

Today many local teachers' organizations, including NEA and AFT affiliates, have won recognition as the official bargaining representatives of their members. Teachers' organizations are also demanding that issues previously considered the prerogatives of local school boards and superintendents be subject to collective bargaining. Among these issues are teacher and paraprofessional salaries, clerical and secretarial assistance, curriculum development, fringe benefits, in-service training, class size, textbook selection, and even the appointment of department heads and other school administrators.

Teachers exercise decision-making power in various ways, such as selecting books to be used in literature classes.
(© Elizabeth Crews)

site-based decision making

Teachers' efforts to negotiate their teaching role and its conditions have not always been welcomed by local school boards and superintendents. However, one recent reform effort to improve schools, **site-based decision making,** has tended to increase teachers' power. The idea behind site-based decision making is that most changes need to occur at the school level, and therefore many administrative and budget decisions should be made at that level, with teachers becoming involved in the decisions that affect them and their students. Site-based decision making transfers much of the budget and decision making from the central school district administration to the individual school level. As a result of such reform efforts, teachers are gaining more authority over important school decisions.

Parents

Ask educators who has the most influence in determining whether children succeed in school, and they will almost always answer "parents." Parents are their children's first and primary teachers, and the only ones who follow a child's progress from year to year. As the two major forces for educating and socializing children in society, parents and teachers should be natural allies. Too often, however, a wide chasm separates them. Some teachers fear that parents will interfere in their classrooms; others feel pressed for time and don't want to spend the extra effort to communicate with and effectively involve parents. Some parents seem too consumed with the problems of work and raising a family to become involved in schools, whereas others actively participate in various school functions. Research is clear that without effective parental involvement in the schools, most students will not succeed academically. In a national survey of school superintendents, 68 percent identified a lack of parental involvement as the biggest roadblock to student achievement.[7]

The local **parent-teacher organization (PTO)** serves as a communications link between parents and the formal school organization, with teachers usually acting as representatives of the schools. Formally, the school system ordinarily operates by means of down-the-line communications, from the superintendent to the principal, to the teacher, and then to the parents. Typically, school systems are less receptive to up-the-line communications from parents or teachers to administrators. But when the formal hierarchy does not respond to up-the-line communications in a satisfactory manner, parents can resort to an informal communications system in an attempt to get a better response.

An instance of informal communications occurred when the energetic principal of a New Haven, Connecticut, school in a low-income neighborhood galvanized the PTO in an attempt to improve the school's facilities. He began by going

A parent is the most important teacher a child ever has.

—JOAN BECK

parental influence

Family support and emphasis on the value of education are extremely important influences on a child's success in school. (© Joan Clifford/The Picture Cube)

to an important neighborhood leader and persuading her that the children in the school needed help. Convinced, the woman helped the principal go to work on the PTO. To stimulate parent involvement, they convinced the PTO to endorse a hot-lunch program; this required the PTO to raise funds and hire kitchen help. As the PTO became more active, the principal began a campaign for a new school to replace the old one. When the city administration raised obstacles, the principal called together the PTO members and other neighborhood leaders to ask their support for the construction of a new school. Within twenty-four hours, they were exerting pressure on the city school board and the administration. Needless to say, the school was built.

ways to improve parental involvement

Most PTOs, however, are comparatively impotent in achieving educational aims. Educational reformers are concerned about the ineffectiveness of parent groups, because they know that reforms will last only if parents are actively involved in the work of their schools. Many strategies can be used to increase parental involvement and improve the partnership between parents and teachers. These strategies include frequent parent-teacher conferences; homework hotlines on which parents can telephone the school to find out about homework assignments or communicate with teachers; workshops for parents that address a variety of topics; school volunteer programs; and school councils on which parents, teachers, and administrators discuss school policies and practices. Teachers and school administrators must be trained to overcome barriers to effective parental involvement and to create school environments where parents of all races, ethnicities, and social classes feel welcome.

Business

historical influence of business

Business influence on education is not a new phenomenon. Whether it was to educate immigrants, gear up for the Industrial Revolution, or catch up with the Soviets after the launch of *Sputnik* in 1957, American business has long sought to shape public schools to meet its needs.

In the early twentieth century, business influenced the way educators thought about schooling by applying many principles of efficiency and standardization to school operations. Schools were compared to factories whose products were students; newly developed tests measured the quality of the school's products; in the name of efficiency, class sizes and teacher loads were increased. In short, the public demanded a profitable return on the money "invested" in schools. Many educators continue to speak of the schools, a child-oriented social institution, in these business terms. The language itself indicates the appeal of standardizing and controlling the schools' outcomes in a business fashion.

business plays leading role in reform

But the relationship between business and education is changing, going beyond school imitation of business practices. Deep concern about the quality of U.S. public education and its ability to produce workers with the knowledge and skills business needs has prompted partnerships between educators and business executives. In particular, during the 1980s and 1990s, the business community was at the forefront of efforts to restructure public education. Business leaders have been substantially involved in almost every educational reform report. As a result, they have become both the strongest critics and the staunchest advocates for public education. The chief executive officers of such major corporations as Procter & Gamble, Xerox, Apple Computer, Eastman Kodak, Coca-Cola, IBM, RJR Nabisco, Exxon, and many others have demanded and pushed for educational reforms in state capitals, the halls of Congress, and the White House. More than 100,000 business-school partnerships have been formed since 1983, and business has donated hundreds of millions of dollars to improve elementary and secondary schools.[8] One major effort on the part of business to influence school reform is the Business Coalition for Educational Reform (BCER), a group of 13 national business organizations and over 400 local and state coalitions seeking to strengthen America's schools by increasing "academic achievement for all students by supporting and expanding business involvement in education at the national, state, and local levels." The BCER supports efforts to raise academic standards for all students and to ensure that standards reflect the knowledge and skill needed for workplace success.[9] Further information on school restructuring efforts appears in Chapter 13.

Why should the business community show such interest? The initiatives to improve the quality of American education go beyond altruistic impulses. One source estimates that the education market represents potential revenue of $600 billion for corporate interests. With that kind of money involved, businesses will make their presence known.[10] In addition, like the nation's governors, many business leaders are convinced that education reform is essential to the health of the American economy. Competition from Asian and European manufacturers in world markets, a massive U.S. trade deficit, and industry's perception that entry-level workers lack proper job skills have focused attention on educating the American work force. In fact, U.S. companies spend more than $50 billion annually on remedial education for their workers.[11]

education/economy link

Not everyone sees business involvement in education as totally positive. Some express concern that financial support from business will lead to business intrusion—that schools may be unduly shaped to meet business needs. Another concern centers on business's provision of free curriculum and instructional materials for teachers. Critics argue that corporate handouts are not just supplementary gifts but sophisticated marketing tools containing subtle and not-so-subtle messages to support the corporation's biases and promote brand identification and product loyalty. Some people cynically view business's push for the expanded use of technology in schools as an attempt to create a new market for computers and other educational technology.

business intrusion?

Among the most controversial business ventures is Channel One, a commercial service that delivers ten minutes of high-quality news programming directly to public school classrooms free of cost in exchange for two minutes of advertising. A school that subscribes to the twelve-minute newscast receives a satellite dish, two videocassette recorders, a television set for every classroom in the building, and schoolwide cabling to hook it all together. By 1999 about 12,000 middle schools and high schools had signed on, reaching an estimated 8 million students, about 40 percent of the nation's twelve- to eighteen-year-olds.[12] Many educators have attacked the concept as gross commercialism and a dangerous

Channel One controversy

Reading, Writing, . . . and Purchasing?

Students are a captive audience in public schools, and they have enormous purchasing power. Elementary-age children have about $15 billion per year to spend, and they influence another $160 billion of spending by their parents. Teenagers spend about $57 billion of their own money yearly. Commercial businesses pitch their wares to these children and youth in schools through a variety of marketing techniques. Here are a few examples from the Center for Commercial-Free Public Education:

▷ An Exxon curriculum teaches young children how the *Valdez* oil spill was an example of environmental protection.

▷ In Colorado Springs, Colorado, 7-Up and Burger King advertise on the sides of school buses.

▷ Clairol distributes free bags of shampoo to students as they leave school, along with surveys asking whether they had "a good or bad hair day."

▷ A Nike program asks young people to devote a week of classroom time to learning the life cycle of a Nike shoe. The curriculum fails to address the sweatshop portion of the manufacturing process.

▷ A Texas school roof features a Dr. Pepper logo that is visible from planes flying overhead.

▷ Dow Chemical's *Chem-TV* and *Chemapalooza* videos feature teenagers dancing and singing about the wonderful world of chemicals.

What other examples of commercialism can you think of that might affect students in public schools? Are you concerned about this trend? Why or why not?

Sources: Henry A. Giroux, "Education Incorporated?" *Educational Leadership* 56, no. 2 (October 1998), p. 16; "A Word from Our Sponsor," *Virginia Journal of Education* (November 1998), p. 13.

> *The classroom is . . . a place in which the claims of various political, social, and economic interests are negotiated. The classroom is both a symbol and a product of deadly serious cultural bargaining.*
>
> —NEIL POSTMAN

privatization

precedent, whereas supporters argue that the program rouses students' interest in current events. In addition, supporters argue, the equipment provided by Channel One enables schools to take advantage of other cable offerings, such as the Discovery Channel, Cable News Network, C-Span, and the Learning Channel. One state superintendent, an opponent of Channel One, states, "The problem is, they want us to sell access to our kids' minds, and we have no right, morally or ethically, to do that."[13] Are the advantages worth the cost? What do you think?

Another way business influences education is through the recent movement toward private management of public schools that has occurred in some urban areas. In a small number of cases, private corporations such as the Edison Schools, TesseracT Group (formerly known as Educational Alternatives, Inc.), and Sylvan Learning, Inc., have contracted with school districts to provide specific educational services, to operate schools whose students have been performing poorly on academic tests, or to begin new schools with promising designs. Advocates of this **privatization** movement argue that private corporations can operate these schools more effectively and less expensively. Opponents, especially teachers' unions, claim that schools operated under a profit motive may shortchange students' welfare in order to make money. They do this, the critics claim, by hiring inexperienced teachers, using unlicensed staff, and eliminating high-cost special education programs. To date, private management of public schools has often led to cleaner buildings, greater access to computers, and more individualized instruction, but has yet to show academic improvement.[14]

There is no question that the role of the business community in educational affairs has greatly expanded since the mid-1980s, and most people see this trend as positive. Businesses and corporations, with a vested stake in the outcomes of public education, will undoubtedly continue to be major players in the reform of our educational system. The challenge for educators will be to walk the line between partnerships and cooperation on the one hand and exploitation for commercial purposes on the other.

cooperation or exploitation?

Standardized Testing

As programs for school improvement proliferated in the 1980s, the trend to assess the quality of schools and teachers by using standardized tests also grew in influence. Many states now require high school students to perform well on tests of general academic competence as a prerequisite for graduation, and almost all states require local public school districts to test students at some point(s) between grades one and twelve. Forty-four states require aspiring teachers to pass a state-prescribed, standardized test before entering a teacher education program and/or before being licensed to teach.[15]

increase of standardized testing

Many educators express grave concerns about what they think is an overemphasis on testing. Measuring school excellence by standardized tests poses a danger arising from the limited and simplistic nature of the tests. Evaluation experts warn that tests external to the schools can be limiting if schools pattern their curricula to conform to the content of the tests. Schools may fail to teach what is difficult to test. In some instances, the content and actual form of a test have become the curriculum itself as weeks of classroom drill have centered on previous versions of tests.

overemphasis on testing?

Others worry that standardized tests overemphasize technical information and underemphasize educators' professional judgments about the worthiness of a school's programs. With a national call to stress more problem solving, critical thinking, and writing skills, educators see a contradiction in using standardized tests that don't measure these outcomes. They are calling for more *authentic assessment,* that is, using such things as actual specimens or examples of students' work to determine educational achievement.

authentic assessment

Currently there is a strong movement in the United States for each state to create standards for student achievement linked to some form of assessment. More and more, policymakers believe that student achievement will not increase markedly until high standards are set and quality work by all students is expected and rewarded. Current standardized tests are seen as reflecting only minimum standards and as being insufficient to measure high learning outcomes. As individual states develop assessment tests that measure what students are expected to learn, the reliance on national standardized tests that are not coordinated with local and state curricula is likely to diminish.

standards movement

The Federal Government

strong court influence

The Federal Courts   One could argue that the most powerful educational policymaking group in the United States is the judicial branch. Many groups, frustrated by local and state school policies, have turned to state and federal courts for relief. The history of education has been shaped by important court decisions on the duties and responsibilities of school officials in such areas as school desegregation, religion in the schools, student rights, and, particularly at the state level, school finance. The U.S. Supreme Court has played a particularly important role in changing educational policy in this country. Because its rulings have altered or reduced the power of state and local educational authorities, some of the Court's decisions have generated deep resentment among those who abhor this "federal intrusion" into states' rights. Other people applaud the Court's decisions as steps to make American education more responsive to broad democratic principles. The Supreme Court has issued rulings affecting such important educational policies as desegregation, public aid to private schools, rights of people with disabilities, gender equity, and sexual harassment. Currently it is poised to review the constitutionality of the controversial Milwaukee voucher plan. (See Chapter 5 for a discussion of vouchers and public funding for private and religious schools.)

However, the courts alone, as powerful as they are, cannot do everything. Often federal administrative action needs to be joined with more detailed judicial rulings and pressures. In the famous 1954 case of *Brown* v. *Board of Education of Topeka,* the U.S. Supreme Court ruled that the doctrine of "separate but equal" had no place in public education. But how was this momentous judgment to be implemented? The Court decided only that "all deliberate speed" should be employed to abolish the dual school system for African Americans and whites, but no judicial guidelines were developed to steer the process. As a result, for a decade

Federal legislation and federal court decisions have significantly affected education, including the education of children with such disabilities as deafness.
(© Will Hart/PhotoEdit)

almost no changes occurred until the 1960s, when a combination of new congressional laws on civil rights and education and strong enforcement of desegregation by President Lyndon Johnson's administration took place.

enforcement necessary

Recent Supreme Court decisions have reversed previous desegregation mandates, effectively diminishing the Court's role in mandating local desegregation efforts. See Chapter 11 for more on desegregation efforts and Chapter 12 for a more detailed discussion of the impact of Supreme Court decisions on American education.

reducing desegregation mandates

The U.S. Department of Education   The Department of Education is a significant part of the federal government, with cabinet-level status and a budget of about $40 billion in fiscal year 2000. The department administers a variety of programs passed by Congress, including programs concerned with elementary and secondary education, postsecondary education, educational research and development, vocational and adult education, special education, and civil rights. It also administers funds devoted to the collection of educational statistics.

Although education is not specifically mentioned in the federal constitution, there has always been some degree of federal involvement in education. The level of involvement often fluctuates depending on whether Republicans or Democrats control the White House and Congress and on the particular ideology professed by the party in power. Republicans generally have sought to decrease the involvement of the federal government in education, even advocating abolition of the U.S. Department of Education, whereas Democrats tend to be more supportive of both the department and federal efforts to improve education.

fluctuating federal involvement

How Are Schools Financed?

The total amount of money available to a school district for education is the sum of locally raised revenues, state aid, federal aid, and miscellaneous revenues. Historically most of the money used to support public elementary and secondary schools has come from local revenue sources, primarily the property tax. But from the late 1970s to the early 1990s, for the first time in American history, the states' share of support for public education exceeded the local share (see Figure 9.3). Increased state revenues have helped to offset the decreases in local and federal funding of the schools. Currently state governments contribute about 49 percent, local governments almost 44 percent, and the federal government slightly less than 7 percent toward the financing of public schools.[16]

The percentage of revenue received from federal, state, and local sources varies considerably from state to state. Federal contributions to state revenues for public education range from a high of 13 percent for Mississippi to a low of 3 percent for New Hampshire and New Jersey. Local contributions to revenues range from a high of 91 percent for New Hampshire to a low of 2 percent for Hawaii, which has a statewide school district. Other than Hawaii, which gets 91 percent of its school funding from the state, the state receiving the highest proportion of revenues from state sources is Michigan at 82 percent, and the lowest is New Hampshire at 6 percent.[17] Let's look in more detail at state and local funding patterns.

funding percentages vary

FIGURE 9.3   Percentage of Revenues Received from Federal, State, and Local
Sources for Public Elementary and Secondary Schools

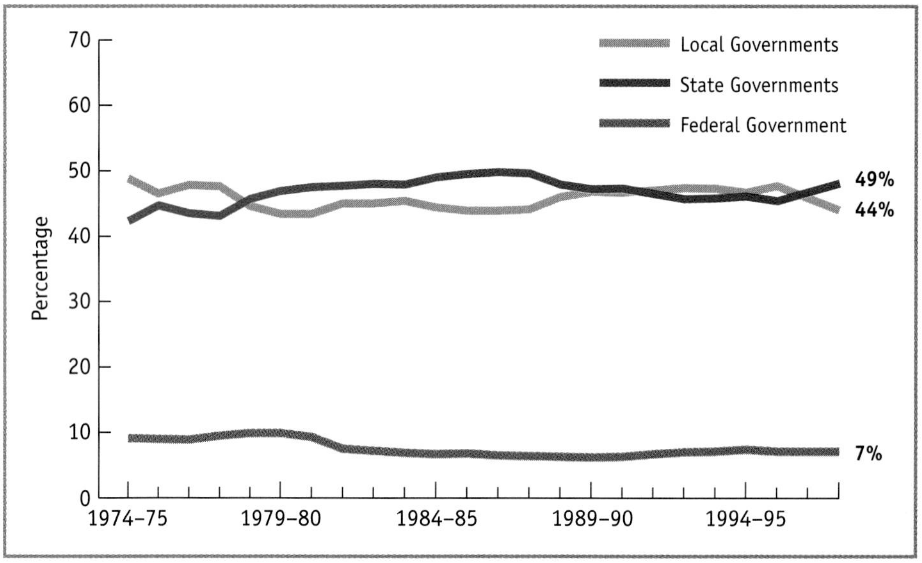

Sources: Thomas D. Snyder, Charlene M. Hoffman, and Claire M. Geddes, *Digest of Education Statistics 1996*
(Washington, DC: U.S. Department of Education, National Center for Education Statistics, 1996), p. 151; "Education Vital Signs," *The American School Board Journal* (December 1998), p. A27.

State and Local Funding

sources of revenue

How is money raised to pay for educational expenditures, and by what systems
of taxation? State revenue systems are as diverse as school finance plans and reflect the socioeconomic makeup, the political climate, and the educational needs
of each state. State governments use a combination of sales, personal income,
corporate income, and excise taxes to generate revenues. Some states fund their
schools partly with income from state-run lotteries. Local governments, in
contrast, rely primarily on the property tax for income. Most states require the
citizens in a school district to vote either on the property tax rate to support
education or on the school budget itself.

rising expenditures per pupil

Figure 9.4 on page 311 shows the upward trend in average expenditure per
pupil in daily attendance. The nationwide average stood at $6,407 per pupil for
1998–99.[18] From state to state, however, the per-pupil expenditures vary widely
(see Figure 9.5 on page 312), ranging from over $10,153 per pupil each year to
$3,732. The reason for these differences is primarily economic. A state's ability to
pay for education depends on the income level of its residents and corporations.
In general, the southern states fund education at lower levels than the northern
states. As a result of lower funding, are students who live in some of the Sunbelt
states being deprived of a quality education? The connection between funding
and excellence of education is often disputed, but a group of researchers from the
University of Chicago, after reanalyzing thirty-two studies on this issue, concluded that higher per-pupil expenditures, better teacher salaries, more educated

FIGURE 9.4   Expenditures per Pupil

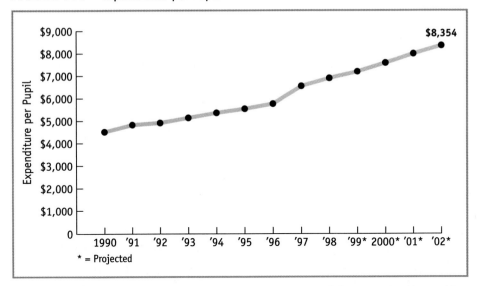

Source: Data in constant 1995–96 dollars from *Projections of Education Statistics to 2008* (Washington, DC: U.S. Department of Education, National Center for Education Statistics, 1998), Table 34; web site at http://nces.ed.gov/pubs98/pj2008/p98t34.html.

and experienced teachers, and smaller class and school sizes—all directly a result of higher funding—are strongly related to improved student learning.[19]

School Finance Reform and the Courts

Many knowledgeable educators and politicians argue that one of the greatest causes of unequal educational opportunity is the method used to finance school systems. Because of local districts' heavy reliance on property taxes, districts where property values are high generate much more money to finance their schools than districts where property values are low. Within the same state, for example, the average amount of money spent per child in one district may be more than three times the amount spent in a nearby district. Such spending differentials result in great educational disparities, as measured by pupil-teacher ratios, training and experience of staff, and availability of facilities, equipment, and counseling services.

unequal funding

Court Rulings   As a result of numerous court decisions, efforts to equalize the disparities in funding within states have shifted some of the responsibility for funding from local school districts to the state level. In 1971, a class action suit, *Serrano* v. *Priest,* was filed by pupils and their parents against California state and county officials concerned with financing public schools. The suit charged that the school-financing scheme was unconstitutional. The Supreme Court of California supported the parents' claim that the quality of a child's education must

Serrano v. Priest

FIGURE 9.5   Average Expenditure per Pupil, by State

not be a function of wealth other than the wealth of the state as a whole. The court also held that the California system of financing schools on the basis of local property taxes violated the Fourteenth Amendment to the U.S. Constitution.

In 1973, however, the Supreme Court of the United States, by a five-to-four vote, reversed a similar decision (known as the *Rodriguez* case) involving the school finance system of the state of Texas. The Court found that the U.S. Constitution was not violated because the right to an education is not guaranteed explicitly or implicitly by the Constitution. Although *federal* law had not been violated, the Court did indicate that the finding should not be interpreted as a victory for the status quo. In effect, issues of inequity in school finance were returned to the province of the state courts and legislatures.

Since the *Rodriguez* case, other state courts have ruled that their school financing systems violate their state constitutions. Many state constitutions, unlike the U.S. Constitution, contain equal protection clauses that can be interpreted to include education as a protected right. Just since 1989, supreme courts in twenty-one states have issued rulings on the constitutionality of their school finance systems. In eleven states the high court has ruled the finance system unconstitutional, and in ten states the system has been upheld. In those states where the finance system has been ruled unconstitutional, the issue has centered on inadequacies in the level of educational opportunities offered to children in the poorer school districts. The courts in those states examined whether the poor children were receiving a sufficient education as required by the state constitution and as measured by contemporary education standards or by comparisons to the best or highest-spending districts. In contrast, in states where the system of school finance was upheld, the courts usually interpreted their state constitutions as guaranteeing only a basic minimum level of funding.[20] As a result of court challenges, more than twenty states have reformed their school finance laws since 1973.

equality as state concern

In an unprecedented move, in 1993 the Michigan legislature voted to eliminate local property taxes as a source of revenue for the public schools. Many observers called the action "bold," while others termed it "reckless." What made the action so controversial was the fact that the Michigan legislature at that time lacked an alternative funding system to replace the $6.3 billion in local property tax funds for schools. State leaders planned to use the self-inflicted crisis to dramatically recast the existing school finance system, which left great gaps in spending power between wealthy and poor school districts. By 1994, the voters of Michigan had voted to increase the state sales tax by 50 percent and raise taxes on cigarettes to replace the greatly reduced property tax, thus permitting the state to reallocate state resources to poorer school districts. Other states are likely to follow the Michigan example of less reliance on local property taxes.

Michigan reform

Educators, parents, and public officials are greatly concerned that the quality of a child's education not depend on whether the child lives in a school district with high property values. Many of these concerned citizens are urging that state governments become responsible for raising educational revenue and distributing the full costs of local schools to the school districts. The school districts would continue to be in charge of the operation of the local schools but would no longer carry the burden of raising needed money.

pressures for equality

Year-Round Schools

One innovative way some school districts are trying to cut costs is to implement year-round schooling to make the best use of school facilities throughout the year. By 1998, about 1.8 million students participated in year-round programs in 2,460 U.S. schools, and the numbers are growing. The major push for year-round schools has occurred mainly in elementary schools and in fast-growing states such as California, Utah, Texas, and Florida.

Year-round schools began in 1968 in Hayward, California, where school was held in session for nine weeks, followed by a three-week break. This pattern was repeated four times a year. Other schools have developed different patterns of attendance, but all keep their facilities open all year and stagger schedules so that some students are always in attendance. That lets schools house 25 to 50 percent more students without increasing class sizes.

Advocates of year-round schooling cite several benefits:

1. Students receive continuous instruction and don't suffer from learning slippage caused by three months' vacation.

2. Students can take enrichment activities or remedial instruction during intersessions.

3. Since one-fourth of the students will be on vacation at any given time, districts can cope with over-enrollments without building new schools. Thus, they save tax dollars.

4. Teachers and students avoid burnout by experiencing more frequent breaks.

5. Teachers can earn more money by serving as substitutes during their vacations or by teaching intersession offerings.

Opponents argue that year-round schooling doesn't save money but actually costs more because schools must pay for additional administrative, utility, maintenance, transportation, and salary costs. Moreover, many older schools lack air conditioning to operate in the summer. One clear disadvantage of year-round schooling is the disruption of established routines. Families may have to alter child care arrangements and vacation schedules, and teachers may have to rearrange their summer pursuits, including graduate studies and second jobs. Other disadvantages include inconvenience to families with siblings on different schedules and the possible limitation of courses available to students.

When year-round schooling is first discussed in a school district, there is often strong opposition. However, in those districts that have tried it, most of the teachers, students, and parents support the move. Even students seem to prefer the shorter and more frequent vacations to the longer, traditional summer vacation.

Would you enjoy teaching in such an arrangement? Why or why not?

Sources: "Year-Round Education," *Education Update* 37, no. 7 (September 1995), pp. 6–8; "Should Kids Go to School Year-Round?" *USA Weekend,* May 29–31, 1998, p. 12.

Federal Funding

Although the federal government may provide less money for public schools than do state or local governments, federal funds are strategically important and have a far greater impact than their proportion of school funding would suggest.

Funding in the Past   Much of federal aid to education traditionally has been in the form of **categorical grants:** that is, the money must be spent for designated purposes (or categories) that are stated generally in the legislation and more

categorical aid

Where Does the United States Stand on Education Funding?

Many politicians, arguing against the need for increased spending on education, assert that the United States already spends more on public education than do most comparable countries, but gets worse results. "Money is not the answer," they claim.

We can shed some light on the debate by comparing U.S. educational spending with that of some other countries. To allow for differences in size of the economies, we can consider public spending on education as a percentage of gross domestic product (GDP), the total value of a country's output. The United States spends 3.5 percent of its GDP on elementary and secondary education. The Scandinavian countries of Denmark and Sweden spend 4.3 and 4.5 percent, respectively, on elementary and secondary education, while France and Great Britain spend 4.0 and 3.8 percent, respectively. Surprisingly, Germany, Australia, and Japan rank below the United States, spending 2.9, 3.2, and 3.0 percent, respectively.

Such figures indicate that the United States devotes more of its resources to elementary and secondary education than do most other industrialized nations.

However, the United States might be expected to spend proportionally more than other countries because of certain characteristics of our school system and society. Our decentralized school system is more expensive than the single, centrally administered system that characterizes many of the other industrialized nations. Our population is more diverse than most countries', thus presenting unique challenges. And the very high number of U.S. children living in poverty creates additional demands for schools. Also, the United States, compared to the other countries, spends a much greater percentage of its public education funds—17 percent—on special education services. Given these factors, our percentage of GDP spent on elementary and secondary education does not seem extravagant.

Sources: Digest of Educational Statistics 1998 (Washington, DC: U.S. Government Printing Office, 1999), p. 469; Richard Rothstein with Karen Hawley Miles, *Where's the Money Gone?* (Washington, DC: Economic Policy Institute, 1995), p. 8.

precisely by the federal agency administering the funds. As a result, the federal government has been able to influence school districts and institutions that have accepted or sought its aid. For example, to qualify for federal funds to improve its reading program, a school district would have to conform to the guidelines and restrictions accompanying the money. Many financially stricken school districts have been grateful for additional funds, regardless of the regulations they carry.

During the period from 1960 to 1980, federal education programs thrived. *strong funding, 1960–80* The federal government's share of elementary and secondary school revenues increased from 4.4 to 9.8 percent during this period.[21] Congressional acts provided money to colleges, cities, states, and agencies to finance a wide variety of projects, including construction of buildings and other educational facilities; improvement of instruction or administration; development of educational personnel, including teachers and paraprofessionals, particularly for high-poverty areas; provision of loans for prospective teachers; and funding for educational research.

During President Reagan's administration (1981–89), categorical grant programs were largely replaced by block grants to state and local education agencies. **Block grants** are sums of money that come with only minimal federal restrictions and are transferred from the federal government to the state governments *block grants*

as a block of money rather than by categories. Moreover, the Reagan administration successfully held the line on federal expenditures for education. These changes reflected the belief of President Reagan, and of many other Republicans, that the federal government should play a reduced role in educational policy-making. In fact, the federal government's share of support for public education fell from 9.8 percent in 1980 to 6.1 percent in 1990, but by 1999 had climbed back to slightly less than 7.0 percent. (See Figure 9.3 on page 310.) Today the federal government employs both categorical and block grant programs.

Compensatory Education   Although the federal government provides money for a variety of educational programs, its most significant efforts have been to address the needs of children from high-poverty areas who are at risk for educational failure. **Compensatory education** is an approach to creating more equal educational opportunities for disadvantaged children. In particular, compensatory education attempts to overcome a student's learning problems by incorporating extra education into the regular school program or, to keep such problems from developing, by providing students with appropriate preschool programs. The most famous preschool initiative is **Head Start,** a federal program that aims to improve the learning skills, social skills, and health status of poor children so that they can begin schooling on an equal basis with their more advantaged peers. For the 2000 fiscal year, the federal government budgeted over $5.3 billion for Head Start programs. Since its inception in 1965, Head Start has served almost 17 million children.[22]

Head Start

Head Start programs target children who are "at risk" of school failure by intervening in their early years to improve their skills. (© Paul Conklin)

Compensatory programs come in many forms. Some programs, like Head Start, emphasize early intervention and target children who are "at risk" for later school failure. Some help parents learn how to interact more effectively with their babies and young children in the areas of cognitive and psychosocial development. Other compensatory programs target older children and focus on basic skill instruction, tutoring, or remediation in a variety of academic areas. Dropout prevention programs, job training, and adult literacy instruction are all attempts to help older individuals improve the quality of their lives through education and to help prevent the cycle of educational disadvantage from being passed down through generations.

varieties of programs

Title I Compensatory education was formalized in Title I of the 1965 **Elementary and Secondary Education Act (ESEA),** which authorizes the federal government's single largest investment in elementary and secondary education. **Title I** was designed to do two things: (1) deliver federal funds to local school districts and schools for the education of students from low-income families and (2) supplement the educational services provided to low-achieving students in those districts. As part of the reauthorization of the ESEA in 1994, several Title I requirements changed. To receive money, states and school districts must submit a state improvement plan that includes the adoption of challenging content standards and aligned assessments for Title I students. Schools are now allowed to use their Title I funds on a schoolwide basis rather than only for the poorest students, and they can combine money from multiple federal programs. However, school districts must now rank their schools based on their percentages of poor students and distribute Title I funds accordingly, with the poorest schools receiving the

Title I requirements

most money per pupil. Although the highest-poverty schools make up only about 15 percent of schools nationwide, they receive 46 percent of Title I funds.[23]

Between 1965 and 1999, Title I provided about $120 billion for educational services in almost all of the nation's school districts. Title I now provides more than $8 billion each year on behalf of over 11 million children in 45,000 schools and is the largest federal investment in our public schools. Of the 11 million Title I students, about two-thirds are enrolled in grades one through six. Hispanic American students make up 30 percent, African American students 28 percent, and white students 36 percent of those receiving Title I support. Title I grants serve about 260,000 preschool children, 167,000 private school children, close to 300,000 migrant children, some 200,000 students identified as homeless, and about 2 million students with limited English proficiency.[24] In spite of what seems like an enormous amount of money, only about 50 percent of all eligible children receive services from Title I funds. Because Title I has never been funded at a high enough level to meet the needs of low-income schools and because its resources are widely dispersed, even the recent funding increases have not checked the growing educational crisis in low-income areas.

insufficient funding

Evaluations and Controversies

Evaluations of Title I programs and Head Start have been mixed. Studies indicating that gains have been made in some programs are often contradicted by other studies. The earliest hopes—that compensatory education would increase student IQ scores and scholastic achievement—have not realized significant results. Many individual Title I programs succeed, but the poor performance of others drags down the effectiveness of the program overall. Long-range studies that have followed students from preschool to age nineteen, like the study of students in the very successful Perry Preschool Program in Ypsilanti, Michigan, provide other indicators of program success. Effective early childhood programs may result in fewer special education placements, more high school graduations, lower teen pregnancy rates, increased employment and earnings, fewer crimes committed, and greater commitment to marriage.[25] *Early intervention*—beginning the program early in the child's life— may provide the key to success in compensatory education programs.

evaluations mixed

early intervention a key

Some observers of compensatory education programs criticize them, however, for not showing evidence of improved IQ scores and scholastic achievement for participating students—the original goals of the programs. They see little point in strengthening programs that they believe have failed in the past. Proponents of compensatory education programs argue that, considering the enormity of the problem, expenditures thus far are a mere drop in the bucket. They also argue that a simultaneous attack must be made on external factors that contribute to low achievement, such as poor housing, family instability, and low income. Some argue that instead of spending the money to hire teachers and aides to provide remedial services, programs they maintain haven't worked effectively, schools receiving Title I money should incorporate proven school improvement models, such as Success for All (see the accompanying box) or James Comer's School Development Program model (see Chapter 4).

Title I reforms called for

Success for All

One compensatory education program that is quite successful is the Success for All program developed by the Center for Research on Effective Schooling for Disadvantaged Students at Johns Hopkins University. The Success for All program restructures the elementary school with one goal in mind: to ensure that all students perform at grade level in reading, writing, and mathematics by the end of third grade.

Success for All schools offer a half-day of preschool and a full day of kindergarten, both focused on providing a developmentally appropriate learning experience for children. The curriculum emphasizes the development and use of language and balances academic readiness with music, art, and movement activities. The program also implements the center's research findings on one-to-one tutoring, regrouping for reading, family support teams, frequent assessments of learning with immediate help on problems, and the use of an effective reading program. Two social workers and one parent-liaison work full-time in the schools to provide parenting education and to encourage parents to support their children's efforts.

The program also includes tutors for children in grades K–3. Each tutor is a certified, experienced teacher who works one-on-one with eleven students per day. First-graders get priority for tutoring.

Evaluation results have been outstanding, much higher than for any other intervention strategy ever tried with at-risk students. Starting with one Baltimore school, the Success for All program had spread to over 1,100 schools in 45 states by 1999, and it has produced dramatic gains in students' reading proficiency. Almost all Success for All programs are in high-poverty, Title I schools. Early programs were more expensive than regular instruction, but that situation seems to have changed. By restructuring elementary schools and reconfiguring the uses of Title I money, special education, and other funds to emphasize prevention and early intervention rather than remediation, the administrators have brought costs in Success for All schools in line with those of other schools that have access to these resources.

The major lesson learned, say Robert Slavin and his colleagues, is that disadvantaged children can routinely achieve substantially greater success in schools that are neither exceptional nor extraordinary. Rather than having to depend on the outstanding principal or charismatic teacher to ensure success, every child, regardless of background, has an excellent opportunity to succeed in school.

In spite of its success in teaching students to read, many teachers don't like the program because it tells them exactly what to do throughout their lessons. In essence, they are asked to follow a fast-paced script written by the Success for All researchers. For some teachers, this process seems contrary to their beliefs about the importance of paying attention to the learning style of each child and varying their instruction accordingly.

Sources: Robert E. Slavin, Nancy A. Madden, Lawrence J. Dolan, Barbara A. Wasik, Steven M. Ross, Lana J. Smith, and Marcella Dianda, "Success for All: A Summary of Research," *Journal of Education for Students Placed at Risk* 1, no. 1 (1996), pp. 41–76; Success for All brochure produced by the Success for All Program, Johns Hopkins University, Baltimore; Jay Mathews, "As Schools Shop for Success, Teachers Rethink Role," *The Washington Post,* June 21, 1999, pp. A1, A8.

Since evaluations of Title I are equivocal, why does Congress so strongly support it? Politicians support Title I because the money reaches almost every school district and thus provides jobs and services in every congressional district. Few members of Congress will vote against providing these benefits to their districts.

Both sides acknowledge that not all programs are equally effective. The best programs achieve desired results, whereas the less effective programs do not seem to have lasting effects on student performance.

Future Outlook   What is the outlook for the future? The long period of economic prosperity during the mid- and late 1990s left the federal government with unanticipated surplus tax revenues. As a result, federal contributions to education have been increasing, including new programs designed to prepare teachers to use technology effectively. Even with the increase in federal money for education, the main action for education reform will continue to be in the states' arenas. The federal government's role in education is likely to be that of an active but minor partner.

States will remain key funders

KEY TERMS

state board of education (292)
chief state school officer (295)
state department of education (295)
local school board (296)
superintendent of schools (296)
site-based decision making (302)
parent-teacher organization (PTO) (303)

privatization (306)
categorical grants (314)
block grants (315)
compensatory education (316)
Head Start (316)
Elementary and Secondary Education Act (ESEA) (317)
Title I (317)

FOR REFLECTION

1. From what you have read about the role of the superintendent, what impressions have you formed about the power of the superintendent and the constraints on that power?

2. Did the schools you attended work in partnership with business and industry? Did your education prepare you for further education and entry into the work force? What, in your opinion, is an appropriate relationship between business and schools?

3. The National Education Association and the National Association of Secondary School Principals make this statement about successful secondary schools: "In good secondary schools, the principal and teachers develop and maintain a variety of cooperative links with the community. Family and community involvement and support complement the efforts of the school." Describe some of the cooperative links you would suggest at either the elementary or secondary level.

4. How involved should the states' governors and legislatures be in public education? What are the advantages and dangers of increased involvement by state governments (as opposed to local governments) in public education?

5. Of the methods of school financing discussed in this chapter (local property taxes, state financing through statewide taxes, and state-run lotteries), which do you believe is most equitable? Why?

6. Do you believe state governments should redistribute money from rich to poor school districts through state taxing power? Why or why not?

7. What role do you think the federal government should play in compensating for educational disadvantages as a result of poverty? Should Title I be continued?

FOR FURTHER INFORMATION

Burrup, Percy E., Vern Brimley, Jr., and Rulon R. Garfield. *Financing Education in a Climate of Change.* **7th ed. Boston: Allyn and Bacon, 1998.**
This comprehensive text examines how schools are financed in this country, the role of the federal government, and significant court cases affecting school finance.

Johnson, Susan Moore. *Leading to Change: The Challenge of the New Superintendency.* **San Francisco: Jossey-Bass, 1996.**
In this text, the author studies twelve superintendents, their models of leadership, and how contexts influence their behavior.

Karp, Stan, Robert Lowe, Barbara Miner, and Bob Peterson. *Funding for Justice: Money, Equity, and the Future of Public Education.* **Milwaukee: Rethinking Schools Ltd., 1997.**
This book gives the facts and opinions of leading researchers and thinkers in the area of school finance. It also features an overview of major court cases on state funding.

Kozol, Jonathan. *Savage Inequalities: Children in America's Schools.* **New York: HarperPerennial, 1992.**
National Book Award winner Jonathan Kozol presents his shocking account of the American educational system in this best-selling book.

U.S. Department of Education. **World Wide Web site at http://www.ed.gov.**
This home page will keep you abreast of educational initiatives of the federal government. Clicking on the National Center for Education Statistics link (under Programs and Services) will give you access to many government publications and statistics on education. For information on Head Start, use http://www2.acf.dhhs.gov/programs/hsb/.

Wirt, Frederick M., and Michael W. Kirst. *The Political Dynamics of American Education.* **Berkeley, CA: McCutchan, 1997.**
This text presents an analysis of the politics of education by two leaders in the field.

What Are the Philosophical Foundations of American Education?

This chapter examines the role of philosophy, a key foundational discipline in the work of the teacher. First, we describe philosophy; then we discuss four different philosophies and analyze their applications to the classroom. This chapter emphasizes that

▶ Philosophical knowledge has a fundamental role in clarifying questions of education.

▶ Philosophical thought has distinct characteristics. Four branches of philosophy—metaphysics, epistemology, axiology, and logic—relate rather directly to the work of the teacher.

▶ Four philosophies of education—perennialism, progressivism, essentialism, and existentialism—have many practical implications for the classroom teacher.

▶ Psychological theories influence modern education, particularly constructivism.

▶ Teachers need to have a philosophy to guide their practice.

A medical student who wants intensely to be a surgeon, has marvelous hands, and displays a high level of technical skill but does not know how the body functions or what constitutes health can hardly be called a doctor.

An aspirant to the ministry who loves to work with people and possesses a marvelous gift of speaking but has no opinion about humanity's relationship to God or about the purpose of religion can hardly be suited for religious ministry.

And a person who has a great desire to be with young people, wants to live the life of a teacher, and possesses great technical skill but lacks purpose and direction is hardly a teacher.

These three individuals are like wind-up toys, moving along blindly without a plan or an intellectual compass. And though this image may be somewhat dramatic, there *are* people who prepare for professions without getting to the core meaning of what those professions are all about. Such directionless behavior can cause problems in any occupation or profession, but particularly in teaching. What kind of a teacher can someone be who lacks a view of what people are and a vision of what they can become? Who cannot clearly define right and wrong in human behavior? Who doesn't recognize what is important and what is unimportant or can't distinguish clear thinking from sloppy thinking? The person who would take on the responsibility for educating the young without having seriously wrestled with these questions is, to say the least, dangerous, for he or she is going against the very grain of what it means to be a teacher. In fact, it is safe to say that such a person is not a teacher but a technician.

> *The educated differ from the uneducated as much as the living from the dead.*
>
> —ARISTOTLE

This chapter introduces you to philosophy, one of the foundational subjects in education, which, along with history and psychology (and, to some degree, economics, political science, sociology, anthropology, and the law), forms the intellectual underpinning on which the practice of education rests. The study of philosophy helps the teacher systematically to reflect on issues that are central to education, including such basic concepts as *learning, teaching, being educated, knowledge,* and *the good life.*

philosophy as foundation

What Is Philosophy?

The word *philosophy* is made up of two root words: "love" (*philo*) and "wisdom" (*sophos*). In its most basic sense, then, **philosophy** is the *love of wisdom.* Although not all people love wisdom in the same way or to the same degree, all humans are questioning beings—seekers of answers. As children, we are preoccupied with such lofty questions as "How do I get fewer veggies and more dessert?" Then we progress to such questions as "How does the teacher always know to call on me when I don't have the answers?" and "What do I need to do to get a decent grade in geometry?" Ultimately, we may move to more fundamental levels of questioning: "Who am I?" "What is the purpose of life, and what am I doing here?" "What does it mean to be a really good person?"

love of wisdom

323

PEANUTS reprinted by permission of United Feature Syndicate, Inc.

Fundamental Questions of Existence

Until about one hundred years ago, most people relied on religion and philosophy for answers to such fundamental questions. Whereas religion is said to represent the revealed word of God, philosophy represents a human attempt to sort out by reason the fundamental questions of existence. Many of the great thinkers of Western civilization—Plato, Aristotle, St. Thomas Aquinas, René Descartes, Jean-Jacques Rousseau, Immanuel Kant, Friedrich Nietzsche, John Locke, John Stuart Mill, William James, Alfred North Whitehead, and John Dewey—have been philosophers. Because education has always been a central human concern, philosophers have thought and written a great deal about education and the questions surrounding it.

Philosophy begins with wonder.
—SOCRATES

Only a few people in our society are professional philosophers who earn their daily bread (usually a rather meager fare) by pursuing answers to the fundamental questions of life. However, all of us who wrestle with such questions as "Who am I?" and "What am I doing with my life?" are engaged in philosophical activity. Although there is a distinction between the few professional philosophers and the great number of us who are amateurs, the questions we ask and the answers we glean usually have a major impact on the practical affairs of our lives and on how we choose to spend our life force.

impact of philosophy on our lives

Sources of Our Philosophy

The very practical decision of whether to become a teacher, or a real estate broker, or a professional bungee jumper almost always has its roots in a person's philosophy of life. In developing a philosophy, we draw on many influences: our experiences in life, our religious views, and our reading of literature, history, and current events. A major difference between professionals and amateurs, however, lies in the precision of their methods.

factors that influence our philosophies

Philosophy is an extremely pure and abstract science. Philosophers work with neither test tubes nor white rats, use neither telescopes nor microscopes, and do not fly off to remote societies to observe the natives. The method or process of philosophers is questioning and reasoning; their product is *thought*.

The Philosopher's Method and Language

Basically, philosophers are concerned with the meanings of things and how to interpret those meanings. Therefore, they have an intense interest in the real meanings of words. Although some philosophical discussion and writing involves technical language, it generally uses "plain language," the ordinary language of people. However, philosophers try to be extremely clear and careful about their use of terms. They do not want their ultimate prey—meaning—to be lost in a thicket of fuzzy language.

Although philosophy appears to deal with simple issues in simple language, behind the philosophers' questions are raging debates about profound issues that can have far-reaching implications. For example, the question "What is a human?" hides other questions, such as "When—if ever—can a fetus be aborted?" and "What rights do severely disabled persons have?"

concern with meanings of words

There is only one subject matter for education and that is life in all its manifestations.

—Alfred North Whitehead

The Terrain of Philosophy

Philosophy covers a large amount of intellectual turf. The terrain of philosophy is divided into several areas, including four that are particularly important to the teacher: metaphysics, epistemology, axiology, and logic. These terms may be foreign to you, but we assure you that these four branches of philosophy are central to the educative process and, in fact, speak directly to the work of the teacher.

four branches of philosophy

Metaphysics

Metaphysics involves the attempt to explain the nature of the real world—the nature of existence. Metaphysics attempts to answer the question "What is real?" without relying on revealed religion, such as the Bible. Further, the metaphysician characteristically believes that it is not adequate to address fundamental matters, such as the nature of a human being or of the universe, simply by collecting data and formulating statistically significant generalizations. From most metaphysical perspectives, the true nature of a person cannot be captured by measuring or counting. A person is more than the sum of his or her height and weight, IQ and SAT scores, and other "vital" statistics.

what is real?

In probing the nature of reality, the metaphysician asks a whole array of questions: "Does life have meaning?" "Are human beings free or totally determined?" "Is there a purpose to life?" "Is there a set of enduring principles that guide the operation of the universe?" "Can these principles be known?" "Is there no such thing as stability—rather, is our world ever-changing?"

Metaphysics and the Curriculum   These abstract questions are ones that the educator cannot dismiss. Ultimately, the purpose of education is to explain reality to the young. The curriculum and how we teach it represent one statement of what that reality is. Although teachers may not actually be metaphysicians, they

teachers take metaphysical stands

Just as the inclusion of something in the curriculum signifies the value placed on it, exclusion bespeaks the culture's devaluation of it.

——*Jane Roland Martin*

do take a stand on metaphysical questions. If a teacher decides to teach because he or she believes the most important thing in the universe is a human mind, that career decision is driven by a metaphysical view: the importance of an individual person. The people on school boards also take stands on metaphysical issues. For example, whether or not a particular school system emphasizes vocational education or makes a major investment in educating individuals with severe mental disabilities depends very much on someone's decision about the nature of the person and the place of work in a person's life.

Epistemology

what is truth?

Epistemology deals with questions regarding knowledge and knowing. The epistemologist, seeking the true nature of knowing, asks such questions as "What is truth?" and "Is truth elusive, always changing and always dependent on the truth seeker's particulars of time, place, and angle of vision?" Some people, whom we call *skeptics,* question our capacity to ever really know the truths of existence. And some, whom we call *agnostics,* are convinced that knowledge of ultimate realities is an empty hope.

how do we acquire knowledge?

Epistemology deals not only with the nature of truth but also with the ways in which we can know reality. There are a variety of ways by which we can know, and each of these ways has its advocates and detractors. Among the ways of knowing are by divine revelation, by authority, through personal intuition, from our own five senses, from our own powers of reasoning, and through experimentation.

impact on teaching methods

Teaching and Ways of Knowing   Questions concerning knowledge and knowing are, almost by definition, of great concern to the teacher. The epistemological question "How do you know this or that?" goes to the heart of teaching methodology. If a teacher wants her students to have a concept of democracy, how does she proceed? Does she explain the characteristics of different forms of government, such as monarchy and oligarchy, and then the characteristics of democracy? Or does she take a more hands-on approach and have the students do a role-playing exercise during which one student is appointed class dictator and the rest must obey the student-dictator's orders? The student who has only read about democracy "knows" it in an *epistemologically* different way than a student who has been bullied and harassed for several days by a teacher-appointed dictator.

It is becoming increasingly clear, in fact, that individuals differ in their degree of comfort with different methods of learning. Much of the teacher's work, then, is helping the student find the most effective way of knowing. Even if the teacher is not very interested in these issues, other people are interested, and sometimes they want to know the teacher's viewpoint.

creationist controversy

For example, many people have strong beliefs about the true origin of humankind and how one knows it. This issue is sometimes called the *creationist controversy,* and it rests on a sharp and fundamental argument over the questions "Who are we?" and "How did we get here?" One faction insists that the public schools should present the evidence of our origin that is given in the Book of Gen-

For many students, outdoor experiences are the key to learning. (© Paul Conklin)

esis, which we know by divine revelation. Others insist that the way to know the origin of the human race is through the scientific theory of evolution. So behind this ongoing educational controversy is a fundamental question of epistemology.

Axiology

Axiology focuses on the nature of values. As human beings, we quite naturally search for the correct and most effective way to live. In doing so, we engage questions of values. Of course, often when different people look at life, they come up with very different sets of values. For instance, *hedonists* believe in seeking pleasure and living for the moment. On the other hand, *stoics* have an austere way of looking at life and seek to be unaffected by pleasure or pain. Many people regard values from a religious perspective, asserting that unless humanity and the rest of the natural world were originally created by God, existence as we know it is just the meaningless coming together of cosmic dust and debris. In this view, the only genuine values derive from God.

what values should we pursue?

Most people would agree with Socrates that schools have a dual responsibility: to make people smart and to make them good. To the degree that teachers accept the second function, they are grappling with an axiological issue. In fact, teachers are intimately involved with questions of moral values. Young people are seeking ways to live lives that are worthwhile, and teachers traditionally have been expected to help students establish moral values both as individuals and as contributing members of society. (See Chapters 12 and 13 for more discussion of this issue.) Moral values such as honesty, respect for other people, and fairness are necessary if we are to live together in harmony. But although a large core of values exists on which a majority of people agree, such as respecting others and avoiding violence in settling disputes, other value issues separate people. Sexual behavior, capital punishment, gun control, and

teachers and moral values

The function of education is to teach one to think intensively and to think critically. Intelligence plus character—that is the goal of true education.

—*Martin Luther King, Jr.*

abortion are examples of contemporary social issues that involve a wide range of viewpoints about what is right.

Ethics and Aesthetics   Axiology has two subtopics: ethics and aesthetics. **Ethics** takes us into the realm of values that relate to "good" and "bad" behavior, examining morality and rules of conduct. At one time, teaching children how to deal with issues of good/bad and right/wrong was the primary purpose of schooling. In recent decades the pendulum has swung the other way, and schools have been more concerned with factual knowledge and skills than with ethical knowledge. There are, however, many signs that schools are being called back to help children deal with ethical issues.[1]

issues of right and wrong

The subject of ethics not only teaches us how we can intellectually ascertain the "right" thing to do but also is often used to help us establish a particular set of standards, such as a code of ethics. In Chapter 12, we will give particular attention to these issues.

The second subtopic of axiology, **aesthetics,** deals with questions of values regarding beauty and art. Many discussions about the value of a particular film, book, or work of art are attempts to come to some aesthetic judgment on the value of the work. Whether or not a person "has good taste" is an example of a common aesthetic judgment.

issues of beauty

Logic

Logic is the branch of philosophy that deals with reasoning. One of the fundamental qualities that distinguishes human beings from brutes is that humans can *think*. Logic focuses on reasoning and modes of arguing that bring us to valid conclusions. The pursuit of logic is an attempt to think clearly and avoid vagueness and contradictions. Certain rules of logic have been identified, and they constitute the core of this branch of philosophy.

the human ability to think

Deductive Reasoning   A primary task of the schools is to help children think clearly and communicate logically. Two types of reasoning are commonly taught in schools: deductive and inductive. In **deductive reasoning,** the teacher presents a general proposition and then illustrates it with a series of particulars. The most highly developed form of this approach is the classic method of the syllogism. In a *syllogism,* one makes two statements, and a third statement, a conclusion, is *deduced* or drawn from them. For instance:

reasoning from general to particular

> All human beings are mortal.
> I am a human being.
> Therefore, I am mortal.

In deductive reasoning, such as in this example, the general proposition, an abstract concept, is followed by a factual statement, which in turn leads to a new factual statement and the creation of new knowledge, at least for the learner.

As another example, imagine that in October Mrs. Wells, a fifth-grade teacher, writes on the board:

All trees that shed their leaves at the end of a growing season are deciduous trees.

As a two-week project, Mrs. Wells asks her class to observe and record data about the trees that surround their school. For two weeks, the students observe the three dozen maple trees shedding their leaves during the fall. The teacher then writes her earlier sentence on the board again:

All trees that shed their leaves at the end of a growing season are deciduous trees.

And, using their observational data (and a little intellectual nudging from Mrs. Wells), the students complete the syllogism:

Maple trees shed their leaves at the end of the growing season.
Therefore, maple trees are deciduous.

Then the students try to identify other types of trees that fit the deciduous classification.

Much of what a teacher does in school is helping children both acquire the intellectual habits of deductive thinking and expand their storehouse of knowledge through this process.

Inductive Reasoning   **Inductive reasoning** works in the opposite fashion. The teacher sets forth particulars, from which a general proposition is derived or *induced.* For instance, the teacher may wish to lead the students to the discovery that water is essential to plant growth. He gives each child two similar plants (a different type, from weeds to flowers, for each child) and then has each student daily feed one plant with water and leave the other plant without water. After ten days the teacher has the students report the condition of their plants, and from all of these individual reports he leads the students to generalize about the necessity of water to plant life. In fact, they have derived or induced their answer.

reasoning from particular to general

One ongoing debate among educators is between advocates of deductive versus inductive teaching. As is true for most controversial issues, good cases can be made for both sides of the argument. Both forms of reasoning are needed. Both have different strengths and weaknesses. For instance, in the plant example, using induction to teach the simple concept "living plants need water" means a good deal of work for the teacher. But the rewards can be great: the student who has closely observed his pet petunia shrivel up and die will hold that concept in a special way.

need for both types of reasoning

Logic, however, is not confined to inductive and deductive reasoning. To use logic means to think clearly, in many different ways. Teachers need logic in many aspects of their work, from trying to understand the behavior of a child who seems to have an erratic learning pattern to developing tests that accurately measure what has been taught in a course. Most of all, teachers need to model this clear, logical thinking for students.

Overall, the four branches of philosophy—metaphysics, epistemology, axiology, and logic—address some of the major concerns of the teacher. The answers they suggest to the teacher and the implications they have for actual classroom practice are areas to which we now turn.

Schools of Educational Philosophy

Answers to the philosophical questions that pepper the preceding section have almost infinite variety. Over the years, however, certain answers by particular philosophers have received more attention and allegiance than others. These more enduring sets of answers or world views represent schools of philosophy. Some started with the early Greek philosophers and have grown and developed through the centuries. Other schools of thought are more recent and offer fresh, new formulations to ultimate questions.

Down through the centuries, philosophers have had a great deal to say about education, and their influences on schooling have been profound. In this section, we describe four philosophies that have had a major impact on education and demonstrate the variety of ways in which teaching and learning can be conceived. It is important to keep in mind, however, that many important philosophies relevant to education—such as neo-Thomism and classical Eastern thought—are not included here. In addition, there are major educational ideas that do not quite qualify as "philosophies" but are having a big impact on schools.

four philosophies influential in American education

The four philosophies we have selected for this chapter are perennialism, progressivism, essentialism, and existentialism. We have selected these not because they are our pick of the "Top Four Philosophical Hits" but because each viewpoint has been influential in educational thought and practice. For each of these philosophies, we present first a brief statement of the core ideas and then a "personal point of view" by a teacher (fictitious) who is committed to that particular philosophy. We have tried to show that these positions are not just windy abstractions or the preoccupations of ivory tower thinkers; rather, they shape what people teach and how they teach it.

Perennialism

nature is unchanging

Perennialism views nature and, in particular, human nature as constant, that is, as undergoing little change. Beneath the superficial differences from one century or decade to the next, the rules that govern the world and the characteristics that make up human nature stay the same. The perennialist, too, is quite comfortable with Aristotle's definition of human beings as rational animals. Education is crucial to perennialists because it develops a person's rationality and thus saves the person from being dominated by the instinctual or animal-like side of life. It is

Kevin and Jim's Guide to Developing Your Own Philosophy of Education

For many readers of this text, developing one's own philosophy of education must seem a daunting task. It is made even more demanding when one realizes that before one can develop a philosophy of education, one needs to do the groundwork of forming or adopting a particular philosophy: that is, one must have a general theory of how the world is put together, what laws regulate the universe and underlie all knowledge and reality. For younger readers in particular, who lack a great storehouse of experience and are relatively new to the world of ideas, the prospect of having to form a philosophy of education is unsettling. But that is as it should be. Something as fundamentally important as a person's basic understanding of reality should not come easily, like buying shoes or going for a walk.

Everyone, at some level, has a philosophy of life. It may be as crude as "Whatever makes me happy is therefore good" or as elaborate as a professional philosopher's own version of enlightened self-interest as the basis for improving the human species. But all philosophies of life ought to be something that individuals have worked out in their own minds and that they use to guide their interpretations of life and their decisions. Their philosophy is the lens through which they observe and interpret reality. As already mentioned, developing a philosophy of education is then a subset of having a guiding philosophy. It is the playing out of the educational implications of one's basic philosophy. But how does one develop a philosophy of education? Here are some suggestions you might consider:

1. Read this chapter carefully, thinking about what the terms mean and how they relate to the different schools of philosophy described. Realize, too, that this chapter is meant only as a door opener—a beginning.

2. As you read, "try on" the ideas. Look at the world through the lens or angle of vision of each philosophy, searching for the one or ones that best "fit" you. Once you have made a tentative decision, start integrating the chosen philosophy into your everyday life ("Well, if I really think 'Humans are alone in a hostile universe,' I ought to do X, Y, and Z"). Discuss your views with your classmates and your teachers. (Be careful, though, how you talk to your parents. From firsthand experience as parents, we can tell you that this topic can panic them!)

3. Take a philosophy course or two as part of your general or liberal education. This will give you a systematic exposure to philosophical thought. Also, it will give you a structured opportunity to explore your own thinking more carefully.

4. Think about how you would want your own child to be educated. Depending on whether you are an inductive or a deductive thinker (see pp. 328–329), start with the child and decide what and how you would want him or her to be taught, or start with your philosophical principles (for example, "Humans are rational beings") and deduce educational principles from them (for example, "The aim of schooling should be to develop a student's capacity for reasoning"). What would a school for your child be like? What would it emphasize? What would it de-emphasize?

5. As you take education courses and read education texts, ask yourself, "What is the teacher's or author's philosophy of education? What does he or she hold as most important? What is the underlying idea that is driving the point being made here?" (We acknowledge that this is difficult, but with practice this ability develops.)

6. As you observe in classrooms during your teacher education program (and even on your own campus), try to figure out what the teachers' philosophies of education are. If you can do it tactfully, ask them questions such as "What do you hope your students become?" "What would be an ideal outcome of your teaching?" "What is the most important thing students should be getting from their education?"

7. Think! (That's what philosophy is all about.)

Socrates *(469–399 B.C.)*

The ancient Greek philosopher Socrates was condemned to death for supposedly corrupting the youth of Athens. Today we know him primarily through the written "dialogues" of his student Plato. How much Plato's portrayal resembled the actual man is open to debate. Nevertheless, the Socrates of Plato's dialogues has had a deep and lasting influence on both philosophy and education, giving us such common terms as Socratic teaching, Socratic questioning, and the Socratic method. The following passage explains some of the basic tenets of Socrates' approach.

Socrates expressly denied that he was a teacher in the commonly accepted sense of that term. What he meant by this—at least in part—was that he was not a sophist, a professional pedagogue who, for a fee, would endeavor to transmit some knowledge that he possessed to someone who lacked it. Not only did Socrates charge no fees, he claimed not to have command of any such knowledge.

The learning that Socrates was concerned with simply didn't fit the information-transmission model of education implicit in the Athenian public mind and the teaching profession. Neither did his pioneering focus on virtue and wisdom square well with the popular attachment to honor, fame, and wealth. As he tries to explain at one point to Anytus in Plato's dialogue *Meno,* "we are inquiring whether the good men of today and of the past knew how to pass on to another the virtue they themselves pos-

sessed, or whether a man cannot pass it on or receive it from another." Since it was clear that wisdom and virtue could not simply be passed on from one person to another, Socrates sought an alternative way of conceptualizing how such excellences of mind and character were acquired. What was the teacher's role in that acquisition, if not simply being a supplier?

As an alternative to the receiving-knowledge-from-another model, Socrates proposed that learning was "recollection"—that is, a process akin to dredging up knowledge from one's own resources. "Teaching" on this model he later compared to acting as a "midwife"—assisting in the birth of knowledge *in* another person rather than serving as a supplier of it *to* another person. This was to be accomplished in conversation, mostly by skillful questioning and cross-examination ("Socratic teaching," "Socratic questioning," "Socratic method").

Socrates admitted to behaving like a "gadfly" in this dialectical pursuit of truth, goading people into serious thinking about human living. And he also confessed to acting like a benumbing "sting ray" or "torpedo fish," referring to his ability to render people tongue-tied about matters that they thought they already knew perfectly well—but actually didn't. Not until people felt the sting of not really knowing about life's really important matters could they be prompted to inquire into them seriously.

Source: Reprinted by permission of Steven S. Tigner.

---

the intellect, not the body or emotions or instincts, that sets a person apart from the beasts. To develop intellect means to learn how to dominate and direct instinctual and emotional energies toward higher, more rational purposes. Therefore, the nourishment of the intellect is believed to be the essential role of the school.

Perennialism in the Curriculum   For the perennialist, the intellect does not develop merely by contact with what is relevant or satisfying. The intellect is

An early introduction to the solar system: "We're the third rock from the sun!" (© David Young-Wolff/PhotoEdit)

nourished only by truth. Since truth resides in the nature of things, it is constant and changeless. Although our grasp of it is incomplete, truth is best revealed in the enduring classics of Western culture. Classical thought, then, should be emphasized as a subject matter in schools. Perennialists believe that schools should teach disciplined knowledge through the traditional subjects of history, language, mathematics, science, and the arts. Perennialists place particular emphasis on literature and the humanities because these subjects provide the greatest insight into the human condition. Although this view of the curriculum is evident in many areas of education, in its most complete form it is known as the "Great Books approach," developed by Robert Maynard Hutchins and Mortimer Adler. The Great Books, which constitute a shelf of volumes stretching from Homer's *Iliad* to Albert Einstein's *On the Electrodynamics of Moving Bodies,* are a perennialist's ideal curriculum.

"Great Books approach"

Since the early 1990s, a controversy has arisen over the content of literature, history, and philosophy courses. Scholars and students have criticized colleges and high schools for promoting a "Eurocentric" view of knowledge and culture, one that ignores the contributions of all but "dead, white, male writers and thinkers." They urge a more inclusive curriculum, one that gives greater attention to women, minorities, and Eastern, African, and Hispanic cultures. Whereas some take this movement as a direct attack on the perennialist's curriculum, others see it as a natural and useful extension of the perennialist's search for the best of the world's wisdom. One perennialist friend of ours, who welcomes this new approach, suggested, "Sure, students should know about Islamic literature and Eastern philosophy, but they should first get to know their own neighborhood, Western culture."

controversy about Eurocentrism

The Paideia Proposal   For the perennialist, then, immersion in these great works helps students reach the perennialist's goal, which is a state of human excellence that the ancients called *paideia*. This is a state not only of enlightenment but also of goodness. As such, it is a goal that perennialists believe all humans should seek.

approach of the Paideia Group

In the 1980s, Mortimer Adler and a group of educators breathed new life into perennialism with the publication of *The Paideia Proposal* and then a series of supporting books.[2] *The Paideia Proposal* presents this educational philosophy not as an austere, joyless curriculum, but as an exciting, involving intellectual and aesthetic journey. Several of the Paideia Group who worked with Adler in formulating this plan are both minority group members and superintendents of big-city school districts serving a large population of poor and minority students. Much of the appeal of *The Paideia Proposal* is that it asserts that *all* children, not just the gifted or the privileged children of the rich, should have this classical education. Members of the Paideia Group see it as providing both quality and equality in education. Although interest in *The Paideia Proposal* has faded somewhat in recent years, another curricular movement has attracted the interest of educators with perennialist leanings. Called the Core Knowledge program, this curriculum spells out in detail what students from kindergarten to eighth grade should know. Based on E. D. Hirsch Jr.'s book *Cultural Literacy,* this content-rich curriculum stresses academics and the learning of specific knowledge. However, because of the curriculum's emphasis on science and the currency of much of literature, it is hardly a pure perennialist curriculum. Currently the Core Knowledge curriculum is being used in over 1,100 schools, and its popularity is spreading rapidly.[3]

Core Knowledge program

Education as Preparation for Life   Education, then, is of great importance to perennialists, but it is an education that is rigorous and demanding. Perennialists hold that education should not attempt to imitate life or be lifelike; rather, education is preparation for life. Students should submit themselves to a disciplined search for the classical wisdom rather than try to discover what might seem to be personally meaningful.

disciplined book learning prepares for life

In summary, the perennialists' view is that one learns by encountering the great works and ideas of the past. It is a view that leans heavily on the authority of the collected wisdom of the past and looks to traditional thought to guide us in the present. Further, it sees education as protecting and conserving the best thought from the past. In this sense, the perennialist favors a very traditional or conservative ("conservative" as in *conserving* the best of the past) view of education. The next section presents the point of view of a more or less typical perennialist teacher.

PERSONAL POINT OF VIEW: A Perennialist Teacher

I came into education twelve years ago for two reasons. First, I was bothered by what I thought was all the nonsense in the curriculum and by all the time I and other students wasted in school. There was so much time given over to elective courses, many of which seemed to be little more than the teacher's hobby. There were so many dis-

electives as wasted time

cussions—discussions that seemed to go nowhere and seemed only vaguely to touch on the supposed content of the course. I often felt as if we were simply sharing our ignorance. My second reason for becoming a teacher is a more positive one. I am convinced that our society, our culture, has great ideas—ideas that have been behind our progress in the last 2,500 years. We need to share these ideas, to vigorously teach these ideas to the young.

Essentially, I see my job as passing on to the next generation, as effectively and forcefully as I can, the important truths: for instance, about human dignity and the capacity of people to do evil. That has always been the teacher's role until recent times, when we seem to have lost our way. I am convinced that a society that doesn't make the great ideas and the great thoughts the foundation of education is bound to fail. Nations and societies do falter and fall. The last fifty years have seen several formerly prominent nations slip to the wayside while other younger, more vigorous countries, like Singapore and Korea, have risen. I am convinced that most of those failed countries fell because of the inadequate education they provided. I am dedicated to the goal of not letting that happen here.

humans not inherently good

I think kids are just great. In fact, I've given my life to working with them. But I don't think it is fair to them or to me or to our country to allow them to set the rules, to decide what they want to learn, or to tell me how to teach it. Sure, I listen to them and try to find out where they are, but I make the decisions. My job is to teach; theirs is to learn. And in my classroom, those functions are quite clear. Really, students are too young to know what are the important things to learn. They simply don't know what they need to know. As a teacher, as a representative of the larger culture and of society, that's my responsibility. Turning that responsibility over to students or giving them a huge say in what is taught just strikes me as wrong.

teachers set the rules

I have another currently unpopular idea: I believe that students should be pushed. School should be very demanding, because life is very demanding. I'm not worried about their so-called self-esteem. Self-esteem is empty unless it is earned. It will come when they discipline themselves. All of us when we are young are lazy. We would much rather play than work. All of this trying to make school like play is just making it more difficult for students to acquire the self-discipline needed to take control of their lives. What schools are turning out right now—and it pains me to say this—are a lot of self-important, self-indulgent kids. And it's not their fault. It's our fault as teachers and parents.

self-discipline needed

And the answer is so simple! We just need to go back to the great ideas and achievements of the past and make them the focal point of education. Also, when we achieve this goal, the students don't mind working. The kids and the other teachers kid me about being a slave driver. I don't really pay attention to that. But I do pay attention to the large number of students, both college bound and not college bound, who come back two or three years out of high school and tell me how much they value having been pushed, how glad they are that I put them in contact with the very best!

focus on great ideas of the past

Progressivism

Progressivism is a relatively young philosophy of education. It came to prominence in the 1920s through the work of John Dewey. The fact that this philosophy rather quickly had a major impact on American education almost guaranteed that it would become controversial.

nature is always changing

Progressivism views nature as being in flux, as ever changing. Therefore, knowledge must continually be redefined and rediscovered to keep up with that change. Whereas other philosophies see the mind as a jug to be filled with truth, or as a muscle that needs to be exercised and conditioned, the progressive views the mind as a problem solver. People are naturally exploring, inquiring entities. When faced with an obstacle, they will try to get around it. When faced with a question, they will try to find an answer.

emphasis on problem solving

The Student as Problem Solver   For the progressive, education aims to develop this problem-solving ability. The student should start with simple study projects and gradually learn more systematic ways to investigate until he or she has finally mastered the scientific method. Method is of great importance to the progressive. On the other hand, knowledge—formal, traditional knowledge—is not given the same honored place. For the progressive, there is really no special, sacrosanct knowledge. The value of knowledge resides in its ability to solve human problems.

Instruction begins when you, the teacher, learn from the learner, put yourself in his place so that you may understand what he is learning and the way he understands it.

— Søren Kierkegaard

Regarding the school curriculum, progressives believe that a student can learn problem-solving skills from electronics just as easily as from Latin, from agronomy just as well as from geometry. Progressive teachers often use traditional subject matter, but they use it differently from the way it is used in a traditional classroom. The problems students are trying to solve are of paramount importance. The subjects contribute primarily through providing methodologies to help solve the problems, but they also provide information that leads to solutions. The focus is on *how* to think rather than on *what* to think.

Learning how to learn from one another is an important educational goal. (© Elizabeth Crews)

John Dewey *(1859–1952)*

John Dewey, the founder of progressivism, is widely considered the single most influential figure in the history of American educational thought.

No prodigy as a child, Dewey attended public schools and the University of Vermont. As a graduate student in philosophy at Johns Hopkins University, he was deeply influenced by the thought of William James, the philosophical pragmatist. Dewey recognized the implications for education of James's argument that ideas are valuable only insofar as they help to solve human problems. Calling his own philosophy *instrumentalism* to emphasize the principle that ideas are instruments, Dewey argued that philosophy and education are identical, both involving the practical, experimental attempt to improve the human condition.

The public school curriculum in the nineteenth century was scholarly and classical, designed to improve the mind by equipping it with large doses of approved culture. Dewey denounced this curriculum as the invention of a parasitic leisure class totally unsuited to the demands of industrialized society. He claimed that the schools were divorced from life and that they failed to teach children how to *use* knowledge. The schools, he said, should teach children not what to think but how to think through a "continuous reconstruction of experience." In *Democracy and Education,* published in 1916, Dewey pointed out that Americans were being called on to make crucial political decisions unprecedented in history and that the schools offered no preparation for the responsibility of citizenship in a democracy. Dewey called for concentrated study of democratic processes as they are manifested in the units of political organization with which the child is familiar—the school, the local community, and the state government—in ascending order of complexity. But his most radical suggestion was that students be given the power to make decisions affecting life in the school in a democratic way. Participation in life, rather than preparation for it, he considered the watchword of an effective education.

In 1893, Dewey established an elementary school at the University of Chicago. It was experimental in two senses: in its use of experiment and inquiry as the method by which the children learned and in its role as a laboratory for the transformation of the schools. The activities and occupations of adult life served as the core of the curriculum and the model teaching method. Children began by studying and imitating simple domestic and industrial tasks. In later years they studied the historical development of industry, invention, group living, and nature. Dewey wrote that we must "make each one of our schools an embryonic community life, active with types of occupations that reflect the life of the larger society and permeated with the spirit of art, history, and science."

The late 1920s to the early 1940s, the era of progressive education, saw a massive attempt to implement Dewey's ideas, but the rigid manner in which they were interpreted led to remarkable extravagances in some progressive schools. For instance, some educators considered it useless to teach geography because maps changed so rapidly. The role of subject matter was gradually played down in progressive schools, replaced by a stress on method and process. The rationale was that it was more important to produce a "good citizen" than a person who was "educated" in the classical sense. Well into his nineties, Dewey fought vehemently against these corruptions of his views.

The centrality of John Dewey's thought to American education has waxed and waned over the years. Traditionally more popular in universities than in actual classroom practice, Dewey is often invoked by people attempting to make the schools more humanistic and the curriculum more relevant to the current world. Whether in favor or out, John Dewey represents the United States' most distinctive contribution to educational thought.

student's concerns most important

Progressive educators believe that the place to begin an education is with the student rather than with the subject matter. The teacher tries to identify what the student's concerns are and tries to shape those concerns into problem statements. The student's motivation to solve the problem is the key. The teacher then helps the student move from hunches about the solution to development of hypotheses and then to methods of testing those hypotheses. Rather than being a presenter of knowledge or a taskmaster, the teacher is an intellectual guide, a *facilitator* in the problem-solving process. Students are encouraged to be imaginative and resourceful in solving problems. They are directed to a variety of methods, from reading books and studying the traditional disciplines to performing experiments and analyzing data.

The School as Training Ground for Democracy   The progressive school has a unique atmosphere. It is not a storehouse of wisdom or a place with clearly defined roles and authority structures. Rather, the school is a small society in itself, a place where students are not only preparing for life but are also living it.

Teaching is itself a sort of political activism. We change lives. To take just three cases that come immediately to mind, activist teaching can help prepare a welfare mother for law school, turn a hockey player into a worker for environmental causes, or divert a young woman of color from her accounting major to a career as a teacher in inner-city schools.

—Nancy J. Holland

Progressive educators believe the school should be democratic in structure so that children can learn to live well in a democracy. Group activity and group problem solving are emphasized. This is one reason many teachers who describe themselves as progressive educators are enthusiastic about cooperative learning, the relatively new approach to classroom instruction discussed in Chapter 8.

Implicit in the progressive approach is the belief that children not only must learn to solve their own problems, but also must develop the view that they can and should be involved in the problems of their neighbors. Often, then, the problem-solving activities of the progressive school spill out into the community, dealing with issues like ecology and poverty. In this way, students learn an important principle of progressive education: knowledge should be used to redesign the world.

Even though it has been with us for more than seventy years, many see progressive education as a new philosophy of education for a new people. As opposed to most other philosophies, it is very American. It has no undue reverence for the past or for authority; rather, it is future oriented and practical. To judge your own sympathy for the progressive approach, see what you think of the following representative statement by a progressive educator.

PERSONAL POINT OF VIEW: A Progressive Educator

I'm a progressive educator and proud of it. I'm not ducking that label just because it is unpopular in many quarters these days, usually among people who don't really understand what it is. Quite honestly, for the life of me, I cannot understand how a teacher can be anything *but* a progressive educator.

Personal Point of View *(cont'd)*

I'm dedicated to a few simple and, I believe, obvious principles. For one thing, children come into the world with a very plastic nature, capable of being molded one way or another. We should therefore work to surround them with activities and opportunities that bring them in contact with good things. Also, by their nature, children are curious. Instead of rejecting their curiosities, I believe we should build on them. Schools should be exciting, involving places where students are caught up in interesting activities.

children molded by environment

I think that I'm a progressive educator because I have looked at my own experiences. I know I learn best when I'm trying to solve a puzzle or a problem that really interests me. And somehow I've always been able to get much more interested in how we're going to solve the problems of our own society than in the affairs of the Athenians and Spartans. I can get much more involved in a research problem about which DVD player gives the best value for the dollar than about some dry economic problem presented to me by a teacher. And I really don't think I'm different from the overwhelming majority of students.

learning through direct experience

I see many of my fellow teachers spending all their energy damming up student curiosity and imposing work on their students. And then the teachers wonder why they themselves are so tired or burned out. I'm sure it's quite tiring to try to convert children into file cabinets and to stuff facts into their heads all day.

One of the things that sets me apart is that I'm not so hung up as others are on what I call the "talky" curriculum. I am convinced that students learn most effectively by *doing,* by experiencing events and then reflecting on and making meaning out of what they have experienced. I think more science is learned on a nature walk than from the same time spent reading a textbook or hearing teacher explanations. I think students learn more abstract principles, such as democracy, from trying to set up and maintain a democratic society in their classroom than from a lot of learned lectures and dusty prose on the subject. I'm trying to get to their hearts and their heads. The traditional approach gets to neither place.

To me, life is a matter of solving problems. New times have new problems and demand new knowledge. I don't want my students to be ready for life in the eighteenth century. I want them to be effective, functioning, curious citizens of the twenty-first century. They are going to need to be able to develop solutions to fit new and unique problems. Although much knowledge is important, they need to realize that knowledge is only today's tentative explanation of how things work. Much of what we know now is incorrect and will have to be replaced.

focus on current and future problems

It's not that I think that ideas and content and the traditional subjects are worthless. Far from it. I teach much of the same material as other teachers. However, I get there by a different route. I let the issues and problems emerge and then give the students a chance to get answers and to solve problems. And, as they quickly learn, they have to know a great deal to solve some of the problems. Often they get themselves involved with some very advanced material. The only difference is that now they want to. Now they have the energy. And, boy, once they get going, do they have energy! No, it doesn't always work. I have students who coast, and I've had projects that failed. But I'd put my track record against those of my more traditional colleagues any day.

Essentialism

Essentialism is another uniquely American philosophy of education, but it has had more impact and meets with more favor outside the United States than does progressive educational thought. Essentialism, in fact, began in the 1930s and 1940s as a reaction to what were seen as the excesses of progressive education.

The Roots of Essentialism   **Essentialism** has its philosophical origins in two older philosophies and draws something from each. From *idealism,* it takes the view of the mind as the central tool for understanding reality and learning the essential ideas and knowledge that we need to live well. From *realism,* it takes the tenet that the mind learns through contact with the physical world; therefore, to know reality, we must learn to observe and measure the physical world accurately.

two origins: idealism and realism

The essentialists believe that there exists a critical core of information and skill that an educated person must have. Further, essentialists are convinced that the overwhelming number of children can and should learn this core of essential material. The school, then, should be organized to transmit this knowledge and skill as effectively as possible.

essential skills and knowledge to be learned

Essentialism begins to sound a good deal like perennialism. Although these two views have much in common, some important differences exist between them. For one thing, essentialists do not focus as intently on "truths" as do perennialists. They are less concerned with the classics as being the primary repository of worthwhile knowledge. They search for what will help a person live a productive life today, and if the current realities strongly suggest that students need to graduate from high school with computer literacy, the essentialist will find a place for this training in the curriculum. In this regard, essentialists are very practical. Whereas the perennialist will hold fast to the Great Books, the essentialist will make more room for scientific, technical, and even vocational emphases in the curriculum. Essentialists see themselves as valuing the past but not being captured by it.

beyond the classics

Essentialist Goals and Practices   For essentialists, the aim of education is to teach the young the essentials they need to live well in the modern world. To realize this goal, schools should focus on the established disciplines, which are the "containers" of organized knowledge. The elementary years should concentrate on the basics—the "three Rs" and the other foundational tools needed to gain access to the disciplined knowledge with which one begins to come in contact in high school.

established disciplines

Although there is some debate about what is "essential" in the curriculum, essentialists believe this is not a debate to which children can contribute fruitfully. Therefore, the role of the student is simply that of learner. The individual child's interests, motivations, and psychological states are not given much attention. Nor do essentialists hold fast to what they would call a "romantic" view of children as being naturally good. They see the students not as evil but as deficient and needing discipline and pressure to keep learning. School is viewed as a place where children come to learn what they need to know. Teachers are not guides but au-

student as learner, teacher as authority

This experiment will make an abstract principle more understandable.
(© Elizabeth Crews)

thorities. The student's job is to listen and learn. Given the imperfect state of the students, the teacher must be ingenious in finding ways to engage their imaginations and minds.

Both progressive and essentialist educators claim their particular approach is the true American philosophy of education. One can make a case that they both are, but each reflects different aspects of the American personality. Progressivism represents our antiauthoritarian, experimental, and visionary side; essentialism speaks to our more conservative, structured side. In recent years, many of the tensions and public debates in American education can be traced to struggles between these two philosophies of education. Clearly, though, essentialist educators gained ground on progressive educators in the 1980s and 1990s. Concerns over the country's global economic competitiveness and the perceived "softness" of our schools have created a receptive climate for essentialist views. The following section offers the perspective of a representative essentialist teacher.

> *If a man empties his purse into his head, no man can take it away from him. An investment in knowledge always pays the best interest.*
>
> —BENJAMIN FRANKLIN

PERSONAL POINT OF VIEW: An Essentialist Teacher

In my view, the world is filled with real problems, and the young people who leave school have to be ready to take up the challenge of life and solve those problems. So for me the watchword in education is *usefulness*. I think everything that is taught has to pass the test of whether or not it is useful. My job as a teacher is to find out what is useful and then to make sure the students learn it.

stress on usefulness

I believe that school should be relevant to the young. However, my view of what is relevant is very different from the views of lots of other people. For me, relevance is

Personal Point of View *(cont'd)*

selecting learning from the past

not what is personally "meaningful" or a "do-your-own-thing" approach. What is relevant is what helps the individual live well and what benefits humanity. For that we need to look very carefully at the past and sort out the most valuable learning. That is what should be taught and what should be learned. I find the back-to-the-classics approach quite valuable. However, most advocates go too far in concentrating on classics. They also stress the humanities and the arts a little too much and tend to underplay science and technology. If children are going to function in today's world, and if our world is going to solve all the problems it's confronted with, we have to give more attention to science and technology than we have in the past. But clearly the past is the place to begin our search for the relevant curriculum.

It's not the most pleasing or satisfying image, but I think the concept of the student as an empty jug is the most accurate one. Certainly kids come to school with lots of knowledge and lots of interests. However, the job of school is to teach them what they don't know and to teach these things in a systematic and organized way. It's not to fill their minds with isolated fragments of information but to fill them with systematic knowledge. They need tools to learn, and, as they get older, they need human insights and skills that come from the disciplines.

task orientation and discipline

Given that there is so much to learn, an emphasis on student "interests" and "projects" and "problem solving" is quite wasteful. There is plenty of time for that outside of school or when school is over. Inside the school, the teachers are the authorities, and the students are there to learn what they don't know. The environment should be task oriented and disciplined. It doesn't have to be oppressive or unjust or any of that. I tell my students that learning is not necessarily going to be fun, but that at the end of the year they will have a great sense of accomplishment. I'd take accomplishment over fun anytime. By and large, most students do too.

Existentialism

the ideas of Sartre

Modern existentialism was born amid the pain and disillusionment of World War II and the period immediately following it. Its founder, the French philosopher Jean-Paul Sartre, broke with previous thinkers by asserting that "existence" comes before "essence." Unlike most philosophers, who defined the nature of humans as rational animals, or problem solvers, or what-have-you and then went on to speak about existence, Sartre believed that our existence comes first, before any definition of what we are. It is up to us to define ourselves in some sort of relationship to that existence.

the existential moment

In other words, **existentialism** proposes that we should not accept any predetermined creed or philosophical system and from that try to define who we are. Instead, we must take personal responsibility for deciding who we are. The process of answering the question "Who are we?" has a start, but really has no ending. It begins at a very crucial event in the lives of young people, what Sartre called the *existential moment*—that point somewhere toward the end of youth when we realize for the first time that we exist as independent agents. Each of us is suddenly struck with the fact that *I am!* With that realization comes the existential question "Okay, I exist, but who am I and what should I do?"

Austere, European Existentialism   The European brand of existentialism tends to be a very austere philosophy. Its practitioners tend to reject all other philosophies. Although there is a vital school called Christian Existentialism, with roots in the work of the Danish minister-philosopher Søren Kierkegaard (some scholars claim Kierkegaard to be the true founder of modern existentialism), "mainline" existentialists reject God and the concept of a benevolent universe. They believe that we live an alien, meaningless existence on a small planet in an unimportant galaxy in an indifferent universe. Whatever meaning a person can make of life has to be his or her own. There is no ultimate meaning.

The only certainty for the existentialist is that we are free. This freedom, however, is wrapped up in a search for meaning. To the existentialist, we define ourselves—that is, we make meaning in our world—by the choices we make. In effect, we are what we choose—no more, no less. No God will throw us a life preserver. No circumstance will shade our responsibility. We are responsible for what we do and what we are.

freedom and responsibility

The one thing the individual can be sure of is death—the complete ending of any kind of existence. Existing in a meaningless world with no afterlife provides the ongoing tension in the existentialist's life. "Why struggle, why continue, if there is no hope?" It is in accepting this question, and the "death dread" buried in it, that the existentialist can gain dignity.

The American Version   Existentialism has affected American education in a somewhat softer version. The *meaningless universe* aspect is downplayed, and the *quest for personal meaning* is emphasized.

Existentialism has entered American education not under the flag of existentialism per se but under several different flags: for instance, the *human potential movement* of the 1960s and 1970s, which stressed the development of all aspects of the person, and an approach to moral education called *values clarification* in which each individual discovers his or her own values. In addition, existentialism's focus on the individual and his or her responsibilities is as American as the Fourth of July.

entrance into American education

Given the fact that by law our schools must be theologically neutral (they cannot advocate any religious creed or world view), there is, by default, an unanswered question about the meaning of existence. In a way, the existentialists' approach of finding meaning through a quest for self has filled this gap. Children are warned not to accept anyone else's answers or values but to search for their own. They learn that they should make their own choices and their own commitments in life rather than being told what they should choose and to what they should commit themselves.

Existentialism in the Classroom   As it exists in the classroom, existentialism is not a set of curricular materials. Rather, it is a point of view that influences all that the teacher teaches and how he or she teaches. It tries to engage the child in central questions of defining life. It attempts to help the child acknowledge his or her own freedom and accept the responsibility for that freedom. It aims to help

students define life for themselves

the child realize that the answers imposed from the outside may not be real answers. The only real answers are the ones that come from inside each person, that are authentically his or her own.

For this reason, the existentialist is against not only the heavy hand of authority but also the group emphasis in education. Homogeneous grouping, group projects, and pressures for social adjustment are always keeping from the child the ultimate truths: you are alone and you must make your own meaning. The group, or a social emphasis in the form and content of education, is an anesthetic that prevents perception of the ultimate nature of the way things are. On the other hand, content and activities that help the child confront his or her own freedom go to the essence of what school should be about. To get a better perspective on these views, consider the following account by an existentialist teacher.

individualized, not group, learning

PERSONAL POINT OF VIEW: An Existentialist Teacher

When I was in college, the last thing I thought I'd become was a teacher. I was really turned off by education—all of that fact cramming and mind bending. I still am quite negative about most of the education that is going on around me. I get along with most of my fellow teachers, and I guess I appear like them on the surface, but I look at the world in a very different way, and that makes some of them uneasy. They are busy trying to give the kids this dogma, that dogma—whether it's democracy or the scientific method. And nothing makes them quite so uptight as students seriously questioning what they have to say. Students who question to see if they have it right so they can get it right on the test are fine. But probing or challenging questions are signs that the students reject what they're getting, and that really makes teachers nervous.

dislike of conventional education

What I'm trying to do is get the kids to listen to their own rhythms. So much of their life is programmed from home, from television, from the crazy peer-group fads and the press of groupthink in the school. I'm trying to get them to break through all that. I want them to begin to find out who *they* are and what *they* feel and what *they* think. I want them to have authentic reactions to things and realize that those are the ones that are important, not what the world's authorities tell them is important. It sounds quite simple, but in fact it is very difficult. Kids find great security in not thinking. I guess we all do. It's so much easier to take someone else's answers and pretend they are ours. But that is just another form of slavery.

personal, authentic thinking

People sometimes call what I do a radical approach. But the aim of education has always been the examined life. Socrates said it long ago: "Know thyself." That's what I'm aiming at. This may sound like I have students look off into space and ask the question "Who am I?" Far from it. I try to get my students passionately involved in life. I try to get them to have peak experiences, whether from watching a sunrise or hearing a Mozart sonata. This often leads to their own insight. Also, they have a lot to learn about the way the world works, and they have lots of skills they have to learn. And I'm busy getting them ready to take on that task. What I don't do is spend a lot of time on all these grouping—or what I call leveling—activities. I let students know that they are

emphasis on involvement

Personal Point of View *(cont'd)*

individuals, and I have a very individualized instructional approach. My students spend a great deal of time on individual tasks, and they always go at their own rate.

If there is anything that I emphasize, it's managing their own freedom. They need to know that freedom is at the core of being a human being. I'm not talking about a "do-your-own-thing," pleasure-oriented freedom. I mean a freedom that fully embraces one's responsibility. The major message of school for me is that you've got lots of choices, but *you* are responsible for what you do with them. This is the reason I stress values clarification, an approach that helps students discover their own values and take the whole issue of values quite seriously.

values clarification

It may sound silly, but I found my educational philosophy at the back end of a car. A couple of years ago I was driving home from school, and at a red light I read the motto on a New Hampshire license plate ahead of me: "Live free or die." That's it. That's the whole ball game.

The Influence of Psychological Theories

Since early in the twentieth century, educational practice has been greatly influenced by the discipline of psychology. Psychology, the scientific study of the mind and human behavior, was a natural influence on the work of teachers, particularly with its focus on how we learn. Over the years, various schools of psychology have emerged, often having roots in particular philosophies. Some of these psychological theories have had a great deal to say to educators. Two in particular have had an impact on our schools: behaviorism and cognitive psychology.

Behaviorism: Conditioning Students or Setting Them Free?

The psychological theory of behavior modification or **behaviorism** is an educational approach that emerged directly from the pioneering research of the late B. F. Skinner. Behaviorists see learning as the learner's response to various stimuli (for example, sounds, words, people) present in the environment. Subscribing to the view that humans learn to act in specific ways based on either reward or punishment, the behaviorist teacher (1) uses clear objectives, spelled out in terms of the behaviors to be learned; (2) gives particular attention to the learning environment and what is rewarded and what is punished; and (3) closely monitors and gives the learner feedback on progress until the goal is achieved. In the 1960s and 1970s, many educators made behaviorism their dominant, organizing educational theory. However, this education movement was criticized as teacher dominated and causing teachers to treat students as passive objects to be conditioned. Nevertheless, behaviorism has made solid contributions to schooling, particularly in the areas of special education and classroom discipline. Further, behaviorist teachers counter the criticism of too much control of learning with the claim that their goal is to eventually put control of learning in their students' hands.

learning by rewards and punishments

Cognitive Psychology: Students as Makers of Meaning

Over the past twenty years, cognitive psychologists, drawing heavily on the trail-blazing research of Swiss psychologist Jean Piaget, have discovered a great deal about how people learn to think and solve problems. Their discoveries have tremendous implications for how teachers teach. One primary research finding is that knowledge cannot be *given* directly from the teacher to the learner, but must be *constructed by the learner* and *reconstructed* as new information becomes available. Instead of seeing students as partially full vessels waiting to be filled, teachers should conceive of their work as creating learning situations where students can build their own knowledge through an active learning process. This perspective, known as **constructivism,** has become so influential in education in recent years that we give it particular attention here.

knowledge constructed

> *Education is not filling a bucket, but lighting a fire.*
> —WILLIAM B. YEATS

Constructivists view individuals as having an aversion to disorder. They believe that we are all continually trying to sort things out, to find clues and patterns amid our impressions that will help us to make sense of the world around us. When we encounter something new—say, a strange sound in the night—we immediately attempt to fit it into the patterns or structures we already possess ("That's the midnight whistle of the Ole Ninety-Eight headin' down to New Orleans"). But when we discover that our constructed knowledge is incorrect or we encounter new information ("Uh-oh! The railroad retired that train two years ago!"), we search for new input from our senses, seeking different patterns and structures ("Maybe that noise was from the hot water boiler and it's about to explode," or "Maybe that creepy guy from the apartment down below is on my fire escape," or "Maybe I shouldn't read Stephen King before going to bed!"). New knowledge about ourselves or the world is constructed. If a teacher asks students to solve a problem about the angle of a triangle, they go through a similar process ("If angle A of a triangle is 35 degrees and angle C is 105 degrees, and I already know that a triangle contains 180 degrees, then angle B has got to be 40 degrees"). Thus, the students construct their answer.

the individual as meaning maker

Cognitive psychologists have also discovered that if learners are to retain new information and find it meaningful, it must be related to what the learners already know. These knowledge structure relationships are called *schemas*, or *schemata*, and change constantly as new information is taken in. Thus, real learning involves moving from the Trivial Pursuit or Jeopardy type of factual or declarative knowledge to use-oriented knowledge—in other words, from "knowing what" to "knowing how." To do this, learners must develop cognitive learning strategies for particular kinds of learning tasks; that is, they have to learn how to think through or go about solving problems.

Implications of Constructivism for Teachers   In the classroom, the constructivist teacher does four things: (1) actively involves students in real situations, (2) focuses on students' perceptions and points of view, (3) uses questions to provoke students' thoughts, and (4) places major value on the process of thought rather than on the answer or product. At heart, the constructivist teacher

POLICY MATTERS!

Standards: High Academic Achievement or Test-Driven Classrooms?

What's the Policy?

Back in January 1996, then president Bill Clinton spoke to the nation in these words: "I challenge every community, every school, and every state to adopt national standards of excellence, to measure whether schools are meeting those standards and to hold them accountable for results."[4] A movement in the 1980s and 1990s to establish national standards had failed. However, many states have since developed and adopted their own sets of standards for what students should know and be able to do.

How Does It Affect Teachers?

Standards are something of an educational two-edged sword. On the one hand, standards provide clarity. Teacher and students know what they are trying to accomplish, and therefore they can focus instruction and attention on achieving those standards (for instance, "At the end of second grade, students will be able to read at X level of proficiency; at the completion of tenth grade, students will have attained Y level of mathematical proficiency").

On the other hand, the focus of instruction often narrows, not to the larger concepts behind the standards but to the tests that claim to measure the standards. Scores on these tests become the criteria for students'—and, yes, the teacher's—success or failure. Given that fact of life, teachers may tend to rely on that infamous educational methodology, teaching-to-the-test.

What Are the Pros?

Supporters of educational standards have positive goals. The "standards movement," as it is called, is driven by the desire of parents and other taxpayers to have the outstanding schools the United States needs to maintain its position in the world.

Also, educators and others naturally desire to have clear targets and to know how well we are doing. Further, the standards movement has been energized by widely published reports of international studies of student achievement, studies that show American students with performance ranging from poor to mediocre.

What Are the Cons?

Philosophical disagreements seem to underlie many of the key objections to the use of standards. Standards, with their emphasis on mastering specific bodies of knowledge that experts believe students should know, appear to emanate from perennialist or essentialist concepts of education. Perhaps because of these emphases, standards seem to work against teachers committed to progressive or constructivist methods of teaching. As discussed earlier, when teachers are under pressure for their students to meet standards of achievement, creative methods such as cooperative learning and projects often go by the board. Direct instruction becomes the rule, followed by much drill and practice. This may help to accomplish high test scores, but these short-term achievements may make education dull, uninspiring, and ultimately counterproductive. In other words, a legitimate public desire for better education may be fostering quite questionable educational practice.

What Do You Think?

1. Are you in favor of national educational standards? Why or why not?

2. Can you think of some effective ways to measure students' problem-solving abilities or the development of their own sense of meaning?

3. How does your philosophy of education influence your views on academic standards?

© Martha Campbell

behaves more like a coach. Such a teacher is interested primarily in helping the child engage problems and issues, search below the surface, try out various possible solutions or explanations, and finally construct his or her own meaning. Constructivist classrooms are active places with many opportunities for discovery and experimentation, often a heavy use of collaborative learning, and teachers who are fellow learners rather than fact givers and drill masters.

Critics of constructivism claim that its qualities of student-centered and self-constructed learning have led to declines in both academic achievement and classroom discipline. If this is true, it represents a poor application of constructivist principles, which are just now making their way into our classrooms. In contrast, we believe that constructivism is the linchpin to truly learning to learn, a key component to the school reform program we turn to in Chapter 13.

Your Philosophy of Education

At this point, you may well be confused and possibly discouraged. To expect to be able to understand and evaluate critically every aspect of each philosophy is to expect of yourself what few professional philosophers are able to do. What you have just finished reading is a précis of some of the major ideas of Western civilization (see Table 10.1 for a summary). Some of these ideas have been around for centuries, and some are the fruits of twentieth-century thinkers. Selecting the philosophy by which you will live and by which you will guide your professional activities takes much more investment of time, thought, and energy than reading our short chapter.

Some teachers, like the teacher-philosophers in this chapter, settle on one philosophical view, and that view structures all of their work. Other teachers lean strongly toward a particular philosophy, even if they may not be fully conscious of their position or be able to give it a proper philosophical label. Typically they have a particular view of the learner, of how the learner should be approached, and of what is most worth knowing.

However, few teachers are philosophical purists. Some teachers, recognizing that they draw ideas from various philosophies, label themselves *eclectics.* But what does it really mean to be an eclectic in contemporary education?

Eclecticism: Not an Excuse for Sloppy Thinking

Eclecticism embodies the idea that truth can be found anywhere and therefore people should select from various doctrines, systems, and sources. The eclectic teacher selects what he or she believes to be the most attractive features of several philosophies. For example, the teacher might take from existentialism a search for the authentic self and from essentialism a curricular viewpoint dominated by the criterion of usefulness.*

Eclecticism is quite popular, but often for the wrong reasons. It sometimes appears as the easy way out of philosophical uncertainty, just taking what you please from the philosophical cafeteria of ideas ("Let's see now: I think I'll begin with a light salad of existential questioning of authority and follow that up with a main course of progressive problem-solving projects, but with some hearty perennialist classics as side dishes. And, oh, yes—let's finish with a popular and tasty dessert of essentialist vocational training.") One problem with this approach is the possibility of inconsistency. To take one's view of society from the existentialist, who gives primacy to individual freedom, and one's teaching methodology from the progressivist, who stresses group membership and democratic process, is liable to make everyone confused. Selecting eclecticism cannot be an excuse for lazy thinking.

the lazy kind of eclecticism

On the other hand, most teachers feel quite free and justified in borrowing teaching methodologies and strategies that are associated with various philosophies of education. The ardent perennialist teacher may choose to involve his or her sixth-grade students in a "hands-on" project constructing a large topographical map of Odysseus's ten years' journey to his home after the fall of Troy. Conversely, the free-spirited existentialist teacher may insist that each student memorize and be able to recite fifty lines of *The Odyssey.* Although this type of eclecticism may, in a narrow sense, seem philosophically inconsistent, at its root

eclecticism as a real teaching strategy

---

*In the process of writing this chapter, we discovered that we are really traditional but progressive essentialists who are searching for a Great Books Club to join.

TABLE 10.1 Four Philosophies and Their Applications to Education

	Perennialism	Progressivism	Essentialism	Existentialism
Metaphysics: What is real? Does it have meaning?	Life has meaning in the context of the collective wisdom of Western culture.	Meaning is in the context of the individual, who is a "problem solver."	What is relevant is what helps an individual live well and what benefits humanity.	"Existence before essence." Reality is always in terms of our relationship to existence—no meaning outside ourselves.
Epistemology: Knowledge and knowing—what is truth?	Truth is changeless, revealed in classics of Western culture.	Truth must be known in the context of individual experience: Nature is ever changing—in flux. Learn how to learn.	Truth exists in the classics *and* modern science. Students must learn process *and* content.	No eternal truths. We are free to make our own meaning.
Axiology: Values, ethics, aesthetics	Changeless. Determined by the very nature of reality.	Determined by each individual in interaction with his or her culture.	Determined by the natural order of things. Values exist in the best of culture.	Determined by the individual. Stress on values clarification.
Logic: How we think, deductive and inductive	Rationality is developed by studying classics.	Emphasis is on inductive thinking and problem solving.	Western culture learned through hard work and regular exposure to essential knowledge.	The only real answers come from within.

is the recognition that no philosophy of education is able to dictate the ideal methodology or learning strategies for all situations or all students. Related to this is the growing realization (discussed in Chapter 4) that different students possess a great range of learning styles and that what works with one student may flop with another. In sum, eclecticism can be a serious philosophical position, and eclecticism in the selection of teaching strategies is quite justified. But, again, the choice to be "eclectic" should not be a substitute for thought.

Philosophy and Liberal Education

Coming to fully understand questions about the true nature of reality or the purpose of existence is a life's work. The great majority of this book's readers are in the college years, and we are not suggesting that you sit yourselves down, think

TABLE 10.1 Four Philosophies and Their Applications to Education *(cont'd)*

	Perennialism	Progressivism	Essentialism	Existentialism
The teacher	Passes on to next generation the accumulated wisdom of the past.	Develops problem-solving abilities. School is a small democracy. Helps children do what they want to do.	Teaches essential knowledge. School is where children come to learn what they need to know. Task oriented.	Helps the child confront his or her freedom. Stresses freedom and the responsibility to choose.
Teaching strategies	Cultivates rational powers through contact with the culture's best and through imitation.	Stimulates students to plan and carry out activities and research projects using group processes and democratic procedures. Teacher is facilitator and resource.	Avoids methodological frills and soft pedagogy and concentrates on sound, proven instructional methods. Teacher is expert.	Promotes freedom and responsibility. Teacher attempts to create a learning environment for students' self-definition.
The child	Is there to learn what is taught.	Is naturally good. Learns by doing and by discovering.	Is there to listen and learn.	Is alone and must make own meaning.
Curriculum	Based on materials reflecting universal and recurring themes that cultivate rationality.	Centered on students' interest in real problems and interdisciplinary solution seeking.	Strong emphasis on basic skills in elementary schools and on disciplined knowledge and scholastic achievement in secondary schools.	Subject matter, particularly liberal education, is a foundation for gaining personal freedom. Emphasizes humanities and the arts while de-emphasizing science.

Source: Adapted from a table suggested by James Hotchkiss. Used by permission of James Hotchkiss.

through all these issues, and come up with a tight set of philosophical answers that will last a lifetime. Rather, we hope that we have focused—or refocused—your attention on some of life's most critical questions and on some issues that are at the very core of teaching. In fact, the college years have always been considered a time of questioning and a time of testing the ideas that have been largely imposed on young people by their education and cultural milieu. The college years should be a time when the questions "What is a good life?" and "How do I live it?" are a major focus.

One purpose of the general education component of teacher education programs (that is, the courses in the arts and sciences required of the prospective

Identifying Your Own Philosophical Leanings

Think of your favorite teacher from elementary or secondary school, or a teacher you have admired during your teacher education. In the left-hand column below, or on a separate piece of paper, list some of that teacher's practices that you admire most. Include instructional techniques, classroom management strategies, ways of relating to the students—anything you think helped that person be an effective teacher.

Now, in the right-hand column, write the philosophical outlook that you think may have underlain each practice you admired. This will take some reflection, and you may well find that no single philosophy matches all the teaching characteristics you listed. Use whatever philosophical labels seem most appropriate.

After completing both columns, what general conclusions can you draw about the philosophy of this teacher you admire? Does your teacher reflect the tenets of a single educational philosophy discussed in this chapter? Or does she or he take an eclectic approach, drawing on different philosophical traditions? Are there ways in which this teacher is too unique to fit any category?

As a final step, reflect on what this tells you about your own philosophical leanings. If you hold this teacher in high regard, presumably you share at least some of his or her philosophical convictions. Is there anything that surprises you about the philosophical beliefs you have deduced? Do they suggest that you are more traditional or more progressive than you supposed? More child centered or subject matter centered? More nicely balanced, or just more muddled? What aspects of your own philosophical base do you need to think about further and clarify?

_____

_____

_____

_____

_____

opportunities to develop your philosophy

teacher) is to provide a chance for future teachers to think through these fundamental questions of human existence. A primary purpose of the college curriculum is to present the student with a spectrum of society's best thinkers and their attempts to understand their own existence. On the other hand, the infamous college bull sessions may be where the real philosophical inquiry goes on; they are frequently thinly veiled discussions of what really counts in life and what one should try to do with one's life. In effect, then, both the formal apparatus of college and its curriculum and the informal opportunities to meet, talk, and test your ideas with a variety of people should help you discover where you stand on some of these essential human questions.

A Final Word

As we said at the beginning of this chapter, the teacher who will be more than a technician has a special obligation to take philosophical issues and questions seriously. Teachers owe it to themselves and to their students to understand where they are going and why they are going there. On the other hand, teachers owe it to themselves to make sure that the schools they work in are hospitable—and certainly not hostile—to their own philosophies of education. It is important, therefore, that you be ready both to discuss your own philosophy of education with prospective employers and to inquire about the district's or school's philosophy. However, do not expect those interviewing you to be able to define their schools precisely according to the particular philosophies described in this chapter. Although educators live out a philosophy of education, we are not always able to capture it in words.

Education makes people easy to lead, but difficult to drive; easy to govern, but impossible to enslave.

——*Henry Brooks Adams*

KEY TERMS

philosophy (323)
metaphysics (325)
epistemology (326)
axiology (327)
ethics (328)
aesthetics (328)
logic (328)
deductive reasoning (328)

inductive reasoning (329)
perennialism (330)
progressivism (336)
essentialism (340)
existentialism (342)
behaviorism (345)
constructivism (346)

FOR REFLECTION

1. At the present time, where are you in your own evolution or development of a philosophy of education? At the beginning of the quest? Just tying up some loose details?

2. What role, if any, does religion play in your philosophy of education?

3. Why do superintendents and principals often ask teaching candidates about their philosophy of education?

4. With which of the four branches of philosophy mentioned in this chapter—metaphysics, epistemology, axiology, or logic—do you feel most at home? What do you believe are the implications of this philosophy for your own teaching?

5. At this point, which of the philosophies of education—perennialism, progressivism, essentialism, or existentialism—appeals to you most? Why? What do you see as the most telling argument against this philosophy of education?

FOR FURTHER INFORMATION

SEARCH

American Philosophical Association (APA). Web site at http://www.oxy.edu/ apa/apa.html.

This excellent web site provides basic information and reference material on many branches and schools of philosophy.

Fenstermacher, Gary D., and Jonas F. Soltis. *Approaches to Teaching.* **New York: Teachers College Press, 1986.**

This slim volume shows how two philosophers can unpack the term *teaching* and explain what is behind several different approaches to instruction.

Gaarder, Jostein. *Sophie's World: A Novel About the History of Philosophy.* **New York: Farrar, Straus and Giroux, 1994.**

This interesting and innovative book is an excellent introduction to philosophy and the history of ideas. The writer is clearly a marvelous teacher, plus a most engaging writer.

Gutek, Gerald L. *Historical and Philosophical Foundations of Education: A Biographical Introduction.* **2d ed. Upper Saddle River, NJ: Prentice-Hall/ Merrill, 1997.**

This textbook is a comprehensive and up-to-date account of the competing schools of educational philosophy and their application to schooling. It provides thumbnail sketches of key figures and leads the reader in investigating their thought.

11

What Is the History of American Education?

American schooling and education did not develop into our current system overnight. The system as we know it has its roots in the social, economic, political, and religious history of the nation. To understand our present educational system, its successes and failures, and the problems it still faces, we must look to our past. There we can identify the forces that have affected and continue to affect the development of American education. This chapter reviews the history of schooling and education in the United States, pointing out six important themes and examining the contributions that significant men and women have made.

This chapter emphasizes that

▶ Education in colonial America was originally religious in orientation but differed in form according to geographical area. Schooling in colonial America was not universal; it was primarily for white males.

▶ During the nineteenth century, influenced by the ideas of Thomas Jefferson and Benjamin Franklin and led by such reformers as Horace Mann, free public education became a reality. Common schools at the elementary level were tax supported and open to all children; the purpose was to cultivate a sense of American identity and loyalty.

▶ The nineteenth century also saw the development of public high schools that were designed to prepare young people, within a single institution, for either vocations or college; this goal of providing comprehensive educational opportunities was unique to American education.

▶ Private education has always played an important role in America, particularly in our nation's early days. Even today, about 11 percent of elementary and secondary school–age children attend private schools. Many private schools have a religious affiliation and thus offer alternatives to the public schools' secular emphasis.

▶ Equal educational opportunities for minorities and women have not always existed in America. Ethnic groups such as African Americans, Hispanic Americans, Native Americans, and Asian Americans, as well as women, have had to fight uphill battles to gain educational rights and treatment equal to those given to white males.

why study educational history?

Rare is the college student who feels a burning urgency to answer the question "What is the history of American education?" Unless you are a history buff, you will probably ask yourself, "Why do I need to know this stuff? How will it help me do a better job in the classroom?" In truth, knowing something about the history of American education probably will not directly affect your classroom practices. So why should you study this aspect of education?

First, understanding American educational history will give you a sense of perspective. As educators, we are sometimes accused of being faddist, which implies that we blindly follow each new approach or idea, thinking it is the greatest thing since sliced bread. On the other hand, we are sometimes accused of reinventing the wheel, spending a great deal of energy discovering something that has been in the educational literature for years or was a significant part of the education program of a different culture.

Second, although studying the history of American education will not give you answers to the immediate problems you are likely to face in your classes, it will enable you to better understand the culture and context in which you will work. It will help you obtain the "big picture" of why things operate as they do in today's schools.

Finally, studying the history of education will help you appreciate its truly noble heritage. Schools have been a progressive instrument in the lives of most people who have attended them. They have freed people from superstition and false information and have given them new skills, positive values, and world-expanding visions of what each individual, as well as what we as a people, can become. Some of the greatest people who have walked the earth—Socrates, Jesus, Gandhi, among others—saw themselves essentially as teachers. Teachers, then, are part of an old, progressive, and inspirational human endeavor. Knowing our educational history and gaining a historical perspective will help you live up to and extend this tradition.

Themes in American Education

Reading this book, surrounded by college classmates and friends, may seem a natural step in your educational career. Kindergarten or nursery school led to elementary school, then to middle school or junior high school, then to high school, and now college. You may have taken this progression for granted, assuming that's the way things have always been.

Actually, you are enjoying a level of education that was available only to the elite of earlier generations. You are already close to the top of an educational pyramid for which the foundation was laid almost 350 years ago. The growth of the pyramid has been shaped and energized by six major themes in American educational history:

six major themes

1. *Local control.* Originating in New England during colonial times, the concept of local control of schools spread during the nineteenth century with the common school district system. Because of a fear of a strong federal government, the framers of the United States Constitution made no reference to education. As a result, state governments assumed the role of educational authorities and then delegated substantial powers to local school boards. Not until the mid-twentieth century did the federal government really become involved in educational matters.

2. *Universal education.* Education for all children has been a developing theme in American education. In the colonial period, education was reserved for a small minority, mainly white males. During the nineteenth and twentieth centuries, children from various groups previously omitted from educational opportunity (girls, minorities, immigrants, people with disabilities) gained access to elementary and secondary education. Today a college education is generally available to all who actively seek it.

3. *Public education.* In the colonial period, education was generally private and primarily for the middle and upper classes. Nationhood brought not only the spread of publicly supported education but, by the early twentieth century, compulsory education as well. Nevertheless, private education remains a small but important part of the overall educational system.

4. *Comprehensive education.* The basic abilities to read, write, and do arithmetic were once sufficient to prepare most children for their adult roles in society. However, the growth of urban, industrial life in America during the nineteenth and early twentieth centuries also demanded that people be educated for work. The result was the comprehensive public high school, which includes both training for trades and preparation for college.

5. *Secular education.* In earliest colonial times, the purpose of education was religious training. Beginning in the eighteenth century and progressing through the twentieth, the function of American education became increasingly secular, concerned with producing socially responsible citizens. Religious study has remained mainly in the private sector.

6. *Changing ideas of the basics.* Literacy and classical learning were the main goals of colonial education, whereas practical skills for a pragmatic, democratic society were the aims of the nineteenth-century schools. Technical and scientific literacy became the basics in the computer- and space-age late twentieth century.

contemporary issues

Many contemporary educational issues have their roots in these six themes, which continue to shape the character of American schooling and education. Consider these examples of current issues:

▌ *Local control.* What should be the role of the federal government regarding education? Should national goals, standards, curriculum, and assessment for elementary and secondary schools be implemented?

▌ *Universal education.* How can we ensure the quality of education regardless of whether students live in wealthy or poor school districts?

▌ *Public education.* Should private schools receive public tax support via school vouchers?

▌ *Comprehensive education.* Should the schools require all students, vocational and college prep, to follow a common curriculum?

▌ *Secular education.* How should public schools treat the fact of religion in American society and world culture?

▌ *Changing ideas of the basics.* Is computer literacy a new "basic" of education, and, if so, how will schools finance programs that train students to use computers?

These are just a few of the issues facing today's policymakers. As you read the rest of this chapter, look for links between historical forces and the key topics and debates in contemporary education. This chapter's tour through history is not a dead-end journey into the past. What happened in earlier generations has had a great impact on the schooling you received and the system you will enter as a teacher.

Elementary Education

Colonial Origins

In the 1600s, some girls received elementary instruction, but formal colonial education was mainly for boys, particularly those of the middle and upper classes. Both girls and boys might have had some preliminary training in the *four Rs*—reading, 'riting, 'rithmetic, and religion—at home. Sometimes, for a small fee, a housewife offered to take in children, to whom she would teach a little reading

dame schools

and writing, basic prayers, and religious beliefs. In these **dame schools,** girls also learned some basic household skills, such as cooking and sewing. The dame schools often provided all the formal education some children, especially girls, ever received.

apprenticeships

Throughout the colonies, poor children were often apprenticed or indentured to local tradesmen or housewives. Apprenticeships lasted three to ten years, generally ending around age twenty-one for boys and eighteen for girls. During that time, an apprentice would learn the basic skills of a trade and might also be taught basic reading and writing, and perhaps arithmetic, as part of the contractual agreement.

Although the lines were not drawn hard and fast, the three geographic regions of the colonies developed different types of educational systems, which were shaped by each region's particular settlement patterns. New England colonists emphasized community-controlled, religiously oriented schools. Settlers in the South tended toward private education and tutors, with community schools seldom getting much support. The Middle Colonies saw the development of private venture and denominational schools.

New England Town and District Schools   In New England, the Puritans believed it was important that everyone be able to read the Bible and interpret its teachings. As early as 1642, Massachusetts passed a law requiring parents to educate their children. That law was strengthened in 1647 by the famous **Old Deluder Satan Act.** Because Satan assuredly would try to keep people from understanding the Scriptures, it was important that all children be taught how to read. Therefore, every town of fifty or more families was obligated to pay a man to teach reading and writing. With these schools, known as **town schools,** New England set the precedent that if parents would not or could not educate their children, the government was obligated to take on that responsibility.

Old Deluder Satan Act

town schools

When settlers spread out, seeking better farmland, the town schools began to disappear. What emerged in their place was the so-called *moving school,* a schoolmaster who traveled from village to village, holding sessions in each place for several months before moving on. One can imagine how much actual learning occurred under such circumstances!

moving schools

Discontent with this system of education led to the development of the **district school.** By this scheme, a township was divided into districts, each having its own school and master and funded by the town treasury. The theme of local control of schooling developed in these various kinds of schools. The district school system soon entrenched itself in New England, since it was inexpensive to finance and gave some measure of schooling to every child. Laws made attendance compulsory, but they were not very strongly enforced.

district schools

Some towns allowed girls to have one or two hours of instruction between 5:00 and 7:00 A.M., when boys were not using the school building. For the most part, however, girls had no access to the town elementary schools until after the American Revolution,[1] and if few girls went to school in the towns, even fewer did so in the outlying districts. The theme of universal education, which would include girls, was not to develop until the next century.

The town and district schools were unlike today's schools in many respects. The schools were usually crude, one-room buildings housing twenty or thirty students. The interiors typically were colorless and cold. Heating was such a problem that students usually had to provide firewood.

Students entered school around age six or seven and stayed in school for only three or four years. They learned their ABCs, numerals, and the Lord's Prayer from a *hornbook,* which consisted of a page that was laminated with a transpar-

New England Primer

ent material made from boiled-down cows' horns and then attached to a flat piece of wood. Having learned the basics, students graduated to the **New England Primer,** an illustrated book composed of religious texts and other readings. Although there were other primers and catechisms, the *New England Primer* was the most famous and remained the basic school text for at least one hundred years after the first edition of 1690.

dreary atmosphere

The learning atmosphere was repressive and grim. Students were under orders to keep quiet and do their work, and learning was characterized by an emphasis on memorization. Group instruction was almost unheard of; each child worked independently, one on ABCs, another on spelling, and another on the catechism. Class recitation was nonexistent. Instead, the master, sitting on a pulpit at the front of the room, called students up to recite to him one at a time.

Foolishness is bound up on the heart of the child; but the rod of correction shall drive it from him.

——New England Primer

If students did well, they were praised and given a new task. If they did poorly, they were criticized harshly and often given a rap across the knuckles or on the seat of the pants. It was believed that if children did not pay attention, that was simply a sign of how easily the devil could distract them from the path of righteousness. Such views continued to serve as a justification for severe classroom discipline throughout the first 250 years of American history.

Education in the South   Conditions in the South were quite different from those in New England. Many upper-class Englishmen emigrated to the South, where they established large estates. As opposed to the more centralized conditions in New England, the great distances between southern settlements encouraged plantation owners to educate their children with private tutors, who were often local ministers or itinerant scholars. In addition, most southern settlers were members of the Anglican church and did not share the Puritan belief that everyone had a religious obligation to learn to read.

private tutors

In the towns of the South, schools were established by governmental authority, but their administration was usually delegated to a group or corporation, which could collect tuition, own property, hire and fire teachers, and decide curriculum content. As in England, education of the poor and orphans was often undertaken by the Anglican church or by religious groups such as the Society for the Propagation of the Gospel in Foreign Parts. The lack of concern for general education of the entire community caused public education in the South to lag behind that in other sections of the country for many generations.

Education in the Middle Colonies   Unlike Puritan New England and the Anglican Southern Colonies, the Middle Colonies were composed of various religious and ethnic groups. Quakers, Catholics, Mennonites, Huguenots, Baptists, and others each wished to train their children in their respective faiths; Dutch, German, and Swedish settlers also wanted a separate education for their children. As a result, **private venture schools,** which were licensed by the civil government but not protected or financed by it, flourished, and the use of public funds to educate everyone's children did not become customary.

private venture schools

In these private schools, parents paid the teacher directly on a contractual basis. The instructor managed the school and curriculum, accepting or rejecting students as desired. The denominational schools in the Middle Colonies shared the New England concern for proper religious training as a primary goal, but they also began early to offer, in addition to the basics, practical subjects such as bookkeeping or navigation.

The Common School

Before the American Revolution, the term **common school** referred to schools that provided education for the average person, but it was not necessarily at public expense or available to all. The Revolution brought a new ideal of the common school that, like the Revolution itself, was nevertheless rooted in the colonial period. The early New England laws had already set the precedent that all children should be taught how to read and that the civil government had authority over education. This implied a communal obligation to provide **universal education,** that is, schooling for everyone.

emerging idea of common school

Even in colonial New England, it was the students' parents who had to pay for the schooling. In the first blush of the new republic, however, conditions began to favor the idea that some sort of elementary education should be provided free, at public expense and under public control, for everyone who could not afford or did not want private schooling. Even though the Constitution had relegated control of education to the states, the impetus for such public schooling came from the federal government, in particular as a result of the enactment of the **Northwest Ordinances** of 1785 and 1787. Concerned with the sale of public lands in the Northwest Territory (from present-day Ohio to Minnesota), Congress passed the Northwest Ordinance of 1785. Every township was divided into thirty-six sections, of which one was set aside for the maintenance of public schools. In the Ordinance of 1787, Congress reaffirmed that "religion, morality, and knowledge, being necessary to good government and the happiness of mankind, schools and the means of education shall forever be encouraged."[2]

Northwest Ordinances

Arguments for the Common School   After the American Revolution, it was recognized that a democratic government would be only as strong as the people's ability to make intelligent choices, which in turn depended on a basic education for all. It was also argued that education was a natural right, just like the very rights for which the Revolution had been fought. During this period, Benjamin Franklin and Thomas Jefferson suggested educational plans, as did other leaders of the Revolution.

The early period of independence saw an increased concern with citizenship and nationhood. The War of 1812, coming so soon after the Revolution, impressed on Americans the idea that their separate regional backgrounds had to be put aside if the new nation was to remain united and free. A system of common schooling would strengthen unity. Similarly, an influx of immigrants in the 1840s and 1850s, following a period of upheaval in Europe, further stimulated demand for an educational

If a nation expects to be ignorant and free, in a state of civilization, it expects what never was and will never be.

—THOMAS JEFFERSON

Noah Webster *(1758–1843)*

Although best remembered today for his *American Dictionary of the English Language,* first published in 1828, Noah Webster was best known in the nineteenth century for his *American Spelling Book* (also known as the *Blue-Backed Speller*). This small, blue-backed booklet appeared in 1783 and became the most widely used schoolbook during the early nineteenth century.

A native of Connecticut and a graduate of Yale University, Webster was a lawyer, schoolmaster, politician, and writer. His intellectual interests were extremely broad. He wrote a paper on epidemic and pestilential diseases, edited John Wingate's historical journal, wrote several scientific treatises, discoursed on banking and insurance, and, along the way, mastered twenty-six languages, including Sanskrit!

An intensely patriotic individual, Webster believed that America had to shed its British influence and develop its own sense of cultural identity and unity. The best way to do this, he believed, was to reshape English language and literature to reflect the unique American culture. The creation of an American language would bind the people together and help produce a strong sense of nationalism. His dictionary contained the first-time appearance of such American words as *plantation, hickory, presidential,* and *pecan.*

Webster knew that if Americans were to develop a sense of national identity and pride, the process should start at an early age. Accordingly, he wrote his blue-backed *American Spelling Book,* one of the most successful books ever written. Roughly 100 million copies were printed, and it is estimated that more than a billion readers used the book—a record surpassed only by the Bible. The *American Spelling Book* was often the only book schoolchildren had, since it served as a combination primer, reader, and speller. The book contained many moral stories and lessons, as well as word lists and guides to pronunciation. Webster must be credited with the fact that Americans differ from the British in writing *color* instead of *colour* and *center* instead of *centre.* Not only did he set the style for American spelling, but he made it the liveliest subject in the classroom. Spelling bees and other spelling games brightened up otherwise typically dull instruction.

Known as the "schoolmaster of the republic," Noah Webster campaigned for free schools for both boys and girls in which children could learn the virtues of liberty, just laws, patriotism, hard work, and morality. He was an educational statesman whose work, more than anyone else's, helped to create a sense of American language and national culture.

system that would serve to "Americanize" the waves of foreigners and keep society stable.

In contrast to European social structure, class membership in America was rather fluid: wealth and social status in this country depended less on the social class into which a person was born. Universal education, one of the key themes of American education, was thus seen by the newly evolving working class as a means of equalizing economic and social opportunities. As a result, another reason given for spreading educational opportunity was that better-educated people would increase productivity and enhance everyone's prosperity while diminishing crime and reducing poverty.

Whereas the *New England Primer* reflected the religious orientation of much colonial education, the textbooks of the nineteenth century began a trend toward secular education (another of the six major themes in the history of American education), emphasizing morality and Americanism. No other book was more popular than the six-volume series of **McGuffey Readers,** which sold more than 100 million copies between 1836 and 1906. Besides training students in (American) English language and grammar, these texts introduced poetry and the writings of statesmen, politicians, moralists, and religious leaders. "They assumed the Fatherhood of God, the brotherhood of man, the wickedness of war, crime, and inhumanity, and above all, they buttressed the concept of the sacredness of property and bulwarked the position of the middle class in society."[3]

McGuffey Readers

Although at this time universal education was meant only for whites, the same arguments advanced by its advocates were used later to extend universal education to include racial and ethnic minorities and children with disabilities, to name just a few groups that have been denied equal educational opportunities. The desegregation efforts of the 1950s and 1960s were based on these very arguments. (For further discussion of the issue of equal educational opportunity, see pages 155–159 in Chapter 5.)

The ladder was there, "from the gutter to the university," and for those stalwart enough to ascend it, the schools were a boon and a path out of poverty.

—DIANE RAVITCH

Arguments Against the Common School   As proper as these thoughts may sound to the modern ear, they often encountered opposition. The arguments against the public common school were based on economics as much as on educational or political principles: why should one family pay for the education of another's children? Many people believed that schooling, especially for the poor, should be the responsibility of religious groups. Still others thought that a free public school would gradually weaken or dilute the particular culture or religion that they had sought to establish in America. If ethnic groups mingled together, what would be the fate of each group's native culture and language? Similar concerns are reflected in the current controversies about multicultural and bilingual education, discussed in Chapter 4.

who pays for universal education?

And what was to be done about religious study? The ability of different religious groups to exist together in one school, as in democracy itself, demanded that no one religious group be favored over another. Although there were many competing proposals, the common schools finally settled on the teaching of basic moral values, such as honesty and sincerity, as a substitute for direct religious instruction. Today the same issues remain with us.

what about religious study?

Victory of the Common School   Between 1820 and 1920, the establishment of common schools made steady progress around the country. By the middle of the nineteenth century and certainly by the end of the Civil War, thanks in large part to the efforts of Horace Mann and other common school advocates, the ideal of universal elementary education was generally acknowledged, if not universally practiced. By 1930, eleven states and the District of Columbia had passed compulsory attendance laws in addition to making common schools generally available.

The Common School is the greatest discovery ever made by man.

—HORACE MANN

Horace Mann *(1796–1859)*

Horace Mann was the radical educational reformer of his day. Though trained as a lawyer, he became eminently successful as an educator and a politician. Asked why he had exchanged the practice of law for education, he answered that "the interests of a client are small compared with the interests of the next generation."

Born in Franklin, Massachusetts, Mann received only the most rudimentary schooling until he was fifteen. Most of his education was self-acquired, a fact that profoundly influenced his philosophy of education. He studied hard to be admitted to Brown University, where he became a brilliant student. In 1827, Mann was elected to the Massachusetts House of Representatives, and a luminous political career lay ahead of him, but he became committed instead to education and to the use of political methods to bring about educational reform.

Mann made it his aim to abolish the cruel floggings that were then routine in the public schools. Schoolmasters believed it their duty to drive the "devil" out of their students, and many schools administered from ten to twenty floggings a day. Most schoolkeepers believed flogging to be an aid to learning. Not only were students treated cruelly, but attendance at school was itself a punishment. Schools were often little better than hovels: the lighting was poor, and many buildings were unsanitary and unsafe. Mann criticized corporal punishment and inadequate facilities in public speeches, lectures, and letters, and lobbied for reform in the state legislature and in Congress.

Horace Mann strongly believed in the ideals of the common school and championed its cause throughout his career. He saw education as a tool of liberation by which the poor could raise themselves, African Americans could become emancipated, and children with disabilities could adjust to their handicaps. After all, Mann reasoned, education had brought him fame and position. Thus, over 150 years ago, the idea of social mobility through education was born in America.

For education to be as powerful a force as Mann envisioned it, he thought the school term must be lengthened and teachers' salaries raised. To make learning more relevant and enjoyable, he helped introduce new textbooks designed to illustrate the relationship between knowledge and the practical problems of society. Mann organized libraries in many schools, making books readily available to students. He believed less in the formal curriculum than in individual learning—undoubtedly because of his own self-education.

Mann was responsible for the establishment of the Massachusetts Board of Education and for the founding in 1839 of the first public *normal school* (a two-year school chiefly for the training of elementary teachers) in Lexington, Massachusetts. Although the normal school opened with only three students, the concept spread and was widely imitated throughout the country. Mann was intensely interested in teacher training, and he believed teachers should be intellectual, moral, and cultural models for their communities.

Many of Mann's ideas were controversial, but he was most violently denounced for his position on religion in the schools. Though a religious man, he believed religious training belonged outside the schools, which should be run by the state. Because of his views, Mann was attacked from many Boston pulpits.

Mann was regarded as a dreamer and a visionary by many of his colleagues. When he took over the presidency of Antioch College in 1852, opened its doors to all races and religious sects, and admitted women on an equal basis with men, some educators predicted that these measures would promote the collapse of higher education. Were he alive today, Mann might still be fighting for ideas he espoused more than a century ago. Many people have yet to accept these ideas.

As a result, between the Civil War and World War I, the number of students in schools grew enormously. In 1870, 57 percent of children between five and eighteen years old were enrolled in some form of schooling. By 1918, more than 75 percent of that age range were enrolled.[4] In 1870, average attendance was forty-five days a year; in 1918, it was more than ninety days. Thus, the hundred years between 1820 and 1920 saw extraordinary growth in the commitment to free, publicly supported, universal education. (See Table 11.1 for a summary of the different types of elementary schooling during our history.)

public school enrollment burgeons

Other Developments in Elementary Education

European Influences   From Europe came new ideas about education. One of the most far-reaching experiments was the **kindergarten** ("children's garden"), where pleasant children's activities, such as songs and stories, were used to lay a foundation before formal education began. Friedrich Froebel of Germany developed the first kindergarten in 1837. In the kindergarten, play helped children express themselves to develop their unique physical, spiritual, emotional, and intellectual selves. The first American experiments were actually made before the Civil War, but in 1873 a public school kindergarten was established in St. Louis, and the idea spread rapidly. Elizabeth Peabody brought Froebel's ideas to the United States and was influential in instituting early childhood education in our country.

Froebel's kindergartens

European influence also resulted in greater emphasis on the interests of the child in elementary education (see Table 11.2). Johann Pestalozzi modeled his educational doctrines in a Swiss experimental school at the beginning of the nineteenth century. Pestalozzi attempted to educate the heads, hearts, and hands of his pupils, relying on attitudes of acceptance and love of the individual student to reach large numbers of poor and handicapped children. Among his instructional techniques were *object lessons,* lessons that focused on actual objects and pictures. He also emphasized learning through sense perceptions and sequencing of learning experiences from the known to the unknown.

Pestalozzi

German educator Johann Friedrich Herbart, influenced by Pestalozzi's thinking, stressed that the primary purpose of education was moral development. For Herbart, the goal of education was to develop cultured human beings guided by the highest ethical principles. Herbart also established a highly structured mode of teaching, thus creating a methodology of teaching that strongly influenced American teachers during the early part of the twentieth century.

Herbart

European thinkers, and American educators influenced by them, believed students could learn best by direct experience, by using their senses and relating new learning to their previous knowledge. As a result, some schools incorporated a lot of physical activity and manual training in their curricula. This innovation was designed not to train technical workers but to complement and round out traditional intellectual instruction. Maria Montessori (profiled in Chapter 5) was particularly influential in developing a curriculum that emphasized learning through the senses for young children.

Montessori

TABLE 11.1   Types of Elementary Schooling

Type of School	Location	Time Period	Purpose
Dame school	Most of the colonies	Seventeenth century	Private school held in housewife's home; taught basic reading, spelling, and religious doctrines
Town school	New England	Seventeenth and part of eighteenth century	Locally controlled institution, public but not free; simple curriculum of reading, writing, catechism, and arithmetic
Moving school	New England	Eighteenth century	Provided schooling for communities spread out over wide areas; an itinerant teacher moved from village to village
District school	Primarily New England	Mid-eighteenth to mid-nineteenth century	Replaced town and moving schools; public but not free; each district hired its own schoolmaster, again with emphasis on basic skills
Private tutoring	Primarily the South	Seventeenth to early nineteenth century	For children of wealthy
Private venture school	Primarily Middle Colonies, but widespread	Eighteenth and nineteenth centuries	Private schools, offering whatever subjects the schoolmaster chose and parents wanted for their children
Common school	New England, Middle Colonies, and the South at first; now universal	1830 to present	Provided free, public, locally controlled elementary schooling; curriculum emphasized basic skills, moral education, and citizenship
Kindergarten	Widespread	1855 to present	Emphasized play and constructive activities as preparation for elementary school

The thoughts of Froebel, Pestalozzi, Herbart, and Montessori, among others, entered American education through their influence on issues of curriculum and instruction. The emphasis on the child's interest and experience, advocated by the progressive educators (described in this chapter and in Chapter 10) and still strong in American elementary education, owes much to these European thinkers.

Curriculum Changes   During the colonial period, it was hardly necessary for one to know anything beyond the four Rs unless one was wealthy and wanted to go on to college. In the early and mid-nineteenth century, the common school curriculum simply expanded on the traditional curriculum. The primary concern was less with religious training and more with obtaining functional knowledge *less religious training* for life after school. Subjects such as spelling, geography, history, and government were added because they were considered important for good citizenship. Natural science, physical training, and mechanical drawing were also included to provide a complete, well-rounded education. The movement toward comprehensive education is one of the key themes of the history of American education.

Consolidation   The growth of school enrollments, especially outside the cities, would not have been possible without the consolidation of smaller school dis- *merging of districts* tricts into larger, unified systems. Although the one-room school had served well in the days of the frontier, as areas developed it became clear that the smaller, poorer districts could not provide the educational opportunities available in larger, wealthier ones. In 1910, more than half the states allowed such unification. By the 1920s, the growth of industry and the invention of the automobile (and the school bus) had helped consolidate the large number of one-room schools around the country into centrally located, modern facilities that could serve larger areas better than the old district schools.

The Progressive Education Association   John Dewey (who is discussed more fully in Chapter 10) and other educators tried to create new, experimental, child-centered schools in the early 1900s. In 1919, the establishment of the Progressive Education Association was a formalized attempt to reform education according to the following principles: *progressive principles*

1. The child should have freedom to develop naturally.

2. Natural interest is the best motive for work.

3. The teacher is a guide, not a taskmaster.

4. A student's development must be measured scientifically, not just by grades.

5. Students' general health and physical development require attention.

6. The school and the home must work together to meet children's needs.

7. The progressive school should be a leader in trying new educational ideas.[5]

TABLE 11.2   Major European Educational Thinkers

Name	Dates	Major Contributions
John Comenius (Czech)	1592–1670	Emphasized sensory experience in learning Materials and instruction should be based on developmental stages of child growth Developed textbooks that were among the first to contain illustrations Stressed that schools should be joyful and pleasant places
John Locke (English)	1632–1704	Believed we acquire knowledge of world through our senses Pioneer of the inductive, or scientific, method Recommended utilitarian and practical learning in a slow, gradual process
Johann Pestalozzi (Swiss)	1747–1827	Stressed the importance of children learning through their senses and concrete situations Advocated love and unconditional acceptance of children; schools should be like warm and loving homes
Johann Herbart (German)	1776–1841	Believed the chief aim of education was moral development Developed the concept of curriculum correlation—each subject should be taught so it relates to other subjects Believed history, geography, and literature were core subjects Developed Herbartian method of instruction: (1) preparation; (2) presentation; (3) association; (4) systematization; and (5) application
Friedrich Froebel (German)	1782–1852	Introduced the kindergarten, or "child's garden," whose goal was the cultivation of the child's self-development, self-activity, and socialization Believed the teacher should be a model of human dignity and cultural values Songs, stories, and games stimulated the child's imagination and transmitted the culture
Maria Montessori (Italian)	1870–1952	Established preschools run on the principle of allowing children freedom within a carefully designed environment Curriculum focused on three types of experiences: practical, sensory, and formal studies Created learning materials designed to develop sensory and muscular coordination Required considerable training of teachers to implement the structured curriculum

The progressive school movement eventually went in several different directions. Some educators argued for letting children be free to do whatever they wanted; others tried to make the school into a community center for recreation, adult education, and even social reform. Critics ranged from traditionalist advocates of the subject-centered curriculum to some progressives, like Dewey himself, who argued that the ties between society and the child would be broken if children were granted total freedom to do whatever they wanted.

The 1940s brought a rather conservative reaction to the progressivism of the previous generation. However, it is good to remember that many ideas we take for granted now—such as teaching through student projects, fieldtrips, and non-lecture methods of instruction—were hotly debated innovations that were introduced by progressive educators.

influence of progressives

Since World War II   After World War II, the role of the United States in world affairs increased tremendously, thus broadening the scope of educational objectives. The use of the single textbook was supplemented by a great variety of learning resources. Other major developments in elementary education included the rapid increase in kindergartens and an emphasis on providing special educational programs for children with disabilities. Between 1948 and 1953, the number of schools offering special education services increased by 83 percent, and enrollments in kindergartens in public schools increased from 595,000 in 1939–40 to 1,474,000 in 1953–54.[6]

special education receives attention

During the 1950s and 1960s, with the stimulus of the Soviet launching of the space satellite *Sputnik,* a number of national curriculum projects were developed and implemented in the elementary schools, particularly in mathematics, science, and social studies.

new curriculum projects

Also during this period, two types of students received major attention from elementary school educators: the gifted and the disadvantaged. Gifted students received attention because of our nation's concern over the Cold War with the Soviet Union and our perceived need to produce scientific breakthroughs to ensure our military superiority over the Soviets. As the movement for civil and human rights gained momentum, more and more curriculum reform movements also focused on the "culturally disadvantaged" child. In response to judicial decisions and to protests by minority groups, the federal government advanced significant financial aid to change schools to better address the needs of these children. Compensatory education programs, such as Head Start and Title I of the Elementary and Secondary Education Act, improved the learning of disadvantaged children. (See Chapter 9 for more details on compensatory education programs.)

education of gifted and disadvantaged

As achievement test and SAT test scores declined during the 1970s, many parents, politicians, and educators argued that the schools had tried to accomplish too much and had lost sight of their basic purposes. A return to the basics seemed to be the cry of the late 1970s and early 1980s. Today academic rigor continues to be emphasized, but more programs have been developed to meet the needs of students who are at risk for dropping out.

back to the basics

Although a public elementary school education is now available universally, the issues of what constitutes a proper education—how comprehensive it should be, how secular it should remain, and how basic learning should be defined—are far from resolved. The changing nature of what constitutes the basics of education has been another one of the key themes of the history of American education.

Secondary Education

four types of secondary institutions

In the history of American secondary education, there have been four major institutions. The first type of secondary school, prevalent in the early colonial period, was the *Latin grammar school,* whose main purpose was to prepare students for college. The *English grammar school,* established in the latter half of the colonial period, was intended to provide a practical alternative education for students who were not interested in college. The third type of school, which flowered in the early national period, was the *academy.* Although its major purpose was to combine the best of both types of grammar schools, the academy gradually took on a college-oriented direction in the nineteenth century. Finally, evolving naturally from the elementary common school, the *public comprehensive high school* became the predominant form of secondary education in America in the twentieth century. A uniquely American institution, the comprehensive high school provides, within a single institution, both preparation for college and a vocational education for students not going on to college. Table 11.3 summarizes these four types of secondary school, together with the modern junior high and middle school.

Early Forms

Latin Grammar Schools   In the colonial period, all secondary education (that is, all education beyond the elementary level) served the sole purpose of training for entrance to college. The earliest secondary institution was the **Latin grammar school,** whose name gradually came to mean "college preparatory school." The term *prep school* still carries that classical connotation today.

emphasis on classical education

A boy entered a Latin grammar school around age seven or eight and spent the next seven years learning Latin texts written by ancient Romans or medieval scholars. Much work was memorized, and over three or four years the student learned composition and writing of Latin verses. Following this, the student studied Greek, moving in the final year to classical Greek writers and the New Testament. He also might have given some attention to the study of the Hebrew language.

The first Latin grammar school in the colonies is generally considered to have been established in 1635 in Boston. It was public, open to boys of all social classes. The Old Deluder Satan Act of 1647, which required communities of fifty or more families to establish elementary schools, also required communities of one hundred or more families to establish Latin schools. At first, Latin grammar schools were found primarily in New England; a bit later they were instituted in the Middle Colonies. Wealthy families in the South generally either hired tutors or sent their sons back to England for college preparation.

TABLE 11.3   Types of Secondary Schooling

Type of School	Location	Time Period	Purpose
Latin grammar schools	New England, Middle Colonies; a few in the South	Seventeenth and eighteenth centuries	Emphasized Latin and classical studies; designed to prepare young men for college
English grammar schools	Middle Colonies, New England; a few in the South	Eighteenth century	Private secondary schools designed to provide practical rather than college preparatory studies
Academies	Middle Colonies, New England; a few in the South	Eighteenth and nineteenth centuries	Private secondary schools designed to prepare young people for business and life; emphasized a practical curriculum, but gradually shifted back to college preparation
High schools	New England, Middle Colonies at first; now universal	1821 to present	Provided public secondary schooling; combined functions of Latin grammar schools and academies (college preparation and preparation for life and business)
Junior high schools	First in California; now universal	1909 to present	Designed to provide students in grades 7–9 with better preparation for high school
Middle schools	Universal	1950 to present	Designed to meet the unique needs of preadolescents, usually grades 6–8; an alternative to junior high schools

Alternative Forms of College Preparation   During the colonial period, many students (especially in the South) received their secondary education from tutors or at private venture schools, which were more common in the Middle Colonies. Instruction provided by a single schoolmaster obviously lacked variety and dependability. Gradually, corporate schools were developed; these institutions were governed by a board of trustees or directors and were able to continue as a corporate endeavor beyond the tenure of any particular teacher.

corporate schools

English Grammar Schools   The growth of middle-class businesses in the 1700s led to the demand for a secondary education that would provide practical instruction in everything from navigation and engineering to bookkeeping and foreign languages. Thus there arose private **English grammar schools,** which catered to the growing number of students who needed more than elementary instruction but were not interested in preparing for college. Classes were offered at various times and places, sometimes to girls as well as to boys. Commercial rather than religious subjects were taught. Some subjects, such as music, art, and dancing, were actually not practical but were meant to train students for socializing in polite company.

commercial subjects

Secondary Education for Females   In the 1700s, private venture English grammar schools were more flexible than the Latin grammar schools and, as a result, were the first secondary institutions to accept female students. Depending on the sophistication of the particular school and the preferences of its clientele, girls typically studied the three Rs, geography, and French, but they also sometimes learned English grammar, history, and Latin. Some practical vocational subjects such as bookkeeping were occasionally taught along with such traditional and socially accepted skills as art and instrumental music.

greater opportunities for girls

Because of the somewhat larger number of private venture schools in the Middle Colonies, girls who lived there probably had greater educational opportunity than girls elsewhere. Quaker leaders, including William Penn and French-born Anthony Benezet, were concerned with and supported the education of several deprived groups, such as African Americans and Native Americans—and women.

In the South, the daughters of wealthy landowners could receive traditional instruction in the various arts and letters, such as music, dancing, and French, which would give them the social skills appropriate for the lady of a household. By the end of the colonial period, there was a double-track education that was as clearly set for middle- or upper-class girls as it was for boys in the English or Latin grammar schools.

The Academy

A new type of secondary school grew up during the second half of the eighteenth century. The **academy** was an attempt to combine Latin and English grammar schools through separate Latin and English departments within one school. Academies were unlike the Latin grammar schools in that the primary language of the academy was English; they were unlike the English grammar schools in that they included classical subjects in the curriculum. Gradually the academy took the place of both types of school.

Growth of Academies   The number of private academies grew rapidly after the American Revolution in response to the growing need for practical business training. Around 1850, about 6,000 academies were in operation.[7] Compared with the Latin grammar schools, the academies included instruction for a larger age range, which on the low end overlapped the curriculum of the common schools and on the upper end sometimes provided instruction that was as extensive as that of colleges. Although academies first focused on practical, useful studies rather than on college preparatory courses, over the years the emphasis shifted back to the classical languages and curriculum. Because they were private institutions, the academies were also at greater liberty to accept girls.

emphasis on practical studies

Female Academies   The real surge of development in education for girls and young women came in the first half of the 1800s with the growth of academies and seminaries that were established especially for young women. Female academies were established by Emma Willard in Troy, New York (1821); by Catharine Beecher in Hartford, Connecticut (1828) (see Chapter 15 for a biographical sketch of Catharine Beecher); and by Mary Lyon in South Hadley, Massachusetts (1837). A secondary education acquired at one of these institutions was often the highest level of education women would ever receive. Eventually, some of these academies themselves became colleges.

surge in education for females

The female academies had to buck the established tradition against formal education for women, who in many quarters were still considered intellectually inferior to men. The schools compromised somewhat by offering courses related to home economics in addition to more classical subjects.

The availability of women teachers at low salaries during the late nineteenth century helped keep education costs down but, at the same time, contributed to the low salary problem that is still with us today. (CORBIS/The National Archives)

practical skills and teacher training

In practical terms, the leaders of the women's education movement were committed to two goals. One was to produce women who could handle the domestic chores and challenges of wives and mothers intelligently and wisely so as to "become companions rather than satellites of their husbands."[8] The curriculum of female academies therefore was designed to include subjects similar, but not identical, to those at men's institutions. Domestic skills were presented as practical applications of the more abstract traditional subjects. The other goal of women's education was to train women as teachers.

The Public High School

Although the private academies reflected the democratic independence of the middle class, their tuition and fees effectively cut out participation by the poorer working class. In the years following the American Revolution, the growing demand for free public elementary education understandably provided a basis on which to argue for free secondary education. Such schooling at public expense was the educational system most appropriate for democracy, it was argued, and the only system that could maintain democracy.

At the beginning of the 1800s, the appeal of the academies had been to provide training in studies that prepared students for a practical livelihood and not necessarily for college. By the 1840s, the same goal was being demanded of public high schools. Seen in retrospect, the academies were really a link between the earlier grammar school and the later high school.

early public high schools

In 1821, Boston created the first public English high school; a second one, for girls, was established in 1826. The number of public high schools throughout the states increased slowly but steadily as an extension of the common school system. Unlike the academies, high schools were governed by the public rather than by private school boards. Although by no means universally accepted, the argument for free public high schools was a logical one, based on the inequality of providing elementary schools for all and secondary schools only for those who could afford tuition.

a luxury or a right?

Opponents of the idea of public high schools did not dispute the need for common elementary schools. They did argue, though, that secondary school was a luxury and was not within the domain of the taxing authorities. In 1874, however, in the famous **Kalamazoo** case (*Stuart and Others* v. *School District No. 1 of the Village of Kalamazoo and Others*), the Michigan courts ruled that the school district could tax the public to support high schools as well as elementary schools. This court case set the precedent for financing public high schools.

multiple purposes

Debate over the Secondary Curriculum   In the late nineteenth century, debate shifted from whether public secondary schools should be supported to what the content of the curriculum should be. Guidelines for the curriculum were derived largely from the goals expressed for the schools. One goal was to reduce social tensions and strengthen the democratic form of government by bringing together all social classes and ethnic groups. Another goal was to provide better preparation for Americans to participate, upon graduation, in the full range of industrial occupations. In addition, the high schools were to offer specialized vocational and technical training. Finally, the high schools were supposed to provide both a terminal educational experience for most students and a bridge to higher education for those who were capable and chose to pursue further studies.

The Comprehensive High School   To meet these varied purposes, the secondary curriculum shifted considerably between the Civil War and World War I. The basic mathematics courses in arithmetic, geometry, and algebra tended to be taught in a more commercial and practical context. American literature began to compete with English literature, and commercial English was added to the study of literary English. The classical languages continued to give way to modern foreign languages. In the sciences, physiology, chemistry, physics, botany, and astronomy were joined by meteorology, zoology, forestry, agriculture, and geology. Physical education was added to the curriculum. In the social studies, the number of courses in American history grew, although European history continued to be central. Civics and citizenship were added to history. Moral philosophy fell away completely and was replaced by purely commercial courses such as typing, stenography, commercial law, home economics, industrial arts, and manual training.[9] The result was the institution known today as the **public comprehensive high school,** which embodies the notion of comprehensive education, another of the key themes of American education.

a more diverse curriculum

During the twentieth century, public comprehensive high schools continued to spread. Between 1890 and 1998, the number of students in public high schools increased as a percentage of all students attending public school from 1.6 percent to 36 percent.[10] This increase is shown graphically in Figure 11.1.

Growth of Junior High and Middle Schools

How to divide grade levels for elementary and secondary training was a widely debated issue for some time. The main question was when to stop teaching basic skills and start teaching content: should there be eight elementary grades and four of secondary school, or six elementary and six secondary, or some other arrangement?

In an attempt to resolve these issues, educators began to experiment with various ways to reorganize the grades. Finally, in the school year 1909–10, in both Columbus, Ohio, and Berkeley, California, a separate program was established for the intermediate grades seven, eight, and nine. The new grouping was called **junior high school.** By 1926, over 800 school systems had a six-three-three organization, and that pattern became the dominant one.[11]

first junior high schools

Since the 1960s, however, the system of five elementary–three intermediate–four secondary grades has become increasingly popular, with a **middle school** for grades six, seven, and eight rather than a junior high school. Advocates argue that middle schools have significant advantages over junior high schools. For one thing, they offer a unique environment where ten- to thirteen-year-olds are free to grow up at their own rates and where attention is focused on the needs of this age group rather than on mimicking the high school's emphasis on academic and sports competition, as is often the case with junior high schools. Because of the earlier onset of puberty in today's children, sixth-graders may be

arguments for middle schools

FIGURE 11.1   Enrollment in Public Elementary and Secondary Schools by Level, 1869–70 to 1998, with Projections to 2008

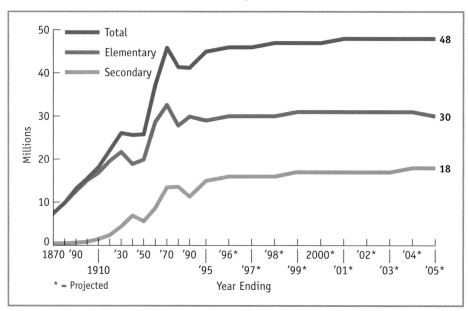

Sources: Thomas D. Snyder, ed., *120 Years of American Education: A Statistical Portrait* (Washington, DC: U.S. Department of Education, National Center for Education Statistics, 1993), p. 26; Debra E. Gerald and William J. Hussar, *Projections of Education Statistics to 2008* (Washington, DC: U.S. Department of Education, National Center for Education Statistics, 1998), Table 2: web site http://nces.ed.gov/pubs98/pj2008/p98t02.html.

better served in a school designed for early adolescents in grades six, seven, and eight than in an elementary school. And giving the ninth grade, which is still considered the first year in the college entrance sequence, to the high school frees middle schools to try new programs and new approaches without having to make them specifically applicable to college preparation.

emphasis on personal growth

Since the middle 1980s, there has been a deepening national commitment to the improvement of the education of early adolescents, with a strong emphasis on personal growth and development. To encourage this kind of personal growth, middle schools often use interdisciplinary team teaching, block scheduling, advisory home rooms, and exploratory activities and courses.

criticisms of middle schools

However, many education officials have become concerned about what they see as a lack of emphasis on academics in the middle school. The Third International Mathematics and Science Study (TIMSS), discussed in Chapter 8, revealed that while American fourth-graders outperform their counterparts in mathematics in all but seven other nations, by the time they reach eighth grade, pupils in twenty other nations do better than U.S. students. As a result of TIMSS and other standardized testing, some critics see the middle schools as having gone "soft," overemphasizing self-esteem building at the expense of academic rigor. These critics see the middle school curriculum as being unfocused, repetitive, and unchallenging. Some critics argue for doing away with middle schools and going to a K–8 elementary school and a 9–12 high school; others want to maintain the middle school but increase its academic focus. In the past, many states permitted teachers with either elementary or secondary teaching licenses to teach in middle school, but more of them are upping the academic coursework required of elementary school teachers who want to teach in middle schools in an effort to refocus the middle school curriculum on academic subject matter. Thirty-three states also offer teacher licenses specifically for middle school that focus on both adolescent development and academic subject-matter preparation.[12]

Middle schools continue to increase in proportion to junior highs. By the late 1990s, only a few more than 1,000 schools called themselves junior high schools, compared to 7,200 in 1968.[13] One researcher concludes, however, that despite the policy talk and incremental changes in curriculum, organization, and instruction, most middle schools, especially those in the cities, still resemble the junior high schools they were designed to replace.[14] These resemblances include departmentalization, teachers teaching separate subjects, teacher-centered instruction, students grouped by ability, and little interdisciplinary teaching. Though many schools exhibit the desired characteristics of a middle school, they are still not the majority.

how different are they?

Secondary Education Today

The most remarkable observation made about secondary education today is how little it has changed over the last one hundred years. There have been changes, of course, but they have been small relative to the changes that have occurred in American living patterns, values, technologies, and careers. The curriculum revolves around subjects that are taught by specialists and are not very different from the subjects offered in schools during World War I. As we pointed out in Chapter 8, instructional practices in high schools have changed very little from 1890 until the present day. Look at the pictures of the two secondary classrooms on this page, one taken in the late 1800s and one from today. In what ways are they similar? How are they different?

high school structure resists change

The reason lies in the basic structure of the high school. Its organizing framework, developed in the nineteenth century, persists today across all regions of the country. High schools are complicated organizations, requiring considerable orchestration to work efficiently. A change in one part of the system means that other parts must also change. As a result, relatively little change occurs. Chapter 13 examines recent efforts at structural or systemwide reform.

Private Education

Private schools have always been part of American education. Historically they have served three major purposes, providing (1) instruction for various religious denominations, (2) an exclusive education for the wealthy, and (3) an alternative for any group that finds the available forms of education unsatisfactory. For more than 150 years, until the growth of the common school movement in the early 1800s, most education in America was private.

Catholic school growth

Since the middle of the nineteenth century, by far the largest private school enrollments have been in parochial schools run by the Roman Catholic Church. The earliest Catholic schools existed primarily in the Spanish-speaking Southwest and in French-speaking Louisiana. After 1840, however, Irish and Italian immigration increased the support of Catholic institutions in the North and East. The total number of Catholic schools grew from about 100 in 1840 to about 3,000 in the 1880s, to 8,000 in 1920, and to over 13,000 in the early 1960s. From that point through the early 1980s, however, many Catholic schools closed. Today, the number of Catholic schools has stabilized at slightly more than 8,200.[15]

In terms of enrollment, Catholic schools now have a total student membership of about 2.5 million, compared with an estimated 1.7 million students in other religious schools and an estimated 770,000 in nonsectarian private schools.[16] The total enrollment for all private schools amounts to about 11 percent of all students in U.S. schools.[17] Chapter 14 offers more information about private schools in the context of job opportunities for teachers.

discrimination against private schools

The steady reduction in the percentage of private school students in the nineteenth and early twentieth centuries was not only a sign of public school strength; it also reflected outright discrimination and pressure against those who wanted to be "different." An extreme case followed World War I, when Nebraska passed a law prohibiting the teaching of German in either public or private schools. However, in 1922, the Supreme Court ruled that a state could not interfere with the prerogative of parents to educate their children as they see fit—in this case, at a private school that taught the German language—simply on the grounds of desiring to "foster a more homogeneous people with American ideals."[18] When, in 1925, an Oregon law required all children to attend public school, a Roman Catholic school and another private school successfully challenged the law on the grounds that their Fourteenth Amendment rights were being threatened.

still an important alternative

But if public schools have clearly become the principal mode of education in America, it is also significant that private education has remained an important alternative for about 10 to 15 percent of the population. This fact reflects a paradox. On the one hand, from the early days, private schools have represented the freedom of immigrant groups to pursue life in America and to educate their children as they choose. That privilege was essential to the young democracy and still represents a basic freedom of choice in America. On the other hand, some argue that private education supports a caste system that is, in principle, not democratic. The very existence of private forms of education can be viewed as an implied criticism either of the quality of public education or of its availability on equal terms to all comers, irrespective of class, religion, or race. As discussed in detail in Chapter 5, this issue has gained in importance as school voucher plans expand to include private and religious school options.

Education of Minorities

Before discussing the education of minorities, it is important to note that members of a minority group are often discussed as though they were a homogeneous subgroup of Americans. However, the terms *African Americans, Asian Americans, Hispanic Americans,* and *Native Americans* actually encompass many ethnic, national, and linguistic groups. Although it is convenient to use these broader terms, we should not forget that within each subgroup great diversity exists.

categories encompass many groups

The picture of American education we've drawn up till now has been quite rosy, because the educational achievements of this country over the past 350 years are indeed impressive. There is, however, a less pleasant side to the picture. The history of education provides insight into people's values in general, and the educational experience of minorities tends to reflect how a society relates to them. The somewhat idealized image of the melting pot begins to break down when we look at the experience of nonwhite groups.

Ethnic minorities such as African Americans, Hispanic Americans, Native Americans, and Asian Americans traditionally have not been given equal educational opportunity in America. Not until the late nineteenth century, for example, did the federal government make any serious effort to provide education for Native Americans. American society is still suffering today from the effects of educational neglect of various minority groups.

minorities excluded from equal educational opportunities

Education of African Americans

Before the Civil War   As is true of colonial education generally, the earliest motivation to educate African Americans was religious. In New England, as early as 1717, the Reverend Cotton Mather started an evening school for slaves. In the South, the first attempts to educate African Americans were carried out by clergy, particularly English representatives of the Society for the Propagation of the Gospel in Foreign Parts. To dubious slave owners, ministers defended the education of slaves not only as a religious duty to save their souls but also because conversion to Christianity, it was believed, would make them more docile.[19]

schools for free African Americans in North

Prejudices, it is well known, are most difficult to eradicate from the heart whose soil has never been loosened or fertilized by education; they grow there, firm as weeds among stones.

—CHARLOTTE BRONTË (JANE EYRE)

education for African Americans prohibited in South

In the North, schools were established for free African Americans. In 1731, Anthony Benezet, a French-born Quaker, started a school for slave and free African American children in Philadelphia. Another school was begun by Benjamin Franklin, as president of the Abolitionist Society, in 1774. In 1787, an African Free School was established in New York City with an enrollment of forty students, which grew to over five hundred by 1820. The city provided funds in 1824 and took over the school in 1834, thus providing education for African Americans before many white children were receiving it.

Yet conditions were not all bright in the North. In 1833, Prudence Crandall, a white schoolmistress in Canterbury, Connecticut, began to take in African American girls. The villagers boycotted the school, threw manure into its well, and tried to burn it down. Finally, a mob broke the windows, and the school was closed.[20]

In the South, following slave rebellions in the early 1800s, states gradually prohibited altogether the teaching of African American children, whether slave or free. Some slaves were taught to read by favorably disposed masters. However, slave owners generally reasoned that reading would lead to thinking, and thinking would lead to the desire for freedom. As the Civil War approached, abolitionist agitation often came from the few liberal colleges, such as Oberlin in Ohio and Bowdoin in Maine, that allowed the enrollment of African American students.

The Late Nineteenth Century   In the period following the Civil War, the seeds for the education of African Americans that had been sown before the war slowly began to sprout. During the period of Reconstruction, from 1865 into the 1870s, the federal government, through the Freedmen's Bureau and the occupying army, attempted to promote African American voting registration and schooling. Help also came from private and religious philanthropies in the North. Because it was hoped that whites also would benefit from these endeavors, schooling was advocated for the general public as well. Yet the common school movement was weakest in the South, and at first most whites there refused to participate not only in integrated schools but also in segregated schools, both of which they believed the northern carpetbaggers were forcing on them.

efforts to promote education

separate schools in South

By the end of Reconstruction, southern whites began to allow the existence of separate schools for African Americans. African American enrollment in the schools, which had been only 2 percent of the school-age children in 1850, was 10 percent by 1870 and 35 percent by 1890, though it dropped somewhat after that during a period of severe repression by the new white state governments.[21] During this period, "Jim Crow" laws were passed separating African Americans from whites in all areas of life. The vote was effectively taken away from the newly enfranchised African Americans by poll taxes and "grandfather rules," which allowed the vote only to those African Americans whose families could vote before the emancipation, thereby excluding all the freed slaves.

Booker T. Washington

Into these conditions, a young African American teacher named Booker T. Washington (1856–1915) was called to start an African American normal school

The Tuskegee Normal School was established in 1881 by Booker T. Washington. (CORBIS/Library of Congress)

in Tuskegee, Alabama, in 1881. Originally named the Tuskegee Normal School for Colored Teachers, it was later renamed the Tuskegee Institute. There Washington found only a few students, no physical plant, and a hostile white community. Washington, who had been born a slave, realized that the traditional curriculum of the classics would neither prepare his students to help other African Americans learn nor help to ameliorate the tensions with the white community. Believing strongly in the idea of learning by doing, Washington instructed his students to build the school themselves. In this process, they learned practical skills, grew produce that could be sold to the white community, and in general showed the whites that African American people could be productive members of society. Booker T. Washington gradually came to be considered the outstanding African American leader of the time by the white establishment.

Tuskegee Institute—practical education

But a growing number of young African Americans who, unlike Washington, had not been born into slavery believed that Washington's policy of conciliatory training for menial positions in white society would not benefit African American people in the long run. They believed that practical training is necessary but there must also be an intellectually sound and academically rich program of study for the "talented tenth" who would form the African American intellectual leadership. This was the view of W. E. B. Du Bois (1868–1963), an African American intellectual and scholar who held a doctorate from Harvard.

Education must not simply teach work—it must teach life.

—W. E. B. Du Bois

W. E. B. Du Bois

In 1862, the U.S. Congress passed the **Morrill Act.** This legislation granted each state a minimum of 30,000 acres of federal land with the proviso that the income from the rent or sale of these lands must be used to establish colleges for the study of agriculture and mechanical arts. A total of 6 million acres of federal land were donated to the states. The resulting land-grant institutions (such as the

University of Illinois, Texas A & M, and Michigan State University) became the great multipurpose state universities that now enroll hundreds of thousands of students from all segments of society.

second Morrill Act

In 1890, Congress enacted a second Morrill Act that increased the endowment of land to the original land-grant colleges but forbade the granting of money to a college with an admission policy that discriminated against nonwhites unless a separate facility for African Americans existed nearby. This second Morrill Act thus provided federal support to states to create "separate but equal" colleges for African Americans. As a result of this legislation, a number of so-called **1890 institutions** were created for the higher education of African Americans. Many of these historically African American colleges (Florida A & M and North Carolina A & T, for example) still exist today as integrated institutions.

1890 institutions

"separate but equal"

In 1896, in the case of ***Plessy* v. *Ferguson,*** the Supreme Court upheld the constitutionality of "separate but equal" accommodations for African Americans. Though the ruling originally referred to seating in a railroad car, it was quickly extended to the schools. The practical significance of this ruling was to add federal sanction to the legal separation of African American schoolchildren from white children, most notably in the South, for almost the next sixty years.

southern African American schools impoverished

The Twentieth Century   The fact that southern schools for African Americans were not equal to those for whites is woefully clear from looking at financial expenditures alone. In 1912, the southern states as a group paid white teachers slightly more than $10 per white child in school but paid African American teachers less than $3 per African American child. In the 1930s, in ten southern states, African American children made up 34 percent of the school population but received only 3 percent of the funds available for school transportation. Discrimination also existed in the distribution of federal funds, particularly in vocational education, the largest and most important educational program subsidized by the federal government.[22]

de jure segregation

de facto segregation

Most northern states did not have **de jure school segregation,** or *segregation by law,* but the crowding of African Americans into isolated neighborhoods often resulted in **de facto segregation,** that is, segregation resulting primarily from residential patterns. Furthermore, the large numbers of southern African American children who migrated with their parents to northern cities often had to be demoted because they had not mastered the same amount of material as their northern counterparts. Generally, even in the North, African American teachers taught African American children.

however, some gains

Although these conditions continued in varying degrees through the 1940s, some gains were nevertheless achieved. The average daily attendance of African American children increased and approached that of white students. The salaries of African American teachers also increased, reducing the economic gap between African American and white teachers with equal training. After African Americans had served in two world wars to "save democracy," the National Association for the Advancement of Colored People (NAACP), founded in 1909, began taking cases to the courts. Beginning with universities rather than elementary schools, the NAACP succeeded in having the courts rule that various law school facilities for African Americans were clearly unequal to those for whites.

The stage was then set for the precedent-shattering case of **Brown v. Board of Education of Topeka** (1954), in which the Supreme Court ruled that separate educational facilities are inherently unequal and that laws requiring white and nonwhite students to go to different schools were illegal. The Supreme Court concluded that de jure school segregation violated the Fourteenth Amendment of the Constitution. Early desegregation efforts therefore were aimed at eliminating de jure segregation.

Brown v. Board of Education

Desegregation Efforts   Throughout the 1960s and into the 1970s, many school systems, often in response to specific court orders, also attempted to reduce or eliminate de facto school segregation. As a result, many school districts underwent desegregation efforts. What have been the results of these efforts? Several researchers have concluded that desegregated schools have accomplished more than mere educational reform; that is, African American students who attended integrated schools experienced desegregation in several aspects of adult life, including attending predominantly white colleges and universities, working in desegregated settings, and living in desegregated neighborhoods.[23]

desegregation results

Busing   Although these long-range findings are quite positive, desegregation efforts have had some negative results. One major problem has concerned busing. Busing students to desegregated schools was one of the most inflammatory issues in education in the 1970s and 1980s. Emotions on the topic often ran very high—so high, in fact, that white parents sometimes slashed bus tires, burned buses, and physically prevented buses from running to avoid having their children bused to other schools.[24]

The federal court system was the prime mover in ordering school districts to employ busing in the desegregation process. For example, the U.S. Supreme Court, in *Swann* v. *Charlotte-Mecklenburg* (1971), concluded that the need to hasten desegregation was great, and busing was deemed an appropriate measure provided the distance of travel was not so great as to risk the health of the children or impinge significantly on the educational process.

court-ordered busing

Busing to achieve desegregation has had mixed success. One of the most successful busing plans began in Berkeley, California, in 1968. Berkeley desegregated its elementary schools by two-way, cross-town busing. A later survey found that the white residents did not leave the community, there was no high teacher turnover rate, and SAT verbal scores indicated that white, African American, and Asian American students all made better progress after desegregation.[25] On the other hand, in many other communities, attempts to desegregate the schools by busing met with tremendous community resistance, for example, in Boston in the fall of 1974.

mixed success

Big-City Desegregation   A major obstacle to desegregating big-city public schools is that the minority percentage of inner-city populations has increased

POLICY MATTERS!

Busing as a Tool for Desegregating the Schools: Is That the Issue?

What's the Policy?

Shortly after the *Brown* v. *Board of Education* decision, the federal government's policy goal was to stop segregation by compelling white and black students to attend school together. For example, busing children from segregated neighborhoods to integrated schools became a major federal court initiative to end desegregation and achieve integration. Today, however, poor student achievement, especially in urban areas, and the exodus of whites with school-age children from our cities has disillusioned many whites and African Americans regarding these desegregation efforts. Recent Supreme Court rulings also seem to signal a policy shift away from forcing school districts to pursue busing and other desegregation plans.

How Does It Affect Teachers?

The Supreme Court's turn away from busing and desegregation efforts means that teachers in certain parts of the country are less likely to find a mixture of black and white students in their classes. Classrooms are more likely to be dominated by single-race representation.

What Are the Pros?

For many whites and African Americans alike, the issue is no longer desegregation for its own sake but higher educational quality. For example, in a 1998 poll of black and white parents, the Public Agenda and the Public Education Network found that almost 70 percent of the African American respondents said the nation had pursued the goal of integration in the wrong way, and just 55 percent supported busing as a means to achieve racial balance. Nearly three-quarters said schools had neglected instructional quality while pursuing integration.

Rather than focusing on putting blacks and whites together in schools hoping good things

will happen, parents want their children to go to good schools where they are safe and where they learn to read and to understand mathematics from well-qualified teachers. They believe the cost of forced busing is too high when the nation's schools face more urgent issues of quality.

What Are the Cons?

Desegregation continues to be an important goal in the minds of many citizens. For instance, the same poll described above also found that eight out of ten African American parents considered it important that their children's schools be racially integrated, as did nearly seven out of ten white parents.

In addition, those who continue to support busing and other desegregation efforts argue that separation of the races has never produced equal and successful schools for African Americans. They find little evidence to suggest that separation will work now. Desegregation proponents also point to research evidence showing a strong correlation between school districts with few whites and those with high rates of poverty, which is known to be linked to lower educational achievement. For these reasons, they believe continued desegregation policies, even busing, are still needed.

What Do You Think?

1. What reasons can you give for the nation's retreat from desegregation efforts?

2. In your opinion, what must happen for minority students in high-poverty areas to receive a quality education? Can it happen in racially separated schools? Why or why not?

3. Do you support busing as a policy for desegregating the schools? Why or why not?

dramatically during the past several decades. In part, this has been due to "white flight": an exodus of white students whose parents have chosen to move to the suburbs or place their children in private schools. (But not only whites are fleeing the city schools: middle-class African Americans are also leaving to give their children a chance to be educated in better schools.) Independent of this population shift, the number of minority students in big-city school systems has also increased. Today cities such as New York, Los Angeles, Chicago, Detroit, Atlanta, Houston, and Dallas have school minority enrollments approaching 90 percent.[26] How can schools in major cities be desegregated when the percentage of racial minority students is growing and the percentage of white students is decreasing?

"white flight"

One solution would be to take the emerging residential segregation as given—minority cities and white suburbs—and attempt to overcome its effects on school segregation with metropolitan-area-wide school desegregation. In this approach, children would be bused over the entire metropolitan area. However, the Supreme Court has ruled that this approach is justified only if racially discriminating acts of either state or local officials are judged to have occurred in the creation of either predominantly white or African American school districts.

metropolitan-area strategies

During the 1980s, court-ordered busing was no longer the preferred method for integrating the schools. Busing, of course, was never an end in itself. It was only one means of integrating society, and polls indicate that even opponents of involuntary busing agree that our society needs to be integrated. Today the principal cause of segregated schools is not legal action but the choices of individuals whose housing patterns segregate our society and our schools. As long as these patterns persist, desegregation of the schools will continue to be problematic.

decline of busing

Recent Developments   After dramatic progress in desegregating our nation's schools during the 1960s and 1970s, evidence suggests that desegregation of African Americans leveled off in the 1980s and resegregation is now fast approaching the levels before 1970.[27] This is particularly true in large urban centers. Although many political and educational leaders remain committed to desegregated schools, others are questioning whether integration is an idea whose time has passed. In many communities, these leaders, typically members of minority groups, call for shifting the emphasis from integrating schools to improving the quality of one-race neighborhood schools. They have lost faith that desegregation is the answer to better schools.

segregation increasing

Several U.S. Supreme Court decisions during the 1990s dramatically reversed school desegregation plans ordered by lower courts, thus eliminating much of the pressure to desegregate schools. In these rulings, the Supreme Court declared that (1) school districts could be released from lower-court desegregation oversight if the school district had complied in good faith with the lower court's decree and eliminated, to the extent practicable, vestiges of segregation in student and staff assignments, transportation, facilities, and extracurricular activities; (2) federal desegregation decrees were never intended to be perpetual, and the day-to-day operations of schools should be returned to local officials as soon as possible; and (3) desegregation decrees cannot eliminate differences in student

Supreme Court reverses direction

> *Segregation was wrong when it was forced by white people, and I believe it is still wrong when it is requested by black people.*
>
> —Coretta Scott King

performance caused by poverty, poor family structure, and other socioeconomic factors, so once the lingering effects of legally enforced segregation are eliminated, school districts may run schools that happen to be all black or all white. In essence, the Supreme Court has said that there are practical limits to what a federal court can do to remedy prior discrimination, and once school districts have corrected initial racial imbalances, they are not required to remedy subsequent imbalances caused by demographic changes.

desegregation does not always lead to integration

Desegregation Versus Integration   Another point needs to be made before closing this discussion: desegregation does not necessarily lead to integration. True integration is a very human process that can occur only after desegregation has gone into effect. It happens when people from different racial and ethnic backgrounds learn to be comfortable with one another and to get along together. It means ending racial prejudice and respecting ethnic differences. Anyone who has spent time in racially mixed schools, especially high schools, knows that African American and white students who attend the same school can still be extremely distant from each other. Just bringing together students from different racial groups, social classes, and neighborhood backgrounds will not automatically lead to friendship, understanding, and appreciation of one another. As long as our society remains segregated, efforts to integrate our schools are likely to produce tension, at least in the short run. Integrating individuals with increasingly diverse racial, cultural, and linguistic backgrounds remains one of the great challenges to schools and society.

At the beginning of the twentieth century, special schools for Native Americans, such as the Carlisle Indian School in Carlisle, Pennsylvania, taught basic skills, such as mending clothes, to students. (CORBIS/Bettmann)

Education of Native Americans

As early as 1622, in an ominous forecast of future policies, one colonist wrote back to England that it was easier to conquer the Indians than to civilize them.[28] The education of Native Americans received less public attention than that of African Americans because Native Americans were considered an impediment to westward expansion, they were far from major population centers, and their dealings were largely with the federal government.

Initially the education of Native Americans, like that of African Americans, had a religious purpose. Once they had been put on reservations, the Native Americans received schooling from missionaries, who attempted to "civilize" them through the three Rs and, of course, the fourth R: religion. In the 1890s, these missionary schools were gradually replaced by government boarding schools, which tried to assimilate Native Americans by prohibiting them from speaking their native language and teaching them skills associated with white society, such as farming and mechanical skills for boys and domestic chores for girls. Little emphasis was placed on academics.

education for religious purposes

The people who had been Native Americans for 20,000 years finally became American citizens in 1924. However, that did not mean they controlled their own education. The federal government, through the Bureau of Indian Affairs, directed the education of Native Americans until the mid-1970s. During this time Native American participation was virtually ignored, as was acknowledgment of their culture in their educational programs. The elimination of Native American languages and culture was an important strategy in the efforts to assimilate Native Americans.

My son, Wind Wolf, is not an empty glass coming into your class to be filled. He is a full basket coming into a different environment and society with something special to share. Please let him share his knowledge, heritage, and culture with you and his peers.

—ROBERT LAKE

By 1965, Native Americans had begun to demand control of their schools, and a few demonstration sites for such tribal schools were funded. These schools were able to include much of the native culture in their curricula, but they were still financially dependent on the federal government, which meant limited instructional materials and lower-paid teachers than in many public schools.

Between 1972 and 1975, Congress enacted three bills that affected Native American education and self-determination. These bills encouraged the establishment of community-run schools, offered grants to develop culturally relevant and bilingual curriculum materials, placed the Office of Indian Education under the U.S. Office of Education (now the Department of Education), and established an advisory council made up of Native Americans. The Bureau of Indian Affairs is still actively involved in educational matters, but now in a supportive rather than directive capacity. The federal government has shifted responsibility for educating Native Americans from the Bureau of Indian Affairs and tribal schools to public schools. As a result, about 90 percent of Native American students in grades K–12 attend public schools.[29] This trend may have helped reduce the isolation of Native American students. However, because Native American community involvement in public education is slight, the move toward public

federal legislation

majority attendance in public schools

schooling has resulted in a loss of the limited control Native Americans had begun to exercise over the education their children receive.

Today the education of the Native American population in the United States, about 500,000 students, is still plagued by poverty, parental alcoholism, underachievement, absenteeism, over-age students, and a high dropout rate of 39 percent.[30] Native American students drop out of school more than any other racial group. Many Native Americans believe that a culturally appropriate curriculum is needed to overcome these deficiencies and reduce the cultural discontinuities between home and school. A 1997 evaluation of Native American schools concluded that they should integrate their programs into a whole-school, standards-based reform effort and increase the participation of the Native American community. A 1998 presidential order on educational opportunities for American Indians and Alaska Natives established an interagency task force to develop a coordinated federal response to help these students, including establishing a research agenda and supporting pilot programs to improve technical assistance.[31]

Education of Hispanic Americans

As with Native Americans, the first contact Spanish-speaking people had with the United States was often a result of annexation and warfare. Although they have lived in the continental United States for over 400 years, Hispanic people came into substantial contact with Anglo-Americans about 200 years ago, and almost from the beginning there was a cultural clash. Hispanic children first attended religious mission schools, which were gradually replaced by secular public schools. In the process, the Spanish language and Hispanic culture were subjected to a type of discrimination that was perhaps less blatant than that against African Americans but just as pervasive. The common school of the nineteenth and twentieth centuries, although it opened educational and social opportunities in Anglo-America, often sealed off those opportunities for Hispanic Americans. Hispanic children tended to receive lower scores than Anglo children on English-language IQ tests, which not only were written in a language that was not their own but also reflected Anglo middle-class values. Thus, an image of Hispanic children's intellectual inferiority was reinforced.

discrimination against Hispanics

Since the 1940s, the courts have acknowledged that de facto segregation exists between Anglo and Hispanic schoolchildren and have required corrective integration plans. The 1965 Elementary and Secondary Education Act provided new support to the education of Hispanics, as it did to the education of Native Americans. Another response has been the establishment of bilingual education programs to provide instruction in the native tongue at the same time students learn English. As a result, students can enter the English-language curriculum at the appropriate age levels for their grades. However, as mentioned in Chapter 4, bilingual education programs are being denounced and replaced with English immersion programs in such states as California and Arizona.

bilingual education

high dropout rates, low academic achievement

Although significant progress has been made, there is still much concern about the education of Hispanics in the United States. For example, the high school completion rate for Hispanics ages twenty-five to twenty-nine is only 62 percent, compared with 93 and 87 percent for whites and African Americans, respectively. About 18 percent of Hispanics have earned bachelor's degrees, compared to 35 and 16 percent for whites and African Americans, respectively.[32] Furthermore, reading and mathematics proficiencies are significantly lower for the Hispanic population in comparison with the white population. The public schools have not served these students well, and the cost in human and economic terms is enormous. Hispanic youth represents the fastest-growing segment of the U.S. population, and Hispanics now account for more than a quarter of all new entrants into the labor force. As demographers project higher and higher percentages of Hispanic students enrolled in public schools in the twenty-first century, the schools' response to these students' needs will have important consequences for society. Without increased educational attainment, Hispanic Americans will be relegated to low-skill jobs and locked in the lowest socioeconomic brackets.

Education of Asian Americans

The diversity of Asian Americans is evident from the historical beginnings of different groups of Asian Americans in the United States, and it persists in educational issues today.

The three largest groups of Asian Americans are the Chinese, the Filipinos, and the Japanese. Chinese immigrants began arriving in the United States in the 1840s. Most of them were poor and largely uneducated. They helped to fulfill a great need for cheap, unskilled laborers in the railroad and other industries in the American West. Intense discrimination was present, however, in part because of competition with white workers for employment. By 1882, Congress passed an exclusionary act halting Chinese immigration. Filipinos began immigrating to the United States in the early 1900s. By 1930, their entry into the United States was also limited by a congressional exclusionary act. Japanese immigrants began arriving in the United States from 1890 to 1920. Many supplied labor for agricultural industries in Hawaii until another exclusionary act was passed in 1924 limiting Japanese immigration.

diverse groups of Asian Americans

Discrimination against early Asian Americans was rampant, especially in the West, where most Asian Americans settled. School segregation of Chinese American children in California lasted until at least 1946. Japanese American children in California were forced to attend segregated schools up until World War II. With the outbreak of World War II, anti-Asian hostility subsided somewhat for immigrants of Chinese, Filipino, and Korean descent. However, the "yellow peril," perceived as emanating from Japanese Americans, resulted in the imprisonment in detention camps of over 110,000 Japanese Americans, most of whom were American-born citizens.

discrimination against Asian Americans

With the end of World War II, discrimination against Asian Americans began to subside. Naturalization rights were extended to resident Asian aliens. With the postwar expansion of the American economy, many Asian Americans benefited from greater job opportunities. Previous immigration restrictions were lifted in 1965, and the influx of Asian immigrants greatly increased. Since the U.S. with-

recent Asian immigration

drawal from Vietnam in 1975, enormous numbers of Indochinese immigrants have come to the United States and entered our school systems. The adaptation of more recent Asian immigrants has varied because of a range of educational levels and previous socioeconomic circumstances. Current census estimates indicate that Asian and Pacific Islanders number roughly 7 million, or about 3 percent of the U.S. population. It is projected that by the year 2020, this group will reach about 20 million.[33]

stereotype misleading

With the higher educational achievement and income levels of some Asian Americans, this group has often been touted as a "model minority" that has overcome discrimination through hard work, perseverance, and industriousness. However, this rosy stereotype is misleading and at times has contributed to misconceptions and complacency in meeting the educational needs and concerns of Asian American students.

language difficulties

Many recent Asian American immigrants to the United States have little or no knowledge of the English language. This creates formidable language and cultural barriers for students entering the U.S. education system, and may lead to serious family-school discontinuities, alienation from school, and dropout problems. The U.S. Supreme Court established in *Lau* v. *Nichols* (1974) that schools must offer students sufficient special instruction to be afforded equal educational opportunity. There is a pressing need for adequate language instruction for this subgroup of Asian Americans, and as immigration continues to increase, this need will likely grow in our school systems.

impediments to parental involvement

Parental and community involvement of Asian Americans in the education process also needs to be fostered. Parents of Asian American students are often noted as being concerned with their children's education. However, because of the respect traditionally given educators, they are hesitant to intervene when they are dissatisfied with their children's educational progress. Another deterrent to parental participation is the fact that a much higher proportion of Asian American families have two parents employed, a situation that makes attendance at traditional teacher conferences or PTO meetings difficult. Many communities are making efforts to organize and voice the needs of Asian American students.

As the number of Asian American students continues to grow, it will become increasingly important for teachers and administrators to be knowledgeable of and sensitive to the special problems and needs of Asian American students and their families. To serve these students adequately in our schools, it is particularly important to keep in mind that Asian Americans are a changing and complex group whose achievement, aspirations, and learning styles should not be stereotyped.

A Final Word

At the beginning of this chapter, we identified six major themes that have shaped the history of American education and schooling: local control, universal education, public education, comprehensive education, secular education, and changing ideas of the basics. If you think back over the issues raised in earlier chapters

TABLE 11.4   Some Significant Dates in the History of American Education

1635	Establishment of the Boston Latin grammar school
1647	Massachusetts Old Deluder Satan Act: towns of fifty families or more must provide instruction in reading and writing; towns of one hundred families or more must establish grammar schools
1687–90	First edition of the *New England Primer*
1783	Noah Webster publishes the *American Spelling Book*
1785, 1787	Northwest Ordinances, requiring new states in that territory to set aside land for educational purposes
1821	First public high school in the United States opens in Boston; Emma Willard establishes first school for women's higher education
1839	First public normal school in the United States established in Lexington, Massachusetts
1860	First English-language kindergarten established in the United States
1862	First Morrill Act provides for land-grant institutions that now enroll hundreds of thousands of students from all segments of society
1890	Second Morrill Act requires that federal funds be available only to colleges with nondiscriminatory admission policies unless separate facilities for African Americans exist nearby. As a result, a number of "separate but equal" institutions are established.
1896	*Plessy* v. *Ferguson,* Supreme Court decision used to support constitutionality of separate schools for whites and blacks
1944	GI Bill of Rights provides federal funding for continued education of veterans of World War II (later extended to veterans of the Korean and Vietnam wars)
1954	*Brown* v. *Board of Education of Topeka* decision of the Supreme Court requiring desegregation of public schools
1957	Soviet Union launches *Sputnik,* leading to criticism and reevaluation of American public education
1965	Elementary and Secondary Education Act provides more federal aid to public schools
1971	U.S. Supreme Court rules unanimously in *Swann* v. *Charlotte-Mecklenberg Board of Education* that busing may be ordered to achieve racial desegregation
1972	Title IX Education Amendment outlaws sex discrimination in educational institutions receiving federal financial assistance
1975	Education for All Handicapped Children Act (Public Law 94–142) passed
1979	Department of Education established in federal government with cabinet status
1990	Congress passes the Americans with Disabilities Act

of this text, you can see the effect of these themes on contemporary education. For example, the universal and public nature of the educational system strikes at the issue of equal educational opportunity and questions of school finance and governance. Current controversies over the content of education—questions about the secular or sacred nature of the curriculum, debate about the need for standards of learning, and efforts to provide excellence in education without sacrificing equality of opportunity—relate to the concepts of secular, universal, and comprehensive education and the definition of what is "basic." Thus, these six themes continue to play themselves out in our evolving educational system. Table 11.4 lists important dates and events in American education, many of which relate to these six themes.

KEY TERMS

dame school (358)
Old Deluder Satan Act (359)
town school (359)
district school (359)
New England Primer (360)
private venture school (360)
common school (361)
universal education (361)
Northwest Ordinances (361)
McGuffey Readers (363)
kindergarten (365)
Latin grammar school (370)

English grammar school (372)
academy (372)
Kalamazoo case (374)
public comprehensive high school (375)
junior high school (375)
middle school (375)
Morrill Act (381)
1890 institutions (382)
Plessy v. *Ferguson* (382)
de jure school segregation (382)
de facto [school] segregation (382)
Brown v. *Board of Education of Topeka* (383)

FOR REFLECTION

1. Why is it important for teachers to know the history of American education? How might you use such knowledge?

2. How did the moral lessons you were taught in school compare with those taught in earlier American schools?

3. Why did the educational development of colonial America differ among the New England, Middle, and Southern colonies? In what ways were the educational systems different?

4. What factors contributed to the development of the common school movement? Who were some of the leading advocates of the movement toward universal, free education?

5. What made the development of the American secondary school so unique in the history of the world?

6. What has been the role of private education in American history?

7. In what ways were the histories of the education of minority groups and women similar and different?

FOR FURTHER INFORMATION

Cuban, Larry. *How Teachers Taught: Constancy and Change in American Classrooms,* **1880–1990. 2d ed. New York: Teachers College Press, 1993.**
This text is a historical examination of instructional practices in American classrooms.

"Lessons of a Century," *Education Week,* **January 27, 1999–December 15, 1999. World Wide Web site at http://www.edweek.org.**
Ten monthly installments examining aspects of the educational landscape of twentieth-century America, including the people, trends, historical milestones, enduring controversies, political conflicts, and socioeconomic forces that shaped education.

Library of Congress. World Wide Web site at http://www.loc.gov.
Users of this site will find easy access to THOMAS (legislative information), the Library of Congress catalog, and much more. Particularly relevant for the history of American education is the "Learning Page," which provides information on using materials in the American Memory historical collections, as well as lesson plans and links to related web pages.

Orfield, Gary, Susan Eaton, and the Harvard Project on School Desegregation. *Dismantling Desegregation: The Quiet Reversal of Brown v. Board of Education.* **New York: New Press, 1996.**
This text explores how the desegregation efforts of the 1960s and 1970s are being reversed, particularly by Supreme Court rulings. The authors contend that our nation is making a serious mistake in doing so.

Spring, Joel. *The American School.* **9th ed. New York: McGraw-Hill, 1999.**
This book focuses on the social, political, and ideological forces that have shaped the evolution of schooling in America from colonial times to the present.

Tyack, David B., and Larry Cuban. *Tinkering Toward Utopia: A Century of Public School Reform.* **Cambridge, MA: Harvard University Press, 1995.**
This important book on school reforms in the United States argues that utopian policy talk about school reform usually has involved only incremental policy action— "tinkering with the system."

Urban, Wayne J., and Jennings L. Wagoner. *American Education: A History.* **2d ed. New York: McGraw-Hill, 2000.**
This book is a relatively brief overview of American education, written by well-known scholars.

12

What Are the Ethical and Legal Issues Facing Teachers?

This chapter aims to sharpen your sense of the ethical dimension of teaching and your understanding of the legal underpinnings of many aspects of school life. We examine several common ethical problems faced by teachers, along with legal issues and recent court rulings that have affected them.

This chapter emphasizes that

▶ Ethics and the law are closely related, but they also differ.

▶ Ethical teaching has six specific characteristics.

▶ In addition to teaching's everyday ethical dimensions, teachers confront certain other, more complex ethical problems.

▶ Teachers need to understand fully how two basic legal terms, *due process* and *liability*, relate to their work.

▶ Broad areas of the law—from contracts to copyright, from self-defense to religion in the classroom—permeate school life.

▶ Students have rights under the law, such as the rights to due process and privacy, and teachers need to understand and respect these rights.

If each of us were the only person on the face of the earth, we could behave exactly as we chose. We would not have to worry about the rights or feelings of anyone else. We would be free of the constraints and demands imposed by others as we went about doing our own will. Quite obviously, though, this is simply not the case. Everyone who walks the earth is bound by real, if unseen, connections with his or her fellow humans. The English poet John Donne said it most succinctly: "No man is an island."

Our systems of ethics and laws are a major part of these invisible connecting fibers. Together they make civilized society in a neighborhood and coexistence on a planet possible. Ethics, as we said in Chapter 10, brings us into the realm of what is the right way to act. **Ethics** refers to a system or a code of morality embraced by a particular person or group. Law is related to, but different from, ethics. A law is a written rule that members of a given community must follow. **The law** is a system of such rules that governs the general conduct of a particular community's citizens.

ethics and the law

Laws and Our Ethics   Whereas ethics may be invisible obligations that we perceive, laws typically are statements that have been hammered out by the legitimate authority of a particular community, state, or nation and are used in court as standards by which to judge, and often penalize, the actual behavior of individuals. As a matter of fact, what someone might refer to as an unstated law is not a law at all, but an ethical statement.

Laws, then, are concrete, made by people and usually written down for the public to see; ethics, on the other hand, consists of ideas and thus are less tangible and observable. Most of our laws are simply the codification of what we see as our moral or ethical obligations to one another. Sometimes, however, laws are unethical (such as the racial segregation laws that existed in this country only a few decades ago), and sometimes ethical obligations are not written into law (such as the ethical obligation to help the weak, the poor, and the sick).

law as codified ethics

The Teacher's Responsibility   What does all this have to do with teachers? First, it is the responsibility of teachers to convey to the young the fundamental moral message that we are all legally and ethically bound to one another. Much of this moral message is embedded in the content of our curricula, from our great stories to the history of our behavior. Second, a unique set of ethical relationships and legal obligations is embedded in teachers' work, and teachers therefore carry a special ethical and legal burden. This second issue is the subject of this chapter.

At the heart of the teacher's unique ethical and legal relationship with students is power. Compared with a corporate executive or a military officer, it may not appear that a teacher has a great deal of power. But in fact the teacher has a special type of power.* This power arises from the fact that the teacher has an

teachers' unique power

---

*As our erstwhile friend Ernie Lundquist once put it, "Show me a guy who claims he was never afraid of a teacher, and I'll show you a damned liar!" Strong words from the normally mild-mannered, congenitally unflappable Ernie, but once again right on target.

impact on people when they are still at a very malleable and impressionable stage. Many careers are open to you, but few offer such truly awe-inspiring power.

Like it or not, power resides in the "office" of teacher. The teacher is in command of the classroom insofar as he or she has the responsibility for what goes on. Teachers evaluate their students. They not only "mark" them with tangible symbols that become part of students' official records; they also mark their minds and hearts. And because of the potential for abuse of this power, there are codes of ethics to guide the teacher and a body of laws governing the work of teaching. Since ignorance of the law (and ethics) is no excuse, we urge you to take the material in this chapter quite seriously.

The Ethics of Teaching

In a sense, individuals lose their "freedom" when they get married. And in a similar sense, people lose their freedom to do as they please when they become teachers. In both situations commitments are made, and ethical constraints come with these commitments. Constrained by ethics, the teacher is not always able to act in a manner that he or she finds most satisfying. For instance, the teacher cannot respond with sarcasm to a student's foolish or rude remark. Even though a child—sometimes even a very small child—can provoke a rush of anger, the teacher cannot act on that anger. In another, more positive sense, though, ethics are principles that call the teacher to higher modes of professional behavior.

The Characteristics of Ethical Teaching

Being an ethical teacher means having a rather special relationship with one's students and with the other people with whom one works. Consider the following situation, as told to educator Kenneth Howe by a practicing teacher:

case of Marilyn Henderson

Marilyn Henderson is a 5th grade language arts teacher at Willoughby Elementary in South Lake, a medium sized city with a population of roughly 150,000. Marilyn is troubled to learn that Connie Severns, a 5th grade social studies teacher, whom Marilyn worked with previously in another school in the South Lake system, will be transferred to Willoughby. Marilyn believes Connie to be incompetent and is uncomfortable with this knowledge, especially in light of the fact that her students will be moving through Connie's class. As Marilyn recalls, "Connie didn't teach anything; she couldn't teach anything." Others in the district share Marilyn's assessment of Connie as a teacher and apparently with good reason. Connie seems totally to lack control. Children cry and complain about the chaos, some steal things from her purse, and on one occasion another teacher discovered a child chasing Connie around the room.

Marilyn had previously tried to do something about Connie's incompetence, but met with little success. The teachers' union advised her that they would have to stand behind a tenured teacher, and the school administration claimed to have to follow procedures (which could take years according to Marilyn). At this point in time (prior to Connie's transfer), the principal of Willoughby called the affected teachers together. He, too, was concerned about Connie's transfer and proposed that they discreetly and surreptitiously "write things down" to build a case which they could use to have Connie fired. Marilyn is asked to be a part of this. What should she do?[1]

This story provides just a peek at the teacher's ethically complex world. Howe suggests that in dealing with issues involving ethical judgment, we as teachers need to exhibit six characteristics: appreciation for moral deliberation, empathy, knowledge, reasoning, courage, and interpersonal skills.[2]

Appreciation for Moral Deliberation   We need, first, to see an ethical dilemma, such as Marilyn's, as a situation characterized by conflicting and competing moral interests (Connie's need for a job, the students' need for a competent teacher, and the other teachers' need to be fair in what they say to and about Connie). We need to see the complex moral dimensions of the problem and appreciate that care must be taken to protect the rights of all parties.

"seeing" competing interests

Empathy   *Empathy* is the ability to mentally "get inside the skin of another." We need to feel what the others in an ethically troublesome situation are thinking and feeling. In the case described, we would need to empathize with the principal who is inheriting a questionable teacher, with the students and their parents, with Connie, and with Marilyn and the other teachers.

feeling what others feel

Warmth and humor are valuable assets in teaching. (© Elizabeth Crews)

knowing all the facts

Knowledge   One of the tools of a teacher who is able to deal effectively with ethical issues is raw knowledge. We need to remember the facts that will enable us to put an issue in context. What does Connie actually do in the classroom? What formal procedures are in place to deal with ineffective or incompetent teachers? We need to be able to formulate reasonable approaches to the problem and then, from experience, anticipate the consequences of each approach. In Marilyn's case, she needs to be able to think clearly about the alternatives—such as participating in the principal's questionable plan or, perhaps, directly confronting Connie—and she must think through, with some degree of accuracy, what the likely consequences of such action would be. This involves knowledge of the context in which she and Connie are working.

thinking systematically

Reasoning   To reason is to reflect systematically on an issue. When we reason about an issue, we move through it step by step and draw conclusions. Or we may compare a particular event or action with some moral principle and come to some conclusion. For instance, Marilyn may hold as a moral principle that people should not deceive others and, further, that spying is deception. Through reasoning, she may come to the conclusion that what the principal has asked her to do is spying. Of course, this leaves Marilyn with another problem: how to tell her principal that his plan is unethical.

Courage   But to feel, to know, and to reason are not enough. To be ethical, we must act—and action sometimes takes courage. To be ethically correct often requires the willpower to act in what we perceive to be the right way rather than in the comfortable way. Frequently, when confronted with a seemingly no-win dilemma like Marilyn's, we tend to ignore it in the hope that it will simply go

confronting, not evading, problems

away. However, as the theologian Harvey Cox sees it, "Not to decide is to decide." Among other things, Marilyn will have to find a way to tell her principal that she simply cannot be a part of his secret reporting network. Besides courage, this will require tact.

acting with sensitivity

Interpersonal Skills   Acting on ethical principles demands sensitivity as well as courage. Therefore, teachers need the communications skills to deal sensitively with issues that demand great tact. They need to be able to call up the right words, with the right feeling and tone, and to address the issue at hand openly and honestly.

Ethical Dilemmas in Teaching

Although teachers spend most of their professional lives working with students in an instructional manner, sometimes ethical concerns break in and demand their attention. Recently, as teacher education students interviewed practicing teachers, they asked them to describe an ethical situation they had encountered in the last few years. The two cases that follow are based on those interviews.

As you read each case, take time to reflect carefully on it. Does the situation really involve ethics? Does it involve unfairness or a breach of ethical standards?

Are there complexities that cause ethical conflicts? If so, what are they? What are the consequences of various courses of action? Who needs to be considered as you try to decide on a course of action? What, specifically, would you say or do? As you work through these situations, keep in mind the six characteristics described by Kenneth Howe. Also, discuss these cases with other people. Frequently we see much more in a situation involving ethics and recognize many other possible courses of action once we have talked to others about it.

CASE STUDY A Big Deal or a Little Fudge?

Recently drugs have plagued your community, and increasingly they are coming into the schools. You are a sixth-grade teacher, and there has been only sporadic evidence of drugs in your building. On the other hand, your principal has been making what seems to you a big deal out of very little in his crusade to stamp out drugs in "his elementary school." He has threatened the student body, first-graders through sixth-graders, in a special assembly about what will happen to them if they are caught with drugs of any kind. Most of your in-service training time this year has been taken up with the subject of drugs. You are concerned about the misuse of drugs in our society. However, you, like most of the other teachers, find the principal's preoccupation with drugs overzealous and slightly laughable, and you are afraid of what will happen to the first offender he catches.

drugs in the classroom

Coming from lunch, you see Alan, one of your sixth-graders, showing two of his friends a plastic bag containing what appear to be three or four marijuana joints. Startled, but unsure that you have actually seen what he has, Alan shoves the bag into his pants pocket. You act as if nothing has happened and usher the boys into class. To gain time to think, you set the students to work on a composition.

Alan is a kid with a spotty record in the school. His family life is rumored to be rather chaotic, but he has behaved well in your class. You have never seen the slightest evidence that he has been high in school. Knowing Alan, you guess he got the dope from one of his brothers and brought it to school to impress his friends. On the other hand, you could be wrong, and the situation could be much more serious. One thing you are sure of is that if you report what you saw to the principal, as you are expected to, he will move in on Alan like a SWAT team. As you mull all this over, Alan and his friends are nervously watching you and anxiously looking back and forth at one another. Then, suddenly, Alan gets up, comes to your desk, and asks if he can go to the boys' room. What do you do?

CASE STUDY Righting Wrongs

You expected to encounter a sour apple or two in the teaching profession, but Kingsley is authentically rotten. He is lazy, way out of touch with his field, hostile to students, and totally uncooperative toward his colleagues and the high school's administrators. He has been tenured for twelve years and has been acting this way for about eleven. He flaunts his behavior, occasionally referring to himself as "the Untouchable One." He is also as smart as he is mean.

a vindictive colleague

For reasons you can only guess at, Kingsley is carrying on some kind of personal vendetta against Ken, one of the best students in the senior class. Ken's father has been

Case Study cont'd

out of work for three years, and Ken has had an after-school and weekend job to help the family stay afloat. Besides carrying a heavy academic load of demanding courses, he has stayed active in a number of the school's key extracurricular activities. This year, as editor of the school newspaper, he took a dull sports and soft-gossip paper and made it genuinely interesting, addressing issues of real concern to the entire high school population and doing it in a mature, evenhanded way. In the process, Ken seems to have gotten on Kingsley's wrong side, and Kingsley, his senior-year English teacher, is making him pay. Ken has told you, as his social studies teacher and friend, about what is going on in English. Besides regular ridicule and baiting, Kingsley has given him very low marks on writing assignments and term papers that you frankly think are across-the-board A work. As a result, Ken is running a low C in English, which has been his best subject, and this could mean he will get no honors at graduation. Worse, it will probably bring his average down just enough that he will lose the state scholarship he needs to go to college next year.

You have tried to talk with Kingsley about the situation, but after smugly telling you about "a teacher's right and responsibility to give the grade he sees fit," he in effect told you to "butt out." In as professional a manner as possible, you have discussed the matter with the principal, but she has told you that although she sympathizes, her hands are tied. Finally, it dawns on you that there *is* something you can do. Ken is running a solid B-plus/A-minus in social studies as you enter the last weeks of the school year. If you were to change a few grades upward so he will receive an A-plus, it could compensate for the unjust grade he is receiving from Kingsley. It would also assure Ken of getting the state scholarship. You would love to see Kingsley's face at graduation, too. What will you do?

The Everyday Ethics of Teaching

As we hope the preceding vignettes make clear, serious ethical issues strongly influence the lives of teachers. Few teachers get very far into their careers without having to deal with situations like these. But these cases do not exhaust the ethical responsibilities of the teacher; everyday events that occur in the classroom and school life have an even greater ethical impact on students.

Although it is clear that parents have the primary responsibility for the ethical training of their children, schools do have an impact on the character and moral lives of students. Classrooms and schoolyards overflow with issues of right and wrong: a child copies someone's homework; a group of girls start a rumor that another girl is pregnant; a teacher continually picks on the same student. Events like these send strong ethical messages to students. How the teacher and the rest of the school respond to this ethical dimension of schooling is what we refer to as *the everyday ethics of teaching*. In particular, teachers ethically influence students in three ways: by example, by the classroom climate they create, and by the dialogue they establish.

three ways to influence ethically

First, the *personal example* provided by teachers includes the care and manner with which they do their work, how they treat students and others, and their use of examples from history and literature to enrich the ethical understandings of students.

A Checklist for Ethics

Paul A. Wagner, a professor at the University of Houston–Clear Lake, recently wrote a fine booklet in which he included a comprehensive, eight-point checklist of ethical considerations for teachers. We recommend these guidelines to you:

1. Never use your students, colleagues, or others for your personal gain. People should not be treated as means to your own ends.

2. Be fair. This means treating equals equally and unequals unequally. For example, school should be a place where every student has the chance to flourish intellectually; but it may cost more for special education students to have the same chance to flourish as regular students.

3. Be sure you understand precisely the meaning of such moral terms as *fairness, rights,* and *duties.*

4. Think through the moral consequences of your actions. Focus on the moral considerations before turning to such other concerns as convenience, political milieu, and so on.

5. Treat each person with respect.

6. Be patient. Do not rush a decision beyond what is necessary. Try to consider all relevant arguments before acting, creating a rule, judging another, or making policy.

7. Have courage. Doing the right thing does not guarantee safety or happiness. Occasionally a teacher gets scolded or even fired for doing the right thing. Still, it is a teacher's professional obligation to make the moral choice.

8. Remember the special duties you have to students, colleagues, and others in the school community.

Source: Paul A. Wagner, *Understanding Professional Ethics* (Bloomington, IN: PDK Educational Foundation, 1996). Copyright © 1996, Phi Delta Kappa Educational Foundation. Reprinted by permission.

Second, teachers can establish a beneficial *classroom climate* by creating an environment of safety and trust where students are free from fear and ridicule, where a spirit of cooperation and friendly competition prevails, and where students are working hard and feeling the satisfaction of learning.

Third, teachers can establish an *ethical dialogue* in their classrooms by discussing with students the core ethical values (such as honesty, respect for others, and responsibility) that come into play in the curriculum and the life of the school.

The *everyday ethics of teaching,* then, means *doing the job as it ought to be done.* It means realizing the preciousness of the minutes and hours that you spend with students and making sure they do not waste their time with you.

Codes of Professional Ethics

Teachers do not struggle alone when they face ethical issues. Besides their own understanding, reasoning, courage, and other qualities, they have the support of a professional group.* Professional groups, such as those of doctors, architects,

---

*The extent to which teaching is or is not a profession is an important question and is the subject of Chapter 15.

and teachers, have special obligations to their clients. Because of their special knowledge and power, they have an ethical responsibility to those they serve.

The way teachers do their work is regulated, then, both by their own ethical standards and by those of the teaching profession. Whereas some professions have formulated their own universal code of ethics (like the Hippocratic oath taken by all medical doctors), there are several published codes of ethics for teachers. The best known is the code of the National Education Association (NEA), which includes such statements as "The educator strives to help each student realize his or her potential as a worthy and effective member of society." The American Federation of Teachers (AFT) has a "Bill of Rights" that deals with the ethical treatment teachers should receive. It contains what it refers to as self-evident truths, for example, "The right of teachers to be secure in their jobs, free from political influence or public clamor, shall be established by law. The right to

NEA Code of Ethics

Preamble

The educator, believing in the worth and dignity of each human being, recognizes the supreme importance of the pursuit of truth, devotion to excellence, and the nurture of democratic principles. Essential to these goals is the protection of freedom to learn and to teach and the guarantee of equal educational opportunity for all. The educator accepts the responsibility to adhere to the highest ethical standards.

The educator recognizes the magnitude of the responsibility inherent in the teaching process. The desire for the respect and confidence of one's colleagues, of students, of parents, and of the members of the community provides the incentive to attain and maintain the highest possible degree of ethical conduct. *The Code of Ethics of the Education Profession* indicates the aspiration of all educators and provides standards by which to judge conduct.

The remedies specified by the NEA and/or its affiliates for the violation of any provision of this Code shall be exclusive and no such provision shall be enforceable in any form other than one specifically designated by the NEA or its affiliates.

Principle I—Commitment to the Student

The educator strives to help each student realize his or her potential as a worthy and effective member of society. The educator therefore works to stimulate the spirit of inquiry, the acquisition of knowledge and understanding, and the thoughtful formulation of worthy goals.

In fulfillment of the obligation to the student, the educator—

1. Shall not unreasonably restrain the student from independent action in the pursuit of learning.

2. Shall not unreasonably deny the student access to varying points of view.

3. Shall not deliberately suppress or distort subject matter relevant to the student's progress.

4. Shall make reasonable effort to protect the student from conditions harmful to learning or to health and safety.

5. Shall not intentionally expose the student to embarrassment or disparagement.

6. Shall not on the basis of race, color, creed, sex, national origin, marital status, political or religious beliefs, family, social or cultural background, or sexual orientation, unfairly:

   a. Exclude any student from participation in any program;

   b. Deny benefits to any student;

   c. Grant any advantage to any student.

teach is a property right, based upon the inalienable rights to life, liberty, and the pursuit of happiness."[3] A third example is the Boston University Educator's Affirmation, which is taken voluntarily in a special ceremony, typically in the junior year. More like the Hippocratic oath taken by physicians, this statement is a positive declaration of the high ideals and professional standards to which teachers commit themselves:

Boston University Educator's Affirmation

one school's code

I dedicate myself to the life of an educator, to laying the living foundations upon which successor generations must continue to build their lives.

I dedicate myself to the advancement of learning, for I know that without it our successors will lack both the vision and the power to build well.

Code of Ethics *(cont'd)*

7. Shall not use professional relationships with students for private advantage.

8. Shall not disclose information about students obtained in the course of professional service, unless disclosure serves a compelling professional purpose or is required by law.

Principle II—Commitment to the Profession

The education profession is vested by the public with a trust and responsibility requiring the highest ideals of professional service.

In the belief that the quality of the services of the education profession directly influences the nation and its citizens, the educator shall exert every effort to raise professional standards, to promote a climate that encourages the exercise of professional judgment, to achieve conditions which attract persons worthy of the trust to careers in education, and to assist in preventing the practice of the profession by unqualified persons.

In fulfillment of the obligation to the profession, the educator—

1. Shall not in an application for a professional position deliberately make a false statement or fail to disclose a material fact related to competency and qualifications.

2. Shall not misrepresent his/her professional qualifications.

3. Shall not assist entry into the profession of a person known to be unqualified in respect to character, education, or other relevant attribute.

4. Shall not knowingly make a false statement concerning the qualifications of a candidate for a professional position.

5. Shall not assist a noneducator in the unauthorized practice of teaching.

6. Shall not disclose information about colleagues obtained in the course of professional service unless disclosure serves a compelling professional purpose or is required by law.

7. Shall not knowingly make false or malicious statements about a colleague.

8. Shall not accept any gratuity, gift, or favor that might impair or appear to influence professional decisions or actions.

Source: From National Education Association, *Code of Ethics of the Education Profession,* adopted by the NEA Representative Assembly, 1985. Used by permission.

I dedicate myself to the cultivation of character, for I know that humanity cannot flourish without courage, compassion, honesty, and trust.

I dedicate myself to the advancement of my own learning and to the cultivation of my own character, for I know that I must bear witness in my own life to the ideals that I have dedicated myself to promote in others.

In the presence of this gathering, I bind myself to this affirmation.[4]

The Teacher and the Law

Once upon a time, teachers were like the kings and queens of small kingdoms. Their authority was wide and their decisions were rarely questioned. Students who would not or could not do the work were "held back" or told not to come back. Students who did not conform to the teacher's standards of behavior were expelled. Students and their parents tended to view education as a special opportunity that put definite responsibilities on their shoulders.

rise in litigation

In the last few decades, however, the attitude toward schooling in our country has changed. The authority of the adults in general and teachers in particular has eroded noticeably, and students are often more fixated on their rights than on their responsibilities. There are many reasons for this change, but suffice it to say that we are a very litigious society. Our country has more lawyers per capita than any other nation in the world. And our increasing tendency to use the courts to settle differences and conflicts has had its impact on the work of the teacher.

On the other hand, it can be argued that our new consciousness of the teacher's legal responsibilities and our heightened sense of students' rights have helped to rid schools of dictatorial practices by teachers and administrators; the systematic denial of rights to students, such as freedom of speech and prayerful assembly (under certain conditions); and the abusive use of corporal punishment. The new presence of the law in educational matters is, like many changes, a mixed bag.

law = collective judgment

Woodrow Wilson once said, "The law that will work is merely the summing up in legislative form of the moral judgment that the community has already reached." Our laws, then, are our collective social judgments and decisions about what is fair. Laws differ from codes of ethics, though, because they apply to all the people, not to a particular group like doctors or teachers. Laws are public, whereas ethics can reflect one's private standards. And laws have judicial teeth, whereas codes of ethics do not. Rarely is a teacher suspended, or expelled, or even sanctioned by the teaching profession for violations of the NEA's Code of Ethics.[5] However, teachers are regularly affected by the law and occasionally are brought to court.

That government is best which governs least, because its people discipline themselves.

——THOMAS JEFFERSON

The Teacher and Due Process

▶ A young junior high teacher, on a lark, changes his "image." He comes to school one Monday morning sporting a shaved head and a diamond stud earring. He is fired on Tuesday.

▶ A teacher gives a speech at a meeting of the local gay and lesbian alliance. The newspaper runs a story on the event, and the superintendent asks her to resign quietly.

▶ A business education teacher who has been teaching for three years has been visited by administrators only twice during that period. He loves teaching, but has only just recently begun to feel competent. Instead of getting the expected letter from the superintendent outlining the upcoming tenure review process, he receives a dismissal notice claiming that his teaching is not up to the district's standards.

All three of these examples represent violations of the teachers' rights to due process. **Due process** is one of the most important principles embedded in our nation's laws. The essential meaning of due process in education is that fairness should be rendered and teachers' rights as individuals should not be violated. Due process protections come directly from two amendments to our Constitution. The Fifth Amendment states that "no person shall . . . be deprived of life, liberty, or property, without due process of law." The Fourteenth Amendment adds, "nor shall any State deprive any person of life, liberty, or property, without due process of law."

due process = fairness

Two Types of Due Process   When judging the fairness of an action, there are two due process concerns. One, *substantive due process,* has to do with the issue itself. The other, *procedural due process,* concerns the fairness of the process followed. For example, if a teacher is fired because he wears a nose ring, this is an issue of substantive due process: Is this matter substantive enough in this particular circumstance to deny a teacher employment? What is a fair decision in this matter? Procedural due process would involve how the case is handled. Suppose the teacher, after hearing several rumors that the nose ring is irking the superintendent, gets a curt letter saying his "services are no longer needed." Is this process fair? Has the teacher had a fair chance to defend himself?

substantive due process

The precise meaning of procedural due process changes from state to state, but the Supreme Court decision in *Goldberg* v. *Kelly* (1970) indicated that "the minimum procedural safeguards . . . demanded by rudimentary due process" would include the following:

procedural safeguards

The opportunity to be heard at a reasonable time and place.
Timely and adequate notice giving details of the reasons for the proposed suspension or dismissal.
An effective opportunity to defend oneself, including oral presentation of evidence and arguments.
An opportunity to confront and cross-examine witnesses.
The right to retain an attorney.
A decision resting solely on the legal rules and evidence adduced at the hearing.
A statement of the reasons for the determination and the evidence relied on.
An impartial decision maker.[6]

The principle of due process and these guidelines reach into many corners of the teacher's life, as we will see in the next section.

Contracts, Tenure, and Dismissal

Few teachers are "independent operators," like painters, novelists, or even some lawyers. Teachers are employees of the local board of education or, in the case of private schools, usually of a board of trustees. As such, they have a legal set of relationships with the board.

Contracts to Teach   All teachers, new or old, sign a contract with their board of education (or trustees) outlining the rights and responsibilities of each party to the agreement. Typically the contract will deal with salary, the area or areas of instruction, class size, length of teaching day, and the procedure teachers should follow if they have a *grievance* (that is, a formal complaint against the employer or a concern about some aspect of their work). Also, if the teachers in a district are represented by a particular teachers' association or union, the contract will acknowledge it as the teachers' bargaining agent.

elements of legal contracts

To be considered a legally enforceable document, a **contract** must do the following:

1. Have a lawful subject matter

2. Represent a meeting of the minds of both parties

3. Include an exchange of something of value (called a *consideration*)

4. Be entered into by parties who are competent to do so

5. Be written in proper form (instead of in vague terms, such as "pay the teacher what he or she is worth")

In addition, the school board must act officially to ratify a teacher's contract.[7] Contracts are for a set period of time. Most new teachers work on a contract that has to be renewed annually if the teacher is to stay on. Even teachers on tenure (to be discussed shortly) sign a yearly contract stipulating the terms of employment. Occasionally teachers work under a **continuing contract,** which states that its terms will remain in force until the teacher is given notice that termination will occur on a particular date.

Sometimes a teacher is dismissed, and sometimes a teacher leaves a position for a different job in or out of education. If either party, the teacher or the board of education, violates any of the terms of the contract, such an action is called a

breach of contract

breach of contract and can lead to a lawsuit. When an injured party successfully sues the other party for breach of contract, the court may order that the contract be fulfilled, that the injured party receive monetary damages, or both. For instance, the district may have to rehire a fired teacher and pay damages. Or a teacher who walks away from a job may have to pay the district's cost of finding a replacement. Since your own contract will govern many important details of your life as a teacher, study it carefully before signing it.

Tenure   The word *tenure* comes from the Latin root "to hold," as in "hold that job." New teachers begin their careers as probationary employees. They are full-fledged teachers in their classrooms, but they are on trial in their school districts. States differ as to tenure, but typically teachers can remain in this temporary status for three years. At that time, they are eligible for tenure.

long-term rights

Tenure represents permanence of position, and the teacher who has tenure has, in effect, a long-term right to a contract with the school district. Once granted tenure, a teacher can be dismissed only "for cause"—that is, for a good reason that will withstand the scrutiny of the courts, such as sexually molesting a student, gross negligence, or gross incompetence. The general purpose of tenure was nicely stated by the Supreme Court of Pennsylvania in 1957: tenure helps to maintain "an adequate and competent teaching staff, free from political or arbitrary interference." In addition, tenure allows "capable and competent teachers" to feel secure and to perform their duties efficiently.[8]

Bear in mind two additional points about tenure laws. First, a teacher is granted tenure not as, say, a third-grade teacher or a vocational education teacher, but simply as a teacher. School boards have the right to transfer and reassign teachers within the district. Second, states differ in their tenuring procedures. In some states, tenure comes automatically with the fourth year's contract. In others, teachers must first pass the formal tenure review process, which examines performance and assesses their professional competence.

Dismissal   Occasionally teachers fail; they simply cannot handle the job. Or they make a big mistake, such as striking a child in anger. Occasionally, too,

special conditions

AUTHORS' DIALOGUE

JIM: Tenure is a pretty hot topic right now.

KEVIN: *I know. Many people charge that tenure protects incompetent teachers and makes it really difficult and expensive for school districts to get rid of poor teachers.*

JIM: On the other hand, there are lots of cases where tenure has protected teachers from capricious or unjust actions of school officials.

KEVIN: *So what do you think should be done with tenure?*

JIM: I think tenure should be harder to get than it is currently. Teachers should have to apply for tenure and present a teaching portfolio that represents their best work and that of their students. This would be reviewed by a committee of administrators, teachers, and parents.

KEVIN: *So each school district would develop guidelines for what these teaching portfolios contained?*

JIM: Right. And for those teachers who chose not to go for tenure, or who were denied, the district could still offer them one-, two-, or three-year contracts that might or might not be renewed, depending on the teacher's performance.

KEVIN: *Tenure might then become a mark of distinction rather than something that is awarded simply for being hired for a fourth year.*

teachers have "philosophical differences" with administrators, sometimes further complicated by mild or severe cases of "personality conflict." These situations, and many more, may result in an attempt to dismiss a teacher, and dismissal procedures are covered by the laws in each state.

If a school district decides in the middle of a school year (and therefore in the middle of a contract) to dismiss an untenured teacher, the teacher always has a right to a full hearing and due process. On the other hand, if the district decides not to extend a second- or third-year contract to a new teacher, the situation is less clear. Although in some states an untenured teacher who is not being rehired can demand a hearing, in most states the school district does not have to justify its reasons for not rehiring.

tenure as "property"

For tenured teachers, the legal situation is different. Tenure is protected under the Fourteenth Amendment and is considered part of the teacher's "property." In a sense, the tenured teacher has "earned" and "owns" the job, and he or she can be separated from it only under very special circumstances. Here the teacher can call on the full protection of the law, as she or he would if someone were trying to take away a home or a car. To justify dismissal, the school district must prove that the tenured teacher has violated some provision of the tenure law. Again, states vary concerning what they consider due cause for dismissal. The most common reasons include immorality, insubordination, incompetence, and unprofessional behavior. It is the responsibility of the courts to weigh the individual situation, to review the law on the subject, and to determine whether the case justifies dismissal.

Reduction in Force   There is one category of dismissal in which the teacher's standing and conduct seem to play a minor part. Called **reduction in force (RIF),** or *riffing* in slang, it occurs when there are more teachers than are needed and a school district, for economic reasons, must let some of the teachers go. Though common in the 1970s and 1980s, when student enrollments were shrinking, riffing is rarely used for this reason today.

reductions for economic reasons

Sometimes the courts allow schools to dismiss teachers as a result of curricular reorganization. For example, a school board might decide to drop its classical language department. Normally, though, riffing occurs in a climate of economic crisis. Although those who select which teachers to rif typically respect the seniority principle (bad news for beginning teachers), states vary in this respect. In some states, the law is relatively silent about whom the school district can let go and how it can do so, leaving the decisions up to the individual boards.

The Teacher and Liability

When you were in elementary or secondary school, did you ever wonder (as we did) why teachers seemed to get so upset with students who ran in the halls, bounded down the stairways, or engaged in a little friendly wrestling? The probable reason behind their concern may be well expressed in one word: liability. **Liability** means blame, as in "The teacher can be held liable for the student's sep-

The school playground can be dangerous . . . and an area of potential teacher liability. (© Myrleen Ferguson/PhotoEdit)

arated shoulder" and other accidents and mistakes; that is, the teacher behaved negligently or intentionally in a way that allowed the injury to happen.

Teachers are responsible for ensuring the safety and well-being of their students in their own classrooms and work spaces and in the activities they oversee. This includes fieldtrips and after-school clubs and activities, such as band, sports, and play rehearsals. Teachers are also liable if they observe a student in some potentially dangerous act that eventually turns out to be harmful and they do nothing. Turning one's back on misbehavior in no way lessens this responsibility. Teachers can be held liable for acts of omission.

areas of liability

A major potential source of liability is the teacher's absence from the classroom. For a variety of reasons, teachers sometimes leave their classrooms unattended and thus their students unsupervised. If an injury occurs during an absence and a suit is brought, the court is quite concerned, first, with whether the teacher's absence contributed to the possibility of the injury (would it have happened if the teacher had been there?) and, second, with what special circumstances surrounded the absence. If some of the students had a history of fighting or if clear evidence suggested that the class might behave irresponsibly, the court will lean toward finding the teacher liable. If the teacher had a good reason to be away from the class or if the incident was a freak event, the teacher will have little to worry about from the courts.

absence from classroom

Liability Precautions   Injuries and accidents are inevitable in schools. With hundreds of students and myriad activities, something unplanned and hurtful is to be expected. From the standpoint of liability, teachers need to be able to show that they have been "reasonably prudent." They need to be able to demonstrate, for example, that

▶ They made a reasonable attempt to anticipate dangerous situations.

▶ They provided proper supervision.

▶ They took precautions.

▶ They established rules.

▶ They gave a warning to minimize the chances of students getting hurt.

liability insurance

Since teachers are vulnerable to legal suit, it is important that they be covered by some form of liability insurance. However, in recent years, many teachers have been scared into buying more insurance than they need or, more commonly, into buying insurance when they are already covered by school district insurance policies. Therefore, the new teacher should check on-the-job coverage with the district's personnel director before beginning work.

automobile liability

One area in which experts claim teachers are particularly at risk is automobile liability.[9] Often teachers volunteer to take students in their own cars to a sports game or on a fieldtrip. Even if teachers have personal insurance, they often do not have enough to cover liability claims if a serious accident happens. Before taking students in a private car, the teacher needs to be sure that the district's insurance policy covers such cases or that his or her own policy is adequate.

In all these issues of liability, it is important for the teacher to use good judgment. Accidents often "just happen," and there may be no liability. As noted earlier, if a school injury results in a legal suit, the courts will try to determine if the teacher was providing reasonable care and, in general, was acting in a prudent and careful manner.

Self-Defense

Schools are very crowded places, and they are crowded, by definition, with immature individuals. Thus, it is not at all surprising that conflicts erupt and teachers find themselves encountering hostile behavior. For instance, a teacher may have to break up a playground fight or stop some students from vandalizing another student's locker. Or a student may strike a teacher in anger.

"reasonable force"

Self-defense is defined broadly here to take in all these situations. In the first two cases, fighting and vandalism, the teacher is expected to intercede in the interest of safety. In a fight, for instance, the teacher must act to stop the students from hurting one another. Strong words usually are effective, but sometimes the teacher must become physically involved. The operating principle here is "reasonable force." If a teacher uses reasonable force, and if, in the process of stopping the fight and separating the students, a student suffers an injury (say, a strained wrist or dislocated arm), the courts typically will find that the teacher is not liable. If the same injuries resulted from a fight the teacher did not act to stop, he or she may be held liable.

In more obvious cases of self-defense, a student threatens or actually strikes a teacher, and the principle of reasonable force applies here too. What constitutes reasonable force is generally a matter of common sense, but the heat of the moment can make good judgment difficult. In one case, a male seventh-grader who weighed 110 pounds struck a 220-pound coach. The coach grabbed the boy, lifted him off the ground, and threw him against a wall, breaking the child's back. When brought to court, the teacher-coach claimed self-defense. He lost—and lost big time. Usually in the court's view, it is the teacher's responsibility to keep a level head.

Assault and Battery   A teacher's recourse against an abusive student is governed by assault and battery laws. In legal terms, *assault* has come to mean a threat to do harm. Threats should always be taken seriously and reported to the principal, but their legal status depends very much on the student's ability to carry through on the threat. An angry fourth-grader's threat to "do something terrible to you" does not have the same status as a high school junior's threat to put sugar in the gas tank of your new car.

assault

Battery means a willful attack on another that results in harm. Being unintentionally knocked to the hall floor by a rushing student is not battery. (It may, however, call for some disciplinary action by the school.) Being intentionally pushed by a student or a parent is an entirely different matter and makes the pusher immediately liable.

battery

Incidents of assault or battery should be promptly reported and disciplinary action demanded or legal charges filed. Often teachers, particularly new teachers, are hesitant about making a fuss or turning offending students in to the proper school authorities. But verbal abuse and physical violence have no place in our elementary and secondary schools.

Freedom of Expression

If an employee of a business "sounds off" in a very public manner about his or her boss, the law provides the employee no protection against being fired. For much of our history, this was the case for public school teachers also. Even throughout most of this century, teachers who publicly criticized administrators' decisions or school board policies received little sympathy from judges. The attitude of the courts was that judges had no business interfering in the legitimate affairs of the schools. Things changed, though, as a result of Marvin Pickering.

Pickering, a high school English teacher, wrote a long and sarcastic letter in the local newspaper about his superintendent and school board. He accused them of, among other things, taking the local taxpayers "to the cleaners," making excessive expenditures on athletics, and forcing teachers to live in an atmosphere of totalitarianism. Pickering was fired. He sued for his job, and the original court verdicts upheld the firing. Although his letter contained factual errors and exaggerations, when the case was appealed before the U.S. Supreme Court in 1968, the Court ruled in Pickering's favor, ordering that he be reinstated and compensated.[10]

Pickering's free speech case

In effect, the Court said in the *Pickering* decision that society needs to balance the interests of a teacher, as a citizen commenting on issues of public concern, and the interests of the state, as the teacher's employer trying to promote

POLICY MATTERS!   School Censorship

What's the Policy?

As information and ideas have increasingly permeated the world of children, the debate over censorship has heated up considerably. Policies about approval of teaching material or about "appropriate material" are rarely called censorship by district or school administrators, but they often forbid the use or display by students and teachers of certain books or academic materials.

Among the most common causes for invoking censorship policies are "the three Ss": swear words, Satanism, and sex. In Monroeville, New Jersey, a parent objected to a school copy of *Webster's Dictionary* because it contains sexually explicit definitions. It was removed. In Texas, schools have banned certain jewelry, clothing, and symbols—including the peace sign and Star of David—that some believe are associated with Satanism.

How Does It Affect Teachers?

New teachers, typically fresh from the freewheeling intellectual environment of the college campus, are often shocked to discover censorship in the schools. Often, too, they discover it the hard way: they are reprimanded when a school newspaper they are supervising contains an off-color joke or vulgar language; a children's book their college teachers were wild about turns up on the district's banned list; they are expected to confront students who have downloaded pornography or racist materials from the Internet during class. No one had told them about censorship, but it is nevertheless there.

Consequences for teachers who choose not to censor their activities or materials can be severe. Recently, for example, an experienced and highly respected journalism teacher was released from her role as advisor to the school newspaper. The school principal in particular was dissatisfied with the tone and much of the content of the school newspaper. Several of the journalism students and newspaper staffers are sure that their advisor-

teacher was released because she supported them in writing such hard-hitting articles as an investigative piece on how easily teenagers can buy cigarettes in the town's local stores. They are convinced that replacing her is an act of censorship, and they are currently suing the school authorities for denying their rights to free speech.

It is useful, then, for a new teacher to inquire about any censorship issues before accepting a new assignment. But since even the word *censorship* sets people's teeth on edge, we recommend that you inquire instead about policies dealing with "controversial material" or policies guiding the selection of "appropriate teaching materials."

What Are the Pros?

Many parents, community members, and even teachers firmly believe children and adolescents are not ready to be exposed to everything. Further, they believe the school board has the responsibility to put in place and monitor censorship policies designed to protect students from exposure to inappropriate material.

The late Albert Shanker, a legendary fighter for teachers' rights, nicely stated the larger issue behind such cases:

> There is a tension between a teacher's academic freedom and a community's right to prescribe an appropriate curriculum for its students, between a teacher's academic freedom and his responsibility not to indoctrinate his students, between the school board's right to set a curriculum and a parent's right to determine what is appropriate for his child, . . . between a student's right to learn whatever he wants and the parent's right to shield his child from potentially harmful ideas.

What Are the Cons?

The limits on academic freedom and free speech that such policies impose may end up being too constricting. As a result, students and teachers might be forbidden to engage in potentially valuable learning experiences. Groups such as the American Association of University Professors have taken strong positions calling for more freedom in all classrooms, not just the college classroom. They report the growing threat of censorship at all levels of education and have called for teachers to be granted the professional right to select the material they believe is useful in promoting teaching and learning.

What Do You Think?

1. Do you believe it is appropriate for precollegiate schools to have censorship rules?

2. What censorship issues, if any, came up during your years in elementary and secondary school?

3. What do you think is the most appropriate way to explore the censorship policies of a potential place of employment?

Sources: David Hill, "Defending Mrs. Halas," *Education Week,* March 10, 1999; "Schools Fend Off More Attempts at Censorship," *USA Today,* August 30, 1990, p. 1D; Commission on Academic Freedom and Pre-College Education, *Liberty and Learning in the Schools* (Washington, DC: American Association of University Professors, 1986); the Shanker statement is from p. 3 of this report.

smoothly running schools. So although the Court affirmed the teacher's right to free expression, it pointed out that this First Amendment protection is not an absolute right. In many possible situations, such as when teachers become disruptive forces in a school or make irresponsible statements, the courts will not support their expression of their views. For instance, in 1981 the courts ruled against a teacher who had claimed that the racially derogatory comments he made to his principal and assistant principal were constitutionally protected.[11]

As with many other legal issues discussed in this chapter, the courts apply a "balancing test," reviewing each case individually and trying to weigh the rights of the teacher or students to free expression against the legitimate interests of the particular community. As a U.S. court of appeals stated in the 1970s *Scoville* v. *Board of Education* case, "Freedom of speech includes the right to criticize and protest school policies in a nondisruptive manner, but it does not include the use of 'fighting' words or the abuse of superiors with profane and vulgar speech."[12]

Scoville *v.* Board of Education

Symbolic Expression   Personal expression is not limited to spoken and written words. Dress styles, arm bands, and buttons have been used in recent years to "make a statement." Typically the courts support teachers (and students) in these cases of free symbolic expression. A key issue here involves the potential of this type of expression to lead to "substantial disruption" within the school. For instance, if a teacher wears a Ku Klux Klan button in a high school with African American students, or if two groups of students are feuding and their wearing their "colors" or jacket insignia provokes fighting, the symbols can be forbidden. On the other hand, these judgments cannot be a matter of a teacher's or an administrator's "taste." Bans on symbolic expression of one's views or preferences must be based on clear indications that the efficiency or safety of the school is endangered.

teaching controversial issues

Academic Freedom   A subcategory of freedom of expression, **academic freedom,** deals largely with issues in the classroom and the teachers' (and students') rights to discuss ideas and read material of their choosing.

Conflict often arises from discussions of controversial issues such as sexual mores, gun control, or abortion. If such issues are a part of the school's curriculum, there is rarely a problem. But when a teacher "adds" them to the curriculum, he or she needs to make a reasonable case that they are relevant to the curriculum. Dismissal for teaching controversial issues may or may not be upheld by the courts. Teaching volatile issues that may disrupt a particular school, such as homosexuality or the alleged characteristics of different races, is frowned on by the courts. So is teaching controversial material considered unsuitable for the age of the students.

Political issues, both local and national, are also a point of tension. In the classroom, teachers may discuss current political controversies, but they must deal with them neutrally and in a balanced way. Away from work, advocating a particular cause or political party is fine, as long as the teacher does not behave as a partisan supporter in the classroom.

the Keefe *case*

Particular essays and books that contain sexually explicit material or even words that are offensive to certain members of a community have been a great source of legal controversy in schools. In one important case, *Keefe* v. *Geanakos* (1969), a Massachusetts English teacher, Robert Keefe, assigned his students an article from the well-respected *Atlantic Monthly* that contained offensive language. Keefe's assignment caused a storm, and he was eventually fired for refusing to agree not to assign the article again. Subsequently, he was reinstated by a circuit court decision because the offending language existed in a number of books already in the school library; because the school board had not notified him that such material was prohibited; and, finally, because that court believed the word in question was not all that shocking to the students. As the decision stated, "With the greatest respect to such parents, their sensibilities are not the full measure of what is proper education."[13]

relevant considerations

Issues of academic freedom often generate a great deal of heat. When they reach the courts, the following considerations, among others, are brought to bear:

1. The teacher's purpose

2. The educational relevance of the controversial publication

3. The age of the students involved

4. The quality of the disputed teaching material and its effects on the class[14]

Perhaps the most important point to remember is that academic freedom is limited: it cannot be used to protect the incompetent teacher or the indoctrinating zealot.

Lifestyle and the Teacher

Teachers bring into their classrooms more than their minds and their lesson plans. They bring their attitudes and values. Elementary and secondary teachers traditionally have been considered extensions of the family in passing on to the young the community's positive values. In past generations, teachers who behaved in ways counter to the community's values were dismissed. Teachers were summarily fired for homosexuality, being pregnant and single, living with someone of the opposite sex, using illegal drugs, being publicly drunk, or committing a crime. However, the late 1960s saw a reconsideration of the community's right to require certain standards of behavior and of individuals' rights to their own lifestyles and values. Although some areas are still legally quite uncertain, on many questions judicial opinion (the way judges are tending to rule) is clear.

teachers and community values

Personal Appearance: Hair, Clothes, and Weight   Although in the late 1960s and early 1970s the courts tended to rule in favor of teachers' rights to do what they wished with their hair, currently the courts are siding more often with school districts' rights to impose reasonable grooming codes for teachers. Teachers, according to the current view, do not have a *constitutional* right concerning their "style of plumage."[15]

less leniency today

The situation is similar for clothing. Courts are upholding districts' judgments on skirts that are considered too short, as well as the requirement (in some districts) that male teachers wear neckties. Courts are asserting that the First Amendment does not extend to "sartorial choice."

For health reasons, obesity may be its own punishment. However, does a school district have a right to fire a teacher because it decides she or he is too fat? A California school district released a forty-two-year-old female physical education teacher because, at 5 feet 7 inches and 225 pounds, the district felt she was "unfit for service." Her principal argued that she "did not serve as a model of health and vigor" and was restricted in her ability to perform on the trampoline, in gymnastics and modern dance, and in other aspects of the program.[16] Here, though, the court sided with the teacher, claiming that the district had not proved that her girth had impaired her performance.

Private Sexual Behavior   In the past, sexual behavior was considered an area in which a community had a complete right to impose its standards on people selected to teach its children. Currently, however, the courts are increasingly viewing teachers' private sexual habits or preferences as separate from their public, professional lives as teachers. A landmark case involved Marc Morrison, who was fired after his former lover, another male teacher, reported their brief relationship to the superintendent. Believing that the state's law requiring teachers to be models of good conduct applied to the case, that teachers are required to impress on their charges "principles of morality," and, further, that homosexual behavior is contrary to the moral standards of the people of California, the school district believed it was on solid ground in dismissing Morrison.

the Morrison *case*

However, in 1969 the California Supreme Court ruled in Morrison's favor. It acknowledged that homosexuality is, for many people, an uncertain or controversial area of morality. But the court made an important distinction between a teacher's private life and his or her professional performance. Since there was no evidence that Morrison's sexual orientation had ever been part of his relationship with his students, or in any way affected the performance of his teaching duties, or, in fact, affected his relationship with his fellow teachers, he was reinstated.[17]

private vs. professional life

Similarly, cases involving pregnancy out of wedlock and unmarried couples living together are being settled in favor of the individual teacher. However, the conditions just cited are required. The behavior must not intrude into the classroom or seriously affect the teacher's professional performance. Flaunting one's deviation from the community's standard tends to increase the chances that the courts will uphold dismissal. In all these cases, though, circumstances play a crucial role in the courts' final opinion.

Conduct with Students   Whereas the courts have become increasingly lenient on issues of private sexual behavior, the line is being held firm with regard to socially unacceptable behavior that spills over into the classroom. One sure way to lose one's teaching position is to make a sexual advance to a student. Usually one incident is enough to sustain a dismissal. The same goes for smoking marijuana, taking other drugs, public drinking to the point of drunkenness, or even using excessively obscene language in the presence of students. In this area, the teacher bears the full weight of the responsibility to be a role model.

teacher held accountable

In general, then, except in matters of personal appearance, the courts are allowing teachers a good degree of freedom in their private and personal lifestyles as long as their choices and their behavior do not adversely affect their performance as teachers. Table 12.1 summarizes the court cases and rulings discussed in this and the previous sections.

Copyright Laws

Good teachers are always on the hunt for effective teaching materials: a story that carries a special message, a poem that captures an idea with beauty and economy, an article that contains the latest information about an issue students are studying. Having found the "perfect" piece, it is difficult to resist the temptation simply to copy it and share it with the class. And the wide availability of photocopying equipment makes this practice all too easy.

Printed matter, however, is the product of someone's labor, the same way a painting or a piece of furniture is. In the law, it is considered intellectual property. The creator or author has a legal right to receive a reward for his or her labor. Without such payment, few could afford to write books, plays, or articles. For this reason, first in 1909 and more recently in 1976, the U.S. Congress passed copyright laws to protect writers and publishers from the unauthorized use of their material.

justification for copyright laws

fair use guidelines

For teachers, the heart of the current copyright law is its **fair use** guidelines, which help specify what printed materials teachers may photocopy and under

TABLE 12.1   Selected Court Cases Dealing with Teachers' Rights and Responsibilities

Issue	Case	Ruling
A teacher's right to free speech (such as criticizing the school authorities)	*Pickering* v. *Board of Education* (1968)	A teacher can criticize the operation of a school as long as this does not interfere with the normal running of the school.
	Scoville v. *Board of Education* (1970)	Freedom of speech does not include the use of "fighting words" or the abuse of superiors with profane and vulgar speech.
A teacher and academic freedom	*Keefe* v. *Geanakos* (1969)	A teacher may not be dismissed only for selecting reading assignments with offensive words.
A teacher and his or her private life	*Morrison* v. *State Board of Education* (California, 1969)	A teacher's sexual orientation is not grounds for revocation of certification, particularly when it in no way affects the performance of professional tasks.

what conditions they may do so. The general principle behind fair use is "not to impair the value of the owner's copyright by diminishing the demand for that work, thereby reducing potential income for the owner."[18] In other words, if people simply copy printed materials whenever they want, they will not buy the books, and publishers and authors will suffer. Some copying is allowed, of course, and it is important for teachers to know what they may and may not do.

Teachers may:

▶ Make a single copy for class preparation of a chapter from a book; a newspaper or magazine article, short story, essay, or poem; or a diagram, chart, picture, or cartoon from a book or magazine

▶ Make a copy for each of their students of a poem if it is fewer than 250 words and printed on not more than 2 pages; and one copy for each student of an article or short story if it is fewer than 2,500 words

Teachers may not:

▶ Make copies of a work for their classes if another teacher in the same building already has copied that same material for his or her class

▶ Make copies of the same author's work more than once a semester or make copies from the same anthology, text, or periodical issue more than three times a semester

▶ Create a class anthology by copying material from several sources (a favorite trick of many teachers!)

▶ Make multiple copies of weekly newspapers or magazines specifically designed for classrooms, or of consumable materials, such as copyrighted games, exercises, and particularly worksheets from workbooks

▶ Charge more for legally permissible copies than it cost to copy them

These guidelines may seem overly restrictive and technical, but teachers actually have more liberal guidelines for copying than the average citizen does.

special rules for TV tapes

Videotapes, Software, and the Internet   There is a great temptation for teachers to tape material "off the air" and to build tape libraries of material to use in instruction. Although this may be effective pedagogy, it may not be legal. Commercially produced videos are intellectual property and are also covered by our copyright laws. Copyrighted television programs (and most of them are copyrighted) can be kept for only forty-five days, after which they must be erased or taped over. Also, during the first ten days after the taping, the teacher may show the tape only twice: once for initial presentation and once when "instructional reinforcement" is called for. Finally, schools cannot routinely record material for potential later use by a teacher. It can be done only at a teacher's request.

The personal computer has helped to revolutionize American life in general and American education in particular. (In Chapter 7, you learned more about how the use of technology can be an effective agent for reform in the schools.) In recent years, it has been possible to link up to nationwide networks of information through a telephone line or other cable. With these links, a world of information is at your fingertips. It is possible to copy information from government agencies, libraries, legal systems, and other schools with the touch of a button. For example, you may be tempted to copy a research report from an online news information service and make copies for all of the students in your class. Unless there are specific stipulations against such usage, this is acceptable practice. However, intellectual property rules are currently a big issue on the Internet and World Wide Web, and the law is still evolving.

Computer software programs are not treated in the same way as text, video clips, or still pictures. Commercially sold software differs from material "taken off" the Internet. Software should not be passed around and copied. In some cases, the software publisher may allow the purchaser to make one backup copy of the software, but making any other copies is a violation of the copyright laws. Although all of this may seem like "overkill," it is important for teachers to follow the rules—not simply because it is the law, but because students will follow their example.

Reporting Child Abuse

The abuse of children by their parents and other adults is a heinous crime. Child abuse includes beating and scarring; it also includes failure to provide a child with enough food, adequate clothing, or even dental care. High on the list too is incest, a frequently secret form of abuse that poisons the lives of many children. As a result of recent efforts in this area, all fifty states now require the reporting of suspected child abuse. Teachers have been a major target of this legislation, since they are often the only ones close enough to see or sense the violation an abused child has undergone.

The laws vary somewhat from state to state, but they are quite specific about the teacher's role. The law says not that teachers *may* report but that they *must* report suspected incidents. The teacher conveys any suspicions to the principal or the social agency that deals with child abuse. To protect a teacher from reaction to an incorrect report or from the anger of an offending parent, the reporting is kept confidential. Further, teachers are granted immunity from accusations of slander or any possible libel suit. Without such protection, many teachers would hesitate to report their suspicions. Child abuse is clearly one of those areas where it is better to act and be wrong than to play it safe. (For a more detailed discussion of child abuse, see Chapter 5.)

teachers must report suspicions

Teachers must be vigilant about possible abuse of their students. (© Bill Aron/PhotoEdit)

Law, Religion, and the School

According to the First Amendment to the Constitution, "Congress shall make no law respecting an establishment of religion, or prohibiting the free exercise thereof." During the past two centuries, the American judicial system interpreted this amendment inconsistently with respect to the place of religion in public schools, a topic of high controversy and much public unrest in recent years. The controversy is not new: the role of religion has been a bone of contention since the beginning of public education in the United States.

Among the questions currently being asked are the following:

▶ May public tax money be spent for support of parochial schools?

▶ What religious observances, if any, are permitted in public school classrooms?

▶ May religious holidays be observed in public schools and, if so, which ones?

▶ Is all prayer, public and private, illegal in our schools?

▶ Are extracurricular religious clubs allowed in public schools?

▶ May parents insist that schools provide alternative textbooks consistent with their religious beliefs?

rulings against prayer

Prayer and Scripture in the School   Until the mid–twentieth century, religious observances, including Bible reading and prayers, were common in the public schools. In fact, Bible reading and the recitation of the Lord's Prayer were required by the Constitution or by statutes in a number of states. In *Abington School District* v. *Schempp* (1963), however, the Supreme Court ruled both to be unconstitutional.

In a 1962 decision (*Engel* v. *Vitale*), the Court had already ruled against the recitation of a nondenominational prayer, holding that Bible reading and prayer violate both clauses of the First Amendment. The Court recognized that the schools involved did not compel a child to join in religious activities if his or her parents objected; nevertheless, the Court held that the social pressures exerted on pupils to participate were excessive. In essence, no distinction was believed to exist between voluntary and compulsory participation in religious activities.

objective use of Bible

The Court did note that the study of comparative religion, the history of religion, and the relationship of religion to civilization were not prohibited by this decision. It would also appear that, although the Bible may not be used to teach religion, it might, if objectively presented, be used in such areas of study as history, civics, and literature. Indeed, most thoughtful people would agree that failure to be conversant with the Old and New Testaments makes understanding of Western history and literature impossible. In the same way, if a student set out to learn about Chinese culture and was not permitted to read Confucius, he or she would be doomed to a very limited understanding.

The Supreme Court has approved the right of public school pupils who so desire to say prayers and read scriptures of their choice in the morning before school starts or after the regular school day has ended. If prayers are said during lunch period, they must be silent.

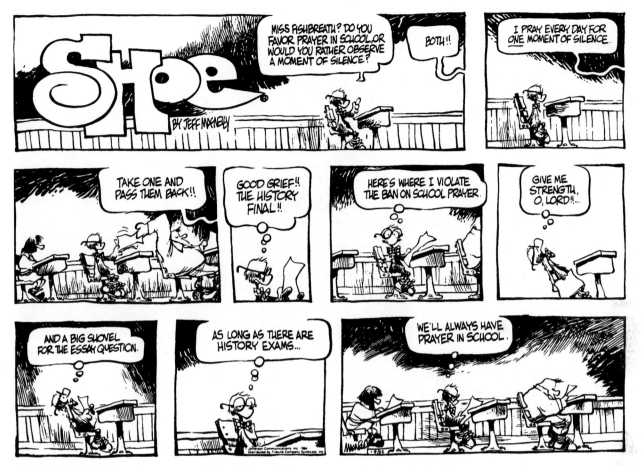

In a more recent decision (*Lee* v. *Weisman,* 1992), the Court determined that the recitation of prayers at a public school function was unconstitutional. A principal of a public middle school, Robert Lee, had invited a rabbi to say a benediction and invocation at the middle school graduation exercises, instructing the rabbi to offer nonsectarian prayers. Student Deborah Weisman and her father filed a suit in court seeking a permanent injunction against including prayers in graduation ceremonies. The Supreme Court used the following facts to reach its decision: (1) public school officials direct the performance of formal religious exercises at graduation ceremonies, and (2) although such exercises do not require attendance, they are in a real sense obligatory for all students, even those who object. As a result, the Supreme Court upheld the decision of the lower court, ruling that it is unconstitutional to include clergy members who offer prayers as part of school graduation ceremonies.[19]

Religious Clubs and Prayer Groups   Are extracurricular religious clubs legal in public schools? Court decisions provide no clear guidelines here. In at least one case, a district judge ruled in favor of such clubs based on students' right to

religious extracurricular clubs

"Meeting at the flag" for morning prayer is a growing movement in our schools. (© Rob Crandall/ The Image Works)

free speech. But a U.S. circuit court of appeals overturned the decision, maintaining that such clubs violated the First Amendment's "establishment of religion" clause. The Supreme Court did not clear the waters: the five-justice majority upheld the district court opinion on a technical point, but declined to comment on the constitutional issues raised.[20]

In yet another case, *Board of Education of Westside Community Schools* v. *Mergens* (1990), the courts ruled that extracurricular religious group meetings held on public school grounds did not necessarily violate the Constitution. The Court stated that if the school provides a limited public access for other noncurriculum student groups, then, under the Equal Access Act, a student religious group may also use the school building for its meetings. Under these circumstances, then, a student religious group meeting in the cafeteria after school does not violate the constitutional separation of church and state.[21] A key point here is that the prayer and scripture-reading groups are student initiated and teachers do not participate.

Religion and Secular Humanism   The many court cases dealing with prayer in school, extracurricular clubs, and the presence of the Bible in schools, and the publicity surrounding them, have had a chilling effect on teachers and administrators. Rather than get involved with what is clearly a controversial set of issues, many public educators have tended to discourage any expression or even mention of religious issues or topics. This, in turn, has caused a reaction from parents and others who think that by ignoring the religious dimension of life, the public schools create a distorted, and ultimately dangerous, view of humankind—a view

secular humanism issue

labeled *secular humanism*. Secular humanism asserts the dignity of human beings but ignores the idea of God and the spiritual.

Objecting to what they see as the prevailing secular humanism of the schools, some parents contend that such fundamental questions as "What is a person's true nature?" can be treated in schools from every perspective except the religious view. They claim that this is not only intellectually unbalanced but a danger to their children. Speaking to this issue, one legal scholar has written, "When government imposes the content of school, it becomes the same deadening agent of repression from which the framers of the Constitution sought to free themselves."[22] Many parents are voting not only with their pocketbooks, by turning down school budgets and tax requests for public schooling, but also with their feet, by walking away from the public school system. This trend has fueled a dramatic growth in religious schools and particularly in home schooling in recent years.

Specific objections to secular humanism in the schools have taken a number of forms. Two examples are the controversies over teaching about the origins of the human race and those over the use of certain textbooks.

The Creationism Versus Evolution Controversy   Major concern over the teaching of evolution dates to the famous 1925 *Scopes* trial in Tennessee. Although at the time the trial came to national attention (and again decades later with the award-winning play and film *Inherit the Wind,* based on that trial), no legal precedents were set. The issue returned to the public eye when citizens asked for equal time for the biblical account of creation. In 1982, the Louisiana legislature passed the Balanced Treatment for Creation-Science and Evolution-Science Act, which quickly came to be known as the Balanced Treatment Act. The act defined *scientific creationism* as "the belief that the origins of the elements, the galaxy, the solar system, of life, of all the species of plants and animals, the origin of man, and the origin of all things and their processes and relationships were created ex nihilo (from nothing) and fixed by God."[23] In addition to requiring that scientific creationism be taught whenever evolution was taught, the act required the development of curriculum guides and research services for teaching creationism. On the other hand, the act provided none of these resources or protections for those teaching evolution.

Balanced Treatment Act

After several challenges and lower court rulings, a case, *Edwards* v. *Aguillard,* reached the U.S. Supreme Court, which in 1987 ruled seven to two against the Balanced Treatment Act. According to the Court, the Balanced Treatment Act was, in fact, not balanced because its provisions favored the teaching of creationism over evolution. Further, the Court asserted, the Balanced Treatment Act was motivated by the legislature's desire to promote a particular religious viewpoint and thereby violated the Constitution's provision against the establishment of a state-sponsored religion. Despite the Court's arguments, few observers think this controversy has been settled. In 1999, the Kansas Board of Education voted on the state's standard and no longer required the teaching of evolution in public schools.[24] Within days, suits were filed challenging the decision. But although 68 percent of Americans believe creationism should be taught in our schools,[25] it appears that the creationism-versus-evolution clash has become the battleground between those who believe the public schools have become antireligious and are promoting secularism and those opposed to the schools teaching a religious point of view.

Tennessee case

The Textbook Controversy   Recent court cases have been launched by fundamentalist Christian parents who argue that texts used in their children's public school classes are anti-Christian and thus a violation of their children's constitutional rights. In a 1986 Tennessee case, a U.S. district judge agreed that students' constitutional rights were violated when they were expelled after they refused to read certain texts. However, the following year a U.S. court of appeals reversed the decision of the lower court and ruled that the texts in question did not promote or require a person to accept any religion.[26]

Shortly after, another challenge to the public schools' choice of textbooks was made in Alabama by fundamentalist parents, students, and teachers. Forty-four textbooks used in history, social studies, and home economics courses were cited as advancing secular humanism. In this case (*Smith* v. *Board of School Commissioners of Mobile County*), the courts followed a pattern similar to that of the Tennessee case just described. Initially the district court ruled that secular humanism is a religion and that some of the textbooks in question did discriminate against theistic religion. On appeal, this decision was reversed, and the court ruled that the textbooks promoted neither secularism nor any other religion.[27]

Guidelines for Religious Neutrality

Table 12.2 summarizes the court rulings on religion and the public schools. Yet with all the cases taken together, teachers may very well remain confused about what they can and cannot do. Thankfully, some attempts have been made to establish guidelines for the teacher and the school.

suggested guidelines

Thomas McDaniel recommends a *religious neutrality principle* in the classroom and offers the following four guidelines for putting it into practice:

1. Students may not be required to salute the flag or to stand for the flag salute if this conflicts with their religious beliefs.

2. Bible reading, even without comment, may not be practiced in a public school when the intent is to promote worship.

3. Prayer is an act of worship and as such cannot be a regular part of opening exercises or other aspects of the regular school day.

4. Worship services (such as prayer and Bible reading) are not constitutional even if voluntary rather than compulsory. Neither consensus, nor majority vote, nor excusing objectors from class or participation makes these practices legal.[28]

This principle of religious neutrality does not mean, however, that the public school must ignore religion. On the contrary, public schools are free to study the history and contributions (pro and con) of individual religions, to read the Bible as literature, and, in general, to expose students to our culture's religious heritage. When teachers cross the line into advocating a particular religion or involving students in prayer, they become vulnerable to legal action.

A few years ago, as debate over such issues continued, the White House asked the Department of Education to issue a directive on religion in the public

TABLE 12.2   Selected U.S. Court Cases Dealing with Religion and the Schools

Issue	Case	Ruling
Teaching evolution and/or creationism Teaching evolution in public schools	*Scopes* v. *State of Tennessee* (1925)	The court upheld the state law permitting the teaching of evolution as an explanation of the origins of the universe.
Balancing the teaching of creationism and evolution in public school curricula	*Edwards* v. *Aguillard* (1987)	Schools teaching the biblical explanation of creation violate the Constitution's provision against teaching a particular religious viewpoint.
Public schooling, prayer, and the Bible The inclusion of Bible reading and prayer	*Engel* v. *Vitale* (1962)	Bible reading and teacher-led prayer in schools are in violation of the First Amendment; because of the social pressures involved, there is no difference between voluntary and compulsory prayer in school. However, private prayer and Bible reading are protected.
	Abington School District v. *Schempp* (1963)	Reading the Bible and reciting the Lord's Prayer in public schools are in violation of the First and Fourteenth Amendments; however, the Bible may be studied for historical, cultural, or other general educational purposes.
Reciting nondenominational prayers at public school ceremonies	*Lee* v. *Weisman* (1992)	It is unconstitutional to include adult-led prayers at public school ceremonies because all students are virtually obligated to attend ceremonies like graduations, even those students who object to the practice.
Public schools and extracurricular religious groups Extracurricular religious clubs meeting on public school property	*Board of Education of Westside Community Schools* v. *Mergens* (1990)	If a public school allows a limited public forum for other extracurricular groups, the Equal Access Act indicates that extracurricular religious groups may meet in public school buildings without violating the Constitution.

schools. The resulting guidelines are an attempt to find a new common ground between religious expression and religious freedom and, further, to correct the perception (or the fact) that schools are hostile to religion. Among the specific points listed in the guidelines are the following:

White House guidelines

▶ Public schools should not interfere with or intrude on a family's religious beliefs.

▶ Public education should be respectful of religion, should be open to appropriate religious expression, and should teach about religion because it is so very much a part of our nation's history.

▶ Advocacy of religion by teachers and administrators has no place in public education.

▶ Students' religious clubs and groups are entitled to hold meetings, to have common prayer, to read scriptures, and to have their meetings publicized through school bulletin boards, newspapers, and public address systems.

▶ Although school-sponsored prayer should not be permitted, it is appropriate to begin the school day with a moment of silence.[29]

> *Teaching about religion is not the same as teaching someone to be religious. In our multicultural, multiethnic society, understanding another person's faith will foster tolerance and harmony, a goal common to all religions.*
>
> —MARGARET BARTLEY

Although this directive from the Department of Education has been well received by many parents and educators, it has not yet been tested in the courts. Nor does it address all of the conflicting issues surrounding religion in public schools.

Students and the Law

Many of the most important legal issues that affect the lives of teachers relate directly to students and their rights. Students, particularly public school students, have a special status under the law. In this section, we will touch on a few of the more significant and current student-related issues that can affect the teacher.

In Loco Parentis: Due Process and the Student

For years, the courts used the legal principle of ***in loco parentis*** in cases involving students. This term literally means that the teacher(s) stands "in the place of the parents" and suggests parental concern and guidance. The teacher is expected to treat the student in a caring and informal manner instead of in the formal and legalistic manner that governs relationships "out in the world." By the same reasoning, since we do not require due process in the home, for a long time it was not valued in the schools.

Gradually, though, in court cases such as *Tinker*[30] and others, the *in loco parentis* principle has eroded, and the courts have come to appreciate that students often need to be protected from the arbitrary use of authority. As a direct result, many schools have developed clear statements governing procedures for expulsion, suspension, student privacy, freedom of speech and publication, and various breaches of discipline. Informing students of the rules, procedures, and consequences of violations in these areas is a major step toward providing due process rights. Still, the most important aspect of due process is the spirit of fair and evenhanded justice with which teachers respond to the daily events of the classroom.

more explicit rules today

Suspension and Expulsion

Schools are crowded, busy places, teeming with growing minds and bodies and throbbing with restless energy. To keep things on track and moving forward, schools have rules and procedures to guide the behavior of students. Amid all the activity and stress of school life and society as a whole, it is surprising that students' conduct breaks down so infrequently. Nevertheless, on occasion it does. Ever since schools began, individual students have had difficulty following the rules and staying out of trouble. In recent decades, as schools have tried harder to keep older youth from dropping out, and as drugs and violence have increased in society as a whole, problems have escalated. One of the most dramatic and horrible examples is the massacre at Columbine High School in Colorado in the spring of 1999.

rising discipline problems

Educators need to keep in mind that some students, having been compelled to stay in school, find little to capture their imaginations and to motivate them. For these students, school continues to be a place of failure and frustration, and trouble is often close behind. Some of the more common forms of school infractions today are stealing; vandalizing school property or someone's private property; bringing a weapon to school; possessing, using, or selling drugs or alcohol; fighting (or encouraging others to fight); and repeatedly disobeying the reasonable directives of teachers and other school personnel.[31]

School districts are not powerless in the face of these kinds of disciplinary breaches. For the good of maintaining a safe and effective academic environment, schools have three alternatives: in-school suspension, out-of-school suspension, and expulsion. Typically in-school suspension is for minor offenses and is brief in duration. Out-of-school suspension and expulsion are, of course, more serious and for a longer period, with expulsion meaning complete separation from the school. This school district power must be wielded in a manner that ensures that students' constitutional rights to due process are protected. And it is here, in the administration of suspension and expulsion, that school administrators in particular have become entangled in the courts.

power of suspension or expulsion

Major Court Cases   One of the most important cases was *Goss* v. *Lopez*,[32] a 1975 suspension case involving Dwight Lopez, a high school sophomore from Columbus, Ohio. Lopez was suspended for ten days for allegedly becoming involved in a cafeteria disturbance. This suspension occurred without a hearing and without any prior notification. Although a suspension of this length and without a hearing or prior notice was in accord with the Ohio statutes, a suit was

Lopez suspension case

filed stating that Lopez's constitutional rights had been violated because there was no notice or hearing. The case went to the U.S. Supreme Court, which ruled in favor of Lopez on the grounds that students facing suspension from a public school have property and liberty interests and therefore are protected by due process. In addition, the Court stated that "longer suspensions (longer than ten days) or expulsions for the remainder of the school term, or permanently, may require more formal procedures."

In a 1988 case with some similar elements, *Honig* v. *Doe,* the Supreme Court ruled against California school officials.[33] A school district had suspended indefinitely two emotionally disturbed students on the grounds that they were dangerous, and the Court ruled that this suspension was a violation of the Individuals with Disabilities Education Act (IDEA) (PL 94–142), which allows school authorities to suspend dangerous students with disabilities for a maximum of ten days. Longer suspensions require either the permission of parents or the consent of a federal judge.

violation of PL 94–142

Pregnancy, Parenthood, and Marriage   As mentioned earlier, not many years ago, unmarried teachers who became pregnant were routinely dismissed from their teaching positions. And once a student was discovered to be either married, pregnant, or both, she was dismissed. With regard to students, this policy of dismissal was standard procedure until relatively recently. Pregnant students were considered to be morally corrupting influences on other students, and their presence in school was seen as legitimizing premature sexual activity and early marriage. Although many people still hold these views, the courts have tended in recent years to see such dismissals as discriminatory to young women and a denial of their rights to an education.[34] The result is that most school districts make arrangements for the education of pregnant students. Nevertheless, vexing issues keep coming up, such as "Should a quite pregnant cheerleader be allowed to continue cheering?"

rights of pregnant students

Guidelines for Educators   Overall, in recent years, the pendulum of judicial decisions seems to be moving away from an emphasis on student rights and back in favor of the authority of the schools.[35] Nevertheless, when dealing with matters that might lead to suspension or expulsion, teachers and administrators should follow these guidelines:

useful guidelines

▶ *Documentation.* First, before suspension and expulsion can take place, students must be notified (either in writing or orally) of the nature of their offense and what the intended punishment is.

▶ *Explanation.* Second, the school must give the students a clear explanation of the evidence on which the disciplinary charges rest.

▶ *Opportunity to defend oneself.* Third, the school must give the students an opportunity to refute the charges before a fair and impartial individual with decision-making authority.

Corporal Punishment

Although few educational theorists living today advocate it, corporal, or physical, punishment is alive and well in American schools. The Supreme Court has regularly refused to rule on corporal punishment, leaving the issue up to the states. The trend among the states is clearly in favor of banning it. In 1979 only two states had banned corporal punishment in public schools, but by 1996 twenty-seven states had prohibited it.[36] A number of other states currently have legislation pending that would abolish corporal punishment. Still, many states leave the decision up to local school districts. Approximately 50 percent of students attend school in districts that do not allow corporal punishment.[37]

What does this situation mean for teachers from a legal point of view? First, they must know the rules of their state and school district. Second, they must be aware that the courts have ruled that corporal punishment can be administered only under certain conditions. Thus, teachers must be sure they are using only "moderate" and "reasonable" corporal punishment and using it only to establish discipline. A teacher who severely punishes a child, especially if any permanent disability or disfigurement results, is highly liable to suit. Also, punishment cannot be administered out of spite, revenge, or anger. In ruling on cases of excessive corporal punishment, the courts scrutinize the teacher's state of mind and motivation. The instruments of corporal punishment and where it can be administered are also matters of concern to the courts. Fists are totally inappropriate; so are switches and canes. Blows must not strike parts of the body where the risk of injury is high. Also, the punishment must be in scale with the crime—no whipping for whispering, for instance. Apparently the days of the principal's dictum "The beatings will continue until the morale improves" are over.

limits on corporal punishment

Corporal punishment, of course, also entails important ethical considerations. Is it better to paddle a schoolyard bully and keep him in school or have legal hearings and separate him from the possibility of further education? One large problem with corporal punishment is that a ruler on the palm provokes terror in one student but is all but meaningless for the next student. On the other hand, noncorporal punishment, such as the prolonged separation of an offending student from classmates, may cause true psychic pain for some children. The entire area of dealing with disruptive and offending students needs careful thought and even more careful actions.

Search and Seizure

As we write this, the newspapers and airwaves abound with news about a study reporting that drug use among school-age children has doubled in four years. Many students, even students of junior high and elementary ages, possess and sell illegal drugs. Schools have drug problems because American youth culture is inundated with images of drug use. And drugs are only one problem relating to search and seizure. Students also bring alcohol, pornography, and even dangerous weapons to school.

locker search rules

A student's locker may be searched by an appropriate school official, usually an administrator, *if there are reasonable grounds* to suspect that the locker contains something illegal or dangerous. The New York State courts have gone further in stating that "not only have the school authorities the right to inspect but the right becomes a duty when suspicion arises that something of an illegal nature may be secreted there."[38] On the other hand, courts have found that it violates students' rights under the Fourth Amendment, and is therefore illegal, for school personnel to systematically spot-check lockers in hunts for drugs, weapons, or other illicit materials. Students' rights are even more closely protected when it comes to clothing and body searches.

Reasonableness and Probable Cause   The most important criterion in cases of search and seizure is *reasonableness,* as shown by the 1985 Supreme Court case *New Jersey* v. *T.L.O.*[39] A teacher found two high school girls smoking in the bathroom and immediately brought them to the assistant vice principal's office. One girl admitted to smoking, but the second denied not only smoking on this occasion but even being a smoker. The administrator asked the second student to come to his office, where he opened her purse and discovered a pack of cigarettes, cigarette-rolling papers, marijuana, a pipe, empty plastic bags, a wad of bills, and a list of "people who owe me money." Enter the police. The student was turned over to the juvenile court, where she was judged to be delinquent. She appealed on the basis that the search of her purse had violated her constitutional rights and therefore the evidence against her had been obtained illegally.

criterion of "reasonableness"

The case went to the U.S. Supreme Court, and the student lost. The Court stated, "The legality of a search of a student should depend simply on the reasonableness, under all the circumstances, of the search." Reasonableness appears to be determined, first, by whether or not the search has been initiated by a "reasonable" suspicion. Having seen rolling papers, it was reasonable to look for marijuana, since the two are so often closely related. The second criterion of reasonableness is that its scope and conduct must be "reasonably" related to the circumstances that gave rise to the search. Further, school officials must take into consideration the age and sex of the student and the nature of the offense.

probable cause

Another way of saying this is that school authorities must have *probable cause* for such strong action, meaning they must have reliable information—not just suspicion—that the individual is hiding dangerous or illegal material. Mistakes here, particularly in the case of unwarranted strip searches, can be not only painfully embarrassing to the students but also very expensive for the school district.

Finally, the police do not have the same *custodial relationship*—the same kind of responsibility toward students—that school officials do. Therefore, as a general rule, police need a warrant and the consent of school officials to search individual students or their lockers.

Freedom of Speech

The right to say what we want, where we want is the cornerstone of a free society, and as such it is near and dear to Americans. Justice William O. Douglas stated,

"Restriction of free thought and free speech is the most dangerous of all subversions. It is the one un-American act that could most easily defeat us." But although our courts vigilantly protect this right, it is not an absolute right. The great Supreme Court justice Oliver Wendell Holmes wrote that freedom of speech does not give a person the right to yell "Fire!" in a crowded theater or to knowingly and maliciously say or write lies that damage the reputation of another. In schools, freedom of expression must be balanced with the school's responsibility to maintain a safe and orderly environment and to protect people's feelings and reputations.

limits of free speech

Students' First Amendment Rights   During the 1960s and early 1970s, many social protests and antiwar demonstrations spilled over into the schools, particularly the high schools. In one case, *Tinker* v. *Des Moines Independent Community School District* (1969), students who had been suspended for wearing antiwar arm bands took the issue to court, claiming that the school had interfered with their right to freedom of expression. The Supreme Court ruled in favor of the students, stating that their black arm bands were a form of symbolic speech in

Tinker case—symbolic protest

Students exercise their free speech at a rally protesting a California educational proposition. (© Jose Carrillo/PhotoEdit)

protest of the Vietnam War and should not be prohibited. A key point in this affirmation of students' First Amendment rights was the passive and nondisruptive nature of the students' protest. According to the Court, there was no evidence that the wearing of arm bands would "materially and substantially interfere with the requirements of appropriate discipline in the operation of the schools."[40]

Fraser case—lewd speech

A Shift in Legal Direction: Restricting Student Speech   During the 1970s and 1980s, the *Tinker* case was often cited, but the tide of court opinion in favor of student rights to free speech soon began to recede. In the 1986 case of *Bethel School District No. 403* v. *Fraser*,[41] Matthew Fraser, a high school student in Bethel, Washington, nominated another student for vice president of the student government in a formal speech at an assembly before 600 students. Despite the warning of two teachers, Fraser built his speech on an elaborate, graphic, and explicit sexual metaphor comparing the nominee to a sexual organ. The court records of this case fail to tell us the outcome of the election, but Matthew Fraser got the ax. He was suspended for three days and removed from the list of candidates to speak at graduation. Fraser sued and won initially, but when the case went to the Supreme Court, he lost by a seven-to-two decision. The Court affirmed the school's right to "establish standards of civic and mature conduct" and to enforce them.

Hazelwood/Kuhlmeier case— school newspapers

School Newspapers and Freedom of the Press   School newspapers have long been the arena for struggles over freedom of speech and freedom of the press. Often the very best efforts to make the paper "vital" and "relevant" draw the newspaper staff into controversies. This is what happened at Hazelwood East High School in the spring of 1983.[42] Attempting to make their paper, *The Spectrum,* speak more directly to the real issues confronting their fellow students, the staff submitted two controversial articles, one dealing with the personal accounts of three Hazelwood students who had become pregnant and the other focusing on divorce and its effect on students.

In line with standard practice, the advisor and teacher of the journalism class that produced the paper passed the issue on to the principal for his approval. The principal eliminated the two pages containing the offending stories and sent the other four pages to the printer. Although the identities of the students were protected and, in the case of the pregnant girls, there were no graphic accounts of sexual activity, the principal believed that, given the small size of the school, the anonymity of the pregnant girls would be violated. He was also concerned about the effect of the articles' frank sexual comments on young readers. Finally, he raised the issue of the one-sidedness of the divorce article, which portrayed an inattentive father as the villain. In response, Kathy Kuhlmeier and the six other journalism students sued, contending that their freedom of speech rights had been violated.

During the next five years, the *Hazelwood/Kuhlmeier* case was first decided in the federal court in favor of the school district, then overturned in favor of the students by the Seventh Circuit Court of Appeals, and finally, in 1988, came before the Supreme Court. By a vote of five to three, the Supreme Court ruled in favor of the school district. Although dissenting justices complained about the potential for "thought control" and the "denuding of high school students of much of the First Amendment protection that *Tinker* in itself prescribed," the majority supported the principal's actions as legal and responsible. As stated in the majority opinion,

> A school may in its capacity as publisher of a school newspaper or producer of a school newspaper or producer of a school play disassociate itself not only from speech that would substantially interfere with its work or impinge on the rights of other students but also from speech that is, for example, ungrammatical, poorly written, inadequately researched, biased, prejudiced, vulgar or profane, or unsuitable for immature audiences. . . . A school need not tolerate student speech that is inconsistent with its basic educational mission even though the government could not censor similar speech outside the school.[43]

students' rights lose ground

Implications of the Court Cases   Taken together, the three cases we have just discussed—*Tinker, Bethel/Fraser,* and *Hazelwood/Kuhlmeier*—suggest that freedom of speech and expression in schools is hardly absolute. Students may be punished for offensive or disruptive speech or publications. Schools, then, are something like Justice Holmes's crowded theaters, and the students' freedom of speech is somewhat limited. Students can and should express themselves, but in an orderly and nonviolent way. And the school has the right and responsibility to be certain that language is not used to hurt or scandalize the students in their charge.

One cutting-edge freedom of speech issue involves use of the Internet. As discussed in Chapter 7, the Internet can be a marvelous educational tool, opening up infinite intellectual resources to students. However, it can also expose students to written and visual pornography, obscenity via email, and chatroom predators. Many school districts have been struggling to respond to these dangers without unduly restricting students' exploration. Among the responses currently in place are orientation programs on appropriate use of the Internet, more careful supervision of computer stations, and special software designed to block forbidden sites. Many districts have or are developing **acceptable use policies** designed to provide rules of the road for students using this technology.

problems with the Internet

Sexual Harassment

A 1993 study entitled "Hostile Hallways" indicated that 81 percent of American students reported they were the subjects of **sexual harassment** at some time during their school lives. However, only 7 percent reported the incident to school authorities. The most common offenses were sexual jokes, gestures, and comments, followed by sexual touching, grabbing, and intentionally brushing up against another person in a sexual way. While most of the offenses were student to student, a quarter of the girls and one-tenth of the boys reported being harassed by a school employee.

sexual harassment

Since the study first appeared, schools have attempted to address this abuse, focusing in particular on student-to-student harassment. The study's definition of sexual harassment is "unwanted and unwelcome sexual behavior which interferes with your life." However, what constitutes sexual harassment in a particular situation can be a thorny issue. For instance, in the fall of 1996, a North Carolina school suspended a *six-year-old* boy who had kissed a female classmate on the cheek for sexual harassment. On the other hand, many readers may know of serious and frightening harassment incidents from their own school experience. One such incident was the subject of a recent Supreme Court ruling in *Davis* v. *Monroe County Board of Education.*[44]

When LaShonda Davis was in fifth grade in Forsyth, Georgia, her harassment nightmare began. A fellow student began groping her, grinding up against her, and declaring that he was "going to get in bed with her." The girl and her parents made repeated complaints to her teacher and the school principal. After five months, the teacher finally agreed to move the boy's desk to the other side of the room. But the sexual taunting and lewd overtures continued, until finally the family sought legal counsel. Six years after the initial incident, and with much legal work, the suit finally made its way to the Supreme Court. The Court, in a controversial five-to-four decision, ruled for the Davises and against the school district.

What has made this case legally controversial is the perceived danger of our courts being flooded with cases ranging from innocuous flirtations to true, hard-core harassment. Further, judges worry that the budgets of school districts will be drained by the legal expenses involved in fighting frivolous suits. However, in the prevailing opinion, the *Davis* decision stresses that school districts are liable only if they were "deliberately indifferent" to information about "severe, pervasive, and objectively offensive" harassment among students. It appears that while the Court has come to the defense of harassed students, the criteria for what actually constitutes an offense have been set quite high. Nevertheless, the problem of sexual harassment in our schools is out of the closet and the high court's ruling is a shot across the bow of schools, which formerly have taken this issue casually. Table 12.3 summarizes the *Davis* case, along with other major students' rights cases discussed in preceding sections.

Records and Students' Right to Privacy

In this information age, most of us probably have a history tucked away on computer disks. For students, the history may consist of school records, various test scores, and ratings by teachers on everything from citizenship to punctuality. Teachers and other staff members judge a student's character and potential, and others use those judgments to decide whether or not the student should go to this school or get that job. Certainly we need some system of exchanging information about one another; otherwise, we would hire only our friends or attend only those schools where enough people knew us to vouch for us. However, the kind of information in school records may be very imperfect, and the danger that it will be misinterpreted or fall into the wrong hands is great.

TABLE 12.3 Selected Court Cases Related to Students' Rights

Issue	Case	Ruling
Students' right to free speech		
Students' right to make a symbolic protest	*Tinker* v. *Des Moines Independent Community School District* (1969)	Students have the right to symbolic protest, if that protest does not interfere with the school's operation.
Students' right to use lewd language for a school speech	*Bethel School District No. 403* v. *Fraser* (1986)	Schools have the right to establish and enforce standards of civic conduct.
Student newspapers and freedom of the press	*Hazelwood School District* v. *Kuhlmeier* (1988)	Because public schools are not public forums, school officials have the right not to publish student articles that may violate the sensibilities of other students.
Students' right to education		
Disabled students with behavior problems	*Honig* v. *Doe* (1988)	Dangerous students with disabilities may not be suspended for more than 10 days without parental consent or permission of a federal judge.
Students' right to freedom from sexual harassment	*Davis* v. *Monroe County Board of Education* (1999)	School held liable for excessive sexual harassment of one student by another student.
Students' right to due process		
Students' right to notification and hearing before a suspension	*Goss* v. *Lopez* (1975)	Schools violate students' constitutional right to due process if they suspend students without a hearing.
Students' rights regarding search and seizure		
Students' protection from school searches of personal items	*New Jersey* v. *T.L.O.* (1985)	Schools can search students' lockers and other private items if there is reasonable cause.

the Buckley amendment

In the early 1970s, a series of situations came to light in which information was poorly used or parents and students were denied access to records (for example, when a diagnosis was used to justify sending a child to a class for students with mental retardation). In response, Congress passed the Family Educational Rights and Privacy Act in 1974. The act, also known as the **Buckley amendment,** outlines who may and who may not see a student's record and under what conditions. A clear winner from this legislation is parents, who previously were kept from many of the officially recorded judgments that affected their children's futures. The amendment states that federal funds will be denied to a school if it prevents parents from exercising the right to inspect and review their children's educational records. Parents must receive an explanation or interpretation of the records if they so request.

However, the Buckley amendment does not give parents the right to see a teacher's or an administrator's unofficial records. For instance, a teacher's private diary of a class's progress or private notes about a particular child may not be inspected without the teacher's consent.

the downside of Buckley

Although the Buckley amendment has undoubtedly reduced the potential for abuse of information, it has had a somewhat chilling effect on teachers' and others' willingness to be candid in their judgments when writing student recommendations for jobs or colleges. Because students may elect to see a teacher's letter of recommendation, some teachers choose to play it safe and write a vague, general letter that lacks discriminating judgments, pro or con, about the student. In effect, some faculty members and other recommenders have adopted the attitude "Well, if a student doesn't trust me enough to let me write a confidential recommendation, I'll simply write an adequate, safe recommendation."

Nevertheless, the Buckley amendment's impact, in our view, has been positive. In the past, many students lost opportunities for higher education and desirable jobs because of inaccurate statements in recommendations or in their school records. One professor reported to us an incident that occurred in his school in 1975, shortly after the Buckley amendment came into being: "Our counselors at the junior high school where I taught were 'purging' the records of subjective comments with black markers. In one student's permanent record folder, a *Playboy* magazine fell out. It seems a grade school teacher took it from Carl and included it in his permanent record because she wanted future teachers to know 'what kind of kid Carl really was.'"

A Final Word

This chapter has been the beginning of what we hope will be your ongoing probe of the important role that two related issues, ethics and law, play in the life of the teacher. Together these issues permeate the school environment. Whereas ethical issues may raise timeless questions, some laws continually change, and even now the courts may be giving a different complexion to some of the decisions cited in this chapter. Also, the chapter has touched on many issues only lightly and has omitted others because of lack of space. We urge you to move on from this introduction to investigate further the work of the teacher in its larger ethical and legal framework.

KEY TERMS

ethics (395)

the law (404)

due process (404)

contract (406)

continuing contract (406)

breach of contract (406)

tenure (407)

reduction in force (RIF) (408)

liability (408)

academic freedom (414)

fair use (416)

in loco parentis (426)

acceptable use policy (433)

sexual harassment (433)

Buckley amendment (436)

FOR REFLECTION

1. Can you remember examples of the "everyday ethics" of teaching shown by the teachers you had in elementary and secondary schools? Can you remember examples in which your teachers' ethical behavior was questionable?

2. Review the two case studies on ethical dilemmas described early in this chapter. Which one do you believe represents the "easier" dilemma for you to solve? Why? Which appears to you to be the more difficult? Why?

3. Do you believe tenure practices are justified and lead to better schools? Why or why not?

4. How do you feel about the current controversies over the place of religion in public schools? Of prayer? Of the Bible and other religious works?

5. Do you understand the concept of due process, and can you recall from your school experience situations in which a student's or teacher's due process rights were violated?

6. Teachers are expected to be people of good character and role models to students. What are the limits of this expectation? What are some points at which the rights of the school district end and the rights of the teacher begin?

FOR FURTHER INFORMATION

Acceptable Use Policies: A Handbook. http://www.pen.k12.va.us/VDOE/ technology/AUP/home.shtml.

SEARCH

This handbook, available on the Internet, is produced by the Virginia Department of Education and is a rich source of information on using the Internet in schools and developing acceptable use policies.

Edwards, Jane. *Opposing Censorship in the Public Schools: Religion, Morality and Literature.* Mahwah, NJ: Erlbaum Associates, 1998.
This recent book summarizes a number of the debates surrounding censorship and reports on several controversies related to specific works of recent literature.

Fischer, Louis, David Schimmel, and Cynthia Kelly. *Teachers and the Law.* 5th ed. New York: Longman, 1999.
This book, written by scholars who are lawyers and professors of education, bridges the worlds of the courts and the classroom with great detail and clarity.

Goodlad, John I., Roger Soder, and Kenneth Sirotnik. *The Moral Dimension of Teaching.* San Francisco: Jossey-Bass, 1990.
This book of readings explores the moral and ethical aspects of teaching from many angles and from the vantage points of several different disciplines.

LaMorte, Michael W. *School Law: Cases and Concepts.* 6th ed. Boston: Allyn and Bacon, 1999.
This current text covers both key legal opinions and dissenting opinions, and adds valuable commentary and explanation.

Strike, Kenneth, and Jonas Soltis. *The Ethics of Teaching.* 3d ed. New York: Teachers College Press, 1998.
This short book is an excellent source for ways to approach the topic of ethics in teaching. It contains a number of practice cases.

2000 Deskbook Encyclopedia of American School Law. Rosemont, MN: Data Research, 2000.
This excellent annual reference book is an easily accessible source on the current law and legal issues surrounding all aspects of public and private education.

Zirkel, Perry. "De Jure" column in *Phi Delta Kappan.*
This recurring magazine column reports on important issues of school law and provides an excellent way to follow recent developments.

13 How Should Education Be Reformed?

This chapter gives you a concentrated look at the educational reform movement. For almost twenty years, politicians and educators have been working vigorously to alter the course of American elementary and secondary education. Though results have been mixed to date, certain patterns and key educational ideas are evident.

This chapter emphasizes that

▶ The educational reform movement is being fueled by a widespread recognition that our schools are inadequate for the demands of the time.

▶ Although educational philosophies may differ, most school practitioners agree that our schools should educate students to be citizens, thinkers, and individuals.

▶ Some key educational ideas *ought* to be at the heart of this current reform movement.

▶ Although the federal government and local communities are involved, the primary source of energy for the school reform movement is at the state level.

▶ Teachers are the crucial element in meaningful reform.

People of every era think that theirs is unique, with the greatest problems and the most formidable challenges. This sense of being in a special moment of crisis and opportunity is particularly true for American schools today. Americans of a wide range of social and economic backgrounds, from all parts of the country, believe our schools are in crisis. This ominous picture of our schools has been supported by numerous statistics, such as the following:

▶ A growing number of students never reach the ninth grade. The dropout rate is approximately 30 percent, and it is substantially higher for Hispanic and African American students.

▶ In many large metropolitan areas, nearly 30 percent of the students who reach ninth grade do not graduate from high school four years later.

▶ At least 25 million adults who should have benefited from our schools are functionally illiterate.

▶ Serious inequalities exist among school districts across the nation, and many districts are operating with growing budget deficits.

▶ In an increasing number of school districts, deteriorating facilities are matched by out-of-date instructional equipment and technologies.

▶ Physical assaults on students, teachers, and administrators are increasing. Many schools and their surrounding environments are unsafe and not conducive to education.[1]

▶ In a 1998 survey of high school students, 70 percent reported cheating during a test and 82 percent admitted lying to a teacher.[2]

Some well-known educators, however, disagree with this picture of our schools. They believe our schools are a great social achievement in that we educate more children to higher levels than any other society in the world. Citing the generous amount of money Americans spend on the education of their young, they argue that dropout rates like those just cited are as low as they have ever been.[3] They are encouraged by snippets of good news, such as the significant gains reported among African American and Hispanic students in mathematics during the early 1990s.[4]

debate about need for reform

Other skeptics believe that the schools, particularly the public schools, are incapable of being reformed. They argue that schools, as institutions, are deeply resistant to change and that unlike corporations, whose effectiveness can be judged by bottom-line profits or losses, the effectiveness of schools is all but impossible to measure. Without a clear bottom line, therefore, schools have little incentive to reform themselves.

Still others oppose all these efforts at change, arguing that childhood is childhood and that school should provide continuity and stability in a society in constant flux. In short, these defenders of the schools ask, "If it ain't broke, why fix it?" Nevertheless, those in favor of serious school reform vastly outnumber these voices of caution and opposition.

Basic Questions   Before addressing the *what* and *how* issues of school reform, we should consider the question of *ought:* What *ought* to be the nature of this reform? Take a moment now and reflect on your own education. Make a short list of current aspects of schooling that cry out for reform.

Your answer should be driven by a view of what we want our schools to achieve, including a set of goals and a realistic plan. (It is crucial for a builder to have goals and a plan before starting a project.) Recently one educator captured the views of many when he wrote that a good school respects and keeps in balance the need "to educate the 'three people' in each individual: the citizen, the worker, and the private person."[5] Using this breakdown, we can categorize the major motivations to reform our educational system as follows:

Children are the messages we will send to a time we will never see.

—NEIL POSTMAN

major motivations for reform

1. To develop a democratic citizen:

    ▶ There are dramatic differences between the schools serving the children of the rich and those serving the children of the poor.

    ▶ Disturbingly high percentages of students know nothing about our democratic traditions and how our government functions.

    ▶ There is little understanding of the world and the global role and responsibility of the United States.

2. To develop the good worker:

    ▶ Our way of life and our individual standard of living are closely linked to our nation's ability to maintain its economic leadership, a leadership that is seriously threatened by the comparatively low level of knowledge and skills demonstrated by the graduates of our schools in mathematics, science, and vocational education.

    ▶ The world of work is rapidly being transformed, and schools are not keeping pace. As Americans cope with the age of the "information highway," many of our schools are still trapped in a horse-and-buggy approach to teaching and learning.

3. To develop the private person:

    ▶ Our schools seem to be failing to help children develop a "moral compass" and the personal habits of responsibility, diligence, kindness, and courage that are associated with mature adulthood.

    ▶ Too many students see schooling primarily as a right rather than an opportunity that entails serious responsibilities.

Keeping in mind these three goals as a basis for reform, we now turn to how our schools ought to be reformed.

What Ought to Be the Elements of Educational Reform?

Underlying all the experimental programs, curriculum innovation, and other efforts for school improvement, a number of elements stand out as essential for true and lasting educational reform: excellence, active learning, authentic assessment, community, learning to learn, character education, and staff development.

Excellence

Although ads for athletic shoes urge young people to high standards in sports ("Just do it!") and ads for the armed services urge us to "Be all that we can be," the call to excellence from our schools is often muted and heard by too few. The reform movement we are witnessing has as its theme and driving force an urgent plea to our schools to excel. The educational wake-up call, *A Nation at Risk*, which in 1983 was the opening salvo of the current reform movement, came from a group named the National Commission on *Excellence* in Education. In clear and forceful language, the commission demanded that the "rising tide of mediocrity" be stemmed by a commitment to excellence. Teachers were challenged to ignite in individual students a desire to excel in all aspects of school life.

the wake-up call

But what does "excellence" mean in schooling? Essentially the **call to excellence** is a demand that high standards be established, that grades reflect real achievement, that evaluations focus on true mastery, and that students adopt a serious task orientation toward their studies. In the past, teachers have been encouraged to raise students' self-esteem through positive reinforcement. Now self-esteem is seen as the direct by-product of excellence. Instead of *giving* self-esteem to students, the teacher ought to set up learning situations in which students *earn* it. An elementary school we know of captures the twin themes of setting high standards and earning self-esteem by challenging its students with the motto "Your best today. Better tomorrow."

the call to excellence

To receive a proper education is the source and root of all goodness.

—PLUTARCH

Helping a child achieve excellence is a high standard for the teacher, too. It requires the teacher to completely understand individual students, to know their weaknesses and strengths, interests, and talents. It demands that teachers not only know their subject matter but also know how to engage students of many different abilities, interest levels, and learning styles.

The theme of excellence has provoked responses throughout the educational community. Behind much of the interest in and efforts expended in the educational standards movement (discussed in Chapter 8) is the desire to ratchet up student performance to achieve excellence. Learned societies are working with teachers to replace inadequate curricula with up-to-date, state-of-the-field knowledge. Teacher education is responding with its own higher standards and enriched curricula. Local school boards are increasing the length of the school day and school year.

Active Learning: The Constructivist's Approach

There is an old saying that all teachers know well: "You can lead a horse to water, but you can't make it drink." Similarly, you can have a child in a classroom, but you can't make him or her learn. Pouring information into students or forcing them to do workbooks or problem sheets won't do it. Nor will the great majority of students learn if simply allowed to wander through a library or laboratory on their own. Something must happen in learners before they learn. Curiosity? A problem that they want or need to solve? And then, with the direct or indirect help of the teacher, the student "constructs" his or her meaning.

Constructivism, as we indicated in Chapters 6 and 10, is an approach that recognizes this process of constructing meaning. It provides a frame of reference, based on how a child learns, for interpreting and organizing classroom practice to enhance a child's ability to learn in any content area.[6] In the constructivist approach to schooling, learners do not passively receive knowledge; rather, they actively "construct" it, building on their bases of prior knowledge, attitudes, and values. In this **active learning** process, learners create patterns, rules, and strategies through hands-on or imagined experimentation. Learners say to themselves, "What makes sense here? What happens when I do this or change that?" A fundamental premise of constructivism is that we humans are "meaning makers" and that we rely heavily on multiple sources of information in the process of learning.[7]

humans as active makers of meaning

How does constructivism embody the goals of educational reform? First, a primary ingredient of the constructivist approach is a learner taking responsibility for his or her own learning. Learners cannot be passive, waiting for the teacher

Three girls who are actively involved in learning Shakespeare's *Macbeth*. "We've heard of green thumbs, but not. . . ." (© Bob Daemmrich)

" HOW DO YOU EXPECT ME TO LEARN ANYTHING
WHEN YOU'RE THE ONE WHO KEEPS ASKING ALL THE
QUESTIONS ? "

Reprinted by permission from *Phi Delta Kappan.*

characteristics of
constructivist classrooms

to teach them or the school to educate them. The teacher and the school play important supporting roles, but the initiative of the learner is essential.

Constructivist classrooms allow experiential learning, encourage open-ended questioning with much wait-time, and provide challenging questions and an atmosphere of intellectual play. In short, constructivism incorporates much of what has been written about in this text, including inductive teaching, student-teacher interaction, cooperative learning, multi- and interdisciplinary teaching, and extensive use of new technologies. While there is more to teaching than constructivism, it is nevertheless a powerful learning tool. It can bridge the gap between teacher-centered drill or rote learning on the one hand and excessively abstract conceptual learning on the other. An ancient Chinese proverb captures well the essence of constructivism: "Tell me and I forget. Show me and I will remember. Make me do it and I learn."

Authentic Assessment

minimum competency tests

During the 1970s and 1980s, a major motivation behind the accountability movement, which called for schools to demonstrate what they were accomplishing, was declining test scores. As discussed in Chapter 9, schools across the country began using standardized achievement tests and so-called *minimum competency tests* to see how they were doing compared with other schools. Results of these tests were often used to make "high-stakes" decisions and judgments. On the basis of the test scores, the performances of school districts, their teachers, and their students were judged; programs were added or dropped and individuals rewarded or punished. The pressure to boost test scores was intense, and many teachers quite naturally responded by emphasizing in their instruction the knowledge and skills that were being tested. In effect, teachers began **teaching to the test.** What was tested became what was taught. Instruction became measurement driven.

As instruction narrowed to concentrate more and more on the basics, student scores seemed to improve. At this point, in state after state and in community after community, what has been called the "Lake Wobegon effect" (see the accompanying box) occurred. Each community interpreted its test results to mean that its children were above average.

Related to this dissatisfaction with minimum competency tests and narrow standardized achievement tests was considerable disillusionment with the use of multiple-choice tests. Educators and the business community began to call for schools to emphasize higher-order thinking skills and problem-solving abilities, qualities that are difficult to measure through multiple-choice and other objective tests. A different type of assessment was called for, one that would directly measure real student performance on important tasks. For example, if we want

new type of assessment demanded

The "Lake Wobegon" Effect: How Can Most Students Be Above Average?

Lake Wobegon is radio humorist Garrison Keillor's mythical town in Minnesota where "all the women are strong, all the men are good looking, and all the children are above average." John Jacob Cannell, M.D., borrowed the name to describe the puzzling fact that school districts across the country have reported their students as above average. On standardized achievement tests, Dr. Cannell discovered, more than 90 percent of the 15,000 elementary school districts and 80 percent of the secondary school districts in the nation reported scores above the national norm instead of the expected 50 percent. How could this be? Dr. Cannell has several explanations.

First, norm-referenced achievement tests compare current student achievement with the achievement of a norm group tested in the past. Current national averages are not computed. The norm groups are supposed to represent an average group of students tested under conditions similar to those used in current testing programs. Dr. Cannell points out, however, that unlike currently tested students, norm groups are "tested cold" without any prepping on exact test questions and without having their curriculum "aligned" with the test questions. The result is that the high scores reported by many school districts, although higher than the norm group scores, are not necessarily higher than the average of all students taking the tests.

Dr. Cannell further charges that because educators are under such tremendous pressure to raise test scores, they sometimes resort to such practices as changing student answers, allowing more time to complete the test, distributing advance copies of the test, and excluding special education and bilingual students from testing. By excluding "at-risk" students from achievement testing, some school districts artificially inflate achievement test scores.

Dr. Cannell's charges have led to a serious examination of practices in the use of norm-referenced achievement tests.

Source: John Jacob Cannell, *How Public Educators Cheat on Standardized Achievement Tests* (Albuquerque: Friends of Education, 1989).

to know how well students can write, we can examine samples of their writing. Or if we want to know how well students understand scientific concepts and can carry out scientific processes, we can ask them to conduct an actual experiment. In other words, the assessment would actually measure what we wanted students to be able to do rather than relying on them to choose the correct response on a multiple-choice test item. This type of assessment is known as **authentic** or **performance assessment.** Advocates claim that authentic assessment involves performance tests that get closer to how students apply knowledge rather than how they store it in their minds.

portfolios

One method of authentic assessment involves having students collect their work over time and assemble it to create **portfolios.** These portfolios can be evaluated by students and teachers to determine progress toward important learning.[8] Instead of testing students with a series of brief, fact-driven questions, teachers inspect the portfolios, repositories of the students' work that have been gathered over several months. In many parts of the country, in fact, student teachers are being urged to assemble portfolios of their own work to show their professional skills when they apply for employment.

unresolved issues

Authentic assessment is not without its critics and unresolved issues. Whether performance assessments will satisfy the validity requirement (answering the question "Is this a true measure of what I want to assess?") and the reliability requirement ("Will this test yield a similar result when administered at different times and under different circumstances?") has yet to be determined. Cost is also a major concern. Evaluating writing samples or judging students' success in conducting a scientific experiment is much more time consuming, and therefore more costly, than machine scoring a multiple-choice exam. Standards of judgment present another difficulty. How, for example, do we judge excellence, originality, and creativity in art and writing, let alone math or science? Though many questions remain, authentic assessment is probably an idea whose time has come. Educators and policymakers will struggle with these issues in the coming years.

Community

"Small is beautiful" has been the slogan for many social activists over the last two decades. Social scientists studying adolescents in our cities found what they labeled "urban sanctuaries," neighborhood organizations that attracted and served inner-city youth, particularly those who were disaffected and drifting toward gangs. These urban sanctuaries had "family-like environments in which individuals are valued and rules of membership are clear. Their activities offer opportunities for active participation and present challenges that result in accomplishments. They are youth driven and sensitive to youth's everyday realities. They assume that youth are a resource to be developed, not a problem to solve."[9] These messages, however, are just beginning to gain a foothold in American education. Recent years have brought a growing realization that the largest of our schools can have some destructive side effects. The schools have an aura of impersonality that results in the disengagement of many students. It is common

urban sanctuaries

disengagement of students

A boy shares his artwork and a poem about his brother with some classmates. (© Nancy Sheehan/PhotoEdit)

to hear such statements as "I'm lost here"; "No one really knows me and no one cares"; "I'm just a name in someone's gradebook." Though these criticisms are directed most often at high schools, they hold for many of our junior highs and middle schools, and even some elementary schools. Clearly, the larger our schools get and the greater the number of classmates and adults with whom students must interact, the more students disengage.

Recent studies have found not only a decline in student engagement, and therefore in academic achievement, in large schools but also a decline in faculty morale and an increase in faculty absenteeism.[10] Further, large schools often tend to keep parents at a distance and therefore uninvolved in their children's school life.

Schools-Within-Schools School-as-community advocates believe that any school whose principal does not know the names of all the students is too big. Reformers such as James Comer of New Haven's School Development Project and Theodore Sizer, formerly of the Coalition of Essential Schools, rely heavily on creating a sense of community to support the development of an academic environment. In these reform projects, large schools are broken up into "houses" of 100 to 200 students; the number of teachers is similarly reduced. The houses

"houses" of students

Class Size: Is Less Always Better?

What's the Policy?

A major achievement of our schools during the twentieth century was reducing class size from fifty and sixty students early in the century to averages in the high teens and twenties today. However, reducing class size even further has been, is, and will continue to be on the reform agenda of the American schools. For example, in the late 1990s, the state of California, as part of a massive movement to fix its ailing schools, initiated a well-intentioned and expensive effort to reduce class size.

How Does It Affect Teachers?

Almost every teacher and administrator we know would enjoy having smaller classes. Teachers with fewer students are often able to spend more time on instruction and less time hassling with the discipline problems that seem to naturally accompany large groups of young people. Fewer students also means less time tending to "administrivia." Teachers have the chance to get to know each student and teach each one in ways that meet his or her individual needs.

What Are the Pros?

There is widespread agreement that public school classes are too large and reducing the student-teacher ratio will substantially improve our schools. Fewer students means more attention to each one. Surely a fourth-grade teacher with seventeen children can know and meet the needs of his class better than one with twenty-five. Surely an algebra teacher with 85 students can zero in on her students better than one with 150 or 160 students. Much of educational theory seems to suggest that increased individual attention can help students with special needs, students at risk for dropping out, students who are not achieving as much as they could—in fact, just about all students.

What Are the Cons?

A key problem for those who wish to make classes smaller is money. Teachers' salaries represent the bulk of most school districts' budgets, and any significant reduction in class size would be extremely expensive. For instance, lowering the pupil-teacher ratio from 20 to 19 in a school district with 100 teachers would mean hiring five new teachers and increasing the school budget by approximately 4 percent or paying for the five teachers by making cuts in the sports program, the computer lab, or the counseling services. But if reducing class size improves student achievement, wouldn't it be worth it? This takes us to the scientific reason for resistance to this reform.

Few educational questions have been more frequently studied than the relationship between class size and student achievement. Several well-executed studies support reducing the pupil-teacher ratio. However, the conclusion of a review of over 300 individual studies found that contrary to expectations, most of the studies suggested that either the fewer educators per student (yes, larger classes!) the better, or that the achievement gains made in smaller classes were trivial.

The explanation for such unexpected research results lies in the answer to the following question: "Would you rather have your child in a twenty-seven-student class with a skillful, experienced teacher or in a fifteen-student class with an inexperienced teacher on an emergency certificate?" During California's recent class reduction push, for example, thousands of people accepted appointments and entered the newly created reduced-size classrooms on emergency teaching certificates. Only then did they learn that an emergency certificate does not make a person a teacher. California's effort to improve early elementary education through reducing class size has been widely judged a failure.

Policy Matters! (cont'd)

What Do You Think?

1. How many students would be in your ideal classroom? Why?

2. Do you think that if qualified teachers could be found for smaller classrooms, research results on student achievement would show greater gains for students in small classes?

3. Do you believe there are any other reasons besides academic achievement that small classes would be better than large ones?

Source: Debra Viadero, "Small Classes: Popular, But Still Unknown," *Education Week,* February 18, 1998.

function as **schools-within-schools.** Since students and teachers stay in the same house for several years, they are able to establish stronger and deeper relationships, which discourages tracking and stereotyping. Each student is a *known* person rather than a name on a class roster.

One obvious advantage of the house plan is that it allows teachers to plan together and to bring to bear their different perceptions of a child who is having difficulties. In addition, these smaller, more intimate school environments provide a more stable emotional climate for students. Faculty advisors have much more knowledge and exposure to students and can offer more help in dealing with students' problems and opportunities.

Learning to Learn

In our global, rapidly evolving social and economic environment, people need more than an education. They must also be capable of continuous learning. The jobs we perform and the tasks we must accomplish today will likely differ ten years from now. Therefore, educational reform must attend to the skills that enable people to *keep* learning throughout their lives. Often the process of acquiring these skills is referred to as **learning to learn.** It has always been important for success in school, and now, more than ever before, it is important for success in later life as well.

need for learning throughout life

The New Basics   The human brain is a glorious instrument capable of enormous feats of creativity, from writing symphonies to making scientific breakthroughs. The average brain can store and manipulate more information, by several hundred times, than the largest computers. But the brain has its drawbacks. It loses or "misfiles" information. Numerous ideas and facts and assorted messages enter it through the eyes, ears, and other senses and somehow get lost. When we want to remember an idea, it often is simply "not there." Or somehow the facts get modified so that when we take the exam, we are sure there are two quarts in a gallon and four pints in a quart. Thus, although the brain is humankind's treasure, it is hardly perfect. And to work well, the brain must be trained.

training the brain

By *trained,* we mean we have to teach people how to use their brains effectively. Most likely the majority of our readers have been urged a time or two by parents and teachers to "Use your brains!" Our meaning is both an extension of that request and a more specialized suggestion. We are urging that we give our brains more power through the use of new tools. In the same manner that reading extends the power of the brain by giving it access to vast amounts of important information, other tools can make the brain more efficient. By *more efficient,* we mean better able to take in, interpret, process, store, and retrieve information.

the New Basics

A fresh focus on the skills of learning can and ought to be a major part of school reform. Of course, we must attend to the three Rs. We are not suggesting that we give a lower priority to subject matter. Rather, to make knowledge (that is, intellectual capital) more useful, we must teach the **New Basics:** advanced reading, remembering, recording, researching, test taking, analyzing, and creating (see the accompanying box for further discussion of the New Basics). These

A Sample of the New Basics

Here is a list of some of the skills—what we are calling the New Basics—that we believe ought to be taught to all students:

- *Various methods for remembering important information.* This largely involves teaching people how not to forget: how to move information from the fleeting short-term memory to the more enduring long-term memory.

- *Two or three methods of taking notes and saving important information.* Definite skills are associated with capturing what another person is saying, and students should systematically learn these skills.

- *Study reading.* One practices study reading when the material is complex and contains information one wants to remember later. It is quite different from reading a novel or reading a telephone book. It is a set of skills that is at the heart of academic success as well as success in many jobs.

- *Preparing for different kinds of tests.* Schools should show students how to study for different types of tests, such as objective and essay tests, and how to deal with test anxiety in various situations. Since examinations and tests do not end with graduation, schools should teach students how to cope with and master these challenges.

- *Doing research.* Students need to learn how to get answers to questions—how to use libraries, expert sources, and data-gathering resources of all kinds. In essence, these are the skills of finding and accessing different data sources and using the information to solve a problem.

- *Thinking through a problem in a systematic way.* Instead of jumping to conclusions or relying on how they feel about an issue, students should learn how to think critically.

- *Generating creative ideas.* Much of life in and out of school requires new solutions or imaginative resolutions. Students need to learn techniques for generating novel and creative ideas individually as well as group-oriented techniques such as brainstorming.

- *Getting the academic job done.* Students need to know how to set goals, develop a work plan, monitor their own behavior, bring a task to successful closure, and gradually become more successful at academic learning. This is important not simply to succeed in school, but because the modern workplace demands these academic skills.

are the tools that students should be taking out of high school into college and into the workplace.

Reclaiming Character Education

Much of the dissatisfaction with schools that has fueled recent educational reform efforts comes from parents and community leaders who believe the schools have not tried to positively affect the character and ethical values of students. Many reformers are convinced that failure to address these needs of students lies at the heart of the schools' problems. A "good student" has come to mean someone who does well on tests and achieves academically rather than someone who is a good person and who demonstrates characteristics such as responsibility, consideration for others, self-discipline, and the ability to work hard. Serious school reform therefore must address the issue of **character education,** which we define as the effort to help the young acquire a *moral compass*—that is, a sense of right and wrong and the enduring habits necessary to live a good life. Character education, then, involves helping the child *to know the good, love the good, and do the good.*[11]

definition of character education

Arguments Pro and Con   Some people argue that the public school has no role in character development and moral education because these are rooted in deeply held religious world views. As such, they are out of bounds to the public school, which should concentrate on cognitive skills exclusively, skills such as reading, writing, and application of the scientific method.[12] These people claim that if parents want attention paid to moral values, they should put their children in private schools.

objections to character education

Others question character education by asking, "*Whose* values should the public schools teach?" In a nation of diverse cultural backgrounds, a nation committed to freedom of thought and expression, is there any one set of values that can be taught without infringing on someone's deeply cherished beliefs? One answer to this objection is that the tax-supported public schools can teach the civic virtues that are necessary for life in a democratic society, such as respect for the rights of others, courage, tolerance, kindness, and concern for the underdog. Another way to approach the answer is to look at a few of the sights we might encounter while walking around some schools:

whose values?

> *Formal education is the playing field on which society vies over values.*
>
> —*Theodore Sizer*

> A counselor is calling a student's home about apparently excused absences, only to find that the parent's letters have been forged. A young boy is in the principal's office for threatening his teacher with a knife. Three students are separated from their class after hurling racial epithets at a fourth. A girl is complaining that her locker has been broken into and all her belongings stolen. A small group of boys are huddling in a corner, shielding an exchange of money for drug packets. In the playground, two girls grab a third and punch her in the stomach for flirting with the wrong boy.[13]

Schools that tolerate such behavior not only are failing to address the character education needs of their students but also have become places where the intellectual goals of schooling are impaired. In addition, such schools win little support from the general public, the people who pay for public education.

We believe that most educators know it is impossible to educate students in a moral vacuum. The process of schooling necessarily affects the way children think about issues of right and wrong. Further, the overwhelming majority of Americans, regardless of religion, class, or racial background, support certain moral values such as respect, persistence, a thirst for justice, honesty, responsibility in our dealings with one another, consideration, compassion, persistence at hard tasks, and courage in the face of adversity.[14] We believe that few people would not wholeheartedly support the schools' vigorous advocacy of these virtues. Teachers and schools can positively influence the development of desirable habits and character formation in numerous ways, but two in particular are worthy of note: using the curriculum and involving students in service activities.

wide support for certain values

Character in the Curriculum   One major approach is to teach more directly and more vigorously the positive moral values that are embedded in our culture. Our history and literature are permeated with value issues and moral lessons from the past. Instead of simply having students study the facts of a historical period or read a story to build vocabulary or appreciate style, the teacher can confront them with ethical issues and moral lessons that are integral to the subject matter. Instead of merely teaching scientific methodologies and findings, the teacher can have students examine the implications of applied science, such as genetic manipulation. They will see that the use of science and technologies, such as nuclear energy, fossil fuels, and high-speed computers, is not neutral but has ethical implications. As teachers, we must see the content of our curriculum as the carrier of our moral heritage and work to engage our students in that moral heritage.

moral issues in subject-matter disciplines

Service Learning   Knowing about justice, compassion, and courage is one thing; making them a part of one's life and practicing them diligently is another. Students need real opportunities to practice these virtues. As many reformers realize, schools can create opportunities for students, from the early grades on, to help one another and the adults in the school building. As students get older, they can be given more and more responsibility for working with and caring for younger students. In the later stages of high school, groups of students can take on projects in the larger community, such as helping a parent whose child has a disability or assisting with an exercise class at a senior citizens' center. Likewise, individual students can provide companionship to elderly shut-ins or peer counseling to troubled youngsters. The emphasis in such programs is not merely on the study of virtues, but also on virtues in action.

move toward social service

Service learning programs are growing rapidly in our schools. In 1984 only 2 percent of high school students were involved, but by 1997 almost one-quarter were participating.[15] An important feature of the much-acclaimed Central Park East, the junior-senior high school in New York City's Harlem, is the requirement that each student perform two hours of service every week. The service can be

Character education in action! (© R. Hutchings/ PhotoEdit)

performed in school by, for example, setting up a science laboratory for an experiment, checking out books at the library's circulation desk, or serving food in the school's cafeteria. In the local community, students do a variety of tasks, such as acting as a guide in one of the city's museums or delivering food to shut-ins.[16]

Several states are considering making a certain number of hours of community service a requisite for high school graduation. In 1993, Maryland became the first state to make service an actual requirement. Currently Maryland high school students are required to perform seventy-five hours of service before they can graduate. We believe schools must succeed in this mission for students' sake and also because a strong program of character education makes teaching a much more satisfying profession.

Staff Development

In the 1980s and 1990s, American business and industry dramatically reformed themselves after decades of inefficiency and loss of markets to their global competitors. The result has been a tremendous growth in national prosperity. An important key to this recovery has been a major investment of time and money in the education and advanced training of the American worker. Individuals from the corporate boardroom to the factory floor learned new ways of doing their work. Today continuing education is a staple in the American workplace.

example of U.S. industry

For many years, the various state departments of education have required teachers to continue their education after their initial teacher preparation. Also, virtually all school districts have salary incentives for advanced training such as college courses, degrees, and workshops. However, these efforts are, at best, minimal and, at worst, the major stumbling block to true educational reform.

an array of activities

Initially called *in-service education,* the effort to extend the education of teachers is usually referred to as **staff development.** As such, the term covers an array of activities, including on-site school- or district-sponsored workshops where teachers come together to learn new skills such as searching the Internet, writing across the curriculum, or a new classroom management technique; college or university courses and programs, often leading to advanced degrees in specialized areas such as reading or guidance counseling; and training experiences provided by textbook companies introducing a new mathematics curriculum to the school. To this list we would add items such as distance learning courses on using technology in the classroom, a teacher-organized book club on women in fiction, an adult education course on yoga and meditation, writing case studies of educational problems or issues that other teachers can use, mentoring new teachers, and a sabbatical year to study the history of Native Americans. The boundaries of what constitutes staff development are often debated, but we believe the essential attribute is that it aids the teacher in becoming a better teacher.

> *We must put knowledge directly in the hands of teachers and seek accountability that will focus attention on "doing the right things" rather than on "doing things right."*
>
> —LINDA DARLING-HAMMOND

For many practicing teachers, the term *staff development* lacks positive connotations. It conjures up memories of trudging off to after-school gatherings where they were lectured to by strangers on topics in which they had little interest, or to state-mandated required courses or workshops that they took under threat of losing their licenses. While a school district that hires a teacher and a state that licenses a teacher have the right to require a teacher's continuing education, such a top-down approach is not likely to serve the needs of children in this new century. For educational reform to truly take hold, several changes are needed:

four needed changes

▶ First, schools should be conceived of as **learning communities,** in which everyone—adults and children alike—learn.

▶ Second, teachers, specialists, and administrators must see their continuing educational growth as an integral part of their workday.

▶ Third, the definition of *staff development* should be broadened to take into account whatever contributes to making an educator more effective.

▶ Fourth, while teachers must be willing to devote their time and energy to staff development, the cost should be borne by the school district or the state.

Mortimer Adler, the force behind the Paideia Proposal mentioned in Chapter 10, once said, "The teacher who has stopped learning is a deadening influence rather than a help to students being initiated into the ways of learning."[17] Educational scholar Michael Fullam suggests that teachers seeking to improve are characterized by four attitudes: they accept that it is possible to improve; they are ready to be self-critical; they recognize better practice than their own; and, most important, they are willing to learn what they have to learn to do what needs to be done.[18] In our view, a teacher who is not learning because of lack of opportunity or lack of personal incentive is stunting his or her own career and is a barrier to the educational reform we need.

We now turn to actual reform initiatives, many of which involve one or more of the elements we have described. As in any other type of reform, certain ideas and principles get attention, while others are ignored or lose ground. As you read about the reforms that have been implemented, compare them in your mind both to what you think ought to be done and to what we have been suggesting here.

Current Reform Initiatives

Most educators agree that the current reform effort started with the 1983 federal report *A Nation at Risk*. This strongly worded report declared that our nation was in serious danger and that our schools had left the nation vulnerable to our military and economic competitors. The report called for longer school days, more homework and effort on the part of students, tougher grading policies, more testing, and more demanding textbooks. It arrived at a time of particularly widespread dissatisfaction with the public schools. Just two years before the report's release, a *Newsweek* poll revealed that nearly half (47 percent) of the American public believed the schools were doing a "poor" or only a "fair" job.[19] The message of *A Nation at Risk* was picked up by the country's newspaper editors and television commentators, and became regular fare on the radio and television talk shows. The public, worried about its young and our country's economic competitiveness, read and listened attentively. The remainder of the 1980s saw a blizzard of national and state reports, most hitting many of the same themes and all calling for massive change. What has been the result?

message of A Nation at Risk

National-Level Reform Efforts

As we discussed in Chapter 9, the U.S. federal government has a very limited role in education. Compared with other modern nations, ours is a highly decentralized system with most of the decision making and financial support coming from

AUTHORS' DIALOGUE

JIM: Hey, isn't that 47 percent dissatisfaction rate somewhat distorting?

KEVIN: *In what way? It was a legitimate poll of a national sample of citizens.*

JIM: But they were talking about the schools in general, not specifically their own community's schools. Over and over again in recent years, the polls have shown support for local schools but little confidence in the nation's schools.

KEVIN: *Maybe what we have here is a variation of the Lake Wobegon effect. All the children—and their local schools—are "above average."*

the state and local governments. Once *A Nation at Risk* had focused the nation's attention on education, President Reagan and his secretary of education, William Bennett, pursued a *bully-pulpit* strategy; that is, the White House staff began using the president's office to call people's attention to the plight of our schools and to advocate change.

National Education Goals for the Year 2000

Nowhere has the bully-pulpit strategy been more evident than in the much heralded Education Summit held in 1989. Then-president George Bush and the state governors together committed themselves and their offices to school reform, adopting a list of goals (shown in Table 13.1) to be reached by the year 2000. A leading figure at the summit was the then-governor of Arkansas, Bill Clinton, who spoke for many when he said, "Not only are we to develop strategies to achieve them [the goals], but we stand here before you and tell you we expect to

TABLE 13.1   Goals 2000: The National Education Goals

Goal 1	By the year 2000, all children in America will start school ready to learn.
Goal 2	By the year 2000, the high school graduation rate will increase to at least 90 percent.
Goal 3	By the year 2000, all students will leave grades 4, 8, and 12 having demonstrated competency over challenging subject matter including English, mathematics, science, foreign languages, civics and government, economics, arts, history, and geography; and every school in America will ensure that all students learn to use their minds well, so they may be prepared for responsible citizenship, further learning, and productive employment in our Nation's modern economy.
Goal 4	By the year 2000, the Nation's teaching force will have access to programs for the continued improvement of their professional skills and the opportunity to acquire the knowledge and skills needed to instruct and prepare all American students for the next century.
Goal 5	By the year 2000, United States students will be first in the world in mathematics and science achievement.
Goal 6	By the year 2000, every adult American will be literate and will possess the knowledge and skills necessary to compete in a global economy and exercise the rights and responsibilities of citizenship.
Goal 7	By the year 2000, every school in the United States will be free of drugs, violence, and the unauthorized presence of firearms and alcohol and will offer a disciplined environment conducive to learning.
Goal 8	By the year 2000, every school will promote partnerships that will increase parental involvement and participation in promoting the social, emotional, and academic growth of children.

Sources: Goals 2000: Educate America Act (March 31, 1994); *The National Education Goals* (Washington, DC: U.S. Department of Education, 1994).

be held personally accountable for the progress we make in moving this country to a brighter future."[20] Few were surprised when, as president, Clinton reaffirmed his commitment to these **National Education Goals,** which were adopted into law as the *Goals 2000: Educate America Act.* However, now that year 2000 has arrived and clearly we have not achieved these benchmark indicators of progress, we are hearing less and less from our leaders about Goals 2000.

Goals 2000

National Standards   Few issues in American education have been debated as heatedly in recent years as whether the federal government should or should not set national standards and develop a national curriculum, along with the testing mechanisms to implement it. Setting broad goals such as those listed in Goals 2000 is one thing, but dictating or even strongly suggesting to our nation's 50 states and 15,000 school districts what they should actually teach is extremely controversial. Advocates of a national curriculum, such as E. D. Hirsch, who popularized the concept of "cultural literacy," say we need a national curriculum because so many students move around from state to state and school to school. Hirsch points to facts such as these: one-fifth of all Americans relocate every year; one-sixth of all third-graders attend at least three different schools between first and third grades; and a typical inner-city school has a 50 percent student turnover between September and May.[21] Others cite the educational excellence attained by France, Germany, and Japan, all countries with national standards and national exams.

advocates of a national curriculum

Others, however, strongly oppose national standards and an accompanying curriculum and testing program, fearing an educational power grab by the federal government. In their view, the idea of Washington bureaucrats instead of locally accountable individuals answering the questions "What should our children know?" and "How well should they know it?" seems both educationally flawed and politically dangerous. Opponents also believe that in a large nation with so many racial and ethnic groups and so many regional traditions, a national curriculum would trample cultural diversity and promote a bland sterility. Further, many are convinced that a national curriculum would put disadvantaged students at an even greater disadvantage.

the critics

So far, Congress has consistently resisted the establishment of a mandatory national curriculum and national subject-matter examinations. On the other hand, the current mood is toward acceptance or rejection of **national curricular standards** on a *voluntary* basis by the states. In sum, the outlook seems to be as follows: national influence, yes; national control, no; national testing, probably not in the near future.

the compromise: voluntary standards

Curriculum Reform   Independently of Goals 2000 and congressional actions, national groups of scholars representing such academic areas as science, history, and mathematics have put out proposals, and in some cases entire curriculum plans, in an effort to have the schools teach the latest subject-matter content. These efforts have aimed to address the complaints of many scholars about the quality and currency of the subject matter offered in our schools.

One such curricular reform effort, *Project 2061* (sponsored by the American Association for the Advancement of Science), was discussed in some detail in

curricular reform projects

Chapter 8. Others include *Becoming a Nation of Readers* (sponsored by the Commission on Reading) and *Science/Technology/Society (S/T/S)* (sponsored by the National Science Foundation). A major breakthrough has occurred in the teaching of writing, spearheaded by the National Writing Project, which promotes a process approach to composition. Likewise, in 1989 the National Council of Teachers of Mathematics developed new curriculum guidelines that stress not just students *knowing* mathematics but *doing* it. The Chicago Mathematics Project is also working on a total revamping of the mathematics curriculum, giving special attention to the average student and to the early grades, where interest in mathematics often begins to drop off. In addition to these efforts, national projects are currently under way in all the major subject-matter areas, including history, geography, and the arts—all working on materials and trying to establish content standards.

These various curriculum reform projects have in common a partnership among scholars in the discipline, teacher-educators, and classroom teachers. Ideas and suggestions flow across lines that were once rigid. University academics observe in elementary and secondary classrooms, and, back on the campus, elementary and secondary school teachers instruct scholars on the realities of teaching their subjects to a wide variety of youthful students.

schools banding together

Ideas move fast when their time comes.

—CAROLYN HEILBRUN

National Voluntary Networks   One of the most interesting recent educational developments is the appearance of networks of schools and school districts. Among these loose, voluntary alliances are two mentioned earlier: the Coalition of Essential Schools begun by Theodore Sizer and the network of schools modeled after James Comer's New Haven School Development Project. Others include John Goodlad's National Educational Network for Reform, Robert Slavin's Success for All schools, Henry Levin's Accelerated Schools (currently involving over one thousand schools in forty states), and a newly established network called Schools of Character, formed by the Character Education Partnership. Schools in these networks commit themselves to a common educational ideal or set of ideals. For instance, the high schools in the Coalition of Essential Schools try to put into practice the following principles:

▶ Helping adolescents to use their minds well

▶ Teaching for the mastery of essential skills and acceleration in certain areas of knowledge

▶ Recognizing the student as worker rather than the teacher as deliverer of information

▶ Provoking students to learn how to learn

▶ Reflecting values of trust, decency, tolerance, and generosity in the tone of the school

▶ Expecting much from students without threatening them[22]

Implications of National-Level Reform Efforts   Overall, two things are clear about education reforms at the national level. First, we are in the middle of a strong push toward national influence on education. Second, there has been a strong response from the states to improve their curricular standards. Still, however, most of the reforms remain voluntary. Local schools and their communities must choose to be a part of them. This fact helps to keep the reform efforts from what some see as the taint of "nationalizing our schools."

summary of current situation

State Educational Reform

As education became more and more of a national issue, reform also became a hot political topic from the state house to the mayor's office. Statewide task forces were formed by governors, state legislatures, and state boards of education, and a large number were formed by citizens' groups and foundations. Some states had several at the same time. Numerous local school districts established their own blue-ribbon commissions to respond to what was increasingly called "the school crisis." As the late Ernest Boyer said, "You could draw a 'Keystone Cops' image here of people charging off in different directions and bumping into each other and, in some instances, having a conflict with one another. There is no overall sense of where the problem is and how we should work together to get there."[23] There was, however, one common theme: the call to excellence.

state task forces and commissions

Throughout both American industry and education, mediocrity was the dominant criticism and excellence became the rallying cry of the reformers. Many of these recent state and local task force reports have *excellence* or *quality* in their titles. Because these task forces and reports were sponsored by state governmental agencies or well-connected citizens' groups, their recommendations were quickly turned into legislative proposals for school reform.

Common Elements in State Reforms   The "search for excellence," then, came down to specific proposals for change. Among the most widely adopted state reforms were the following.

1. *An increase in graduation requirements.* Instead of one or two years of English and history, states began requiring three and four years in core subjects. For academic high school diplomas, science and advanced mathematics courses were required. The idea of "social promotion," moving students through the grades to stay with their own age groups, independently of their performance came under great pressure and was eliminated in many places.

more courses in core subjects required

2. *Longer days, more days.* In the minds of many educators, the short school day and the long, academically fallow period between June and September are major causes of the poor performance of American students. Recent research confirms that in nine out of ten instances, students achieve more when they spend more time in class.[24] School days, which in many locales were only five-and-a-half to six hours, were lengthened to six-and-a-half to seven hours. The school year, which in many states was between 170 and 175 days or fewer, has

more time in school

Increased graduation requirements and calls for more testing are part of many states' educational reforms. (© Bob Daemmrich/Stock Boston)

increase in statewide tests

been lengthened to 180 days or more in thirty-four states.[25] Though many of the reform reports recommended that our schools follow the example of Japan (240 days) and Germany (216 to 240 days),[26] no states and relatively few school districts have taken such a major step in lengthening the school year. One reason is that lengthening the amount of schooling is extremely costly.

    3. *Statewide testing.* Reform groups and state legislatures want to make certain that the effort and monies going into their reform efforts are paying off, and they are demanding accountability. The result has been a huge growth in interest in testing and assessment. In the 1970s, relatively few states had a statewide testing program, a system that assessed how students did or did not meet the state's minimum curriculum standards. But by 1998, as a result of the new testing movement, forty-six states had such programs.[27]

    The movement for statewide testing has been a mixed blessing. The statewide tests have been used as educational "report cards" to allow policymakers and the public to see how the schools are doing.[28] But a danger lurks, as captured in the old saying "What gets measured gets taught; what gets reported gets taught twice as well." As we stated when discussing teaching to the test, many be lieve the demand for testing and accountability has increased measure-driven instruction. During this reform period, schools massively increased their use of objective tests—largely multiple-choice tests—which are easy to administer, score, and report. And because the educational stakes were high, teachers began to "teach to" those narrowly focused tests. Although there has been a call for authentic assessment, progress toward it appears to be slow.

4. *Higher standards for teachers.* One of the major state-driven reform efforts of the 1980s and 1990s was the move to improve the quality of America's teaching force. Three initiatives in particular were notable: teacher competency testing, stiffening requirements for entering teacher education, and career ladder programs.

The first initiative, **teacher competency testing,** was not new, but it underwent massive growth during the last two decades of the twentieth century. Currently forty-three states have some form of teacher testing, typically taking place when candidates are leaving their teacher education programs or before they receive state licensure.[29] One vexing issue that has plagued the movement for teacher competency testing has been the low cut-off scores that have often been established. In effect, teachers are supposed to demonstrate their proficiency by jumping over a hurdle, but the hurdle has been so low as to be meaningless. Nevertheless, teacher competency tests have run into strong opposition from the organized teaching profession. As one commentator has stated, "Not only are the majority of the state teacher tests absurdly easy, the scores needed to pass them are astonishingly low. . . . Nonetheless, the failure rates on the test have been extraordinarily high."[30]

testing teachers

The second initiative had to do with teacher education. Legislatures across the country have been making changes in the licensure requirements for teaching and in the process of approval for universities and colleges that prepare teachers. In general, the call has been for an increase in liberal education (for instance, the elimination of education as a major in favor of an academic subject such as mathematics or English) and for fewer and better education courses. In recent years, all but two states have raised admission standards for teacher education programs, reevaluated teacher education programs, or developed unified course requirements for students in such programs.[31] Also, several states, such as Connecticut, have established loan programs for college students who wish to prepare for careers in teaching. Some of the most constructive criticisms have come from the profession itself. In 1996, the Report of the National Commission on Teaching and America's Future offered the nation a blueprint to guide the reform of teacher education. To date, progress in making the recommended changes has been slow.

changes in teacher education

The third initiative involved **career ladders.** Critics have long complained about the "flatness" of the career structure in teaching. The criticism goes something like this: "Beginners have too much responsibility at the beginning of their careers and too little opportunity to make the most of their abilities once they really learn to teach. The only way to get promoted in education is to be promoted *away from students,* to become a guidance counselor or an administrator." With the encouragement of state legislatures, a variety of teacher specialty programs,

changes in the career ladder

such as master teacher programs, differentiated staffing, and mentoring programs for new teachers, have appeared on the scene. Typically these programs give experienced teachers new roles, new responsibilities, and usually new rewards. Although these innovations have had somewhat limited adoption, the assumption that "a teacher is a teacher is a teacher" has been dispelled, and new roles, such as mentor teacher and team leader, have been opened to teachers who want new challenges but also want to stay in the classroom, close to students.

rising salaries

5. *Higher salaries for teachers.* A key problem revealed by the blizzard of reports published in the 1980s and 1990s was the weak reward system for teachers. Career ladders and other schemes, which expand and enrich the teacher's role, are one way to reward teachers, but more was needed if teaching was to become an attractive professional option for talented students. Salaries were an obvious target. From 1983 to 1993, the average teacher salary increased at a rate twice that of inflation. In some states, the increases were even more dramatic. From 1982–83 to 1988–89, the average teacher salary increased by 98 percent in Connecticut, 75 percent in Vermont, 55 percent in Virginia, 53 percent in South Carolina, and 50 percent in California.[32]

performance pay

Further, all across the country the lock-step pay scale by which teachers were rewarded only by years of service and number of courses taken has been altered to allow for **performance pay,** a form of recognition and reward for special service. Closely linked to this change has been a substantial move to make teaching more attractive by increasing the starting salaries of teachers. Ten years ago, beginning teachers earned $12,000 to $13,000. By 1998, the national average for beginning teachers was almost $26,000. In fact, a number of school districts around the country have established starting salaries of $30,000 and above.

> *The politics of education is complex and ever changing. At various times and places it can appear to be an asset or a liability. But it is real. Only through understanding and making proper use of politics can education be improved.*
>
> —WENDELL H. PIERCE

Although there has been a good deal of commonality among the reform movements from state to state, a few states have distinguished themselves for their energetic and innovative responses to the call to excellence. Among those states are Kentucky, South Carolina, and, in particular, California (see the accompanying box).

Local-Level School Reform

The late Speaker of the House of Representatives, Tip O'Neill, was fond of saying, "All politics are local." The same is true of education. Children are educated at their local schools, not at the state capitol or in Washington, DC. Though some school reform efforts, such as the Coalition of Essential Schools Project, are national in scope, they are implemented in local schools under the supervision of a school district.

shortage of local funding for reform

At present, however, the great majority of changes being made in schools are coming at the direction of the various states' departments of education. Since the 1980s, the state houses have had the money and the muscle to dictate educational reform. Locally initiated reform efforts, although in no way stopped, have slowed down, partly because of a shortage of local funds. Growing competition for municipal tax dollars—from police and fire departments, and agencies serving the

California's School Reform: A Giant Tsunami or Just a Lot of Ripples?

Once upon a time, California, the Golden State, had a golden school system. The state's public elementary and secondary schools were the envy of its forty-nine sister states. Its student achievement scores, per-pupil expenditures, and teacher salaries were among the nation's highest. That was thirty years ago, however, and now California's public school system is struggling.

Today California's schools face a flood of problems, including one of the nation's lowest high school graduation records (close to one in three ninth-graders drop out before getting a diploma); average reading scores well below the national average, along with per-pupil expenditures; and a chronic shortage of good teachers (approximately half of the state's teachers quit in five years).

One needs to be sympathetic with California educators, though, because they have had to cope with mammoth problems in recent decades. One problem has been money. Beginning in the 1980s, California suffered a taxpayer revolt that drastically cut educational funding. During the same period, California schools welcomed a huge influx of new students. While many of these newcomers came from other states, many more came from Mexico and Asia, presenting the schools with special language instruction problems. During the next few decades, California's current enrollment of 6 million students is expected to reach one-fifth of the nation's school population.

California voters recently sent the politicians of both parties a clear, loud message: fix the schools. The current governor responded by announcing that "Education is my first, second, and third priorities." The legislature, often stingy with education, has now opened its checkbook to the reform cause.

It is inaccurate, however, to refer to what is happening as the California reform effort, since in reality there are many different reform programs and proposals. Among them is an effort to address poorly performing schools through a statewide performance index whereby the worst-performing schools would receive special staff help and additional financial aid. One of the most novel aspects of this school assessment plan is that the evaluators will be not the usual suspects—administrators, educational experts, bureaucrats, and politicians—but specially recruited classroom teachers.

Another major reform addresses the very high student-teacher ratios that exist in many California schools. This $1.5-billion-a-year effort has been targeted at the early grades. Thousands of teachers have been recruited to reduce class sizes to twenty students or fewer, often from thirty or more. However, critics of this program claim that because many of the newly recruited teachers are inadequately prepared, students' education has suffered.

Among the other reform efforts are

- Tightening up academic standards by reducing the use of social promotion and putting in place a high school graduation examination system

- Releasing poorly performing tenured teachers

- Establishing charter schools

- Possibly implementing a voucher program enabling students to attend private schools with tuition paid with public funds

Struggling to sort out and put in place these various, sometimes conflicting proposals has given many California politicians and educators what is being called "reform fatigue." But again, the message from the citizenry is loud and clear: "fix our schools!"

Sources: Rene Sanchez, "A Tough Lesson Plan: Fixing Schools," *The Washington Post,* August 18, 1999, pp. 1, A4–A5; John W. Myres, "Why Reforms Won't Work in California," *Education Week on the Web,* June 9, 1999.

poor and the elderly—and a citizenry increasingly critical of public education have made it difficult to start new, locally supported reform efforts.

Currently state funds are given out or withheld on the basis of compliance with state-level directives, and this means less real power for the local school boards. The Kentucky Educational Reform Act is a case in point. Through this plan, the state-level judges, legislators, and education officials are telling the local Kentucky schools how they must change. What we are witnessing is a classic shift in power, with the state house dictating more and more what should be taught and how it should be taught.

shifting power to state level

On the other hand, the local school boards—those 15,000 centers of power and decision making in our highly decentralized educational system—have been extremely busy responding to the reform initiatives emanating from the state house and from national educational groups. Though the center of gravity may be elsewhere, the local school district is deeply involved in the current reform movement. Furthermore, the overwhelming percentage of reform ideas that have made their way onto the agendas of national and state reform groups existed first at the local level. They became statewide or national because they succeeded at the local level. In the future, more innovative ideas, such as block scheduling, year-round schooling, single-sex schools, school uniforms, and site-based decision making, will continue to come up "from the trenches"—from our local schools.

ideas emerge at local level

School Reform and the Teacher: Concluding Thoughts

Although we clearly have a new set of educational reform priorities, goals, and expectations, most schools have been relatively untouched by educational reform. Some have made fundamental changes in the way they engage children and in what they teach. Most have adopted pieces of reform, such as a new districtwide mathematics curriculum, or a computer lab, or a career ladder for teachers. Some states have pushed through serious changes that affect the great majority of their schools, but they are the rarities. The school experience of the first-grader or the high school senior is pretty much the same today as it was in 1983, when the current reform era began.

piecemeal reform

American education is not like an individual who, after a few life failures, looks in the mirror and says, "That's it; I'm going to get my act together starting today," and from that moment on is a "new" person. American education is a giant institution, involving some 15,000 centers of decision making (school boards), well over 50 million people (students, teachers, and administrators), and influences from many quarters of society. And most important, like any institution, it has a standard operating procedure, or SOP. Everyone starting a school year in September (except for the newcomers, the kindergartners) has a clear set of expectations about what school ought to be like. Without this chaos would result. But because of these expectations, altering the course of schooling is quite a demanding task.

Perhaps a better parallel than an individual trying to change the course of his or her life is a large luxury liner plowing through the ocean. Someone convinces the captain that dangerous icebergs lie ahead. The captain first has to be assured that the reports are reasonable, then decide where the safe water is, and then turn the wheel. But because of its size and momentum, the ship may need miles to truly change course. This is where we believe American schools are today. They have heard the message; they have committed to change course and avoid the hazards; they have begun to turn the wheel. Whether the ship actually turns and misses the dangers we must wait to see.

Since 1983, Americans have seen their industries "reengineered" and "restructured," making them much more competitive in the global marketplace. Educational researchers are now suggesting that schools follow the example of outstanding private-sector firms, guiding their reform efforts by five principles: *principles from private sector*

▶ Ensure that all front-line workers (that is, teachers) understand the problem.

▶ Design jobs so that all front-line workers have both incentives and opportunities to contribute to solutions.

▶ Provide all front-line workers with the training needed to pursue solutions effectively.

▶ Measure progress on a regular basis.

▶ Persevere and learn from mistakes; there are no magic bullets.[33]

Clearly it is the teacher who stands at the center of true school reform. It is the teacher who actually delivers educational services, who creates or fails to create an environment for learning, who either knows or does not know how to engage students in their own pursuit of excellence. *teachers at the center*

The final decisions about educational reform are, by necessity, made by teachers. Although it is discouraging (and even threatening) to know we do not have better schools, we Americans are often at our best when challenged. And clearly school reform is part of the unfinished business of America and the American teacher. A job of critical importance to all of us awaits you.

KEY TERMS

call to excellence (442)	New Basics (450)
constructivism (443)	character education (451)
active learning (443)	staff development (454)
teaching to the test (445)	learning communities (454)
authentic (performance) assessment (446)	National Education Goals (457)
portfolios (446)	national curricular standards (457)
schools-within-schools (449)	teacher competency testing (461)
learning to learn (449)	career ladders (461)
	performance pay (462)

FOR REFLECTION

1. What do you believe are the most compelling reasons to reform American schools?

2. What current strengths of our schools could be weakened by the current reform trends?

3. Are any of the reform initiatives described in this chapter evident in your local schools?

4. Which of the reform efforts described in the chapter most interests you? Why?

5. If monies for schooling continue to be tight, which educational reforms will be most weakened? Which will be least weakened?

6. What do you believe teachers should do to take a more active role in the reform process?

FOR FURTHER INFORMATION

SEARCH

Carvin, Andy. *EdWeb: Exploring Technology and School Reform.* **World Wide Web site at http://edweb.cnidr.org: 90.**
This book is devoted to school reform, the spread of educational technology, and the interconnections between these two trends. It includes information on such topics as school choice, accountability, school restructuring, and the Coalition of Essential Schools.

Cawelti, Gordon. *Portraits of Six Benchmark Schools: Diverse Approaches to Improving Student Achievement.* **Alexandria, VA: Association for Supervision and Curriculum Development, 1999.**
This well-written report offers portraits of excellent public schools with high standards, multiple changes, strong leadership, collaborative teams, and committed teachers—in other words, reform success stories.

Kanstoroom, Marci, and Chester E. Finn, eds. *New Directions: Federal Education Policy in the Twenty-First Century.* **Washington, DC: Thomas B. Fordham Foundation, 1999.**
This collection of essays on various federally sponsored efforts at school reform points out both past failures and new directions for our reform efforts.

Ryan, Kevin, and Karen Bohlin. *Building Character in Schools: Practical Ways to Bring Moral Instruction to Life.* **San Francisco: Jossey-Bass, 1999.**
This book offers teachers both a theory and a set of practical steps to infuse their teaching with our core moral values. In addition, the book has many practical lists and materials to promote character in classrooms and schools.

Sizer, Theodore, and Nancy Sizer. *The Children Are Watching.* **Boston: Beacon Press, 1999.**
This short book by two veterans of the school reform wars focuses on the personal side of the reform effort. The Sizers describe schools and students the way they currently are and then suggest ways teachers need to respond.

THE TEACHING PROFESSION

This section deals with both practical and theoretical questions: Will there be job openings in teaching? How do you go about obtaining a teaching position? What kind of salary can you expect to make? What does it mean to be a professional teacher?

It is anticipated that during the next ten years, over 2 million new teachers will have to be hired to offset rising student enrollment and replace retiring teachers. Yet finding the teaching position in the school that is right for you can be a complex and challenging prospect. This section explores the teaching profession: what it is and how to become part of it.

14

What Are Your Job Options in Education?

This chapter provides you with information regarding the availability of teaching positions in elementary, middle, and secondary schools. The chapter also explores other career opportunities both within and outside the educational field. Study the information carefully and discuss it with your instructors and your career planning and placement office. Your program of study may offer more job options than you have realized.

This chapter emphasizes that

▶ Many factors influence the availability of teaching jobs. Although an oversupply of teachers exists in a few teaching fields, other fields face a severe shortage of teachers.

▶ Teacher salaries have made some gains in recent years, with the average salary of classroom teachers in 1998–99 being over $40,500 and the average salary of *beginning* teachers in 1997–98 being just over $25,700. However, salaries vary tremendously from state to state and from school district to school district.

▶ Certain job-hunting strategies will increase your chances of locating the right job for you. You may have to spend considerable time and energy preparing materials for your job search.

▶ Licensure requirements differ from state to state for both general and specialized areas of teaching.

▶ A wide variety of careers are available to people trained as teachers. Should you be unable to secure a teaching position or wish to change careers after you have taught, the skills you have acquired in teacher education can be transferred to related occupational areas.

▎ No matter what the job market may be at a particular moment, there has never been a surplus of good teachers. Better-prepared teachers will find it easier to gain employment and will improve the teaching profession and its public image.

"Pupil Enrollment Exceeds Estimates"

"State Grants Emergency Teaching Licenses to Scientists"

"School Bond Issue Defeated by Voters"

"Schools Scramble to Hire Teachers"

"College Enrollments in Teacher Education Up"

"Teachers Face Worst Layoffs in Decade"

You have probably read newspaper headlines similar to these and may have wondered whether you will be able to obtain a teaching position when you graduate. Although we would like to answer this question for you personally, we obviously cannot. We can, however, provide you with information that may help you increase your chances of obtaining the kind of teaching position you are seeking.

Will There Be Job Openings in Education?

Factors Influencing Teacher Supply and Demand

Will there be a shortage of teachers in the near future? Many people think so, but estimates of shortages are based on rapidly changing situations influenced by unpredictable factors. The following sections discuss a number of these factors.

Student Enrollment in Schools   Obviously, when more students are enrolled in schools, more teachers are needed. The good news is that enrollment is rising, eclipsing the previous record set in the early 1970s, and it is expected to continue climbing for at least the next eight to ten years. Enrollments in public and private schools are projected to reach 53.4 million students by the fall of 2000 and almost 54.3 million by 2008. As a result, the number of classroom teachers is expected to increase from 3.2 million in 2000 to 3.5 million by 2008[1] (see Figures 14.1 and 14.2).

rising student enrollments

Ratios of Students to Teachers   During the 1980s, the demand for new teachers was boosted by declining pupil-teacher ratios, which now hover around seventeen or eighteen students per teacher in the public schools and around fifteen students per teacher in private schools. However, the changes in the pupil-teacher ratio during the next few years are expected to be small, and they will not likely affect the demand for new teachers in any significant fashion. One exception to this prediction is the state of California. In 1996, California

stable pupil-teacher ratios

469

FIGURE 14.1   Enrollment in Public and Private Schools (in millions)

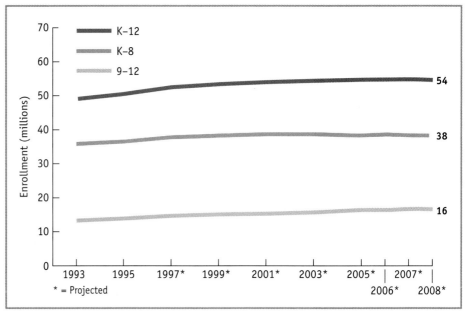

Source: William J. Hussar and Debra E. Gerald, *Projections of Education Statistics to 2008* (Washington, DC: National Center for Education Statistics, 1998), Table 1 at web site http://nces.ed.gov/pubs98/pj2008/ p98t01.html.

provided over $.75 billion to cut class sizes in grades K–3 from as many as 30 students to 20, requiring an estimated total of 26,000 additional primary school teachers.[2]

Enrollment in Teacher Education Programs   Enrollments in teacher education programs have been growing, but not sufficiently to offset the anticipated need for more teachers. Enrollments in teacher education programs often lag behind the need for teachers; that is, by the time college students learn there is a shortage of teachers and decide to enroll in teacher education programs, the shortage will have grown more acute. Although more than 200,000 teachers will be hired annually over the next decade, teacher education programs are graduating between 150,000 and 200,000 each year.[3]

Geographical Location   Location significantly influences the teaching job market. Some communities have far more applicants than available teaching positions. University towns, for example, usually have a great surplus of teachers. Although large urban areas historically have had more teachers available than they needed, they are now experiencing significant teacher shortages. In 1996, nearly a quarter of central-city schools in the forty-seven largest urban areas had vacancies they could not fill with a qualified teacher.[4] Rural America traditionally has had difficulty attracting and holding on to teachers because of lower salaries and a more sedate lifestyle than that sought by many young teachers.

teacher shortages in urban areas

FIGURE 14.2   Classroom Teachers in Public and Private Schools (in thousands)

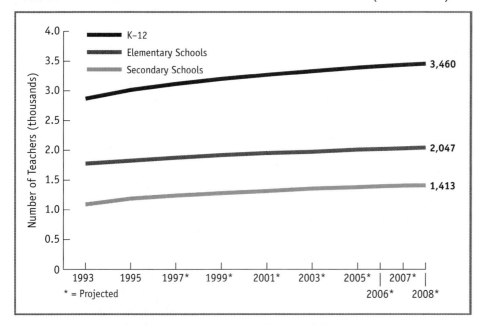

Source: William J. Hussar and Debra E. Gerald, *Projections of Education Statistics to 2008* (Washington, DC: National Center for Education Statistics, 1998), Table 32 at web site http://nces.ed.gov/pubs98/pj2008/p98t32.html.

Generally speaking, teacher vacancies are greatest in the West (California, Arizona, Nevada, and Utah), the Great Plains/Midwest (the Dakotas, Minnesota, Iowa, Nebraska, and Missouri), and the south central states (Texas, Oklahoma, Arkansas, and Louisiana). There are fewer vacancies and/or more competition in the northeastern states (Maine, Vermont, New Hampshire, Massachusetts, Rhode Island, and Connecticut), the Southeast (Virginia, the Carolinas, Mississippi, Alabama, Georgia, Florida, Tennessee, Kentucky, and West Virginia), the Middle Atlantic states (Delaware, District of Columbia, Maryland, New Jersey, New York, and Pennsylvania), and the Northwest (Washington, Oregon, and Idaho).[5]

jobs available in Sunbelt and Midwest states

Teachers tend to be more "place bound" than many other professionals; that is, because of family commitments or the importance of geographical location, many teachers seeking jobs are reluctant to stray far from home. So even though teaching jobs may be available in Las Vegas (which they are!), teachers from the Northeast, for example, may not want to relocate in Nevada.

Subject Matter and Grade Levels Taught   Teachers are not interchangeable units. They are prepared for different specialties (special education, primary grades, art, or high school social studies, for example), and the job market in each of these subfields is different. Moreover, the job market for specific subfields may change often. It is unwise, therefore, to decide whether or not to become, say, an English teacher because you have heard that today there is in general either a surplus or a shortage of such teachers.

job availability depends on teaching field

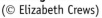

fields with teacher shortages

There have been and continue to be chronic teacher shortages in certain subjects, including speech pathology, special education (all areas), bilingual education, audiology, mathematics, science (physics, chemistry, earth and physical science, biology), English as a second language, and languages (including Spanish and Japanese). Subjects for which there is less demand include social studies, physical education, health education, and elementary education.[6] This does not mean there are no jobs in these subjects. It means, rather, that job seeking is more competitive and that you may have to relocate in a different community or commute some distance to work.

shortage of minority and male teachers

In addition to looking for teachers in the subjects just listed, schools are seeking increased numbers of minorities and males. Because 73 percent of all teachers are female, schools want to increase the number of males in the teaching force, especially at the elementary school level, where fewer than 12 percent of the nation's 1.3 million public school teachers are men.[7]

Retiring Teachers, Teacher Dropouts, and Returning Teachers   An estimated 2.2 million new teachers will be needed during the next ten years in the face of rising school enrollments and teacher retirements. A factor that bodes well for the long-term job outlook is that the teaching profession, like much of the rest of the American work force, is getting older, partly because teachers are remaining in teaching longer and partly because older people are becoming teachers. The average age of all public school teachers is forty-three years, and 67 percent are forty years of age or older.[8] It is estimated that half of our nation's teachers will retire during the next decade.

aging of teacher work force

There is a demand for male teachers at the elementary school level, where they compose less than 12 percent of the teaching force.
(© Elizabeth Crews)

Another factor influencing job availability concerns the percentage of new teachers who elect to leave teaching after a few years. Of the college graduates who began teaching by the 1993–94 school year, nearly one in five had left within three years. Sadly, the brightest novice teachers, as measured by their college-entrance exams, were the most likely to leave. Factors influencing the high turnover included poor working conditions, dissatisfaction with student discipline, lack of mentoring, and unhappiness with the school environment.[9]

What is difficult to estimate is the number of licensed teachers, currently not teaching, who might re-enter the teaching force if jobs are readily available. When teacher shortages have been predicted in the past, these returning teachers have filled the anticipated shortages. Whether this pattern will continue remains to be seen. Teachers licensed through alternative routes (alternative licensure is discussed later) have thus far made up only a small percentage of the available pool of teachers, but that situation could change if states promote these programs more vigorously.

Economic Conditions   In spite of the positive long-term outlook for teaching positions, in times of economic hardship school districts may find it necessary to reduce the size of their teaching forces to balance budgets. During the 1990–91 recession, for example, school districts in a number of states found it necessary to issue RIFs—reduction-in-force notices—to teachers, informing them that they were in danger of not being rehired for the following fall. Although painful in the short run, such layoffs will probably be only temporary and will have little overall effect on the long-term demand for new teachers. RIF notices do show, however, that the demand for teachers is greatly influenced by school district budgets, which in turn are affected by the health of the state and local economies.

job availability affected by economy

Summary   What, then, are the job prospects for the future? The situation is very promising, because the number of classroom teachers in elementary and secondary schools is projected to rise at least until 2008, primarily because of increased school enrollment and teacher retirements. Recruitment of teachers recently has become so competitive that many districts are offering incentives to qualified teachers, including paying bonuses ranging from $1,500 to $20,000, closing costs on home purchases, and relocation expenses. Some states are even considering offering state income tax breaks for teachers. However, if the supply of qualified teachers doesn't keep up with the demand, states and local school districts may, as they have in the past, increase class size, hire less-than-qualified personnel, and issue emergency teaching licenses to fill vacancies.

demand for teachers promising

Keep in mind, too, that demographic projections and supply-and-demand forecasting are not only hard to apply but also very inexact and short-lived. With difficulty, forecasters try to take into account factors such as retirement rates, supplies of former teachers re-entering the field, and programs that may attract individuals from nonteaching fields into the profession. What seems to be true for a particular geographic area, a particular teaching field, or a particular year may be out of date at the moment you are reading it.

obtain recent information

Therefore, you ought to make every effort to get the most up-to-the-minute information possible about teacher supply and demand. You should consider such information carefully before making a choice about a career in education and, in particular, about a specific subfield within education. This is especially true for people who are unable to wait for openings in their areas of teaching interest or unable to relocate. Sources of data with which to begin your search are your school's career counseling office, the department chairperson's or dean's office, and your state department of education. Also, see the listing of useful references at the end of this chapter.

The bottom line is that demand for teachers is high and is expected to continue to be high in the coming years, and there has never been a surplus of *good* teachers in any field.

The Severe Shortage of Minority Teachers

One of the greatest teacher supply-and-demand problems concerns minority teachers. At a time when the minority school-age population is increasing rapidly, the number of minority teachers is decreasing. The shortage is severe now and appears likely to become worse.

fewer minority teachers

> *[Emma Belle Sweet] taught me many things. . . . But nothing could be so important to me and of such enduring quality as her simple, human act of figuratively leading me gently by the hand to a sense of self-respect, dignity, and worth.*
>
> —RALPH BUNCHE (NOBEL PEACE PRIZE WINNER)

As you saw in Chapter 4, enrollments of students from minority groups are increasing and currently are estimated to be 36 percent. Teaching staffs, on the other hand, are becoming more and more white. Almost 91 percent of public school teachers are white, 7 percent are African American, and only 2 percent come from other minority groups, including Hispanic American, Asian American or Pacific Islander, and Native American or Native Alaskan.[10] Most minority teachers are located in central cities rather than in suburban or rural areas. During most of the 1990s, the graduation rates of minority students from teacher education were lower than their percentage distribution in the teaching force. Although minority enrollment in teacher education has been increasing in recent years, the need is still acute.

This shortage of minority teachers is problematic for several reasons. First, the growing number of minority children deserve to have positive minority role models who can help guide them in a world still plagued by racism. Second, white children also need to have minority teachers as positive role models to help them overcome the effects of stereotyping and racism. Third, it is important for our country's well-being to have a teaching staff that reflects the diversity of racial and ethnic backgrounds in our country's population.

factors affecting shortage of minority teachers

The shortage of minority teachers exists for a number of reasons. Before desegregation efforts, nearly one-half of African American professional workers were teachers. When schools desegregated in the 1960s and 1970s, resulting in the consolidation of formerly all-black and all-white schools, thousands of African American teachers were dismissed. Today other professions that pay more and have higher status are actively recruiting minority college students. Another causal factor has been the increasing use of competency tests at either the be-

The shortage of minority teachers deprives both white and minority students of positive role models. (© Chip Henderson/Tony Stone Images)

ginning or the end of teacher education programs. Minority college students traditionally have not performed as well on standardized tests as white college students. As a consequence, many minority teaching candidates are either failing to pass these tests or are being discouraged from even considering teaching as a career.

What can be done to address this problem? Teaching salaries must continue to improve if teaching is to compete with other professions for well-qualified candidates. Assistance programs to help minority candidates perform well on competency tests have been effective in a number of universities and need to be expanded to other colleges. Active recruitment programs for minority candidates must be developed and implemented, and they must reach down into the middle and high schools to encourage minority students to consider teaching as a career. Scholarship and loan-forgiveness programs are needed for students who want to teach but cannot afford college. And the American public must communicate, in a variety of ways, that it values teachers and the work they do.

Employers Besides the Public Schools

Department of Defense schools

U.S. Government A large employer of teachers is the U.S. government. The Department of Defense operates 231 schools in seven states, Puerto Rico, Guam, and fourteen countries around the world, making it the twentieth largest school district in the United States. These schools enroll approximately 115,000 students and employ about 9,000 educational personnel.* Salaries are comparable to those in the United States, but preference is given to applicants who have at least one year of successful full-time employment as a professional educator.[11]

private schools a significant employer

Private Schools Although much of the data presented in this chapter refer to public elementary and secondary schools, private education is a highly significant part of the American educational system. Projections indicate there are more than 26,000 private schools with an enrollment of over 6 million preschool, elementary, and secondary school students and a staff of 413,000 teachers. About 11 percent of the children in elementary or secondary schools attend a private school, with the overwhelming majority attending religion-affiliated schools.[12]

salaries in private schools

Since private schools employ about 13 percent of all elementary and secondary teachers, they obviously offer an employment opportunity for new teachers. Many teachers who work in religion-affiliated schools do so because of religious motives. These teachers are often willing to work for less money than their public school counterparts, and, as a result, the average teacher salary in private schools is considerably lower than that in public schools. But lower salaries tend to be offset by favorable working conditions. Compared with public schools, private schools have fewer disciplinary problems, stricter discipline, smaller classes, fewer students using drugs, students who are absent less often, parents who are more supportive, more assigned homework, and more time spent in instruction in the central academic subjects. Although private school teachers tend to work about two more hours per week than their public school counterparts, they believe they have more influence over important school policies.[13] Thus, for many individuals, teaching in a private school is an attractive alternative to teaching in the public schools. Helpful references for finding teaching jobs in nonpublic schools are provided at the end of this chapter.

What Are Teachers Paid?

We might answer this question by saying, "Not nearly enough." No one ever went into teaching because of the lure of big money. As we noted in Chapter 1, most of the rewards for teaching are personal rather than monetary. Most of teachers' satisfactions come from being of service to others and helping students learn. That does not mean, however, that you have to be a pauper to enjoy the satisfactions

---

*For more information on applying for a job with the Department of Defense overseas schools, write U.S. Department of Defense, Office of Dependents Schools, Personnel Center, 4040 North Fairfax Drive, Arlington, VA 22203-1635, or call the office at 703-696-3068.

**AUTHORS'
DIALOGUE**

KEVIN: *Some people argue that we shouldn't require prospective teachers to spend much time in preservice teacher education but should put them into teaching situations right away where they can learn practical things on the job.*

JIM: Sure, they can learn much of what they need to know, but it's going to be trial and error, and lots of elementary and secondary students will receive less than adequate instruction while their teacher is learning.

KEVIN: *What about those people who argue that you can't learn to be a teacher in a college classroom? The faster our prospective teachers get into the classroom, they say, the better, especially given the projected need for new teachers. Those in favor of alternative licensure make this argument.*

JIM: I'm in favor of early immersion in the classroom, and most teacher education programs are already getting students out into the schools early in their programs. But I also believe that there are many things that new teachers need to learn before they are given full responsibility for a classroom.

KEVIN: *How about those people who point to teachers in private schools, many of whom have had no formal teacher preparation? If teachers in private schools don't need formal teacher preparation, why should we require it of public school teachers?*

JIM: I think the circumstances are very different. Private schools accept only those students whom they want, whereas public schools have to take every student who shows up. That means that private schools can dismiss students who don't follow rules, try hard, or behave themselves. Private schools also don't have to accept students with disabilities unless they're well equipped to work with them. Public school teachers need to know how to work with a much greater diversity of students.

KEVIN: *So you're saying that because public school teachers are likely to work with a greater variety of students, they need more teacher preparation. Is that right?*

JIM: Yes, and for other reasons. Public school teachers are affected by many school reform efforts that don't touch private school teachers, such as state standards for student learning that dictate what teachers must teach, high-stakes student testing, and required technology competencies for teachers. In other words, states require much more of future public school teachers than private school teachers, so more teacher preparation is needed.

KEVIN: *Thank goodness for that, Jim—we need to sell these books!*

that come from teaching. Salaries are a legitimate concern for a prospective teacher; after all, everyone must have sufficient income to meet the costs of living. You will have to decide whether the salary you are likely to make as a classroom teacher will allow you to establish the lifestyle you want. This section will give you some objective facts with which to make your decision.

average teacher salaries

The 2000–01 average salary of classroom teachers in the United States is estimated to be about $42,400.[14] Figure 14.3 shows the substantial rise in average salaries since the mid-1980s, and Table 14.1 shows how salaries vary by state and region. The "Average Salary" column in the table represents the average

FIGURE 14.3   Average Public School Teacher Salaries

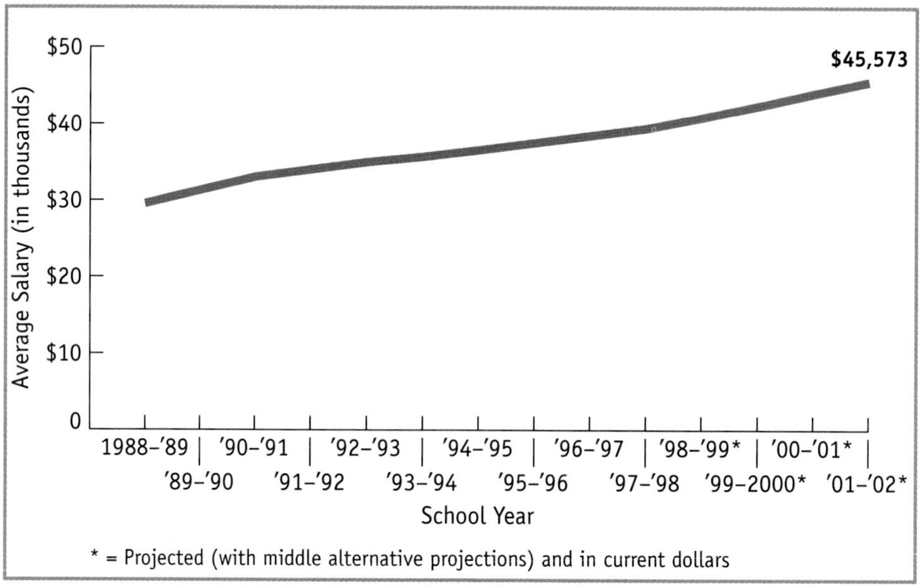

* = Projected (with middle alternative projections) and in current dollars

*Projected (with middle alternative projections) and in current dollars.

salary schedules

for *all* public elementary and secondary school teachers, and the "Beginning Salary" column indicates the average for *first-year* teachers. For teachers in their first year, the average pay across the nation as a whole was $25,735 in 1997–98, ranging from a low of $19,146 (North Dakota) to a high of $33,162 (Alaska).[15]

Most public school salary schedules are usually determined by two factors: years of teaching experience and amount of education, usually expressed in terms of college credit-hours or advanced degrees. Thus, the longer you teach and the more college education you receive, the more money you will make (see Table 14.2 on page 480 for an example of a school district salary schedule). In addition, some states and school districts have used various forms of merit or performance pay plans to reward teachers for exceptional teaching or for assuming more professional responsibilities.

As you can see from Table 14.1, salaries vary considerably from state to state. Each school district determines what it will pay its teachers, with many states setting a minimum base salary below which the school district cannot go. Generally, the large and middle-size school districts pay better than the small ones, and urban and suburban school districts pay better than rural ones. Many school districts offer extra pay for special duties such as directing the band or coaching athletic teams. Some offer summer teaching or curriculum development jobs.

fringe benefits

Most states and school districts provide public school teachers with a number of fringe benefits, including sick leave, health and life insurance programs, and retirement benefits. When applying for a teaching position, be sure to ask about these benefits.

TABLE 14.1   Average and Beginning Teacher Salaries, by State and Region

State	Average Salary (1998–99)	Beginning Salary (1997–98)	State	Average Salary (1998–99)	Beginning Salary (1997–98)
New England			**Southeast**		
Connecticut	$51,584	$29,506	Georgia	$39,675	$26,706
Rhode Island	45,650	26,300	Virginia	37,475*	25,272
Massachusetts	45,075*	27,238	Tennessee	36,500	22,140
New Hampshire	37,405	23,927	Florida	35,916	25,266
Vermont	36,800	25,183	Kentucky	35,526	23,536
Maine	34,906	21,554	South Carolina	34,506	23,427
			West Virginia	34,244	22,529
Mideast			North Carolina	36,098	22,150
New Jersey	$51,193*	$28,319	Alabama	35,820	27,388
New York	49,437*	30,204	Arkansas	32,350*	21,000
Pennsylvania	48,457	29,581	Louisiana	32,510	22,843
D.C.	47,150*	27,234	Mississippi	29,530	20,630
Delaware	43,164	25,493			
Maryland	42,526	27,010	**Rocky Mountains**		
			Colorado	$38,025*	$24,867
Great Lakes			Utah	32,950*	22,241
Michigan	$48,207*	$27,064	Idaho	34,063	20,248
Illinois	45,569	28,183	Wyoming	33,500	22,230
Indiana	41,163	24,716	Montana	31,356	21,045
Minnesota	39,458	26,266			
Ohio	40,566	22,535	**Far West**		
Wisconsin	40,657	24,077	Alaska	$46,845	$33,162
			California	45,400*	27,852
Plains			Oregon	42,833	26,098
Missouri	$34,746	$24,125	Nevada	38,883	28,641
Iowa	34,927	22,475	Washington	38,692	23,860
Kansas	37,405	22,445	Hawaii	40,377	26,744
Nebraska	32,880	21,949			
North Dakota	28,976	19,146			
South Dakota	28,552	20,340	**U.S. average**	$40,582*	$25,735
Southwest					
Arizona	$35,025*	$24,917			
Texas	35,041	24,736			
Oklahoma	31,149*	23,676			
New Mexico	32,398	23,297			

*estimated

Sources: Average salaries from "Average Salaries of Public School Teachers, 1998–99" (Washington, DC: National Education Association, 2000) (http://www.nea.org/publiced/edstats/salaries.html). Beginning salaries from F. Howard Nelson, *Survey and Analysis of Salary Trends, 1996, 1998.* Table I-8. Copyright © 1998. Reprinted by permission of American Federation of Teachers.

TABLE 14.2   Teacher's Salary Schedule for Arlington, VA, Public Schools, 1999–2000 (200 Days)

Step	Bach.	Bach. + 15 sem. credit-hours	Master's	Master's + 30 sem. credit-hours	Doct.
A	$30,230	$31,741	$33,328	$34,995	$36,744
B	31,741	33,328	34,995	36,744	38,581
C	33,328	34,995	36,744	38,581	40,511
D	34,995	36,744	38,581	40,511	42,536
E	36,744	38,581	40,511	42,536	44,663
F	38,581	40,511	42,536	44,663	46,396
G	40,511	42,536	44,663	46,896	49,240
H	42,536	44,663	46,896	49,240	51,703
I	44,663	46,896	49,240	51,703	54,287
J	46,896	49,240	51,703	54,287	57,003
K	46,896	51,703	54,287	57,003	59,853
L	46,896	54,287	57,003	59,653	62,844
M	46,896	57,003	59,853	62,844	65,989
N	46,896	59,853	62,844	65,989	69,286
L1	48,067	61,348	64,415	67,637	71,018
L2	49,269	62,883	66,025	69,329	72,794
L3	50,500	64,455	67,675	71,061	74,612

Note: Movement from lower levels to higher levels occurs annually, except there is a four-year waiting period between steps N and L1, L1 and L2, and L2 and L3.
Source: Payroll Office, Arlington Public Schools, Arlington, VA. Reprinted with permission.

How Do You Obtain a Teaching Position?

The job market is very encouraging for beginning teachers. But no matter how great the demand for teachers is or how effective you may be as a teacher, school district personnel are not likely to walk up to you and offer you a job unless you have taken a number of steps that we will outline in this section. We will suggest several courses of action that will greatly increase your chances of finding the best teaching job for you.

Campaign Actively

First, you must be determined to campaign actively for a teaching position. Draw up a plan, in writing, of how you will proceed. Don't wait for happenstance. You might get lucky and land a job on your first try, but why take a passive attitude when you can do much to increase your chances of obtaining satisfying employment? For example, try attending job fairs sponsored by various colleges, universities, or school districts.

develop a plan

Job seekers often make two common mistakes.[16] One is to try one strategy, wait for results (positive or negative), then try something else. What you should do is pursue many avenues or strategies simultaneously. The second common error is to block oneself out at the wrong stage in the process. Some teachers only halfheartedly write for information or never complete the application form. Others withdraw their applications prematurely. Remember: you can always say no to a job offered to you, but you can never say yes to one that has not been offered. Keep your options open.

The great aim of education is not knowledge but action.

—Herbert Spencer

Prepare Materials

Next, you need to get certain materials ready. These include your résumé, cover letter, credentials, and transcripts. Your résumé allows you to present yourself the way you want to be presented to prospective employers. Its purpose is to help you get an interview with school district officials. You should make several copies of your résumé.

prepare a good résumé

Many sources are available to help you write your résumé. The office of career planning and placement at your college or university is a good place to start. These offices often run workshops on résumé writing and frequently have samples of well-written résumés for you to examine. The AAEE annual *Job Search Handbook for Educators* listed in the For Further Information section at the end of the chapter is an excellent source on how to write résumés as well as on other job search strategies.

Another set of materials that more and more teachers are using to help them obtain jobs is called a **teaching portfolio.** Just as artists, actors, architects, and journalists use portfolios to display the products of their work, so can teachers. A teaching portfolio can include an organized collection of such items as research papers, letters of commendation or recommendation, pupil evaluations, teaching units, and videocassettes of lessons you have taught. There is no set format; you are limited only by your common sense and your own imagination. Remember, the purpose of the portfolio is to market yourself effectively, so don't be modest. A properly constructed portfolio will say much more about you than your résumé ever can. Many beginning teachers are constructing electronic portfolios either as web sites or on disk. The advantage of an electronic portfolio is that it is easily accessible by potential employers and can be changed or added to as needed.

teaching portfolios

The National Board for Professional Teaching Standards (discussed in Chapter 15) has advocated teaching portfolios as a means of assessing a teacher's work for national certification. As the board's standards are developed, the teaching portfolio may become an essential part of a teacher's repertoire. (See the AAEE *Job Search Handbook for Educators* for specific recommendations on portfolio construction.)

cover letters

Your cover letters, written to prospective school districts, should be addressed individually. The letters may all have the same or similar content, but the recipients should not feel they are receiving a standard letter. And, incidentally, be sure to ask for an interview. That's why you are writing the letter.

establish your credential file

Almost all school districts require credentials, that is, the whole package from your college recommending you for licensure. Be sure to check with the career planning and placement office about how to establish your **credential file** and what should go into it. Typically this file will include letters of recommendation, a copy of your transcript, and a résumé. Career planning and placement office personnel will help you assemble this file, and they will send copies of your file to school districts on your request. You should start on the file early in your program so you will have time to accumulate the required materials. Be familiar with the Family Educational Rights and Privacy Act, also known as the Buckley amendment, which affords you certain kinds of legal protection regarding what goes into your file.* Your letters of recommendation should be recent and from people who can testify to your teaching ability.

Buckley amendment

Reproduce unofficial copies of your official transcript. Many applications require that transcripts accompany them. Since colleges charge several dollars per transcript, you can save money by reproducing the transcript yourself. Most school districts will accept unofficial transcripts (those sent from you rather than directly from the college) for the initial screening process. If you receive a job offer, you will then have to provide the school district with an official copy.

Develop Interview Skills

prepare for interviews

The success of your personal interview with the school district representative is one of the most important determinants of whether you get hired, so be prepared. Try to anticipate the kinds of questions that might be asked (see the accompanying box for some sample questions). Try role playing with a friend who plays the role of the interviewer while you play the candidate. Audiotape your "interview" so the two of you can criticize it.

empathy for children important

One survey indicated that the major factor school officials look for is whether the candidate has empathy for children. Be prepared to show your empathy, not by saying you have it but through the examples you give from your own experience. You should also ask those who write letters of recommendation for you to emphasize this aspect.

---

*A copy of this law appears in the *Federal Register* 53, no. 69 (April 11, 1988), pp. 11942–11949. It can also be obtained by writing the U.S. Government Printing Office, Washington, DC 20402.

Remember, you are also interviewing the school district or specific school. You should look for a good fit between you and your style of teaching and what the school or district expects from you. Don't be so eager to get any position that you ignore the issue of fit. As charter schools continue to develop (see Chapter 5), new teachers will have more options to choose from in terms of work climate, educational philosophy, and learning goals.

Determine Job Availability

Your next major task is to find out what jobs are available and where. Several strategies are possible. Your college's career planning and placement office receives hundreds of notifications of position vacancies. Contact that office frequently to see if there are any vacancies that might interest you. Another source may be the teacher employment office operated by the state department of education. About one-third of the states run such offices, and you can register with them for free or for a slight charge. These offices send registered candidates a listing of openings in their specialty area for both state and out-of-state vacancies.

use your college placement center

There are also private organizations that keep current nationwide teacher vacancy lists and will try to match your qualifications with those vacancies for a nominal fee. Personal contacts too are often very effective in securing a position. Don't hesitate to call friends and acquaintances who might be able to help you obtain interviews. They probably can't get you a job, but they may be aware of vacancies and know whom you should contact. Contacting specific school districts directly is another way to determine what positions are available. Call, write, or visit the personnel office of the school districts in which you are interested. This will ensure that you get current information directly from the school district. Alternatively, use the World Wide Web to see if the school districts that interest you have home pages. If they do, they may very well list their job openings on their pages. Again, the AAEE *Job Search Handbook for Educators* lists and discusses a number of Internet sources with teaching and other educational job opportunities. We have cited a few of these sources at the end of the chapter.

personal contacts important

Gain Experience Through Substitute Teaching

Many teacher education students develop valuable experience, earn some money, and establish an entrée into a school district by serving as substitute teachers. Some universities even offer coursework in becoming an effective substitute. Besides giving you the opportunity to refine your teaching skills, substitute teaching can provide a competitive advantage in the job market. Some school districts are apt to hire full-time teachers from their substitute ranks if the substitutes have done a good job. After all, school officials would rather hire a known teacher in whom they have confidence than take a chance on a new teacher whom they don't know. If you're interested in being a substitute teacher, visit the district personnel office to find out the requirements and attend substitute-teacher training sessions if they are offered.

advantages of substitute teaching

Typical Questions Asked During Job Interviews

Most interviews follow a simple question-and-answer routine. Your ability to communicate effectively with a stranger in a stressful situation is critical. Being prepared is the best way to avoid a disorganized answer. Sometimes the interviewer plays "devil's advocate," disagreeing with a position you articulate to see if you will back down from it in deference to an authority figure. You should be aware of this possibility; be prepared to assess your position straightforwardly, and then stand behind it. Avoid "waffling." Your success in interviewing depends on how convincingly you can convey your ability to teach.

Interviews are often subjective, so your enthusiasm, self-confidence, eagerness, and believability will affect the outcome of your interview. Be sincere and mean what you say. First impressions are important, so dress conservatively. At the conclusion of the interview, restate any important points you want to emphasize. Ask the interviewer for a business card, and ask when the selection decision will be made. Send the interviewer a thank-you note; courtesy can make a difference.

Questions you may be asked include the following:

Motivation/Experience/Education

- Tell us about yourself.
- Why do you want to teach?
- Why do you want to work in our school district?
- What grade levels or subjects are you most interested in teaching?
- What do you consider to be your strongest attributes as a teacher? Weaknesses?
- What was your biggest problem in student teaching? How did you resolve it?
- How would you work with students who perform below grade level, especially those from poverty backgrounds?

Teaching Skills

- What is your philosophy of education?
- What are the most important learning outcomes you want your students to achieve?
- What skills and experience do you have in employing cooperative learning strategies or computers for instructional purposes?
- How can you motivate unmotivated learners?
- How would you involve parents to help students learn?
- How do you individualize your teaching?
- What is your grading philosophy?

Classroom Management

- What ideas do you have regarding maintaining classroom control?
- What rules for students would you establish in your classroom?
- How would you enforce these rules?
- Describe the most difficult student discipline situation you've faced and how you handled it.

Professional Responsibilities

- How do you plan to keep growing as a professional?
- What professional journals do you read?
- What added school responsibilities are you willing to accept?

Hypothetical Questions

- What would you do if you caught a student cheating?

**Typical Questions Asked
During Job Interviews** *(cont'd.)*

▶ If money were unlimited, how would you improve education?

▶ How would you handle a student who refused to do the work you assigned?

During a job interview, you will answer many questions. But to gain the information that will help you choose among the jobs offered to you, you will also need to *ask* questions. Remember, you are interviewing the prospective employer, too. Before you accept a position, you will need to know about the following:

▶ Instructional assignment

▶ Characteristics of the school district and student population

▶ Curriculum and resources available

▶ Typical class size

▶ Salary and benefits (medical and dental coverage and retirement)

▶ District's expectations and reimbursement policies for professional development

▶ Orientation or support services available for beginning teachers

These are just a few suggestions. For additional information on interview questions, see "Interview Questions from Both Sides of the Desk," *1999 Job Search Handbook for Educators* (Evanston, IL: American Association for Employment in Education, 1999), p. 30.

How Do You Become Licensed?

All fifty states and the District of Columbia require public elementary and secondary school teachers to be licensed to teach by the department of education in the state in which they work. The terms *licensure* and *certification* are often confused or misused. **Licensure** is the official recognition by a state governmental agency that an individual meets state requirements, whereas **certification** is the process by which the profession grants special recognition to an individual who has met certain qualifications specified by the profession. Often, however, the term *certification,* as in "I'm going to get my certification to teach," is used when *licensure* is meant. This usage is a carryover from earlier times. Today some states continue to use *certification* as a synonym for *licensure,* but in this book we have tried to distinguish the terms.

state license required to teach

Traditional Licensure Programs

Traditionally, to qualify for licensure, a teacher has had to complete an approved teacher education program. Besides conferring a bachelor's degree, which provides the necessary liberal arts background, teacher education programs fulfill the state requirement that prospective teachers take certain education courses or demonstrate certain competencies.

state exams for teachers

Since the mid-1980s, many states have increased the requirements for licensure, adding test requirements such as the PRAXIS examinations or, in some cases, state-developed minimum competency tests of basic skills. Often prospective teachers are examined on their content-area knowledge. Increasingly, competency testing is being used to screen candidates for licensure. In addition, some states require U.S. citizenship, some criminal background checks, some an oath of allegiance, and several a health certificate. And some local school districts may require teacher applicants to take written examinations or meet other requirements to be hired.

differences among states . . .

Because the requirements for licensure differ from state to state, you should become aware of the requirements for the state in which you will seek employment. Someone in your placement office or your school of education most likely will be able to acquaint you with licensure requirements. Your education library probably contains books that list the licensure requirements for all the states. Should you not be successful there, you can call or write directly to the teacher licensure office in the states in which you are interested. A directory of state teacher licensure offices in the United States appears as an appendix at the end of this book. A number of states have reciprocal agreements to accept one another's licenses as valid. If you move from one state to another, you may want to check whether your teaching license is accepted by the state to which you are moving.

. . . and specialization areas

Besides the basic licenses for teaching at the elementary and secondary levels, many states require different licenses, or *endorsements,* for such specialization areas as special education, bilingual education, and kindergarten. If, as you gain experience, you want to move out of teaching into a supervisory, administrative, or counseling position, you will need a special license.

pursue more than one licensure area

If at all possible, you would be wise to become licensed or endorsed in more than one teaching area. Adding a second field of licensure will make you more attractive to prospective employers, particularly in smaller school districts, which have less flexibility to hire specialists who teach in only one area. If you are going to be an elementary school teacher, having an additional license in reading, special education, early childhood education, or bilingual education would be very worthwhile. Another way to increase your appeal to prospective employers would be to take a major or minor in mathematics, one of the sciences, or instructional technology. Elementary school teachers with expertise in these areas are in short supply. If you are going to teach at the secondary level, you can broaden your appeal by being licensed to teach in two or more subject fields. For example, if you are a Spanish major, minor in French; if you are a chemistry major, minor in physics or mathematics. Any doubling up of teaching fields will work to your advantage.

> *Teaching was the hardest work I had ever done, and it remains the hardest work I have done to date.*
> —ANN RICHARDS (FORMER GOVERNOR OF TEXAS)

In summary, individual states use licensure requirements to assure the public that the teachers teaching the youth of our society have been adequately prepared. Licensure requirements should present you with little difficulty as long as the teacher education institution you attend meets the general regulations of the state department of education and as long as you maintain contact with the college official responsible for coordinating the education program with the state licensure requirements. But in many states, the traditional route to licensure—graduation from an approved teacher education program—is no longer the sole route to gaining a teaching license.

Alternative Licensure

Many states offer alternative routes to licensure, and there is tremendous variation among these options. For example, some states permit **alternative licensure** routes only when there is a shortage of traditionally licensed teachers. Other states permit alternative routes only at the secondary level. Still other states allow institutions of higher education to design alternatives to their college-approved teacher education programs.

Generally, those licensed through alternative means hold a bachelor's degree in the subject area they will teach but have taken fewer credit-hours in professional education courses than are normally required. Often these candidates are required to have at least a B college grade average and to have passed a basic skills test and a test in a subject or specialty area. Alternative programs are a response to (1) teacher shortages and (2) the perception on the part of some lawmakers that courses in education contribute little.

alternative licensure requirements

One alternative program that has gained considerable attention is *Teach for America*. The program recruits motivated undergraduate students with arts and science majors from select colleges and universities to teach for two years in rural or urban areas that have had difficulty recruiting teachers. Although the program has been successful in attracting significant numbers of minority teachers, its dropout rate is high. Also, the number of teachers produced through the Teach for America program is very small compared to the number graduated through approved teacher education programs.

Teach for America program

pluses and minuses

How successful are these alternative licensure programs? Although forty-one states had some form of alternative licensure option by 1997, only about 75,000 teachers in the entire nation had been licensed through alternative routes since 1985.[17] That's fewer than 3 percent of the 2.6 million teachers now working in public elementary and secondary schools. Formal evaluation studies of alternative licensure programs have been few and have sometimes been conducted by persons with vested interests in the outcomes.

alternative programs—how successful?

One positive feature of alternative licensure programs is that, like Teach for America, they seem to attract minorities more than do traditional teacher preparation programs. For example, in Texas, whereas 91 percent of all public school teachers are white, 43 percent of teachers entering through the state's alternative programs are minority.[18]

Nevertheless, tensions exist between those who want to break college-based teacher education's monopoly and professional educators who believe that completion of an approved teacher education program is the public's best guarantee that a teacher is "safe to practice." The variety of alternative licensure programs across the various states is testimony to the differing views on how teachers should be prepared. One thing seems certain: alternative licensure programs will continue to grow to meet the projected need for teachers.

Preparing Teachers: High Standards, Large Numbers, or Both?

What's the Policy?

The United States will need a projected 2.2 million new teachers in the next decade, approximately 220,000 each year. College- and university-based teacher education programs are expected to produce between 75 and 100 percent of the nation's new teachers, but many teacher education graduates choose never to teach. Where will the shortfall come from? State policymakers are now grappling with this problem. One popular solution is to create alternative routes to the traditional teacher education program for licensing prospective teachers.

How Does It Affect Teachers?

Recently several new avenues have opened up for those interested in teaching. Some see retiring military personnel as a source of new teaching talent, especially in the sciences and mathematics. To capitalize on this population source, Congress has created a Troops to Teachers program to help military personnel who want to teach to acquire teaching licenses. Many states allow liberal arts graduates with academic majors to bypass regular teacher education programs and be hired directly into teaching positions without having had any supervised teaching experience. Usually these programs require that the schools provide mentor teachers to work with the neophyte teacher for a year or two. Another highly publicized program, Teach for America, recruits liberal arts graduates to undertake a two-year commitment to teach in either an urban or a rural setting where teachers are desperately needed.

What Are the Pros?

Programs such as Troops to Teachers and Teach for America are helping to fill a need that otherwise would soon grow desperate. In addition, they are targeting especially high-need areas, including the disciplines of math and science and geographical locations that find it particularly hard to recruit teachers.

In addition, alternative licensure methods may offer opportunities to some extremely gifted potential teachers who would have been put off by the requirements of a standard teacher preparation program. People older than the traditional college-age student, for example, may welcome the chance to enter the teaching field without spending several unpaid years returning to college.

What Are the Cons?

Research indicates that having a well-qualified, competent teacher is one of the most important factors in whether or not students learn the school's curriculum. Toward this end, most states have increased standards for prospective teachers entering the field via traditional teacher preparation programs. States have begun requiring graduates of such programs to have higher grade point averages, more preparation in the subjects they will teach, more experiences in schools, and higher scores on tests of subject-matter knowledge and teaching competence. In contrast, many observers wonder about the qualifications and commitment of teachers prepared in alternative programs. Does student learning suffer while these teachers are learning on the job? How long will these teachers stay in the classroom compared to regularly prepared teachers?

Other concerns involve the reasons at the root of the teacher shortage and whether they stem from the nature of teaching as a profession. Is the shortage of well-qualified teachers a factor of inadequate pay and working conditions, problems that won't be solved with short-term solutions?

As policymakers and the public grapple with these questions, one thing seems certain: school districts will always have a warm body in front of

Policy Matters! *(cont'd)*

each classroom. Whether that warm body can inspire students to learn and teach them what they need to know is another question.

What Do You Think?

1. How would you propose to address the gap between the number of teachers needed and the number produced through teacher education programs?

2. What are the advantages and disadvantages of the various kinds of alternative teacher education programs? What concerns, if any, do you have about them?

3. What are some ways for policymakers to increase the number of bright and committed college students in college-based teacher education programs?

If You Don't Teach, What Then?

Suppose that despite all your job-seeking efforts you are unsuccessful in finding the position you want. Or suppose that after teaching a few years, you decide that teaching is not for you. What will you be prepared to do after your teacher education? Has your preparation equipped you with skills that are in demand in fields outside education? For many different reasons, a substantial number of teachers each year find themselves looking for jobs outside education.

Transferable Skills

What generic or transferable skills—that is, skills that are needed in most businesses and professions—are you likely to have developed in your preparation as a teacher? Among the skills and abilities that teachers acquire are the following:

teaching skills transferable to other jobs

- Planning and decision making

- Working under pressure

- Conducting performance evaluation

- Keeping records and organizing materials

- Using technology

- Establishing and maintaining good interpersonal relations

- Communicating effectively in oral and written form

- Managing groups of people

In short, many of the skills required of teachers are also required for other types of work. Naturally, additional training may be necessary, depending on the exact type of work. Now let's examine some alternative careers.

Work in recreation or leisure activities are among the careers available for people prepared as teachers. (© Dana White/PhotoEdit)

Other Jobs

In addition to teaching, schools and school districts offer a number of other educational occupations, including librarian, counselor, supervisor, administrator, and school psychologist. Although these roles don't involve full-time teaching of children, they usually require a minimum of two or three years of teaching experience and additional licensure. All these roles are important in the educational enterprise. If you decide that you are interested in education but not necessarily in long-term elementary or secondary school teaching, one of these other occupations may be right for you.

jobs requiring teaching experience

You might also investigate employment in early childhood education and day care centers. Because early childhood education is a growing field, numerous new occupations are developing within it, such as reading specialists to help diagnose learning abilities and curriculum specialists to help plan the studies. State, local, and federal government agencies need researchers, planners, evaluators, and others to administer the growing number of early childhood projects they fund.

training and development in corporations

Large businesses also conduct extensive training programs for their employees, and they require the services of people who can design and implement such programs. Many people who have been trained as teachers find their way into such jobs. Several hundreds of thousands of people are employed (full- and part-time) in training and development in the United States.*

recreation and leisure jobs

The field of recreation and leisure activities attracts many people trained as teachers. Workers in this field plan, organize, and direct individual and group activities that help people enjoy their leisure hours. They work with people of various ages and socioeconomic groups, the sick and the well, and those with emotional and physical disabilities. Employment settings range from wilderness to rural to suburban and urban, including the inner city. Examples of recreation program jobs include playground leaders; program specialists in dance, drama, karate, tennis, the arts, and other physical activities; recreation center directors; therapeutic recreation specialists; camp counselors and wilderness leaders; senior citizen program leaders; civilian special services directors in the armed forces; and industrial recreation directors. Recreation workers held about 233,000 jobs by 1996, not including summer workers. The majority worked in local, public tax–supported agencies such as municipal and county park and recreation departments.[19] Employment of recreation workers is expected to grow faster than the average for all occupations through the year 2006 as growing numbers of people possess both the time and the money to enjoy leisure services.

jobs in publishing

The publishing industry affords numerous job opportunities for education-oriented writers, editors, and salespeople. If you have good writing and analytic skills, you might be interested in helping to develop or edit textbooks for use in elementary and secondary schools and in colleges. If you enjoy meeting people and traveling, being a textbook sales representative might appeal to you. Another growing area is the development of computer software related to education. Individuals who combine computer skills with an understanding of classroom instruction will have a distinct advantage in the job market.

working for professional organizations

Preparation as a teacher is also important for work related to professional organizations such as the National Education Association and the American Federation of Teachers, Phi Delta Kappa and Kappa Delta Pi, and the National Association of Mathematics Teachers and the National Council for the Social Studies. These organizations and others like them hire people for fieldwork, writing, research, and other staff positions.

A Final Word

Many indicators point to a strong demand for teachers in the coming years. Impending retirements in the current teaching force and increased school enrollments are encouraging signs for prospective teachers. However, we don't know how many former teachers will re-enter the job market to compete with recently

*The American Society for Training and Development, 1640 King St., Box 1443, Alexandria, VA 22313, can provide more information about corporate career opportunities for teachers. Web site at www.astd.org.

graduated teachers for the job openings. Successful job searches may require special steps, such as relocating to another area or state to secure a teaching position in your field.

To those bright young people who want to enter the profession that has been so good to many of us—education—I say "good choice!" My advice to them is not "You're too smart to be a teacher," but rather, "You're too smart not to be one."

—JAMES R. DELISLE

As we stated earlier, there has never been a surplus of good teachers. If you and your credentials are good, and you are willing to go where the jobs are, you can find a teaching job. Preparing yourself well for school districts' needs, especially gaining expertise in more than one teaching field, can expand your job options and make you more attractive to prospective employers.

America has become an education-oriented society. We are realizing that reaching our individual and national goals depends on achieving high levels of education. This means we are committed to more and better education, to lifelong learning in and out of schools. Over seventy years ago, President Calvin Coolidge said, "The business of America is business." Today and into the future, the business of America is education. Teaching is where the action is and will continue to be!

KEY TERMS

teaching portfolio (481)
credential file (482)
licensure (485)
certification (485)
alternative licensure (487)

FOR REFLECTION

1. What are the present and projected teacher supply in the field that currently interests you most? In the geographic area you desire? How do you expect these figures to affect your ability to find a position you want?

2. Are you prepared to leave your current location to find a teaching position? Are you willing to teach in an urban school? A rural school? A private school?

3. What ways can you think of to increase your chances of being hired when you are ready to begin teaching?

4. What are some effective job-hunting strategies?

5. Do you have any opinions about the alternative licensure programs currently offered in many states?

6. Are there any education-related occupations other than teaching that might interest you?

FOR FURTHER INFORMATION

Anthony, Rebecca, and Gerald Roe. *From Contact to Contract: A Teacher's Employment Guide.* **Woodmere, NY: Sulzburger & Graham Publishing, Limited, 1994.**

This book provides sample cover letters, information on various types of teacher contracts, and additional professional advice.

Bolles, Richard Nelson. *What Color Is Your Parachute? 2000.* **Berkeley, CA: Ten Speed Press, 1999.**

This practical manual for job hunters and career changers is updated yearly.

Council of Chief State School Officers. World Wide Web site at http://www. ccsso.org.

SEARCH

This organization of the chief state school officers has a useful and informative home page, including links to each state education agency. Click on "Links to State Education Agencies" and choose the state in which you're interested. Some states list telephone numbers and web sites of different school districts in the state.

Edelfelt, Roy A. *Careers in Education.* **3d ed. Lincolnwood, IL: NTC Contemporary Publishing, 1998.**

This book explores various educational careers in teaching, administration, higher education, and business and industry.

Job Search Handbook for Educators. **Evanston, IL: American Association for Employment in Education.**

This annual publication is designed to assist both new and experienced educators in their job searches, and is the single most important reference on this topic. The *Handbook* is usually distributed through career planning and placement offices in colleges and universities, but it may also be obtained from the AAEE office at 820 Davis Street, Suite 222, Evanston, IL 60201-4445; 847-864-1999. AAEE's web site at www.aaee.org also provides links to public school systems and educational organizations.

References for Locating Sources of Job Vacancies

General Information

Directory of Public School Systems in the U.S. **American Association for Employment in Education, 820 Davis Street, Suite 222, Evanston, IL 60201-4445. Order online at www.aaee.org.**

SEARCH

Published annually.

Education Week. **4301 Connecticut Avenue, N.W., Suite 250, Washington, DC 20008.**

SEARCH

An independent newspaper published forty times per year, available online at http://www.edweek.org.

Project Connect. **Connect through AAEE's web site at www.aaee.org.**
A national cooperative venture among school districts and university schools of education, Project Connect provides lists of teaching vacancies, either through college placement offices or directly via the web site. You can register online for a password; no fees are involved.

Teaching Opportunities Catalog.
This publication contacts all 2,800 public school districts in sixteen states on the eastern seaboard and lists openings for teachers. It is published nine times per year and costs $48 for four issues or $94.50 for a full year. Teaching Opportunities, 637 Georges Road, North Brunswick, NJ 08902-3331; 1-800-969-4001.

Private Schools

Independent School Management, Inc.
This organization carries job vacancy listings for teaching in independent schools on its web site at http://www.isminc.com/pubs/mart/mm.html. Ads are changed every three weeks.

National Association of Independent Schools (NAIS).
This organization represents more than 1,000 independent schools nationwide. Contact: Associate Director of Academic Services, NAIS, 1620 L Street, N.W., Washington, DC 20036; 202-973-9700. Also see its web site at http://nais-schools.org/ for information on how to secure a teaching job at one of its schools.

Peterson's Private Secondary Schools 1999–2000. **Peterson's Guides, P.O. Box 2123, Princeton, NJ 08543-2123. Order online at www.petersons.com.**
This guide provides descriptions and contacts for hundreds of independent or private schools across the country.

Teaching Opportunities Abroad

U.S. Department of Defense Dependents Schools
Teachers in these American schools are U.S. government employees. Contact: Office of Dependents Schools, Recruitment/Assignment Section, 4040 North Fairfax Drive, 6th floor, Arlington, VA 22203-1635; 703-696-3054.

European Council of International Schools (ECIS).
This organization can provide information about schools in Europe. Contact: 21B Lavant Street, Petersfield, Hampshire GU32 3EL, UK (44-730-68244) or the North American office at 908-903-0552.

Fulbright Teacher Exchange Program
This program provides a booklet and list of programs on opportunities to teach or study overseas. Contact: Bureau of Educational and Cultural Affairs, U.S. Information Agency, Room 353, E/ASX, 301 4th Street, S.W., Washington, DC 20547; 202-619-4555.

International Schools Services (ISS)

This resource contains names, addresses, and other information on nearly 500 international elementary and secondary schools. Ask for the *ISS Directory of Overseas Schools*. Contact: 609-452-0990.

The Peace Corps

Several months of training are provided prior to living in the host country. Following a stint in the Corps, members have access to a range of programs intended to help them become teachers in the United States. Contact: Peace Corps Recruiting Office, 1990 K Street, N.W., Suite 9102, Washington, DC 20526; 800-424-8580.

Private Schools with U.S. State Department Affiliation

Each of these schools does its own hiring. Children native to the host country make up part of the student population. Contact: Office of Overseas Schools, Room 245, SA-29 A/OS, U.S. Department of State, Washington, DC 20522-2902; 703-875-7977.

International Recruiting Fair

The College of Education at The Ohio State University sponsors an annual recruiting fair usually held in mid-February. Contact: College of Education, Ohio State University, 110 Arps Hall, 1945 North High Street, Columbus, OH 43210-1172; 614-292-2741.

15

What Does It Mean to Be a Professional?

In this chapter, we focus on the teacher as a professional, that is, as a member of an occupational group. We will see how this rather abstract concept of *professionalism* affects the daily life of the classroom teacher. In effect, we put the role of the individual teacher in the larger context of being a member of a profession.

This chapter emphasizes that

▶ Teachers can become involved in different types of situations and conflicts in which they will need counsel or support.

▶ The education of the American teacher has evolved substantially since colonial times.

▶ Teachers have become more powerful in recent years, but they don't have the same kinds of power that members of some other professions have.

▶ The question of whether teaching is a profession can be judged by reference to specific criteria. Furthermore, cases can be made both for and against teaching being a profession.

▶ The National Board for Professional Teaching Standards and its standards for certification may have a substantial effect on teachers.

▶ The National Education Association and the American Federation of Teachers, the most influential teacher organizations, have quite different origins and are competing for the support of classroom teachers.

▶ The teaching profession is still defining itself, and much depends on its capacity to maintain the public's trust.

▶ Current educational demands require the teacher to be a continuous learner. Teachers can continue their professional growth in various ways.

The essence of a career in teaching is close, hands-on work with the young. When people think about becoming teachers, their thoughts and daydreams usually revolve around working with students. Rarely do they bother with hypothetical issues beyond the scope of the classroom. This is both natural and appropriate, since the teacher's success or failure depends on his or her effectiveness with students. Nevertheless, there is much more to being a teacher than this. Teachers work within a system that exposes them to pressures from many quarters. Prospective teachers are frequently somewhat naive about the pressures and forces that will affect them—and naiveté can be dangerous, both in making a career decision and in making a successful career.

teaching within a system

To help you see this point, we would like you to indulge in a set of daydreams for a few moments. We will offer you a few brief scenarios, and, after reading each one, you should reflect on how you might react. As you read each scenario, imagine yourself teaching in that ideal classroom you carry around in your head. Assume that you appear to be doing a fine job. You are really enjoying it. Your students are making nice progress. They seem to be interested in their work. A few parents have indicated that although they were initially worried that their precious child was to have a new (read "untested") teacher, they are thrilled with the child's progress in your class. OK. Things are going very well, until . . .

1. You get a special-delivery letter from a group called PAP (Patriotic American Parents). You have heard they are very active in your area and are especially interested in schools. Their letter informs you that their lawyer is preparing a case against you for using books that are on their disapproved list. (You didn't know there was such a list—but, sure enough, there is, and you have!) They claim they have evidence that you are waging a subtle but nevertheless vicious war against the cause of justice and liberty and have succeeded in temporarily deflecting the minds of some of your students from the truth. Furthermore, they want to know why you display the U.N. flag. Finally, you are said to recite the Pledge of Allegiance in a much too hasty fashion, which is clearly a sign of your disrespect for your country. This is the first you have heard of these charges or even of the Patriots' interest in you. You think of yourself as patriotic and are shocked by the letter. They have requested that you respond in writing by next week or they will begin legal proceedings.

target of pressure groups

2. In late January, the superintendent, who holds a conference with each new teacher, told you she thought you were doing a fine job and that she wanted you to return next year. In passing, she remarked that she would be getting a contract to you in the spring. Toward the end of April, you got a little nervous and called her. You spoke to her executive secretary, who said not to worry, that you were on the list, and that a contract would be coming before long. You stopped worrying.

the invisible contract

Today is the last day of school, and you find a very nice personal note from the principal in your school mailbox. He thanks you for your fine work during the year and says he is sorry you will not be back next year. You call the superintendent's office. She is in conference, and her executive secretary says they are not renewing your contract. She cannot remember speaking to you in April. She knows nothing about the case. She does know, however, that the board of education has put on a lot of pressure for cuts in next year's personnel budget. She ends by telling you, "You must be very disappointed, dear. I know how you feel."

conflict with colleagues

3. You noticed something peculiar when you sat down at the faculty dining table one lunch hour. Conversations stopped, and you had the distinct impression your colleagues had been talking about you. A few days later, an older teacher stopped you in the hall after school and said, "I don't want to butt in, but you really are upsetting Mrs. Hilary and Mr. Alexandra." Mrs. H. and Mr. A. have the classrooms on either side of yours. Apparently they claim your class makes so much noise that they can't get anything done. Both are very traditional in their approach to education, whereas you believe in a more activity-oriented approach. Although your class is rather noisy occasionally, it is never chaotic, and its noise is usually a byproduct of the students' involvement in the task. Twice Mr. Alexandra has sent messengers with notes asking that your class be more quiet. You have always complied. You hardly know either teacher. You have never really talked to Mr. Alexandra except to say hello. Mrs. Hilary, with whom you've chatted, prides herself on being a strict disciplinarian. What she means, you have inferred, is that she is able to keep the children quiet. You know Mr. Alexandra is chummy with Mrs. Hilary. You go to the vice principal, who seems to know all about the case, but only from the Hilary-Alexandra angle. Inexplicably, the vice principal gets quite angry and claims that until you came along, the faculty got along beautifully. Furthermore, you are being very unprofessional in making complaints against experienced teachers. You feel as if you are trapped in a bad dream.

These horror stories, of course, are not everyday occurrences. Also, keep in mind that entrance into any profession has its trials. These accounts are intended to help you realize that you can be an effective teacher and still have trouble keeping your job. What is the common theme running through each of these anecdotes? You, the teacher, were succeeding in your work with children, but forces outside the classroom began to impinge on you. The Patriotic American Parents wanted to make a target case of you. The school system bureaucracy was ready to put you on the unemployed rolls. Two of your colleagues damaged your reputation with the faculty and administration. Other than that, it was a super year.

Although you may feel confident that you could handle some of these situations, it is doubtful that you could cope with all such cases that might arise. In some instances you would be powerless to respond effectively to your adversaries, and you might end up a helpless victim of circumstance. Fortunately, a teacher is

organizational support

not alone. Like people in many other occupational groups, teachers have organizations that protect them from such indignities and injustices. These organizations function on several levels, from the local to the national, and usually their very existence keeps situations like those described from occurring. When they do occur, these organizations are there to support the teacher, even though seniority usually rules. At least, that is the way they should work.

It is important to realize that in becoming a teacher, you are not just committing yourself to work with children. You are joining an occupational group composed of other individuals with similar responsibilities, concerns, and pressures whose help you may need and who, in turn, will need your help. It is also an occupational group with a long and rich history in American society.

The Upward Road to Professionalism

The education of teachers for their profession has made great strides since the colonial period, when often the only real criterion was that a teacher had to know more than the students. In the nineteenth century, the expansion of the common schools called for larger numbers of teachers, and the development of public high schools required that the quality of elementary teaching be improved. By the 1900s, new theories about psychology, learning, and the nature of teaching made professional training even more necessary. Normal schools, colleges, and universities began to take more seriously the needs of those who would teach society's children.

The Colonial Period

Qualifications   Although much emphasis was placed publicly on the religious, political, and moral worthiness of teachers, the public had very low expectations concerning teachers' professional training. There were no specialized schools to train teachers; the only educational training any teacher had was simply having been a student. Generally, a teacher was expected to know just enough about the subject matter to be able to pass along this knowledge to the pupils. Thus began the teacher's revered tradition of being only one page ahead of the students. *no professional preparation*

Throughout the colonial period, much attention was paid to ensuring that teachers lived up to the expectations of the people who controlled education. In New England, teachers were approved by town meetings, selectmen, school committees, and ministers. In the Middle Colonies and the South, governors and religious groups issued teachers' certificates. Before the American Revolution, teachers were required to sign oaths of allegiance to the crown of England; once the revolution started, they had to sign loyalty oaths to the various states. *oaths of allegiance*

Salaries and Status   The highest salaries and status were granted to college teachers, the next highest to secondary school teachers, and the lowest to elementary school teachers. Salaries were often paid irregularly and were frequently supplemented with payment in produce or livestock. Essentially the colonial teacher received wages equivalent to those of a farmhand. *poor pay*

Teaching was hardly considered a profession in colonial America. Schools were poorly equipped, and students attended irregularly. The school term was *undesirable conditions*

Kay Toliver

"I'm a teacher. What else would I do?" Kay Toliver asks.

Kay Toliver teaches at P.S. 72 in Spanish Harlem, where she has been instilling a love of knowledge in middle school students for over twenty-five years. Toliver teaches on the cutting edge of mathematics, stressing thinking and application over computation, and weaving history and art through class discussions into the study of mathematics. Because many of her students come from poor, unstable backgrounds and have poor language skills, she emphasizes writing, reading, and research. Her students must always be prepared to explain their solutions orally, in complete and clear sentences. They are required to keep daily journals, in which they write about what they have learned in class, ideas about how to apply the concepts they study, or simply observations about the class or the teacher. Toliver believes that the students' ability to express themselves in well-written English must be acquired hand-in-hand with mathematical discovery. In addition to enhancing writing skills, the journals allow the teacher to gain a glimpse of her students' confusions in mathematics. "A teacher can stand in front of the class and think she's giving a great lesson. But, that's not always the truth," she explains.

Kay Toliver's influence is spreading beyond her classroom to videos. In 1995, she was featured in a Peabody award–winning PBS special, "Good Morning Miss Toliver." Also, with Jaime Escalante, Toliver contributed to "Interactions: Real Math—Real Careers," a multimedia tool that connects prealgebra math principles to real life in scenarios featuring career professionals. Along with Escalante, Toliver sees the way to future jobs through mathematics, especially for students from the inner city.

In addition to the mathematical tools, P.S. 72 children use computers. Toliver feels her students must be technologically competitive. With money she received from one of her many awards, the Presidential Award for Excellence in Science and Mathematics Teaching, she purchased software and computers for her school's computer lab.

Toliver has seen many students who have been exposed to drugs or crime, or both. Frequently, one parent is gone, or a child may be in foster care. Too often a sibling is in jail, and the students' peers are dealing with everyday street life in East Harlem. But having grown up in the South Bronx and East Harlem, she is well acquainted with the world of her students. As a result, discipline is not a problem in Toliver's class. Students understand she is serious and works hard to make math interesting. "We don't need different methods to teach so-called 'disadvantaged children.' We just need teachers who are dedicated and who believe their students can succeed," she says.

Kay Toliver hopes some of her students will share her love of teaching and become teachers themselves. Recently, after she had appeared on a television special, five students told her they wanted to become teachers. She had become a real-life role model after the television appearance. She likes being recognized for her work, but mainly she finds rewards in the changes brought to the lives of her students by mathematics.

Source: From "Inspiring Young Minds: Kay Tolliver," by Arwen Larson, *Technos* Quarterly, Vol. 2 No. 4. Used by permission.

short, in many cases making teaching a part-time occupation. Many patrons of education believed teaching was a fairly undemanding task, and they would add to the duties of the teacher such custodial chores as cleaning out the church, ringing the assembly bell, providing for the baptismal basin, running errands, serving as messenger, digging graves, assisting the pastor in reading the Scriptures, leading the singing at church services, keeping records, issuing invitations, writing letters, visiting the sick, and generally making themselves useful. The teacher was often "boarded round," living with a different family every few weeks to stretch out meager school funds.

As a result of these and other indignities, the turnover rate among teachers was high, and this turnover contributed to keeping the status and quality of teachers low. In many ways, the idea of teachers being a professional group, with a "calling" to their vocation, did not develop until the 1800s.

The Nineteenth Century

Teachers for the Common Schools   The common school movement of the early nineteenth century (described in Chapter 11), with its consequent demand for better-trained elementary school teachers, was one of the most exciting periods in the history of American education. Speeches and pamphlets called for placing education at the center of the endeavor to maintain democracy and for raising the professional qualifications for teaching as well as teacher salaries. The vocation of teaching was put forth as an intellectual, religious, and patriotic calling. In the period between 1820 and 1865, educators began to urge special training for teachers that coupled academic secondary education for teachers with education in the principles of teaching.

call for better teachers

Women Teachers   As in colonial times, teachers' salaries were quite low. Wages continued to reflect a general attitude that teachers were people who were unable to hold a regular job, or were a bit eccentric, or had nothing much else to do anyway. Indeed, it was at this time that a shift from men to women teachers began in the elementary schools. The result of that trend is still evident today, since more than two out of three teachers are women. Among the reasons women were actively recruited into the teaching ranks was the clear financial benefit to the community. Women could be hired for less than men—in some places, for only about one-third the salary paid to male teachers.

women teachers cheaper

Other factors also encouraged the greater involvement of women in education from the 1830s on. In formerly handcrafted production, such as embroidery, industry was gradually replacing housewives with machines. The arrival of the machine decimated the handicraft industries such as embroidery, displacing large numbers of women. Seeking a higher standard of living, men began to move either westward or to the industrializing cities. As a result, when the common schools began to require better-quality teachers, the female academies, seminaries, and normal schools began to provide them.

Catharine Beecher *(1800–1878)*

Catharine Beecher believed strongly that for women to be properly prepared as teachers, they needed special training institutions similar to the model of men's colleges and universities. She spent nearly fifty years improving the quality of women's education and raising women's status in the teaching profession.

Born in Connecticut, Catharine Beecher received her first formal education from her father, the well-known clergyman Lyman Beecher. After the untimely death of her fiancé, Beecher decided to devote her life to service as a teacher. Not long afterward, in 1828, she founded the Hartford Female Seminary. The establishment of this institution for the education of females set the pattern for her life's work.

At a time when women had to leave the teaching profession upon marriage, Beecher urged them to become teachers before fulfilling their calls to be wives and mothers. However, she emphasized that the quality of women's education needed to be improved, pointing out that the model of female loveliness that included fainting and playing the "pretty plaything" was not adequate for the roles women were expected to assume. Beecher called upon the leading female schools in the country to establish a uniform course of education adapted to the character and circumstances of women, corresponding to what was done in colleges for young men, and she urged the benefactors of female institutions to provide suitable facilities for instruction, such as libraries and scientific equipment. She also saw the need for teachers who were not generalists, but specialists in academic disciplines.

As she spoke and wrote extensively on ways to improve the education of women, Beecher established female seminaries in New England and across the Midwest. Each of these seminaries was attached to a model school supported financially by the children who attended it. The faculties were prepared to teach at other seminaries in order to establish a regular and systematic course of education throughout the country. For women who were unable to pay for their preparation as teachers, Beecher urged that alternative public institutions be maintained. At a time when it was uncommon to campaign for educational reform and defend the needs of women, Catharine Beecher spent her life striving to do both.

rise of "normal schools"

Normal Schools and Colleges   The first true teacher education institutions were called **normal schools.** The idea of the normal school originated in Europe. The term *normal* referred to teaching teachers the norms, or rules, of teaching. The first two normal schools in the United States were established in 1823 in Vermont and in 1827 in Massachusetts. The normal schools were essentially private academies that offered additional training in teaching methods and classroom discipline. A decade later, in 1837, Catharine Beecher became a full-time advocate of normal schools to train women for teaching. In addition, Beecher established the National Board of Popular Education, which sent more than 400 eastern women teachers to the West. Besides these newly developing normal schools, there were informal teachers' institutes offered for six-week sessions between teaching schedules, and colleges even began to offer an odd course or two on teaching methods.

An American classroom circa 1900. What will the 2100 classroom look like? (CORBIS/Bettmann)

Growing Professionalization   Following the Civil War, the greater demand for public secondary education carried with it the inherent demand for more highly trained teachers. At the same time, new educational theories and techniques and the development of the field of child psychology required that teachers receive greater training if they were to use the new strategies in the classroom. It became less and less tolerable that many reasons other than educational criteria were used to judge applicants for teaching positions.

more demand, more training

By the end of the nineteenth century, balanced teacher-training programs had been developed that included instruction in the academic content the teacher was going to teach, the foundations of educational theory, the administrative aspects of teaching, child psychology, and pedagogical strategies. Every state had at least one public normal school. Most schools accepted students who had about two years of high school background. Most graduates became elementary school teachers after two years, although some took a four-year program to become high school teachers and administrators.

College-level teacher training grew with impetus from two directions. One was the expansion of normal school course offerings into four-year curricula; the other was the development of university courses in education and, eventually, entire departments of education. Both were stimulated by the increasing demand that high school teachers have some college training. Thus, by 1900 and well into the new century, there were several ways to acquire teacher training: normal schools, teachers' colleges, university departments of education, and the less formal teachers' institutes.

college training increases

The Twentieth Century

After World War I, normal schools continued to evolve into four-year colleges, which quadrupled in number between 1920 and 1940 from about forty-five to more than two hundred. The Great Depression of the 1930s actually helped to raise the standards for teachers, simply as a function of supply and demand. With more people than jobs available, school districts could require additional training for teachers.

rising standards

A number of major changes in teacher training can be traced over the first fifty years of the twentieth century. The most important change was the move from teacher training to *teacher education*. This change in labels was not merely empty symbolism. It signaled a change in the substance of what teachers were expected to know. By 1950, most teachers had at least a four-year college degree, with a specific content area of instruction; professional courses in teaching methods and educational psychology; and some period of practice through observation, laboratory experience, and student teaching. It was also recognized that elementary as well as secondary school teachers needed four years of college.

from training to education

The four-year time period has been the norm until the present. Today only a small percentage of states require teachers to have five years of college education before they can be licensed. But many teacher educators, believing that adequate teacher preparation cannot be accomplished in four years of college, are calling for extended teacher preparation programs that combine a baccalaureate degree in a discipline with a master's degree in professional coursework. This is not a totally new idea, since many of the nation's best universities have had master of arts in teaching (MAT) programs for many decades. These MAT programs typically are designed for liberal arts graduates who are preparing to be high school teachers. The new effort is to make all teacher education extend into the graduate level.

extending the education period

While the work of the teacher has, from its beginnings, been among the nation's most important and most noble, this brief historical account shows that the career of teaching has been a bumpy road for many. In earlier times, the low status of teachers hindered their ability to do their work with children. But in recent years, this condition has led to a drive to make elementary and secondary school teaching not just a job or a career but a profession.

The Status of Teaching: A Profession or Not?

The question "Is teaching a profession?" probably arouses little interest in many of our readers. Most people thinking about a career in teaching are more interested in whether it will be a personally rewarding way to spend their time than in whether or not it is a true profession. Will teaching bring me personal satisfactions? Will it provide an outlet for my talents and energies? Will I be effective with kids? These questions are, we suspect, closer to your skin. Nevertheless, the question of professionalism and the related issues are important to teachers and

professionalism a key question

influence the quality of education teachers provide for children. They will also affect the quality of your life as a teacher. So what actually is a profession?

A **profession** is more than a group of individuals all engaged in the same line of work. Professions have a more or less recognizable set of characteristics that distinguish them from nonprofessions.[1] As you read the following list of characteristics, check whether or not you think teaching qualifies on each premise.

does teaching qualify?

First, a profession renders a unique, definite, and essential service to society. *yes* ❏ *no* ❏
Only the people in the particular profession render the service; for instance, only lawyers practice law. The service rendered must be considered so important that it is available to all the people in a society.

Second, a profession relies on intellectual skills in the performance of its ser- *yes* ❏ *no* ❏
vice. This does not mean that physical actions and skills are not needed; rather, the emphasis in carrying on the work is on intellectual skills and techniques.

Third, a profession entails a long period of specialized training. Because pro- *yes* ❏ *no* ❏
fessional work requires special intellectual skills, it requires specialized intellectual training. General education, such as that represented by a bachelor's degree, is valued but is not considered adequate. The specialized training must cover a substantial period and not be obtained in cram courses or correspondence schools.

Fourth, both individual members of the profession and the professional group *yes* ❏ *no* ❏
enjoy a considerable degree of autonomy and decision-making authority. Professional groups regulate their own activities rather than having outsiders set policies and enforce adherence to standards. Whereas factory workers have very limited decision-making power and are closely supervised in the performance of their work, professionals are expected to make most of their own decisions and be free of close supervision by supervisors.

Fifth, a profession requires its members to accept personal responsibility for *yes* ❏ *no* ❏
their actions and decisions and, in general, for their performance. Since the professional's service is usually related to the client's human welfare, this responsibility is an especially serious one.

Sixth, a profession emphasizes the services rendered by its practitioners more *yes* ❏ *no* ❏
than their financial rewards. Although the personal motives of any individual professional are not necessarily any higher than any other worker's, the professional group's public emphasis is on service.

Seventh, a profession is self-governing and responsible for policing its own *yes* ❏ *no* ❏
ranks. This means there are professional groups that perform a number of activities aimed at keeping the quality of their services high and looking out for the social and economic well-being of the professional members. Also, these self-governing organizations set standards of admission and exclusion for the profession.

Eighth, a profession has a code of ethics that sets out the acceptable standards *yes* ❏ *no* ❏
of conduct for its members. To regulate the quality of service, the professional group needs a code of ethics to aid it in enforcing high standards.

These characteristics, then, are the major requirements of a profession. Few professions satisfy all of them fully. However, the list does serve as a benchmark by which occupational groups can measure themselves and direct their development if they wish to enjoy professional status. With this in mind, let's look at the arguments for and against teaching as a profession.

The Case *Against* Teaching as a Profession*

The roots of teaching as an occupation go back to ancient Greece, where slaves called *paidagogos*, or pedagogues, taught children to read and write and helped them memorize passages of poetic history. Despite this long history, however, a careful look at current practices reveals that teaching does not qualify as a profession.

teaching not a unique service

A Child's Many Teachers   If education is a teacher's unique function, the teacher certainly has a great deal of competition. Children today learn a tremendous amount from media offerings, including *Sesame Street,* public affairs specials, MTV, *Sassy,* and *Sports Illustrated.* The nonteacher-educators include parents, ministers, older friends, neighbors, employers, best friends, coaches, scout leaders, playground and camp counselors, and grandparents. The world is bursting with teachers, and those who hold forth in school buildings have only a small piece of the action.

training not rigorous

Limited Training   Although teaching has intellectual and theoretical foundations, it requires a rather short period of specialized training (considerably less than some of the skilled trades), and entrance into the occupation is not especially competitive, particularly on intellectual grounds. If it is a profession, it is one largely composed of college graduates with a wide range of academic abilities, levels of commitment, and motivations for becoming teachers.

little decision-making power

Constraints on Autonomy   Although there is a good deal of talk about teachers' autonomy and decision-making power, both exist at a very low level. Teachers are at the second rung from the bottom (superior only to students) of the hierarchy commanded by the local board of education. Unlike lawyers and doctors, who can reject clients, teachers have students assigned to them. They also have a supervisor, their principal, lead teacher, or department head. They teach a curriculum that has been chosen or developed largely by others.

If their supervisors do not like the results, teachers are only rarely protected by their professional group from being fired (or, more gently, "not rehired") by the local school board. Teachers do not formally evaluate other teachers; administrators do that. Moreover, most of the important decisions that affect teachers' daily lives, even those that bear directly on the standards of their own profession, are made by nonteachers (administrators and citizen school board members). Although teachers are beginning to get more involved in teacher preparation pro-

*To be read with *attitude.**

Sometimes a teacher's best work is done outside the classroom. (© Tony Freeman/PhotoEdit)

grams and are acquiring some say in the licensing and certification of teachers, laypeople and bureaucrats still wield a great deal of decision-making power. Some teachers, like factory workers, even have to punch a time clock (or, more genteelly, they "sign in and sign out"). In sum, they have very little to say about what goes on in their "shop."

Responsibility for Their Profession   Teachers rarely lose their jobs because Johnnie can't read or Samantha failed calculus. After a teacher achieves tenure, it takes some form of gross negligence, clear incompetence, or serious sexual offense for him or her to be fired. As professionals, teachers do very little policing of their own ranks. Their professional organizations are just like other self-serving organizations, whether composed of teamsters or autoworkers: the primary energies of teacher associations and unions go to their own survival and growth. Secondarily, they attempt to protect their members, increase their salaries, and expand their benefits.

little accountability

Most teachers, in fact, are minimally involved in professional organizations and their activities. Except when the organization calls a strike—a somewhat contradictory activity for a "profession" supposedly dedicated to serving children—teachers generally just pay their dues. Most teachers claim they are too busy to take an active role in professional affairs. This lack of real involvement in professional activities may stem from the fact that so many teachers have second jobs, either as homemakers or in the labor market. They are unenthusiastic about working for higher standards because one of the first sacrifices to professionalism would be their second job.

little involvement

Job Security and Salary   In reality, teachers work in circumstances very different from those of other professionals. Like other public servants, they are hired rather than operating as independent agents. They are on a fixed salary schedule and are protected by tenure laws rather than having to find a market for their services independently. In effect, teaching is a low-pay, relatively high-security job rather than a high-pay, low-security profession. Seniority as a teacher appears to be more important than competence. Talk about professionalism may be personally satisfying to teachers, but it does not conform to the reality of the teacher's occupational life.

> *When teachers come to regard themselves as persons of key importance in the society, they will retain much longer than at present something of the respect in which the young should naturally hold them.*
>
> —J. GLENN GRAY

The Case *for* Teaching as a Profession

The very nobility of the teacher's work is evidence in favor of its status as a profession. Society has entrusted teachers with its most important responsibility: the education of its young. Throughout history, many great thinkers have acknowledged how crucial the work of the teacher is to the fulfillment of personal and national goals. And, as this realization has spread in recent decades, opportunities and rewards for the teacher have continued to improve.

. . . teach difficult skills

The Teacher's Unique Skills   Although children learn from many people—from parents to television personalities—teachers are the specialists who pass on to the young the key skills necessary to participate effectively in the culture. They aid the young in acquiring the most difficult, if not the most important, skills: those that involve thinking and manipulating ideas. Neither reading nor geometry is often learned on the street. Although teachers do not undergo a particularly lengthy period of specialized training, they are in a sense continually educating themselves. Teachers are expected (and, in most states, required by law) to upgrade their teaching skills and knowledge periodically.

. . . have a domain of control

The Teacher's Autonomy   Teachers have an immense area of personal control. They normally determine the method of instruction. They decide which aspects of the curriculum they will highlight and which they will cover quickly. The limits on their creativity in the classroom are few or nonexistent. After the initial few years of teaching, they are seldom observed and evaluated. Teachers' classrooms are their castles.

> *What office is there which involves more responsibility, which requires more qualifications, and which ought, therefore, to be more honourable than that of teaching?*
>
> —HARRIET MARTINEAU

If teachers believe they do not have enough autonomy or do not agree with their administrators, they are free to move to another school. However, a teacher's autonomy is accompanied by a responsibility to teach effectively. Like other professionals, teachers must be able to justify the manner in which they render their social services, whether it be grading or disciplinary actions. Teachers take responsibility for their actions and, like other professionals, are open to criticisms of their performance.

A Third Possibility: An Evolving Profession

Like most other complex questions, our query about whether teaching is a profession cannot be answered satisfactorily with simple pro-and-con arguments such as those just offered. Also, teachers differ so much in the conditions under which they work and they possess such varying degrees of knowledge, commitment, and expertise that it is difficult to come up with a definitive answer. In some schools, teachers fulfill many of the criteria of professionals. In other schools, they seem to function as clerks and technicians. Perhaps we could say, as some others do, that teaching is a *semiprofession*.

teaching as a semiprofession

In certain ways teaching clearly is eligible for professional status, and in certain other ways it deviates sharply from accepted canons of professionalism. On the one hand, teachers provide an intellectual service to the community. They undergo specialized training to master the theoretical basis of their work. Ethical standards guide their work with students. On the other hand, they too often function like many other lower-level white-collar workers and civil servants. Too often seniority and job security are the rule rather than excellence and independence. Like many other occupational groups that are called professional, teachers, at this moment in history, only partially qualify.

Another way to look at the issue, and one we favor, is to think of teaching as an *evolving profession*; that is, it is in the process of becoming a profession. As shown by the historical descriptions of the work and living conditions of teachers presented earlier in this chapter, the life, status, and education of teachers have changed dramatically. What will determine whether teaching becomes a full-fledged profession during your lifetime? Among the factors are the trends toward greater self-determination, better preparation, and recognizing excellence in teaching.

teaching as an evolving profession

Greater Self-Determination It may be true that a teacher lacks the autonomy of, say, a small-town lawyer. Yet every profession has limits on its autonomy. For example, today more and more doctors and dentists are employed by HMOs (health maintenance organizations) and are forming unions to protect their rights. The crucial point is the direction in which teaching is moving.

need more self-determination

To make teaching a full profession, teachers must take on a larger role in the governing of their career affairs. Whereas the direction of education and the schools should be in the hands of many groups (parents, community leaders, and students as well as teachers), control over the teaching profession per se should be largely in the hands of teachers. Up to now, the great majority of teachers have taken the attitude of "Let George do it," allowing others to make the major decisions about who should teach, how teachers should be trained, and under what conditions they should render their services. This situation will not substantially change until teachers take a major role in making it change.

Better Preparation To make teaching a full profession, teachers must also demand better preparation requirements. As long as the public believes that any college graduate with a smattering of education courses can walk in off the street and do a teacher's job, people will not treat teachers as professionals. We are definitely not suggesting that teachers should adopt artificial trappings, like a doctor's smock or a general's uniform, to appear more distinctive and impressive. Rather, teachers must appear better because they *are* better. Like architects and surgeons, teachers must know their work, and it must be imbued with a sense of high purpose. When that happens, the public will decide whether or not teachers should be treated as professionals.

Recognizing Excellence in Teaching We need to realize that not all of the 3 million plus people working in the American schools are interested in and, in some cases, capable of measuring up to the standards of professionalism discussed earlier. At present, what we are calling (and, incidentally, will continue to call) the *teaching profession* is a mixed bag, with a great many transients "just passing through," a great many rather uncommitted teachers, and a great many truly excellent, dedicated career teachers.

recognizing the best

Over thirty years ago, an educator captured what we believe to be the essence of the professional teacher:

> Let us define a career teacher as one who plans to, and actually does, make a life occupation of teaching; one who is philosophically, emotionally, and spiritually committed, who is never satisfied with what he does and how well he's doing it, and who fully intends to keep on growing for the rest of his life.[2]

> *To erect fine buildings and to seek to meet the needs and abilities of all individuals who desire to avail themselves of the opportunities so generously offered without providing teachers with qualifications commensurate with the ideal is a sham.*
>
> —I. L. KANDELL

This educator went on to estimate that only about one out of four practicing teachers fit his definition. And herein lies the difficulty: until the great majority of teachers qualify by this educator's definition, or until there is a qualitative regrouping of those presently identified as "teachers," teaching will not be called a profession. Currently, however, a move is afoot to recognize and provide greater support to superior teachers, and, in the process, to strengthen the claim of professionalism for the career of teaching. The National Board for Professional Teaching Standards aims to play a leading role in this effort.

The National Board for Professional Teaching Standards

The lack of recognizable high standards has discouraged some potentially outstanding people from entering teaching and has lowered the level of aspiration of others. On the other hand, high standards tend to focus people's attention and harness their energies. For example, in long-distance running, the four-minute mile was long considered the unbreakable barrier. For years and years, sports commentators pontificated that it was beyond the capacities of humans to run a mile in four minutes or less. Then, in 1957, Roger Bannister, a relatively obscure medical student, broke the magic barrier. A new standard was set, and runners

standards stimulate achievement

reset their sights. The following year, thirty-seven runners broke that "unbreakable barrier." Today breaking the four-minute barrier is commonplace. The reason is that a new standard has been set and people have risen to it in great numbers. The **National Board for Professional Teaching Standards (NBPTS)** intends to perform a similar function for the teaching profession.

Formed in 1987, the NBPTS is currently establishing standards for teaching practice and developing a series of board certification assessments based on these standards. In turn, board advocates believe that these standards will allow teachers to gain a highly regarded, professional credential like that available to physicians, accountants, architects, and other professionals.

You have not done enough, you have never done enough, as long as it is still possible that you have something of value to contribute.

—Dag Hammarskjöld

Core Propositions and Characteristics   The NBPTS is dedicated to and directed by five core propositions:

five core propositions

1. Teachers know the subjects they teach and how to teach these subjects to students.

2. Teachers are committed to their students and their learning.

3. Teachers are responsible for managing and monitoring student learning.

4. Teachers think systematically about their practice and learn from experience.

5. Teachers are members of a learning community.[3]

In addition, the organization has five distinguishing characteristics.

First, the NBPTS is for experienced teachers, teachers with a baccalaureate or an advanced degree, who have graduated from an accredited college or university and have at least three years of experience.

five distinguishing characteristics

Second, "taking the boards" is completely voluntary. It is not intended to be a condition of work, like state licensure, but an achievement testifying to an individual teacher's attainment of a high level of professionalism.

Third, "taking the boards" involves submitting oneself to a set of examinations and assessments in particular areas or subject matters, such as early childhood, English language arts, and physical education and health.

Fourth, these assessments are not typical paper-and-pencil tests. Teaching, by its very nature, is a mixture of thought and action and is not measured well by traditional "sit-down" testing. Among the means of assessment are videotapes of one's teaching and an evaluation of one's professional portfolio. Such a portfolio might include examples of students' work, sample lesson plans, and other items that the teacher believes will support his or her candidacy.

Fifth, the primary control of the NBPTS is in the hands of practicing teachers. Although administrators, teacher educators, and the general public are represented on the NBPTS, two-thirds of the board members are teachers—a further step toward achieving professionalism in teaching.

POLICY MATTERS!   # A Two-Tiered Profession?

What's the Policy?

For years, competition has been a hallmark of most occupations and careers—except for teaching. If anything, careers in teaching have been characterized by a lack of competition. In fact, most teachers believe cooperation among teachers is important and shun any competitive model that might destroy that cooperation. With the advent of the National Board for Professional Teaching Standards, however, a new and controversial element of competition has emerged.

How Does It Affect Teachers?

National board certification is still in its infancy. Varying degrees of interest and enthusiasm exist for this innovative staffing designation among different states and school districts. Besides the substantial prestige associated with being board certified, those few teachers who achieve this distinction often receive salary increases, job flexibility and mobility, and increased opportunities for leadership within the profession. And, of course, those who don't, won't.

What Are the Pros?

Some believe that an element of competition, which features recognition and extra compensation for outstanding performance, is needed to attract talented new teachers to the field—and keep them there. Traditionally, a teacher's salary has depended on degrees earned and years of service rather than competence. If a teacher wanted recognition in education, he or she had to move out of the classroom into administration or college teaching.

What Are the Cons?

The overriding question concerning any new program is "Will it improve the education we provide for our children?" In the case of national board certification, there are a host of other policy questions as well: "Who will pay the $2,300 examination fee?" "How will districts foot the bill for salary increases and benefits for certified teachers?" "Will board-certified teachers be assigned to the students in greatest need or to the most advanced and gifted? Or will they decide whom they teach?" And, finally, "Will this new distinction enhance the career of teaching, making it more attractive, or will it bring into teaching a poisoning division of first team/second team, a new antagonism between the teacher ranks of haves and have-nots?"

What Do You Think?

1. In your school experience, have the truly outstanding teachers been adequately recognized and rewarded?

2. Other than those mentioned above, what do you see as the advantages and disadvantages of a two-tiered teaching profession?

3. Would you personally be interested in working toward board certification? Why or why not?

Advantages to Board Certification   Advocates believe NBPTS certification will mean higher salaries for those teachers so designated. And it will mean, in effect, that school boards have a recognizable basis on which to award merit pay other than arbitrary and impressionistic criteria such as "Her children do well on tests" or "He seems to work long hours and is popular with the brightest students." More than twenty states are offering board-certified teachers a bonus of

$5,000 in each year of the ten-year period that their National Board Certification is valid.[4]

Besides raising salaries, board certification offers a number of other advantages. Teachers who have achieved NBPTS certification may be professionally "more portable," that is, able to move more freely across state lines. Also, this effort promises to stimulate research on what constitutes superior teaching. And it should trigger more attention to this research-based knowledge within teacher education and throughout the teaching force. Most of all, it should contribute to the essential but difficult mission of creating a system of recognition for highly skilled and dedicated professionals.

advantages of the NBPTS

Criticisms of NBPTS   The National Board for Professional Teaching Standards, however, is not without critics. Some educators claim that there is no solid knowledge base in teaching (as opposed to medicine or architecture) on which to ground the board's assessments. Others see the NBPTS as a public relations move to enhance the status and salaries of teachers with artificial trappings ("Fillmore got himself board certified, but we all know he couldn't teach a duck!"). Still others, suspicious that the NBPTS is controlled by its majority of teacher members, see it becoming a vehicle primarily to serve the economic interests of teachers and to insulate them further from their "clients," the students. Finally, some caution a wait-and-see attitude, acknowledging the strengths in the idea of a board but waiting to see it in full operation before passing judgment.

arguments against the NBPTS

As we will see in the next section, the two largest professional organizations, the National Education Association and the American Federation of Teachers, have been involved in promoting NBPTS certification, as well as performing other important functions.

Professional Associations

Like other occupational groups, such as doctors and teamsters, teachers have associations that protect their interests and attempt to improve their lot. For example, teacher salaries (which are the major cost of schooling) and other educational expenses come out of the taxpayers' pockets. Tax revenues are used for many purposes and are heavily competed for by groups attempting to fight crime and delinquency, to increase aid to the elderly and the poor, and so on. In the rough-and-tumble of a democracy, teachers need someone or something to look out for their interests and the interests of the recipients of their services: children. This is the avowed function of many teachers' associations.

the need for an advocate

The protection of teachers' rights and improvement in their rewards and working conditions will not just happen. In the words of the distinguished educational policy wonk, our friend Ernie Lundquist, "Nobody gives you nothin' for nothin'. " The advances teachers make will occur largely as a result of their hard work and readiness to stand up for what they believe.

Our primary focus in this section is on the large umbrella organizations of teachers, the **National Education Association (NEA)** and the **American Federation of Teachers (AFT),** since these have the most immediate and sustaining effects on the lives of teachers. In the 1990s, over 70 percent of all public school teachers reported belonging to the NEA. The AFT represents slightly fewer than 25 percent. These two large associations claim to represent teachers to the federal, state, and local governments, to educational authorities at the state and local levels, and, finally, to the general public. It is important to know something about them, because if you become a teacher, they will claim to be speaking for you. In fact, many new teachers report being asked to join their professional association their first day on the job.

two competing alternatives

As you read the following pages, be aware that the NEA and the AFT are and have been in a struggle for the hearts, minds, and membership dues of teachers. Further, each is concerned about putting its case before and gaining the support of future teachers. Bob Chase, president of the NEA, and the late Albert Shanker, formerly president of the AFT, each agreed to write a special letter to the readers of this book, and we urge you to read these inserts. In addition, there is a short insert about one of the newer, smaller professional associations, the American Association of Educators, which is taking a very different tack than the major professional organizations of teachers.

The National Education Association

Founded in 1857, the National Education Association today is a complex institution that operates on the national, state, and local school district levels and serves a diverse clientele of rural, suburban, and urban teachers. The bulk of its 2.2 million–plus members are classroom teachers, but also included are teacher aides, administrators, professors, retired educators, and college students preparing to become teachers. In addition, the NEA has some 13,520 local affiliates in some 80 percent of the nation's school districts.[5]

a range of support services

Services to Members   The NEA offers its members a wide range of services, from an extensive array of publications to research on issues such as comparative salary scales and the attitudes of teachers. In addition, its UniServ program has some 1,500 professionals in the field working with teachers, ready to give local teachers help in such specialized areas as collective bargaining. In addition to these support services, a number of special services are available to members, such as travel programs, insurance policies, mutual fund programs, and book club programs. Also, the NEA (as does the AFT) comes to the aid of teachers, like those in the vignettes that began this chapter, whose legal rights are being violated or who are being treated unethically.

The NEA and Political Issues   Since the NEA's inception, its goal has been "to elevate the character and advance the interests of the profession of teaching and to promote the cause of education in the United States." In advancing this goal, it

Why Join NEA?

Bob Chase, President, NEA

The only constant in the teaching profession today is change. Every key factor that determines the success or failure of a teaching career—from training to tenure—is undergoing fundamental change or is on the cusp of change. Consequently, every new teacher faces a big decision regarding how he or she will relate to change. Essentially, it comes down to this: Do you want change done *to* you or *by* you?

The teachers who belong to the National Education Association have opted for a less passive, more interactive approach. They are networking with their colleagues to shape change. They are taking responsibility for their professional lives. For too long, too many teachers were treated like assembly line workers, rather than professionals. They were expected to follow, mindlessly, decisions from on high, even when those decisions adversely affected their students.

Today, working through their local NEA associations, our members are increasingly becoming partners, with management, in the education enterprise. Our members are taking on professional responsibilities that were unheard of a decade ago and unimaginable two decades ago.

There are now NEA members who choose their own principals and who take part in decisions that determine curricula, discipline policy, scheduling, and how instructional budgets are spent. Some NEA members are mentoring new teachers, and through peer review, some are helping veteran teachers improve their teaching skills or leave the profession. There are now NEA members who receive a bonus in their paycheck for having achieved national teacher certification, a program our organization has long promoted.

NEA members are also breaking new ground when it comes to professional development. Every profession has had a system through which its members can sharpen skills, improve practices, and keep abreast of the latest advances in knowledge or technology. Every profession, that is, except teaching. Professional development for teachers has been haphazard and lacking in rigor. As NEA's National Foundation for the Improvement of Education has urged, teachers need to "take control" of their own learning.

A number of NEA locals are taking up that challenge and are now partnering with universities and school districts to provide professional academies for teachers. Because these academies are close to home and well grounded in the realities of real classrooms, teachers find them extremely useful.

Parents, employers, and the public are demanding students who are better educated and better prepared for the workplace. Often, however, it takes more than the dedication and inspired work of an individual teacher to improve student achievement. It takes teachers working together, as NEA members are doing, to reduce class size and pupil load, to focus our schools on high academic standards, and to integrate information technologies into our teaching. It takes us working together to improve the licensing and assigning of teachers to ensure that there is a fully qualified teacher in every classroom.

When teachers join NEA, they join an organization dedicated to helping them succeed in the classroom. Through our teacher-to-teacher books, our Web page on the Internet, our profession-building projects in specific school districts, and many other teacher services, NEA helps teachers help themselves.

In the final analysis, teachers join the NEA for the same reason they became teachers in the first place: They want to make a difference in children's lives.

Source: "Why Join NEA?" by Bob Chase. Reprinted by permission of National Education Association.

regularly comes out against issues such as standardized testing of children and any type of competency testing of teachers. And it has often supported the most current movements in education, such as special programs for linguistic and ethnic groups within schools.[6]

If one is going to change things, one has to make a fuss and catch the eye of the world.

—ELIZABETH JANEWAY

Further, it has taken forceful positions on such issues as public monies for private schools and various voucher plans. (The NEA is opposed to supporting private schools with public funds or vouchers, even though 22 percent of its members send their own children to private schools.)

In the 1950s and 1960s, the NEA was influential in improving the preservice training of teachers and raising the entrance qualifications for teaching. But although the NEA is currently supporting the National Board for Professional Teaching Standards, it has expended most of its energies and monies on service for its membership: practicing teachers. To do this, the NEA has increasingly devoted its attention to political action at the local, state, and national levels. In 1976, the NEA for the first time formally backed a presidential candidate (Jimmy Carter), and since then it has consistently backed Democratic candidates for national and most state offices.

NEA as a political force

a power on the national scene

The NEA has become a strong political player for various reasons. One political commentator referred to teachers as "bright, articulate, and reasonably well informed, making them naturals for political activism."[7] Also, teachers have the best record of any occupational group in registering to vote: well over 70 percent.[8]

Further, the NEA is big, having recently passed the teamsters in numbers. Its sheer size and presence in many congressional districts, not to mention its substantial political war chest, give it great clout in Washington, DC.

I ask for philosophy from my union and it gives me politics, partisanship and public relations. Teachers learn to be pragmatists or they don't survive. Underneath their veneer of practicality, they are dreamers. Truck drivers and longshoremen might not need a philosophical guiding light from their union leaders, but teachers do. Teachers yearn for commitment, for caring and for conscience.

—SUSAN OHANIAN

The NEA's relatively recent alignment with one political party is not without risks. Former secretary of education William Bennett accused the NEA of being "the absolute heart and center of the Democratic Party."[9] Republicans frequently criticize the NEA as a lobbying group that is more interested in the welfare of teachers than in the education of children. Further, the NEA does not always reflect the political views of its members, since teachers as a whole do not have deep attachments to either the political left or the political right. It has been reported that the teaching profession "has almost as many Republicans and independent members as Democrats. In other words, about two-thirds of its members have differed in their party preference."[10]

Shortly after taking over the presidency of the NEA, Bob Chase announced a course change for his organization. Acknowledging a number of the criticisms of the NEA cited earlier, Chase called on his association "to transfer its focus from the old style of labor-management antagonism to a new emphasis on professionalism and collaboration."[11] Drawing on a metaphor widely used by industry and government, he called on members to "reinvent" the NEA, to take leadership in school reform and return the focus to improving the education of children.

TABLE 15.1   Nationwide Organizations of Interest to Teachers

Specialized Associations of Teachers

▶ The Council for Exceptional Children (http://www.cec.sped.org)

▶ The National Science Teachers Association (http://www.nsta.org)

▶ The National Council of Teachers of English (http://www.ncte.org)

▶ The National Council for the Social Studies (http://www.ncss.org)

▶ Music Teachers Association (513-421-1420)

▶ The National Association for the Education of Young Children (http://www.naeyc.org)

▶ The American Vocational Association (http://www.avaonline.org)

▶ The International Reading Association (http://www.reading.org)

▶ The National Council of Teachers of Mathematics (http://www.nctm.org)

▶ The American Council on the Teaching of Foreign Language (http://www.actfl.org/index/htm)

▶ The National Art Education Association (http://www.naea-reston.org)

▶ American Alliance for Health, Physical Education, Recreation and Dance (http://www.aahperd.org)

▶ Association for Education Communications and Technology (http://www.aect.org)

Nationwide Special-Interest Groups in Education

▶ The National School Boards Association (http://www.nsba.org)

▶ The American Association of School Administrators (http://www.aasa.org)

▶ The Association for Supervision and Curriculum Development (http://www.ascd.org)

▶ The American Educational Research Association (http://www.ipd.edu.hk/cric/cies99/aera.htm)

▶ The Council of Chief State School Officers (http://www.ccsso.org)

▶ The Association of Teacher Educators (http://www.siu.edu/departments/coe/ate)

▶ The American Association of Colleges for Teacher Education (http://www.aacte.org)

AFT, and the Democratic party have tinged teacher professionalism with a certain political gloss.

Professionalism can also be a cover for quite self-serving ends. Occasionally teachers use their "professional status" as a barrier against criticism by children and parents ("How dare you question what I have done? I am a professional!"). Further, in the interest of protecting and expanding the rights of its members, a professional group can ride roughshod over the needs and rights of the client group. For instance, insisting on tenure rights for all teachers who have taught

Sometimes teachers take to the streets, but with decreasing frequency.
(© Bob Daemmrich)

for three years or more makes it difficult to get rid of those teachers who turn out to be genuinely incompetent. In the big cities, basing eligibility for transfer to more congenial schools on seniority may be robbing the most difficult schools of exactly the experienced teacher talent they need. Behind the jargon of professionalism, then, one often finds naked self-interest that can do harm to the teachers' clients: children.

Wanted: A New Professionalism

behind the jargon

In recent years, while teachers adopted a labor-management stance (with the "management" being their administrators and the local school board), American industry has seen a decline in aggressive trade unionism. In its place a new, co-operative spirit has brought about a revival of many of our industries. Following slogans of "excellence" and "re-engineering," workers and management have changed the economic landscape. We see the beginnings of a similar revival in the "educational excellence" movement and the "restructuring" efforts currently sweeping through our schools. In our view, the issue of teacher professionalism is very much wrapped up in these broader school reform efforts. Whether or not teachers are treated as professionals will depend on the bottom line: the performance of our schools. To promote that performance, teachers need to begin with a personal commitment to excellence. Your satisfaction as a teacher and your impact on students will be strongly influenced by the effect of this next topic on your career.

Your Own Professional Development

At one time, as we have seen, it was considered adequate for a teacher to obtain an undergraduate education and a teaching license and then have no further training. However, forces both inside and outside the teaching profession have since adopted the stance that the teacher must be a continuous learner. Many states have legislated continuing education for teachers. In fact, in more than one-half of the states, it is no longer possible to gain permanent licensure. More and more states are requiring teachers to keep up with developments in their fields or specific areas of education.

Central to this drive for the continuing education of teachers—or **professional development,** as it is often called—is the growth of new knowledge and the demand for new skills. A dramatic example is the rising interest in technological literacy. As American society has become increasingly dependent on electronic information services, the needs and advantages of being comfortable and competent with computers, the Internet, CD-ROMs, videodiscs, and networking have become clear. Therefore, elementary and secondary schools and colleges are rushing to provide students with this new competence. And to keep up with the rapidly widening "information superhighway," teachers, like their students, need to become continuous learners.

> *Education must not any longer be confined to the young. The young must not look forward to its completion; the old must not look back on it as an accompaniment of immaturity. For all people, education must be made to seem a requirement of humanlife as long as that endures.*
>
> —Isaac Asimov

Types of Continuous Learning Opportunities

Independent Study   One aim of education is to develop the ability to engage in independent study. *Independent study* is jargon for being able "to go it alone." Although this approach is much discussed among educators, students seem to get little actual practice in choosing and systematically investigating their own areas of interest. Independent study, though, is one of the most important means for continual self-renewal available to you as a teacher. Teachers are confronted daily with things they do not understand about children and knowledge and human learning: "Is there anything to this talk about learning styles and how I can apply it in my classroom?" "What does the new brain research suggest about teaching X and Y?" "What are the fundamental skills of composition that children should know?" "How can I help my students use history for their own benefit?" Such questions are daily grist for the teacher's independent study mill. Of course, your study should not be confined to professional problems. Your own personal interests may lead into such areas as organic gardening, physical fitness, classic movies, the politics of colonial America, the humanizing of the corporate state, or harnessing the media. Not by professional problems alone doth the teacher live!

self-renewal through study

> *The more we know, the more we want to know; when we know enough, we know how much we don't know.*
>
> —Carol Orlock

"INSTEAD OF LEARNING TO ORGANIZE MY PRIORITIES I'VE BECOME COMFORTABLE WITH PANIC."

© Mark Litzler

forming study groups

Group Study   Group study is another common form of continuous learning for the teacher. It frequently takes the form of committee work. When a problem arises in the school for which there are no apparent solutions, a group of people take on themselves the task of exploring the problem with a view toward recommending an enlightened course of action. In recent years, to obtain opinions from outside the school, teachers and administrators have begun inviting community residents to these study groups. Typical issues these groups might take on are alternatives to a second-grade reading program, an analysis of the unused education resources in the community, a writing across the curriculum program, and the potential benefits and costs of using paraprofessionals in a high school.

graduate courses

Graduate Study   A third way for you to continue to learn is to take courses or to work toward an advanced degree. Most colleges and universities offer courses suitable for and interesting to teachers. Special and regular courses are offered in the evening, on weekends, and during the summer vacation. Some universities are pioneering in computer-based distance-learning courses, which enable teachers (and others) to do advanced study without leaving their homes. These courses and degree programs not only allow teachers to gain a deeper understanding of their work but also make it possible for some teachers to train for other jobs in education, such as guidance counseling, administration, or college teaching.

In-Service Programs   A fourth opportunity you will have to grow and learn is to attend an in-service program or a professional development program sponsored by the school or school district. In-service programs are often targeted at school- or districtwide problems or issues. For instance, if students in a particular school are getting unsatisfactory grades on standardized achievement tests, the district may choose to provide special in-service training for the faculty. Or the district may decide to switch to a new, supposedly better mathematics program, a change that will also require special training for the faculty. In-service training often takes place weekly or monthly, before or after school. Also, special days are sometimes set aside on which school is canceled or students are dismissed early so teachers can participate in in-service training.

programs sponsored by district

So to all of you who teach, hats off. Yours is an invaluable profession, a calling sure and high and noble, a model we cannot live without if we expect to remain strong and free. Don't quit. Don't even slack off. If ever we needed you, we need you today.

—CHARLES SWINDOLL

Supervision   A fifth form of continuous learning comes through supervision. During a teacher's early years in the profession, school districts provide professional advice that amounts to one-on-one help. For instance, if you are a new high school teacher, your department head may observe your classes regularly and discuss the observations with you. Or if you are an elementary school teacher, your building principal may make regular visits and follow them with feedback sessions. Although supervision can sometimes be quite threatening, particularly to nontenured teachers, it offers an opportunity to obtain valuable information about your teaching techniques and skills.

observation and feedback

Good colleagues make professional growth a pleasure. (© Elizabeth Crews)

mentoring

Mentoring   In recent years, many school districts around the country have instituted **mentoring** programs whereby more experienced teachers are assigned to assist beginners. Along with special training, the mentors receive a reduction in teaching responsibilities, a salary increase, or both. Mentoring programs formalize and make more systematic a time-honored process in which an experienced teacher takes a rookie under his or her wing, helping the beginner make the theory-into-practice transition and serving as a nonjudgmental colleague.

the teacher as both object and artist

A Perspective on the Teacher as Learner   Becoming a teacher may be compared to sculpting a work of art from a piece of stone. The difference is that the teacher is both the sculptor and the stone. The teacher begins with a vision of what he or she wants to be and then sets to work transforming the vision into a reality. The process requires an understanding of the material with which one is working—the self—and of the tools one can use. It also requires a vision of what one needs to become. Finally, it takes long hours of chipping away and then smoothing the surfaces. To be a teacher, particularly a teacher who is continuously moving forward, is a lifelong commitment to be an artist.

KEY TERMS

normal schools (502)
profession (505)
National Board for Professional
  Teaching Standards (NBPTS) (511)
National Education Association
  (NEA) (514)

American Federation of Teachers
  (AFT) (514)
professional development (523)
mentoring (526)

FOR REFLECTION

1. What basic changes have taken place in teacher education in America's history?

2. Do you think it is important for teachers to devote themselves to becoming professionals? If so, what must they do? Are you willing to do it? How do you feel about the description of the "career teacher" on page 510?

3. Does certification by the National Board for Professional Teaching Standards appeal to you? When you have completed three years or more of teaching, do you see yourself applying for NBPTS certification?

4. Do teachers need a professional organization? What essential functions does such a group perform?

5. At this moment, what seem to you to be the most important issues with which teachers should concern themselves? Increased power? Higher salaries? Better training? Something else? Be prepared to defend your choice. What can you do to help bring about the changes you consider most important?

6. Do you believe it is right for teachers to strike? Why or why not?

7. Which of the ideas for lifelong professional development described in this chapter appeal to you most?

FOR FURTHER INFORMATION

American Federation of Teachers. Home page on the World Wide Web: http://www.aft.org.
The AFT's web site provides information on the organization and its programs, commentary on current issues, and links to other interesting web pages. If you don't have access to the Web, you can write to the AFT at 555 New Jersey Ave., N.W., Washington, DC 20001.

Darling-Hammond, Linda. "Teachers and Teaching: Signs of a Changing Profession," in *The Handbook of Research on Teacher Education*, ed. Robert Houston, pp. 267–290. New York: Macmillan, 1991.
This article summarizes much recent research on various factors and trends affecting the teaching profession, from the demographic composition of the teaching force to supply-and-demand factors.

Grant, Gerald, and Christine Murray. *Teaching in America: The Slow Revolution*. Cambridge, MA: Harvard University Press, 1999.
This book traces the progress of two groups, college professors and precollegiate teachers, pointing out the similarities and differences in the evolution of professions. Drawing lessons from the development of the professoriate, the authors point out the steps teachers need to take to continue their progress.

Lortie, Dan C. *Schoolteacher: A Sociological Study*. Chicago: University of Chicago Press, 1975.
This book presents a sociological view of the ethos of the teaching profession, that pattern of orientations and sentiments that are peculiar to teachers.

National Education Association. Home page on the World Wide Web: http://www.nea.org.
This web site offers a great deal of information about the NEA and its programs. Or you can write to the NEA at 1201 16th St., N.W., Washington, DC 20036; phone: 202-822-7200; fax: 202-822-7292.

National Education Association. *Status of the American Public School Teacher: 1995–96*. Washington, DC: National Education Association, 1996.
This report is one in a series of studies conducted every four years. It contains a massive amount of information on who teachers are, what is on their minds, and the conditions of their work. Information on the 2000 report was not available when this book went to press, but you can contact NEA directly at the address above.

Provenzo, Eugene F., and Gary McCloskey. *Schoolteachers and Schooling: Ethoses in Conflict*. Norwood, NJ: Ablex, 1996.
This short book gives a thoughtful and detailed picture of how teaching has changed in the last third of the twentieth century and the forces at play in a teacher's life.

SEARCH

SEARCH

Endnotes

Chapter 1

1. Metropolitan Life Insurance Company, *The American Teacher 1984–95: Old Problems, New Challenges* (New York: Metropolitan Life Insurance Company, 1995), p. 47.
2. Ibid., p. 62.
3. Sharon Feiman-Nemser and Robert E. Floden, "The Cultures of Teaching," in *Handbook of Research on Teaching*, 3d ed., ed. Merlin C. Wittrock (New York: Macmillan, 1986), pp. 510–511.
4. David Haselkorn and Louis Harris, *The Essential Profession: A National Survey of Public Attitudes Toward Teaching, Educational Opportunity and School Reform* (Belmont, MA: Recruiting New Teachers, Inc., 1998), p. 2.
5. Ibid., p. 13.
6. Dan Lortie, *Schoolteacher* (Chicago: University of Chicago Press, 1975), p. 102.
7. Mihaly Csikszentmihalyi and Jane McCormack, "The Influence of Teachers," *Phi Delta Kappan* 67, no. 6 (February 1986), pp. 415–419. The article is reprinted in this text's companion volume of readings: *Kaleidoscope: Readings in Education*, 8th ed., ed. Kevin Ryan and James M. Cooper (Boston: Houghton Mifflin, 1998).
8. John Goodlad, *A Place Called School* (New York: McGraw-Hill, 1984); Judith W. Little, "The Persistence of Privacy," *Teachers College Record* (Summer 1990), pp. 509–536.
9. Leslie A. Swetnam, "Media Distortion of the Teacher Image," *The ClearingHouse* (September/October 1992), p. 30.
10. Ibid., pp. 30–32.

Chapter 2

1. *Education Week*, March 17, 1999, p. 1.
2. Estelle Fuchs, *Teachers Talk: Voices from Inside City Schools* (Garden City, NY: Doubleday, 1969), p. 21.
3. T. M. Wildman and J. A. Niles, "Reflective Teachers: Tensions Between Abstractions and Realities," *Journal of Teacher Education* 38, no. 10 (1987), pp. 25–31.
4. From Gary Cornog, "To Care or Not to Care," in *Don't Smile Until Christmas: Accounts of the First Year of Teaching*, edited by Kevin Ryan, pp. 18–19. Copyright © 1970. Reprinted by permission of Kevin Ryan.
5. Jeff Archer, "New Teachers Abandon the Field at High Rate," *Education Week*, March 17, 1999, pp. 1, 20–21.

6. *Teacher Quality: A Report on the Preparation and Qualifications of Public School Teachers*, U.S. Department of Education, 1999.

Chapter 3

1. Task Force on Teaching as a Profession, *A Nation Prepared: Teachers for the 21st Century* (New York: Carnegie Corporation, 1986), pp. 14–15.
2. Susan Moore Johnson, *Teachers at Work* (New York: Basic Books, 1990), p. 142.
3. Elliot Eisner, *The Educational Imagination: On the Design and Evaluation of School Programs*, 3d ed. (New York: Macmillan, 1994), p. 87.
4. Ibid., p. 89.
5. James Shaver and William Strong, *Facing Value Decisions: Rationale Building for Teachers* (Belmont, CA: Wadsworth, 1976).
6. Among the leading spokespersons for this position are Michael Apple and Henry Giroux. See Michael Apple, *Education and Power*, 2d ed. (New York: Routledge, 1995), and Henry Giroux, "Critical Pedagogy: Cultural Politics and the Discourse of Experience," *Journal of Education* 67, no. 2 (1987), pp. 23–41.
7. Paulo Freire, *The Pedagogy of the Oppressed* (New York: Herder and Herder, 1970).
8. Thomas L. Friedman, *The Lexus and the Olive Tree* (New York: Farrar, Straus and Giroux, 1999).
9. Philip W. Jackson, *Life in Classrooms* (New York: Teachers College Press, 1990).
10. Ibid., p. 16.
11. Joyce Epstein, "What Matters in the Middle Grades—Grade Span or Practices?" *Phi Delta Kappan* 71 (February 1990), pp. 438–444.
12. Ibid., p. 438.
13. Ernest L. Boyer, *High School: A Report on Secondary Education in America* (New York: Harper and Row, 1983).
14. Henry J. Becker, "Curriculum and Instruction in Middle-Grade Schools," *Phi Delta Kappan* 71 (February 1990), pp. 450–457.
15. James McPartland, "Staffing Decisions in the Middle School Grades: Balancing Quality Instruction and Teacher/Student Relations," *Phi Delta Kappan* 71 (February 1990), p. 466.
16. Ibid., p. 468.
17. Boyer, *High School*.

18. Ibid., pp. 21–22.

19. Ibid., p. 57.

20. Ibid., p. 79.

21. Arthur G. Powell, Eleanor Farrar, and David K. Cohen, *The Shopping Mall High School: Winners and Losers in the Educational Marketplace* (Boston: Houghton Mifflin, 1985).

22. Ibid., p. 76.

23. Ibid., p. 173.

24. Laurence D. Brown, "A New Metaphor for U.S. High Schools Provides Fresh and Powerful Insights," *Phi Delta Kappan* 67 (May 1986), p. 685.

25. Larry Cuban, *How Teachers Taught: Constancy and Change in American Classrooms 1890–1980* (New York: Longman, 1984).

26. Boyer, *High School,* pp. 141–142.

27. *Education Week,* February 28, 1996, pp. 1, 9.

28. In preparing this section, we have drawn on the following studies: W. B. Brookover, *Effective Secondary Schools* (Philadelphia: Research for Better Schools, 1981); R. Edmonds, "Effective Schools for the Urban Poor," *Educational Leadership* 32 (1979), pp. 15–17; M. Rutter et al., *Fifteen Thousand Hours* (Cambridge: Harvard University Press, 1979); J. Stallings and G. Mohlman, *School Policy, Leadership Style, Teacher Change and Student Behavior in Eight Secondary Schools* (Mountain View, CA: Stalling Teaching and Learning Institute, for the National Institute of Education, 1981); R. Blum, *Effective Schooling Practices: A Research Synthesis* (Portland, OR: Northwest Regional Education Laboratory, April 1984); H. J. Walberg, "Productive Teaching and Instruction: Assessing the Knowledge Base," *Phi Delta Kappan* 71 (February 1990), pp. 470–478; T. Toch, *In the Name of Excellence* (New York: Oxford University Press, 1991); Richard J. Murname and Frank Levy, "What General Motors Can Teach U.S. Schools About the Proper Role of Markets in Education Reform," *Phi Delta Kappan* 78 (October 1996), pp. 113–116.

29. David C. Berliner, "Effective Classroom Teaching: The Necessary But Not Sufficient Condition for Developing Exemplary Schools," in *Research on Exemplary Schools,* ed. Gilbert R. Austin and Herbert Garber (Orlando: Academic Press, 1985), pp. 127–154. Copyright 1985.

30. Edward A. Wynne, "Looking at Good Schools," *Phi Delta Kappan* 62 (January 1981), pp. 377–381.

31. John W. Gardner, from a speech entitled "Fall of the Twentieth Century," *Chicago Sun-Times,* June 16, 1968.

Chapter 4

1. Ask NCBE No. 8, "How Has the Limited English Proficient Student Population Changed in Recent Years?" *National Clearinghouse for Bilingual Education* (http://www.ncbe.gwu.edu/askncbe/faqs/08leps.htm).

2. *1998 Summary Report of the Survey of the States' Limited English Proficient Students and Available Educational Programs and Services 1995–1996,* National Clearinghouse for Bilingual Education (http://www.ncbe.gwu/ncbepubs/seareports/95-96/2enroll.htm).

3. Catherine Minicucci, Paul Berman, Barry McLaughlin, Beverly McLeod, Beryl Nelson, and Kate Woodworth, "School Reform and Student Diversity," *Phi Delta Kappan* 77 (September 1995), p. 77.

4. *Resident Population of the United States: Estimates, by Sex, Race, and Hispanic Origin, with Median Age,* U.S. Bureau of the Census Internet Release Date: December 28, 1998 (http://www.census.gov/population/estimates/nation/intfile3-1.txt); *Digest of Education Statistics 1998* (Washington, DC: National Center for Education Statistics, 1998), p. 80.

5. Harold Hodgkinson, "American Education: The Good, the Bad, and the Task," *Phi Delta Kappan* 74 (April 1993), p. 620.

6. William Glasser, *The Quality School* (New York: Harper and Row, 1990).

7. Howard Gardner, *Frames of Mind* (New York: Basic Books, 1985), and *Multiple Intelligences: The Theory in Practice* (New York: Basic Books, 1993).

8. Kathy Checkley, "The First Seven . . . and the Eighth," *Educational Leadership* 55 (September 1997), p. 12.

9. Harvey Silver, Richard Strong, and Matthew Perini, "Integrating Learning Styles and Multiple Intelligences," *Educational Leadership* 55 (September 1997), pp. 22–23. Reprinted with permission from ASCD. All rights reserved.

10. *Twentieth Annual Report to Congress on the Implementation of the Individuals with Disabilities Education Act* (Washington, DC: U.S. Department of Education, 1998), pp. II-5, II-11, III-42.

11. Sarah Wernick, "Hard Times for Educating the Highly Gifted Child," *New York Times,* May 30, 1990, p. B8.

12. *National Excellence: A Case for Developing America's Talent* (Washington, DC: U.S. Department of Education, Office of Research and Improvement, October 1993), p. 17.

13. Christine E. Sleeter, "Curriculum Controversies in Multicultural Education," in *Issues in Curriculum: A Selection of Chapters from Past NSSE Yearbooks, Ninety-eighth Yearbook of the National Society for the Study of Education,* ed. Margaret J. Early and Kenneth J. Rehage (Chicago: University of Chicago Press, 1999), p. 261.

14. M. Donald Thomas, "The Limits of Pluralism," *Phi Delta Kappan* 62 (April 1981), pp. 589, 591–592.

15. James A. Banks, "Multicultural Education: Characteristics and Goals," in *Multicultural Education: Issues and Perspectives,* 3d ed., ed. James A. Banks and Cherry A. McGee Banks (Boston: Allyn and Bacon, 1997), p. 7.

16. Russell Gersten and John Woodward, "A Case for Structured Immersion," *Educational Leadership* 43 (September 1985), p. 75.

17. Lynn Schnaiberg, "Calif.'s Year on the Bilingual Battleground," *Education Week,* June 2, 1999, p. 9.

18. Raul Yzaguirre, "What's Wrong with Bilingual Education?" *Education Week,* August 5, 1998, pp. 72, 46.

19. Richard Rothstein with Karen Hawley Miles, *Where's the Money Gone?* (Washington, DC: Economic Policy Institute, 1995), p. 8.

20. "Some Thoughts on Assistive Technology Devices and Services," *The Special Educator* 8, no. 2 (September 22, 1992), pp. 17–19.

21. *The Link* (Charleston, WV: The Appalachia Educational Laboratory), vol. 14, no. 1 (Spring/Summer 1995), p. 21.

22. *The 1994 State of the States Gifted and Talented Education Report* (Council of State Directors of Programs for the Gifted, 1994), pp. 3, 28–32.

23. Harriet Tyson, "A Load Off the Teachers' Backs: Coordinated School Health Programs," *Phi Delta Kappan* (January 1999), pp. K1–K8.

24. As cited in Lisbeth Schorr, *Within Our Reach* (New York: Doubleday, 1988), p. 5.

25. *Mini-Digest of Education Statistics 1997* (Washington, DC: U.S. Department of Education, National Center for Education Statistics, February 1998), p. 29.

Chapter 5

1. Lisbeth Bamberger Schorr, "Effective Programs for Children Growing Up in Concentrated Poverty," in *Children in Poverty,* ed. A. C. Huston (Cambridge, UK: University of Cambridge Press, 1991), pp. 261–262.

2. *Kids Count Data Book 1999* (Baltimore: Annie E. Casey Foundation, 1999), pp. 6, 10.

3. Harold L. Hodgkinson, *The Same Client: The Demographics of Education and Service Delivery Systems* (Washington, DC: Institute for Educational Leadership, 1989), p. 3.

4. Federal Interagency Forum on Child and Family Statistics, *America's Children: Key National Indicators of Well-Being, 1998* (Washington, DC: U.S. Government Printing Office, 1998), p. 6.

5. Ibid.

6. U.S. Bureau of the Census, "Money Income in the United States: 1997," *Current Population Survey,* Table F (http://www.census.gov/hhes/income/income97/in97def.html).

7. Federal Interagency Forum on Child and Family Statistics, *America's Children,* p. 12.

8. Thomas D. Snyder and Linda Shafer, *Youth Indicators 1996: Trends in the Well-being of American Youth* (Washington, DC: National Center for Education Statistics, 1996), p. 48.

9. U.S. Bureau of the Census, *Current Population Reports,* P60-200, *Historical Income Tables—Families,* Table F.2, 1998 (http://www.census.gov/hhes/income/histinc/f02.html).

10. Joseph Dalaker, U.S. Bureau of the Census, *Current Population Reports,* P60-207, *Poverty in the United States: 1998* (Washington, DC: U.S. Government Printing Office, 1999), p. v.

11. Ibid., p. vi.

12. Ibid., pp. vii, 2, 4.

13. *Kids Count Data Book 1999,* p. 7.

14. Ralph da Costa Nunez and Kate Collignon, "Creating a Community of Learning for Homeless Children," *Educational Leadership* 55, no. 2 (October 1997), p. 56.

15. Yvonne Rafferty, "Meeting the Educational Needs of Homeless Children," *Educational Leadership* (January 1998), p. 49.

16. The Alan Guttmacher Institute, *Teenage Pregnancy: Overall Trends and State-by-State Information,* Summary, April 1999 (http://www.agi-usa.org/pubs/teen_preg_stats.html).

17. *When Teens Have Sex: Issues and Trends* (Baltimore: Annie E. Casey Foundation, 1999), p. 8.

18. National Clearinghouse on Child Abuse and Neglect Information (http://www.calib.com/nccanch/pubs/infact.htm).

19. Cynthia Crosson Tower, *The Role of Educators in the Prevention and Treatment of Child Abuse and Neglect* (Washington, DC: National Center on Child Abuse and Neglect, 1992), pp. 22–27 (http://www.calib.com/nccanch/pubs/educator/index.htm).

20. *The 1998 National Household Survey on Drug Abuse* (Washington, DC: U.S. Department of Health and Human Services, August 1999) (http://www.samhsa.gov/).

21. University of Michigan, Institute for Social Research, *Monitoring the Future Study,* Table 1b, December 1998 (http://www.isr.umich.edu/src/mtf/pr98t1ba.html).

22. "U.S.A. Suicide: 1997 Official Final Data" (Washington, DC: American Association of Suicidology, 1999) (http://www.suicidology.org/suicide_statistics97.htm).

23. Ibid.; John Kalafat, "Adolescent Suicide and the Implications for School Response Programs," *The School Counselor* 37 (May 1990), p. 360.

24. Jessica Portner, "Increased Suicide Rate for Blacks Puts Prevention Efforts in Doubt," *Education Week,* April 1, 1998 (http://www.edweek.com).

25. From Deborah Burnett Strother, "Suicide Among the Young," *Phi Delta Kappan* 67 (June 1986), p. 759.

26. U.S. Department of Education, *Crime and Violence in Our Schools: An Overview of Statistics,* Update on Legislation, Budget, and Activities (http://www.ed.gov/updates/fact-209.html).

27. Ibid.

28. *Indicators of School Crime and Safety, 1998* (Washington, DC: National Center for Education Statistics, 1998), Figure 14.2 (http://nces.ed.gov/pubs98/safety/environment.html#reports).

29. Laura Sessions Stepp, "Cliques or Gangs?" *The Washington Post,* January 4, 1996, p. C5.

30. R. Craig Sautter, "Standing Up to Violence," *Phi Delta Kappan* 76 (January 1995), p. K8.

31. *Dropout Rates in the United States: 1997* (Washington, DC: National Center for Education Statistics, 1997), p. iv.

32. Thomas M. Smith et al., *The Condition of Education 1996* (Washington, DC: National Center for Education Statistics, 1996), p. 48.

33. Marvin Lazerson, "Access, Outcomes, and Educational Opportunity," *Education Week,* January 27, 1999, p. 46.
34. "Choice and Vouchers," *Education Week on the Web* (http://www.edweek.org/context/topics/choice.htm).
35. Susan Black, "The Pull of Magnets," *The American School Board Journal* (September 1996), p. 35; Peter Schmidt, "Magnets' Efficacy as Desegregation Tool Questioned," *Education Week,* February 2, 1994, p. 17.
36. "Developing Magnet Programs," *Education Digest* 54 (February 1989), pp. 22–24. Condensed from *Research in Brief,* September 1988, published by U.S. Department of Education Office of Educational Research and Improvement, Washington, DC.
37. Caroline Hendric, "Magnets' Value in Desegregating Schools Is Found to Be Limited," *Education Week,* November 13, 1996, pp. 1, 27.
38. Black, "The Pull of Magnets," p. 36.
39. Ibid.
40. Center for Education Reform, *About Charter Schools* (http://edreform.com/pubs/chglance.htm).
41. Thomas D. Snyder, Charlene M. Hoffman, and Claire M. Geddes, *Digest of Education Statistics 1998* (Washington, DC: National Center for Education Statistics, 1999), p. 35.
42. American Association of University Women (AAUW), *How Schools Shortchange Girls* (Washington, DC: American Association of University Women, 1992).
43. Myra Sadker, David Sadker, and Susan Klein, "The Issue of Gender in Elementary and Secondary Education," in *Review of Research in Education* 17, ed. Gerald Grant (Washington, DC: American Educational Research Association, 1991), pp. 269–334.
44. Myra Sadker and David Sadker, *Failing at Fairness: How America's Schools Cheat Girls* (New York: Charles Scribner's Sons, 1994), p. 44.
45. "The Educational Progress of Women," findings from *The Condition of Education, 1995* (Washington, DC: U.S. Department of Education, National Center for Education Statistics, 1995), p. 1.
46. *Hostile Hallways: The AAUW Survey on Sexual Harassment in America's Schools* (Washington, DC: American Association of University Women, 1993).
47. AAUW, *How Schools Shortchange Girls,* p. 73.
48. Mark Walsh, "Harassment Ruling Poses Challenges," *Education Week,* June 2, 1999, pp. 1, 22.
49. Lena Sun, "Gay Students Get Little Help with Harassment," *The Washington Post,* July 20, 1998, p. A8.
50. *When Teens Have Sex: Issues and Trends, KIDS COUNT Special Report* (Baltimore: Annie E. Casey Foundation, 1998), p. 14.
51. Ibid., p. 14.
52. Ibid., p. 9.
53. Ibid., p. 14.
54. William A. Firestone, "Joycelyn Elders Is Almost Right," *Education Week,* September 8, 1993, p. 42.

Chapter 6

1. David Ryans, *Characteristics of Teachers* (Washington, DC: American Council on Education, 1960).
2. J. W. Getzels and P. W. Jackson, "The Teacher's Personality and Characteristics," in *Handbook of Research on Teaching,* ed. N. L. Gage (Chicago: Rand McNally, 1963), p. 574.
3. Gloria Ladson-Billings, *The Dreamkeepers: Successful Teachers of African-American Children* (San Francisco: Jossey-Bass, 1994), p. 34.
4. Thomas L. Good and Jere E. Brophy, *Looking in Classrooms,* 8th ed. (New York: Longman, 2000), pp. 95–96; Gloria Ladson-Billings, "What We Can Learn from Multicultural Education Research," *Educational Leadership* (May 1994), pp. 22–26.
5. Good and Brophy, *Looking in Classrooms,* p. 88.
6. Ibid., p. 79.
7. Carl Rogers, *Freedom to Learn* (Columbus, OH: Merrill, 1969).
8. Lee S. Shulman, "Knowledge and Teaching: Foundations of the New Reform," *Harvard Educational Review* 57 (February 1987), p. 8.
9. C. Argyris and D. A. Schon, *Theory in Practice: Increasing Professional Effectiveness* (San Francisco: Jossey-Bass, 1974), pp. 3–19.
10. B. O. Smith et al., *Teachers for the Real World* (Washington, DC: American Association of Colleges for Teacher Education, 1969), p. 44.
11. Wilford A. Weber, "Classroom Management," in *Classroom Teaching Skills,* 6th ed., ed. J. M. Cooper (Boston: Houghton Mifflin, 1999), p. 223.
12. David C. Berliner, "Effective Classroom Teaching: The Necessary But Not Sufficient Condition for Developing Exemplary Schools," in *Research on Exemplary Schools,* ed. Gilbert R. Austin and Herbert Garber (Orlando: Academic Press, 1985), pp. 136–138.
13. Jacob S. Kounin, *Discipline and Group Management in Classrooms* (New York: Holt, 1970).
14. Alfie Kohn, "Beyond Discipline," *Education Week,* November 20, 1996, pp. 37, 48.
15. Good and Brophy, *Looking in Classrooms,* pp. 394–395.
16. Ibid., pp. 393–395.
17. Ibid., pp. 389–395; William W. Wilen and Ambrose A. Clegg, Jr., "Effective Questions and Questioning: A Research Review," *Theory and Research in Social Education* (Spring 1986), pp. 153–161.
18. Greta Morine-Dershimer, "Instructional Planning," in *Classroom Teaching Skills,* 6th ed., ed. J. M. Cooper (Boston: Houghton Mifflin, 1999), p. 28.
19. Ibid.
20. Mardell Raney, "*Technos* Interview with Jonathan Kozol," *Technos* 7, no. 3 (Fall 1998), p. 10.

Chapter 7

1. This example is loosely based on a class at Ligon Middle School in Raleigh, NC (http://www.ncsu.edu/midlink/gis/hazardous_waste.htm).
2. Marsha Alibrandi, "GIS as a Tool in Interdisciplinary Environmental Studies: Student, Teacher, and Community Perspectives," *Meridian* 1, no. 2 (June 1998) (http://www2.ncsu.edu/unity/lockers/project/meridian/jun98/feat2-3/feat2-3.html).
3. David A. Dockterman, "A Teacher's Tools," *Instructor* 100, no. 5 (January 1991), pp. 58–61.
4. Gene White, "From Magic Lanterns to Microcomputers: The Evolution of the Visual Aid in the English Classroom," *English Journal* 73, no. 3 (March 1984), p. 59.
5. Paul Saettler, *The Evolution of American Educational Technology* (Englewood, CO: Libraries Unlimited, Inc., 1990), p. 98.
6. The Children's Partnership, *America's Children and the Information Superhighway: A Briefing Book and National Action Agenda* (Santa Monica, CA, and Washington, DC: The Children's Partnership [TCP], September 1994) (http://www.childrenspartnership.org/bbar/techin.html).
7. David Moursund, Talbot Bielefeldt, Siobhan Underwood, and Daniel Underwood, "Foundations for the Road Ahead: An Overview of Informational Technologies in Education," for the National Foundation for the Improvement in Education (Eugene, OR: ISTE, 1998) (http://www.iste.org/Research/RoadAhead/pd.html).
8. David H. Jonassen, *Computers in the Classroom: Mindtools for Critical Thinking* (Englewood Cliffs, NJ: Prentice Hall, 1996), p. 3. The concept of a computer application as a cognitive tool follows from the idea that "learning is a consequence of thinking"; see David Perkins, *Smart Schools: Better Thinking and Learning for Every Child* (New York: Free Press, 1992), p. 8.
9. Thomas C. Reeves, "Technology in Teacher Education: From Electronic Tutor to Cognitive Tool," *Action in Teacher Education* 17, no. 4 (1996), p. 74.
10. David H. Jonassen, Chad Carr, and Hsiu-Ping Yueh, "Computers as Mindtools for Engaging Learners in Critical Thinking," *TechTrends* 43 (March 1998), pp. 24–32.
11. Cleborne D. Maddux, D. LaMont Johnson, and Jerry W. Willis, *Educational Computing: Learning with Tomorrow's Technologies* (Boston: Allyn and Bacon, 1992), pp. 204–205.
12. Matthew Maurer, "Supporting Language and Literacy Development with Technology," in *Leadership in Instructional Technology,* ed. Matthew Maurer and George Steven Davidson (Upper Saddle River, NJ: Merrill, 1998), p. 79.
13. Ibid., p. 76.
14. Andrew Trotter, "Teaching the Basics: Beyond Drill and Practice," *Technology Counts '98* in *Education Week* (October 1, 1998), pp. 25–27 (http://www.edweek.org/sreports/tc98/cs/cs1.htm).
15. Diann Boehm, "I Lost My Tooth!" *Learning and Leading with Technology* 24 (April 1997), pp. 17–19.
16. Dennis M. Adams and Mary Hamm, *Collaborative Inquiry in Science, Math, and Technology* (Portsmouth, NH: Heinemann, 1998), p. 99.
17. Yvonne Marie Andres, "Scientist on Tap: Video-Conferencing Over the Internet" (1995) (http://www.globalschoolhouse.org/teach/articles/sot.html).
18. Millicent Lawton, "Making the Most of Assessments: New Windows into a Child's Mind," *Technology Counts '98,* in *Education Week* (October 1, 1998), pp. 59–62 (http://www.edweek.org/sreports/tc98/cs/cs9.htm).
19. Paul G. Geisert and Mynga K. Futrell, *Teachers, Computers, and Curriculum: Microcomputers in the Classroom,* 2d ed. (Needham Heights, MA: Allyn and Bacon, 1995), pp. 119–124.
20. Jonassen, Carr, and Yueh, *Computers in the Classroom,* pp. 49–59.
21. Candy Beal and Cheryl Mason, "Virtual Fieldtripping: No Permission Notes Needed. Creating a Middle School Classroom Without Walls," *Meridian* 2, no. 1 (January 1999) (http://www.ncsu.edu/meridian/jan99/vfieldtrip/index.html).
22. Hollylynne Stohl Drier, Kara M. Dawson, and Joe Garafalo, "Not Your Typical Math Class," *Educational Leadership* 56 (February 1999), p. 21.
23. David Perkins, Gavriel Salomon, and Tamar Globerson, "Partners in Cognition: Extending Human Intelligence with Intelligent Technologies," *Educational Researcher* 20, no. 3 (1991), pp. 2–9.
24. National Council of Teachers of Mathematics, *Curriculum and Evaluation Standards for School Mathematics* (Reston, VA: The National Council of Teachers of Mathematics, 1989), p. 124.
25. Ann M. Farrell, "Teaching and Learning Behaviors in Technology-Oriented Precalculus Classrooms," Ph.D. dissertation, Ohio State University, *Dissertation Abstracts International* 51 (1990), p. 100A.
26. Peter West, "Support Pilot Distance-Learning Projects, Congress Urged," *Education Week,* March 17, 1993, p. 16.
27. Sharon Goldman Edry, "High-Tech High," *Newsweek,* April 3, 1999 (http://newsweek.washingtonpost.com/nw-srv/issue/14_99a/tnw/today/cs/cs02fr_1.htm).
28. U.S. Congress, Office of Technology Assessment, *Teachers and Technology: Making the Connection,* OTA-EHR-616 (Washington, DC: U.S. Government Printing Office, April 1995), p. 1103.
29. Carole Bagley and Barbara Hunter, "Restructuring, Constructivism, and Technology: Forging a New Relationship," *Educational Technology* 32 (July 1992), pp. 24–25.
30. Rena B. Lewis, "Assistive Technology and Learning Disabilities: Today's Realities and Tomorrow's Promises," *Journal of Learning Disabilities* 31 (January/February 1998), pp. 16–26.
31. "Some Thoughts on Assistive Technology Devices and Services," *The Special Educator,* September 22, 1992, pp. 17–19.
32. Mary Ann Zehr, "The State of the States," *Technology Counts '98,* in *Education Week* (October 1, 1998), pp. 69–71 (http://www.edweek.org/sreports/tc98/st/st-n.htm).

33. National Educational Technology Standards for Students (http://cnets.iste.org/).

34. Mary Ann Zehr, "Preparing Students for a Digital World," *Technology Counts '98,* in *Education Week* (October 1, 1998), pp. 33–35 (http://www.edweek.org/sreports/tc98/cs/cs3.htm).

35. Bagley and Hunter, "Restructuring, Constructivism, and Technology," pp. 684–689.

36. Sarah M. Butzin, "Using Instructional Technology in Transformed Learning Environments: An Evaluation of Project CHILD (Computers Helping Instruction and Learning Development)" (1999) (http://www.ifsi.org/lehmanreport.html).

37. Henry Jay Becker and Jason Ravitz, "The Influence of Computer and Internet Use on Teachers' Pedagogical Practices and Perceptions," *Journal of Research on Computing in Education* 31, no. 4 (Summer 1999), pp. 356–384.

38. U.S. Congress, Office of Technology Assessment, *Teachers and Technology: Making the Connection,* OTA-EHR-616 (Washington, DC: U.S. Government Printing Office, April 1995), p. 41.

39. Bess Keller, "Forging the Home-School Connection: For More Information, Press 1. . . ," *Technology Counts '98,* in *Education Week* (October 1, 1998), pp. 49–51 (http://www.edweek.org/sreports/tc98/cs/cs7.htm).

40. Brett T. Jones, "The Lighthouse Project" (1998) (http://www.soe.unc.edu/lighthouse/home.htm).

41. Ronald E. Anderson and Amy Ronnkvist, "The Presence of Computers in American Schools," *Teaching, Learning and Computing: A National Survey* (1998) (http://www.crito.uci/edu/tlc/findings/computers_in_american_schools/html/startpage.htm).

42. Rockman et al., "Powerful Tools for Schooling: Second Year Study of the Laptop Program," Executive Summary (San Francisco, 1998) (http://rockman.com/execs/laptop2exec.htm).

43. Mickey Revenaugh, "Are You Ready for E-rate II?" *THE Journal—Technological Horizons in Education* 26, no. 7 (February 1999), pp. 8–10.

44. Craig D. Jerald, "By the Numbers," *Technology Counts '98,* in *Education Week* (October 1, 1998), pp. 102–105 (http://www.edweek.org/sreports/tc98/data/exsum.htm).

45. Anderson and Ronnkvist, "Computer Presence in Schools."

46. Ibid.

47. Ibid.

48. Zehr, "The State of the States."

49. Jeff Archer, "The Link to Higher Scores," *Technology Counts '98,* in *Education Week* (October 1, 1998), pp. 10–14+ (http://www.edweek.org/sreports/tc98/ets/etc-n.htm).

50. Richard J. Coley, John Cradler, and Penelope K. Engel, *Computers and Classrooms: The Status of Technology in U.S. Schools* (Educational Testing Service, 1997) (http://www.ets.org/research/pic/compclass.html).

51. Lin Foa, Richard Schwab, and Michael Johnson, "Upgrading School Technology: 'Support the Zealots' and Other Pointers for Entering a Strange New Land," *Education Week,* May 1, 1996, p. 52.

52. Task Force on Technology and Teacher Education, *Technology and the New Professional Teacher: Preparing for the 21st Century Classroom* (Washington, DC: National Council for Accreditation of Teacher Education, 1997) (http://ncate.org/projects/tech/TECH.HTM).

53. Milken Exchange on Education Technology, "Information Technology Underused in Teacher Education, New Study Reports" (1998) (http://www.milkenexchange.org/article.taf?_function=detail&Content_uid1=131).

54. Task Force on Technology and Teacher Education, *Technology-Based Student Work: The Creation of "Billie's Story"* (Washington, DC: National Council for Accreditation of Teacher Education, 1997) (http://ncate.org/projects/tech/TECH.HTM;http://ncate.org/projects/tech/ci4.html).

55. Milken Exchange on Education Technology, "Information Technology Underused in Teacher Education."

56. Zehr, "The State of the States."

57. Ibid.

58. U.S. Congress, Office of Technology Assessment, *Teachers and Technology: Making the Connection* (Washington, DC: Office of Technology Assessment, 1995).

59. Milken Exchange on Education Technology, "Progress of Technology in the Schools: Report on Twenty-one States" (1998) (http://www.milkenexchange.org/progress/).

60. "Indiana's Buddy System Links Families with the Classroom Through Technology: Kids and Computers 'Buddy-Up'" *Parent Power Newsletter* 5, no. 1 (August 1996).

61. "Frequently Asked Questions About Information Technology in Education" (Eugene, OR: ISTE, 1998) (http://www.iste.org/Research/Background/FAQ08.html).

62. Anderson and Ronnkvist, "Computer Presence in Schools."

63. Zehr, "The State of the States."

64. Jeff Archer, "The Link to Higher Scores" (http://www.edweek.org/sreports/tc98/ets/etc-n.htm).

65. Janice Weinman and Pamela Haag, "Gender Equity in Cyberspace," *Educational Leadership* 56, no. 5 (February 1999), pp. 44–49.

66. Cornelia Brunner, Dorothy Bennett, and Margaret Honey, "Technology, Gender, and Education: Defining the Problem," paper prepared for the AAUW Commission on Gender, Technology, and Teacher Education, October 1998.

67. Cornelia Brunner, "Opening Technology to Girls," *Electronic Learning* 16, no. 4 (February 1997), p. 55.

68. "Essential Conditions to Make It Happen" (Eugene, OR: ISTE, 1998) (http://cnets.iste.org/condition.htm).

69. Larry Cuban, "High-Tech Schools and Low-Tech Teaching," *Education Week* 16 (May 21, 1997) (http://www.edweek.org/ew/vol-16/).

70. Larry Cuban, "Techno-Reformers and Classroom Teachers," *Education Week* 16 (October 9, 1996) (http://www.edweek.org/ew/vol-16).

71. Judi Harris, *Virtual Architecture: Designing and Directing Curriculum-Based Telecomputing* (Eugene, OR: International Society for Technology in Education, 1998).

Chapter 8

1. Jerome S. Bruner, *The Process of Education* (New York: Random House, 1960).
2. Karin Chenoweth, "Reading Wars, Take 2," *The Washington Post Magazine,* May 16, 1999, p. 17.
3. Jay Mathews, "Study Faults Computers' Use in Math Education," *The Washington Post,* September 30, 1998, p. A3.
4. *Science for All Americans* (Washington, DC: American Association for the Advancement of Science, 1989).
5. Arthur W. Foshay, "Knowledge and the Structure of the Disciplines," in *The Nature of Knowledge: Implications for the Education of Teachers,* ed. William A. Jenkins (Milwaukee: University of Wisconsin Press, 1961).
6. Scott Willis, "Foreign Languages," *Curriculum Update* (Alexandria, VA: Association for Supervision and Curriculum Development, Winter 1996), p. 6.
7. *What Work Requires of Schools* (Washington, DC: U.S. Department of Labor, Secretary's Commission on Achieving Necessary Skills, 1991).
8. Larry E. Suter, ed., *Indicators of Science and Mathematics Education 1995* (Arlington, VA: National Science Foundation, 1996), pp. 14, 29.
9. Paul Williams et al., *NAEP 1994 U.S. History: A First Look* (Washington, DC: National Center for Education Statistics, 1995), p. 19.
10. *The Nation's Report Card* (http://nces.ed.gov/nationsreportcard/site/home.asp).
11. *Policy Brief: What the Third International Mathematics and Science Study (TIMSS) Means for Systematic School Improvement* (Washington, DC: The National Institute on Educational Governance, Finance, Policymaking, and Management and Consortium for Policy Research in Education, U.S. Government Printing Office, 1998), p. 3.
12. Robert B. Schwartz, "Lesson from TIMSS," *Hands On* (Spring 1998), a publication of TERC, Cambridge, MA.
13. William Schmidt, "Are There Surprises in the TIMSS Twelfth Grade Results?" *TIMSS United States, Report No. 8* (East Lansing, MI: United States National Research Center [TIMSS], April 1998), p. 4.
14. *Splintered Vision: An Investigation of U.S. Mathematics and Science Education, Executive Summary* (East Lansing, MI: U.S. National Research Center for the Third International Mathematics and Science Study, 1996), pp. 5–9.
15. *Prisoners of Time: A Report of the National Education Commission on Time and Learning* (Washington, DC: U.S. Government Printing Office, 1994), p. 23.
16. Gerald W. Bracey, "Tinkering with TIMSS," *Phi Delta Kappan* 80, no. 1 (September 1998), pp. 32–36.
17. Larry Cuban, *How Teachers Taught: Constancy and Change in American Classrooms, 1890–1980* (New York: Longman, 1984).
18. Robin Rogarty, "Ten Ways to Integrate Curriculum," *Educational Leadership* 49, no. 2 (October 1991), p. 61.
19. Robert E. Slavin, *Cooperative Learning,* 2d ed. (Boston: Allyn and Bacon, 1995), pp. 3–4.
20. Ibid., pp. 14–70.
21. Joyce L. Epstein, "What Matters in the Middle Grades—Grade Span or Practices?" *Phi Delta Kappan* 71 (February 1990), 438–444.
22. *Prisoners of Time,* pp. 10, 31, 34.
23. Meg Sommerfield, "More and More Schools Putting Block Scheduling to Test of Time," *Education Week,* May 22, 1996, pp. 1, 14.
24. E. D. Hirsch, Jr., *Cultural Literacy* (Boston: Houghton Mifflin, 1987).
25. Debra Viadero, "On the Wrong Track," *Teacher Magazine* (January 1999), pp. 22–23.
26. Dominic Brewer, Daniel Rees, and Laura Argys, "Detracking America's Schools: The Reform Without Cost?" *Phi Delta Kappan* 77 (November 1995), pp. 210–212+.

Chapter 9

1. "Education Vital Signs," *American School Board Journal* 186, no. 12 (December 1999), p. A15.
2. Larry Cuban, "Conflict and Leadership in the Superintendency," *Phi Delta Kappan* 67 (September 1985), p. 28. See also Arthur Blumberg with Phyllis Blumberg, *The School Superintendent: Living with Conflict* (New York: Teachers College Press, 1985), p. 32, and Susan Moore Johnson, *Leading to Change: The Challenge of the New Superintendency* (San Francisco: Jossey-Bass, 1996), pp. 77–78.
3. "Education Vital Signs," *American School Board Journal* 183, no. 12 (December 1996), p. A21.
4. Mary Jordan, "Big City School Chiefs Learn Reform Is Not 1 of the 3 Rs," *The Washington Post,* February 13, 1993, p. 1; *Urban Indicator* 4, no. 1 (October 1997), Figure 2 at web site http://www.cgcs.org/newslett/indicator/1997/october/html/article_3.htm.
5. William L. Rutherford, "School Principals as Effective Leaders," *Phi Delta Kappan* 67 (September 1985), pp. 31–34.
6. "Education Vital Signs," *American School Board Journal* 185, no. 12 (December 1998), p. A14.
7. Ibid., p. A13.
8. Brian Dumaine, "Making Education Work," *Fortune,* special issue: "Saving Our Schools," Spring 1990, p. 12.
9. Business Coalition for Education Reform web site at http://www.bcer.org/.
10. Henry A. Giroux, "Education Incorporated?" *Educational Leadership* 56, no. 2 (October 1998), p. 13.
11. Reagan Walker, "The Education of Business," *Teacher Magazine* (January 1990), p. 67.
12. Mark Walsh, "Nader, Schlafly Lambaste Channel One at Senate Hearing," *Education Week,* May 26, 1999, p. 20.
13. Thomas Moore with Nancy Linon, "The Selling of Our Schools," *U.S. News & World Report,* November 6, 1989, p. 40.
14. Mark Walsh, "Private Control Has Yet to Show Improved Test Scores, Report Finds," *Education Week,* May 29, 1996, p. 11.

15. Ann Bradley, "Researchers Find Teacher Tests Short on Covering College Content," *Education Week,* June 2, 1999, p. 5.

16. "Education Vital Signs," *American School Board Journal* 185, no. 12 (December 1998), p. A27.

17. Ibid., pp. A22–A27.

18. "Education Vital Signs," *American School Board Journal* 186, no. 12 (December 1999), p. A27.

19. Rob Greenwald, Larry V. Hedges, and Richard D. Laine, "The Effect of School Resources on Student Achievement," *Review of Educational Research* (Fall 1996), pp. 361–396.

20. Deborah A. Verstegen, "Judicial Analysis During the New Wave of School Finance Litigation: The New Adequacy in Education," *Journal of Education Finance* 24 (Summer 1998), pp. 51–52.

21. Thomas D. Snyder, Charlene M. Hoffman, and Claire M. Geddes, *Digest of Education Statistics 1998* (Washington, DC: U.S. Department of Education, National Center for Education Statistics, 1998), p. 169.

22. U.S. Department of Health and Human Services web site at http://www2.acf.dhhs.gov/programs/hsb/html/hs_98_fact_sheet.htm.

23. "The Educational Excellence For All Children Act of 1999," *Education Week,* June 9, 1999, p. 32.

24. Ibid., p. 31.

25. Deborah L. Cohen, "Perry Preschool Graduates Show Dramatic New Social Gains at 27," *Education Week,* April 21, 1993, pp. 1, 16–17; Lawrence J. Schweinhart et al., "The Promise of Early Childhood Education," *Phi Delta Kappan* 66 (April 1985), pp. 548–553.

Chapter 10

1. In a recent national survey of deans and department chairpersons of education schools and departments, 91.4 percent "agreed" or "strongly agreed" with the statement "There exists a set of core values/virtues upon which most Americans agree, regardless of race, creed, class or culture, which can and should be taught in schools." See Emily Nelsen Jones, Kevin Ryan, and Karen E. Bohlin, *Teachers as Educators of Character: Are the Nation's Schools of Education Coming Up Short?* (Washington, DC: Character Education Partnership, 1999), p. 7; Association of Supervision and Curriculum Development, *Moral Education in the Life of the School* (Alexandria, VA: ASCD, 1989). Also, President Clinton, in his 1996 and 1997 State of the Union addresses, pointedly called on American schools to give greater attention to character education.

2. Mortimer J. Adler, *The Paideia Proposal: An Educational Manifesto* (New York: Macmillan, 1982); *Paideia Problems and Possibilities* (New York: Macmillan, 1983).

3. Lynn Olson, "Kudos for Core Knowledge," *Education Week,* March 17, 1999, p. 44.

4. *Education Week,* January 31, 1996, p. 21.

Chapter 11

1. Willystine Goodsell, ed., *Pioneers of Women's Education in the United States* (New York: AMS Press, 1970/1931), p. 5.

2. R. Freeman Butts and Lawrence A. Cremin, *A History of Education in American Culture* (New York: Holt, 1953), p. 245.

3. Charles W. Coulter and Richard S. Rimanoczy, *A Layman's Guide to Educational Theory* (New York: Van Nostrand, 1955), p. 130.

4. Butts and Cremin, *A History of Education in American Culture,* p. 408.

5. John D. Pulliam, *History of Education in America,* 3d ed. (Columbus, OH: Merrill, 1982), pp. 157–159.

6. Gene D. Shepherd and William B. Ragan, *Modern Elementary Curriculum,* 6th ed. (New York: Holt, 1982), p. 440.

7. Butts and Cremin, *A History of Education in American Culture,* p. 260.

8. Merle Curti, *The Social Ideas of American Educators,* 2d ed. (Totowa, NJ: Littlefield, Adams, 1959), p. 183.

9. Butts and Cremin, *A History of Education in American Culture,* p. 443.

10. Thomas D. Snyder, *120 Years of American Education: A Statistical Portrait* (Washington, DC: U.S. Department of Education, National Center for Education Statistics, 1993), pp. 36–37; *1997–98 Estimates of School Statistics* (Washington, DC: National Education Association, 1998), p. 7.

11. William T. Gruhn and Harl R. Douglass, *The Modern Junior High School,* 3d ed. (New York: Ronald Press, 1971), pp. 46–53.

12. "Teachers Train for Tough Years," *USA Today,* October 6, 1998, p. D1.

13. Debra Viadero, "Middle School Gains over 25 Years Chronicled," *Education Week,* May 29, 1996, p. 7.

14. Larry Cuban, "What Happens to Reforms That Last? The Case of the Junior High School," *American Educational Research Journal* 29, no. 2 (Summer 1992), p. 246.

15. Thomas D. Snyder, Charlene M. Hoffman, and Claire M. Geddes, *Digest of Education Statistics 1998* (Washington, DC: U.S. Department of Education, National Center for Education Statistics, 1998), p. 73; Jeanne Ponessa, "Catholic School Enrollment Continues to Increase," *Education Week,* April 17, 1996, p. 5.

16. Snyder, Hoffman, and Geddes, *Digest of Education Statistics 1998,* p. 71.

17. Ibid., p. 12.

18. Herbert M. Kliebard, ed., *Religion and Education in America: A Documentary History* (Scranton, PA: International Textbook, 1969), p. 119.

19. Earle H. West, ed., *The Black American and Education* (Columbus, OH: Merrill, 1972), pp. 7–8.

20. Eric Lincoln and Milton Meltzer, *A Pictorial History of the Negro in America,* 3d ed. (New York: Crown, 1968), pp. 108–109.

21. *Historical Statistics of the United States, Colonial Times to 1970,* vol. I, Table Series H 433–441 (Washington, DC: U.S. Government Printing Office, 1975), p. 370.

22. Franklin Frazier, *The Negro in the United States,* rev. ed. (New York: Macmillan, 1957), pp. 427, 432–436, 438.

23. Gary Orfield, Susan E. Eaton, and the Harvard Project on School Desegregation, *Dismantling Desegregation* (New York: The New Press, 1996), pp. 105–106; Jomills Henry Braddock II, Robert L. Crain, and James M. McPartland, "A Long-Term View of School Desegregation: Some Recent Studies of Graduates as Adults," *Phi Delta Kappan* 66 (December 1984), pp. 259–264.

24. See J. Anthony Lukas, *Common Ground* (New York: Knopf, 1985), for a Pulitzer Prize–winning description of desegregation efforts in Boston, Massachusetts.

25. Howard Ozmon and Sam Craver, *Busing: A Moral Issue* (Bloomington, IN: Phi Delta Kappa Educational Foundation, 1972), pp. 33–34.

26. Snyder, Hoffman, and Geddes, *Digest of Education Statistics 1998,* pp. 99–107.

27. Ethan Bronner, "After 45 Years, Resegregation Emerges in Schools, Study Finds," *The New York Times National,* June 13, 1999, p. 31.

28. R. Freeman Butts, *The Education of the West: A Formative Chapter in the History of Civilization* (New York: McGraw-Hill, 1973), p. 279.

29. Lynn Schnaiberg, "Presidential Order on Indian Education Calls for Comprehensive Federal Policy," *Education Week,* September 9, 1998, p. 35.

30. Ibid.

31. "The Educational Excellence For All Children Act of 1999," *Education Week,* June 9, 1999, p. 47.

32. U.S. Department of Commerce, Bureau of the Census, March Current Population Surveys, web site at http://www.nces.ed.gov/pubs98/condition98/c9822a01.html.

33. *The State of Asian Pacific America: Policy Issues to the Year 2020,* Executive Summary (Los Angeles: Leadership Education for Asian Pacifics, 1993), p. 2.

Chapter 12

1. Reprinted with permission. Copyright by the American Association of Colleges for Teacher Education. Kenneth R. Howe, "A Conceptual Basis for Ethics in Teacher Education," *Journal of Teacher Education* 37 (May/June 1996), p. 6.

2. Ibid., p. 6.

3. American Federation of Teachers, "Bill of Rights" (Washington, DC: AFT).

4. Steven Tigner, *Educator's Affirmation,* Boston University and University of Toledo, 1989. Reprinted by permission of Steven S. Tigner

5. John Martin Rich, "The Role of Professional Ethics in Teacher Education," *Journal of the Association of Teacher Educators* 7 (Fall 1985), p. 22.

6. *U.S.L. Week 4223,* March 24, 1970, quoted in Louis Fischer and David Schimmel, *The Rights of Students and Teachers* (New York: Harper and Row, 1982), p. 323. Much of this chapter is drawn from the material presented in this excellent and highly readable book, and also from Louis Fischer, David Schimmel, and Cynthia Kelly, *Teachers and the Law,* 4th ed. (New York: Longman, 1995).

7. Fischer, Schimmel, and Kelly, *Teachers and the Law,* p. 17.

8. *Smith* v. *School District of the Township of Darby,* quoted in Fischer, Schimmel, and Kelly, *Teachers and the Law,* p. 31.

9. Robert L. Monk and Ernest I. Proulx, "Legal Basics for Teachers, Fastback 235" (Bloomington, IN: Phi Delta Kappa, 1986), p. 35.

10. *Pickering* v. *Board of Education,* 225 N.E.2d 1 (1967); 391 U.S. 563 (1968).

11. *Anderson* v. *Evans,* 660 F.2d 153 (6th Cir. 1981).

12. *Scoville* v. *Board of Education,* 425 F.2d 10 (7th Cir. 1970).

13. Fischer, Schimmel, and Kelly, *Teachers and the Law,* p. 169.

14. Ibid.

15. Ibid., p. 413.

16. Ibid., p. 304.

17. Ibid., pp. 282–283.

18. Thomas R. McDaniel, "The Teacher's Ten Commandments: School Law in the Classroom, *Phi Delta Kappan* 60, no. 10 (June 1979), p. 707.

19. Perry A. Zirkel, "A Bedeviling Message from Providence," *Phi Delta Kappan* 74, no. 2 (October 1992), pp. 183–184.

20. Benjamin Senor, "Even After the Supreme Court Ruling, We're Still in the Dark About Religion Clubs at School," *American School Board Journal* 173 (August 1986), p. 17.

21. Cheryl D. Mills, "Important Education-Related U.S. Supreme Court Decisions," in *Challenges and Achievements of American Education,* ed. Gordon Cawalti (Alexandria, VA: Association for Supervision and Curriculum Development, 1993), p. 192.

22. Stephen Arons, "Separation of School and State," *Education Week,* November 17, 1984, p. 24.

23. Thomas J. Flygare, "Supreme Court Strikes Down Louisiana Creationism Act," *Phi Delta Kappan* 69, no. 1 (September 1987), pp. 77–79.

24. Associated Press, "Science Standard Debates in Kansas," August 11, 1999.

25. "ABC Nightly News," August 25, 1999.

26. *A. Mozert* v. *Hawkins County Board of Education,* U.S. Dist. Ct. (E.D. Tenn.), 647 F Supp. 1194 (1987).

27. *Smith* v. *Board of School Commissioners of Mobile County,* no. 87–7216 (11th Cir., 26 September 1987).

28. Thomas R. McDaniel, "The Teacher's Ten Commandments: School Law in the Classroom," *Phi Delta Kappan* (June 1979), p. 703. Used by permission.

29. Richard Riley, secretary of education, and Walter Dellinger, assistant attorney general, White House press release, July 12, 1995, pp. 2–4.

30. *Tinker* v. *Des Moines Independent Community School District,* 393 U.S. 503 (1969).

31. M. M. McCarthy and N. H. Cambron-McCabe, *Public School Law: Teachers' and Students' Rights,* 3d ed. (Boston: Allyn and Bacon, 1992).

32. *Goss* v. *Lopez,* 95 S.Ct. 729 (1975).

33. *Honig* v. *Doe,* 108 S.Ct. 592, 605 (1988).

34. Title IX of the Education Amendments (1972), which addresses issues of prohibiting sexual discrimination in any education program receiving federal funds, is the basis for most court decisions supporting a pregnant young woman's right to stay in school.

35. See, for instance, *Newsome* v. *Batavia Local School District,* 842 F.2d 920 (6th Cir. 1988).

36. Thomas R. McDaniel, "The Teacher's Ten Commandments: School Law in the Classroom" (revised version), in *Kaleidoscope,* 8th ed., ed. Kevin Ryan and James M. Cooper (Boston: Houghton Mifflin, 1998).

37. Temple University Center for the Study of Corporal Punishment and Alternatives in the School, cited in John Johan-sen, Harold W. Collins, and James A. Johnson, *American Education,* 6th ed. (Dubuque, IA: Wm. C. Brown, 1990), p. 71.

38. Fischer, Schimmel, and Kelly, *Teachers and the Law,* p. 268.

39. *New Jersey* v. *T.L.O.,* 105 S.Ct. 733 (1985).

40. *Tinker* v. *Des Moines Independent Community School District.*

41. *Bethel School District No. 403* v. *Fraser,* 106 S.Ct. 3159 (1986).

42. *Hazelwood School District* v. *Kuhlmeier,* 56 U.S.L.W. 4079, 4082 (12 January 1988).

43. Ibid.

44. American Association of University Women, *Hostile Hallways: The AAUW Survey on Sexual Harassment in America's Schools* (New York: Louis Harris Associations, 1993), p. 6.

45. Mark Walsh, "High Court Addresses Harassment," *Education Week,* July 8, 1999, pp. 1, 30–31.

46. *Ray* v. *School District of DeSoto County,* 666 F. Supp. 1524 (M.D. Fla. 1987).

Chapter 13

1. Hal A. Lawson, *Toward Healthy Learners, Schools and Communities: Footprints in a Continuing Journey* (Seattle: Institute for Educational Inquiry, July 1993), p. 4.

2. Study by the Josephson Institute of Ethics, reported in *Education Week,* November 4, 1998, p. 4.

3. Jon W. Wiles, *Promoting Changes in School* (New York: Scholastic, 1993), pp. 1–2.

4. Editors of *Education Week, From Risk to Renewal* (Washington, DC: Editorial Projects in Education, 1993), p. xiv.

5. Conway Dorsett, "Multicultural Education: Why We Need It and Why We Worry About It," *Network News and Views* 121, no. 3 (March 1993), p. 31.

6. For further information on portfolios and authentic assessment, see Susan Black, "Portfolio Assessment," *The Executive Educator* 15 (February 1993), pp. 28–31.

7. Lawrence Feinberg, "Standards and Reform," *Network News and Views* 12, no. 8 (August 1993), p. 54.

8. Quoted in Theodore Sizer and Nancy Faust Sizer, *The Students Are Watching* (Boston: Beacon Press, 1999), p. 6, from

Milbrey W. McLaughlin, Merita A. Irby, and Juliet Langman, *Urban Sanctuaries: Neighborhood Organizations in the Lives and Futures of Inner-City Youth* (San Francisco: Jossey Bass, 1994), p. 216.

9. Anthony Bryk and Yeow Meng Thum, "The Effects of High School Organization on Dropping Out," unpublished paper, University of Chicago, 1988, pp. 54–68. See also Anthony Bryk and Mary Erina Driscoll, "An Empirical Investigation of the School as a Community," unpublished paper, University of Chicago, 1988, pp. 54–63.

10. Kevin Ryan and Thomas Lickona, eds., *Character Development in Schools and Beyond* (Washington, DC: Council for Research on Values and Philosophy, 1987), pp. 21–26.

11. See Chapter 6, "Against Moral Education," in Barry Chazan, *Contemporary Approaches to Moral Education* (New York: Teachers College Press, 1985).

12. William Damon, quoted by Amitai Etzioni, *The Spirit of Community* (New York: Crown, 1993), pp. 100–101.

13. "Values Education: Time for Greater Emphasis?" *Phi Delta Kappan* 75, no. 2 (October 1993), p. 145.

14. Julie Blair, "Kellogg Begins Program to Boost Service Learning," *Education Week,* May 26, 1999.

15. Thomas Toch, *In the Name of Excellence* (New York: Oxford University Press, 1991), p. 260.

16. Mortimer Adler, *The Paideia Proposal: An Educational Manifesto* (New York: Macmillan, 1982), p. 59

17. Quoted by Mark Edwards in "Turbo-Charging Professional Development," *The School Administrator* (December 1998), p. 36.

18. Toch, *In the Name of Excellence,* p. 9.

19. Editors of *Education Week, From Risk to Renewal,* p. 4.

20. E. D. Hirsch, as quoted by Sara Mosle, *The New York Times Book Review,* September 29, 1996, p. 15.

21. Theodore Sizer, *Horace's School: Redesigning the American High School* (Boston: Houghton Mifflin, 1992), pp. 207–208.

22. Quoted by the editors of *Education Week, From Risk to Renewal,* p. 187.

23. Herbert Walberg, *U.S. News & World Report,* January 11, 1993, p. 60.

24. Editors of *Education Week, From Risk to Renewal,* p. 64.

25. Ibid., p. 70.

26. *Digest of Education Statistics 1998* (Washington, DC: U.S. Department of Education, National Center for Education Statistics, 1999), p. 167.

27. Editors of *Education Week, From Risk to Renewal,* p. 102.

28. *Digest of Education Statistics 1995,* p. 149.

29. Toch, *In the Name of Excellence,* p. 164.

30. Emeral A. Crosby, "The 'At-Risk' Decade," *Phi Delta Kappan* (April 1993), p. 603.

31. Toch, *In the Name of Excellence,* p. 186.

32. Richard J. Murname and Frank Levy, "What General Motors Can Teach U.S. Schools About the Proper Role of Markets in Education Reform," *Phi Delta Kappan* 78, no. 2 (October 1996), p. 114.

Chapter 14

1. William J. Hussar and Debra E. Gerald, *Projections of Education Statistics to 2008* (Washington, DC: National Center for Education Statistics, 1998), pp. 9, 72.
2. Ann Bradley, "Class-Size Cuts Set Off Hiring Spree in Calif.," *Education Week,* September 4, 1996, pp. 1, 29.
3. Recruiting New Teachers, Inc. web site at http://www.rnt.org/publications/urban.html; C. Emily Feistritzer, *The Making of a Teacher* (Washington, DC: Center for Education Information, 1999), p. 5.
4. Ibid.
5. *The 1999 Job Search Handbook for Educators* (Evanston, IL: American Association for Employment in Education, 1999), pp. 12–13.
6. Ibid., p. 13.
7. David Hill, "Odd Man Out," *Education Week,* September 11, 1996, p. 30.
8. Anne Meek, "America's Teachers: Much to Celebrate," *Educational Leadership* 55, no. 5 (February 1998), pp. 12–16.
9. *Quality Counts 2000: Who Should Teach?* Fourth annual edition of *Education Week*'s 50-state report card on public education, January 13, 2000. Web site at http://www.edweek.org/sreports/qc00/.
10. Thomas D. Snyder, Charlene M. Hoffman, and Claire M. Geddes, *Digest of Education Statistics 1998* (Washington, DC: National Center for Education Statistics, 1998), p. 80.
11. *Department of Defense Education Activity: Fiscal Year 1997–98,* Executive Summary (Arlington, VA: Department of Defense Education Activity, 1998); web site at http://www.odedodea.edu/.
12. Hussar and Gerald, *Projections of Education Statistics to 2008,* Tables 1 and 32; Snyder, Hoffman, and Geddes, *Digest of Education Statistics 1998,* p. 73.
13. Thomas M. Smith et al., *The Condition of Education 1996* (Washington, DC: U.S. Department of Education, National Center for Education Statistics, 1996), p. 34; James Coleman, T. Hoffer, and S. Kilgore, *Public and Private Schools,* Report to the National Center for Education Statistics, 1981.
14. Hussar and Gerald, *Projections of Education Statistics to 2008,* Table 36.
15. Ibid.
16. Most of the ideas in this section are taken from John William Zehring, "How to Get Another Teaching Job and What to Do If You Can't," *Learning* 6 (February 1978), pp. 44, 46–51.
17. C. Emily Feistritzer, *Alternative Teacher Certification—An Overview* (Washington, DC: National Center for Education Information); web site at http://www.ncei.com/Alt-Teacher-Cert.htm.
18. C. Emily Feistritzer and David T. Chester, *Alternative Teacher Certification: A State-by-State Analysis 1996* (Washington, DC: National Center for Education Information, 1996), p. 5.
19. *1998–99 Occupational Outlook Handbook* (Washington, DC: U.S. Department of Labor, 1999); web site at http://stats.bls.gov/ocohome.htm.

Chapter 15

1. We have drawn heavily on one of the classic texts on this subject: Myron Lieberman, *Education as a Profession* (Englewood Cliffs, NJ: Prentice-Hall, 1956).
2. Walter Boggs, quoted at 1963–64 convention of the National Commission on Teacher Education and Professional Standards, in Myron Brenton, *What's Happened to Teachers?* (New York: Coward-McCann, 1970), p. 242.
3. National Board for Professional Teaching Standards, *What Teachers Should Know and Be Able to Do* (Washington, DC: NBPTS, n.d.).
4. National Board for Professional Teaching Standards web site at http://www.nbpts.org/nbpts/about/pr=oklahoma.html/.
5. *NEA Fact Sheet* (Washington, DC: National Education Association, October 1996).
6. Rene Sanchez, "Teachers Unions Struggle to Pass Reformers' Muster," *The Washington Post,* June 3, 1996, pp. A1, A5.
7. Steven Chauffman, "The NEA Seizes Power: The Teachers' Coup," *The New Republic,* October 11, 1980, pp. 9–11.
8. Stanley Elam, "The National Education Association: Political Powerhouse or Paper Tiger," *Phi Delta Kappan* 63 (November 1981), pp. 169–174.
9. Peter Brim Low and Leslie Spencer, "The National Extortion Association?" *Forbes,* June 7, 1993.
10. "NEA: Does It Still Speak for Teachers?" *Teachers in Focus* (April 1994), p. 4.
11. Jeanne Pones, "Seeking 'Reinvention' of NEA, Chase Calls for Shift in Priorities," *Education Week,* February 12, 1997, p. 1.
12. Letter from Bella Rosenberg, assistant to the president, American Federation of Teachers, January 18, 1991.

Appendix

Directory of U.S. State Teacher Certification Offices

A teaching license is valid only in the state for which it is issued, and licensure and testing requirements are never static. If you are planning to move to another state, you should contact that state's licensure office, as listed below. The number code following each entry indicates the types of testing that the state required at the time of publication. The key to the codes follows the state listings.

When you write or call the state licensure office, indicate the type of license you are receiving from your current state and which national tests you have taken, and ask for application materials and procedures for obtaining licensure in the new state. Another source of information about licensure requirements will be the actual districts to which you apply.

Alabama
Department of Education
Division of Instructional Service
5108 Gordon Persons Building
50 North Ripley Street
Montgomery 36130-2101, 334-229-4271

Alaska
Department of Education
Teacher Education and Certification
Goldbelt Building
801 West 10th Street, Suite 200
Juneau 99801-1894, 907-465-2831
www.educ.state.ak.us/teachercertification

Arizona   1
Department of Education
Teacher Certification Unit
1535 West Jefferson
Phoenix 85007, 602-542-4367
www.ade.state.az.us/certification

Arkansas   3
Department of Education
Teacher Education and Licensure
#4 State Capitol Mall, Rooms 106B/107B
Little Rock 72201, 501-682-4342

California   2
Commission on Teacher Credentialing
1812 9th Street
Sacramento 95814-7000, 916-445-0184

Colorado   1
Department of Education
Educator Licensing, Room 105
201 East Colfax Avenue
Denver 80203-1704, 303-866-6628
www.cde.state.co.us/edlic.htm

Connecticut   3
State Department of Education
Bureau of Certification and Professional
    Development
P.O. Box 2219
Hartford 06145, 860-566-5201
www.state.ct.us/sde/cert

Delaware   3
State Department of Education
Office of Certification
Townsend Building, P.O. Box 1402
Dover 19903-1402, 302-739-4686

District of Columbia   3
Teacher Education and Certification Branch
Logan Administration Building
215 G Street, N.E., Room 101A
Washington 20002, 202-724-4246

Florida   1
Department of Education
Bureau of Teacher Certification
Florida Education Center
325 West Gaines Street, Room 203
Tallahassee 32399-0400, 904-488-5724

Georgia 1 & 3
Professional Standards Commission
1454 Twin Towers East
Atlanta 30334, 404-657-9000
www.gapsc.com

Hawaii 3
State Department of Education
Office of Personnel Services
P.O. Box 2360
Honolulu 96804, 800-305-5104

Idaho
Department of Education
Teacher Certification and Professional
    Standards
P.O. Box 83720
Boise 83720-0027,
    208-332-6884

Illinois 1
State Teacher Certification Board
Division of Professional Preparation
100 North First Street
Springfield 62777-0001, 217-782-2805
www.isbe.state.il.us/homepage.html

Indiana 3
Professional Standards Board
251 East Ohio Street, Suite 201
Indianapolis 46204-2133,
    317-232-9010

Iowa
Board of Educational Examiners
Teacher Licensure
Grimes State Office Building
East 14th and Grand
Des Moines 50319-0146, 515-281-3245
www.state.ia.us/educate/depteduc/elseced/
    praclic/license/index.html

Kansas 3
State Department of Education
Certification and Teacher Education
120 South East 10th Avenue
Topeka 66612-1182, 913-296-2288
www.ksbe.state.ks.us/cert/cert.html

Kentucky 3
Office of Teacher Education and
    Certification
1024 Capital Center Drive
Frankfort 40601, 502-573-4606

Louisiana 3
State Department of Education
Bureau of Higher Education, Teacher
    Certification, and Continuing Education
626 North 4th Street
P.O. Box 94064
Baton Rouge 70804-9064, 504-342-3490

Maine 3
Department of Education
Certification Office
23 State House Station
Augusta 04333-0023, 207-287-5944

Maryland 3
State Department of Education
Division of Certification and Accreditation
200 West Baltimore Street
Baltimore 21201, 410-767-0412

Massachusetts
Department of Education
Certification and Professional Development
    Coordination
350 Main Street
P.O. Box 9140
Malden 02148-5023, 781-388-3300
www.info.doe.mass.edu/news.html

Michigan 1
Department of Education
Office of Professional Preparation and
    Certification Services
608 West Allegan, 3rd Floor
Lansing 48933, 517-335-0406
www.mde.state.mi.us

Minnesota 3
State Department of Children, Families, and
    Learning
Personnel Licensing
610 Capitol Square Building
550 Cedar Street
St. Paul 55101-2273, 612-296-2046

Mississippi 3
State Department of Education
Office of Educator Licensure
Central High School Building
359 North West Street
P.O. Box 771
Jackson 39205-0771, 601-359-3483
http://mdek12.state.ms.us/OVTE/License/
    license.htm

Missouri   3
Department of Elementary and Secondary
   Education
Teacher Certification Office
205 Jefferson Street
P.O. Box 480
Jefferson City 65102-0480, 573-751-0051
http://services.dese.state.mo.us/
   divurbteached/teachcert

Montana   3
Office of Public Instruction
Teacher Education and Certification
1227 11th Avenue East, Room 210
Box 202501
Helena 59620-2501, 406-444-3150

Nebraska   3
Department of Education
Teacher Education and Certification
301 Centennial Mall South, Box 94987
Lincoln 68509-4987, 402-471-0739
http://nde4.nde.state.ne.us/TCERT/TCERT.html

Nevada   3
Department of Education
Licensure Division
700 East 5th Street
Carson City 89701, 702-687-9141

New Hampshire
State Department of Education
Bureau of Credentialing
101 Pleasant Street
Concord 03301-3860, 603-271-2407
www.state.nh.us/doe/education.htm

New Jersey   3
Department of Education
Office of Professional Development and
   Licensing
Riverview Executive Plaza, Building 100,
   Rte. 29
Trenton 08625-0500, 609-292-2045

New Mexico   3
State Department of Education
Professional Licensure Unit
Education Building
Santa Fe 87501-2786, 505-827-6587

New York   1
State Education Department
Office of Teaching
Cultural Education Center, Room 5A47
Nelson A. Rockefeller Empire State Plaza
Albany 12230, 518-474-3901
www.nysed.gov/tcert/homepage.htm

North Carolina   3
Department of Public Instruction
Licensure Section
301 North Wilmington Street
Raleigh 27601-2825, 919-733-4125

North Dakota
Department of Public Instruction
Educational Standards and Practices Board
600 East Boulevard Avenue
Bismarck 58505-0540, 701-328-2264

Ohio   3
Department of Education
Division of Professional Development and
   Licensure
65 South Front Street, Room 412
Columbus 43215-4183, 614-466-3593
www.ode.ohio.gov/www/tc/teacher.html

Oklahoma   1
State Department of Education
Professional Standards Section
Hodge Education Building
2500 North Lincoln Boulevard, Room 212
Oklahoma City 73105-4599, 405-521-3337
www.sde.state.ok.us

Oregon   2
Teacher Standards and Practices
   Commission
Public Service Building, Suite 105
255 Capitol Street, N.E.
Salem 97310, 503-378-3586

Pennsylvania   3
State Department of Education
Bureau of Teacher Preparation and
   Certification
333 Market Street, 3rd Floor
Harrisburg 17126-0333, 717-787-3356
www.cas.psu.edu/pde.html

Puerto Rico   3
Department of Education
Certification Office
P.O. Box 190759
San Juan 00919-0759, 787-754-0060

Rhode Island   3
Department of Education
Office of Teacher Preparation, Certification,
   and Professional Development
Shepard Building
255 Westminster Street
Providence 02903, 401-222-2675

South Carolina   3
State Department of Education
Office of Organizational Development
Teacher Certification Section
Rutledge Building, Room 702
Columbia 29201, 803-734-8466

South Dakota
Division of Education and Cultural Affairs
Office of Policy and Accountability
Kneip Building, 700 Governors Drive
Pierre 57501-2291, 605-773-3553
www.state.sd.us/state/executive/deca/
   account/certif/htm

Tennessee   3
State Department of Education
Teacher Licensing and Certification
Andrew Johnson Tower, 5th Floor
710 James Robertson Parkway
Nashville 37243-0377, 615-532-4880

Texas   1
State Board of Educator Certification
1001 Trinity Street
Austin 78701-2603, 512-469-3001
www.sbec.state.tx.us/sbec/txcert.htm

Utah
State Office of Education
Certification and Personnel Development
250 East 500 South
Salt Lake City 84111, 801-538-7741
www.usoe.k12.ut.us/cert/regs.html

Vermont
State Department of Education
Licensing and Professional Standards
120 State Street
Montpelier 05620, 802-828-2445

Virginia   3
Department of Education
James Monroe Building
P.O. Box 2120
Richmond 23218-2120, 804-371-2522
www.pen.k12.va.us/Anthology/VDOE/
   Compliance/TeachEd

Washington
Superintendent of Public Instruction
Professional Education and Certification Office
Old Capitol Building
600 South Washington Street
P.O. Box 47200
Olympia 98504-7200, 360-753-6773
http://inform.ospi.wednet.edu/CERT/
   welcome.html

West Virginia   3
Department of Education
Office of Professional Preparation
1900 Kanawha Boulevard East
Building #6, Room B-252
Charleston 25305-0330, 304-558-7010

Wisconsin   3
Department of Public Instruction
Teacher Education and Licensing Teams
125 South Webster Street, P.O. Box 7841
Madison 53707-7841, 608-266-1879
www.dp.state.wi.us/tcert

Wyoming
Professional Teaching Standards Board
Hathaway Building, 2nd Floor
2300 Capital Avenue
Cheyenne 82002, 307-777-6248
www.k12.wy.us

St. Croix District   3
Department of Education
Educational Personnel Services
2133 Hospital Street
St. Croix, Virgin Islands 00820, 340-773-1095

St. Thomas/St. John District   3
Department of Education
Personnel Services
44–46 Kongens Gade
St. Thomas, Virgin Islands 00802,
   340-774-0100

**United States Department of Defense
Dependent Schools**   3
Certification Unit
4040 N. Fairfax Drive
Arlington, Virginia 22203-1634
703-696-3081, ext. 133
www.tmn.com/dodea

Key to State Codes for Testing Requirements

No Code	No testing is required.
1	State requires successful completion of its own examination.
2	State requires successful completion of its own examination *plus* completion of one or more national tests.
3	State requires successful completion of one or more national tests. The Praxis Series is administered by the Educational Testing Service (ETS). States set their own minimum scores.

Source: "Directory of State Teacher Licensure Offices," from *The 1999 Job Search Handbook for Educators.* Copyright © 1998. Used by permission of American Association for Employment in Education.

Glossary

academic engaged time   The time a student spends on academically relevant activities or materials while experiencing a high rate of success.

academic freedom   The freedom of teachers to teach about an issue or to use a source in teaching without fear of penalty, reprisal, or harassment.

academy   A type of secondary school during the early national period that tried to combine the best of the Latin and English grammar schools. During the nineteenth century it took on a college preparation orientation.

acceptable use policy   A statement of rules governing student use of school computers, especially regarding access to the Internet.

active learning   Learning in which the student takes control of or is positively involved in the process of his or her education; strongly associated with constructivism.

aesthetics   A branch of philosophy that examines the perception of beauty and distinguishes beauty from that which is moral or useful.

alternative licensure   A procedure offered by many states to license teachers who have not graduated from a state-approved teacher education program.

American Federation of Teachers (AFT)   The nation's second largest teachers' association or union. Founded in 1916, it is affiliated with the AFL-CIO, the nation's largest union.

assimilation   The absorption of an individual or a group into the cultural tradition of a population or another group.

assistive technology   The array of devices and services that help people with disabilities to perform better in their daily lives. Such devices include motorized chairs, remote control units that turn appliances on and off, computers, and speech synthesizers.

at-risk students   *See* Students at risk.

authentic assessment   A recent trend in student evaluation that attempts to measure real student performance on significant tasks; the focus is on what we want the student to be able to do. Also called *performance assessment*.

axiology   The philosophical study of values, especially how they are formed ethically, aesthetically, and religiously.

back-to-basics movement   A theme in education reform during the 1970s and early 1980s. Proponents called for more emphasis on traditional subject matter such as reading, writing, arithmetic, and history.

behaviorism   A psychological theory asserting that all behavior is shaped by environmental events or conditions.

bilingual education   A variety of approaches to educating students who speak a primary language other than English.

block grant   Federal aid to education that comes with only minimal federal restrictions on how the funds should be spent; *compare* Categorical grant.

block scheduling   An approach to class scheduling in which students take fewer classes each school day but spend more time in each class.

breach of contract   A failure to fulfill the requirements of a legal agreement.

Brown* v. *Board of Education of Topeka   U.S. Supreme Court ruling in 1954 holding that segregated schools are inherently unequal.

Buckley amendment   The shorthand name for the Family Educational Rights and Privacy Act, which outlines who may and may not have access to a student's records.

call to excellence   An educational slogan pointing students to high standards.

career ladder   A series of steps in an occupation. Usually the higher steps ("rungs" on the ladder) bring new tasks, more responsibility, increased status, and enhanced rewards.

categorical grant   Federal aid to education that must be spent for purposes that are specified in the legislation and by the federal agency administering the funds.

CD-ROM   An acronym for Compact Disc–Read-Only Memory, a type of computer disk that stores several hundred megabytes of data and is currently used for many kinds of multimedia software.

certification   Recognition by a profession that one of its practitioners has met certain standards. Often used as a synonym for *licensure,* which is governmental approval to perform certain work, such as teaching.

character education   Efforts by the home, the school, the religious community, and the individual student to help the student know the good, love the good, and do the good and, in the process, to forge good qualities such as courage, respect, and responsibility.

charter schools   Public schools in which the educators, often joined by members of the local community, have made a special contract, or charter, with the school district. Usually the charter allows the school a great deal of independence in its operation.

chief state school officer The executive officer of a state's board of education who is usually responsible for the administration of that state's public education. This person is also the head of that state's department of education. Also called *superintendent of education, commissioner of education,* and *superintendent of public instruction.*

child-centered curriculum A curriculum that tends to stress the needs and development of the individual student rather than the mastery of fixed subject matter; also called *society-centered curriculum.*

choice theory A theory articulated by psychiatrist William Glasser holding that humans have fundamental needs such as survival, love, power, freedom, and fun, and that throughout our lives our actions are attempts to satisfy these needs.

civic learning A part of social studies that emphasizes preparing students to be good citizens by becoming aware of our common heritage and engaging issues related to character and values. Students learn to apply principles of democracy to everyday concerns they will face as citizens.

classroom management The set of teacher behaviors that create and maintain conditions in the classroom permitting instruction to take place efficiently and effectively.

cognitive tools Computer applications that are used to engage and enhance thinking.

common schools Public elementary schools that are open to children of all classes. During the nineteenth century, the common school became the embodiment of universal education.

compensatory education Educational support to provide a more equal opportunity for disadvantaged students through such activities as remedial instruction and early learning.

constructivism A theory, based on research from cognitive psychology, that people learn by constructing their own knowledge through an active learning process rather than by simply absorbing knowledge directly from some other source.

continuing contract An agreement between a school district and a teacher outlining the conditions and terms of work.

contract A binding agreement between parties.

cooperative learning An instructional approach in which students work together in groups to achieve learning goals. A variety of cooperative learning strategies exist.

core curriculum A common course of study for all students, often called for by essentialist reforms in the 1980s.

core knowledge *See* Cultural literacy.

credential file A file established by college students—typically with the school's career planning and placement office—that contains materials important for securing a teaching job, for example, letters of recommendation, a transcript, and a résumé.

critical thinking A general instructional approach intended to help students evaluate the worth of ideas, opinions, or evidence before making a decision or judgment.

cultural literacy Being aware of the central ideas, stories, scientific knowledge, events, and personalities of a culture; also known as *core knowledge.*

cultural pluralism An approach to diversity of individuals that calls for understanding and appreciating cultural differences.

culture shock The feeling of disorientation experienced by individuals when initially immersed in a society with different values, customs, and mores.

curriculum All the organized and intended experiences of the student for which the school accepts responsibility. *See also* Formal curriculum; Informal curriculum.

dame school A school run by a housewife during early colonial days.

database A software program that organizes and stores complex sets of information in the form of records that can be sorted according to different criteria.

deductive reasoning A type of reasoning from the general to the particular; reasoning in which the conclusion follows from the premise stated.

de facto school segregation Segregation in the schools resulting primarily from residential patterns.

de jure school segregation Segregation in the schools that occurs by law.

democratic reconstructionists Subscribers to an educational perspective that focuses on developing students who are prepared to make positive changes in a democracy.

distance education The use of technology to link students and instructors who are separated in terms of location.

district school The type of school that succeeded the town school and moving school in New England. A township was divided into districts, each with its own school, its own schoolmaster, and funding from the town treasury.

drill and practice In educational technology, software programs that give students a series of tasks to reinforce a concept or to initially diagnose a student's level. These programs monitor progress, provide feedback, and present tasks accordingly.

due process The deliberative process that protects a person's constitutional right to receive fair and equal protection under the law.

economic reconstructionists Subscribers to an educational perspective or motivation that focuses on developing students who take a critical stance toward the dominant social and economic status quo.

education   The process by which humans develop their minds, their skills, and their character. It is a lifelong process marked by continual development and change.

effective schools   Schools that provide a significantly better education (usually measured by student test scores) for a much larger percentage of their students than do other schools serving similar student populations.

1890 institutions   Colleges and universities created for African Americans as a result of the second Morrill Act passed by Congress in 1890.

Elementary and Secondary Education Act (ESEA)   The federal government's single largest investment in elementary and secondary education, including Title I. Originally passed in 1965, Congress reauthorizes it periodically, most recently in 1999.

English grammar school   A form of secondary education in the latter half of the colonial period that provided a practical alternative education for students who were not interested in college.

epistemology   A branch of philosophy that examines the nature of knowledge, its origins, its foundations, its limits, and its validity.

equality of educational opportunity   A concept that students from less advantageous backgrounds should have equal opportunities to experience success in school. Disagreement exists on whether this implies simply providing equal resources or ensuring equal success as more privileged students.

essentialism   An educational philosophy that emphasizes a core body of knowledge and skills necessary for effective participation in society. Proponents believe that an educated person must have this core of knowledge and skills and that all children should be taught it.

ethics   A branch of philosophy that examines the right and wrong of human conduct. The term can also refer to a particular moral code or system.

existentialism   A philosophical doctrine emphasizing that individuals must create their own meaning and purpose in life. In education, an existentialist believes that each student must ultimately make meaning through individual learning, not group learning.

extrinsic rewards   Rewards to an individual that are external to the activity itself, such as grades, gold stars, and prizes.

fair use   A legal principle defining specific, limited ways in which copyrighted material can be used without permission from the author.

formal curriculum   Those subjects that are taught in school and the instructional approaches used to transmit this knowledge; also known as *explicit curriculum*.

gifted and talented children   Children who demonstrate or give evidence of potential for high achievement or performance in academic, creative, artistic, or leadership areas. The term *gifted* typically includes high intellectual ability; the term *talented* usually applies to creative or artistic abilities.

Goals 2000   *See* National Education Goals.

Head Start   A federally funded compensatory education program, in existence since the mid-1960s, that provides additional educational services to young children suffering the effects of poverty.

hidden curriculum   *See* Informal curriculum.

inclusion   The commitment to educate each child, to the maximum extent appropriate, in the regular school and classroom, rather than moving children with disabilities to separate classes or institutions.

individualized education program (IEP)   A management tool required for every student covered by the provisions of the Individuals with Disabilities Education Act. It must indicate a student's current level of performance, short- and long-term instructional objectives, services to be provided, and criteria and schedules for evaluation of progress.

individualized family services plan (IFSP)   Similar to an individualized education program for school-aged children, the IFSP specifies the services to be provided to developmentally delayed children from birth through age two. The IFSP is authorized by PL 99–457, the Education of the Handicapped Act Amendments.

inductive reasoning   A type of reasoning, from the particular to the general, in which one can make a general conclusion based on a number of facts.

informal curriculum   The teaching and learning that occur in school but are not part of the formal, or explicit, curriculum; also called the *implicit* or *hidden curriculum*.

in loco parentis   The responsibility of the teacher to function "in the place of the parent" when a student is in school.

integrated curriculum   *See* Interdisciplinary curriculum.

interdisciplinary curriculum   A curriculum that integrates the subject matter from two or more disciplines, such as English and history, often using themes such as inventions, discoveries, or health as overlays to the study of the different subjects. Also known as *integrated curriculum*.

Internet   A worldwide computer network that individuals can access to communicate with others and to retrieve various kinds of information stored electronically in many locations throughout the world.

intrinsic rewards   Rewards to an individual that come from within, such as personal satisfaction or happiness.

junior high school A separate kind of school created typically for grades 7, 8, and 9. The first junior highs were founded in 1909–10. In recent years, they have been gradually replaced by middle schools.

Kalamazoo case The 1874 U.S. Supreme Court decision (*Stuart and Others* v. *School District No. 1 of the Village of Kalamazoo and Others*) that upheld the right of states to tax citizens to create public high schools.

kindergarten A division of school for children below the first grade, usually for children between ages four and six; the concept, which means "children's garden," was imported to the United States from Germany during the nineteenth century.

Latin grammar school First type of secondary school in the American colonies, whose main purpose was to prepare students for college.

law The system of rules that governs the general conduct of a particular community's citizens.

learning communities Organizations in which all members are engaged in continuous learning and improvement efforts.

learning style Characteristic way a student learns, including such factors as the way an individual processes information, preference for competition or cooperation, and preferred environmental conditions such as lighting or noise level.

learning to learn Acquiring a set of skills or competencies that enable one to learn more and to learn with greater efficiency.

least restrictive environment (LRE) A requirement of the Education for All Handicapped Children Act that students with disabilities should participate in regular education programs to the greatest extent appropriate.

liability A legal obligation.

licensure The approval given to an individual by a governmental agency, usually the state, to perform a particular work, such as teaching.

limited English proficient (LEP) Term for students whose native language is not English and who have difficulty understanding and using English.

local school board The policymaking body of a school district, which represents the citizens of the district in setting up a school program, hiring school personnel, and generally determining local policy related to public education.

logic A branch of philosophy that involves the study of reasoning or of sound argument. In a more specific sense, logic is the study of deductive inference.

looping An educational practice of multiyear teaching in which the teacher follows students to the next grade level and stays with the group for several years.

magnet school An alternative school that provides instruction in specified areas such as the fine arts; for specific groups such as the gifted and talented; or for using specific teaching styles such as open classrooms. In many cases, magnet schools are established as a method of promoting voluntary desegregation in schools.

mainstreaming The practice of placing special education students in general education classes for at least part of the school day while also providing additional services, programs, or classes as needed.

McGuffey **Readers** A six-volume series of readers developed by William Holmes McGuffey that sold more than 100 million copies between 1836 and 1906. The readers served to create a common curriculum for many students.

mentor A person who gives both personal and professional guidance to a novice.

metaphysics A branch of philosophy devoted to exploring the nature of existence or reality as a whole rather than to studying particular parts of reality as the natural sciences do. Metaphysicians try to answer questions about reality without referring to religion or revelation.

middle school A school that bridges the grades between elementary school and high school, usually grades 6–8. It differs from a junior high school in that it is specifically designed for young adolescents, with a strong emphasis on personal growth and development, rather than mimicking the high school's emphasis on academics and sports, as junior high schools often did.

Morrill Act Federal legislation passed in 1862 that granted each state federal land to establish colleges for the study of agriculture and mechanical arts. A second Morrill Act, passed in 1890, provided similar federal support to create "separate but equal" colleges for African Americans.

multicultural curriculum Several approaches to multicultural curriculum exist, but at its essence it promotes an understanding of and appreciation for cultural pluralism. It attempts to address issues of social injustice related to racism, sexism, and economic inequality by reducing prejudice and fostering tolerance through the formal curriculum.

multicultural education An approach to education that recognizes cultural diversity and fosters cultural enrichment of all children and youth.

multiple intelligences A theory of intelligence put forth by Howard Gardner that identifies at least seven dimensions of intellectual capacities that people use to approach problems and create products.

National Board for Professional Teaching Standards (NBPTS) A professional agency that is setting voluntary standards for what experienced teachers should know and be able to do in more than thirty different teaching areas.

national curricular standards Nationally dictated or recommended curriculum and levels of educational achievement.

National Education Association (NEA) The nation's largest teachers' association, founded in 1857 and having a membership of over 2.2 million educators.

National Education Goals Goals for U.S. education, established by the president and the fifty state governors and legislated by Congress, that were intended to be reached by the year 2000.

New England Primer The basic text used in schools during the eighteenth century. It was an illustrated book composed of religious texts and other readings.

New Basics A label given to a proposed agenda of curricular reforms that hope to teach students how to *apply* knowledge.

news group A worldwide electronic network of users who share a common interest and post messages to one another.

normal school A two- or four-year institution devoted entirely to preparing teachers that gained great popularity in the nineteenth century and faded out in the twentieth century.

Northwest Ordinances Passed by Congress in 1785 and 1787, these ordinances were concerned with the sale of public lands in the Northwest Territory (from present-day Ohio to Minnesota). Every township was divided into thirty-six sections, one of which was set aside for the maintenance of public schools. The 1787 ordinance reaffirmed that religion, morality, and knowledge were necessary to good government.

Old Deluder Satan Act A Massachusetts law passed in 1647 that strengthened an earlier law requiring parents to educate their children. It required every town of fifty or more families to pay a teacher to teach the children reading and writing so they could read the Bible and thwart Satan, who would assuredly try to keep people from understanding the scriptures.

parent-teacher organization (PTO) A local organization, usually centered around each school, that consists of both parents and teachers at that school. Its purpose is to serve as a communication mechanism between the school and the parents of the school's students.

participant observation In teacher education, the process of observing a class, recording one's observations, and comparing notes with other observers.

pedagogical content knowledge Teachers' knowledge that bridges content knowledge and pedagogy with an understanding of how particular topics can best be presented for instruction given the diverse interests and abilities of learners.

perennialism A particular view of philosophy that sees human nature as constant, with few changes over time. Perennialism in education promotes the advancement of the intellect as the central purpose of schools. The educational process stresses academic rigor and discipline.

performance assessment *See* Authentic assessment.

performance pay A financial reward given to teachers, based on the special quality of their work.

philosophy The love or search for wisdom; the quest for basic principles to understand the meaning of life. Western philosophy traditionally contains five branches of philosophy: metaphysics, ethics, aesthetics, epistemology, and logic.

phonics An approach to reading that teaches the reader to "decode" words by sounding out letters and combinations of letters.

Plessy v. Ferguson A Supreme Court decision in 1896 that upheld the constitutionality of separate but equal accommodations for African Americans. The ruling was quickly applied to schools.

portfolio A collection of a person's work. For students, portfolios are being used as a relatively new form of authentic assessment. They can contain a great range of work, from paper and pen work to sculpture.

private venture school A type of school in the middle states during colonial times, licensed by the civil government but not protected or financed by it.

privatization A movement to contract with private organizations, often for-profit, to operate particular public schools whose students have been performing poorly on academic tests, or to provide specific educational services to public schools. The Edison Schools and Sylvan Learning Centers are examples of such providers.

problem solving The process of either presenting students with a problem or helping them to identify a problem and then observing and helping them become aware of the conditions, procedures, or steps needed to solve the problem.

profession An occupation or occupational group that fulfills certain criteria. Among other things, it must require training and knowledge, must perform a social service, must have a code of ethics, and must have a sense of autonomy and personal responsibility.

professional development *See* Staff development.

progressivism A form of educational philosophy that sees nature as ever changing. Because the world is always changing and new situations require new solutions to problems, learners must develop as problem solvers.

public comprehensive high school The predominant form of secondary education in America in the twentieth century. It provides both preparation for college and a vocational education for students not going on to college.

real encounters Face-to-face experiences that are powerful sources of learning.

reduction in force (RIF) The elimination of teaching positions in a school system because of declining student population or funding.

reflection Conscious and analytical thought by an individual about what he or she is doing and how the action impacts others.

reflective teaching A teacher's habit of examining and evaluating his or her teaching on a regular basis.

scaffolding Providing assistance—some structure, clues, help with remembering certain steps or procedures, or encouragement to try—when a learner is on the verge of solving a problem but can't complete it independently.

school choice Allowing parents to select alternative educational programs for their children, either within a given school or among different schools.

school culture The prevailing mores, values, and rituals that permeate a school.

schooling Formal instruction typically conducted in an institution, adhering to standardized practices.

schools-within-schools In large schools, the establishment of "houses" of teachers and 100 to 200 students.

school vouchers A type of educational choice plan that gives parents a receipt or written statement that they can exchange for the schooling they believe is most desirable for their child. The school, in turn, can cash in the received vouchers for the money to pay teachers and buy resources.

search engine A large database that has searched and indexed millions of web pages and helps users navigate the World Wide Web and pinpoint the information they need.

self-fulfilling prophecy Students' behavior that comes about as a result of teachers' expectations that the students will behave in a certain way. Teachers expect students to behave in a certain way; they communicate those expectations by both overt and subtle means; and students respond by behaving in the way expected.

sexual harassment Unwelcome sexual attention.

simulation A technique for learning or practicing skills that involves dealing with a realistic but artificial problem or situation. Typically, it provides an opportunity for safe practice with feedback on performance.

site-based decision making A school reform effort to decentralize, allowing decisions to be made and budgets to be established at the school-building level, where most of the changes need to occur. Usually teachers become involved in the decision-making process. Also known as *site-based management, school-based management,* or *school-based decision making.*

social distance The psychological relationships between individuals.

socialization The general process of social learning whereby children learn the many things they must know to become acceptable members of society.

social reconstructionists Proponents of the theory of education that schools and teachers need to engage in the restructuring and reforming of society to eradicate its ills and shortcomings.

society-centered curriculum *See* Child-centered curriculum.

socioeconomic status (SES) A system for measuring the economic conditions of people using the family's occupational status, income, and educational attainment as measures of status.

special education Educational programming provided by schools to meet the needs of students with disabilities.

spreadsheet An interactive software program allowing users to perform multiple calculations and view more than one answer at a time.

staff development The efforts by a school or school district to improve the professional skills and competencies of its professional staff. Also called "in-service" training in education.

standard Exemplary performance that serves as a benchmark.

state board of education The state's primary education policymaking body for elementary and secondary education.

state department of education The state bureaucracy, operating under the direction of the state board of education, whose responsibilities typically include administering and distributing state and federal funds, licensing teachers and other educational personnel, providing educational data and analyses, and approving college and university educational licensure programs.

structure of disciplines approach An approach to teaching subject matter that emphasizes understanding the structure of a discipline—the concepts and methods of inquiry that are the discipline's most basic part—by learning the principles that constitute the heart of a discipline. Popularized by Jerome Bruner during the 1960s.

students at risk Students judged to be in serious jeopardy of not completing school or not succeeding in school.

subject-matter–centered curriculum A curriculum that focuses on bodies of content or subject matter, usually the traditional subject disciplines.

submersion model A method of learning English in which students receive instruction in all-English-speaking classes.

superintendent of schools Typically, a professional educator selected by the local school board to act as its executive officer and as the educational leader and chief administrator of the local school district.

teacher competency testing Examinations given to teachers to assess their professional knowledge and skills.

teaching journal A professional record of reflections, instructional ideas, and observations by a teacher or future teacher.

teaching portfolio Collection of such items as research papers, pupil evaluations, teaching units, and videocassettes of lessons to reflect the quality of a teacher's teaching. Portfolios can be used to illustrate to employers the teacher's quality or to obtain national board certification.

teaching to the test   Instruction that is driven by the requirements or characteristics of a test, rather than the needs of students or the substance of a particular subject.

telecollaborate   To use telecommunications technology, such as the Internet, telephone, or television, to bring individuals from remote locations together to work on a project.

telecommunication   Communication through electronic transmission of messages, as by telephone, television, or computer network.

tenure   A legal right that confers permanent employment on teachers, protecting them from dismissal without adequate cause.

TIMSS   The Third International Mathematics and Science Study, the largest and most extensive international study of academic achievement in mathematics.

Title I   The section of the 1965 Elementary and Secondary Education Act that delivers federal funds to local school districts and schools for the education of students from low-income families and supplements the educational services provided to low-achieving students in those districts.

Title IX   A provision of the 1972 federal Education Amendment Act that prohibits discrimination on the basis of sex for any educational program or activity receiving federal financial assistance.

town school   A New England elementary school during the early colonial period, required in every town of fifty or more families.

tracking   The homogeneous grouping of students for learning tasks on the basis of some measure(s) of their abilities.

tutorial   A software application designed to provide initial instruction in a given topic, check for understanding throughout the process, and evaluate the learner's grasp of the topic once the program is completed.

universal education   Schooling for everyone.

vicarious experiences   Learnings gained not through direct experiences, but through observations or readings.

virtual fieldtrip   Computer software that simulates the experience of an actual fieldtrip with the use of digital images and multimedia tools.

wait-time   The time a teacher spends waiting for an answer after posing a question. Research indicates that good questioning practices involve giving students sufficient time to think about and respond to each question.

whole language approach   A teaching approach emphasizing the integration of language arts skills and knowledge across the curriculum. It stresses the provision of a literate environment and functional uses of language.

word processor   A software application that allows users to create, store, and edit text. These programs often come with additional writing aids such as on-screen dictionaries or spell checkers.

World Wide Web (WWW)   A collection of sites on the Internet that users can access using a graphical interface called a web browser. In addition to text, the sites often contain graphics, sound, video, or other multimedia applications, and many are connected to one another by hypertext links.

writing across the curriculum   An instructional approach using writing as a tool for learning in all subject areas.

zone of proximal development   A range of tasks that a child cannot yet do alone but can accomplish when assisted by a more skilled partner. This zone is the point at which instruction can succeed and real learning is possible.

Index

Chapter 7, **"What Should Teachers Know About Technology and Its Impact on Schools?"** provides examples of applications and methods within the context of subject-matter disciplines. In addition, new technology resources, such as software programs, URLs, and references to standards appear throughout the text.

TABLE 7.1 Types of Technology Tools

Technology Tool	Educational Benefits	Example
Word processor	• Easy cut-and-paste procedures and the ability to save and return to a document later encourage editing. • On-screen spell checkers, dictionaries, and thesauruses aid accuracy.	*Alpha Smart,** a portable and user friendly word processor, is especially popular with teachers who work with younger writers.
Multimedia presentation software	• Combining text, audio, video, and virtual environments helps to communicate complex ideas. • Caters to a variety of learning styles.	*PowerPoint* allows students to easily combine a variety of media or even publish a presentation on the Web.
Drill and practice	• Similar to an interactive worksheet that provides feedback for the user and teacher. • Progress through the program depends on mastery of previous level. • Effective at reinforcing a concept.	*Reader Rabbit* is a popular program to reinforce letter recognition, rhyming words, and word families.
Database	• Organizes and stores complex sets of information. • Users can sort through information and filter unwanted data.	The *Valley of the Shadow* web site offers students access to a variety of searchable databases from two communities during the Civil War.
Simulation	• Interactive in nature, simulations allow students to reenact an event. • Students assume roles in the story, making decisions to which the software responds appropriately.	*Decisions, Decisions: Local Government* lets students play the role of a mayor facing a dilemma about the city's economic future.
Spreadsheet	• Allows users to form multiple calculations and to see all answers simultaneously. • A powerful tool to manipulate large sets of data. • Includes easy tools to graph.	Students can study a graph of population demographics in a community and use a spreadsheet program, like *Excel,*[†] to predict future changes in that society.

AlphaSmart is a product of IPD, Inc. (web site: http://www.alphasmart.com/; phone: 1-888-274-0680).
[†]Microsoft produces *Excel* (web site: www.microsoft.com; phone: 425-882-8080).